VERBAL PERIPHRASIS IN ANCIENT GREEK

Verbal Periphrasis in Ancient Greek

Have- and Be-Constructions

KLAAS BENTEIN

OXFORD
UNIVERSITY PRESS

Great Clarendon Street, Oxford, OX2 6DP,
United Kingdom

Oxford University Press is a department of the University of Oxford.
It furthers the University's objective of excellence in research, scholarship,
and education by publishing worldwide. Oxford is a registered trade mark of
Oxford University Press in the UK and in certain other countries

© Klaas Bentein 2016

The moral rights of the author have been asserted

First Edition published in 2016

All rights reserved. No part of this publication may be reproduced, stored in
a retrieval system, or transmitted, in any form or by any means, without the
prior permission in writing of Oxford University Press, or as expressly permitted
by law, by licence or under terms agreed with the appropriate reprographics
rights organization. Enquiries concerning reproduction outside the scope of the
above should be sent to the Rights Department, Oxford University Press, at the
address above

You must not circulate this work in any other form
and you must impose this same condition on any acquirer

Published in the United States of America by Oxford University Press
198 Madison Avenue, New York, NY 10016, United States of America

British Library Cataloguing in Publication Data
Data available

ISBN 978-0-19-874709-3

Links to third party websites are provided by Oxford in good faith and
for information only. Oxford disclaims any responsibility for the materials
contained in any third party website referenced in this work.

For Elisabeth

Foreword

This book constitutes a completely rewritten version of my doctoral dissertation, *Verbal Periphrasis in Ancient Greek: Cognitive and Diachronic Studies*, which was submitted at Ghent University (2012) and supervised by Mark Janse and Wolfgang de Melo. My dissertation was composed in the so-called 'PhD-by-publication' format: it consisted of a number of articles that I had published over a period of time on the subject of verbal periphrasis. In these articles, I did not intend to give a coherent analysis of verbal periphrasis in Ancient Greek: rather, I intended to explore the value of different Cognitive Linguistic theories for our understanding of both the synchrony and the diachrony of specific periphrastic constructions, particularly perfect periphrases formed with εἰμί. The articles were based in part on pre-existing collections of examples, such as that of Kontos (1898), and partly on my own, corpus-based research.

This book has an entirely different purpose: in it, I present a coherent study of periphrasis with εἰμί and ἔχω to a more general public, bringing together both old and new ideas about periphrastic constructions. For both Archaic/Classical and Post-Classical/Byzantine Greek, I provide an exhaustive analysis of a large corpus of texts. As a result, this study contains much new material. The presentation of the book is also completely different from my doctoral dissertation: the three diachronic chapters are based on the threefold distinction between perfective, imperfective, and perfect aspect, which helps us better understand the continuities and discontinuities between Archaic/Classical Greek and Post-Classical/Byzantine Greek.

It is a pleasure to thank all the people who have shaped my ideas on verbal periphrasis over the years. They include Rutger Allan, Gunnar de Boel, Marc de Groote, Jesús de la Villa, Wolfgang de Melo, Kristoffel Demoen, Trevor Evans, Benjamin Fortson, Thanasis Giannaris, Geoffrey Horrocks, Mark Janse, Marjolijne Janssen, Brian Joseph, Leonid Kulikov, John Lee, Amalia Moser, Sander Orriens, Anna Pompei, Albert Rijksbaron, Arthur Verhoogt, Gerry Wakker, and Andreas Willi. Oxford University Press's anonymous referees have also provided me with many valuable suggestions concerning various aspects of this book.

A special word of thanks goes to the editor of *Journal of Greek Linguistics*, Brian Joseph: although the ninth chapter of my dissertation, 'Transitivity and the diachrony of εἰμί with present participle in Post-Classical and Early Byzantine Greek', had already been accepted for publication in *JGL* (2014), he agreed that it would be better to incorporate it in revised and extended form here. John Hilton, the editor of *Acta Classica*, granted permission to reuse some of the material previously published in *AClass* 56 (2013).

A special word of thanks also to my father, Gilbert Bentein, who has helped me with the technical side of my research projects for many years now. Without his help, the analysis presented here would have been unimaginable.

Matt Newman read through an early version of the manuscript and made many helpful comments on language and style, as well as contents, for which I thank him wholeheartedly. At Oxford University Press, working with Charlotte Loveridge, Annie Rose, and the other members of the editorial team has been a real pleasure. Any shortcomings in this book remain entirely my own responsibility.

Most of the research for this book was executed at Ghent University (Belgium). Smaller parts of it were done at Macquarie University (Australia) and the University of Michigan (United States). My work at these universities was funded by the Special Research Fund of Ghent University (2009–13), the Belgian American Educational Foundation (2013–14) and the Fund for Scientific Research—Flanders (2013–14).

Klaas Bentein

Ann Arbor
January 2014

Contents

Figures   xi
Tables   xiii
Abbreviations   xv

Introduction to Verbal Periphrasis in Ancient Greek   1
   0.1 Preamble   1
   0.2 Objectives   3
   0.3 Previous research   5
   0.4 Data collection and presentation   6
   0.5 General outline   9

1. Theoretical Background   11
   1.1 Introduction   11
   1.2 Factors motivating the use of periphrasis   11
   1.3 Register and genre   19
   1.4 Aspect   29
   1.5 Language change   51

2. 'Verbal' and 'Adjectival' Periphrasis   59
   2.1 Introduction   59
   2.2 Background to the debate   60
   2.3 A prototype-based approach towards verbal periphrasis   69
   2.4 Adjectival periphrasis   79
   2.5 Conclusion   102

3. Perfect Aspect   105
   3.1 Introduction   105
   3.2 Archaic Greek (VIII–VI BC)   107
   3.3 Classical Greek (V–IV BC)   113
   3.4 Early Post-Classical Greek (III–I BC)   152
   3.5 Middle Post-Classical Greek (I–III AD)   168
   3.6 Late Post-Classical and Early Byzantine Greek (IV–VIII AD)   182
   3.7 Conclusion   201

x Contents

4. Imperfective Aspect 205
   4.1 Introduction 205
   4.2 Archaic Greek (VIII–VI BC) 208
   4.3 Classical Greek (V–IV BC) 211
   4.4 Early Post-Classical Greek (III–I BC) 238
   4.5 Middle Post-Classical Greek (I–III AD) 254
   4.6 Late Post-Classical and Early Byzantine Greek (IV–VIII AD) 276
   4.7 Conclusion 289

5. Perfective Aspect 293
   5.1 Introduction 293
   5.2 Functional complexity of εἰμί with the aorist participle in the Classical period 294
   5.3 Transitivity and the diachrony of periphrasis in Classical (Ancient) Greek 302

Conclusion to Verbal Periphrasis in Ancient Greek 305

Appendix 311
Glossary 335
Bibliography 343
Index locorum 371
Index nominum et rerum 387

Figures

Fig. 1.1	Malchukov's (2006: 333) Transitivity Scale	50
Fig. 2.1	The noun-to-verb continuum (after Givón 1984: 55)	91
Fig. 2.2	The adjectival (property-referring) participle on the noun-to-verb continuum	98
Fig. 3.1	'Aoristic drift'	107
Fig. 4.1	Frequency of occurrence of εἰμί with the present participle (from EPG to EBG)	277
Fig. 4.2	PROG-imperfective drift (revised)	291

Tables

Table 0.1	Synthetic vs. periphrastic pairs	2
Table 1.1	The aspecto-temporal system in Ancient (Classical) Greek	29
Table 1.2	Actionality (Vendler 1957)	42
Table 1.3	Transitivity parameters (Hopper & Thompson 1980: 252)	46
Table 1.4	Processes of grammaticalization (after Croft 2000: 157)	52
Table 2.1	Parts of speech as typologically unmarked combinations (Croft 2001: 88)	89
Table 2.2	Transience of the property-referring perfect/present participle	95
Table 2.3	Scores on Pustet's (2003) parameters	99
Table 3.1	Distribution of ἔχω with the aorist participle (CG)	124
Table 3.2	Distribution of εἰμί with the perfect participle in CG (aspect, voice)	133
Table 3.3	Distribution of εἰμί with the perfect participle in CG (mood)	135
Table 3.4	Distribution of εἰμί with the perfect participle in CG (aspect)	139
Table 3.5	Distribution of ἔχω with the (medio-passive) perfect participle in CG	148
Table 3.6	Distribution of εἰμί with the perfect participle in EPG	158
Table 3.7	Distribution of εἰμί with the perfect participle in EPG (mood)	159
Table 3.8	Distribution of εἰμί with the perfect participle in EPG (aspect, voice)	160
Table 3.9	Distribution of ἔχω with the (medio-passive) perfect participle in EPG	164
Table 3.10	Distribution of εἰμί with the aorist participle in MPG	169
Table 3.11	Distribution of εἰμί with the perfect participle in MPG	172
Table 3.12	Distribution of εἰμί with the perfect participle in MPG (aspect, voice)	173
Table 3.13	Distribution of ἔχω with the (medio-passive) perfect participle in MPG	176

Table 3.14	Distribution of εἰμί with the perfect and the aorist participle in LPG & EBG	183
Table 3.15	Distribution of εἰμί with the perfect participle in LPG & EBG (aspect, voice)	187
Table 3.16	Distribution of εἰμί with the aorist participle in LPG & EBG (aspect, voice)	188
Table 3.17	Distribution of εἰμί with the perfect participle from CG to EBG (aspect, tense)	191
Table 4.1	Developmental stages of Bertinetto et al.'s PROG imperfective drift	207
Table 4.2	Distribution of εἰμί with the present participle in CG (stative)	213
Table 4.3	Distribution of εἰμί with the present participle in CG (progressive)	222
Table 4.4	Distribution of τυγχάνω with the present participle in CG (indicative)	230
Table 4.5	Distribution of εἰμί with the present participle in EPG (stative)	249
Table 4.6	Distribution of εἰμί with the present participle in EPG (progressive)	251
Table 4.7	Distribution of εἰμί with the present participle in MPG (stative)	262
Table 4.8	Distribution of εἰμί with the present participle in MPG (progressive)	264
Table 4.9	Some passages (possibly) imitating the LXX/NT	283
Table 4.10	Distribution of εἰμί with the present participle in LPG and EBG (progressive)	287
Table 5.1	Distribution of εἰμί with the aorist participle in CG	295

Abbreviations

A	Agent
ACT	Active
ANT	Anterior
AOR	Aorist
ASV	American Standard Version
CEV	Contemporary English Version
CG	Classical Greek
CURR	Perfect of current relevance
DDBDP	Duke Databank of Documentary Papyri
DUR	Durative progressive
EBG	Early Byzantine Greek
EPG	Early Post-Classical Greek
EXP	Experiential perfect
FOC	Focalized progressive
FP	Focalization point
GNB	Good News Bible
IMP	Imperative
IMPF	Imperfect
IND	Indicative
INF	Infinitive
KJV	King James Version
LPG	Late Post-Classical Greek
LXX	Septuagint
MED	Middle
MPG	Middle Post-Classical Greek
NETS	New English Translation of the Septuagint
NRO	Normed rate of occurrence
NT	New Testament
O	Object
OPT	Optative
PART	Participle
PASS	Passive
PERS	Perfect of persistence
PIE	Proto-Indo European
PRES	Present
PROG	Progressive
RES	Resultative

SG	Singular
STAT	Stative
SUBJ	Subjunctive
TOT	Total
TTR	Type-token ratio
V	Verb
WEB	World English Bible

Introduction to Verbal Periphrasis in Ancient Greek

> The Greek language has ample facilities for a large number of periphrastic tenses. With its many participles and its various auxiliaries, the possible combinations are almost inexhaustible, while the existing combinations show at once the resources and the moderation of the language. Few languages capable of ἔμελλε οὐ τὸ δεύτερον διαφυγὼν ἔσεσθαι (Hdt. 7, 194), and of ἔμελλε... ἔσεσθαι δεδωκώς (Ps.-Dem. 52, 24) would have shown such self-restraint.
>
> (Gildersleeve 1980 [1900-11]: 122)

0.1 PREAMBLE

Together with Latin, Ancient Greek is often considered a prime example of a so-called 'synthetic' language.[1] According to Farrar (1867: 2), for example, Ancient Greek even constitutes 'the most perfect specimen of an inflectional or synthetic language', a characteristic which apparently entails a number of aesthetic advantages, such as 'compactness', 'precision', and 'beauty of form'. Studies have shown, however, that this view must be nuanced, both from a synchronic and a diachronic point of view.

---

[1] For a history of the concepts 'synthetic' and 'analytic', see e.g. Schwegler (1990: 3-28). For our present purposes, we can say that a synthetic language has a high *morpheme-per-word* ratio, while an analytic language has a low *morpheme-per-word* ratio. Contrast, for example, the Ancient Greek form λυθήσομαι with its English counterpart *I shall be released*.

With respect to synchrony, it was recognized already in the nineteenth century that a binary distinction between 'synthetic' and 'analytic' languages is hard to maintain.[2] This insight was elaborated more fully in the work of Sapir (1921: 120–46) and later Greenberg (1960 [1954]), who first proposed a quantitative approach to morphological typology.[3] From a diachronic point of view, scholars have argued that languages[4] tend to become more synthetic or analytic,[5] a process for which Sapir (1921) devised the term 'drift'. This is a process which should be conceived of as 'cyclical' or 'locally progressive',[6] rather than globally progressive, that is, changing continuously in a single direction.[7]

Analyticity can refer to a number of linguistic areas. Consider, for example, the following pairs from Ancient Greek:

Table 0.1. Synthetic vs. periphrastic pairs

Synthetic	Periphrastic
εἶπεν αὐτῷ (Gen. 3.9)	εἶπεν πρὸς αὐτόν (Gen. 15.7)
φίλτερον (Eur., *Hipp.* 185)	μᾶλλον φίλον (Eur., *Hel.* 92)
λέγω (Mt. 3.9)	ἐγὼ λέγω (Mt. 21.27)
φράσω (Hdt. 2.51.1)	ἔρχομαι φράσων (Hdt. 1.194.1)

In the second item of each pair, a multi-word, 'periphrastic'[8] form is used (for a variety of reaons): (a) πρός + accusative instead of the

---

[2] See e.g. Humboldt (1979 [1827–29]: 317–18).

[3] Deriving a degree of syntheticity by dividing the total number of morphemes by the total number of words. See Schwegler (1990: xii) for the difficulties associated with this approach.

[4] In recent years, however, attention has mostly gone to the cyclical change of individual linguistic items (van Gelderen 2013: 234 speaks of 'microcycles', in contrast to 'macrocycles'). In fact, Heine *et al.* (1991: 246) argue that 'there appears to be more justification to apply the notion of a linguistic cycle to individual linguistic developments'.

[5] See e.g. Hodge (1970) with regard to Egyptian. For some observations with regard to Ancient Greek, see e.g. Joseph (1987: 429); Kramer (2004); Christidis (2007: 19).

[6] For a modification of the linguistic cycle as traditionally conceived, see Oesterreicher (2001: 1577–9).

[7] See Croft (2000: 80–1). Note that in the nineteenth century scholars already recognized a historical tendency from synthesis to analysis; they considered this as a non-cyclical, unidirectional process, however (Schwegler 1990: 7–8).

[8] The terms 'periphrasis' and 'analysis' overlap to some extent, though the latter tends to be used with reference to languages in general, while the former with reference to specific constructions.

Introduction

dative case, (b) μᾶλλον + adjective instead of stem + comparative morpheme -τέρ(ος), (c) ἐγώ + verb (1SG) instead of verb (1SG), and (d) ἔρχομαι + future participle instead of stem + future morpheme -σ(ω).

In the present study, I focus on tense and aspect. I shall attempt to improve our understanding of (the development of) the Ancient Greek verbal system by studying (the diachrony of) constructions consisting of the verbs 'to be' (εἰμί) and 'to have' (ἔχω) and a participle. From a (Indo-)European perspective, the choice for focusing on these two verbs is self-evident: both are known to be particularly frequently used for verbal periphrasis.[9] Consider, for example, formations of the type 'amatus sum' (Lat.), 'I am going' (Engl.), 'j'ai lu' (Fr.), 'sono arrivato' (It.), 'ik heb gewandeld' (Dutch), etc.

0.2 OBJECTIVES

This study has four general objectives. First, I intend to clarify the central notion of 'verbal periphrasis' from a synchronic point of view. At present, there is no consensus about which constructions in Ancient Greek form 'proper' instances of verbal periphrasis, and on the basis of which criteria: while the standard account of Aerts (1965: 1–3) acknowledges constructions formed with both εἰμί and ἔχω, more recently Porter (1989: 452–3) has argued that only those formed with εἰμί qualify as periphrastic. Dietrich (1973a, 1973b), on the other hand, discusses a broad variety of 'periphrastic' constructions, formed with verbs such as γίγνομαι 'I become, am', ἔρχομαι 'I go', and τυγχάνω 'I happen to be, am'.

Specifically with regard to constructions formed with εἰμί, a second issue has come under debate: Björck (1940: 17–40) and Aerts (1965: 5–17) argue that only some of the examples are 'truly' periphrastic. In particular, they claim that in cases like πρέπον ἐστί 'it is fitting' or ἀνεῳγμένον ἐστί 'it is open(ed)', the participle should be considered 'adjectivized', as a result of which they ought not be labelled as 'true' (that is, verbal) periphrases; they refer to such cases with the term 'adjectival periphrasis'. Again, however, there is no general consensus on the matter: Porter (1989: 454) claims that we are dealing with

---

[9] See e.g. Benveniste (1960); Kuteva (1998).

verbal periphrasis in all cases. A second objective is therefore to investigate how 'adjectival' periphrasis relates to 'verbal' periphrasis. Third, I aim to present an in-depth investigation of the diachrony of periphrastic constructions with εἰμί and ἔχω. While previous studies, particularly those of Björck (1940), Aerts (1965), and Dietrich (1973a), have greatly advanced our knowledge of the use and development of periphrastic constructions, they are not entirely satisfactory from a modern point of view, for two main reasons. First, in general these studies adopt a somewhat selective approach, as they do not treat perfect periphrases, are based on a selective corpus of texts,[10] do not go into the interrelationship between different periphrases, and pay little attention to less frequently used periphrastic constructions. Second, they are rather static in nature: next to the 'adjectival' use mentioned above, they generally recognize only a single aspectual value for each periphrastic construction, which is described for extensive periods of time.[11] As a result, the semantic development of the constructions under analysis remains unclear. Furthermore, in the absence of large-scale lemmatized databases, the older studies do not present any statistical data but rely entirely on a qualitative analysis, which gives their accounts an impressionistic outlook.

Fourth, I attempt to complement earlier investigations into Greek periphrasis with recent findings in diachronic linguistics. From a historical point of view, most earlier work on periphrasis was written before there was renewed interest in diachronic linguistics in the 1970s and 1980s. Since then, scholars have greatly enhanced our understanding of linguistic change. By applying these recent insights, we can not only refine the findings of some of the older studies, but also contribute to other issues that are currently under debate in diachronic linguistics, especially in the subfield of diachronic typology (cf. Cook 2012). As Haspelmath (1992: 187) among others observes, Ancient Greek, because of its long history of written sources, provides a unique opportunity for diachronic linguistic research.

---

[10] Especially when it comes to Post-Classical and Byzantine Greek.
[11] Dietrich (1973a: 189-232), for example, categorizes εἰμί with the present participle under the heading of 'Winkelschau' (which can be compared to progressive aspect), limiting his treatment to an enumeration of examples from Homer to the tenth century AD.

Introduction 5

In summary, these are the general research questions that I aim to answer:

1. Which constructions in Ancient Greek that consist of a finite and a non-finite verb (participle) qualify as 'periphrastic', and on the basis of which criteria?
2. What validity does the notion of 'adjectival periphrasis' have, and how should it be related to 'verbal periphrasis'?
3. What does the diachronic development of periphrastic constructions formed with εἰμί and ἔχω from Archaic to Early Byzantine Greek look like?
4. What can the study of periphrastic constructions formed with εἰμί and ἔχω in Ancient Greek contribute to current diachronic research, especially as regards typology?

0.3 PREVIOUS RESEARCH

When it comes to verbal periphrasis formed with εἰμί and/or ἔχω,[12] there are three foundational studies: the doctoral theses by Björck (1940), Aerts (1965), and Dietrich (1973a). Björck (1940) and Dietrich (1973a) are mainly concerned with the construction of εἰμί with the present participle; Björck focuses specifically on the evidence from the New Testament. Aerts (1965), on the other hand, discusses constructions formed with both εἰμί and ἔχω, ranging 'from Homer up to the present day'. All three studies address the definition of verbal periphrasis, and its relationship to 'adjectival' periphrasis.

Besides these three seminal works, a number of books and articles have appeared during the nineteenth and more so the twentieth centuries, most of which concentrate on the construction of εἰμί with the present participle in a particular author/corpus. These studies include those of Barbelenet (1913: 84–94), Rosén (1957), Gonda (1959), and Rydbeck (1969) on Herodotus, Verboomen (1992) on the Septuagint, and Regard (1918: 109–85), Hartman (1963), and Porter (1988, 1989: 441–92, 1999: 20–49) on the New Testament. Pouilloux (1957) treats the combination of ἔχω with the aorist participle in

---

[12] For an overview of research on participial periphrasis more generally, see Bentein (2012a).

6   *Verbal Periphrasis in Ancient Greek*

Sophocles. Various studies have also appeared that enumerate periphrastic examples,[13] most importantly Laroche (1893: 161–73, 218–20, 230), Kontos (1898), and Harry (1905, 1906). In recent years, there has been renewed interest in the subject of verbal periphrasis. One issue that has received much attention is the role of language contact in the history of the Greek periphrasis, a topic that was first engaged by Coseriu (e.g. 1971, 1977) and his disciple Dietrich (1973a, 1973b). Relevant recent studies in this area are Evans (2001) (on Greek and Hebrew), Amenta (2003) (on Greek and Latin), Drinka (2003a, 2003b, 2007) (on Greek, Latin, and the European languages), and Bruno (2012) (on Greek and Latin). Another element that has received significant attention is the analysis of verbal periphrasis within Grammaticalization Theory, a framework that will also be referred to in the present study. The works of Moser (1988), Amenta (2003), and Giannaris (2011b) engage with this topic.

0.4 DATA COLLECTION AND PRESENTATION

Since my aim is to present an in-depth analysis of verbal periphrasis with εἰμί and ἔχω, I shall concentrate on the period from the eighth century BC to the eighth century AD, rather than from 'Homer up to the present day', as Aerts (1965) did. For organizational purposes, this period can be further subdivided[14] into Archaic Greek (VIII–VI BC), Classical Greek (V–IV BC), Early Post-Classical Greek (III–I BC), Middle Post-Classical Greek (I–III AD), Late Post-Classical Greek (IV–VI AD), and Early Byzantine Greek (VII–VIII AD).[15] I have chosen to cut off the investigation at the eighth century AD for two reasons. First, owing to the Arab presence in Egypt and the production of less costly writing materials such as paper, Greek documentary papyri cease to be found after this date. In comparison with earlier periods, literary texts are also less frequently produced,[16] especially

---

[13] Mostly of εἰμί with the perfect participle.
[14] The subdivision of the Post-Classical period in an 'early', 'middle', and 'late' period is based on a suggestion by Lee (2007: 113) (cf. also Evans & Obbink 2010: 12).
[15] As the analysis showed a large degree of similarity between Late Post-Classical and Early Byzantine Greek, it was decided, for reasons of space, to discuss these two periods under one and the same heading.
[16] Cf. Markopoulos (2009: 87–8).

Introduction 7

lower-register ones such as chronicles and hagiographical texts,[17] which can be connected to the so-called 'Dark Age'.[18] On the other hand, the obsolescence of the participle[19] obviated further development of participial periphrastic constructions in the Byzantine period.[20] This gradual process affected the perfect, present, and aorist active participles in particular, as well as the aorist passive participle, which were being reduced to indeclinable forms, functioning adverbially.

Particularly with regard to the Post-Classical and Byzantine period, scholars have stressed the need to limit ourselves to 'authentic', spoken-like texts, in an attempt to 'reconstruct' the spoken language.[21] Such a view, however, entails a number of methodological difficulties: among others, the spoken language is likely to have varied considerably, and probably made use of archaisms just as literary idioms did. Moreover, any 'reconstruction' of the spoken language must necessarily remain approximate. Therefore, I propose that we approach Ancient Greek as a 'corpus language',[22] and try to acquire a comprehensive image of the variation that occurs in our written sources, including high-register texts.[23] With that in mind, I compiled a 'register-balanced'[24] corpus of texts,[25] which is as representative as possible of the different linguistic levels encountered in our written sources.

The corpus, which comprises about ten million words, was analysed for periphrastic constructions formed with εἰμί and ἔχω by means of two online lemmatized databases, the *Thesaurus Linguae Graecae* (TLG) and the *Duke Databank of Documentary Papyri* (DDBDP).[26] I focused specifically on combinations of εἰμί and ἔχω with the

---

[17] See e.g. Horrocks (1997: 179): 'after the disruption of the seventh and eighth centuries, however, a general stylistic elevation set in, facilitated by the collapse of literacy among the wider population.'
[18] Cf. Eftymiadis (2011: 96) with regard to hagiography.
[19] See further §3.4.1.   [20] See e.g. Horrocks (2010: 181-3).
[21] See e.g. Browning (1983: 4-5), and specifically with regard to the Greek verb, Mirambel (1966: 169-70) and Moser (1988: 17).
[22] Cf. Fleischman (2000).
[23] For a similar approach, see e.g. Manolessou (2008); James (2008); Horrocks (2010); Lee (2013).
[24] Cf. O'Donnell (2000).
[25] See appendix for an overview of the literary sources.
[26] These databases can be found online at <http://stephanus.tlg.uci.edu> and <http://www.papyri.info>. The DDBDP has been updated since my own research in 2009-10.

perfect, present, and aorist participles: as a number of scholars have noted, εἰμί and ἔχω are almost never used periphrastically with a future participle,[27] since tense in periphrastic verbal constructions is marked on the finite verb, rather than on the participle.[28] An Excel file containing an overview of my findings is available from the OUP catalogue webpage for this title at <http://www.oup.com>. This file consists of six spreadsheets, one for each historical period.

Unlike older scholarship, the present study combines qualitative and quantitative approaches: I provide considerable statistics throughout. The statistical data presented in the following chapters are twofold in nature. First, the tables contain purely formal data with regard to tense, voice, mood, etc. In order to be able to compare frequency and productivity of periphrastic constructions across authors, genres, and periods, most tables also contain a 'normed rate of occurrence' (NRO),[29] which indicates the number of instances per 10,000 words, and a 'type-token ratio' (TTR), which specifies the ratio of the number of different non-finite verbs (the 'types') to the *total* number of non-finite verbs (the 'tokens') appearing in each construction.[30] The examples referred to in these tables can be considered either unquestionably periphrastic or very likely to be so on contextual grounds.[31] This does not mean, however, that all combinations of εἰμί or ἔχω with a present, perfect, or aorist participle are always clearly periphrastic:[32] diachronic research has shown that ambiguity plays an integral part in linguistic change in general,[33] and this is certainly also the case with verbal periphrasis in particular. Second, the tables contain

---

[27] Some exceptional examples can nevertheless be found. See e.g. Björck (1940: 88); Aerts (1965: 60).

[28] Cf. Duhoux (2000: 295); Campbell (2008: 33).

[29] Normed rate of occurrence does not concern the papyri, as the DDBDP does not mention the number of words for each papyrus. To get a rough image of the number of papyri per period studied, we can rely on the study of Habermann (1998) (see further Dickey 2003), according to whom the Early Post-Classical papyri represent 20% of the total number of papyri, the Middle Post-Classical ones almost 50%, the Late Post-Classical ones 23%, and the Early Byzantine ones only 7%.

[30] For example, if in a given century εἰμί with the present participle would be attested fifty times with thirty different verbs, the type-token ratio would be 30/50 or 0.6.

[31] With 'context' is meant here both the sentential and discourse context.

[32] On periphrasis and ambiguity (from a synchronic point of view), see e.g. Björck (1940: 13–6, 89–95); Aerts (1965: 7–12); Karleen (1980: 125–31); Fanning (1990: 311); Bailey (2009: 194–206).

[33] See e.g. the four-stage model by Marchello-Nizia (2006: 261).

Introduction 9

functional information—that is, the different aspectual functions of a given construction. While the inclusion of this type of information is crucial to capturing the process of diachronic change that the different constructions underwent, it may wrongly suggest that the difference between aspectual categories such as 'stative' and 'progressive' is self-evident. While this is often the case, it is certainly not always so. Hundreds of examples are therefore discussed *in extenso*, and the factors that suggest a certain aspectual interpretation are explicitly indicated and situated within a larger theoretical framework.

0.5 GENERAL OUTLINE

This study consists of five chapters. In the first chapter, I introduce a number of theoretical concepts that are necessary for a good understanding of what follows. These include (a) the motivation for periphrasis, (b) genre and register, (c) aspect, and (d) grammaticalization (theory). In the second chapter, the concepts of 'verbal' and 'adjectival' periphrasis are discussed, as well as their interrelationship. After an overview of previous research, an alternative approach is presented, whereby it is noted that Grammaticalization Theory, the framework that is used for the diachronic analysis, also has relevance to evaluations of synchrony. In Chapters 3 and 4, which constitute the centrepiece of this book, I investigate the diachrony of periphrastic constructions with εἰμί and ἔχω from the Archaic to Early Byzantine period, first with respect to the functional domain of perfect aspect (§3), and afterwards with respect to that of imperfective aspect (§4). In these chapters, I focus primarily on the functional aspects of grammaticalization, applying in particular the notions of 'grammaticalization path' and 'transitivity' to the diachronic analysis. In the fifth and final chapter, I discuss periphrases in the domain of perfective aspect, as well as how these constructions fit into the overall development of verbal periphrasis during the period under analysis.

1

Theoretical Background

> One objection that I have against many studies of aspect in Ancient Greek is that Ancient Greek is focused upon exclusively, and no reference is made to any other languages. Hellenists have a tendency to act as if verbal aspect is a phenomenon absolutely unique to Ancient Greek, which is the case for only a few minor issues.
>
> (Slings 1988: 66, originally in Dutch)

1.1 INTRODUCTION

In this first chapter, I discuss some of the theoretical concepts that lie at the heart of the present study: (a) the factors that motivate the choice to use a periphrastic form (§1.2); (b) the relevance of 'register' and 'genre' (§1.3); (c) how 'aspect' can be conceived of (§1.4); and (d) how language change takes place (§1.5). Obviously, these are very broad topics. As such, it lies beyond the scope of this book to provide an exhaustive overview of present and past discussions of these issues. Rather, the main purpose is briefly to introduce the framework within which I conducted the analysis.

1.2 FACTORS MOTIVATING THE USE OF PERIPHRASIS

Unlike in some languages, such as English and the Modern Romance languages, most periphrastic constructions in Ancient Greek are not compulsory and are used alongside synthetic forms. What motivates

12 Verbal Periphrasis in Ancient Greek

the choice for one or the other has been, as Rijksbaron (2002: 127) notes, a contentious issue. The standard account by Aerts (1965: 3) addresses the issue by distinguishing three main types of periphrasis: (a) substitute periphrasis, 'when the periphrasis replaces a monolectic form without any, or scarcely any distinguishable change in meaning'; (b) suppletive periphrasis, 'when the periphrasis is used to replace a non-, or no longer extant, monolectic form'; and (c) expressive periphrasis, 'when the periphrasis appears to be used with a special purport'. This typology, however, which is still followed in modern discussions of periphrasis,[1] has its disadvantages: (a) the category of 'substitute' periphrasis appears to be rather subjective: how is one to know whether there is no change in meaning?; (b) the category of 'suppletive' periphrasis assumes that periphrasis can only become obligatory in the domain of morphology, but the example of English periphrases formed with 'do', which is obligatory for certain questions and negations, shows that this is not necessarily the case; (c) the category of 'expressive' periphrasis leaves unspecified with what kind of 'special purpose' a periphrastic form could be used.

In what follows, I supply an alternative approach which concentrates to a greater extent on the different linguistic levels at which the motivation for periphrasis may be situated, that is, morphology, syntax, semantics, and pragmatics.[2]

1.2.1 Morphology

The most obvious case of periphrasis motivated at the morphological level is when it replaces a no longer existing synthetic form (i.e. what Aerts calls 'suppletive' periphrasis), as in (1):[3]

(1) δεῖ τοίνυν ὑμᾶς κἀκεῖνο σκοπεῖν, ὅτι πολλοὶ τῶν Ἑλλήνων πολλάκις εἰσὶν ἐψηφισμένοι τοῖς νόμοις χρῆσθαι τοῖς ὑμετέροις (Dem. 24.210)
'You ought also to consider this point, that many Hellenic nations have often resolved by vote to adopt your laws.' (tr. Murray)[4]

---

[1] See e.g. the recent overview-article by Haspelmath (2000: 656).
[2] For the possible factors motivating periphrasis, compare García-Hernández (1980) with regard to Latin, and from a cross-linguistic point of view, van der Auwera (1999) and Jäger (2006).
[3] Here and in the remainder of this book, periphrastic forms (including ambiguous examples) are underlined for the sake of clarity.
[4] Translations are my own unless otherwise indicated.

While some synthetic perfect forms exist of the verb ψηφίζομαι 'I vote' (such as ἐψήφισται in Dem. 19.288), no such form was available in the third person plural.[5]

In other cases, periphrasis can be considered an 'avoidance' strategy, for example, when the synthetic form is morphologically complex (e.g. the medio-passive perfect imperative).[6] In poetry, periphrasis can also be adopted because it fits the metre better than the synthetic alternative, as in (2):

(2) {Πη.} ὦ μοῖρα, γήρως ἐσχάτοις πρὸς τέρμασιν / οἷα με τὸν δύστηνον ἀμφιβᾶσ' ἔχεις (Eur., Andr. 1081-2)
'Peleus. Ah fate, how you have overwhelmed me, unhappy man that I am, on the farthest edge of old age!' (tr. Kovacs)

As Aerts (1965: 140) notes, synthetic ἀμφιβέβηκας does not fit the iambic trimeter, which is overcome by using the periphrastic form ἀμφιβᾶσ' ἔχεις 'you have overwhelmed'.

Similarly, Björck (1940: 32-3) observes that periphrastic forms may be preferred to their synthetic alternative in order to avoid hiatus.[7] Consider the following example:

(3) τοιοῦτόν που πρέπον ἂν εἴη καὶ περὶ τὰς τοιαύτας ᾠδὰς γιγνόμενον, καὶ δὴ καὶ στολή γέ που ταῖς ἐπικηδείοις ᾠδαῖς οὐ στέφανοι πρέποιεν ἂν οὐδ' ἐπίχρυσοι κόσμοι, πᾶν δὲ τοὐναντίον, ἵν' ὅτι τάχιστα περὶ αὐτῶν λέγων ἀπαλλάττωμαι (Pl., Leg. 800e)
'Such music would also form the fitting accompaniment for hymns of this kind; and the garb befitting these funeral hymns would not be any crowns nor gilded ornaments, but just the opposite, for I want to get done with this subject as soon as I can.' (tr. Bury)

Quite noticeably, Plato uses a periphrastic form for the third person singular (instead of synthetic πρέποι ἄν, where two vowels come together), and a synthetic form for the third person plural.[8]

---

[5] See further §3.3.1.
[6] In the sense of its being infrequently used.
[7] On (the avoidance of) hiatus in prose, see e.g. Dover (2003: 703-4).
[8] Note that other factors may have motivated the choice for periphrasis in this case, since Plato could have simply written τοιοῦτόν που ἂν πρέποι. In any case, hiatus avoidance is typical for the later dialogues (see e.g. Brandwood 1990, ch. 17 (discussing the work of G. Janell)).

1.2.2 Syntax

The choice for periphrasis may also be situated at the level of syntax. For example, an author might use periphrasis in order to maintain coordination with one or more adjectives.[9] Consider example (4) in this regard:

(4) ἡ δὲ Ἱπποδάμεια ἡ καὶ Βρισηὶς <u>ἦν</u> μακρή, λευκή, καλλίμασθος, εὔστολος, σύνοφρυς, εὔρινος, μεγαλόφθαλμος, κεχολλαϊσμένα <u>ἔχουσα</u> βλέφαρα, οὐλόθριξ, ὀπισθόκομος, φιλόγελως, <u>οὖσα ἐνιαυτῶν κα</u>' (Jo. Mal., *Chron.* 101.16-9)

'Hippodameia Briseis was tall, fair-skinned, with beautiful breasts, a good figure, eyebrows that met, a good nose, large eyes with painted eyelids, and curly hair which was combed back; she was fond of laughing, and she was twenty-one years old.' (tr. Jeffreys *et al.*)

In this long description, various adjectives are used to characterize the (beautiful) appearance of Briseis. Two properties are not typically expressed by adjectives, her having painted eyelids (κεχολλαϊσμένα ἔχουσα βλέφαρα) and being twenty-one years old (οὖσα ἐνιαυτῶν κα'), but these are also included in the enumeration through the use of participles (instead of using separate sentences with main verbs).

Also attested is the coordination of multiple participles forming periphrastic combinations. In (5), for example, the present and the perfect participle are both combined with the verb ἦσαν:

(5) συνιδών τε ἦλθεν ἐπὶ τὴν οἰκίαν τῆς Μαρίας τῆς μητρὸς Ἰωάννου τοῦ ἐπικαλουμένου Μάρκου, οὗ <u>ἦσαν</u> ἱκανοὶ <u>συνηθροισμένοι</u> καὶ <u>προσευχόμενοι</u> (Acts 12.12)

'Thinking about that, he came to the house of Mary, the mother of John whose surname was Mark, where many were gathered together and were praying.' (WEB)

In this example, the use of (ἦσαν) συνηθροισμένοι '(they were) gathered' must have been motivated at the morphological level, while (ἦσαν) προσευχόμενοι '(they were) praying' appears to be motivated at the syntactic level.

Recently, Hauspie (2011: 127) has suggested that periphrasis (especially with the present participle) 'disconnects the verb from its

---

[9] Cf. Björck (1940: 32); Aerts (1965: 17).

Theoretical Background 15

complements, thus emphasizing the verb'. Kahn (1973: 137) similarly stresses the 'stativizing' effect of periphrasis with εἰμί,[10] noting that 'even verbs that are formally transitive may be used periphrastically without an expressed object', as in (6):

(6) δεινῶς ἀθυμῶ μὴ <u>βλέπων</u> ὁ μάντις <u>ᾖ</u> (Soph., *OT* 747)
'I fear the prophet may not be blind after all.' (tr. Kahn)

As Kahn (1973: 137) observes, the omission of the object serves to focus attention on the subject of the construction, that is, the blind seer Teiresias. While there indeed seems to be an interesting connection between valence reduction and periphrasis, it must be stressed that this is only the case in particular circumstances,[11] which will be further explored in Chapters 2 and 4.

1.2.3 Semantics

The semantic difference between synthetic and periphrastic forms has been the subject of much discussion. Several scholars have suggested that a periphrastic form may be more 'emphatic' in one way or another. Rijksbaron (2002: 127), for example, notes with regard to example (6) that periphrasis may suggest a subtle difference in conceptualization, the participle bringing forward the adjective-like quality of βλέπω 'I see' to a greater extent. Kühner & Gerth (1976 [1898]: 38) similarly find a greater emphasis in a progressive form such as δρῶν... ἦν 'he was doing' (uttered by Agamemnon, in defense of his words to Teucer):[12]

(7) {Αγ.} ἤκουσεν αἰσχρά· <u>δρῶν</u> γὰρ <u>ἦν</u> τοιαῦτ' ἐμέ (Soph., *Aj.* 1324)
'Agamemnon. He heard shameful words, because his acts towards me were shameful.' (tr. Lloyd-Jones)

Other scholars, however, have criticized the subjectivity inherent in the notion of verbal emphasis in cases such as these.[13] In this context,

---

[10] Compare the observations by Risselada (1987: 128–32) on the middle voice.
[11] Contrast Hauspie (2011: 139): 'such periphrases [with the present participle, KB]...*always* highlight the verb by dissociating it from its complements' (my emphasis).
[12] On this particular example, cf. similarly Hilhorst (1976: 72).
[13] See e.g. Coseriu (1975: 11): 'es muß darauf hingewiesen werden, daß der Rückgriff auf "Emphase" ein beliebtes Mittel ist, wenn die genaue Bestimmung

Rosén (1957, 1975, 1987, mostly focusing on Herodotus) has drawn attention to the connection that seems to exist between periphrasis and constituent focus[14] in many instances.[15] Consider the following example:

(8) ἥντινα δὲ γλῶσσαν ἵεσαν οἱ Πελασγοί, οὐκ ἔχω ἀτρεκέως εἰπεῖν... εἰ τούτοισι τεκμαιρόμενον δεῖ λέγειν, ἦσαν οἱ Πελασγοὶ βάρβαρον γλῶσσαν ἱέντες (Hdt. 1.57.1-2)

'What language the Pelasgians spoke I cannot say definitely... if, as I said, one may judge by these, the Pelasgians spoke a language which was not Greek.' (tr. Godley)

In 1.57.1, what language the Pelasgians spoke is established as a topic. In 1.57.2, the narrator concludes that it was not Greek, but a barbarian tongue. As Rosén (1957: 147) notes, in 1.57.2, where the speaking of a language is backgrounded and focus lies on βάρβαρον 'barbarous', a periphrastic form is used (ἦσαν... ἱέντες 'they were speaking'), while this is not the case in 1.57.1 (ἵεσαν). While Rosén suggests considering (non-suppletive) periphrasis a dedicated constituent-focus device, Gonda (1959) and Rydbeck (1969) have shown that this view is too strong, and cannot account for all instances.

1.2.4 Pragmatics

Recent studies have stressed the importance of the pragmatic level of grammar in accounting for the use of periphrasis. In the Septuagint, for example, in many cases the choice for a periphrastic construction seems to be motivated by the presence of a similar construction in the Hebrew original.[16]

---

einer besser definierten Funktion nicht gelingen will' ('it must be noted that reference to "emphasis" is typical when the precise determination of a better defined function is unsuccessful').

[14] There are three main types of focus structure (see e.g. Bailey 2009 with regard to Ancient Greek): constituent focus (as in '[it's not the cat that smells] *The dog* smells'), sentence focus (as in '*There once was a princess*') and predicate focus (as in '[remember Anna?] She *went to a concert*').

[15] As one of the reviewers notes, the connection between periphrasis and information structure could also be discussed under the heading of pragmatics (§1.2.4).

[16] See further §4.4.2.

Theoretical Background

Register[17] can also often be related to the presence of a particular periphrastic form. Consider example (9):

(9) μή τῳ δὲ χαλεπὸν εἶναι δόξῃ, ὅτι τινὰς τῶν εἰρημένων αἱρέσεων ἢ ἀρχηγοὺς ἢ σπουδαστὰς γενομένους <u>ἐπαινέσας ἔχω</u> (Soz., H.E. 3.15.10)
'Let it not be accounted strange, if I have bestowed commendations upon the leaders or enthusiasts of the above-mentioned heresies.' (tr. Hartranft)

In this example, the historiographer Sozomenus (fifth century AD) uses ἔχω with the aorist participle, which, as Aerts (1965) among others has argued, had disappeared already in the fourth century BC. It seems likely that Sozomenus, who is known for his 'Atticizing' language,[18] uses this archaic construction in order to imitate the Classical authors.[19]

Those periphrastic forms that have been chosen in order to achieve a particular stylistic effect are also motivated by pragmatics. Conybeare and Stock (1995 [1905]: 68) refer to Plato in this regard, who in their opinion makes use of periphrastic forms 'for the sake of philosophical precision, and partly, it must be confessed because in his later style he preferred two words to one'. Ruijgh (1970: 76) similarly considers the occurrence of periphrastic forms in the work of Herodotus to be a sign of 'abundant style'. One clear pragmatic motivation for the use of periphrasis is to achieve variation,[20] which is evidenced by its appearing alongside a synthetic form:

(10) ὅπως, ἂν μὲν ὑμῖν ἑκατὸν δέῃ τριήρων, τὴν μὲν δαπάνην ἑξήκοντα τάλαντα <u>συντελῇ</u>, τριήραρχοι δ' ὦσι δώδεκα, ἂν δὲ διακοσίων, τριάκοντα μὲν ᾖ τάλαντα τὴν δαπάνην <u>συντελοῦντα</u>, ἐξ δὲ σώματα τριηραρχοῦντα, ἐὰν δὲ τριακοσίων, εἴκοσιν μὲν ᾖ τάλαντα τὴν δαπάνην <u>διαλύοντα</u>, τέτταρα δὲ σώματα τριηραρχοῦντα (Dem. 14.20)
'Thus, if you want a hundred war-galleys the cost of each will be covered by the sixty talents and there will be twelve trierarchs for each; if you want two hundred, there will be thirty talents to cover the cost and six persons

---

[17] On the notion of 'register', see further §1.3.
[18] See e.g. Treadgold (2007: 145–55).
[19] As we shall see in Chapter 3, similar forms can be found in authors such as Dionysius of Halicarnassus, Plutarch, Cassius Dio, etc.
[20] Cf. Björck (1940: 27), who refers to Hdt. 1.57.1–2 (our example (8)). Compare the use of nominal periphrasis (as in φυγὴν ποιέομαι for φεύγομαι) in order to achieve variation (Ros 1938: 129–30).

to serve as trierarchs; if you want three hundred, there will be twenty talents for the cost and four persons to serve.' (tr. Vince & Vince)

It seems quite clear here that Demosthenes strives after variation: first he uses synthetic συντελῇ 'it will cover', afterwards periphrastic ᾖ... συντελοῦντα, and in the third instance periphrastic ᾖ... διαλύοντα (with διαλύω instead of συντελέω).[21]

Finally, it is worth noting that the choice for periphrasis may also be motivated on the level of discourse. As noted by Luraghi (1995, esp. 373–9), in narrative texts, fronted verbs often organize the discourse by indicating important background information. A form of εἰμί in particular can often signal new participants or a new situation, as in (11):

(11) ἦσαν δὲ ἐν Ἰερουσαλὴμ κατοικοῦντες Ἰουδαῖοι, ἄνδρες εὐλαβεῖς ἀπὸ παντὸς ἔθνους τῶν ὑπὸ τὸν οὐρανόν (Acts 2.5)

'Now there were dwelling in Jerusalem Jews, devout men, from every nation under the sky.' (WEB)

In this case, ἦσαν... κατοικοῦντες 'they were dwelling' may have been chosen because it signals more clearly than synthetic κατῴκουν would have the existence of a situation that is novel to the discourse (Jews living in Jerusalem), which is highly relevant to what is to follow (note the use of English 'now'), that is, the hearing of a sound by these people and their being confused.[22]

In conclusion, the motivation for verbal periphrasis is complex. Crucially, in any given instance, multiple factors may motivate the choice for periphrasis, even if one of them can be considered the primary motivation. As such, periphrasis ought to be considered a 'multi-purpose' or 'multi-functional' phenomenon. From a diachronic point of view, the primary motivation for periphrasis can, of course, change: for example, it may be situated at the semantic level first (being used for its expressive force), and afterwards at the morphological level (having come to replace synthetic forms).

---

[21] As one of the reviewers notes, this example could also be explained in terms of Rosén's argument focus hypothesis: first the topic of costs is established; the subsequent clauses are about the specific costs.

[22] γενομένης δὲ τῆς φωνῆς ταύτης συνῆλθεν τὸ πλῆθος καὶ συνεχύθη (Acts 2.6) 'when this sound was heard, the multitude came together, and were bewildered' (WEB).

1.3 REGISTER AND GENRE

1.3.1 Introduction

Given the considerable attention that I dedicate to the notion of 'register' in this study, it is worth further clarifying the concept, and specifying how it can be applied to the corpus under study.

With the establishment of sociolinguistics as a discipline in the second half of the twentieth century, it has come under renewed attention that language both in its spoken and written forms is not homogeneous: rather, variation is ubiquitous.[23] According to one influential linguistic model,[24] language can be connected to its social context by taking into account three main 'vectors of context', that is, *field* (concerning the nature of the social activity, e.g. 'science'), *tenor* (concerning the interactants and their social relation, e.g. 'close friends') and *mode* (concerning the ways in which interactants come in contact, e.g. 'written communication').[25] The term 'register' is used to denote a variety of language use according to one of these three vectors.

In what follows, I shall attempt to situate the various texts that are under investigation in relation to each other in terms of register, indicating along the way a number of typical linguistic characteristics *other than* verbal periphrasis.[26] The tenor vector is of particular importance in this regard, since the mode of discourse remains relatively stable (that is, written communication), and the field of discourse mainly influences lexical, rather than grammatical, choice.[27] For practical purposes, we can distinguish between two larger periods ('Archaic/Classical Greek' and 'Post-Classical/Byzantine Greek')[28] and a number of traditional '(macro-)genres'.[29] As is often the case, some texts fall into

---

[23] See e.g. the seminal study by Weinreich *et al.* (1968).
[24] See e.g. Halliday (1978).
[25] Each of these vectors of context can be further subdivided into a number of dimensions, but this will not further concern us here.
[26] For the need for such a description, see Joseph (2009, esp. 198).
[27] Cf. Biber & Conrad (2009: 46).
[28] There are some noticeable differences between these two larger periods: (a) from a registerial point of view, the Post-Classical/Byzantine textual witnesses differ to a much greater extent—particularly when it comes to lower-register language, the evidence is scanty for Archaic/Classical Greek (cf. Jannaris 1897: 5; Dover 1987); (b) dialect plays a much more prominent role in the Archaic/Classical texts: each literary genre is typically associated with a specific dialectal group (e.g. oratory with the Attic dialect).
[29] Note, however, that 'documentary papyri' is not in itself a generic category.

a grey area, both chronologically and generically. Furthermore, within different genres and even texts, there are often also important linguistic differences.[30]

Previous studies on register in Ancient Greek, which have concentrated mostly on Post-Classical and Byzantine Greek,[31] have recognized a number of tenor-related registers and usually distinguish between three or four registers. Porter (1989: 152–3) and O'Donnell (2000: 277), for example, identify four registers: (a) 'vulgar' (e.g. papyri concerned with personal matters); (b) 'non-literary' (e.g. official business papyri, Epictetus); (c) 'literary' (e.g. Philo, Iosephus, Polybius); and (d) 'Atticistic' (e.g. Dionysius of Halicarnassus, Plutarch). This kind of typological work is at an early stage, however, and at present it remains unclear with what linguistic and contextual features these categories ought to be associated. With that in mind, I shall not explicitly refer to these pre-established and mutually exclusivizing categories of register, but rather to the notion of a register-continuum.[32]

1.3.2 Archaic/Classical Greek

1.3.2.1 Epic poetry[33]

Our oldest written texts[34] belong to the category of 'epic poetry', at the core of which lie the *Iliad* and *Odyssey*, which are traditionally ascribed to Homer (eighth century BC?), next to the cosmogonic and didactic epics known as the *Theogony* and *Works and Days*, which were composed by Hesiod (around 700 BC?). Additionally, we have the so-called *Homeric Hymns*, the longer of which were written between 650 and 400 BC.[35]

---

[30] See e.g. Rydbeck (1967: 24–5) with regard to the New Testament.

[31] See e.g. Jannaris (1897: 4); Browning (1978); Sevčenko (1981); Adrados (1981); Porter (1989: 152–3); O'Donnell (2000); Høgel (2002: 22–3); Horrocks (2007); James (2008); Markopoulos (2009). For Classical Greek, see Willi (2010).

[32] Compare e.g. Hudson (2000: 477); Biber & Conrad (2009: 33), and, with regard to Ancient Greek, Porter (1989: 152); Horsley (1994: 64); O'Donnell (2000: 277).

[33] While it would have been preferable to concentrate exclusively on prose, it is a remarkable fact of Ancient Greek literature that no prose texts can be found until the fifth century BC, while a poetical tradition developed at a much earlier stage (cf. Palmer 1980: 142). Note that early lyric and elegy are not further investigated in this study.

[34] Not including the Mycenaean tablets.   [35] Kirk (1985b: 111).

As Adrados (2005: 89) notes, the language of the *Iliad* and *Odyssey* is an artificial one, a 'Kunstsprache' that uses both Ionic and Aeolic elements, both archaisms and more recent forms.[36] This idiomatic hybridity can be connected in part with the oral background of the poems, more specifically the central importance of a fixed metre, which encourages the retention of archaic and extra-Ionic dialect forms that have convenient metrical properties.[37] Hesiod's epics and the *Homeric Hymns* follow the language of the *Iliad* and *Odyssey* closely, though attention has been drawn to some innovations.[38]

1.3.2.2 Drama

Greek drama was also composed in verse, but in a dialect different from that of epic poetry. In accordance with their subject, tragedy and comedy differ quite radically from each other from a linguistic point of view: while tragedy can be characterized by its elevated language, and is thereby positioned towards the right (that is, high-register) end of the register-continuum, comedy is often considered one of the main sources for 'colloquial' language in the Classical period. Some elements of elevated language in tragedy include the use of rare or unique words such as μελισσοτρόφος 'bee-nurturing', the use of abstract nouns in -μα (e.g. δούλευμα for δοῦλος 'slave'), the poetic plural (e.g. φόνοι 'murder'), the omission of the definite article, etc.[39] Examples of lower-register language in comedy (i.e. Aristophanes) are the tendency of diminutives to replace the base word (e.g. ἀδελφίδιον for ἀδελφός 'brother'), the use of prepositional phrases instead of cases, the use of the sigmatic future next to the contract form (e.g. βαλλήσομεν next to βαλοῦμεν 'we will throw'), parataxis instead of hypotaxis, etc.[40] It should be noted, however, that in tragedy, too, one finds instances of 'colloquial' language, for example, with characters of lower social status. Similarly, in comedy, higher-register language (e.g. tragic and epic) is often parodied.

---

[36] Two typical archaisms are the optionality of the augment in preterite forms and the incomplete use of the demonstrative pronoun as the definite article (Hackstein 2010: 405).
[37] Cf. Horrocks (2010: 45-6). As one of the reviewers remarks, however, a fixed metre may also further the creation of new forms to fit it.
[38] See e.g. Adrados (2005: 98-9).   [39] See e.g. Rutherford (2010: 442-8).
[40] See e.g. López Eire (1986).

1.3.2.3 Historiography

The first substantial prose texts are attested only in the fifth century BC. These first prose texts, including historiography as well as scientific prose, were written in the Ionic dialect (Herodotus). Later on, this was extended to Attic (Thucydides, Xenophon), following the military and material success of Athens. Already in antiquity, the language of Herodotus was contrasted with that of Thucydides, especially with respect to syntax: while Herodotus often uses relatively simple sentences, characterized by parataxis ('λέξις εἰρομένη'), Thucydides often writes long and complex sentences, with much more subordination ('λέξις ἐστραμμένη').[41] Thucydides' language is also characterized by other high-register features such as the present/past perfect endings -αται/-ατο, abstract nouns in -μα, nominal periphrases, the choice of archaic words, and the use of ὅπως rather than ἵνα.[42] It should be noted, however, that Herodotus' idiom tends to vary according to context: in direct discourse, for example, it may show poetic (i.e. Homeric) influence.[43] As for Xenophon, it has been noted that his language seems to lie toward the left (low-register) end of the register-continuum.[44] This is the case not only for his vocabulary,[45] but also in terms of morphology and syntax: he uses a number of innovative forms that will reappear in Koine texts.[46]

1.3.2.4 Scientific prose

Like the earliest historiographic texts, early scientific prose is written in the Ionic dialect, although Attic forms do show up. One of the first specialized scientific languages is medical language, which is well attested in the so-called 'Hippocratic corpus', a heterogeneous collection of about sixty texts, most of which can be dated to the fifth and more so the fourth century BC.[47] As one might expect given the

---

[41] This may be related to a difference in composition/audience, on which see e.g. Bakker (2006: 109).
[42] See e.g. Rosenkranz (1930, esp. 168–70); Björck (1940: 109); Wille (1965: 686–7).
[43] Cf. Schick (1956: 357).   [44] See e.g. Gautier (1911: 142).
[45] Cf. Gautier (1911: 12).
[46] e.g. second aorists in -α, as in εἶπαν (Gautier 1911: 82).
[47] Note, however, that some texts are of a later date. See Jouanna (1992: 527–63) for a detailed overview of the texts and their date.

subject matter, a number of the texts included in this collection are written in a lower register, with little or no literary pretension.[48] In the *Epidemics*, for example, syntactic features such as unmarked change of subject, absence or infrequency of predicates and connecting particles, infrequency of articles, predominance of parataxis, use of a *nominativus pendens*, etc., indicate that we are dealing with 'brachylogic' language, intended for private use or for circulation among specialists.[49] Other texts, however, are more elaborate linguistically and were probably intended for a broader audience. Even within the *Epidemics*, one observes a tendency towards greater stylistic and syntactic organization, a feature which is taken to indicate an increasing awareness of a broader, perhaps literary-minded audience.[50]

1.3.2.5 Philosophical prose

'Philosophical prose' in this study refers to the work of two authors, Plato and Aristotle, both of whom wrote in the Attic dialect. Plato's works are mostly composed in the form of dialogues,[51] although he himself is never a participant. Various scholars refer to Plato's dialogues, especially the earlier ones, as a source for everyday language. One observes lexical items from the Attic vernacular (e.g. κανθήλιος 'pack-ass', ναυτιάω 'suffer from seasickness'), short paratactic sentences, frequent ellipsis, attenuative expressions (as in ἴσως ἂν οὖν εἴποι τις 'so perhaps one could say'), the use of interactive 'affective' language (e.g. ὦ μακάριε 'my dear sir', εἰπέ 'say', φέρε 'come', ἴθι δή 'come now', ὁρᾷς 'you see'), etc.[52] Many scholars note, however, that elsewhere Plato adopts higher-level language.[53]

While Aristotle is reported to have written dialogues, too, his surviving works mainly take the form of treatises, which have some affinity with what we have called 'scientific prose'. While

---

[48] Cf. Palmer (1980: 143).
[49] Cf. Thesleff (1966: 108–9); van der Eijk (1997: 102–6).
[50] Cf. van der Eijk (1997: 106).
[51] Some letters are attributed to Plato too. These have not been taken into account for this study.
[52] See e.g. Campbell (1894: 280–6); Trenkner (1960); Thesleff (1967: 63–6); Adrados (1992b).
[53] See e.g. Campbell (1894: 166); Sandbach (1985: 495). Thesleff (1967) distinguishes between as many as ten 'stylistic registers'.

some scholars have noted that Aristotle's works 'were not written to charm the ear',[54] others have detected the presence of both 'literary' and 'non-literary' styles in his writings.[55] Stevens (1936) has drawn attention to some interesting non-literary innovations in the works of Aristotle with regard to the use of prepositions, including a tendency to use 'improper' prepositions[56] and combinations of prepositions with adverbs, such as ἐπάνω 'above' + gen., ὑποκάτω 'under' + gen., ἕως 'up to' + gen., etc.

1.3.2.6 Oratory

Like philosophical prose, Classical oratory is considered a thoroughly 'Attic' genre. Adrados (2005: 155) characterizes the language of oratory as a 'middle language', which was neither vulgar nor poeticizing.[57] It must be stressed, however, that there are some major differences, not only between the different structural parts of the orations,[58] but also among the different types of oratory, that is, deliberative (or political), epideictic (or display), and forensic (or judicial).[59] Unsurprisingly, the language of epideictic oratory could be more elevated, as is illustrated by Isocrates' long, periodic sentences[60] and his choice of words. This may be contrasted with Lysias' language in his predominantly forensic speeches: relatively short sentences[61] and simple vocabulary. Demosthenes, on the other hand, employed both lower- and higher-register linguistic features, and he absorbs Lysian and Isocratean traits in what has been called a 'protean' way.[62] On occasions, Demosthenes even uses features reminiscent of comedy, such as animalic epithets, diminutives, and neologisms.[63]

---

[54] Long (1985: 531).
[55] According to Verdenius (1985), this may be due to the fact that he first expressed his ideas in lecture notes, which he continually worked up to a series of books (though he never completed the task).
[56] Stevens (1936: 215) defines improper prepositions as 'adverbs and nouns used as prepositions'.
[57] For an overview of the different orators' language-use, see Edwards (1994).
[58] Trenkner (1960: 2) points out that especially the narrative part, the *diegesis*, is linguistically less elevated.
[59] For an application of this tripartition, see e.g. Edwards (1994: 74–9).
[60] See Webster (1941: 409).   [61] See Webster (1941: 408).
[62] On Demosthenes' linguistic range, cf. Rowe (1983).
[63] See e.g. Ronnet (1951: 9–22); Rowe (1983: 177).

1.3.3 Post-Classical/Byzantine Greek

1.3.3.1 Documentary papyri

The value of the non-literary, documentary papyri for linguistic research has often been stressed,[64] because they allow us to study linguistic change in the lowest register. A few noteworthy examples include the interchange of η with ι and ει, the accusative ending -ν for consonantal stem nouns, the expansion of pronominal forms such as ἐμένα/ἐσένα 'me/you', the replacement of contract futures with sigmatic ones (e.g. καλέσω 'I will call', τελέσω 'I will pay'), the use of the accusative or genitive for the dative case, the loss of particles, etc.[65] It should be stressed, however, that documentary papyri do not constitute a linguistically homogeneous corpus;[66] scholars often distinguish between 'private' documents (e.g. private communications, records of transactions, documents of piety) and 'official documents' (e.g. petitions to officials, tax receipts, pronouncements of the government/administration).[67] Even in the case of private documents, the educational level of the individual authors varies considerably.[68]

1.3.3.2 Biography/hagiography

A broad range of texts is categorized under 'biography/hagiography' in this study, including *acts, apocalypses, encomia, gospels, homilies, miracles, laudations, lives,* and *passions.*[69] Many of these are written in a low register; they are aimed at a wider audience and often describe the lives of persons of low social standing.[70] Some characteristics include the use of parataxis instead of subordination, the use of the active voice instead of the middle, the omission of the optative, confusion of the endings of the imperfect and aorist (e.g. ἐλάλουσαν 'they talked'), and extension of the use of prepositions (e.g. ἐν 'in' with

---

[64] See e.g. James (2014).   [65] See e.g. Gignac (1985); Dickey (2009).
[66] Cf. Lee (1985: 9); Horsley (1994: 64–5); Bentein (2015b).
[67] Cf. Palme (2009).   [68] See Salonius (1927: 3).
[69] Compare Høgel (2002: 21).
[70] Cf. Høgel (2002: 25, 28). Note, however, that the authors of hagiographical texts did not necessarily come from the lower social strata. As Høgel notes (2002: 30), 'the social diversification of authors attested in hagiography is hardly matched in any other form of literature in late antiquity.'

an instrumental or causal force).[71] It should be noted, however, that especially in praise texts, such as encomia, homilies, and laudations, one finds more rhetorical elaboration. Thus, we can identify them as positioned more towards the right end of the register-continuum.[72] Moreover, the biographical genre was not immune to diachronic change: when Christianity became the Roman state religion in the fourth century AD, members of the elite, who, as Browning (1978: 108) puts it, had received a 'long and rigorous training in grammar and rhetoric', introduced the higher registers of their curriculum into Christian literature.[73] Lastly, it should be noted that the biographical work of Plutarch also falls under this category; his register is high.[74]

1.3.3.3 Historiography

As opposed to documentary papyri and the corpus of biographical and hagiographical texts, Post-Classical historiographic texts tended to be written in a high register, dealing as they did with glorious events of the past and being aimed at the well-educated men of the cultural and political elite.[75] Some typical linguistic characteristics include the use of the optative, the use of the dual, the preservation of the full paradigms of the future and perfect, the use of the classical participial construction with τυγχάνω in the sense of 'happen to be doing', etc.[76] As in §1.3.3.2, however, we can nuance our characterization. Under the umbrella of historiography, scholars usually distinguish[77] between more traditional historiographical works,[78] which, like the works of Herodotus and Thucydides, claim to give an impartial treatment of shorter, discrete periods of time, and so-called 'world chronicles' (also 'chronographies'),[79] which begin with the creation of the world and chronicle peoples and events up to the time of the

---

[71] See e.g. Ljungvik (1926); Ghedini (1937); Tabachovitz (1943).
[72] Cf. Høgel (2002: 22).
[73] As noted by Høgel (2002: 27), however, 'apart from the writings of the fourth-century fathers and high-style enkomia for translations of relics, examples of Greek high-style hagiographical writings from late antiquity are few.'
[74] Compare §1.3.3.3.   [75] See Adrados (2005: 196); Croke (2010).
[76] See e.g. Horrocks (2007).
[77] Rosenqvist (2007: 10–11) notes that a third type can be distinguished—that is, Church Histories.
[78] e.g. Zosimus' *New History*, Theophylact Simocatta's *Histories*.
[79] e.g. John Malalas' and Theophanes Confessor's *Chronography*; the *Chronicon Paschale*.

author, often with the purpose of showing how God is involved in historical events.[80] These world chronicles, which were written for a broader audience, were composed in a much less elevated language than the Atticizing histories of the Post-Classical period.

1.3.3.4 The Greek novel

Unlike the other Post-Classical and Byzantine genres, the surviving Greek novels come down to us almost solely from the period between the first and the fourth centuries AD. Like historiographical texts, the Greek novel was written in a linguistically high level, and was likely intended as 'lighter reading for the intelligentsia'.[81] Some noteworthy linguistic characteristics include the use of words and phrases from Classical authors, the use of the optative, the use of the preposition ἀμφί 'around' (which had disappeared in lower-level Greek), the use of the dual, deictic -ί, etc.[82] There seems, however, to be variation among the Greek novels; the work of Chariton in particular, who is the oldest of the novelists,[83] was not affected by Atticism and did employ lower-level language.[84] Scholars also stress the variation within individual novels: with regard to Longus' *Daphnis and Chloe*, for example, Hunter (1983: 84–98) notes that a contrast must be made between narrative passages 'written in a simple, apparently artless style' and ornate passages such as the prologue, the descriptions of the seasons, the description of Eros, etc.

1.3.3.5 Scientific prose

As in the Classical period, later scientific prose includes medical texts, next to mathematical and geographical ones. Scholars generally stress that these texts are not written in a high register,[85] and for obvious reasons: to some extent at least, they were intended for practical

---

[80] See e.g. Rosenqvist (2007: 10–13); Horrocks (2010: 223). Horrocks (2010: 223) notes that the distinction became blurred during the Iconoclastic period.
[81] Bowie (1985: 688).   [82] See e.g. Papanikolaou (1973).
[83] Bowie (1985: 684) dates Chariton's *Chaereas and Callirhoe* to the mid-first century BC/AD.
[84] Cf. Papanikolaou (1973); Bowie (1985: 685).
[85] See e.g. Browning (1978. 107, 110 11); Wifstrand (2005: 89). Rydbeck (1991: 196–7) notes that Atticism did have some impact on scientific prose. On Galen and Atticism, see Swain (1996: 56–63).

purposes.[86] In this context, Rydbeck (1967, 1991) compares the language of the biographical/hagiographical texts, papyri of a relatively decent level, and scientific prose. Some typical linguistic characteristics of what Horrocks (2007: 630–1) calls the 'official and scientific/technical level of writing' are the use of unclassical (technical) vocabulary, the use of the articular infinitive,[87] the use of ὅτι after verbs of thinking and perception (instead of the Classical accusative and infinitive/participle), quoted speech rather than a subordinate clause after verbs of saying, the use of the impersonal passive of the type 'it is said [that X]' (rather than Classical 's/he is said [to X]'), etc. Again, however, we see some differences among authors. Hutton (2005: 177), for example, stresses that Pausanias' language is 'not commonplace, colloquial or vernacular, nor does it conform to the dominant stylistic trends of the day'.[88] Instead, he seems to make a conscious effort to achieve novelty, using, among others, Herodotus as a model.[89]

To conclude, it should be noted that 'genre' itself can have an impact on the use of particular periphrastic forms. Smith (e.g. 2001, 2003), who has recently stressed the importance of micro-genres[90] or 'discourse modes' when it comes to the use of tense and aspect, argues that five main types can be distinguished: 'narrative', 'report', 'description', 'information', and 'argument'. The first three of these modes are temporal: they primarily introduce events that are ongoing (description) or concluded (narrative and report). The last two modes, on the other hand, are 'atemporal': they primarily consist of statives. While none of the macro-genres discussed limits itself to a single 'discourse mode', all of them tend to show preference for one mode of discourse.[91] For example, in scientific texts, 'information' tends to predominate, while in historiographical texts or novels, 'narrative' and 'description' are the main modes of discourse. Thus,

---

[86] See e.g. Rydbeck (1991: 195): 'the authors of technical prose wanted to communicate facts, describe things, argue for or against something; they have no literary pretensions.'

[87] That is, the infinitive preceded by an article; also called the 'substantivized' infinitive.

[88] Contrast Porter (1989: 153), who classifies Pausanias under the 'non-literary' register.

[89] Hutton (2005: 234) speaks of a 'new archaism'. On Pausanias' language, see further Strid (1976).

[90] I use the term 'micro-genre' since the level of analysis is typically the paragraph.

[91] Compare Smith (2001: 184).

unsurprisingly, while we find (present) stative forms more often in scientific texts, we see (past) progressive forms more often in historiography and the novel.

1.4 ASPECT

Ancient Greek aspect has been studied from many different perspectives, too many to outline here.[92] Generalizing, one could say that three main dimensions have been taken into account, which, following Halliday (1978), can be called 'ideational' (or 'semantic', concerning propositional content), 'textual' (concerning the organization of discourse), and 'interpersonal' (or 'expressive', concerning the social world, in particular the relationship between speaker/writer and hearer).[93] Since this study is primarily investigating the ideational dimension (more in particular the diachronic semantic development of periphrastic constructions), I shall not go further into the textual and interpersonal dimensions of aspect in this introductory chapter.[94]

Before discussing the ideational dimension of aspect in further detail, it is worth addressing two issues. As is well known, Ancient Greek grammatically encodes both tense and aspect in verb forms, as is shown in Table 1.1:[95]

Table 1.1. The aspecto-temporal system in Ancient (Classical) Greek

	Past	Present	Future
Imperfective	Imperfect	Present	Future
Perfective	Aorist	Ø	Future
Perfect	Past Perfect	Present Perfect	Future Perfect

---

[92] Online bibliographical overviews have been compiled by Robert Binnick (<http://www.utsc.utoronto.ca/~binnick/TENSE/OnGreek.htm>) and Michel Buijs (<http://vkc.library.uu.nl/vkc/antiquity/knowledgeportal/Wiki/A%20Bibliography%20of%20Ancient%20Greek%20Linguistics.aspx>). For a thoroughgoing discussion on the various definitions given in modern scholarship of the aspectual opposition in Ancient Greek, see Fanning (1990: 8–85).

[93] Compare Fleischman (1989, 1990).

[94] On these dimensions, see e.g. Rijksbaron (1988) and Bakker (1997). I further elaborate on the interplay between these dimensions in Bentein (2015a, 2016).

[95] Cf. Joseph (1987: 428–9).

It should be stressed, however, that languages that do not do the same (such as Dutch) do not lack aspect, as is implied by the oft-made distinction between 'aspectual' and 'non-aspectual' languages.[96] Maslov (1985: 16), for example, has argued that aspect can be expressed not only through morphological but also through lexical and syntactic information, and that different languages achieve aspect differently. Therefore, aspect should in the first place be approached from a *functional* rather than a *formal* point of view.[97]

A second, related issue concerns the subfunctions that will be discussed in each of the major aspectual domains, as, for example, perfect aspect, which can be subdivided into resultative [perfect] aspect and anterior [perfect] aspect. Some scholars have argued that such aspectual subdistinctions belong to the domain of pragmatics, rather than verbal semantics.[98] In my view, this is not a binary matter: frequent use of a given construction, be it periphrastic or integrated into the verb form, in a given context will lead to its association with this context, as a result of which contextual elements no longer need to be present in all cases; in other words, the construction itself will index the context. Thus, the distinction between semantics and pragmatics is a difficult one to make, especially for a corpus language such as Ancient Greek. For the sake of efficiency, I shall say that a verb/periphrastic construction has this or that aspectual function, but it should be kept in mind that the context may (still) make a rather important contribution.

1.4.1 Aspect and Temporality

The concept of 'aspect' has often been contrasted with that of 'tense' on the basis of the fact that only the latter is deictic (that is, referring to the

---

[96] Alternatively, Zhang (1995) speaks of languages that are 'aspectually prominent' or 'highly aspectual' (e.g. Chinese), versus those that are 'relatively non-aspectual' (e.g. German).
[97] Compare Brinton (1988: 52); Zhang (1995); Michaelis (1998: 16); Bohnemeyer & Swift (2004). With regard to Ancient Greek, see especially Friedrich (1974).
[98] See e.g. Porter (1989: 260–70); Olsen (1994: 77); Sicking & Stork (1996); Evans (2001: 27–8). Haspelmath (2003: 212) outlines three positions vis-à-vis the debate on aspect and multifunctionality—that is, the 'monosemist' position, the 'intermediate polysemist' position, and the 'polysemist' position. Depending on one's position, scholars discuss aspectual subdistinctions in terms of 'uses', 'values', 'interpretations', 'meanings', etc. I follow Haspelmath (2003) in using 'function' as a neutral term.

communicative situation). Aspect, on the other hand, is typically taken to involve 'different ways of viewing the internal temporal constituency of a situation'.[99] Nevertheless, as several scholars point out, an important similarity exists between tense and aspect, as both are principally involved with time, one of the major conceptual categories of the human mind. As Michaelis (1998: 1) observes, 'in studying tense and aspect, we focus on the set of linguistic devices used by the speakers of a given language to specify the temporal features of a situation'.

In what follows, I outline the temporal characteristics of the three main types of aspect, that is, imperfective aspect, perfective aspect, and perfect aspect. The illustrations given below all contain synthetic verb forms: periphrastic forms will be discussed in greater detail in the following chapters. As I noted above, I believe aspect should be approached from a functional, rather than formal, point of view, and I do not see the point of distinguishing between 'synthetic' and 'analytic' aspect, as Hewson (1997: 14) proposes; while synthetic and periphrastic constructions do not necessarily cover the same functional domain, in principle they can be described in terms of the same (cross-linguistically attested) aspectual categories.

1.4.1.1 Imperfective aspect

Imperfective aspect can be defined in terms of temporal 'unboundedness',[100] meaning that no explicit attention is paid to the boundary transition phases of the event. Three main subfunctions can be distinguished: 'progressive [imperfective] aspect', 'stative [imperfective] aspect', and 'habitual [imperfective] aspect'.

Progressivity describes an event that is in the midst of happening ('in progress'), for example, the event of eating in 'he was eating when she arrived'. As such, Bertinetto (1997: 223) considers progressive to be a prototypical exponent of ('unbounded') imperfective aspect. As many scholars have observed,[101] progressives generally do not occur with stative predicates (as in *I am knowing).[102] According to some scholars, this can be explained by the fact that progressive aspect

---

[99] Comrie (1976: 3).
[100] See e.g. Zhang (1995: 32); Boogaart (2004: 1174); Sasse (2006: 535); Croft (2012, ch. 3). Compare e.g. De Boel (1991: 393); McKay (1994: 29-30); Rijksbaron (2002: 1); Bary (2009: 11-13) with regard to Ancient Greek.
[101] See e.g. Comrie (1976: 35); Bybee et al. (1994: 126).
[102] See further §1.4.2.1.

'stativizes', as a result of which it would be superfluous with predicates that are already stative.[103] Other scholars believe that progressive aspect 'detelecizes' (i.e. removes their natural endpoint or 'telos') rather than stativizing.[104]

In recent cross-linguistic work,[105] a further distinction is made between two types of progressive aspect,[106] that is, 'focalized progressive aspect'[107] and 'durative progressive aspect'. Both types express an event that is ongoing, but with focalized progressives there is a temporal coherence relation of overlap[108] with another foregrounded event, with which it is narrowly connected.[109] Durative progressives, on the other hand, refer to an event that is not evaluated with regard to a single point in time and that typically occurs in a broad(er) time frame.[110] Consider the following two examples:

(12) ταῦτα δὲ αὐτῶν λαλούντων αὐτὸς ἔστη ἐν μέσῳ αὐτῶν καὶ λέγει αὐτοῖς, εἰρήνη ὑμῖν (Lk. 24.36)

'While they were saying these things, Jesus himself appeared in their midst and said to them, "peace be with you".'

---

[103] See e.g. Langacker (1995: 179).

[104] See e.g. Castelnovo (1993); Bertinetto (1997: 83).

[105] See Bertinetto (1995, 2000); Bertinetto *et al.* (2000).

[106] As Pusch (2003: 183) notes, in Italian there seems to be a specialization of periphrases in one of these subtypes of progressivity, *stare* + *gerund* being used for focalized progressivity, while *andare* + *gerund* is used for durative progressivity.

[107] The notion of 'focalized progressive' can be compared to that of 'Inzidenzschema'/'schème d'incidence' outlined in earlier publications (Pollak 1976; with regard to Ancient Greek, see Strunk 1971: 201; Hettrich 1976: 28), which is defined by Strunk (1971: 201) as follows: 'werden zwei Handlungen der Vergangenheit so miteinander in Beziehung gesetzt, daß die eine Handlung in den Ablauf der anderen hineinfällt, sie unterbricht oder ablöst, so liegt nach einem treffenden modernen Terminus ein "Inzidenzschema" vor' ('when two past actions are related to each other in such a way that one action occurs during the termination of the other, or when it interrupts or supersedes it, then we are dealing, according to a felicitous modern term, with an "incidence scheme"'). It should be noted, however, that the two notions are not entirely similar, as durative progressives can also be used in such an 'incidence' scheme (without there being strong semantic/pragmatic connectivity, however; see further Chapter 4).

[108] For different types of coherence relations, see esp. Givón (1995). Givón takes coherence to be a 'multi-strand' phenomenon: next to temporal coherence, he refers to *spatial coherence*, *thematic coherence*, and *referential coherence*.

[109] Intra-clausal coherence relations are often considered 'semantic' (or 'local'), while inter-clausal ones are considered 'pragmatic' (or 'global'). The distinction is somewhat arbitrary; with Givón (2001: 2.328) we can postulate a functional continuum ranging from (semantic) 'event integration' (e.g. 'I saw him reading') to (pragmatic) 'cross-event coherence' (e.g. 'I saw him there. He was reading').

[110] Cf. Bertinetto *et al.* (2000: 527).

(13) ἔτι παῖς ὤν, ὅτ' ἐπαιδεύετο καὶ σὺν τῷ ἀδελφῷ καὶ σὺν τοῖς ἄλλοις παισί, πάντων πάντα κράτιστος ἐνομίζετο (Xen., An. 1.9.2)
'While he was still a boy and was being educated with his brother and the other boys, he was regarded as the best of them all in all respects.' (tr. Brownson)

In (12), while the apostles are talking about the events that had happened, they are interrupted by the appearance of Jesus, who addresses them. Progressive λαλούντων 'while they were saying' is narrowly connected to foregrounded ἔστη 'he appeared' (and by extension λέγει 'he said'), which serves as what Bertinetto et al. refer to as a 'focalization point'. This can be contrasted with (13), where the event of being educated occurs in a broader time frame and there is no strict connection of this event with a single point in time. As Bertinetto et al. (2000: 565) note, examples of the second type are less often discussed in the literature on progressive aspect, perhaps under the influence of English, where the 'to be V-ing' construction is largely restricted to focalized progressivity. Depending on the type of verb that is used, durative progressives may convey a sense of iteration, though not necessarily.[111]

A second imperfective subtype is stative aspect, which refers to temporally stable events. The use of the term 'stative' as an aspectual category occurs somewhat less often than 'progressive',[112] since it is mostly used with reference to actionality.[113] It should be stressed, however, that there is not necessarily a one-to-one relationship between stative predicates and stative aspect, as shown in (14) and (15):

(14) οὐκ οἶδας ὅτι ἐξουσίαν ἔχω ἀπολῦσαί σε καὶ ἐξουσίαν ἔχω σταυρῶσαί σε (John 19.10)
'Don't you know that I have the power to let you go free or to nail you to a cross?' (CEV)

(15) πυνθανόμενος γὰρ τὸ ἄεθλον ἐὸν στέφανον ἀλλ' οὐ χρήματα, οὔτε ἠνέσχετο σιγῶν εἶπέ τε ἐς πάντας τάδε· «Παπαί, Μαρδόνιε, κοίους ἐπ' ἄνδρας ἤγαγες μαχησομένους ἡμέας, οἳ οὐ περὶ χρημάτων τὸν ἀγῶνα ποιεῦνται ἀλλὰ περὶ ἀρετῆς» (Hdt. 8.26.3)

---

[111] Cf. Bertinetto (1997: 227, fn. 8), and with regard to Ancient Greek Fanning (1990: 244-9).
[112] Compare e.g. Jones (1996: 140); Croft (2012: 149-52).
[113] See further §1.4.2.

'When he heard that the prize was not money but a crown, he could not hold his peace, but cried, "Good heavens, Mardonius, what kind of men are these that you have pitted us against? It is not for money they contend but for glory of achievement!"' (tr. Godley)

In both cases, the sentence expresses a situation that remains constant over time. However, while in (14) a predicate whose lexical semantic value is stative is used (i.e. ἔχω 'I have'), in (15) a non-stative ('dynamic') predicate is used (i.e. ποιέω 'I do'). Sentences of the latter type are often called 'gnomic' or 'generic'.[114]

A third and final subtype is habitual aspect, which expresses the repeated occurrence of an event over an extensive period of time, so much so that it becomes characteristic, mostly of the subject of the sentence. One such example is given in (16),[115] where the regularity of the event is reinforced by the frequency adverbial κατ᾽ ἔτος 'every year':

(16) καὶ ἐπορεύοντο οἱ γονεῖς αὐτοῦ κατ᾽ ἔτος εἰς Ἰερουσαλὴμ τῇ ἑορτῇ τοῦ πάσχα (Lk. 2.41)

'Every year the parents of Jesus went to Jerusalem for the Passover Festival.' (GNB)

It is worth noting that habituals can resemble both durative progressives and statives. To be more specific, habituals resemble durative progressives when the latter have an iterative character; however, as we shall discuss further in §4.4.1, habituals generally describe situations that are characteristic of extended periods of time, with greater emphasis on the temporal boundaries between the subevents. Habituals also resemble statives, in particular generics, as both can be considered to 'characterize' the subject: in (15), for example, the Greeks are assigned the trait, by way of understood habit, of fighting not for money but for glory, and in (16), the habitual nature of Jesus' parents' going to Jerusalem each year can be understood as a stable characterization of them. I follow Bertinetto (1997: 84, 88), who argues that habituals have an 'eventive' character (referring to specific occurrences), while generics/statives do not, at least explicitly; while in (16) the separate occasions of going to Jerusalem are singled out (κατ᾽ ἔτος), no information in (15) demarcates different occasions in which Greeks can be said to fight in the manner they are said to.

---

[114] See e.g. Rijksbaron (2002: 4-5) with regard to Ancient Greek.
[115] I borrow this example from Fanning (1990: 246).

1.4.1.2 Perfective aspect

Perfective aspect can be defined in terms of temporal boundedness,[116] meaning that explicit attention is paid to the boundary transition phases of the event (i.e. its beginning and end).[117] Again, a number of subfunctions can be distinguished, most importantly 'constative [perfective] aspect', 'ingressive [perfective] aspect', 'generic [perfective] aspect', and 'habitual [perfective] aspect'.

Most commonly, perfective aspect indicates the simple occurrence of an event, as in (17), a use that is known as 'constative':[118]

(17) καὶ ἐγὼ τοιαῦτα πεπυσμένος τῆς ἐπιούσης νυκτὸς διέπλευσα Μέγαράδε (Lys. 12.17)

'Thus apprised of his fate, I sailed across on the following night to Megara.' (tr. Jebb)

In some cases, sentences containing an aorist form may seem to express a perfect-like event,[119] as in (18):

(18) πάντα δ' ἠπίστατο τὰ ἐν τῷ ἱρῷ ὅσα λόγου ἦν ἄξια Ξέρξης, ὡς ἐγὼ πυνθάνομαι, ἄμεινον ἢ τὰ ἐν τοῖσι οἰκίοισι ἔλιπε, πολλῶν αἰεὶ λεγόντων, καὶ μάλιστα τὰ Κροίσου τοῦ Ἀλυάττεω ἀναθήματα (Hdt. 8.35.2)

'[Xerxes] who (as I have been told) knew of all the most notable possessions in the temple better than of what he had left in his own palace, and chiefly the offerings of Croesus son of Alyattes; so many had ever spoken of them.' (tr. Godley)

The Persians are about to plunder the temple at Delphi, intending to lay its wealth before Xerxes. Herodotus adds that Xerxes knew very

---

[116] See e.g. Zhang (1995: 32); Lindstedt (2001: 775); Boogaart (2004: 1174); Sasse (2006: 535); Croft (2012, ch. 3). Compare e.g. De Boel (1991: 393); McKay (1994: 30); Rijksbaron (2002: 1); Napoli (2006: 28-31); Bary (2009: 11-13) with regard to Ancient Greek.

[117] As Rijksbaron (2002: 2-3) notes, indicative of this semantic opposition between perfective and imperfective aspect is the fact that only the forms of the present stem can be combined with verbs meaning 'to interrupt', 'to stop' (as in παῦσαι σπεύδων τὰ σπεύδεις (Hdt. 1.206.1) 'stop striving after the things that you are striving after' (tr. Rijksbaron)), and that the adverb μεταξύ 'in the middle of' can only modify present stem forms (as in ἔπειτα ὁ Μενέξενος ἐκ τῆς αὐλῆς μεταξὺ παίζων εἰσέρχεται (Pl., Ly. 207b) 'Menexenos stepped in from the court, in the middle of his game' (tr. Rijksbaron)).

[118] See e.g. Fanning (1990: 255); Rijksbaron (2002: 28).

[119] Cf. Gildersleeve (1980 [1900-11]: 107-9); Mandilaras (1972: 14); Horrocks (2007: 627).

well of the notable possessions in the temple, even more so than of those he had left in his own palace. The verb ἔλιπε 'he had left' can be said to function as an anterior perfect,[120] expressing a past event with relevance at a later point in time (the time of knowing, and by extension the time of the Persians being about to plunder the temple). In such cases, scholars generally take it that the verb maintains its perfective value, and that the perfect-like value is a contextual effect (often triggered through subordination).[121]

When a predicate whose lexical-semantic value is stative is used, emphasis can only be put on the beginning, as illustrated in (19):

(19) ἐπισχόντες δὲ ἐν τούτῳ τῷ χώρῳ μέχρι μέσου ἡμέρης, τὸ ἀπὸ τούτου ἔπλεον ἐς Ἱστιαίην· ἀπικόμενοι δὲ τὴν πόλιν ἔσχον τῶν Ἱστιαιέων, καὶ τῆς Ἐλλοπίης μοίρης, γῆς δὲ τῆς Ἱστιαιώτιδος, τὰς παραθαλασσίας κώμας πάσας ἐπέδραμον (Hdt. 8.23.1)

'Here they waited till midday and then sailed to Histiaea. Upon their arrival they took possession of the Histiaeans' city and overran all the villages on the seaboard of the Ellopian region, which is a district belonging to Histiaea.' (tr. Godley)

While ἔχω typically has the stative value of 'I have, possess', in the aorist stem it comes to mean 'I take possession of'. This use is known as 'ingressive', and can be considered complementary to the former, constative use.

As with the imperfective aspect, perfective aspect can be used to express situations that remain constant over time. With perfective aspect this typically concerns generic/gnomic expressions of the type found in (20):[122]

(20) μεγάλοι δὲ λόγοι / μεγάλας πληγὰς τῶν ὑπεραύχων / ἀποτείσαντες / γήρᾳ τὸ φρονεῖν ἐδίδαξαν (Soph., Ant. 1350-3)

'The great words of boasters are always punished with great blows, and as they grow old teach them wisdom.' (tr. Lloyd-Jones)

The relationship between perfective aspect and gnomicity/genericity has been explained in a variety of ways. Gildersleeve (1980 [1900–11]: 109) draws the comparison between the gnomic/generic aorist and the definite article: 'a single specific instance is taken as typical of all such occurrences and thus gives expression to the

---

[120] See further §1.4.1.3. [121] See e.g. Keil (1963: 31-2).
[122] I borrow this example from Kühner & Gerth (1976 [1898]: 160).

general truth.'[123] According to de la Villa (2014: 384), this use can be seen as the result of an inference: 'if something happened in the past, it can happen again.'

Perfective aspect can also be used for habitually occurring events, as illustrated in (21):[124]

(21) πολλάκις γὰρ καὶ δεσπόται ὀργιζόμενοι μείζω κακὰ ἔπαθον ἢ ἐποίησαν (Xen., Hell. 5.3.7)
'For often even masters have, in rage, suffered more damage than they inflicted.' (tr. Rijksbaron)

This example can be compared with (16), where imperfective aspect was used to express a habitually occurring event. The difference between imperfective and perfective habitual aspect lies in the fact that with the latter the multiple occurrences are seen as a whole (focus lies on the 'macro-event'), with less attention to the individual events (the 'micro-events').[125] In addition, the imperfective aspect does not exclude the idea that the habitually occurring event is still going on.

1.4.1.3 Perfect aspect

There has been much discussion about the semantics of perfect aspect, some scholars even arguing that it does not constitute a third basic aspect.[126] In terms of boundedness, perfect aspect indeed constitutes an intermediate category. Perfects typically refer to both a bounded (past) event and the unbounded situation resulting from this event, and either of these components may be highlighted. When the unbounded situation is focused upon, perfects resemble imperfective aspect, while when the bounded event is focused upon, they

---

[123] See further Humbert (1972: 145-6); Bakker (2001: 18-23); Rijksbaron (2002: 31-3).
[124] I borrow this example from Rijksbaron (2002: 33). On the (diachronic) relationship between the 'generic' and the 'habitual' aorist, see Humbert (1972: 145-6); Rijksbaron (2002: 33).
[125] Cf. Bertinetto (1997: 205-8), and with regard to Ancient Greek Moorhouse (1982: 193-4); Fanning (1990: 258-9).
[126] See e.g. Evans (2001: 32), who considers it as 'a special type of imperfectivity'. Friedrich (1974: 19) and Olsen (1994: 321), on the other hand, classify it under perfective aspect. As I have argued before (Bentein 2014b), diachrony should be taken into account in discussions of this type (cf. also Moser 2008): as will be argued in Chapter 3, the semantics of the synthetic perfect changed quite dramatically throughout the history of Ancient Greek.

resemble perfective aspect. Rosemeyer (2012: 139) describes the semantic difference between these two main types, which are called 'resultative' and 'anterior' in the literature,[127] as follows:

> Resultatives and anteriors can thus be distinguished with regard to which part of a complex situation is highlighted. Whereas resultatives highlight the situation resulting from an event, anteriors highlight the event causing the situation.

In illustration, consider the following two examples:

(22) τότε δὴ τρίποδι βροτοὶ ἶσοι, / οὗ τ' ἐπὶ νῶτα ἔαγε, κάρη δ' εἰς οὖδας ὁρᾶται· / τῷ ἴκελοι φοιτῶσιν, ἀλευόμενοι νίφα λευκή (Hes., *Op.* 533-5)
'Then, like the Three-legged One whose back is broken and whose head looks down upon the ground, like him, I say, they wander to escape the white snow.' (tr. Evelyn-White)

(23) νῦν δ' ἃ μὲν ἦν πλεύσασι σῶσαι, βαδίζειν κελεύων ἀπολώλεκεν, ἃ δ' εἰπούσι τἀληθῆ, ψευδόμενος (Dem. 19.181)
'What might have been saved by sailing, he has lost by insisting on travel by land; and what might have been saved by telling the truth, he has lost by telling lies.' (tr. Vince & Vince)

In (22), the perfect ἐπὶ ... ἔαγε 'it is broken' serves to characterize the present state of the back of the 'Three-legged One' (that is, an old man walking with a staff).[128] In (23), on the other hand, the perfect ἀπολώλεκεν 'he has lost' denotes an event which occurred in the past (losing what might have been saved), and which has relevance at a later point in time (the time of speaking).

---

[127] With regard to Ancient Greek, see e.g. Haspelmath (1992); Slings (1994); Haug (2008). Unfortunately, in cross-linguistically inspired works such as these (as well as the present study), the term 'resultative perfect' has come to be used in a sense that is almost opposite to that proposed in major studies such as Wackernagel (1953 [1904]) and Chantraine (1927) (where the term 'resultative perfect' refers to those perfects which stress the state of the object rather than that of the subject; see further §3.3.1). When the term is used in the Wackernagel–Chantraine sense, this will be explicitly indicated. Furthermore note that I use the term 'resultative' in a broad sense (cf. Nedjalkov & Jaxontov 1988: 7), which also encompasses purely stative perfects, including perfects of experiential verbs such as γηθέω 'I rejoice', ἔλπομαι 'I hope', ῥιγέω 'I shiver', etc. (cf. Haspelmath 1992: 201-5).

[128] As we can see in this example, this renders the present perfect similar to the simple present (ὁρᾶται 'he looks').

Various scholars[129] have suggested that the anterior perfect itself may be further subdivided into a number of subtypes.[130] Next to the most common type of anterior perfect, which is called the 'perfect of current relevance' (as in (23)), a distinction can be made between an 'experiential perfect', a 'perfect of persistence', and a 'perfect of recent past'.[131]

The experiential perfect, which next to the perfect of current relevance occurs most often, indicates that an event took place a number of times in the past, rather than just once (as with the perfect of current relevance).[132] In our example (24), this is explicitly indicated by the adverb ἤδη πολλάκις 'already often':[133]

(24) οὐ δεῖ δὴ τοιοῦτον, ὦ ἄνδρες Ἀθηναῖοι, παραπεπτωκότα καιρὸν ἀφεῖναι, οὐδὲ παθεῖν ταὐτὸν ὅπερ ἤδη πολλάκις πρότερον πεπόνθατε (Dem. 1.8)

'Men of Athens, you must not let slip the opportunity that offers, nor make the blunder you have so often made before.' (tr. Vince)

An example of the 'perfect of persistence' is given in (25):[134]

(25) ἀλλὰ ὑμᾶς τοῦτο οὐ πείθω· ὀλίγον γὰρ χρόνον ἀλλήλοις διειλέγμεθα (Pl., Ap. 37a)

'But I cannot convince you of this, for we have been conversing with each other only a little while.' (tr. Fowler, slightly modified)

---

[129] See e.g. Comrie (1976: 56-60); Bybee et al. (1994: 61-3); Schwenter (1994a, 1994b); Lindstedt (2000). With regard to Ancient Greek, see e.g. Slings (1988, 1994); Isebaert (1991: 106); Ruijgh (1991, 2004); Gerö & von Stechow (2003); Haug (2008). For a critique, see Sicking & Stork (1996: 151-70).

[130] Identifying these subtypes is not always unproblematic. For some criteria to distinguish between them, see Bentein (2012b: 181-2).

[131] It should be noted that 'current relevance' is characteristic for each of these subtypes. However, with the experiential perfect and the perfect of persistence there is relatively more emphasis on the subject as the 'locus of relevance', whereby the anterior event is less salient, while with the perfect of recent past the anterior event is much more salient, as a consequence of which the present result/effect is less emphasized (see Carey 1996; cf. Dahl & Hedin 2000 for current relevance as a graded concept).

[132] Bybee et al. (1994: 62) use a more narrow definition of this type of perfect, which presupposes an animate agent ('certain qualities or knowledge are attributable to the agent due to past experiences').

[133] Note that the aorist can be used in a similar way, as, for example, in καὶ πολλάκις ἤδη παρ' ἐκείνων πολιτῶν ὄντων δίκην τὴν μεγίστην ἐλάβετε, ὅτι οὐχ οἷοί τ' ἦσαν τῆς τούτων πονηρίας ἐπικρατῆσαι (Lys. 22.16) 'and often you have been known to inflict the extreme penalty on those officials, who were citizens, for having failed to defeat the villainy of these men' (tr. Lamb).

[134] I borrow this example from Gerö & von Stechow (2003: 274).

Rather than denoting a temporally bounded past event, this type of (anterior) perfect indicates that an event which started in the past (here Socrates' talking to the Athenian jury) continues up to a later point in time (here the time of speaking).[135]

The final subtype, the 'perfect of recent past', indicates that a past event has just occurred, and thus implies a certain emphasis on account of its recency.[136] An illustration is given in (26):[137]

(26) τεκμαίρομαι δὲ ἔκ τινος ἐνυπνίου ὃ ἑώρακα ὀλίγον πρότερον ταύτης τῆς νυκτός (Pl., Crit. 44a)

'And my reason for this is a dream which I had a little while ago in the course of this night.' (tr. Fowler)

In this example, the adverbial phrase ὀλίγον πρότερον ταύτης τῆς νυκτός 'a little while ago in the course of this night' specifies the occurrence of a recent past event—that is, Socrates having a dream.[138]

1.4.2 Actionality

1.4.2.1 'Aspect' versus 'actionality'

In recent years, it has become common to make a further distinction between 'aspect' and 'actionality' (also called *Aktionsart, lexical aspect*), the latter being concerned with the *phrasal*, rather than the *sentential*, level:[139]

> Aktionsart (lexical aspect) is an aspect of meaning contributed by the meaning itself of the words that make up the predicate constituent (i.e. the verb phrase, including the complement(s) and necessary adverbial(s), if any).
>
> (Declerck 1997: 191)[140]

---

[135] Note that in Ancient Greek the present and imperfect could be used with a similar function, as in πάλαι θαυμάζω 'I have been wondering for a long time'. Cf. Smyth (1984 [1920]: 422-3); Gerö & von Stechow (2003: 274-81); Haverling (2009: 355).

[136] Cf. Bybee et al. (1994: 62).

[137] I borrow this example from Gerö & von Stechow (2003: 252).

[138] Thus detracting attention from the present result, and focusing rather on the time of the past event, cf. Dahl & Hedin (2000: 395).

[139] There has been much discussion about exactly which representational level to associate actionality with (see e.g. Smith 1997; Sasse 2002: 216), but I shall not go further into this complex matter here.

[140] The distinction between aspect and actionality is sometimes made on the basis of the fact that the former belongs to the morphological domain, while the latter

Boogaert (2004: 1166) shows the importance of making this distinction by means of the notions of 'telicity' (a semantic notion situated at the level of actionality)[141] and 'perfectivity' (a semantic notion situated at the level of aspect).[142] Consider the following two examples:

(27) He ate an apple.
(28) He was eating an apple.

There is a clear distinction between these two examples in terms of aspect: (27) is perfective, referring to a temporally bounded event (an endpoint being reached), while (28) is imperfective, referring to a temporally unbounded event (an endpoint not explicitly being reached). As regards actionality, however, both examples can be considered telic: they both refer to a situation with a potential endpoint. In other words, eating an apple has a conceivable point of cessation.

1.4.2.2 The Vendlerian classification

One of the most influential classificatory proposals with regard to actionality has been that of Vendler (1957). Although the important distinction between actionality and aspect had already been made at the beginning of the twentieth century, until Vendler there was a tendency 'to multiply categories of Aktionsarten and draw over-fine (and idiosyncratic) differences'.[143] Vendler was the first scholar to draw up a workable distinction of *Aktionsarten*, distinguishing between verbs of state, activity, accomplishment, and achievement.

The characteristics of these different types can be summarized by means of the binary features of dynamicity (is the situation denoted by the verb eventive or stative? does it require a constant input of energy?), durativity (does the situation denoted by the verb persist

---

belongs to the semantic domain (see e.g. Boogaert 2004: 1166–7; Napoli 2006: 32; in this case, the terms 'grammatical' and 'lexical' aspect are often used). Such a definition is difficult to apply to 'non-aspect languages', however. Other scholars have noted that actionality can be characterized as 'objective' and aspect as 'subjective' (see e.g. Moser 2008: 8). This position too is difficult to maintain. As Boogaert (2004: 1166) writes, 'the Aktionsart distinction between "he ate" and "he ate an apple" is no less a matter of speaker choice than is the aspect distinction between "he ate an apple" and "he was eating an apple"'.

[141] See §1.4.2.2.   [142] See §1.4.1.2.   [143] Fanning (1990: 43).

during an interval of time?), and telicity (does the situation denoted by the event have an inherent endpoint?),[144] as outlined in Table 1.2:

Table 1.2. Actionality

	Telic	Dynamic	Durative
State	−	−	+
Activity	−	+	+
Accomplishment	+	+	+
Achievement	+	+	−

Source: Vendler 1957.

In English, verbs such as 'to know', 'to love', and 'to believe' are *states*: they do not have an inherent endpoint, there is not much action involved, and they last for an interval of time. Verbs such as 'to run', 'to walk', and 'to swim' are *activities*: in contrast to states they involve an action, which lasts for a certain interval of time. These verbs do not have an inherent endpoint, however. Verbs such as 'to draw' (as in 'to draw a circle'), 'to paint' (as in 'to paint a picture'), and 'to build' (as in 'to build a house') are *accomplishments*: contrary to states and activities, they have an inherent endpoint. They involve an action that lasts for an interval of time. Lastly, verbs such as 'to recognize', 'to reach', and 'to realize' are *achievements*: they have an inherent endpoint and involve an action, as do accomplishments, but they do not last for an interval of time (rather, they are punctual).

One insight that Vendler (1957) presents but does not emphasize concerns the fact that actionality is not limited to the verb on its own. Scholars have pointed out a number of elements which may influence actionality,[145] among others (a) singular vs. plural reference of the object, (b) durational vs. non-durational adverb-phrases, (c) count vs. mass nouns, (d) directional adverb-expressions, and (e) the presence of an effected vs. affected object.

---

[144] Note that these features involve—to a large extent—temporality, similarly to aspect. Vendler (1957) himself speaks of his *Aktionsart*-classes as 'time schemata'. Cf. also Tomasello (2003: 218); Boogaert (2004: 1165); Croft (2012, ch. 2).

[145] See Mateos (1977: 32) and Fanning (1990: 163–79) with regard to Ancient Greek.

1.4.2.3 Diagnostic tests

Vendler determines the actionality of a verb (predicate) on the basis of three kinds of 'diagnostic tests':[146] tests based upon (a) possibility of use in a certain construction, (b) different truth-entailments, and (c) the compatibility with certain adverb(ial)s. I limit myself to giving some representative examples of each of these types of tests. A well-known test of the first type is whether a verb can occur in the progressive construction: as shown in (29), states cannot be used in the progressive construction in English:[147]

(29) What are you doing?
   I am running.
   *I am knowing.

The second type of test involves truth-entailments. This type of test can be used, among others, to distinguish activities from accomplishments. Consider the following two examples:

(30) He is pushing a cart.
(31) He is running a mile.

In the first example, the situation denoted by the verb proceeds in a homogeneous way, but in the second, it does not:[148] we can say of the subject in (30) when he stops pushing the cart that he has pushed the cart, but if the subject of (31) stops running a mile (before having run a mile), we cannot say that he has run a mile.

A last type of test looks at the compatibility of a verb with adverbs such as 'deliberately' and 'carefully'. As shown in (32) and (33), accomplishments can co-occur with the adverb 'deliberately' but states cannot:

(32) I deliberately trashed his car.
(33) *I deliberately believe her.

---

[146] Cf. Shain (2009: 16) for this threefold distinction.
[147] Cf. Vendler (1957: 144). As one of the reviewers notes, however, some verbs are nevertheless used in the progressive construction, as in McDonald's slogan 'I'm loving it'.
[148] Cf. Vendler (1957: 146).

1.4.2.4 Difficulties of application to Ancient Greek

In the last few decades, the Vendlerian classification has been referred to in various studies of Ancient Greek aspect[149] (sometimes with modifications), as it will also be in the present study, and its advantages have been recognized.[150] However, other scholars have been more critical of its applicability[151] and have drawn attention to various disadvantages it poses. I shall briefly outline these criticisms here.[152]

One issue concerns the applicability of criteria such as those outlined in §1.4.2.3 to the classification of predicates. Obviously, for a corpus language such as Ancient Greek, we cannot rely on 'native' intuition by applying tests ourselves; rather we must search for evidence in our texts, which is often scarce.[153] Furthermore, some of the tests are explicitly designed for English (e.g. the use of a verb in the highly grammaticalized progressive construction to test for stativity),[154] and at this point it is unclear whether other tests should/could be applied to Ancient Greek.[155]

A second issue is that while some verbs are easily classified under one of Vendler's four categories (e.g. βασιλεύω 'I rule' as a state or θνῄσκω 'I die' as an achievement), others are much less so (e.g. verbs such as κελεύω 'I order' or λέγω 'I say').[156] Since similar comments have been made with regard to other languages, including English, it seems that this is not a language-specific issue, but rather a problem inherent in linguistic categorization. Difficulties of this nature can be handled by not assuming a strict division between different types of actionality. Zhang (1995: 15), for example, has proposed an alternative representation of the Vendlerian categories, that is, as circles with overlapping or 'fuzzy' areas. In addition, it may be helpful to refer to

---

[149] See e.g. Mateos (1977); Stork (1982); Fanning (1990); Olsen (1994); Napoli (2006); Shain (2009). For some different classificatory proposals of actionality in Ancient Greek, see e.g. Ruipérez (1979 [1954]: 60); Sicking & Stork (1996: 138–46).
[150] See esp. Stork (1982: 35–6).
[151] See e.g. Porter (1989), who does not refer to actionality in his book on verbal aspect in the New Testament.
[152] With regard to English too, a number of issues have been raised. See e.g. Croft (2012: 33–7).
[153] Cf. Stork (1982: 36–7).   [154] Cf. Boogaert (2004: 1169–70).
[155] Stork (1982: 37) proposes to test for stativity in Ancient Greek by analysing whether a verb receives an ingressive interpretation when used in the aorist tense.
[156] Cf. Stork (1982: 36); Ruijgh (1985: 20–1).

Theoretical Background 45

higher- and lower-order categorizations (as will be done in this study), such as the general distinction between 'states' and 'events', which is taken to be primary by most scholars,[157] or the very specific verb classes proposed by Levin (1993),[158] which include 'verbs of perception', 'verbs of communication', 'verbs of change of state', etc.

A third problem raised by several scholars is the fact that modern categorizations of Ancient Greek verbs are often based on traditional lexical definitions, rather than advanced lexicographical methods. Apart from the fact that these may be problematic (e.g. the glosses advanced by LSJ), they may obscure the fact that a verb can belong to more than one actionality category. McKay (1994: 28) gives the example of νικάω, which is often translated with 'I conquer' (that is, as a telic verb), but can also be understood as 'I am being victorious' (that is, as an atelic, state verb).

1.4.3 Transitivity

1.4.3.1 Hopper & Thompson (1980)

So far, we have discussed grammatical aspect (and to some extent also actionality) in terms of temporality. While such an analysis is standard, it is not entirely satisfactory,[159] since it does not clarify a number of elements that will be of some importance in this study. First, it remains unclear exactly which sentential elements determine aspectual interpretation, or why certain elements tend to occur with perfective or imperfective aspect (e.g. the negation, constituent focus, definite objects).[160] Second, it has been observed that aspectual categories (such as 'progressive') are prototypically organized.[161] By using an approach that is based purely on temporality, however, we have no means to deal with this. Third, from a more general, conceptual point of view, we are unable to compare aspectual categories

---

[157] See e.g. McKay (1994: 28) with regard to Ancient Greek.
[158] Note, however, that Levin's (1993) verb categorization is based on English.
[159] Compare Michaelis (1998: 2), who calls it 'limited'.
[160] With regard to Ancient Greek, see e.g. Friedrich (1974: 23); Sicking (1991, 1996); Oréal (2000).
[161] Meaning that not all members of the category are as typical (see further §2.3). The following phrases, for example, can be ranked from most to least typical instances of progressive aspect: 'I'm reading it' > 'I'm loving it' > *'I'm knowing it'. On aspect and prototypicality, see further Galton (1997).

and subcategories to each other (e.g. how does 'perfective' aspect relate to 'imperfective' aspect?).

As noted by Michaelis (1998: 2), 'aspectual meaning involves not only the temporal make-up of a situation, but a number of other notions that are not strictly temporal.' One of these is transitivity.[162] With respect to the notion of transitivity, the work of Hopper & Thompson (1980) is crucial. They argue that transitivity should be understood as a prototypical concept,[163] which can be broken down into ten component parameters,[164] as shown in Table 1.3:

Table 1.3. Transitivity parameters

Parameter	High	Low
A. Participants	Two or more participants, A and O	One participant
B. Kinesis	Action	Non-action
C. Aspect[165]	Telic	Atelic
D. Punctuality	Punctual	Non-punctual
E. Volitionality	Volitional	Non-volitional
F. Affirmation	Affirmative	Negative
G. Mode	Realis	Irrealis
H. Agency	A high in potency	A low in potency
I. Affectedness of O	O totally affected	O not affected
J. Individuation of O	O highly individuated	O non-individuated

Key: 'A' = agent; 'O' = object
Source: Hopper & Thompson 1980: 252. Reproduction of this table has been granted by the Linguistic Society of America.

Hopper & Thompson (1980) connect transitivity as a semantic notion with the morpho-syntactic properties of the clause: they argue that a clause with a low score on any of their parameters is more likely to diverge morpho-syntactically from the prototypical transitive clause than a clause that does not have a low score.[166] Conti (2014: 424–6)

---

[162] Other phenomena mentioned by Michaelis (1998: 2) are evidentiality, modality, individuation, granularity of perspective, etc.

[163] Contrast with the more traditional sense of transitivity, which refers to the presence of two syntactic arguments in the clause (one nominative and the other accusative in Ancient Greek). See e.g. Lazard (2002: 150–5); Kittilä (2002: 20–5); De Boel (2004).

[164] Compare Lakoff (1977: 244); Rice (1987: 145).

[165] Hopper & Thompson (1980: 252) discuss aspect in terms of 'telicity', seemingly also with the value of 'perfectivity' or 'boundedness'.

[166] Cf. Lazard's (2002: 152) 'major biactant construction' as the morpho-syntactic reflex of the 'prototypical action': 'the MAJOR BIACTANT CONSTRUCTION... in any language, is the construction used to express a prototypical action.'

Theoretical Background

gives a number of examples from Ancient Greek: in (34), for example, we see that a low degree of affectedness of the second argument (parameter I) is associated with dative (i.e. Ἀγαμέμνονι δίῳ 'noble Agamemnon') rather than accusative marking (contrast e.g. a verb such as κτείνω 'I kill (someone)', which takes an affected, accusative object).

(34) ἐξ οὗ τὰ πρώτισθ' ἑπόμην Ἀγαμέμνονι δίῳ / Ἴλιον εἰς εὔπωλον
(Hom., Od. 11.168-9)
'From the day when first I went with noble Agamemnon to Ilium, famed for its horses.' (tr. Dimock-Murray)

Hopper & Thompson (1980) furthermore formulate a so-called 'transitivity hypothesis', which predicts that transitivity-parameters will co-vary: 'in the grammars of all the languages we have examined, we find that these component features of Transitivity co-vary extensively and systematically.'[167] A standard example in this regard would be Finnish, where the object can be placed either in the accusative or in the partitive case. This distinction also serves to encode the aspect of the clause: the accusative case gives the clause perfective value, while the partitive case gives it imperfective value.[168]

Perhaps most germane to our study is Hopper & Thompson's (1980: 280-94) connection of transitivity with aspect,[169] the latter of which they refer to in terms of discourse, more specifically 'grounding'.[170] They argue that grounding is inferred not on the basis of a single morpho-syntactic feature (e.g. the choice of the present or the aorist stem in Ancient Greek), but rather on the basis of a cluster of properties. It is exactly this cluster of properties that characterizes transitivity. In this context, they contend that:

> Foregrounding is not marked absolutely, but is instead indicated and interpreted on a probabilistic basis; and the likelihood that a clause will receive a foregrounded interpretation is proportional to the height of that clause on the scale of Transitivity.
>
> (Hopper & Thompson 1980: 283)

---

[167] Hopper & Thompson (1980: 254).
[168] Cf. Hopper & Thompson (1980: 330).
[169] As a functional notion, that is.
[170] In a number of studies, the insight was developed that events can be placed on a continuum ranging from most foregrounded to least foregrounded. See esp. Longacre (1989: 445, 1996: 24), who divides discourse into different 'bands' according to 'saliency'.

They furthermore argue that 'from the performer's viewpoint, the decision to foreground a clause will be reflected in the decision to encode more (rather than fewer) Transitivity features in the clause'.[171]

1.4.3.2 Criticism of Hopper & Thompson (1980)

Since 1980, various scholars have criticized Hopper & Thompson's (1980) proposal. In what follows, I briefly discuss some of the most relevant points of criticism. A first criticism concerns the relative importance of the transitivity parameters. Hopper & Thompson (1980) seem to assume that these are of equal importance in all languages, but Kittilä (2002a: 128) argues otherwise:[172]

> Languages differ crucially from each other in which of the properties associated with the basic transitive sentence can be lacking in structurally transitive sentences without causing any changes in their marking.[173]

A case in point would be Greek verbs of seeing:[174] for 'I see something' we typically find ὁράω with the bare accusative, and for 'I look at something' βλέπω with the preposition πρός and an accusative.[175] According to Hopper & Thompson's (1980) transitivity hypothesis, it is difficult to explain why ὁράω takes the bare accusative (which indicates higher transitivity) and not βλέπω, as the latter verb typically expresses the intentional character of the event (cf. the volitionality-parameter).[176] In other languages, however, a different pattern is found: in some Polynesian languages, 'look' takes a transitive, ergative-absolutive case frame, while 'see' takes an absolutive-oblique case marking.[177] This finding

---

[171] Hopper & Thompson (1980: 283). As Thompson & Hopper (2001) note, however, this must be related to discourse mode: in non-narrative discourse, foregrounded clauses will typically be of a lower transitivity than those found in narrative discourse.

[172] Cf. also Lazard (2002: 179–80).

[173] In this context, Kittilä (2002a: 112) observes that 'one can say that parameters that relate to the inherent semantic transitivity of the event described (for example, changes in the affectedness of the Patient or the agentivity of the Agent) are more likely to cause changes in the marking of sentences typologically than those that are associated with the conceptualization of the event (e.g. mood and tense)'.

[174] See esp. De Boel (1987), (1988).

[175] Less frequently, ὁράω occurs with a prepositional object (e.g. Hom., *Il.* 10.239), and βλέπω with the bare accusative (e.g. Soph., *Aj.* 1042).

[176] As one of the reviewers notes, however, βλέπω may also be used in the non-intentional sense of 'to be seeing, to have eye-sight'.

[177] See Naess (2007: 193–4).

indicates that in Ancient Greek, the parameter of volitionality plays a less important role than that of the affectedness[178] of the object.[179]

In this study, I shall focus on a specific number of parameters of transitivity:[180] (a) participants (is there one or more participants?); (b) kinesis (are we dealing with a single action or a repeated one? with an action or state?); (c) aspect (is the event telic or atelic? is it bounded or unbounded?); (d) volitionality (is the subject an agent?); (e) mode (did the event actually occur, or did it not (yet) occur/take place in a non-real world?);[181] and (f) affectedness of the object (how strongly is the object affected by the verbal event? Is the object a patient?).

A second criticism concerns the nature of the criteria listed by Hopper & Thompson (1980). Several scholars have criticized the fact that they present a rather heterogeneous list of parameters, which can be classified in groups: on the one hand, most of the parameters are semantically oriented, but some of them (e.g. affirmation, mode) are more pragmatic in nature.[182] On the other hand, some of the parameters (such as animacy) can be considered subject-related, while others are verb-related (such as aspect), and still others object-related (such as individuation).[183] This has inspired Malchukov's (2006) revision of the transitivity parameters in the form of a transitivity-scale, as in Fig. 1.1. Note that while some features are closely related to the domains of A (agent), O (object), or V (verb), others are intermediate, forming a 'semantic bridge' between domains:

---

[178] On affectedness with the verb 'see', cf. Tsunoda (1985: 389): 'the patient of say, *see* "to form a complete visual image"... is more affected than that of look'. Tsunoda notes that with *see* the patient is more 'attained'.

[179] Cf. Naess (2007: 194), who notes that a more general distinction can be made between ergative and accusative languages: 'it is certainly striking that the more controlled event tends to be encoded as more transitive in ergative languages, while the event with the more affected experiencer is typically encoded as more transitive in accusative languages'.

[180] Compare Givón (2001: 1.126), who singles out agentivity ('having a deliberate, active agent'), affectedness ('having a concrete, affected patient'), and perfectivity ('involving a bounded, terminated, fast-changing event in real time') as three crucial properties.

[181] Hopper & Thompson (1980: 252) concentrate on the distinction between realis and irrealis (contrast e.g. 'he went to a party' (more transitive) with 'he would have gone to a party' (less transitive)). More broadly, the mode-parameter can be applied to future and negated events as well (contrast e.g. 'he went to a party' (more transitive) with 'he did not go to a party'/'he will go to a party' (less transitive)).

[182] Cf. Kittilä (2002b: 26–9).

[183] Cf. Cooreman *et al.* (1984: 3); Desclés (1998: 163).

A-features	V-features	O-features
[animacy] [volitionality]	[kinesis] [factivity]	[tense/aspect] [affectedness] [(O-)individuation]

Fig. 1.1. Malchukov's (2006: 333) Transitivity Scale.

Reproduction of this figure has been granted by John Benjamins.

Other scholars have gone even further and argued that Hopper & Thompson's (1980) parameters should be related to a so-called 'conceptual archetype' or 'transitive prototype'.[184] Rice (1987: 8), for example, formulates the prototypical action as follows:

> The prototypical transitive clause describes an event in which two entities are involved in some activity; the activity is conceived of as being unilateral, thus, the two entities are nonequivalent or asymmetrical; because there is movement and effect, contact between the two entities is presumed to be important; the second entity is directly affected in some way by the contact; and finally, the entities are taken to be distinct from each other, from their locale or setting, and from the speaker/conceptualizer.

Third, it has been argued that the predictions made by Hopper & Thompson's (1980) transitivity hypothesis are too strong. Lazard (2002: 175) gives the example of 'kick at the ball' and 'kick a ball': in the former sentence the object is more definite, but the action is also less complete. Malchukov (2006: 334) has recently proposed a weaker form of the hypothesis, which predicts that 'only parameters that are semantically related (and placed adjacently on the Transitivity Scale)[185] will show a systematic co-variation'.[186]

1.4.3.3 Application of transitivity

How can the work of Hopper & Thompson (1980) on transitivity contribute to the difficulties outlined under §1.4.3.1 and, consequently, to the description of verbal periphrasis? A first element is the specification of which sentential elements determine aspectual interpretation. As we shall see in the third chapter, an (affected) object, agent phrase, or a locating adverb typically occur in sentences

---

[184] See e.g. Delancey (1987: 60); Langacker (1991: 13–14); Kemmer & Verhagen (1994: 125–6); Desclés (1998: 164–73); Naess (2007).

[185] Cf. again Fig. 1.1.

[186] An example would be affectedness and O-individuation. As Malchukov (2006: 333) notes, 'total affectedness is easier to envisage in case of definite objects.'

Theoretical Background 51

that express anterior perfect aspect (as in English 'I have cut the tree down some time ago'), while sentences expressing resultative perfect aspect (as in 'the tree is cut down') typically do not present these characteristics. Using Hopper & Thompson's (1980) transitivity framework, anterior perfect aspect can be related to higher transitivity than resultative perfect aspect.

Second, the transitivity parameters outlined by Hopper & Thompson (1980) offer a framework to deal with prototypicality, explaining why specific examples are more or less prototypical. In the domain of imperfective aspect, for example, we find periphrases of the type ἦν εὖ φρονῶν 'he was wise' next to those of the type ἦν ἔχων ταῦτα 'he had these things'. Such periphrases, which have proven very difficult to describe from a semantic point of view in previous studies, can now be described and contrasted on the basis of parameters such as participants, volitionality, individuation of O, etc.

Third, from a more general, conceptual point of view, Hopper & Thompson's (1980) transitivity continuum offers a means to compare general aspectual categories to each other (or more correctly, the verb forms/clauses expressing these aspectual categories). For example, we can say that perfective aspect is more transitive than imperfective aspect (cf. the aspect parameter), which in turn is more transitive than perfect aspect (cf. the kinesis parameter). Within each of these functional domains, we can now compare aspectual categories to each other: for example, 'resultative' can be considered less transitive than 'anterior', and 'stative' less transitive than 'progressive'.

1.5 LANGUAGE CHANGE

1.5.1 Approaches Towards Language Change

In the past three decades, scholars have significantly enhanced our understanding of linguistic change, in both formal and functional terms. It is likely that the two most important contributions to the field are Principles and Parameters and Grammaticalization Theory.[187] The primary difference between these two approaches is that a functionalist model such as Grammaticalization Theory is interested in the

---

[187] Cf. Fischer (2007).

use of language, rather than the underlying system.[188] As such, it seems better suited to the analysis of a corpus language such as Ancient Greek.

The starting point for Grammaticalization Theory is commonly acknowledged to be the work of Meillet (1921 [1912]), although references to grammaticalization phenomena appear as early as the eighteenth century.[189] Grammaticalization is generally defined as:

> The change whereby lexical items and constructions come in certain linguistic contexts to serve grammatical functions and, once grammaticalized, continue to develop new grammatical functions.
> (Hopper & Traugott 2003: xv)

Grammaticalization is typically conceived as a set of concurrent[190] phonological, functional, and morpho-syntactic processes, which can be further subdivided along paradigmatic and syntagmatic dimensions. An overview of the so-called 'processes of grammaticalization', which were first outlined by Lehmann 1995 [1982], is given in Table 1.4:

Table 1.4. Processes of grammaticalization

	Paradigmatic	Syntagmatic
Phonological	Attrition (reduction)	Coalescence (fusion)
Functional	Generalization	Idiomaticization/Semantic integration[191]
Morpho-syntactic	Decategorialization/ Paradigmaticization	Rigidification

Source: after Croft 2000: 157.

Phonologically, reduction takes place (e.g. Lat. *ille* > Fr. *le*), as well as fusion of the component parts (e.g. Engl. *out of* > *outta*). Functionally, there is a generalization of meaning (e.g. Engl. *can* (< *cunnan* 'to know'), which went through three stages: (a) mental ability; (b) ability; (c) root

---

[188] Cf. Fischer & Rosenbach (2000: 12).
[189] Cf. Heine (1997: 27, 2003: 575–6).
[190] As noted by Markopoulos (2009: 6), this need not necessarily be the case. For example, a construction can be fully grammaticalized from a functional point of view, without any phonological consequences.
[191] Note that the term 'semantic integration' (for which, see e.g. Langacker 2005) is not included in the overview given by Croft (2000: 157). There is a slight difference in emphasis between the two terms: 'idiomaticization' primarily refers to the construction in its entirety, while 'semantic integration' refers to the component parts.

possibility),[192] and the informational contribution of the grammaticalizing elements becomes less transparent (e.g. *go*, *-ing*, and *to* in the 'going to V-' construction). Morpho-syntactically, verbs or nouns tend to lose their canonical verbal or nominal properties (e.g. with regard to tense, aspect, mood, person, argument structure, etc., as in Engl. *can*: *to can *canning *I can that) and linear order becomes more rigid.

1.5.2 Cognitive Factors Underlying Grammaticalization

Although, as Heine (2003: 577) notes, virtually all authors working within the grammaticalization paradigm subscribe to the same general definition of the process, namely that it involves the development from lexical to grammatical and from grammatical to even more grammatical, in the past three decades a number of different currents of thought have arisen. One of these currents, which is of particular relevance to the present book, emphasizes the cognitive factors that underlie the process of grammaticalization by explicitly comparing data from several languages. Haiman (1994) and Bybee (2009a: 26–30), for example, have suggested that grammaticalization be thought of in domain-general terms as an instance of 'ritualization' or 'automatization'.[193] The key factor in this process is (increased) frequency or repetition.

Scholars working within Grammaticalization Theory have discovered the universality of both the source constructions of grammaticalizing items and their paths of development,[194] thus opening up what has been a 'problem area in orthodox methods of historical linguistics'[195]—that is, semantic change.[196]

When it comes to the cognitive sources, scholars have drawn attention to the human tendency to use linguistic forms expressing meanings 'that are concrete, easily accessible, and/or clearly delineated' to

---

[192] Cf. Bybee (2003b: 606).
[193] See e.g. Bybee (2007: 969): 'grammaticalization is the process of automatization of frequently occurring sequences of linguistic elements.' An example of non-linguistic ritualization given by Bybee (2009a: 26) is saluting in the army: initially saluting began in the Middle Ages when metal armour was worn: when greeting, soldiers lifted their faceplate to identify themselves as friendly. Nowadays, this originally functional act continues to exist, even though metal armour is no longer worn.
[194] See esp. Bybee & Dahl (1989); Bybee *et al.* (1994).
[195] Heine (2003: 597).
[196] Bybee (2007: 966–7), in fact, argues that this is 'one of the most important consequences of recent research into grammaticalization'.

also express meaning contents that are much less concrete, easily accessible, and/or clearly delineated.[197] According to Heine (2003: 578), the main motivation for this strategy lies in our wish to communicate successfully. In his 1997 study, Heine (1997: 31) singles out a number of 'event schemas' as responsible for expressions of tense and aspect, including location ('X is at Y'), motion ('X moves to/from Y'), volition ('X wants Y'), and possession ('X has Y').

As for the development of grammaticalizing items, Bybee & Dahl (1989: 57) note that 'the paths along which grams[198] develop may be the same or similar across languages'. Bybee (2009a: 27–8) gives an overview of a number of common paths of development or 'grammaticalization paths': in many European languages, for example, the indefinite article has developed out of the numeral 'one': Dutch 'een', English 'an', German 'ein', French 'un/une', etc. Similarly, in many languages, demonstratives turn into definite articles, a development which is also known to have occurred with Ancient Greek ὁ, ἡ, τό (compare English 'that', which became 'the', and Latin 'ille/illa', which became French 'le/la' and Spanish 'el/la'). Verbs denoting 'movement towards' frequently develop into future markers, as in English 'going to' or French 'aller'.

One final issue worth mentioning here is the correlation between form and function.[199] To be more specific, scholars of grammaticalization have found that across the languages of the world morphologically bound (i.e. synthetic) expression is typically associated with perfective aspect, while periphrastic expression is associated with imperfective and perfect aspect, particularly progressive and anterior subaspects.[200] This can be explained by the processes of grammaticalization which I outlined in §1.5.1: when a construction grammaticalizes, its meaning becomes more general and its form reduced ('generalization' and 'reduction'/'fusion'). Since perfective aspect looks at the event as a whole, with no attention to the internal temporal constitution of the event,[201] it also expresses less

---

[197] See Heine (2003: 578). Cf. also Bybee & Dahl (1989: 57).
[198] The term 'gram' is short for 'grammatical morpheme'. Bybee & Dahl (1989: 51) define grammatical morphemes as 'morphemes which belong to closed classes and exhibit grammatically regular distributional properties' (contrast with 'lexical' morphemes), distinguishing between bound and periphrastic expression.
[199] Cf. Bybee (1985: 145); Bybee & Dahl (1989); Bybee et al. (1994: 20).
[200] See e.g. Bybee (1985: 145); Bybee & Dahl (1989: 56); Bybee (1994).
[201] Cf. §1.4.1.2.

specific aspectual meanings than imperfective and perfect aspect, and therefore is less likely to be expressed periphrastically.

1.5.3 Constructions

In recent years, much attention within linguistics has been paid to the notion of 'constructions' as 'pairings of form and meaning'.[202] Within diachronic linguistics, too, the relevance of this notion has been stressed.[203] While grammaticalization is often defined as the process whereby lexical items become more grammatical, scholars have drawn attention to the fact that these lexical items 'grammaticalize only in certain highly specifiable morphosyntactic contexts, and under specifiable pragmatic conditions'.[204] As Markopoulos (2009: 3) notes, it would be quite meaningless to say that the English verb 'have' grammaticalized, without specifying the context in which this occurred, since the verb can be used in a number of different constructions, each conveying a different meaning.[205]

1.5.4 Criticism

Grammaticalization Theory has faced criticism from a number of different angles.[206] In what follows, I briefly discuss three particularly relevant criticisms.

1.5.4.1 The epiphenomenality of grammaticalization

The first major point of criticism, voiced by Newmeyer (1998, 2001), Campbell (2001), Campbell & Janda (2001), and Joseph (2001, 2004: 61, 2009: 200), among others, is that grammaticalization is 'epiphenomenal', in that it involves the coincidence of various kinds of changes and mechanisms of change that occur independently. Most grammaticalizationists nowadays agree with the view that grammaticalization consists of various types of changes.[207] However, they

---

[202] See e.g. Goldberg (2003: 219).
[203] See e.g. Traugott (2003); Joseph (2004: 61); Bergs & Diewald (2008).
[204] Traugott (2003: 624).   [205] Compare Bybee (2009a: 27).
[206] For an overview, see e.g. Heine (2003: 581–4); Bybee (2010: 112–14).
[207] See e.g. Bybee (2010: 112). According to Haspelmath (1999: 1063), the view that grammaticalization is 'a distinct process', 'an encapsulated phenomenon, governed by

stress the need of studying the *interaction* of these individual phenomena (McMahon 1994: 161 speaks of 'cross-componential change'), and draw attention to the general factors that underlie the individual processes. Bybee (2006, 2009b: 353), for example, stresses that 'frequency of use is one of the major links among the changes that occur in phonology, morphology, syntax, semantics and pragmatics'. Heine (2003: 583) argues that grammaticalization should in the first place be considered a semantic process, and considers desemanticization (generalization) to be responsible for decategorialization and reduction.

1.5.4.2 Grammaticalization paths

A second point of criticism concerns the notion of grammaticalization paths.[208] As noted by Janda (2001), this metaphor assumes a sense of continuity which is not empirically real (language transmission across generations being discontinuous).[209] As noted by Fischer (2008: 340):

> Grammaticalization linguists concerned with diachrony look at form as well as function (or meaning), but they do so mainly from the point of view of the language as a historical object that floats through time, as if it were divorced from speakers and from their system of grammar... such a view can be observed, for instance, in the typological approach to grammaticalization as seen in the work of Haspelmath, Bybee, Heine & Kuteva and others.

While this is indeed one of the disadvantages of the cross-linguistically informed approach, it certainly does not render it worthless,[210] as it offers a number of guiding principles in a problematic area of historical linguistics. However, especially when studying individual languages, we must attempt to embed language change as much as possible in its linguistic and social context.[211]

---

its own set of laws' has been wrongly attributed to mainstream grammaticalization studies.

[208] See §1.5.2.

[209] Janda (2001: 271) attributes this in part to the existence of a 'chronologically broad spectrum of representative writings' for some languages (including Ancient Greek), which may give the impression that the language had an unbroken existence of over a millennium.

[210] Cf. Oesterreicher (2001: 1585).   [211] See further §1.5.4.3.

Related to this issue is the criticism raised against the principle of 'unidirectionality', which posits that grammaticalization works in a single direction—that is, that lexical items and constructions achieve a grammatical function, and not vice versa.[212] Scholars such as Campbell (2001: 127-8), Janda (2001: 291-304), and Newmeyer (2001: 205-13) have noted that this certainly cannot be considered exceptionless, a view which was defended by Haspelmath (1999) among others. Most scholars of grammaticalization nowadays assume a weaker position, according to which unidirectionality represents a tendency rather than an absolute principle.[213] Heine (2003: 582) notes that while the unidirectionality principle might not be exceptionless,[214] the exceptions are relatively few in number, and that no instances of 'complete reversals of grammaticalization' have been discovered so far.[215]

1.5.4.3 The social dimension of language change

The third and final point of criticism (which is related to the second one) concerns the fact that the social dimension of language change has not been particularly prominent within Grammaticalization Theory, thus rendering it 'ahistorical'.[216] As noted by Janda (2001: 266):

> References to socio-linguistic considerations of even the most elementary sort (other than, occasionally, social deixis) are absent from the index of virtually every book-length treatment of grammaticalization.

In recent years, however, especially those scholars who work within the (sub)discipline of 'socio-historical linguistics' have attempted to integrate the findings of sociolinguistics and grammaticalization,[217] paying attention to the role of sociolinguistic variables in linguistic variation and change (e.g. social status, gender, education). With regard to language change in Ancient Greek, Markopoulos (2009) has recently stressed the importance of the notion 'register', which

---

[212] See e.g. Marchello-Nizia (2006: 47).   [213] Cf. Markopoulos (2009: 5).
[214] For an example see e.g. Janda (2001: 299), who notes that the English preposition 'off' has now also ended up as a verb ('to off'), at least in informal speech. On the topic of 'degrammaticalization', see further the recent book by Norde (2013).
[215] Cf. also Bybee (2010: 113). A complete reversal of grammaticalization would include the regaining of phonetic substance.
[216] Joseph (2004: 47).
[217] See e.g. Nevalainen & Palander-Collin (2011).

will also play a prominent role in this study. Markopoulos (2009: 232) suggests adding another dimension to the commonly recognized parameters / processes of grammaticalization,[218] that is, '[sociolinguistic] acceptability', which predicts that 'the further grammaticalized an AVC [auxiliary verb construction, KB] becomes, the higher up it rises in terms of sociolinguistic (register) acceptability'. In other words, when a construction becomes grammaticalized, it will be found in a higher number of registers; this happens both from above and below on the register-continuum.

[218] Cf. Table 1.4.

2

'Verbal' and 'Adjectival' Periphrasis

> In linguistics ... categorization is of paramount importance.
> (Aarts 2006: 362)

> If linguistics can be said to be any one thing it is the study of categories.
> (Labov 1973: 342)

2.1 INTRODUCTION

As I noted in the introduction to this book, various studies of verbal (participial) periphrasis in Ancient Greek have been conducted. Surprisingly, however, scholars have yet to reach a consensus on exactly which constructions can be considered periphrastic, as a result of which periphrasis is often considered a problematic issue in the relevant literature.[1] While some scholars limit the use of the term 'periphrasis' to those constructions with εἰμί 'I am', other scholars also take into account constructions with the verb ἔχω 'I have', and some even with verbs such as γίγνομαι 'I become', ἔρχομαι 'I go', τυγχάνω 'I happen to be, am', and ὑπάρχω 'I am'.

In this second chapter I shall attempt to clarify the nature of the concept of 'verbal periphrasis'. I focus on the Classical period, since this scope will best allow me to draw explicit comparisons with previous studies; however, what I shall argue is also relevant to Post-Classical and Byzantine Greek. After summarizing the current

---

[1] See e.g. Kahn (1973: 126–7); Dietrich (1973a: 21); Porter (1989: 452); Adrados (1992a: 450–1); Evans (2001: 221); Campbell (2008: 32).

status of the debate (§2.2), I present an alternative proposal (§2.3), which is based on the so-called 'prototype' model of linguistic categorization. To illustrate this model, I discuss the 'periphrasticity'[2] of three constructions, διαγίγνομαι 'I continue' with the present participle, ἔχω 'I have' with the aorist participle, and ἔρχομαι 'I go' with the future participle. In the final part of the chapter (§2.4), I address the notion of 'adjectival' periphrasis, which has been introduced by some scholars to distinguish true, 'verbal' periphrasis from constructions of the type πρέπον ἐστί 'it is fitting', where the participle denotes a property. I argue that in this regard, too, the prototype model offers a viable alternative, one which allows us to include the perfect and aorist participles in the discussion.

2.2 BACKGROUND TO THE DEBATE

2.2.1 'Periphrastic' Constructions

Various participial constructions are considered 'periphrastic' in the scholarly literature. Three types of constructions are generally distinguished: (a) constructions with verbs of state, (b) constructions with verbs of motion, and (c) constructions with phasal verbs.[3] These labels refer to the semantics of the finite verb when it is used independently, for example, εἰμί 'I am, exist' or ἔρχομαι 'I go'. A few issues should be noted by way of preface. First, the basic semantic value of γίγνομαι 'I become' and τυγχάνω 'I obtain' cannot be called stative. However, when these verbs are combined with a participle, the semantic value of these constructions becomes similar to that of the other constructions discussed under §2.2.1.1. Second, the verb στήκω 'I stand' (a present formed from ἕστηκα) strictly speaking is a 'postural verb', which bears some similarity to both verbs of state and verbs of movement; in §2.2.1.1 it is classified as a verb of state. Third, some phasal verbs also have a spatial semantic value, of which the temporal value may be considered an extension (e.g. διάγω 'I carry over or across' > 'I pass (life)', 'I continue').

---

[2] That is, the degree to which these constructions can be considered periphrastic.
[3] Phasal verbs are verbs that highlight the beginning, continuation, or ending of the event (as in 'to begin V-ing', 'to continue V-ing', 'to stop V-ing').

2.2.1.1 With verbs of state

Under this first and largest group,[4] we include constructions with the verbs εἰμί 'I am', ἔχω 'I have', γίγνομαι 'I become', στήκω (ἕστηκα) 'I stand', κυρέω 'I prove to be, am', πέλομαι 'I am', ὑπάρχω 'I am', and τυγχάνω 'I happen to be, am'. These can be combined with a present, perfect, or aorist participle, as in ἦν οἰκεομένη (Hdt. 4.204.1) 'it was (being) inhabited', ὑπῆρχον δύναμίν τινα κεκτημένοι (Dem. 3.7) 'they had acquired some power', or ἀντειπὼν ἐτύγχανε (Lys. 12.27) 'he happened to have spoken in opposition'. These constructions realize a number of values which can be characterized as aspectual.[5]

2.2.1.2 With verbs of movement

A second group of constructions[6] is formed with verbs of movement such as βαίνω 'I go', εἶμι 'I go', ἔρχομαι 'I go', and ἥκω 'I have come'. These verbs are typically combined with a present or future participle, as in ἥκεις δὲ ὀλίγον ὕστερον λέγων (Pl., Grg. 518a) 'a little bit later you come telling (me)', or ἔρχομαι ἐρέων (Hdt. 2.40.1) 'I am going to speak'. In addition, scholars have mentioned the combination of some of these verbs with an aorist or perfect participle, drawing attention to their similarity with constructions that are found in the Romance languages.[7] The value of these constructions can be characterized as 'aspecto-temporal'; especially those constructions that are combined with a future participle are said to realize a temporal (futural) value.[8]

2.2.1.3 With phasal verbs

The third group[9] discussed here consists of constructions with phasal verbs such as ἄρχομαι 'I begin', διάγω 'I continue', διαγίγνομαι

---

[1] On this group of constructions, see e.g. Thielmann (1891); Björck (1940); Aerts (1965); Dietrich (1973a, 1973b); Moser (1988); Amenta (2003); Giannaris (2011a, 2011b).

[5] Note, however, that the constructions with τυγχάνω also carry a modal value. See further §4.3.3.

[6] On this group of constructions, see e.g. Thielmann (1898); Dietrich (1973a, 1973b); Létoublon (1982); Adrados (1992: 453–4); Wakker (2007: 178–80).

[7] See e.g. Thielmann (1898: 58); Dietrich (1973a: 242).

[8] See e.g. Adrados (1992a: 453).

[9] On this group of constructions, see e.g. Jannaris (1897: 490); Mateos (1977: 32–3); Dietrich (1973a, 1973b); Adrados (1992: 453).

62 Verbal Periphrasis in Ancient Greek

'I continue', διατελέω 'I continue', ἐπιμένω 'I continue', λήγω 'I stop', and παύομαι 'I stop'. These are typically combined with a present participle, as in καὶ τὰς ἰδίας οὐσίας προσαναλίσκοντες διετέλουν (Dem. 20.10) 'they continued lavishing even their own fortunes'. The value realized by these constructions can be described as 'aspectual', as they emphasize the beginning (ἄρχομαι), ending (λήγω, παύομαι), or continuation (διάγω, διαγίγνομαι, διατελέω, ἐπιμένω) of the action.[10]

2.2.2 Previous Proposals to Define Verbal Periphrasis

In what follows, I discuss some previously proposed definitions of verbal periphrasis. The discussion does not include the studies by Létoublon (1982), de la Villa (1989), and Wakker (2006): while these studies are to some extent relevant to our present purposes, they take a different approach by concentrating exclusively on the notions of 'auxiliary' and 'auxiliarity', without making much reference to 'verbal periphrasis' and 'periphrasticity'.[11]

2.2.2.1 Björck (1940)

Björck (1940: 9) defines periphrastic constructions by making reference to their synthetic counterparts:

> Unter Periphrase möchte ich jede solche Verbindung der Kopula mit einem prädikativen Partizip verstanden wissen, die ohne Änderung des Tatsacheninhalts gegen eine einfache Verbalform vertauscht werden kann.[12]

Whether such complete synonymy of two different forms exists, however, is problematic, and difficult to assess.[13]

In distinguishing between true 'verbal' combinations of εἰμί with the present participle (as in ἦν προάγων αὐτούς (Mc. 10.32) 'he was

---

[10] Compare Brinton (1988) with regard to English, who refers to verbs such as 'to begin' and 'to stop' with the term 'aspectualizers' (distinguishing between 'ingressive', 'egressive', and 'continuative' aspectualizers).
[11] For the difference between these two approaches, see de la Villa (1989: 196).
[12] 'Under periphrasis I understand each combination of the copula with a predicative participle which is such that it can be replaced by a synthetic verbal form without a change in meaning.'
[13] Compare Porter (1989: 453–4).

'Verbal' and 'Adjectival' Periphrasis 63

going before them') and 'adjectival' ones (as in πρέπον ἐστί 'it is fitting'), Björck (1940: 17–40) seems to adopt, albeit implicitly, a second criterion for periphrasticity: he notes that the latter are not periphrastic because there is no semantic integration of the finite verb and the participle (as the participle is adjectivized). Björck claims that such combinations also violate his first (main) criterion, as a form such as συμφέρει 'it is fitting' should not be considered 'equivalent' to συμφέρον ἐστί (Björck 1940: 29), but this is less convincing.[14]

2.2.2.2 Aerts (1965)

Aerts (1965: 2) largely follows Björck (1940) in noting that the term 'periphrasis' must be limited to combinations of εἰμί and ἔχω and a participle expressing 'an elementary verbal conception', as in ἦν διδάσκων = ἐδίδασκεν 'he was teaching' or γεγραμμένον ἐστί = γέγραπται 'it is written'. Surprisingly, however, Aerts (1965: 150) seems to adopt a much broader definition of the term elsewhere in his book. For example, he writes of Herodotus that 'we find all sorts of nominal and verbal periphrases, for example, with εἶναι, γίγνεσθαι, ποιεῖν, ποιεῖσθαι, μέλλειν, ἔρχεσθαι, ἰέναι etc.' Aerts (1965: 3, 12–17) also adopts the term 'adjectival periphrasis' for those combinations of εἰμί with a (present) participle where the participle refers a property to the subject of the verb; these combinations are not considered periphrastic.

The novelty of Aerts' (1965) treatment is his introduction of three main types of periphrasis,[15] namely, *substitute*, *suppletive*, and *expressive periphrasis*.[16] While this classification helps us understand the relationship between synthetic and periphrastic forms, it does raise the question whether the third, expressive type still corresponds to Aerts' initial definition of periphrasis, that is, combinations of εἰμί and ἔχω and a participle expressing an elementary verbal conception.[17]

2.2.2.3 Kahn (1973)

Kahn (1973: 126–42) stresses the need to define verbal periphrasis in purely syntactic terms, for which purpose he turns to Harris'

---

[14] Contrast, for example, Gildersleeve (1980 [1900–11]: 81), who explicitly equates προσῆκόν ἐστι with the synthetic form προσήκει.
[15] See Aerts (1965: 3).   [16] Cf. §1.2.
[17] Compare Evans (2001: 221–2).

'transformational' grammar. Focusing on the participial constructions with εἰμί, Kahn (1973: 127) proposes the following definition:

> The occurrence of εἰμί + participle in a given sentence is periphrastic whenever there is only one kernel sentence underlying both forms in the transformational source of the given sentence.[18]

This formulation, as Kahn himself notes, essentially corresponds to Aerts' (1965) earlier criterion of an 'elementary verbal conception' (as in ἦν διδάσκων = ἐδίδασκεν 'he was teaching'). Contrary to Aerts (1965) and Björck (1940), however, Kahn follows this criterium through and considers most cases of 'adjectival periphrasis' periphrastic (for example, ἀρέσκον ἐστί = ἀρέσκει 'it is pleasing'). Kahn (1973: 133–6) nevertheless agrees that in some cases the participle resembles an adjective and therefore proposes to distinguish between 'unitary' and 'copulative' periphrasis. These, however, should be conceived of 'not as distinct kinds of construction but as distinct tendencies within a single construction'.[19]

Kahn's (1973) treatment suffers from two major weaknesses. First, Kahn does not discuss how his approach can be applied to other constructions; in other words, are there participial combinations that never correspond to a single kernel sentence?[20] Second, even with such a 'syntactic' formulation of the problem, judging whether the combination of a finite verb and a participle corresponds to one or two kernel sentences is a subjective matter,[21] as Kahn himself (1973: 130) admits:

> This definition cannot produce mechanical agreement, since the kernels which a reader is willing to recognize in transformational decomposition will depend upon his understanding of the sentence in the first place.

2.2.2.4 Dietrich (1973a, 1973b)

Unlike most scholars, Dietrich (1973a: 56–7, 1973b: 192) provides criteria for the identification of verbal periphrasis that are situated at

---

[18] Kernel sentences are simple affirmative constructions containing only one verb, from which other more complex constructions can be derived.
[19] Kahn (1973: 135).
[20] For some observations with regard to ἔχω, see Kahn (1973: 128–30).
[21] Cf. also Porter (1989: 448–9).

different linguistic levels.[22] For Dietrich, the term 'verbal periphrasis' refers to a construction that comprises at least two component parts and meets the following criteria: (a) it forms a syntactic unit; (b) its meaning cannot be derived from the component parts; (c) it stands in functional opposition to a synthetic verb form. These criteria are reminiscent of the so-called 'processes of grammaticalization' outlined in §1.5.1, which were later formulated by Lehmann (1995 [1982]).

Dietrich's discussion is of a general nature, as it is intended as diagnostic not only of Ancient Greek but also of Latin and the Romance languages. The practical application of his criteria to Ancient Greek is somewhat less evident, however, and it is surprising to find that Dietrich takes into account a much broader range of constructions than most authors (with constructions belonging to all of the groups outlined under §2.2.1). Whether there is, in cases such as εὐαγγελιζόμενοι ἦσαν (Acts 14.7) 'they were preaching the gospel' or προσαναλίσκοντες διετέλουν (Dem. 20.10) 'they continued lavishing',[23] complete semantic non-compositionality seems debatable, for example. In many of the examples Dietrich (1973a, 1973b) provides, the component parts are also syntactically non-contiguous. At first sight the third criterium seems comparable to what Björck (1940) and Aerts (1965) argue for, when they posited that a periphrastic form ought to be 'roughly equivalent' to a synthetic form; however, this does not seem to be entirely the case, as Dietrich (1973b: 192) explicitly notes:

> Es handelt sich also nicht um die 'Umschreibung' einer einfachen Verbalform (wie z.B. griech. πεπαιδευκὼς ὦ statt πεπαιδεύκω), sondern um eine neue, zusätzliche Funktion, die nur so ausgedrückt wird (z.B. das deutsche Fut.).

While this may justify taking into account a large number of 'periphrastic' constructions, it leads to the paradoxical situation wherein the one construction that virtually all other scholars consider periphrastic (that is, εἰμί with the perfect participle) is excluded by Dietrich.

---

[22] Cf. also Hopper & Traugott (2003: 124).
[23] Both examples are mentioned as periphrastic by Dietrich (1973a).

2.2.2.5 Basset (1979)

Basset's (1979: 1–7) treatment focuses specifically on infinitival periphrases formed with μέλλω 'I am destined to', but it remains relevant for our present discussion. Basset focuses on the semantic and paradigmatic aspects of periphrasis, which, as he shows, change over time. Only when the finite verb has acquired a more general meaning, that is, when it functions as an auxiliary, and when the construction as a whole can be considered an expressive variant of a synthetic form (or when it is paradigmatically integrated) can we speak of verbal periphrasis. Although he advances a three-stage model, which he applies to the development of Latin *habeo* 'I have' with the infinitive,[24] he notes that the actual difference between these three stages is one of degree, and that the nuances are often difficult to grasp. He also notes that even within the periphrastic stage, properly speaking, an evolution is possible.

2.2.2.6 Moser (1988)

Moser's (1988: 19–45) discussion of the definition of verbal periphrasis is primarily of theoretical importance. She starts from the observation that in traditional accounts, verbal periphrasis is often defined as consisting of an auxiliary and a 'simple' verb.[25] She argues, however, that this does not solve the question, since which verbs qualify as auxiliaries is a thorny issue and can only be determined by analysing the construction as a whole, rather than the auxiliary in isolation.[26] Some relevant criteria in this regard are the position of the construction in the verbal system, and the degree of bondedness between the component parts of the construction.[27] She notes, however, that this is not an all-or-nothing matter. For example, 'it is possible to have constructions with a relatively small degree of

---

[24] In the first stage, we are dealing with a Hellenism, whereby habeo = ἔχω 'I can', as in *adhuc multa habeo vobis dicere* (John 16.12) 'I still have many things to say to you'. In the second stage, the periphrasis appears with a modal nuance, the value of habeo + INF being similar to that of Ancient Greek μέλλω + INF, as in *deus enim est qui habet videri* (Iren. 4.38.3) 'For God is He who is yet to be seen'. In the third stage, the periphrasis has the value of a simple future, as in *qui sedent vel sedere habent* 'those who are sitting or will be sitting'.

[25] As in 'to have' or 'to be' with a participle, e.g. 'I have eaten'.

[26] Moser (1988: 30).   [27] Moser (1988: 31, 36).

bondedness, but undoubtedly forming part of the verbal system.'[28] In this context, she notes the possibility of applying so-called 'prototype theory', which she finds 'intuitively very satisfactory', and which she suggests would combine well with Grammaticalization Theory.[29]

2.2.2.7 Porter (1988, 1989, 1999)

Porter (1988, 1989: 452–4, 1999: 45–9) provides the fullest discussion of our topic. Reacting against Björck (1940) and Aerts (1965), Porter (1989: 454) notes that the delimitation of periphrasis on the basis of the adjectivization of the participle must be dismissed. He argues that while a participle may function as an adjective, it is not necessarily adjectivized, and notes that translational choices may influence the individual scholar's interpretation.

Porter (1988: 158, 1989: 452–3, 1999: 45) provides two main formal criteria for defining verbal periphrasis. In his opinion, a periphrastic construction must contain (a) an 'aspectually vague' auxiliary verb,[30] so as to avoid an 'aspectual conflict' with the participle, and (b) a participle in grammatical agreement with its referent. This participle may follow or precede the auxiliary verb, but it can only be separated from it by elements complementing the participle (e.g. adjuncts or complements). The only constructions that comply with these two criteria are those formed with εἰμί 'I am'. Participial constructions with verbs such as ἔχω 'I have' or γίγνομαι 'I become' are not considered periphrastic, since these verbs are not 'aspectually vague';[31] hence, 'the auxiliary inherently maintains its integrity as an independent contributor to the semantics of the clause'. Both of Porter's (1989) criteria have attracted criticism in recent years: for example, it has been shown that the participle and the finite verb can be separated by elements other than complements of the participle.[32] Scholars have also argued that even with verbs that are not aspectually vague, there is not necessarily an 'aspectual conflict' between the

---

[28] Moser (1988: 36). [29] Moser (1988: 38).

[30] On this notion, see e.g. Porter (1988: 158): 'aspectually vague verbs are those very few verbs which "lack choice" in their formal paradigm, in that they are confined to a single stem form and hence offer no corresponding aspectual opposition.'

[31] Porter (1989: 487–92) uses the term 'catenative construction' for these constructions.

[32] See e.g. Evans (2001: 232).

auxiliary and the participle, since the participle is the main contributor of aspectual semantics.[33]

2.2.2.8 Evans (2001)

In his study on verbal syntax in the Greek Pentateuch, Evans (2001: 220–57) discusses 'periphrastic' verb forms, in particular combinations of εἰμί 'I am' and γίγνομαι 'I become' with a participle, and μέλλω 'I am destined to' and θέλω 'I want' with an infinitive. Evans (2001: 256) offers the following definition of verbal periphrasis, which is strongly reminiscent of Aerts (1965):

> Verbal periphrasis is defined here as the combination of auxiliary verb plus participle or infinitive as near equivalent to (substitute periphrasis) or replacement for (suppletive periphrasis) a synthetic tense form.[34]

Evans (2001) provides an in-depth discussion of the previous contributions by Aerts (1965) and especially Porter (1989), but he does not entirely clarify his own definition. More specifically, he does not explain how 'near equivalence to a synthetic form' can be determined, and especially how the problematic notion of 'auxiliarity' can be defined.

Evans (2001: 230–1) also engages in the debate on the adjectivization of the participle when it is combined with εἰμί.[35] He agrees with Porter (1989: 454) that translational choices may influence one's interpretation, but, on the basis of his definition of verbal periphrasis, believes the following:

> An attempt must be made on the grounds of contextual probabilities to isolate the genuine εἰμί periphrases from cases where the participle in close proximity and grammatical agreement to a form of εἰμί is fully adjectivized.

This observation must refer to the 'auxiliary' part in Evans' definition, the precise interpretation of which, however, was left implicit. Exactly which contextual probabilities are meant is also not further specified. Thus, it remains unclear why in phrases such as ἐστιν ζῶν (Gen. 9.3)

---

[33] See e.g. Duhoux (2000: 295); Campbell (2008: 33).

[34] Evans does not recognize Aerts' third category, as he considers it 'over-subjective' (Evans 2001: 221).

[35] Note that Evans (2001) takes into account both adjectivized present and perfect participles.

'it is alive' or κεκλεμμένον ἔσται (Gen. 30.33) 'it will be stolen', Evans considers the participle adjectivized, while this would not be the case in phrases such as ἔσῃ εὐφραινόμενος (Deut. 16.15) 'you will be happily disposed' or ἀφωρισμένη ἐστίν (Lev. 14.46) 'it [the house] is set apart'.[36]

2.3 A PROTOTYPE-BASED APPROACH TOWARDS VERBAL PERIPHRASIS

2.3.1 Linguistic Categorization

Following the suggestion made by Moser (1988) that the so-called 'prototype model' of linguistic categorization can be applied to the category of verbal periphrasis, I present such an alternative approach here.

Stimulated by the research of Eleanor Rosch and her colleagues in the 1970s on human categorization,[37] linguists working within Functional and Cognitive approaches[38] proposed the prototype model as an alternative to the classical, criterial-attribute model of linguistic categorization, which had prevailed since the time of Aristotle.[39] According to the more traditional view, (a) categories can be defined in terms of necessary and sufficient features, (b) all members of a category are equivalent representatives of the category, and (c) categories have clear-cut boundaries. By contrast, Rosch's research showed that (a) necessary and sufficient conditions for category membership cannot always be defined, (b) some entities may be better examples of the category than others, and (c) category boundaries may be blurred at the edges or 'fuzzy'.[40] A typical example would be the category 'bird'.[41] While robins possess most of the attributes found across members of this category and are thus considered highly

---

[36] Note that Evans (2001: 232) himself classifies ἐξεικονισμένον (Exod. 21.23) 'fully formed' as 'adjectivized', but later on considers the example an instance of suppletive periphrasis (Evans 2001: 243).
[37] See e.g. Rosch (1978).
[38] See e.g. Langacker (1987); Lakoff (1987); Givón (1989); Taylor (1998, 2003); Geeraerts (2006 [1989]).
[39] For discussion of approaches towards linguistic categorization, see Aarts (2006).
[40] See Taylor (1998: 179); Geeraerts (2006 [1989]: 146–7).
[41] I borrow this example from Evans & Green (2006: 267).

prototypical, ostriches have many fewer of these attributes: they cannot fly, they do not chirp, and they are not small.[42] As such, they constitute less prototypical, more peripheral representatives of the category.

In recent years, prototype theory has been applied to linguistic domains other than lexical semantics.[43] Taylor (2003: 200–21) notes in this regard that traditional grammatical categories such as 'noun', 'adjective', and 'verb' are prototypically organized. Some adjectives, for example, cannot be used in attributive or predicative position (*my husband is former, *the asleep child), or cannot be graded (*a very only child).[44] A prototype-based approach has also been applied to verbal periphrasis in other languages,[45] and has, it seems, a number of distinct advantages. First, it allows us to situate different periphrastic constructions on a continuum of 'periphrasticity', without having to draw any arbitrary lines. Second, while it is synchronically oriented, it allows for diachronic analyses: particular constructions may become more or less prototypical over time.[46] Third, it also explains the considerable amount of confusion in previous studies of verbal periphrasis. It seems likely that all of the constructions that have been considered 'periphrastic' resemble the prototype to some extent, some scholars adopting a more rigid approach than others.

2.3.2 Criteria of 'Periphrasticity'

As suggested by Moser (1988) and others, the criteria adopted to identify prototypical periphrastic constructions can be derived from Grammaticalization Theory.[47] While Grammaticalization Theory in essence provides a theory of language change, many scholars have pointed out its synchronic relevance.[48] Different linguistic items can be situated on a 'grammaticalization scale' (synchrony),[49]

---

[42] Note that this feature is not a binary one like the other two.
[43] For an overview, see e.g. Luraghi (1993).   [44] See Taylor (2003: 211).
[45] See esp. Bertinetto (1990) with regard to Italian.
[46] Cf. Luraghi (1993: 512).   [47] See e.g. Haspelmath (2000: 660–1).
[48] See e.g. Lehmann (1985: 303): 'from the synchronic point of view, grammaticalization provides a principle according to which subcategories of a given grammatical category may be ordered.'
[49] Cf. Lehmann (1985: 305–6).

corresponding to the degree to which they have been grammaticalized (diachrony).

While it goes beyond the scope of this book to offer an in-depth synchronic analysis of the periphrasticity of all constructions that are mentioned in the literature, it is useful to briefly illustrate the prototype approach which I am advocating here. To that end, I have analysed all instances in Classical Greek of three constructions representing the three different groups I outlined under §2.2.1: ἔχω 'I have' with the aorist participle (constructions with verbs of state), ἔρχομαι 'I go' with the future participle (constructions with verbs of motion), and διαγίγνομαι 'I continue' with the present participle (constructions with phasal verbs). Before starting the analysis, however, it is worth outlining those processes of grammaticalization that are particularly relevant for our present purposes. As we saw in §1.5.1, a distinction can be made between *phonological, functional,* and *morpho-syntactic* processes/criteria, which can be situated on *syntagmatic* and *paradigmatic* axes.

With respect to phonology, focus lies on the syntagmatic axis, since attrition (reduction) is typical for the later stages of grammaticalization. To be more specific, I shall analyse the coalescence of the component parts, or in other words their degree of continuity/adjacency.[50]

As regards function, attention will be paid to the *generalization* of the finite verb. Two specific indicators of generalization that can be referred to in this regard are (a) lexical class expansion of the participle, and (b) compatibility with inanimate subjects. Narrowly connected to generalization is idiomaticization or semantic integration on the syntagmatic axis: when the construction becomes more idiomatic, or in other words when the semantic contribution of the finite verb becomes less substantial,[51] the integration of the component parts increases.[52] Attention will be drawn in this regard to the functional (aspecto-temporal) range of the constructions under analysis.

---

[50] Fusion too can be considered typical for the later stages of grammaticalization. Moreover, it seems debatable whether in case of fusion we are still dealing with a (prototypical) periphrastic construction. Compare Moser (1988: 44).

[51] A good example would be the 'going to V'-construction in English. While some cases retain a sense of motion (as in 'I am going to have lunch'), in many others the contribution of *going to* is much less transparent (as in 'I am going to read the newspaper').

[52] Cf. Langacker (2005: 177–8).

Morpho-syntactically, I shall examine both paradigmatic and syntagmatic processes, particularly the following: paradigmaticization, which describes the process of a construction becoming integrated into the conjugational paradigm, obligatorification, which assesses whether there are other constructions available for the same function, and rigidification, which determines the degree of syntagmatic variability of the component parts of the construction. Since decategorialization—that is, the loss of canonical verbal properties[53]—is indicative of a later stage of grammaticalization, it will not be further discussed here.

In addition to evaluating periphrases according to the above criteria, I shall also attend to the use of the construction in different registers, as Markopoulos (2009) suggested we do.[54]

2.3.3 Application of the Prototype Model

2.3.3.1 διαγίγνομαι with the present participle

The construction of διαγίγνομαι with the present participle occurs relatively infrequently in Classical Greek, with only ten instances in our entire corpus. Eight of the ten examples are found in Xenophon, including the following example (35):

(35) καὶ μάχῃ τε ἐνίκησε καὶ ἀπὸ τούτου δὴ ἔφερε καὶ ἦγε τούτους καὶ πολεμῶν διεγένετο μέχρι Κῦρος ἐδεήθη τοῦ στρατεύματος (Xen., An. 2.6.5)

'He defeated them in battle and from that time on plundered them in every way, and he kept up the war until Cyrus wanted his army.' (tr. Brownson)

In examples such as these the construction expresses the value of 'to continue V-ing', which can be considered aspectual (though note that no synthetic form explicitly expresses such a value).[55] A relatively strong semantic integration of the component parts of the

---

[53] e.g. with regard to tense, aspect, mood, person, argument structure, etc., as in Engl. *can*: **to can *canning *I can that.*
[54] Cf. §1.5.4.3 for the pragmatic criterion of 'acceptability'.
[55] Cf. Brinton (1988: 59) with regard to English, who distinguishes between two systems of aspect marking, that is, the primary system of simple, progressive, and perfect forms and the secondary system of 'aspectualizers' such as 'to begin', 'to stop', 'to continue', etc.

construction is also indicated by the fact that there is temporal, spatial, and referential identity between πολεμῶν 'waging war' and διεγένετο 'he continued' (that is, both verb forms refer to the same person, as well as the same time and place).[56] The participle following phasal verbs such as διαγίγνομαι is compared by Rijksbaron (2002: 117–22) with that following 'verbs of perceiving and knowing' such as οἶδα 'I know', but it is worth noting the difference with an example from Thucydides (36):[57]

(36) τόν τε γὰρ Μῆδον αὐτοὶ ἴσμεν ἐκ περάτων γῆς πρότερον ἐπὶ τὴν Πελοπόννησον ἐλθόντα ἢ τὰ παρ' ὑμῶν ἀξίως προαπαντῆσαι (Thuc. 1.69.5)

'For example, the Persian, as we ourselves know, came from the ends of the earth as far as the Peloponnesus before your forces went forth to withstand him in a manner worthy of your power.' (tr. Forster Smith)

There is weak referential, temporal, and spatial cohesion in (36): ἴσμεν 'we know' refers to different persons as well as a different time and place than ἐλθόντα '[that] he came'.

Nevertheless, it should be pointed out that διαγίγνομαι as a finite verb has generalized to a limited extent, as is indicated by the fact that it is used only with animate subjects and atelic lexical verbs. Moreover, the construction is limited to a 'continuative' aspectual meaning, and has not generalized to a progressive one, a development which is cross-linguistically attested.[58] The semantic contribution of the two parts of the construction is also relatively clear. The participial complement can be seen as an extension of a nominal complement, in which case διαγίγνομαι as a lexical verb has the meaning of 'go through (something)', as illustrated in (37):

(37) ταύτην μὲν οὖν τὴν νύκτα οὕτω διεγένοντο (Xen., An. 1.10.19)

'Thus it was then that they got through this night.' (tr. Brownson)

In seven out of ten examples the component parts of the construction are syntactically contiguous. However, this is not always the case, as can be seen in (38):

---

[56] Compare Givón (2001: 2.54–8) on English 'modality verbs' such as 'to want', 'to finish', 'to begin', 'to try', etc.
[57] I borrow this example from Rijksbaron (2002: 117).
[58] See Bybee et al. (1994: 164–6).

(38) μετὰ ταῦτα τοίνυν ὅσον μὲν χρόνον ἡ ὑμετέρα δύναμις παρῆν ἐν Ἑλλησπόντῳ, κολακεύων καὶ φενακίζων ὑμᾶς διαγέγονεν (Dem. 23.179)
'Since that time, so long as you had forces in the Hellespont, he has continually flattered you and cozened you.' (tr. Murray)

Roughly the same is valid for the order of the participle and the finite verb: there is a tendency for the participle to precede the finite verb (7/10), but this order has not become rigid.

During the Classical period, several variant constructions realized more or less the same aspectual value, particularly διάγω 'I continue', διατελέω 'I continue', and ἐπιμένω 'I continue' with the present participle.[59] At no time did the construction become part of the conjugational paradigm.

2.3.3.2 ἔχω with the aorist participle

Compared with διαγίγνομαι with the present participle, the construction of ἔχω with the aorist participle is much more frequently attested (with sixty-two clearly periphrastic examples), and in a much broader range of texts. Already in antiquity, however, it was noted that the construction occurs particularly frequently in tragedy, especially in the work of Sophocles: the construction was known as the σχῆμα Σοφόκλειον 'Sophoclean form'.[60]

The construction tends to be used with verbs that have telic content, as in (39):

(39) {Χο.} οἴμ᾽ ὡς ἔοικας ὀψὲ τὴν δίκην ἰδεῖν. / {Κρ.} οἴμοι, / ἔχω μαθὼν δείλαιος (Soph., Ant. 1270-2)
'Chorus. Alas, you seem to have seen justice only late! Creon. Alas, I have learned, unhappy as I am.' (tr. Lloyd-Jones)

However, the construction is not limited to verbs that have telic content, and is also used with verbs that Vendler (1957) categorizes as 'activities' and 'states', such as ἔραμαι 'I love', ταρβέω 'I am frightened', and θαυμάζω 'I wonder'. Similarly, while the construction

---

[59] See Dietrich (1973a: 243-6). According to Dietrich (1973a: 245-6), the construction of διάγω with the present participle can be considered semantically closest to that of διαγίγνομαι with the present participle, though he stresses the need for further research.

[60] See e.g. Rijksbaron (2002: 130).

'Verbal' and 'Adjectival' Periphrasis 75

occurs predominantly with animate subjects, this is not always the case, as shown in (40):

(40) {*Io.*} ηὐδᾶτο γὰρ ταῦτ' οὐδέ πω λήξαντ' ἔχει (Soph., *OT* 731)
'Iocasta. Yes, that was the story, and it has not ceased [to be told].' (tr. Lloyd-Jones, modified)

In terms of idiomaticization, it is worth noting that the construction can be found both with an older, resultative value and a younger, anterior value. The development from resultative to anterior is well attested across languages,[61] and will be discussed at much greater length in Chapter 3. In illustration, consider examples (41) and (42):

(41) {*Κρ.*} ἐμοὶ γὰρ ὅστις πᾶσαν εὐθύνων πόλιν / μὴ τῶν ἀρίστων ἅπτεται βουλευμάτων, / ἀλλ' ἐκ φόβου του γλῶσσαν ἐγκλῄσας ἔχει, / κάκιστος εἶναι νῦν τε καὶ πάλαι δοκεῖ (Soph., *Ant.* 178–81)

'Creon. Yes, to me anyone who while guiding the whole city fails to set his hand to the best counsels, but keeps his mouth shut by reason of some fear seems now and has always seemed the worst of men.' (tr. Lloyd-Jones)

(42) τὴν μὲν τοίνυν προῖκα τοῦτον τὸν τρόπον ἔχει λαβών (Dem. 27.17)
'The dowry then he has gotten in this way.'

In (41), Creon sets out his principles as a ruler to the citizens of Thebes. The form ἐγκλῄσας ἔχει does not refer to a past event, but rather characterizes a present state in which the subject (who is not further specified) finds himself: 'he keeps his lips closed'. In (42), on the other hand, the periphrastic form ἔχει λαβών 'he has gotten' is used to relate a past event, Aphobus' receipt of the dowry, which has relevance at the time of speaking. In the former case the semantic contribution of the component parts is most transparent (lit. 'having his lips closed, he keeps [them] so'), and in fact it seems that the construction is best considered non-periphrastic.[62]

As with constructions of διαγίγνομαι 'I continue' with the present participle, there is no fixed order to the component parts, although there is a tendency for the participial complement to precede the main verb (49/62 = 79%). There is a remarkably high degree of bondedness between the component parts (56/62 = 90%).

---

[61] See e.g. Bybee *et al.* (1994: 68–9).
[62] Compare Aerts (1965: 148–9).

As I shall argue in the third chapter, the construction may be considered at least partially integrated into the verbal paradigm; it was used as an alternative (present/past) perfect formation for verbs for which no active (present/past) perfect was available,[63] for example, ἀπειλέω 'I threaten', κηρύσσω 'I proclaim', and προτίω 'I prefer in honour'. It was also used, however, with verbs for which a synthetic form was available, for example, ἀποσπάω 'I drag away from', γαμέω 'I marry', and μανθάνω 'I learn'.

During the Classical period, a number of periphrastic constructions were available that effected a similar aspectual value, most importantly εἰμί with the perfect participle. Constructions such as ὑπάρχω 'I am' with the aorist or the perfect participle and γίγνομαι 'I become' with the aorist or the perfect participle were used with less frequency.

2.3.3.3 ἔρχομαι with the future participle

The construction of ἔρχομαι with the future participle occurs only slightly more frequently (twenty-one examples) than that of διαγίγνομαι with the present participle. Next to these examples, where periphrastic interpretation seems to be preferable, there are also various ambiguous cases, as in (43):

(43) {Ιφ.} ὡς σωτηρίαν / Ἕλλησι δώσουσ᾽ ἔρχομαι νικηφόρον (Eur., IA 1472–3)

'Iphigenia. For I am departing to give the Greeks salvation and victory!' (tr. Kovacs)

This statement is uttered by Iphigeneia, who has consented to be sacrificed to Artemis so that the Greek fleet can sail to Troy. While one could interpret δώσουσ᾽ ἔρχομαι 'I am going to give' as a future periphrasis, a non-periphrastic interpretation, where the future participle functions primarily to convey the purpose of Iphigenia's going, is more likely. After all, Clytaemnestra's question (ὦ τέκνον, οἴχῃ; (Eur., IA 1463) 'oh child, are you going away?') emphasizes the motion.

Almost half of the examples can be found in Herodotus, who uses the construction only with verbs of saying (λέγω 'I say', φράζω 'I tell', μηκύνω 'I talk at length about', σημαίνω 'I tell'), as in (44):[64]

---

[63] Cf. Aerts (1965: 129). [64] Cf. Létoublon (1982: 185).

(44) τὴν δ' ὧν μεγίστην τε δαίμονα ἥγηνται εἶναι καὶ μεγίστην οἱ ὁρτὴν ἀνάγουσι, ταύτην ἔρχομαι ἐρέων (Hdt. 2.40.1)

'I shall now, however, speak of that goddess whom they consider the greatest, and in whose honor they keep highest festival.' (tr. Godley)

The construction can also be found in the work of other authors, most notably Xenophon and Plato, where it is used with a broader range of verbs, mostly those with telic content. The construction is never used with an inanimate subject.[65]

In terms of semantics, the value of the construction can be called 'immediative':[66] it indicates what is going to happen immediately afterwards, as in (45), where Socrates states he intends to explain how the rhapsode Ion excels in speaking about Homer, but does not have much to say about other things:

(45) καὶ ὁρῶ, ὦ Ἴων, καὶ ἔρχομαί γέ σοι ἀποφανούμενος ὅ μοι δοκεῖ τοῦτο εἶναι (Pl., *Ion* 533c)

'I do observe it, Ion, and I am going to point out to you what I take it to mean.' (tr. Lamb)

In most of the examples, there is also a strong sense of intention,[67] which is reflected in the fact that a large percentage of the examples (16/21 = 76%) occur in the first person. According to Bybee *et al.* (1994: 269), this may be related to the originally spatial meaning of the construction: 'when the speaker announces that s/he is going somewhere to do something, s/he is also announcing the intention to do that thing'. Cross-linguistically, the value of 'imminence' also typically occurs in the early stages of grammaticalization.[68]

In most of the examples the finite verb and the future participle are syntactically contiguous (14/21 = 67%). There is a strong tendency for the participle to follow the finite verb (20/21 = 95%).

This construction, which occurs rather infrequently, was not integrated into the paradigm. Various alternative expressions were available, such as εἶμι 'I go' with the future participle, ἥκω 'I have come'

---

[65] Cf. Wakker (2007: 253).
[66] Compare Wakker (2007: 178-80) with regard to Herodotus. Bybee *et al.* (1994: 244) offer the following definition: 'a future gram restricted to referring to events which are imminent or about to occur is an immediate future.'
[67] Cf. Adrados (1992a: 453-4).
[68] See Bybee *et al.* (1991: 29-32); Bybee *et al.* (1994: 243-80).

with the future participle, and μέλλω 'I am destined to' with the future infinitive.[69]

2.3.4 The Periphrastic Continuum

It seems that none of the constructions analysed in §2.3.3 can be considered prototypically periphrastic:[70] they occur (relatively) infrequently, they are not (or only partially) integrated into the paradigm, and there is no fixed order to the component parts of the construction. Moreover, there are various alternative periphrastic constructions available. This can be considered a major difference of Ancient Greek from modern European languages such as English, in which highly grammaticalized periphrastic constructions can be found (such as the 'I am going to V' or the 'I have V-ed' constructions), corresponding much more closely to the periphrastic prototype. Binnick (1991: 32) notes the following in this regard:

> The classical languages had complex [periphrastic, KB] forms, but the use of complex forms was sporadic and played no essential role in the grammatical systems, so that the periphrastics of the classical languages parallel those of the modern languages little in regard either to form or to content.

Even so, the approach adopted here allows us to explicitly compare different constructions. Of the three constructions that have been investigated, the construction of ἔχω with the aorist participle corresponds most closely to the periphrastic prototype: besides the fact that it is used most frequently of the three and in a variety of genres/registers, the component parts of the construction are syntactically contiguous in a large percentage of the examples (up to 90%), there are clear signs of generalization/idiomaticization (the construction being used with different types of content verb, animate and inanimate subjects, and with different aspectual functions), and the construction is partially integrated in the paradigm.

The two other constructions under discussion should be considered (much) less prototypical, particularly διαγίγνομαι with the present participle. Although the construction realizes an aspectual

---

[69] Cf. Dietrich (1973a, 1973b); Wakker (2007).
[70] For a different use of the term 'periphrastic continuum', see Jäger (2006: 72–4).

value, it achieves a relatively low degree of generalization/idiomaticization, since the construction does not occur with inanimate subjects, always retains the value of 'to continue', and is only used with verbs whose content is atelic. Moreover, the construction occurs infrequently (being almost entirely limited to a single author), its component parts are contiguous to a lesser extent, and it is not integrated into the verbal paradigm.

The construction of ἔρχομαι with the future participle may be situated in between these two extremes, although it seems to resemble διαγίγνομαι with the present participle more than ἔχω with the aorist participle with respect to degree of periphrasticity. The construction also shows a low degree of generalization/idiomaticization, as it does not occur with inanimate subjects and is limited to an 'immediative' value. The component parts are contiguous more or less to the same extent as with διαγίγνομαι with the present participle, and the construction is not integrated into the verbal paradigm. However, there are signs that the construction was grammaticalizing during the Classical period, as it can be found in several authors (mainly Herodotus, Xenophon, and Plato), and while it was initially limited to verbs of saying, it also came to be used with other verbs.[71]

2.4 ADJECTIVAL PERIPHRASIS

2.4.1 The Property-referring Participle

In various languages, it has been observed that the participle in BE-periphrases can have an 'adjective-like' (or more correctly 'property-referring') function. Scholars differ, however, in the conclusions they draw with regard to the *categorial status* of the participle[72] as a result of its quasi-adjectival capability: (a) some scholars limit themselves to function, and do not make any explicit statements about categorial status; (b) other scholars simply assume that a property-referring function also entails adjectival categorial status; and (c) still other scholars explicitly argue that the property-referring participle is an adjective.

---

[71] Compare Létoublon (1982: 187).
[72] That is, its categorization in terms of word class or 'part of speech'.

Scholars working on periphrasis in Ancient Greek to a large extent belong to this third group:[73] already in Smyth (1984 [1920]: 414), for example, we read that participles such as συμφέρων 'useful' and διαφέρων 'superior' are 'completely adjectivized'. As mentioned under §2.2.2, this view was further elaborated by Björck (1940) and Aerts (1965), and has become common in many discussions of verbal periphrasis.[74] It has particular relevance for the present study, since it is argued (by Björck and Aerts among others) that such 'adjectival' constructions should be excluded from the discussion of true, verbal periphrasis.[75] Some scholars, however, such as Porter (1989: 454) maintain that 'reference to a property' and 'adjectivization' should not be equated, and hence that we are still dealing with verbal periphrasis.

The basis for the recognition of 'adjectival periphrasis' lies in the semantic difference perceived between examples such as (46) and (47):

(46) {Αγ.} οὐ γὰρ κλυόντες ἐσμὲν αἰσχίστους λόγους, / ἄναξ Ὀδυσσεῦ, τοῦδ' ὑπ' ἀνδρὸς ἀρτίως; (Soph., Aj. 1320-1)

'Agamemnon. For were we not just hearing the most shameful words from this man, lord Odysseus?'

(47) ὑπόλοιπόν μοί ἐστιν ἔτι πρὸς ταύτην τὴν ἐπιστολὴν τὴν εὖ ἔχουσαν καὶ τοὺς λόγους τῶν πρέσβεων γράψαι τὴν ἀπόκρισιν, ἣν ἡγοῦμαι δικαίαν τ' εἶναι καὶ συμφέρουσαν ὑμῖν (Dem. 7.46)

'It now remains for me, in answer to this precious letter and to the speeches of the ambassadors, to propose the resolution which I conceive to be just and expedient for you.' (tr. Vince, slightly modified)

While in (46) the particle in combination with the verb εἰμί denotes an action, that is hearing something, in (47) the participle denotes a property, as also indicated by the coordination with the adjective δικαίαν 'just'. Björck (1940: 25-6), referring to Kühner & Gerth (1976 [1898]: 39), notes in this context that:

> Das Wesen der adjektivischen Periphrase liegt darin beschlossen, dass 'das Partizip in der Weise eines Adjektivs dem Subjekte ein charakteristisches

---

[73] As an illustration of the first group see e.g. Mitchell (1985: 272-80; 410-12) (Old English), and as an illustration of the second group Núñez-Pertejo (2003) (Early Modern English).

[74] See e.g. Karleen (1980: 118-20); Ceglia (1998: 26-7); Evans (2001: 231).

[75] As such, the term adjectival *periphrasis* is somewhat badly chosen (cf. Ceglia 1998: 26).

Merkmal, eine dauernde Eigenschaft, einen bleibenden Zustand beilegt' (K.-G. I S. 39).[76]

Under the notion 'adjectival' periphrasis, Björck (1940: 16, 23-5), as well as other scholars, also categorizes examples such as (48):

(48) ἔστιν δὲ τοὺς μὲν Ἕλληνας παρακαλῶν ἐπὶ τὴν τῶν βαρβάρων στρατείαν (Isoc. 15.57)
'It (the speech) summons the Hellenes to make an expedition against the barbarians.' (tr. Norlin, slightly modified)

In this example, the property-referring function of the participle may be somewhat less clear, given that we are dealing with a verb whose content is non-stative (dynamic), παρακαλέω 'I invite'. However, the context makes it clear that a previously delivered speech is being discussed, rather than one which is ongoing. Since examples of this kind are much less frequent than those of the kind illustrated under (47), Björck (1940) proposes to make a distinction between two main types of adjectival periphrasis—that is, *Daueradjektivierungen* (frequently occurring adjectivizations) and *Gelegenheitsadjektivierungen* (infrequently occurring adjectivizations). Björck stresses, however, that in both cases the participle is 'adjectivized', and that neither type can be identified as true (verbal) periphrasis.

Before further investigating the formal criteria used to argue for adjectivization of the participle, it is worth noting that other types of participle (in combination with εἰμί) could also be used with such a property-referring function. This is an element which has received very little attention in the relevant literature, which has almost entirely concentrated on the present participle. Consider the following two examples:

(49) κεχωρισμέναι μὲν γάρ εἰσι καὶ πλήρεις περιττώματος, ἐξ ἑνὸς δ' ἤρτηνται τοῦ στομάχου καὶ τελευτῶσι πρὸς μίαν ἔξοδον τὴν τοῦ περιττώματος (Aristot., *Part. an.* 680a)
'But although they are separated from each other and are full of residue, they all spring from the gullet and they all terminate in the residual vent.' (tr. Peck)

---

[76] 'The essence of adjectival periphrasis lies in the fact that "the participle attributes to the subject in the way of an adjective a characteristic feature, a lasting property, an enduring situation" (K.-G. I S. 39).'

(50) οὔτε γὰρ θρασὺς / οὔτ᾽ οὖν προδείσας εἰμὶ τῷ γε νῦν λόγῳ (Soph., OT 89–90)
'Oedipus. So far, I am neither bold nor prematurely fearful at your words.'

In (49), we find the perfect participle (κεχωρισμέναι) 'removed' with a property-referring function, and in (50) we see that even the aorist participle could be used in this way (προδείσας 'prematurely fearful'), though much less frequently. Moreover, some combinations of the verb ἔχω with a perfect participle are also relevant for our present discussion. Consider example (51):

(51) ὁ μὲν οὖν ἄνθρωπος ἀπολελυμένην τε καὶ μαλακωτάτην ἔχει μάλιστα τὴν γλῶτταν καὶ πλατεῖαν (Aristot., Part. an. 660a)
'So man has his tongue the most free and soft and broad.'

This example closely resembles our previous example (49), as the perfect participle again expresses a property (ἀπολελυμένην 'released, free'). With this type of construction, however, the property is not predicated of the subject, but rather of the object (τὴν γλῶτταν 'the tongue'). This may be considered roughly equivalent to ἡ γλῶττα τοῦ ἀνθρώπου ἐστὶ μάλιστα ἀπολελυμένη κτλ. 'the tongue of man is the most free'.

2.4.2 Criteria for the Adjectivization of the Present Participle

In the literature, various criteria have been proposed for adjectivization of the present participle, though never systematically.[77] In what follows, I critically discuss these various criteria, distinguishing between 'phonological' (§2.4.2.1), 'morphological' (§2.4.2.2) and 'syntactic' (§2.4.2.3) criteria.

2.4.2.1 Phonological criteria

The first set of criteria is of a phonological nature. Amenta (2003: 32) notes that in cases where there is phonological reduction of the participle (as in Latin *prudens* < *providens < *providere*) or where the verbal stem from which the participle is derived is no longer

---

[77] For a systematic overview with regard to Latin, see Vester (1977: 272–9).

recognizable (as in Latin *frequens* < *frequo), we can assume adjectivization of the participle. While these indeed can be considered robust criteria of adjectivization,[78] in practice they are of little use, since only a very small number of forms are attested. Most often cited in this context are ἄκων 'unwillingly' and ἑκών 'purposely'.[79]

2.4.2.2 Morphological criteria

The next set of criteria are morphological. Contrary to the phonological and most of the syntactic criteria, these criteria do not pertain to the combination of the participle with εἰμί, but rather analyse indirectly whether a participle is used in the same morphological environments as true adjectives. As such, we have to assume that the relevant forms are always adjectivized (that is, also in their combination with εἰμί), an assumption which may not be entirely unproblematic. Moreover, it remains unclear what the consequences are for those participles that are not used in these environments.[80]

The first morphological criterion, which was advanced by Björck (1940: 17) and Amenta (2003: 30) among others, addresses whether an adverb is attested of the participle. This appears to be the case for various lexically stative participles, such as ἀγαπώντως 'gladly', ἀρκούντως 'abundantly', ἐπισταμένως 'skilfully', θαρρούντως 'boldly', λυσιτελούντως 'profitably', πρεπόντως 'fittingly', etc.[81] As already mentioned, it is unclear whether we can generalize on this basis that these participles are adjectivized. As Chanet (1986: 36) notes, these adverb formations occur rather infrequently, much less so than those based on perfect participles.[82] It should also be noted that,

---

[78] Cf. also Kahn (1973: 135).
[79] See e.g. Stahl (1907: 681); Schwyzer (1950: 408). For the perfect participle, reference can be made to ἄσμενος 'well-pleased' and ἴκμενος 'fair' (of a breeze).
[80] Compare Heine (1972: 235) on the Latin participle: 'sicherlich ist ein Partizip dann, wenn es im Komparativ erscheint, adjektivisch, aber dies erlaubt generell weder einen positiven Rückschluß auf die Grundform noch einen negativen auf diejenigen Partizipien, die keine Steigerungsformen bilden' ('it is certainly the case that a participle used in the comparative degree is adjectival, but in general this does not permit a positive conclusion with regard to the base form, nor a negative conclusion with regard to those participles which do not have comparative/superlative forms').
[81] For further examples, see Kühner & Blass (1983 [1892]: 300).
[82] See e.g. ἀνειμένως 'carelessly', ἀπονενοημένως 'desperately', ἐντεταμένως 'vigorously', κεχαρισμένως 'acceptably', κεχυμένως 'profusely', πεφοβημένως 'timorously', πεφυλαγμένως 'with due caution', τεθορυβημένως 'tumultuously', τεταγμένως 'in orderly manner', etc. (Kühner & Blass 1983 [1892]: 300).

unsurprisingly, there are no attested adverbs of lexically dynamic verbs, and that this is also the case for various lexically stative verbs. Whether we should conclude on this basis that the latter were not adjectivized is unclear: it seems that semantic factors also have to be taken into account when it comes to adverb formation, as with regular adjectives.[83]

A second morphological criterion, which was advanced by Amenta (2003: 30), deals with whether the participle could appear in the comparative and superlative degrees. Apart from the fact that there seem to be very few examples for (Classical) Greek,[84] it seems that semantic factors again must be taken into account, as will be discussed at greater length under §2.4.2.3.

2.4.2.3 Syntactic criteria

The large majority of the criteria mentioned in the literature are syntactic in nature. The first of these resembles the morphological criteria in that it does not pertain directly to the combination of the participle with the verb εἰμί. Both Björck (1940: 17) and Aerts (1965: 15–16) mention 'frequent attributive and substantival use of the participle' (as in τὸ πρέπον 'that which is fitting') as a criterion for adjectivization, again under the assumption that the relevant participles will be adjectivized in all cases. As pointed out by Kahn (1973: 135–6), the main problem with this criterion is that 'frequent use' is a matter of degree: how many times must a participle accompany a noun before it becomes completely adjectivized?

After the example of English, Karleen (1980: 120) has proposed the combination of the participle with adverbs of degree (i.e. λίαν 'very') as a criterion of the adjectivization of the participle. As pointed out by Hamann (1992: 659–60), among others, 'adjectives... are marked for gradability... nouns and verbs, on the other hand, are not inherently gradable'. This syntactic potential can be explained on semantic grounds: semantically, adjectives are less complex than verbs and nouns (expressing only a single property, contrast e.g. 'thin' with

---

[83] See e.g. Dixon (1977: 39): 'adjectives differ as to whether or not they form adverbs.' With regard to Ancient Greek, see Crespo et al. (2003: 30-2).

[84] Amenta does not cite any. συμφερώτερος 'more expedient' and συμφερώτατος 'the most expedient' are attested in Post-Classical and Byzantine Greek.

'Verbal' and 'Adjectival' Periphrasis 85

'house'),[85] and therefore more easily gradable. There are two major problems with Karleen's suggestion, however: first, as there are only a few examples, Karleen proposes to add an adverb of degree himself, as one would do for modern-day English. The validity of this type of approach for a corpus language such as Ancient Greek seems questionable. In our corpus of periphrastic constructions, around fifteen examples can be found of 'adjectival' participles combined with an adverb of degree such as ἥκιστα 'least', μάλιστα 'most', μᾶλλον 'more', (οὐκ) ὀλίγον '(not) a little', πολύ 'much', and σφόδρα 'very much'.[86] In the large majority of the cases, we find the present participle of lexically stative verbs (ἁρμόζει 'it is fitting', δέομαι 'I am in need of', διαφέρω 'I differ', ὀργίζομαι 'I am angry', πρέπει 'it is fitting', συμφέρει 'it is expedient') as in the following passage from Plato, where πολύ is combined with πάνυ:

(52) ἀλλ᾽ ἐγώ σοι, ἔφη, λέγω, ὦ Σώκρατες, ὅτι ταῦτα πάντα μόρια μέν ἐστιν ἀρετῆς, καὶ τὰ μὲν τέτταρα αὐτῶν ἐπιεικῶς παραπλήσια ἀλλήλοις ἐστίν, ἡ δὲ ἀνδρεία πάνυ πολὺ <u>διαφέρον</u> πάντων τούτων (Pl., *Prot.* 349d)
'Well, Socrates, he replied, I say that all these are parts of virtue, and that while four of them are fairly on a par with each other, courage is something vastly different from all the rest.' (tr. Lamb)

There is one example in Euripides, (53), where an adverb of degree is combined with a participle (διδοῦσα) that does not belong to Björck's class of *Daueradjektivierungen*:

(53) ἀλλ᾽ <u>ἔστιν</u>, ἔστιν ἡ λίαν δυσπραξία / λίαν <u>διδοῦσα</u> μεταβολάς, ὅταν τύχηι (Eur., *IT* 721-2)
'Great misfortune can offer great reversals, when it is fated; it can indeed.' (tr. Potter)

In this particular example, however, it seems that what is graded is not the property expressed by the participle, but rather the μεταβολαί, the reversals.[87] That λίαν 'very' is nevertheless repeated and combined with διδοῦσα seems to be emphatic, and may be compared with the repetition of ἔστιν.

---

[85] Cf. Wierzbicka (1986: 362); Hamann (1992: 659); Givón (2001: 1.50-4).
[86] See e.g. Aristoph., *Plut.* 49 (σφόδρα); Aristot., *Mund.* 391a (μάλιστα); Isoc. 6.72 (μᾶλλον); Lycurg. 1.27 (ἥκιστα); Pl., *Alc.* 2, 149b (πολύ), *Leg.* 723c ((οὐκ) ὀλίγον).
[87] England (1883: 188) notes with regard to this passage that 'it is only with a verbal noun (the name of an action or state) that λίαν can be thus joined'.

A second problem, which was already mentioned under §2.4.2.2 ('use in the comparative and superlative degree'), concerns the fact that semantic factors must also be taken into account when considering which participles are attested with an adverb of degree: as noted by Crespo et al. (2003: 30–2), a subclass of the adjectives (so-called 'relational adjectives', typically expressing time-stable properties such as material, sex, location, etc.) is non-gradable. To complicate matters further, scholars have shown that some verbs are gradable, such as English 'to love [very much]' or 'to respect [greatly]'.[88] As such, it could be argued that the possibility to combine a participle with an adverb of degree should be related to the semantics of the verb from which it is formed, rather than to its supposed adjectivization, as Borer (1990: 98–9) suggests with regard to the English participle:

> The distribution of *very* and *rather* in V + *ing* combinations can be traced back directly to the properties of the verbs from which they [the relevant participles, KB] are derived and cannot be treated as a test for the adjectival nature of the result.

A third syntactic criterion, suggested by Boyer (1984: 168) and Amenta (2003: 31–2), deals with the coordination of the participle with a regular adjective, as in (54), where ἔχουσα 'having' is coordinated with the adjectives ὑψηλή 'high' and μεγάλη 'large':

(54) πυργομαχοῦντες δὲ ἐπεὶ οὐκ ἐδύναντο λαβεῖν τὴν τύρσιν (ὑψηλὴ γὰρ <u>ἦν</u> καὶ μεγάλη καὶ προμαχεῶνας καὶ ἄνδρας πολλοὺς καὶ μαχίμους <u>ἔχουσα</u>), διορύττειν ἐπεχείρησαν τὸν πύργον (Xen., *An.* 7.8.13)
'And when they found themselves unable to take the tower by storm (for it was high and large, and furnished with battlements and a considerable force of warlike defenders), they attempted to dig through the tower-wall.' (tr. Brownson)

While some scholars take this as an indication of adjectivization, it is unclear whether coordination indicates categorial identity, or simply functional likeness. Examples such as (50), where the aorist participle (προδείσας 'prematurely afraid') is coordinated with a regular adjective (θρασύς 'bold') seem to indicate that the latter is the case.[89] While this needs further research, it could be argued that even functional

---

[88] See Thesleff (1954) with regard to Ancient Greek.
[89] Compare Núñez-Pertejo (2003: 145) with regard to early Modern English.

similarity is not an absolute requirement when it comes to coordination in Ancient Greek. Consider the Post-Classical example (55):

(55) καὶ ἦν ὀργιζόμενος σφόδρα καὶ λέγων πρὸς τοὺς ἱερεῖς· Τί ὅτι τὴν ἐμὴν ἐμάγευσαν γυναῖκα; (A. Phil. (Vat. Gr. 824) 124.2–3)
'And he was very angry and said to the priests: what about the fact that they bewitched my wife?'

In this exceptional example, there is no functional likeness between the two participles: ὀργιζόμενος 'angry' denotes a property, while λέγων 'saying' an action.

Moreover, if in an example such as (54) the participle were really adjectivized, it would be surprising to find that it retains its argument structure, which is, after all, a typically verbal characteristic. Björck (1940: 20) and Aerts (1965: 13) both refer to combinations such as νοῦν ἐχόντως 'sensibly' (< νοῦν ἔχων) and λόγον ἐχόντως 'reasonably' (< λόγον ἔχων) to show that 'the accompaniment of an object does not prevent the adjectivization of a participle'.[90] That προμαχεῶνας καὶ ἄνδρας πολλοὺς καὶ μαχίμους ἔχουσα 'furnished with (lit. having) battlements and a considerable force of warlike defenders' should be considered on a par with such fixed combinations seems questionable, however, and the same may be said with regard to many other examples.

Continuing on the same topic, Kahn (1973: 136) has argued that argument structure provides a good indication of the categorial status of the participle, adjectives typically taking only a single argument:[91]

> The only formal test I see for deciding when a participle acquires the syntax of an adjective or noun would be when it loses the verbal construction with accusative or dative object, as sometimes happens with the articular participle, e.g. οἱ προσέχοντες τούτου.

As Kahn (1973: 136) notes, however, such shifts in argument structure do not seem to be attested. As will be discussed at greater length under §2.4.3, various property-referring participles take two arguments, and occasionally we even find an example with three arguments, as in the

---

[90] Aerts (1965: 13).
[91] See e.g. Hamann (1992: 661). For Ancient Greek adjectives taking more than one argument, see Crespo et al. (2003: 35–7).

following example, where the present participle of the verb ἀποδίδωμι 'I give back' is used:

(56) ἱκανὸς δὲ καὶ περὶ μονῳδίαν εἷς, μὴ ἔλαττον ἢ τριάκοντα γεγονὼς ἐτῶν, εἰσαγωγεύς τε <u>εἶναι</u> καὶ τοῖς ἁμιλλωμένοις τὴν διάκρισιν ἱκανῶς <u>ἀποδιδούς</u> (Pl., *Leg.* 765a)
'And for solo performances one umpire, of not less than thirty years, is sufficient, to act as introducer and to pass an adequate judgment upon the competitors.' (tr. Bury)

To conclude this discussion, it is worth making some brief comments on word order. Ceglia (1998: 26, 28–9) and Amenta (2003: 33) have observed that when the participle is adjectival (adjectivized) the copula tends to follow the participle, and that the participle and the verb εἰμί are much more autonomous in terms of syntactic contiguity than in 'truly' periphrastic constructions. While these observations indeed have some validity, it should be stressed that they cannot serve as criteria of adjectivization, since they represent tendencies which are not without exception: for example, when there is coordination, as in our previous example (54), the participle generally follows εἰμί. There also seems to be a substantial difference between participles of lexically stative and lexically dynamic verbs: the latter typically follow εἰμί, as our previous examples (48) and (53) show.

2.4.3 A Prototype-based Account

It may be clear that none of the criteria proposed in the literature for adjectivization are entirely satisfactory, except for the phonological criteria, which, however, have little relevance for our discussion. Furthermore, it has become clear that the 'adjectival' or property-referring present participle does not constitute a homogeneous category: lexically stative present participles, especially of impersonal verbs, have turned up much more often in our discussion than dynamic ones: they can often be found as adverbs, combined with an adverb of degree, or coordinated with a true adjective.

The alternative approach that I propose is based on the prototype model. As I hope to show, it provides not only a more satisfying account of the above-mentioned difficulties, but also offers an *integrated* account, since I involve the perfect and aorist participle in my evaluation.

2.4.3.1 Two recent proposals towards the parts-of-speech issue

My proposal is based on two major contributions to the parts-of-speech issue, both of which explicitly allow for prototypicality. The first is the typologically oriented one by Croft (1991, 2001), which is based on markedness theory. Croft observes that in the languages of the world unmarked (prototypical) nouns are used for reference to an object or identity, unmarked (prototypical) verbs for predication of an action, and unmarked (prototypical) adjectives for reference to a property, as shown in Table 2.1:

Table 2.1. Parts of speech as typologically unmarked combinations

	Reference	Modification	Predication
Objects	UNMARKED NOUNS	Genitive, adjectivalizations, PPs on nouns	Predicate nominals, copulas
Properties	Deadjectival nouns	UNMARKED ADJECTIVES	Predicate adjectives, copulas
Actions	Action nominals, complements, infinitives, gerunds	Participles, relative clauses	UNMARKED VERBS

Source: Croft 2001: 88. Reproduction of this figure has been granted by Oxford University Press.

In this innovative matrix, Croft separates the semantic categories of objects, properties, and actions from the pragmatic categories of reference, modification, and predication. Note that Croft somewhat generalizingly locates participles at the intersection of 'action' and 'modification', while in reality their function is more complex: the Ancient Greeks, who are known as φιλομέτοχοι or 'participle-lovers',[92] made a much broader use of the participle, including reference and predication.[93] The main importance of Croft's proposal, however, is that it offers a way to compare parts of speech across

---

[92] See e.g. Jannaris (1897: 505) for the use of this term.
[93] For an overview of the functions of the participle, see e.g. Crespo et al. (2003: 306–17).

languages, in addition to clearly demarcating the non-prototypical nature of the participle.[94]

As Pompei (2006) recently demonstrated of the Ancient Greek conjunct participle,[95] it is possible to take the analysis one step further by investigating the internal organization of the participle, which may similarly be organized prototypically. To that end, one can refer to the work of Givón (1979, 1984), which has had a massive impact on the parts-of-speech debate in the last two decades of the twentieth century.[96] Givón's proposal is oriented towards semantics, focusing in particular on the parameter of 'time-stability'. For Givón, categories such as 'noun', 'adjective', and 'verb' are conceptualizations of the time-stability of real-world phenomena:[97] while nouns such as 'house' or 'tree' denote phenomena that remain stable over time, verbs such as 'to eat' or 'to run' refer to phenomena that do not remain stable over an extended period of time. Adjectives are of an intermediate time-stability: the most prototypical adjectives denote relatively time-stable properties such as size, shape, colour, weight, etc.[98]

Givón's proposal not only allows us to put the major parts of speech on a continuum of time-stability, but also enables us to further categorize the different members within each category from most to least prototypical, as shown in Fig. 2.1:

---

[94] This is also indicated by the label 'μετοχή' (compare Latin 'participium', Dutch 'deelwoord').

[95] The conjunct participle is typically defined as specifying the circumstances under which the main action occurs, syntactically agreeing with a noun or pronoun (as in ἐπαιάνιζον...ἅμα...πλέοντες (Thuc. 2.91.2) 'they were singing a paean of victory while rowing'; example borrowed from Rijksbaron 2002: 122). Pompei (2006) shows that the conjunct participle is functionally more complex and distinguishes between three main types: (a) *the appositive participle*, where the participle functions as an adnominal modifier (as in μετὰ ταῦτα Κῦρος ἐξελαύνει...ἐπὶ τὸν Χάλον ποταμόν, ὄντα τὸ εὖρος πλέθρου (Xen., An. 1.4.9) 'after this Cyrus marched to the Chalus river, which is a plethrum in width'; example borrowed from Rijksbaron 2002: 133); (b) *the subordinative participle*, where the participle functions as an adverbial modifier (cf. the example given above, Thuc. 2.91.2); (c) *the co-subordinative participle*, where the participle indicates a link between predications (as in καὶ νῦν, ἔφη, μὴ μέλλωμεν, ὦ ἄνδρες, ἀλλ' ἀπελθόντες ἤδη αἱρεῖσθε οἱ δεόμενοι ἄρχοντας (Xen., An. 3.1.46) '"and now, gentlemen", he went on, "let us not delay; withdraw and choose your commanders at once"'; example borrowed from Pompei 2006: 366).

[96] Cf. Pustet (2003: 21).   [97] Cf. Fox (1983: 27).

[98] As Dixon (1977) has shown, when a language has a category of 'adjectives', these properties are always expressed.

NOUNS	ADJECTIVES		VERBS	
MOST TIME-STABLE	INTERMEDIATE STATES		RAPID CHANGE	
Stone (noun) Red (adj.)	Young (adj.)	Know (verb)	Walk (verb)	Kick (verb)

Fig. 2.1. The noun-to-verb continuum (after Givón 1984: 55)

Minor parts of speech can also be located on this continuum. Ross (1972: 316), for example, has made the following proposal (what he calls a 'linear squish'): verb > present participle > perfect participle > passive participle > adjective > preposition (?) > 'adjectival noun' > noun.

Givón's proposal has received some criticism, however, as it does not make correct predictions in all cases: on the basis of time-stability, a noun such as 'explosion' would have to be classified as a verb, while a verb such as 'to last' as a noun.[99] As Pustet (2003: 21) points out, this does not mean that the time-stability hypothesis should be entirely abandoned:

> The amount of lexemes that contradict the hypothesis is extremely small if compared to the amount of those that support it. It would be premature to discard a hypothesis with high predictive power because there are some exceptions to it.

A second problem with Givón's classification, specifically concerning adjectives, is mentioned by Thompson (1989: 250–1): prototypical adjectives, as shown by Dixon (1977), express time-stable properties.[100] It remains, therefore, unclear whether adjectives really occupy the middle of the time-stability scale.

Building on Givón, Pustet (2003, ch. 3) has recently proposed a four-parameter model, which includes the parameters of dynamicity, transience, transitivity, and dependency. In what follows, I shall discuss the first three of these parameters and apply them to the Ancient Greek property-referring participle.[101]

---

[99] Cf. Hopper & Thompson (1984: 705–6); Pustet (2003: 21).
[100] Cf. also Givón (2001: 1.81–3).
[101] The parameter of 'dependency' is not relevant for our present purposes, since we can assume that all participles are always [+dependent].

2.4.3.2 Application to the property-referring participle

a. Dynamicity

The first parameter to be discussed is that of 'dynamicity', which Pustet (2003: 96) phrases in terms of 'homogeneity' vs. 'inhomogeneity through time', that is, the presence vs. absence of intrinsic change.[102] A lexeme (and by extension a participle) can thus be classified as [+dynamic] if it involves at least two disparate component states (e.g. English 'jump', 'sneeze', 'explosion'), while [-dynamic] if it does not (e.g. English 'sad', 'exist', 'live', 'belief').[103]

For our present investigation, we need to take into account not only lexical semantics, but also the effects of verbal morphology, aspect in particular. The 'adjectival' perfect participle, for example, is typically formed on the basis of verbs that are [+dynamic], for example, μονόω 'I desert'; ὁρίζω 'I determine'; διασκεδάννυμι 'I scatter'; θνήσκω 'I die'. Perfect participles formed of these verbs are [-dynamic], however, and indicate a state: μεμουνωμένοι (Hdt. 1.102.2) 'deserted'; ὡρισμένον (Aristot., *Mag. mor.* 1.17.10) 'determined'; διεσκεδασμένοι (Hdt. 1.63.2) 'scattered'; τεθνηκυῖα (Pl., *Phd.* 106b) 'dead'.

The present participle does not interfere with dynamicity to a similar extent: if a content verb is [+dynamic], it will also be so when combined with the present participle, for example, προσποιούμενος (Dem. 29.13) 'pretending'; γιγνόμενα (Aristot., *Rhet.* 1369a) 'happening'; ἐναντιούμενος (Isaeus 11.28) 'opposing'. The large majority of the 'adjectival' present participles are formed with a lexically stative verb, however, and as such can be classified as [-dynamic]: for example, ἁρμόζοντα (Hippoc., *Acut.* 1.14) 'suitable'; εὖ φρονῶν (Soph., *Aj.* 1330) 'wise'; ἔχον (Aristoph., *Ran.* 1396) 'having'; δυναμένη (Xen., *An.* 2.2.13) 'able'.

As I noted in §2.4.1, there are only few examples of 'adjectival' aorist participles. Since perfective aspect inherently profiles boundaries, these participles are always [+dynamic], even when combined with lexically stative verbs such as προδείδω 'I fear prematurely' (cf. our earlier example (50)). In most cases however, we find content verbs which involve disparate component states, such as ὑφίσταμαι (Dem. 21.114) 'I bring myself to' or γίγνομαι (Pl., *Leg.* 711c) 'I become'.

---

[102] Compare the traditional distinction made between 'states' and 'processes'.
[103] Pustet (2003: 97) also allows for a class of [+-dynamic] lexemes, but this will not further concern us here.

b. Transitivity

A second parameter is 'transitivity', which is used by Pustet (2003: 114–20) in the traditional sense of 'valency'.[104] Prototypical adjectives have valency value 1 (e.g. 'sad', 'solid'), while verbs typically have either valency value 1 or 2 (e.g. 'to go', 'to have'). Valency value 3 is exceptional for verbs, and can be found, for example, with 'to give'.[105]

'Adjectival' perfect participles resemble prototypical adjectives in that they are typically limited to a single argument, the subject. The perfect has a valency-changing effect with transitive content verbs, as noted by Haspelmath & Müller-Bardey (2004), who consider the resultative perfect a 'valency-decreasing category': verbs such as ἀντιτάσσω 'I position (someone/something) against', ἀνθίζω 'I adorn (something) with flowers', or δέω 'I bind, fasten (someone/something)' become limited to a single argument as 'adjectival' perfect participles (taking the passive voice): ἀντιτςταγμέναι (Xen., *Hell.* 1.6.31) 'positioned against'; ἠνθισμένοι (Hdt. 1.98.6) 'adorned with flowers'; δεδεμένα (Pl., *Men.* 97d) 'fastened'. Intransitive verbs such as βαίνω 'I go', συμπίπτω 'I fall together', and ἀπόλλυμαι 'I perish' are also used to form 'adjectival' perfect participles (taking the active voice): βεβακώς (Eur., *Heracl.* 910–11) 'gone'; συμπεπτωκότα (Pl., *Tht.* 195a) 'crowded together'; ἀπολωλός (Dem. 35.36) 'perished, lost'. In these cases, there is no valency change.

As I noted in §2.3.2, the present participle is not limited to a single argument. Particularly often used with valency value 2 is the verb ἔχω, which is combined with objects such as γνώμην (Hippoc., *Morb. sacr.* 16.10–1) 'intelligence', διαίρεσιν (Pl., *Soph.* 229d) 'division', δύναμιν (Isoc. 15.117) 'power', ἡλικίαν (Pl., *Prm.* 141a) 'age', λευκὴν τρίχα (Xen., *Cyn.* 4.8) 'white hair', λόγον (Aristot., *Mag. mor.* 1.34.3) 'reason', οὐσίαν (Pl., *Crat.* 386e) 'reality', πάντα ταῦτα (Aristot., *Mag. mor.* 2.11.40) 'all these things', and σπλῆνα μέγαν (Hippoc., *Epid.* 2.2.7) 'a big spleen'. Other examples of participles with valency value 2 are ἀποδεχόμενος (Pl., *Hp. mai.* 289e) 'accepting', γιγνώσκοντες (Dem. 13.15) 'knowing', θέλουσα (Soph., *OT* 580) 'wanting', and κλύων (Soph., *OT* 1389) 'hearing'. In a large number of cases, however, 'adjectival' present participles with valency value 1 are used, such as ἁρμόττοντα (Xen., *Cyr.* 1.4.18) 'fitting', ἀσφαλέως ἔχον (Hdt. 1.86.5) 'being safe', χλοάζουσα (Aristot., *Mir.* 846b) 'bright green', and ἀκμάζουσα (Hdt. 2.134.2) 'being at her height'.

---

[104] Contrast with Hopper & Thompson's (1980) notion of 'prototypical transitivity' (on which, see §1.4.3).
[105] Contrary to the traditional accounts, Pustet (2003: 114) does not take into account the coding strategy for the second argument; as such, English 'worth' and 'devoid of' are both accorded valency value 2.

Because there are only a few examples with the 'adjectival' aorist participle, it is hard to draw any conclusions. It is mostly used with valency value 1 (as in γενόμενον (Aristot., *MXG* 975a) 'generated'), though an example with valency value 2 is also attested (πᾶν ἂν ὑποστὰς εἰπεῖν (Dem. 21.114) 'ready to do or say anything' (tr. Murray)).

c. Transience

Next to dynamicity and valency, Pustet (2003: 105–14) also refers to 'transience', which resembles Givón's (1984, 2001.1) earlier-mentioned concept of 'time-stability'. Pustet proposes a different approach, however, by focusing on likelihood of termination (during the lifetime of the entity of which something is predicated) rather than duration in itself. This provides a more satisfactory account of the 'intermediate time-stability' of adjectives: according to Givón, these have a duration that is intermediate between that of nouns and verbs, but this is somewhat hard to explain for properties that have been found to be prototypical, such as colour and dimension. For Pustet (2001: 109), however, the intermediate status of adjectives lies with the fact that termination and non-termination are both possible:

> 'Redness' can change, 'smallness' can change, and 'goodness' can change. But 'dog-ness', 'stone-ness', or 'house-ness' are non-terminable. Thus, the assumption that the time-stability of adjectivals is 'intermediate' can be rephrased by stating that with adjectivals, termination and non-termination are equally possible.

On Pustet's account, prototypical verbs are [+transient], prototypical nouns [-transient], and prototypical adjectives [+-transient]. However, this cannot be generalized: some English verbs, such as 'to have' or 'to love', can be classified as [+-transient], and the same is true for nouns such as 'friend' or 'cook'. English also has adjectives which can be classified as [+transient], such as 'nervous' or 'thirsty', and [-transient], such as 'female' or 'colour-blind'.

When it comes to the Ancient Greek adjectival participle, a distinction can be made between the perfect and present participle on the one hand, and the aorist participle on the other: only with the latter is an endpoint explicitly profiled. A further division can be made, however, between adjectival present participles formed on the basis of lexically dynamic verbs, which are [+transient], and those formed on the basis of stative content verbs. Even the group of 'stative' participles (that is, perfect participles, and present participles based on lexically stative content verbs), is not homogeneous, as is shown in Table 2.2:

Table 2.2. Transience of the property-referring perfect/present participle

Transience	Property[1]	Perfect participle	Present participle
[-transient]	Body feature/bodily state	e.g. τεθηηκώς (Soph., *Phil.* 435) 'dead'; τετελευτηκώς (Xen., *Hell.* 3.5.23) 'dead'	e.g. βλέπων (Soph., *OT* 747) 'seeing'; ζῶν (Aristoph., *Thesm.* 77) 'alive'; κλύων (Soph., *OT* 1389) 'hearing'
	Colour	e.g. κεχρωματισμένος (Aristot., *Mete.* 374a) 'coloured'	e.g. χλοάζων (Aristot., *Mir.* 846b) 'bright green'
	(Physical/metaphorical) distance	e.g. ἀπολελειμμένος (Isocr. 12.263) 'distanced (from)'; κεχωρισμένος (Dem. 22.22) 'separated from'	e.g. ὁμορέων (Hdt. 8.47.1) 'bordering upon'; προέχων (Thuc. 4.109.2) 'jutting out'; ὑπερέχων (Pl., *Leg.* 696b) 'being above'
	Mental property		e.g. ἐπιστάμενος (Aristot., *An. pr.* 51b) 'knowing'; εὖ φρονῶν (Soph., *Aj.* 1330) 'wise'; μαινόμενος (Pl., *Prt.* 350b) 'mad'
	Personality feature	e.g. εἰθισμένος (Dem. 58.34) 'used to'; ἐξωγκωμένος (Hdt. 6.126.3) 'puffed up'; πεπαιδευμένος (Pl., *Leg.* 840a) 'educated'	e.g. δυνάμενος (Aristot., *An. pr.* 51b) 'able'; εὔβουλος ἔχων (Aesch., *Cho.* 696) 'prudent'
	Physical property	e.g. ἐγγεγραμμένος (Aesch., *Supp.* 946) 'inscribed'; ἐσχομένος (Aristot., *Hist. an.* 578з) 'split up'; τετρημένος (Aristoph., *Vesp.* 127) 'perforated'; ὡδοποιημένος (Xen., *An.* 5.3.1) 'constructed (of a road)'	
	Social relation	e.g. γεγονώς (Hdt. 7.11.2) 'descendant'; ὠρφανισμένος (Soph., *Trach.* 941–2) 'orphaned'	e.g. προσήκων (Dem. 48.6) 'related to'
[+-transient]	(Physical/metaphorical) absence/presence		e.g. ἀπών (Soph., *OT* 1285) 'absent'; ἐνών (Pl., *Resp.* 431e) 'present in'; περιών (Hdt. 1.92.1) 'left remaining'; ὑπάρχων (Hdt. 5.124.2) '(being) at hand'

(*continued*)

Table 2.2. Continued

Transience	Property[1]	Perfect participle	Present participle
	Bodily state	e.g. ἀπηλλαγμένος (Xen., Hell. 5.2.7) 'freed from'; ἀφειμένος (Aristot., Pol. 1278a) 'released'; καταλελειμμένος (Xen., An. 3.1.2) 'left behind'	
	Emotional state	e.g. ἀναπεπτωκώς (Dem. 19.224) 'supine'; πεπεισμένος (Aristot., Metaph. 1011a) 'convinced'	e.g. βουλόμενος (Dem. 23.194) 'wanting'; θέλων (Xen., Mem. 2.6.4) 'wanting'; μισῶν (Dem. 19.312) 'hating'
	Evaluative	e.g. ἡμαρτημένος (Aristot., Pol. 1301a) 'erroneous'; κεχαρισμένος (Pl., Leg. 805c) 'dear to'; συμπεπλεγμένος (Aristot., De int. 23b) 'complex'; ὑπερβεβλημένος (Pl., Leg. 719d) 'excessive'	e.g. ἀναγκαίως ἔχων (Aesch., Cho. 239) 'necessary'; ἀρέσκων (Soph., OT 274) 'pleasing'; πρέπων (Pl., La. 188d) 'fitting'; προσῆκον (Isoc. 5.110) 'proper'; συμφέρων (Dem. 16.10) 'expedient'
	(Physical/metaphorical) position	e.g. ἀποδεδειγμένος (Pl., Leg. 758e) 'appointed'; καθεστηκώς (Xen., Cyr. 8.6.9) 'appointed'	e.g. ἐπιστατῶν (Pl., Plt. 261c) 'being in charge of'; ἡγεμονῶν (Pl., Leg. 631c) 'having authority'
	Possession	e.g. ἐπαμμένος (Hdt. 1.199.5) 'in possession of'; ἐσκευασμένος (Hdt. 7.95.2) 'equipped'; ὡπλισμένος (Xen., Cyr. 2.1.11) 'equipped'	e.g. ἔχων (Eur., Bacch. 471) 'having'; κατέχων (Pl., Ti. 52b) 'occupying'
	Resemblance	e.g. ἐοικώς (Xen., Symp. 4.32) 'resembling'	e.g. διαφέρων (Xen., Mem. 4.3.11) 'different from'; ὁμολογούμενος (Isoc. 6.14) 'in accordance with'; συνεπόμενος (Pl., Criti. 117a) 'in accordance with'
	Social behaviour		e.g. ἐλεῶν (Dem. 21.185) 'feeling pity'; ὁμονοῶν (Pl., Leg. 759b) 'being of one mind'

[+ transient]	Bodily state	e.g. ἀντιτεταγμένος (Xen., Hell. 1.6.31) 'positioned against'; ἐρρωμένος (Xen., Oec. 10.5) 'strong'; πεποδισμένος (Xen., An. 3.4.35) 'hobbled'; ᾠνωμένος (Soph., Trach. 268) 'intoxicated'
		e.g. ἀκμάζων (Hdt. 2.134.2) 'being at one's height'; μεθύων (Aristot., Pr. 953b) 'drunk'; νοσῶν (Pl., Alc. 2, 139d) 'sick'; σφριγῶν (Pl., Leg. 840a) 'vigorous'; ὑγιαίνων (Xen., Oec. 10.5) 'healthy'
	Emotional state	e.g. ἐκπεπληγμένος (Xen., An. 5.6.36) 'panic-struck'; ἐπηρμένος (Thuc. 7.51.1) 'eager'; τεθηγμένος (Xen., Cyr. 1.6.41) 'sharpened (of one's spirit)'; ὠργισμένος (Eur., Hipp. 1413) 'enraged'
		e.g. ἁλύων (Hippoc., Epid. 5.1.64) 'agitated'; ὀργιζόμενος (Lycurg. 1.27) 'angry'
	Physical property	e.g. ἀνεῳγμένος (Xen., Cyr. 7.4.6) 'open(ed)'; ἠνθισμένος (Hdt. 1.98.6) 'painted'; κεκλῃμένος (Thuc. 5.7.5) 'closed'

---

[1] Note that the terms for the different properties have not been chosen at random: they are based on the cross-linguistically informed studies of Dixon (1977), Givón (2001: 1.82–3), and Pustet (2003).

This table shows that while 'adjectival' present and perfect participles represent a whole range of properties, they do not often express prototypical properties such as size, shape, colour, weight, etc.[106] In terms of transience, we see that the perfect participle is particularly often used for [-transient] and [+transient] properties (e.g. 'personality feature', 'bodily state'), while the present participle is most often used for [+-transient] properties (e.g. 'evaluative', 'resemblance'). Most properties can be expressed by both the present and the perfect participle, although in some cases one of the two participles predominates, as is the case with 'mental property' (present participle), 'physical property' (perfect participle), 'physical/metaphorical absence/presence' (present participle), 'bodily state' (perfect participle), and 'social behaviour' (present participle).

2.4.3.3 The noun-to-verb continuum

Based on our application of Pustet's (2003) three parameters in §2.4.3.2, we can now locate the different 'adjectival' (property-referring) participles on a continuum ranging from most noun-like to most verb-like, as illustrated in Fig. 2.2:[107]

N   V

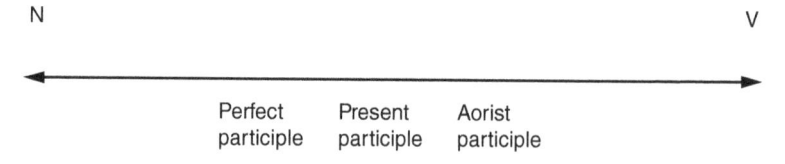

⟵——————————————————⟶

                 Perfect   Present   Aorist
                 participle participle participle

Fig. 2.2. The adjectival (property-referring) participle on the noun-to-verb continuum

As we have argued, the perfect participle is least verb-like: it is [-dynamic], limited to valency value 1, and grammatically [-transient], as no right temporal boundary is profiled.[108] A more in-depth analysis of transience has shown, however, that the adjectival perfect participle

---

[106] Cf. Dixon (1982); Givón (2001: 1.82–3). Note, however, that Dixon lists 'value' as one of the universally attested adjectival properties, while Givón considers 'evaluative' less prototypical.

[107] Compare Pompei (2006: 386) with regard to the conjunct participle.

[108] In other words, the event is not inherently temporally limited.

can express not only [-transient] properties, but also [+-transient] and [+transient] ones.

The present participle is more verb-like than the perfect participle: it can be either [-dynamic] (in the case of verbs whose content is lexically stative) or [+dynamic], and is not limited to valency value 1. Like the perfect participle, the present participle in general can be considered [-transient], since a right boundary is not explicitly profiled. However, a more in-depth analysis has shown that the present participle can also express [+transient] and especially [+-transient] properties.

Since there are only a limited number of examples available, it is difficult to make any firm conclusions with regard to the aorist participle. However, we may be justified in considering it most verb-like, since it is [+dynamic], not limited to valency value 1, and [+transient], as it explicitly profiles a right boundary.

The results of our analysis are summarized in Table 2.3:

Table 2.3. Scores on Pustet's (2003) parameters

	Dynamicity	Transitivity	Transience
Perfect participle	[-dynamic]	[-transitive]	[-transient]
Present participle	[+-dynamic]	[+transitive]	[-transient]
Aorist participle	[+dynamic]	[+transitive]	[+transient]

2.4.4 An Alternative Classification of 'Adjectival Periphrasis': Default vs. Non-default Construal

In conclusion of our discussion of adjectival periphrasis, I would like to introduce a classification of constructions formerly discussed under the heading of 'adjectival periphrasis' which forms an alternative to Björck's distinction between *Daueradjektivierungen* and *Gelegenheitsadjektivierungen*, which concentrates exclusively on the present participle. This novel classification is based on the distinction between 'default' and 'non-default' construal,[109] as advanced

---

[109] Often, one and the same form can receive two distinct semantic construals, with the context determining the intended construal. Consider, for example, the sentences 'I had only one beer' and 'I had a lot of beer', where the same form

by Croft & Cruse (2004: 103–4) and Croft (2012: 13–9) among others.[110] This distinction starts from the idea that while in principle no type of 'adjectival' participle should be considered adjectivized, some types are more easily used for adjectival periphrasis, as is also reflected in frequency of occurrence (a point of resemblance between my own proposal and Björck's).

The principle that lies behind the distinction between 'default' and 'non-default construal' is (scalar) transitivity (along the lines of Hopper & Thompson 1980): I take it that those examples that are commonly referred to as 'adjectival periphrasis' are indicative of low transitivity. Up until now, scholars have mostly focused on the finite verb and the participle, but examples such as (57) (our earlier example (48)) show that other sentential factors play a role as well: if not, ἔστιν ... παρακαλῶν might well be given a progressive interpretation ('he/it is (in the process of) inviting'). Therefore, I believe it is more correct to discuss examples such as these in terms of a 'property reading'.[111]

(57) ἔστιν δὲ τοὺς μὲν Ἕλληνας <u>παρακαλῶν</u> ἐπὶ τὴν τῶν βαρβάρων στρατείαν (Isoc. 15.57)

'It (the speech) summons the Hellenes to make an expedition against the barbarians.' (tr. Norlin, slightly modified)

As may be clear at this point, there is some similarity between the parameters proposed by Pustet (2003) for prototypical verbhood and the parameters of prototypical transitivity proposed by Hopper & Thompson (1980),[112] not unsurprisingly of course. As such, those participles that are most adjective-like may also be considered the most suitable for a property reading, or in other words, they have a property reading as a default construal. This particularly concerns the perfect participle, which, as we have seen, expresses a property that remains stable over time, and is limited to a single non-agentive argument. The aorist participle, on the other hand, does not have a property reading as its default construal: since it is situated at the right

---

('beer') is used in a count noun construction and a mass noun construction respectively. When one type of construal is more typical, we can speak of a 'default construal'.

[110] Compare Allan (2003: 68) with regard to the Ancient Greek middle voice.
[111] For a similar use of this term, cf. Doiz-Bienzobas (2002).
[112] Cf. §1.4.3.

side of the noun-to-verb continuum, it is indicative of high transitivity. In examples with the aorist participle, we often find 'de-transitivizing' elements.[113] Consider the following example from Plato:

(58) καὶ γὰρ οὖν ἡμῖν οὐ τοῦτ' ἐστὶν ἀδύνατον οὐδὲ χαλεπῶς ἂν γενόμενον
(Pl., Leg. 711c)
'Indeed, that is not impossible or difficult to bring about for us.'

In this example we find three typical de-transitivizing elements:[114] (a) the choice for an inanimate subject, (b) coordination with a regular adjective, and (c) the use of the finite verb in the present tense.[115]

In terms of the distinction between 'default' and 'non-default' construal, the present participle is the most complex. With participles of lexically stative verbs, a property reading can be considered the default construal. This is especially true for those verbs which are referred to by Fanning (1990: 135) with the term 'verbs with lexicalized predication of qualities', such as ἄπειμι 'I am absent', ζῶ 'I live, am alive', πένομαι 'I am poor', πρέπει 'it is fitting', and συμφέρει 'it is expedient'. As we have seen in §2.4.3, the participles of these verbs typically express time-stable properties, and mostly only take a single, non-agentive argument. Other lexically stative verbs, such as as γιγνώσκω 'I know', ἔχω 'I have', θέλω 'I want', μισέω 'I hate', etc., also have a property reading as their default construal, but here such a reading comes slightly less natural, since they often have two participants, possibly with an agentive first argument. Present participles of lexically dynamic content verbs, on the other hand, do not have a property reading as their default construal: as noted with regard to ἦν παρακαλῶν, in such cases one would expect a progressive interpretation. As such, we often find the same de-transitivizing elements as with the aorist participle: in (57), for example, we observe the use of the present tense and an inanimate subject, although it is worth noting that there is no coordination.

---

[113] On the notion of 'detransitivization strategy', see Naess (2007: 140).
[114] Another de-transitivizing element is object omission. See e.g. Aristot., Pr. 939a.
[115] Hopper & Thompson (1980) do not explicitly connect transitivity to tense, though a distinction can be made between present/past and future on the basis of the 'mode' parameter. Givón's (2001: 1,126) formulation ('involving a bounded, terminated, fast-changing *event*') does seem to emphasize pastness to a greater extent.

2.5 CONCLUSION

Much of this chapter has been negative: I have discussed current definitions of verbal periphrasis, and have argued that these are largely unsatisfactory. With regard to the notion of 'adjectival' periphrasis, which is advanced by some scholars to distinguish constructions with an 'adjectival' (adjectivized) participle from truly periphrastic constructions, I have attempted to show that the criteria proposed for adjectivization of the present participle are inconclusive. Moreover, I have drawn attention to the fact that these scholars do not discuss the perfect and aorist participle, which can similarly be used with a property-referring function.

In both cases, I have advanced the prototype model of linguistic categorization as an alternative approach. Scholars working within this paradigm assume that there are no sharp boundaries between categories, and that some category members may be more prototypical than others. Therefore, I have argued that constructions considered 'periphrastic' in the literature may be located on a continuum of 'periphrasticity', the most prototypical periphrastic constructions being syntactically contiguous, paradigmatically integrated, semantically idiomatic, etc. One of the main advantages of this approach is that it is also compatible with a diachronic analysis of the evidence, in that it accords with the tendency of constructions to become more periphrastic over time.

Similarly, I have argued that those participles with a 'property-referring' function (also called 'adjectival' participles) can be located on a noun-to-verb continuum, with the perfect participle being most adjective-like and the aorist participle being most verb-like. The present participle is most complex, and occupies an intermediate position, with participles of lexically stative verbs resembling the perfect participle, and participles of lexically dynamic verbs the aorist participle. In this context, I have suggested an alternative classification of 'adjectival' (property-referring) participles, distinguishing between those participles for which a 'property reading' constitutes the 'default construal' and those for which it does not.

One last question worth briefly addressing is what the relationship between verbal and adjectival periphrasis looks like: in particular, should the two notions be conceived of as mutually exclusive, as previous studies have argued? It may be clear that I do not believe this to be the case: verbal periphrasis, as we have seen, is a complex notion, to be analysed in terms of three interrelated dimensions—that is, the phonological, functional, and morpho-syntactic dimensions (both paradigmatically and syntagmatically). The notion of adjectival periphrasis, on the other hand, is limited to the functional dimension, more in particular the semantic integration of the component parts of the construction. Even if the participle is situated towards the left of the noun-to-verb continuum, a construction such as εἰμί with the perfect participle can still be considered relatively periphrastic, since it is paradigmatically integrated and relatively often syntactically contiguous.

3

Perfect Aspect

> Given that it has been established that the same function, that of denoting a state, appears at both ends of the continuum, Homeric and present-day Greek, and that the εἰμαι construction is the oldest of the periphrastic forms under investigation, it seems probable that it has always fulfilled this function.
>
> (Moser 1988: 229)

3.1 INTRODUCTION

Now that we are oriented to some crucial theoretical concepts (§1), and the notions of 'verbal' and 'adjectival' periphrasis have been given a more precise description (§2), we can focus on the actual diachronic development of verbal periphrasis in the following three chapters. We first turn to the functional domain of perfect aspect, where, as previous studies have noted,[1] periphrases were first formed.

While the entire study constitutes an analysis of *periphrastic* forms, especially in this third chapter will I attend to the synthetic tenses, the perfect[2] in particular.[3] During the period under consideration, the synthetic perfect itself developed semantically (and morphosyntactically), a process that brought it into competition with the aorist and ultimately led to its demise. In this regard, Ancient Greek displays an interesting divergence from what is the case in most European languages, where the aorist, rather than the perfect, was lost.[4]

---

[1] See e.g. Aerts (1965: 14); Kahn (1973: 131).
[2] With 'the (synthetic) perfect' I refer to the (synthetic) present/past/future perfect.
[3] On the importance of this, see also Gonda (1959: 111).
[4] See further §3.4.1.

Previous research by Aerts (1965) and Moser (1988) among others has identified three main perfect periphrases: εἰμί with the perfect participle, εἰμί with the aorist participle, and ἔχω with the aorist participle. A common argument in these studies is that in terms of semantics εἰμί with the perfect participle was mainly limited to a 'stative' ('situation-fixing') function, while εἰμί with the aorist participle and ἔχω with the aorist participle fulfilled a more 'eventive' function. While this is true to some extent, in this chapter we shall nuance the picture somewhat. A second issue which I shall focus upon, and which has received little attention so far, is the occurrence of various 'minor' constructions—that is, constructions which occur relatively infrequently in comparison with the three 'major' constructions. Aerts (1965: 161–7) briefly discusses the constructions of ἔχω with the (medio-passive) perfect participle and an object, and ἔχω with the aorist participle and a temporal adjunct, but his treatment is limited because, among other reasons, he considers neither of these constructions periphrastic.

As we reconsider the evidence, the notion of 'grammaticalization paths', which I summarized in §1.5.2 as universal semantic paths along which relevant forms develop, will be of particular importance. The specific grammaticalization path that is relevant here has recently been called 'aoristic drift',[5] and mainly consists in a shift from 'resultative' to 'anterior' perfect aspect, i.e. a shift in emphasis from the situation that results from a past event to the past event that causes this situation.[6] Eventually, the past component may become even more dominant, with the construction acquiring an 'aoristic' or perfective value.[7]

At present, there is some debate as to whether the development from resultative to anterior could be described in an even more detailed way. In an influential study, Harris (1982) has hypothesized that before periphrastic perfects are used as perfects of current relevance, they will typically first be used in more specific contexts[8]—that is, with an 'experiential' function (as in 'I have visited Greece twice') or 'perfect of persistence' function (as in 'I have been coughing for

[5] Squartini & Bertinetto (2000).
[6] For relevant cross-linguistic studies, see e.g. Harris (1982); Bybee & Dahl (1989); Bybee, Perkins & Pagliuca (1994); Schwenter (1994a, 1994b); Carey (1994, 1995, 1996); Schwenter & Cacoullos (2008).
[7] Cf. Comrie (1976: 60–1); Schwenter (1994a, 1994b).
[8] Cf. also Carey (1994, 1995, 1996).

Perfect Aspect

several days').[9] Squartini & Bertinetto (2000: 419), on the other hand, consider the use of periphrastic perfects with such an experiential or perfect of persistence function 'a totally independent development'. Similarly, Comrie (1976: 60-1) and more recently Schwenter (1994a, 1994b) have suggested that the 'perfect of recent past' (as in 'I've just seen him!') constitutes an important intermediate step in the development from anterior (with current relevance) to perfective past.

A schematic overview of 'aoristic drift', with its hypothesized intermediary stages, is given in Fig. 3.1.

Resultative ⟶ Anterior ⟶ Perfective

Experiential/Persistence --?--> Current relevance --?--> Recent past

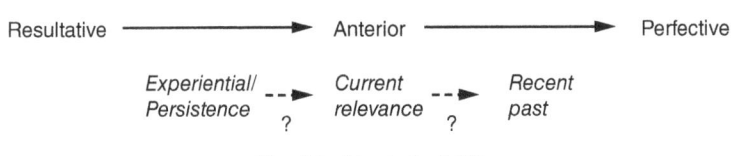

Fig. 3.1. 'Aoristic drift'

3.2 ARCHAIC GREEK (VIII–VI BC)

3.2.1 Verbal Periphrasis as an Emergent Phenomenon

Already in Archaic Greek sources, we find the first examples of participial constructions with εἰμί and ἔχω, particularly εἰμί with the perfect participle, ἔχω with the aorist participle, and ἔχω with the (medio-passive) perfect participle.[10] These constructions occur infrequently, and as such constitute what Harris & Campbell (1995: 72-5) call 'exploratory expressions'.

With some sixty examples, the construction of εἰμί with the perfect participle is by far the most frequently attested. Most of the examples can be found in the Homeric epics,[11] as in (59):

(59) τῷ νῦν μή ποτε καὶ σὺ γυναικί περ ἤπιος εἶναι / μηδ' οἱ μῦθον ἅπαντα πιφαυσκέμεν, ὅν κ' ἐῢ εἰδῇς, / ἀλλὰ τὸ μὲν φάσθαι, τὸ δὲ καὶ κεκρυμμένον εἶναι (Hom., Od. 11.441-3)

---

[9] See §1.4.1.3 for the different perfect subfunctions.
[10] One construction which may go back to PIE is εἰμί with the verbal adjective in -τός (Meiser 2004; Drinka 2009). The construction will not be further discussed in this chapter.
[11] The construction appears slightly more frequently in the *Odyssey* (with a normed rate of occurrence (NRO) of 2.6 instances per 10,000 words) than in the *Iliad* (with an NRO of 2.1 instances per 10,000 words).

'Therefore in your own case never be gentle even to your wife. Do not declare to her every thought that you have in mind, but tell her some things, and let others also be hidden.' (tr. Dimock-Murray)

The shade of Agamemnon advises Odysseus never to treat women kindly, and never to tell them everything that is on one's mind. In accordance with the grammaticalization path stipulated by Squartini & Bertinetto (2000), in this early example periphrastic κεκρυμμένον εἶναι is used with a resultative aspectual function, expressing the state of being hidden, rather than referring to a past event with current relevance.

A remarkable characteristic of the construction in Archaic Greek, in Homer in particular, is its low type-token ratio:[12] almost half of the examples occcur with the verb τελέω 'I accomplish' (twenty-four examples),[13] as in (60), where Penelope grants Odysseus, who is disguised as a beggar, the right to string his own bow:

(60) ἀλλ' ἄγε οἱ δότε τόξον ἐΰξοον, ὄφρα ἴδωμεν. / ὧδε γὰρ ἐξερέω, τὸ δὲ καὶ <u>τετελεσμένον ἔσται</u>· / εἴ κέ μιν ἐντανύσῃ, δώῃ δέ οἱ εὖχος Ἀπόλλων, / ἕσσω μιν χλαῖνάν τε χιτῶνά τε (Hom., Od. 21.336-9)

'No, come, give him the polished bow and let us see. For thus will I speak out to you, and this word shall truly also be brought to pass; if he shall string the bow, and Apollo grant him glory, I will clothe him with a cloak and tunic.' (tr. Dimock-Murray)

The construction with τετελεσμένον 'accomplished' mostly occurs paratactically (less often hypotactically) connected with ὧδε γάρ (or ἀλλ' ἔκ τοι) ἐξερέω 'thus will I speak out', and with εἰμί in the future tense, as in our example (60).[14] Three other contexts in which it occurs are as follows: (a) in a relative clause introduced by ὃ δή or ἃ δή;[15] (b) in a wish preceded by αἲ γὰρ τοῦτο, ξεῖνε, ἔπος 'if only this word, stranger' (only in the *Odyssey*), paired with εἰμί in the optative mood;[16] and (c) in a conditional clause preceded by εἰ δύναμαι τελέσαι 'if I can fulfil it', paired with εἰμί in the indicative present.[17]

---

[12] Cf. Keil (1963: 44) on the 'formulaic' character of the construction in Homer.
[13] Cf. also Giannaris (2011b: 123).
[14] For similar examples, see *Il.* 1.212, 2.257; *Od.* 16.440, 17.229. *Il.* 9.310 presents an interesting variant.
[15] See e.g. *Il.* 1.388, 18.4; *Od.* 19.547. Note that a similar example occurs in the *Homeric Hymn to Aphrodite* (line 26).
[16] See e.g. *Od.* 15.536, 17.163, 19.309.
[17] See e.g. *Il.* 14.196, 18.427; *Od.* 5.90. Note that in this context the participle can acquire the value of a verbal adjective (see e.g. Ameis & Hentze 1920: 154 with regard

In all cases, the periphrastic construction occurs at the end of the line, after the hephthemimeral caesura.

Two constructions that occur less frequently than εἰμί with the perfect participle, and which will be discussed in much greater detail with respect to Classical and Post-Classical/Byzantine Greek, are ἔχω with the aorist participle and ἔχω with the medio-passive perfect participle. In Homer, the former combination occurs in the phrase ἑλὼν γὰρ ἔχει γέρας 'having taken the prize, he has it',[18] but most scholars argue that ἔχω in this context maintains its full possessive value, and that the construction as such is not periphrastic.[19] More interesting in this regard is the following example from Hesiod:

(61) κρύψαντες γὰρ ἔχουσι θεοὶ βίον ἀνθρώποισιν / ῥηιδίως γάρ κεν καὶ ἐπ' ἤματι ἐργάσσαιο, / ὥστε σε κεῖς ἐνιαυτὸν ἔχειν καὶ ἀεργὸν ἐόντα (Hes., Op. 42–4)

'For the gods keep hidden from men the means of life. Else you would easily do work enough in a day to supply you for a full year even without working.' (tr. Evelyn-White)

Hesiod narrates how the gods have concealed the 'means of life', so that man has to work hard to supply himself with food. Although some scholars seem to believe that κρύψαντες ἔχουσι should be interpreted as a perfect of current relevance,[20] indicating a past event with relevance at the time of speaking, it may be more viable to accord ἔχω the value of 'I keep or hold in a certain state'[21] (which is intermediate between pure possession and the semantically bleached auxiliary value), and to take κρύψαντες 'having hidden' as a conjunct participle, as suggested by Thielmann (1891: 297) (as well as Evelyn-White in his translation of this passage). On this interpretation, the construction

---

to Od. 5.90, who suggest to translate with 'erfüllbar' and note that 'beim griechischen Part. Pass. ist die Bedeutung der Möglichkeit etwas Seltenes' ('with the Greek passive participle, the meaning of possibility seldomly occurs')).

[18] See Il. 1.356, 1.507, 2.240, 9.111.

[19] See e.g. Thielmann (1891: 294); Aerts (1965: 128); Moser (1988: 237). Schwyzer (1953: 812), on the other hand, does seem to consider the construction periphrastic.

[20] See e.g. Pouilloux (1957: 129), who refers to Mazon's translation: 'les dieux ont caché ce qui fait vivre les hommes' ('the gods have hidden that which makes men live'). Aerts (1965: 129–30) refers to the scholia (Schol. Eur. Hippol. 932), where κρύψαντες ... ἔχουσι is compared to the synthetic form κεκρύφασι.

[21] Cf. West (1980: 153): 'the ἔχειν keeps some of its proper force, as in other early examples of its combination with an aorist participle.'

would have a resultative-like value, stressing the hidden state of the object βίον 'the means of life' ('having hidden the means of life the gods keep them [in a hidden state]' > 'the gods keep the means of life hidden'). Such an interpretation fits well within the context, where the fact that the means of life are still hidden is stressed.[22] In the absence of any other examples of the construction with an anterior function in Archaic Greek, such an interpretation also takes into account the general diachronic development of the construction.[23]

The second construction that deserves mention here is ἔχω with the medio-passive perfect participle. While this construction is generally taken into account only with regard to Post-Classical Greek,[24] some instances can already be found in Archaic Greek,[25] as in (62), where the Trojan Asius drives his chariot to the Greek camp, and is surprised to find the gates open:[26]

(62) τῇ ῥ' ἵππους τε καὶ ἅρμα διήλασεν, οὐδὲ πύλῃσιν / εὗρ' ἐπικεκλιμένας σανίδας καὶ μακρὸν ὀχῆα, / ἀλλ' <u>ἀναπεπταμένας ἔχον</u> ἀνέρες (Hom., Il. 12.120–2)
'There he drove on his horses and chariot, and at the gate he did not find the doors shut nor the long bar drawn, but men were holding them flung wide open.' (tr. Wyatt-Murray)

Similarly to what we have seen in our previous examples, the construction expresses a state, in this particular case of the object σανίδας 'the door'. In comparison with (61), this is expressed more directly, through the concord between the object and the medio-passive perfect participle; this type of resultative HAVE-construction can be encountered in many of the European languages.

---

[22] That a state still obtains may be implied by the anterior perfect, but as Bybee & Dahl (1989: 68–9) point out, this is not necessarily the case: '[anterior] perfects... typically do not imply the presence of a direct result: they can be used both in cases where no such result can be defined at all (e.g. with statives and 'activities') or where a former result has been cancelled at the point of reference (as in *Poland has been divided by her neighbors several times*).'
[23] See further §3.3.2.1.
[24] See e.g. Aerts (1965: 161–7); Moser (1988: 239).
[25] Cf. Thielmann (1891: 305–6).
[26] For a similar example, see Hom., Il. 21.531.

3.2.2 Innovative Tendencies in Archaic Greek?

As has been pointed out by several scholars, the synthetic perfect in Archaic (Homeric) Greek generally has a resultative character,[27] as is illustrated in (63):

(63) μαινόμενε φρένας ἠλὲ διέφθορας· ἦ νύ τοι αὔτως / οὔατ' ἀκουέμεν ἐστί, νόος δ' ἀπόλωλε καὶ αἰδώς (Hom., Il. 15.128-9)

'You madman, deranged in mind, you are doomed! Surely it is for nothing that you have ears for hearing, and your understanding and shame are gone from you.' (tr. Wyatt-Murray)

Athena addresses Ares, who has decided to partake in the battle, despite Zeus' interdiction. Two synthetic perfects are used, διέφθορας 'you are lost' and ἀπόλωλε 'it is gone', both of which express the present 'lost' state of their subject, respectively Ares and his understanding and sense of right. In examples such as these, the perfect expresses a state which is the result of an unemphasized and implicit past event. As is shown in (64), however, this is not always the case:

(64) καὶ τὰ μὲν ἠλασάμεσθα Πύλον Νηλήϊον εἴσω / ἐννύχιοι προτὶ ἄστυ· γεγήθει δὲ φρένα Νηλεύς, / οὕνεκά μοι τύχε πολλὰ νέῳ πόλεμον δὲ κιόντι (Hom., Il. 11.682-4)

'These then we drove into Neleian Pylos by night into the town, and Neleus rejoiced at heart, since much booty had fallen to me when I went to war as a stripling.' (tr. Wyatt-Murray)

Nestor recounts how after a dispute with the Eleans he drove home a great amount of beasts, bringing joy to Neleus, the king of Pylos. The (past) perfect form that is used, γεγήθει, is based on a lexically stative form, γηθέω, 'I rejoice', and as such cannot be considered the result of a past event. Cases such as these, which may be considered remnants of an older PIE-situation, are perhaps best characterized as 'stative'.[28]

More interesting for our present purposes is that already in Homer traces can be found of innovation.[29] Consider (65):

---

[27] Cf. Haspelmath (1992); Slings (1994: 240-1); Gerö & von Stechow (2003: 262-9); Haug (2008).
[28] Cf. Slings (1994: 240-1). Haspelmath (1992: 201-4), on the other hand, referring to Nedjalkov & Jaxontov (1988), argues that we can still speak of resultatives.
[29] See e.g. Haspelmath (1992: 209-10); Slings (1994: 241-3); Duhoux (2000: 427); Ruijgh (2004: 32).

(65) ὢ πόποι ἦ δὴ μυρί᾿ Ὀδυσσεὺς ἐσθλὰ ἔοργε / βουλάς τ᾿ ἐξάρχων ἀγαθὰς πόλεμόν τε κορύσσων (Hom., Il. 2.272-3)
'Well, now! Surely Odysseus has before this performed good deeds without number as leader in good counsel and setting battle in array.' (tr. Wyatt-Murray)

In this passage, the past event expressed by the perfect form (ἔοργε) is more salient: the Greek soldiers stress the many good deeds done by Odysseus. Observe how this correlates with transitivity, ἔοργε 'he has done' taking an accusative object and a volitional subject (agent). It is worth noting, however, that the second participant is not affected, and that multiple events are expressed, rather than a single one (as such, we are dealing here with an 'experiential' (anterior) perfect).[30]

When it comes to the periphrastic constructions I discussed in §3.2.1, such innovative, more transitive uses in general do not seem to be attested, although it is worth briefly discussing two instances of εἰμί paired with the perfect participle. Consider (66):[31]

(66) ἦ σύ γ᾿ ἄνακτος / ὀφθαλμὸν ποθέεις, τὸν ἀνὴρ κακὸς ἐξαλάωσε / σὺν λυγροῖσ᾿ ἑτάροισι, δαμασσάμενος φρένας οἴνῳ, / Οὖτις, ὃν οὔ πώ φημι πεφυγμένον ἔμμεν ὄλεθρον (Hom., Od. 9.452-5)
'Surely you are sorrowing for the eye of your master, which an evil man blinded along with his miserable fellows, when he had overpowered my wits with wine, Nobody, who, I tell you, has not yet escaped destruction.' (tr. Dimock-Murray)

In this famous scene from the ninth book of the *Odyssey*, the giant Polyphemus addresses his ram, asking why he lags behind when he normally does not. As in (65), the construction is accompanied by an accusative (ὄλεθρον 'destruction'), which renders the past event more salient.[32] The relative clause refers to a time-range that started in the past and continues up to the present; thus, we can speak of a 'perfect of persistence',[33] although we are certainly dealing with a less

---

[30] Chantraine (1927: 13) and Sicking & Stork (1996: 161) stress the state that results from the combined past events (Odysseus being a reliable leader). On the subject-orientedness of the experiential perfect, see fn. 131 (Chapter 1) and §3.3.3.

[31] Note that there are two more examples of εἰμί + πεφυγμένος + accusative object in Archaic Greek: Hom., Il. 6.488 and H. Hom. 5.34.

[32] Alternatively, Ameis & Hentze (1922: 95) suggest to take πεφυγμένον as a passive participle (meaning 'entronnen, sicher vor' ('escaped, safe from'), cf. similarly Liddell & Scott 1968: 1925), but under this interpretation the accusative is difficult to explain (compare Od. 1.18, where πεφυγμένος ἦεν 'he was free from' is followed by a genitive).

[33] Compare Michaelis (1998: 183).

Perfect Aspect

prototypical instance, since the event is negated and as such has not occurred (contrast with more common examples such as 'he has been coughing since Tuesday').

A second example comes from the *Homeric Hymn to Aphrodite*:

(67) φιλομμειδὴς δ' Ἀφροδίτη / ἕρπε μεταστρεφθεῖσα κατ' ὄμματα καλὰ βαλοῦσα / ἐς λέχος εὔστρωτον, ὅθι περ πάρος <u>ἔσκεν</u> ἄνακτι / χλαίνῃσιν μαλακῇς <u>ἐστρωμένον</u> (H. Hom. 5.155–8)

'And laughter-loving Aphrodite, with face turned away and lovely eyes downcast, crept to the well-spread couch which was already laid with soft coverings for the hero.' (tr. Evelyn-White)

Anchises is filled with sweet desire to sleep with the goddess Aphrodite, who is apparently willing to fulfil his desire. Evelyn-White suggests interpreting ἔσκεν... ἐστρωμένον as a resultative perfect ('[the bed] was laid'), with πάρος meaning 'already' and ἄνακτι being taken as a dative of advantage. Perhaps, however, we should not exclude the possibility that we are dealing with an anterior perfect, with πάρος referring to an earlier, not specified time and ἄνακτι being a dative of agent. Crudden (2001: 70) has recently made such a suggestion, although he does not take ἄνακτι as a dative of agent ('where for the lord it had already with blankets been softly spread').[34]

3.3 CLASSICAL GREEK (V–IV BC)

3.3.1 Periphrasis and the Paradigm

During the Classical period, the frequency of constructions of ἔχω with the aorist participle and εἰμί with the perfect participle increases quite spectacularly, with nearly two thousand examples in our corpus,[35] the large majority of which are εἰμί with the perfect participle. The increase in frequency of these two constructions may be connected with certain developments in the synthetic paradigm, the perfect in particular.

---

[34] Contrast Faulkner (2008: 226), who specifically notes that 'the dative ἄνακτι is best understood as a "dative of agent"'.

[35] To be more specific, the combined NRO of ἔχω with the aorist participle and εἰμί with the perfect participle in Archaic Greek is 2.67, and in Classical Greek 5.55.

The development of the synthetic perfect was first treated in detail by Wackernagel (1953 [1904]) and Chantraine (1927), both of whom focused heavily on whether an accusative (affected) object accompanied the synthetic perfect. To be more specific, they suggested that the perfect underwent a semantic development, which can be phrased in terms of a shift of emphasis from the state of the subject to that of the object. Thus, the 'resultative perfect'[36] expressed the continuing state in which the object finds him/her/itself,[37] as in λέλυκα αὐτόν 'I have freed him [and he continues to be free]'.[38] Wackernagel (1953 [1904]: 1002) and Chantraine (1927: 140–1) connect the rise of this resultative perfect, which they situate in the Classical period, to the spread of perfect formations with the suffix -κ- (for perfects with stems ending in vowels, liquids, or nasals),[39] which occur infrequently in Archaic (Homeric) Greek.[40]

While the Wackernagel–Chantraine view was quite influential during the twentieth century and was adopted by many scholars (including Aerts 1965 with regard to periphrasis), it also received criticism. For one thing, it is often unclear in what sense the state of the object is emphasized. McKay (1965: 9–10), for example, finds that in a sentence such as ὃν Ἀθηναῖοι πολλάκις ἑαυτῶν στρατηγὸν ᾕρηνται ξένον ὄντα (Pl., *Ion* 541c) '(Apollodorus of Cyzicus) whom the Athenians have often chosen as their general, though a foreigner', about which Chantraine (1927: 165) notes that 'l'état exprimé est celui de l'object',[41] emphasis lies on the Athenians and their attitude of appointing foreigners such as Apollodorus of Cyzicus as general, rather than on the object, whose current state of generalship is unclear.[42] Rijksbaron (1984) has furthermore posed the question of how the passive perfect fits into the picture sketched by Wackernagel (1953 [1904]) and Chantraine (1927): he notes that in order to emphasize

---

[36] Note that 'resultative perfect' is not used here in the same sense as it is throughout this chapter (cf. fn. 127 (Chapter 1)).

[37] Cf. Wackernagel (1953 [1904]: 1001): 'das Perfekt von einer vergangenen Handlung... deren Wirkung im oder am Objekt noch in der Gegenwart fordauert' ('the perfect of a past action... which continues to affect the object in the present').

[38] Cf. Chantraine (1927: 122, 152).

[39] Cf. Kimball (1991: 142).

[40] There are a few examples in Homer, but there does not seem to be any connection with transitivity. Cf. Kimball (1991: 144).

[41] 'The state expressed is that of the object.'

[42] Cf. similarly Rijksbaron (1984); Sicking & Stork (1996: 146–50); Duhoux (2000: 428); Willi (2010: 129).

the state of the object/patient, one could use the passive perfect, which renders the notion of 'resultative perfect' superfluous.

Partly due to these criticisms, a number of scholars have abandoned the Wackernagel–Chantraine view, and stressed that 'stativity' should be considered the sole defining feature of the synthetic perfect throughout its history.[43] I agree with Willi (2003: 129–30), however, who notes the following:

> Although Wackernagel and Chantraine failed to explain clearly *what* was new, it is impossible to deny that there *was* something new about the perfect in fifth-century Greek.

In fact, the work of Wackernagel and Chantraine fits well with the findings of cross-linguistically oriented studies, where two main types of perfect are typically distinguished,[44] called 'resultative' and 'anterior'.[45] Within the present approach, which does not view aspectuality solely in terms of temporality but also transitivity, the insights of Wackernagel and Chantraine can be rephrased by saying that the semantic development of the perfect was indeed one of increased transitivity, but in the *scalar* sense.[46] From this point of view, the presence of an accusative object is an important indicator of transitivity, but not the only one; two participants can also be involved with the passive voice, with a dative of agent or ὑπό with the genitive alongside the subject. Moreover, other parameters such as volitionality, affectedness, etc. need to be taken into account.

As noted by Haspelmath (1992: 212–13), the development of the synthetic perfect from resultative to anterior entailed an increase in lexical generality: while resultatives are typically restricted to verbs whose content is telic (indicating the final 'resultant' state of the event), anteriors do not have such lexical restrictions. In the fifth century BC, however, an active perfect form was not available for all

---

[43] See e.g. McKay (1980); Porter (1989: 245–90); Sicking & Stork (1996); Evans (2001: 26–32); Rijksbaron (2002: 1, 4–6, 35–9).

[44] Cf. §1.4.1.3.

[45] This is not to say that these categories should be equated with the two types of perfect distinguished by Wackernagel and Chantraine. One important difference, which was already mentioned in footnote 22, is that the state of the object does not necessarily still obtain with the anterior perfect, as Wackernagel and Chantraine would have it.

[46] For a similar proposal, see Kavčič (2014).

verbs, and in this respect the construction of ἔχω with the aorist participle provided 'temporary relief', as noted by Aerts (1965: 129):

> It appears repeatedly that the construction is used with verbs of which there is no perfect active whatsoever, or of which the perfect active only came into being in or after the fifth century B.C.

Thielmann (1891: 302) has argued that this primarily concerned so-called 'aspirated' perfects (which were still relatively infrequent in fifth-century Classical Greek)[47] such as ἀπήλλαχα 'I have freed', κεκήρυχα 'I have announced', τετάραχα 'I have disturbed', etc., but this seems to be an overgeneralization. Aerts (1965: 128–60) cites many other examples with verbs that do not belong to this class, including ἀτιμάζω (Soph., Ant. 22) 'I dishonour', ἀπειλέω (Soph., OC 817) 'I threaten', and καταισχύνω (Eur., Ion 736) 'I put to shame'. The periphrastic construction could also be used with verbs that did have a synthetic form, such as βάλλω (Soph., Ant. 1068) 'I throw', γαμέω (Soph., OT 577) 'I marry', and μανθάνω (Eur., Ion 230) 'I learn'.[48]

Porter (1989: 489) has argued against the connection made by Aerts (1965) and others between ἔχω with the aorist participle and the 'resultative' perfect on the grounds that the Wackernagel–Chantraine view is problematic, but within the present approach such an argument no longer holds relevance.

The spread of εἰμί with the perfect participle can also be related to the development of the synthetic perfect, but it concerns the passive, rather than the active voice. While there are no problems in the formation of perfects with vocalic stems, in the formation of the third person plural of perfects with consonantal stems there was an accumulation of consonants, which in Archaic Greek led to the regular vocalization of the nasal in interconsonantal context (e.g. with κρύπτω 'I hide': kekrupʰn̥tai > κεκρύφαται). Towards the Classical period, however, the periphrastic construction of εἰμί with the perfect participle was increasingly more often used as an alternative formation, first in the third person plural of verbs with consonantal stems (e.g. κρύπτω: κεκρυμμένοι εἰσί). Later on, the use of periphrasis was extended to the third person singular and to verbs with vocalic stems, and it also came to be used in the subjunctive and optative moods.[49] This

---

[47] For some early examples, see Ringe (1984: 132–5).
[48] Cf. Thielmann (1891: 303); Rijksbaron (2002: 130–1).
[49] For further details, see §3.3.2.

Perfect Aspect   117

development is well observed in the Attic inscriptions, where, as noted by Aerts (1965: 41), no more forms in -αται and -ατο can be found after 410 BC.[50] Ionic seems to have been more resistant: in Herodotus, for example, we see that the endings -αται and -ατο are extended to verbs with vocalic stem (as in πεπονέαται (Hdt. 2.63.1) 'they are occupied with'), and are even used in the present tense (as in προτιθέαται (Hdt. 1.133.1) 'they set before themselves'). Whether the loss of the old endings stimulated the rise of periphrasis, or periphrasis rather contributed to the loss of the endings, is unclear. As Rosén (1992: 17) notes, periphrastic forms already existed at an early stage, so that the latter possibility should not be entirely excluded.

To conclude this section, the connection between periphrasis and the paradigm also needs to be taken into account when considering the decline of ἔχω with the aorist participle towards the end of the Classical period. As Chantraine (1927: 29) notes, in the fourth century BC a perfect could be formed from almost any verb, which entailed the loss of a *raison d'être* for the construction of ἔχω with the aorist participle. Porter (1989: 490) has suggested a somewhat different scenario. According to him, the increased usage of synthetic perfect forms should be attributed to the fact that the periphrastic construction at a certain point was felt to be 'insufficient to capture the stative sense that already existent Perfect forms conveyed',[51] but given the relative frequency of the synthetic and the periphrastic perfect, this seems rather unlikely. Porter's (1989) account also does not explain why the periphrastic form would have become 'insufficient'.

3.3.2 The First Major Perfect Periphrases: ἔχω with the Aorist Participle and εἰμί with the Perfect Participle

In the present section, we shall look into the use of ἔχω with the aorist participle and εἰμί with the perfect participle in somewhat greater detail. As noted in the introduction, the difference between these two constructions is often represented as one of 'eventivity' versus 'stativity', but this picture must be nuanced.

---

[50] Cf. also Rijksbaron (2002: 129).
[51] Note that Porter (1989) defines perfect aspect in terms of stativity.

3.3.2.1 ἔχω with the aorist participle

While Proto-Indo-European used the 'BE + dative' construction to express possession,[52] already in the earliest stages of Ancient Greek ἔχω is attested next to ἔστι μοι, which it gradually came to replace. As noted by Kulneff-Eriksson (1999: 5), 'the introduction of "have" into a "be" language causes considerable structural changes', and indeed already in the fifth century BC ἔχω is attested with some frequency as an auxiliary in combination with the aorist participle. Although Drinka (2003b: 13, 2007: 106) has recently noted that in this period ἔχω can be considered a 'full-fledged auxiliary', it should be pointed out that traces of diachronic development are still clearly visible.

This development does not entirely follow that of the cross-linguistically more usual HAVE-perfect—that is, HAVE + object + passive past (perfect) participle (as in Engl. 'he has it written down'), although it shows some similarities. The development of the latter construction is typically described in terms of a form-function reanalysis,[53] whereby [[HAVE$_{POSS}$ + object] + participle] came to be interpreted as [HAVE$_{AUX}$ + [object + participle]].[54] Carey (1994: 33) has argued, however, that too much attention has gone to the possessive construction, and that other intermediate stages must be recognized. Consider the following Latin examples:[55]

(68) qui eum vinctum habebit (*Lex XII Tab.* 3.4)

'Who shall hold him in bonds.' (tr. Pinkster)

(69) (Flamines)... caput cinctum habebant filo (Varro, *L.L.* 5.84)

'The Flamines had their hair girt with a woollen fillet.' (tr. Pinkster)

(70) cum cognitum habeas quod sit summi rectoris... numen (Cic., *Fin.* 4.11)

'When you have realized what is the will of the supreme Lord.'

---

[52] As one of the reviewers notes, Proto-Indo-European also had a BE + genitive construction to express possession. For discussion and references, see Bauer (2000: 190–3).

[53] A form-function reanalysis involves the reanalysis of the 'mapping' between form and meaning (see e.g. Croft 2000: 117–21). An example would be the 'be going to'-construction in cases such as '[I am going] [to buy cake]': the semantic feature of future intention may be analysed as inherent in the construction and that of spatial motion dropped: '[I am going to buy cake]'.

[54] Compare with Heine's (1993: 31) 'possession schema' (cf. §1.5.2), formulated as 'X has Y'.

[55] I borrow these examples from Pinkster (1987).

Carey (1994) refers to these three different types as the 'secondary predicate construction' (ex. (68)), the 'resultant state object construction' (ex. (69)), and the 'resultant state process construction' (ex. (70)). As she shows, these constructions differ in a number of respects, concerning (a) the obligatoriness of the participle, (b) the role of the subject, (c) the 'target' of HAVE,[56] and (d) the status of the object.

In our first example, (68), the participle can be considered non-obligatory: 'to have or hold someone' makes sense, while 'to have a head' 'is so evidently true that it is pointless'[57] and 'to have what is the will of the supreme Lord' is impossible. The subject in (68) is not necessarily the agent of the event denoted by *vinctum* 'captured', and the 'have' relation can be described as one of ownership/possession. We are dealing with an 'external' (or 'pre-existing') object, the final state of which is expressed by the participle. In the second example, (69), the subject is not necessarily the agent of the event denoted by *cinctum* 'girt', and the object is also external. Importantly, however, the participle is no longer non-obligatory, and as such the target of HAVE can be described as 'a stative relation between the object and a process', of which the subject is in control. In our third example, (70), the subject is the agent (or more correctly experiencer) of the process denoted by the verb, and the object is internal ('non-pre-existent'), so that there can be no question of physical ownership or possession. While in some examples of the resultant state object construction a pragmatic inference[58] is possible, whereby the participle refers to a completed process rather than a resultant state (e.g. 'he had his eyes opened' > 'he had opened his eyes'), in examples of the resultant state process construction such as (70) such an inference is necessary, as it would be non-sensical to focus on the resultant state of the object.[59]

---

[56] The term 'target' stems from Langacker (1991: 170–1), who describes possessive constructions in terms of a 'reference point' (the possessor) and a 'target' (the possessed).

[57] Pinkster (1987: 197).

[58] The context in which an utterance is made may stimulate the addressee/reader to understand more than was intended by the speaker/author. In that case, we are dealing with a 'pragmatic inference'. See further Traugott & Dasher (2002), who stress the role of pragmatic inference for language change.

[59] Note, however, that in the absence of concord between the participle and the subject, we are formally still dealing with a resultative construction.

Thus, the target of HAVE can be described as a completed process which involves the subject.

To return to ἔχω with the aorist participle, one factor that needs to be taken into account is that the participle always agrees with the subject, rather than the object of the verb.[60] Thus, we cannot speak of 'secondary predicate constructions', although examples where the verb ἔχω denotes the possession of an external object by the subject abound, as in (71), where a concubine of a certain Persian addresses the Spartan king Pausanias, and (72), where Philoctetes laments his fate:[61]

(71) εἰμὶ δὲ γένος μὲν Κῴη, θυγάτηρ δὲ Ἡγητορίδεω τοῦ Ἀνταγόρεω· βίῃ δέ με λαβὼν ἐκ Κῶ εἶχε ὁ Πέρσης (Hdt. 9.76.2)

'I am by race of Cos, the daughter of Hegetorides the son of Antagoras; and the Persian took me by force in Cos and kept me a prisoner.' (tr. Macaulay)

(72) {Φι.} προσθείς τε χεῖρα δεξιάν, τὰ τόξα μου / ἱερὰ λαβὼν τοῦ Ζηνὸς Ἡρακλέους ἔχει (Soph., Phil. 942-3)

'Philoctetes. And having given his right hand as pledge, he has taken and is keeping my sacred bow of Heracles the son of Zeus.' (tr. Lloyd-Jones)

Interestingly, there are also various examples that approach Carey's 'resultant state object construction' (cf. already ex. (61)),[62] as in (73), where Antigone informs Ismene that she will bury her brother 'in accordance with what the gods have established', (74), where the function of the heart is discussed, and (75), where the Athenian Stranger draws a parallel between unwritten laws and ancestral customs:

(73) {Αν.} σὺ δ᾽ εἰ δοκεῖ / τὰ τῶν θεῶν ἔντιμ᾽ <u>ἀτιμάσασ᾽ ἔχε</u> (Soph., Ant. 76-7)

'Antigone. But if you so choose, continue to dishonor what the gods in honor have established.' (tr. Jebb)

(74) ἐξ ἅπαντος γὰρ τοῦ σώματος φλέβες ἐς αὐτὴν συντείνουσι, καὶ <u>ξυγκλείσασα ἔχει</u> ὥστε αἰσθάνεσθαι, ἤν τις πόνος ἢ τάσις γίνηται τῷ ἀνθρώπῳ (Hippoc., Morb. sacr. 17.14-16)

---

[60] Cf. Moser (1988: 236).
[61] For other examples, see Thielmann (1891: 295-6).
[62] Cf. also Thielmann (1891: 297-8); Kühner & Gerth (1976 [1904]: 61-2).

'Coming from the entire body, veins run to it [the heart], which keeps them tied together, so that it feels whatever distress or tension takes place in man.' (tr. Jouanna, originally in French)

(75) οἷον πάτρια καὶ παντάπασιν ἀρχαῖα νόμιμα, ἃ καλῶς μὲν τεθέντα καὶ ἐθισθέντα πάσῃ σωτηρίᾳ περικαλύψαντα ἔχει τοὺς τότε γραφέντας νόμους (Pl., Leg. 793b)

'Exactly like ancestral customs of great antiquity, which, if well established and practiced, serve to wrap up securely the laws already written.' (tr. Bury)

In these examples, the participle can no longer be considered optional: it does not make sense to say 'have what the gods in honor have established', 'the heart has the veins', or 'the ancestral customs have the laws'. Thus, the stative relation between the object and the participle can be thought of as the target of HAVE, even though the participle formally agrees with the subject.

Both the possessive construction and the 'resultant state object construction' provided suitable contexts for a form-function reanalysis to take place (as in '[he has the bow] [having taken it]' > '[he has taken the bow]' or '[he has [it honoured]]' > '[he has honoured it]'), leading to the use of ἔχω with the aorist participle as an anterior perfect.[63] Carey (1994) seems right in drawing attention to the role of the 'resultant state object construction', since this type of construction provides an important intermediary step towards the use of an anterior perfect construction,[64] especially concerning the target of HAVE, and the relation between the object and the participle. Whether yet another intermediate step should be recognized—that is, Carey's 'resultant state process construction'—is impossible to say for Ancient Greek, in the absence of concord between the object and the participle. In any case, already in the fifth century BC we find unambigous examples with what Carey (1994) calls 'mental state verbs' (e.g. English 'learn', 'perceive', 'remember'), where a possessive interpretation of HAVE is excluded, since these verbs take internal

---

[63] Dover (1968: 88) and Kulneff-Eriksson (1999: 7, 36) have (independently) suggested that intransitive ἔχω + adverb may have served as a source-construction. I do not consider this very likely, for the following reasons: (a) there is no semantic similarity between the adverb and the aorist participle, so there is little motivation for a direct analogical extension; (b) the construction of ἔχω + adverb never presents any ambiguity, so that a development via inference also seems unlikely; (c) ἔχω + adverb does not occur with particular frequency, as Kulneff-Eriksson (1999: 33) notes.

[64] Cf. already Thielmann (1891: 297).

objects, and a resultative interpretation is more or less non-sensical. Consider (76):

(76) {Οι.} ὦ παῖδες, ἥκει τῷδ' ἐπ' ἀνδρὶ θέσφατος / βίου τελευτή, κοὐκέτ' ἔστ' ἀποστροφή / {Αν.} πῶς οἶσθα; τῷ δὲ τοῦτο <u>συμβαλὼν ἔχεις</u>; (Soph., OC 1472-4)

'Oedipus. Children, the end of life that was prophesied has come upon this man, and there is no way of putting it off! Antigone. How do you know? How have you inferred this?' (tr. Lloyd-Jones, slightly modified)

Oedipus has arrived at the village of Colonus. After he has spoken to his son, Polynices, there is a thunderstorm, which he interprets as a sign of his impending death. Antigone wants to know how Oedipus has come to this conclusion, using a periphrasis. συμβαλὼν ἔχεις functions as an anterior perfect: it refers to Oedipus' coming to a conclusion about his death, which has relevance at the time of Antigone's question.

In terms of transitivity, examples such as (76) are indicative of relatively high transitivity, since it involves two participants. Even more transitive examples can be found, however, where the first participant is volitional and the second affected. This includes examples with verbs of destroying such as διόλλυμι 'I destroy utterly', verbs of killing such as κτείνω 'I kill', and psych-verbs[65] such as ταράσσω 'I trouble'. Consider, for example, (77):[66]

(77) {Οι.} ἐκμάνθαν'· οὐ γὰρ δὴ φονεὺς ἁλώσομαι. / {Κρ.} τί δῆτ'; ἀδελφὴν τὴν ἐμὴν <u>γήμας ἔχεις</u>; (Soph., OT 576-7)

'Oedipus. You shall learn all you wish; I shall not be proved to be the murderer. Creon. Well, have you married my sister?' (tr. Lloyd-Jones, slightly modified)

After Tiresias has revealed that Oedipus himself is the murderer of King Laius, Oedipus accuses Creon. Creon enters the scene to face the accusations, and claims the right to interrogate Oedipus, starting with the (obvious) question as to whether Oedipus has indeed married his (Creon's) sister. Periphrastic γήμας ἔχεις 'you have married' refers to

---

[65] The term 'psych-verbs' stands for 'verbs of psychological state' (Levin 1993: 188-93). Examples are English 'to anger', 'to annoy', 'to admire', 'to hate', etc.

[66] As one of the reviewers notes, in this example γήμας could function as a conjunct participle, ἔχω having the lexical value of 'I have as a wife'. This is not the standard interpretation, however (compare Aerts 1965: 135; Dawe 2006: 123).

Perfect Aspect 123

the earlier event of getting married, which has relevance for the current discourse situation. Relatively high-transitivity examples such as these led Pouilloux (1957) to the controversial hypothesis that Sophocles (who uses the construction with particular frequency) coined the construction to denote responsibility or a 'rupture of εὐκοσμία'.[67]

The presence of intransitive verbs as participial complement, which also unambiguously signal an anterior perfect, is still limited in the Classical period: we only have two examples, with ταρβέω (Soph., *Trach.* 37) 'I fear' and λήγω (Soph., *OT* 731) 'I stop'. The presence of such verbs can, however, be considered a clear sign of the extension of the construction in the Classical period. Another sign of extension is the fact that the construction is also used in the passive voice.[68] As will be discussed further on in this chapter, while in principle the passive voice does not de-transitivize (at least not when an agent is explicitly mentioned), it does constitute a less prototypical representation of the event,[69] reversing the action-chain.[70]

For a more detailed overview of the use of the construction, consider Table 3.1:

---

[67] See e.g. Pouilloux (1957: 128, 134): 'la périphrase verbale marque la rupture de l' εὐκοσμία, l'ordre du monde avec lequel les hommes se doivent de découvrir un accord, une harmonie. Où paraît cette expression rare, se révèle une faute des hommes'; 'une notion de faute ou de responsabilité transparaît constamment derrière cette forme verbale si rarement employée' ('the verbal periphrasis marks the rupture of εὐκοσμία, the order of the world with which men have to find an agreement, a harmony. Where this rare expression appears, a fault of men is revealed'; 'a notion of fault or responsibility appears constantly through this verbal form so rarely employed').

[68] See e.g. Hdt. 1.83.1 (ambiguous); Pl., *Crat.* 404c, *Leg.* 958a (ambiguous).

[69] Compare Wistrand (1972: 72): 'der voll entwickelte Passivsatz hat inhaltlich denselven Sinn wie der entsprechende aktive Satz. Es besteht jedoch ein wichtiger Unterschied formaler Natur. Der aktive Satz folgt dem Verlauf einer Handlung von deren Ausgangspunkt zu ihrem Ziel, der passive Satz such sich von dem Endpunkt einer Handlung nach ihrem Ursprung zurück' ('the fully developed passive sentence has the same meaning as the corresponding active sentence. There is, however, an important formal distinction. The active sentence follows the course of an action from its point of origin to its goal, while the passive sentence runs back from the endpoint of the action to its origins').

[70] The notion of 'action-chain' is well established in Cognitive Linguistic theory, where it refers to the conceptualization of the energy flow, typically with the subject as 'energy source' and the object as 'energy sink'. See e.g. Langacker (1991: 283, 292).

Table 3.1. Distribution of ἔχω with the aorist participle (CG)[1]

Genre/Author	TOT (ANT)	NRO	TTR
Drama[71]	37	1.00	0.86
Sophocles (b. 496/5 BC?)	21	3.28	0.90
Euripides (b. 480s BC?)	14	0.89	1.00
Historiography	10	0.15	0.80
Herodotus (b. 484 BC?)	10	0.53	0.80
Philosophy	5	0.03	0.80
Plato (b. c.429 BC)	4	0.07	0.75
Scientific prose	0	0	0
Oratory	10	0.16	0.50
Demosthenes (b. 384 BC)	9	0.31	0.55

Key: 'TOT' = total; 'ANT' = anterior perfect; 'NRO' = normed rate of occurrence (per 10,000 words); 'TTR' = type/token ratio.
[1] The dates of birth are based on the Oxford Classical Dictionary (third edition).

As noted in §2.3.3.2, ἔχω with the aorist participle was also known as the σχῆμα Σοφόκλειον. This table confirms that Sophocles indeed used the construction much more often than any other writer, with a (remarkable) NRO of 3.28 instances per 10,000 words. Euripides and Herodotus too used the construction quite frequently, though less so than Sophocles. Occasional examples can also be found in philosophy (Plato) and oratory (Demosthenes), though to a much lesser extent.

Thielmann (1891: 301–2) has suggested that we interpret these data in terms of the 'vulgar' origins of the construction.[72] He notes that the construction occurs only rarely in higher prose such as oratory, and that Plato and Herodotus are known for their use of lower-level linguistic features. With regard to the tragedians, Thielmann furthermore notes that the construction is mostly used in dialogue, rather than in lyric parts, which he considers 'ein deutlicher Hinweis auf den vulgären Charakter der Verbindung' (Thielmann 1891: 302).[73]

There may be some truth to Thielmann's theory, although the frequent appearance of the construction in tragedy remains a

[71] Various examples can also be found in the fragments (see e.g. Aerts 1965: 130–50). These have not been included in Table 3.1, as they do not form part of the main corpus.
[72] Cf. Thielmann (1891: 301): 'unsere Perfektumschreibung muß in der Volkssprache erwachsen sein' ('our perfect periphrasis must originate from the vulgar language').
[73] 'A clear sign of the vulgar character of the construction.'

difficulty.[74] The more important observation regarding the distribution of the construction seems to be made by Aerts (1965: 129), when he notes the following:

> It is... remarkable that especially Sophocles, Euripides and Herodotus were the ones who used it [the construction of ἔχω with the aorist participle, KB], that is the writers of the period immediately preceding the enormous expansion of the use of the transitive and resultative perfect in -κα.

3.3.2.2 εἰμί with the perfect participle

When it comes to εἰμί with the perfect participle, previous scholarship has generally stressed the 'stativity' of the construction,[75] Moser (1988: 229) even hypothesizing that the construction maintained this characteristic throughout the history of the language.[76] While it cannot be denied that examples with a resultative aspectual function play a prominent role in all stages of the language investigated here, we should be careful about overgeneralizing.

In the literature on resultative constructions, a distinction is commonly made between two types of resultative, called 'subject-oriented' (or 'subjective') and 'object-oriented' (or 'objective') resultative:[77] in the former case, the subject of the resultative construction corresponds to the direct object (or better patient/theme) of the base verb (as in 'the window is opened' < 'X opens the window'), while in the latter the underlying subject is retained (as in 'John is gone' < 'X goes'). Subject-oriented resultatives, which occur least frequently, can be found with a number of verb classes,[78] including verbs of motion and verbs of assuming a position (e.g. ἔρχομαι 'I go', πίπτω 'I fall'), verbs of change of state (e.g. γίγνομαι 'I become', φύομαι 'I grow'), and verbs of appearance, disappearance, and occurrence

---

[74] As one of the reviewers notes, if we follow Thielmann's (1891) theory through, this means that we consider oratory a 'higher' genre than tragedy. Thielmann (1891) also notes that metre may be considered an important stimulus for the use of the construction in tragedy (cf. §1.2.1), but the importance of metre should not be overestimated: the dramatists certainly had enough 'métier' to use another construction that fitted the metre. Compare e.g. Kulneff-Eriksson (1999: 106).

[75] See e.g. Aerts (1965: 36–51); Kahn (1973: 138); Smyth (1984 [1920]: 182); Karleen (1980: 131–3); Rijksbaron (2002: 128–9).

[76] See the introductory quote to this chapter.

[77] See Nedjalkov & Jaxontov (1988: 9); Nedjalkov (2001: 928).

[78] The categorization of verb classes used here is based on Levin (1993).

(τελευτάω 'I die', φαίνομαι 'I appear'). They typically take active endings, as for example in μὴ ἀναπεπτωκότες ἦτε (Dem. 19.224) '[I am afraid] that you are supine (lit. that you have fallen back)'; εἶ... γεγώς (Eur., *IT* 509) 'you are born'; ὡς τεθνεὼς εἴη (Hdt. 4.14.2) 'that he was dead'; ἀποπεπηδηκὼς... ἐστιν (Hippoc., *Art.* 47.8) 'it is displaced'; βεβὼς ἦν (Soph., *Trach.* 247) 'he was gone'. Object-oriented resultatives occur with a broader variety of verb classes, including verbs of communication (e.g. λέγω 'I say', τάσσω 'I order'), verbs of change of possession (e.g. δίδωμι 'I give', λαμβάνω 'I take'), verbs of creation and transformation (e.g. δράω 'I do', κατοικίζω 'I establish'), verbs of combining and attaching (e.g. κεράννυμι, συντίθημι), and verbs of sending and carrying (e.g. πέμπω 'I send', φέρω 'I carry'). They typically take medio-passive endings, as for example in λελευκωμένον... ἐστιν (Dem. 46.11) 'it is whitened'; ἐσκευασμένοι ἦσαν (Hdt. 7.68.1) 'they were equipped'; ἢν τετρωμένον ἔῃ (Hippoc., *Fract.* 4.2) 'if it is broken'; πεπερασμένον ἂν εἴη (Pl., *Prm.* 144e) 'it would be limited'; ἐκπεπληγμένοι ἦσαν (Xen., *An.* 5.6.36) 'they were panic-stricken'.

It should be noted, however, that the relationship between subject/object-oriented resultative and voice is more complex.[79] Object-oriented resultatives in the active voice, for example, are not entirely absent,[80] as in ὅτι ἀπολωλὸς εἴη (Dem. 35.36) 'that it was lost'; ἐπὴν συμπεπηγὸς ᾖ ἢ ξυνσεσηπὸς (Hippoc., *Loc. Hom.* 29.4) 'when it is clothed together or putrefied into a mass' (tr. Potter); κατεαγὼς ἔσται (Pl., *Grg.* 469d) 'it will be broken'; εἰσὶ καθεστηκότες (Xen., *Cyr.* 8.6.9) 'they are appointed'. Subject-oriented resultatives in the medio-passive voice are less common. Some examples are εἶναι... γεγενημένα (Aristot., *Rhet.* 1370a) 'to be past'; ὅταν ὠργημένον ᾖ (Hippoc., *Septim.* 122.17) 'when it is ready'; δεδογμένον... ἐστι (Pl., *Ap.* 34e) 'it is believed'. In his work on the synthetic perfect, Chantraine (1927) has argued that these forms can be thought of in terms of distinct diachronic layers: active object-oriented resultatives constitute an archaic layer, while passive subject-oriented resultatives represent a newer, innovative stage.[81] Also belonging to an older layer are perfects formed of lexically atelic

---

[79] Compare Chantraine (1927) with regard to the synthetic perfect.

[80] As one of the reviewers notes, however, some of the examples could also be interpreted as being subject-oriented: ἀπολωλὼς εἴη, for example, can be taken as the perfect of ἀπόλλυμαι 'I am lost', rather than active ἀπόλλυμι 'I destroy'.

[81] As Chantraine (1927: 117) notes, diachronically these represent opposite movements, during which active versus medio-passive endings respectively are given more prominence.

content verbs,[82] including verbs of mental state such as γιγνώσκω 'I (come to) know', verbs of perception such as δέρκομαι 'I see', and psych-verbs such as καταφρονέω 'I look down upon'.

Some verb classes are used with both medio-passive and active endings, but here semantic factors may need to be taken into account. This particularly concerns verbs of change of state, with which the resulting state can be either externally or internally motivated. In a phrase such as ἦν... εὖ δὲ αἱ πολεμικαὶ τέχναι μεμελετημέναι ὦσιν (Xen., Cyr. 1.6.41) 'if the arts of war are well studied', for example, μελετάω can be thought of as a transitive (causative) verb, while in ἦν δὲ τὸ μὲν τῶν Θηβαίων ἱππικὸν μεμελετηκός διά τε τὸν πρὸς Ὀρχομενίους πόλεμον (Xen., Hell. 6.4.10) 'the cavalry of the Thebans was well trained through the war with the Orchomenians', it can be considered an intransitive verb.[83] The same may be true for phrases such as τοῖσι δὲ πίνουσι σπλῆνας μὲν αἰεὶ μεγάλους εἶναι καὶ μεμυωμένους (Hippoc., Aer. 7.10–11) 'for those who drink the spleen is always very big and obstructed' vs. καὶ ἢν μὲν μεμυκὸς ᾖ, ἀναστομῶσαι (Hippoc., Mul. 11.15) 'if it [the orifice] is closed, open [it]', though the difference in these examples is less clear.

Both types of resultative are often used in coordination, for example, to express a notion that is contrary to that expressed by a regular adjective, as in the following pairs: ἄτακτον εἶναι καὶ τεταγμένον (Aristot., Cael. 280a) 'to be unordered and ordered'; εἰσὶ οἱ μὲν ἁπλοῖ οἱ δὲ πεπλεγμένοι (Aristot., Poet. 1452a) 'some are simple and some are complex'; ἐλευθέρην εἶναι ἢ δεδουλωμένην (Hdt. 9.60.1) 'to be free or enslaved'; καὶ μήτ' ἀνεσπασμένον ἔστω μήτε προπετές (Hippoc., Prorrh. 2.24) 'let it be neither retracted nor inclined forwards'. Even more often, we find the perfect participle coordinated with an adjective that expresses a semantically similar notion, as in (ὅταν) ἄπαις ᾖι καὶ λελειμμένη τέκνων (Eur., Ion 680) 'when she is childless and deprived of children'; ἐάν τι ἡδὺ μὲν ᾖ καὶ κεχαρισμένον (Pl., Grg. 502b) 'if something is pleasant and gratifying'; ἐρρωμένον ἦν καὶ ἐνεργόν (Xen., Ages. 1.24) 'it was strong and vigorous'; οὐ νόμιμον οὐδ' εἰθισμένον ἐστίν (Lycurg., 1.141) 'it is neither lawful nor customary'. Examples such as these indicate that the origins of resultative εἰμί with the perfect participle lie with Heine's (1993: 31) 'equation schema' (formulated

---

[82] Cf. our earlier observations in §3.2.2.
[83] Note that the terms 'transitive' and 'intransitive' are used here in their traditional sense (that is, referring to the presence of two arguments in the clause).

as 'X is (like) a Y'),[84] whereby copulative εἰμί was combined with the perfect participle, after the example of the regular adjective.[85]

In connection with the claim that the construction of εἰμί with the perfect participle would have been predominantly stative, Rijksbaron (2002: 129) notes that 'the periphrastic perfect is mainly formed with the passive perfect participle, and, in the active, with participles of intransitive verbs' (corresponding to the two resultative types outlined above). There would only be a few instances 'with an active participle of a fully transitive verb'. My own research shows that this claim must be rejected: almost 30% (233/867) of the examples of (anterior) εἰμί with the perfect participle are accompanied by an accusative object (either in the active or the middle voice). These objects can be found with participles of various lexical classes, among others verbs of destroying (e.g. ἀναιρέω 'I destroy', ἀπόλλυμι 'I destroy', καταστρέφω 'I ruin');[86] psych-verbs (e.g. πάσχω 'I suffer');[87] verbs of communication (e.g. ἀποκρίνομαι 'I answer', δείκνυμι 'I show', λέγω 'I say');[88] verbs of change of possession (e.g. δανείζω 'I lend', δίδωμι 'I give', πιπράσκω 'I sell');[89] and verbs of creation and transformation (e.g. ἐργάζομαι 'I work at', ἑτοιμάζω 'I prepare', ποιέω 'I make').[90] Some of these verbs are used with particular frequency in combination with an accusative object, such as ἐργάζομαι (17 ex.), ποιέω (21 ex.), and πάσχω (29 ex.).[91]

---

[84] Flobert (1975: 480) has argued for a second source-construction—that is, εἰμί with the verbal adjective in -τός, which would have been used as a periphrasis at an even earlier stage, and analogically extended to the medio-passive perfect participle (cf. Drinka 2009: 154–5).

[85] Compare Rosenkranz (1930: 163): 'da aber die Verbindung Adjektiv + εἶναι durchaus geläufig war, konnte natürlich jeden Augenblick die Verbindung Partizip + εἶναι gebildet werden' ('since the combination of adjective + εἶναι was very familiar, the combination participle + εἶναι could be built at any moment').

[86] See e.g. Aristoph., *Plut.* 867; Aristot., *Top.* 102a, 102b, 109b; Dem. 58.31; Hdt. 1.45.1, 3.64.2, 4.66.1; Xen., *Hell.* 5.2.27, 5.2.38.

[87] See e.g. Aristot., *Rhet.* 1380b; Dem. 24.107, 30.31, 47.41; Hdt. 1.44.2; Isoc. 14.9, 21.3; Lys. 9.7, 18.10, 32.18.

[88] See e.g. Antiph. 1.8; Aristot., *Rhet.* 1419a, *Top.* 108b, 143a; Dem. 55.8, 57.66; Isoc. 12.130; Pl., *Prt.* 358a, *Hp. mai.* 288a.

[89] See e.g. Aristot., *Oec.* 1348b, *Top.* 131b; Dem. 19.16, 31.14, 35.36, 36.6, 48.19; Isaeus 3.40; Isoc. 19.44; Lys. 12.82; Pl., *Alc. 2*, 140c, *Phd.* 76b; Xen., *Hell.* 4.8.35.

[90] See e.g. Dem. 21.169, 23.209, 35.26, 43.68; Hdt. 3.119.1; Isoc. 12.128; Thuc. 3.52.4, 6.29.1; Xen., *An.* 4.8.26, 6.6.25, *Hell.* 1.5.2, *Vect.* 4.17.

[91] Compare Chantraine (1927: 175ff.) and Willi (2010: 133; 2016) with regard to the synthetic perfect.

Perfect Aspect 129

While the 'patienthood' of the accusative object differs with each of these verb classes, the presence of a second participant increases the transitivity of the clause, inclining us to interpret the periphrastic construction as an anterior perfect.[92] As noted in §3.3.1, however, I believe we should not entirely focus on the presence of such an accusative object, as Wackernagel and Chantraine did. Consider the following example:

(78) ἔλεγεν ὅτι οὔτε τὰ χρήματα ἔνθοιτο εἰς τὴν ναῦν οὗτος κατὰ τὴν συγγραφήν, οὔτε τὸ χρυσίον <u>εἰληφὼς εἴη</u> παρ' αὐτοῦ ἐν Βοσπόρῳ τότε (Dem. 34.11)

'He [Lampis] said that he [Phormio] did not put the goods on board the ship according to our agreement, nor had he himself [Lampis] received the gold from him [Phormio] at that time in Bosporus.' (tr. Murray)

The speaker notes how Lampis, the captain of a merchant ship sailing to Bosporus, testified that Phormio (who stands accused) had neither loaded any goods on board of his ship, nor given him any money. While it is true that the accusative object, τὸ χρυσίον 'the gold', draws attention to the event denoted by the participle εἰληφώς, thus increasing the transitivity of the clause, the same can be said of the temporal adverb τότε 'at that time', as well as the locative adverb ἐν Βοσπόρῳ 'in Borporus', both of which specify the past event.

Adverb(ial)s of manner play a similar role. Consider in this regard another example from Demosthenes, (79), where we read how the plaintiff reacts at Lacritus' announcement that all his goods were lost, and therefore he would not be able to repay a loan:

(79) οὐδὲν δ' ἧττον ἠρωτῶμεν αὐτούς, ὅντινα τρόπον <u>ἀπολωλότα εἴη</u> τὰ χρήματα (Dem. 35.31)

'Nevertheless we asked them in what way the goods had been lost.' (tr. Murray)

Although ἀπολωλότα εἴη could be interpreted as a (object-oriented) resultative, meaning 'they were lost', the adverbial of manner ὅντινα

---

[92] Compare Duhoux (2000: 430): 'les complements d'object direct qui dépendent du verbe ont tendance à jalonner la trajectoire chronologique qui conduit à l'état exprimé par le parfait, et donc à davantage attirer l'attention sur la zone passée' ('direct object complements which depend from the verb have a tendency to mark the chronological trajectory leading to the state expressed by the perfect, and thus to draw attention primarily to the past component').

130 *Verbal Periphrasis in Ancient Greek*

τρόπον 'in what way' clearly indicates that reference is made to a past event—that is, the actual losing of the goods.

Especially in the authors of the earlier part of the fifth century, one finds many examples of these periphrases in the passive voice; here the presence of an agent indicates increased transitivity, or in other words, anteriority. Such an agent can be expressed either in the dative, or by a prepositional phrase (mostly ὑπό 'by' + gen.),[93] as in (80), where Herodotus describes how Darius had decided to leave behind the weakest men and depart with the stronger part of the army during the night:[94]

(80) ἡμέρης δὲ γενομένης γνόντες οἱ ὑπολειφθέντες ὡς <u>προδεδομένοι εἶεν</u> ὑπὸ Δαρείου χεῖράς τε προετείνοντο τοῖσι Σκύθῃσι καὶ ἔλεγον τὰ κατήκοντα (Hdt. 4.136.1)

'But when it was day, those who were left behind perceived that they had been betrayed by Dareios, and they held out their hands in submission to the Scythians, telling them what their case was.' (tr. Macaulay)

In this example ὑπὸ Δαρείου 'by Darius' unambiguously refers to the agent of the past action that has relevance at the later point in time (when the weaker soldiers notice that they have been abandoned). In examples where εἰμί with the perfect participle is accompanied by a dative, this is not always the case.[95] Consider the following three examples:

(81) {Χο.} ἡμεῖς μέν, ὦ πρεσβῦτα, συμβουλεύομεν, / εἴ σοι τις υἱός ἐστιν <u>ἐκτεθραμμένος</u>, / πέμπειν ἐκεῖνον ἀντὶ σαυτοῦ μανθάνειν (Aristoph., *Nub.* 794–6)

'Chorus Leader. What we advise, old man, is that if you have a son grown-up, send him to school in your place.' (tr. Henderson, slightly modified)

(82) {Βλ.} καὶ μὴ παραλείψεις μηδέν', ἀλλ' ἐλευθέρως / καλεῖς γέροντα, μειράκιον, παιδίσκον· ὡς / τὸ δεῖπνον αὐτοῖς <u>ἔστ' ἐπεσκευασμένον</u> / ἁπαξάπασιν (Aristoph., *Eccl.* 1145–8)

---

[93] On the use of agent expressions with the passive synthetic perfect, see esp. George (2005: 78–102).
[94] For similar examples, see e.g. Aristot., *Hist. an.* 606b; Dem. 35.53; Hdt. 2.152.3, 6.23.5, 7.229.1; Thuc. 3.52.2; Xen., *An.* 7.7.1, *Cyr.* 4.5.14., *Hell.* 1.3.17.
[95] Compare Aerts (1965: 42–4); Rijksbaron (2002: 31).

Perfect Aspect   131

'Blepyrus. Leave no one out. Be liberal, invite the old man, the boy, the little child: dinner is specially made for all of them.' (tr. Henderson, slightly modified)

(83) ἡμῖν δὲ εἰ μηδὲν ἄλλο <u>ἐστὶ ἀποδεδεγμένον</u>... ἀλλὰ καὶ ἀπὸ τοῦ ἐν Μαραθῶνι ἔργου ἄξιοί εἰμεν τοῦτο τὸ γέρας ἔχειν καὶ ἄλλα πρὸς τούτῳ (Hdt. 9.27.5)[96]

'But if by us no other deed has been displayed ... yet even by reason of the deed wrought at Marathon alone we are worthy to have this privilege and others besides this.' (tr. Macaulay)

In (81), where the chorus advises Strepsiades, interpreting the predicate as anterior would not be entirely misguided ('if a son has been raised by you'), but the main point seems to be that Strepsiades has a son of age, not that he has raised a son in the past: thus, this example must be considered non-periphrastic. Context also makes it clear that an anterior interpretation is not correct in (82), where Blepyrus invites the audience to join him in the communal feast: since αὐτοῖς ... ἁπαξάπασιν refers to the persons who are invited to dinner, it seems unlikely that they would also have prepared it. The example can still be considered periphrastic, however, since ἐστ' does not have a possessive value. In (83), too, where the Athenians and Tegeans both claim the right to hold the second wing of the army on the basis of past deeds, a resultative interpretation is available. However, since ἡμῖν ('us, the Athenians') corresponds to the agent of the event denoted by ἀποδεδεγμένον, and since past deeds are being discussed, an anterior interpretation seems preferable.

These examples provide a suitable context for the reanalysis of εἰμί with the perfect participle as an anterior perfect (as in '[there is a son for you] [who is raised]' > '[you have raised a son]'). They bear an obvious similarity to the examples we discussed under §3.3.2.1 as 'secondary predicate construction' (also possessive construction) and 'resultant state object construction', which, I have suggested, lie at the basis of the anterior use of ἔχω with the aorist participle. Thus, it seems likely that the earlier reanalysis of ἔχω with the aorist participle as an anterior perfect stimulated the reanalysis of εἰμί with the perfect participle. In a similar vein, Drinka (2003a: 112) has recently argued that 'the creation of a new HAVE perfect entailed the creation of a BE passive upon the old BE intransitive pattern'.

---

[96] Note that the reading ἐστὶ is considered suspect by Stein (1962.5: 146).

A second influence must have been the development of the synthetic perfect from resultative to anterior during the Classical period.[97] Since εἰμί was accompanied by a *perfect* participle (rather than an *aorist* participle, as with ἔχω), it seems likely that the two developments were interrelated, to some extent at least. Interestingly, Chantraine (1927) has also argued that the development of the synthetic perfect to an anterior should be connected with the passive voice,[98] although it remains unclear in his account whether passive resultative perfects were first reanalysed as anterior perfects. This possibility seems *a priori* excluded, since Chantraine's 'resultative' perfect is entirely dependent on the presence of an accusative object, a possibility that only exists for the active and middle voice.

The general development of εἰμί with the perfect participle may be clear: like the synthetic perfect, εἰμί with the perfect participle underwent a development from resultative (Archaic Greek) to anterior (Classical Greek), with retention of the earlier resultative use. For a more detailed overview, consider Table 3.2.

On the basis of this table, a number of observations can be made. First, the construction of εἰμί with the perfect participle was much more frequently used than that of ἔχω with the aorist participle, with an average frequency of over five instances per 10,000 words in all genres, the orators using the construction with particular frequency.[99] The dramatists and Thucydides represent an exception to this pattern, which may be explained in terms of a resistance vis-à-vis periphrasis as an innovative formation. On this account, however, it remains unclear why Aristophanes did not make more frequent use of the periphrastic construction.[100] Moreover, the dramatists do not show such a resistance when it comes to other innovative periphrastic constructions. Second, in terms of diachrony we do not see a sharp

---

[97] On which, see §3.3.1.

[98] See e.g. Chantraine (1927: 70): 'comme le système de la conjugaison se complétait et s'achevait, sur le modèle βάλλω : βάλλομαι, on a créé en face de βέβλημαι un parfait transitif et résultatif βέβληκα' ('as the conjugational system became complete and final, after the model of βάλλω : βάλλομαι the transitive and resultative perfect βέβληκα was built corresponding to βέβλημαι'). Chantraine (1927: 140–1) argues that -κα perfects are typically built on the medio-passive voice, e.g. ἔσταλκα after ἔσταλμαι, and ἔφθαρκα after ἔφθαρμαι. Cf. also Wackernagel (1953 [1904]: 1012); Ruijgh (2004: 32–3).

[99] Note, however, the relatively low type/token ratio in oratory and philosophy.

[100] Compare Lopez Eire (1986: 252) on the use of the synthetic and periphrastic formation in Aristophanes.

Table 3.2. Distribution of εἰμί with the perfect participle in CG (aspect, voice)

Genre/Author/Text	TOT	NRO	RES	TTR (RES)	RES (ACT)	RES (MED/PASS)	ANT	TTR (ANT)	ANT (ACT)	ANT (MED)	ANT (PASS)
Drama	91	2.46	56	0.75	13	43	35	0.80	5	5	25
Aeschylus (b. 525/4 BC?)	18	4.19	11	0.91	1	10	7	1	1	1	5
Sophocles (b. 496/5 BC?)	18	2.82	10	0.80	5	5	8	1	2	0	6
Euripides (b. 480s BC?)	25	1.59	17	0.94	5	12	8	0.88	0	2	6
Aristophanes (b. 460/50 BC?)	30	2.82	18	0.83	2	16	12	0.92	2	2	8
Historiography	362	5.45	172	0.59	26	146	190	0.62	56	49	85
Herodotus (b. 484 BC?)	104	5.49	45	0.80	7	38	59	0.56	16	11	32
Thucydides (b. 460/55 BC?)	41	2.68	18	0.83	4	14	23	0.87	4	8	11
Xenophon (b. c.430 BC)	219	6.82	111	0.61	15	96	108	0.78	36	30	42
Philosophy	886	5.62	541	0.37	82	459	345	0.33	134	44	167
Plato (b. c.429 BC)	317	5.58	186	0.52	37	149	131	0.53	67	25	39
Aristotelic corpus (IV BC)	569	5.63	355	0.39	45	310	214	0.26	67	19	128
Scientific prose	195	5.28	171	0.65	20	151	24	0.92	8	3	13
Oratory	395	6.42	122	0.48	28	94	273	0.48	124	66	83
Lysias (b. 459/8 BC?)	45	7.68	12	0.58	1	11	33	0.76	10	13	10
Isocrates (b. 436 BC)	59	5.34	19	0.84	5	14	40	0.73	24	6	10
Isaeus (b. c.420 BC)	32	9.70	6	0.66	4	2	26	0.77	13	9	4
Demosthenes (b. 384 BC)	215	7.30	75	0.55	17	58	140	0.55	61	34	45

Key: 'TOT' = total; 'NRO' = normed rate of occurrence (per 10,000 words); 'TTR' = type/token ratio; 'RES' = resultative perfect; 'ANT' = anterior perfect; 'ACT' = active; 'MED' = middle; 'PASS' = passive.

increase in the use of εἰμί with the perfect participle as an anterior perfect, indicating that the reanalysis discussed in the preceding sections must have taken place at an early stage: the percentage of anteriors in Isocrates (b. 436 BC), for example, is comparable to that in Demosthenes (b. 384 BC), and in Herodotus (b. 484 BC?) it is even slightly higher than in Xenophon (b. c.430 BC). An overall increase in frequency of the construction is noticeable, however: some of the earliest writers of the Classical period use the construction markedly less often than others (see esp. Sophocles, Euripides, Thucydides, and Aristophanes). Third, a diachronic development can be seen in the use of active vs. passive anterior perfects: it is only with later authors such as Isocrates, Xenophon, Plato, Isaeus, and Demosthenes that anterior perfects come to be expressed more often in the active voice. This corresponds to the observations of earlier studies such as Chantraine (1927), where it is noticed that especially in the fourth century, active (synthetic) perfects came to be more frequently used.[101] As already noted with regard to anterior ἔχω with the aorist participle, in principle such passive examples are not less transitive than their active counterparts (that is, when an agent is explicitly expressed), but they are non-prototypical since they bring with them a reversal of the common action-chain (a first participant (agent) exerting force on a second participant (patient)). In practice, however, it turns out to be much more common for passive anteriors to omit a second participant (the agent), than it is for active anteriors, so that the former can be thought of as less transitive in general. This difference in transitivity can be situated within the larger development of increasing transitivity (*transitivization*) described in §3.3.1, whereby anterior examples become more and more transitive. Fourth, when it comes to the use of the construction as a resultative vs. anterior perfect, there is a noticeable though unsurprising generic difference, which comes to the fore most prominently when we compare scientific prose such as the Hippocratic corpus to oratory: in the former almost 90% of the examples are resultative, while in the latter almost 70% of the examples are anterior. This can be explained by reference to Smith's (2001, 2003) discourse modes:[102] texts classified as 'scientific

---

[101] Cf. similarly Slings (1994: 243–4); Ruijgh (2004: 32). For (some) statistical information, see Cloud (1910), Sicking & Stork (1996: 187–245), Duhoux (1996, esp. 63) and Willi (2010: 130, 2016).

[102] Cf. §1.3.

Perfect Aspect 135

prose' typically have 'information' as their primary discourse mode, such that resultative perfects are very frequent. Texts classified under 'oratory' are more varied in terms of discourse modes, but in any case 'narrative' and 'report' play a more prominent role, such that we can expect anterior perfects to be more frequent.[103] Unsurprisingly, we see that 'historiography' resembles 'oratory', while 'philosophy' resembles 'scientific prose'.

As noted in §3.3.1, the development of periphrases with εἰμί and the perfect participle was stimulated by phonological difficulties in the formation of the third person (plural) of the synthetic perfect in the Classical period. This primarily concerned the indicative mood, but as can be seen in Table 3.3, the use of the construction also spread to other moods:

Table 3.3. Distribution of εἰμί with the perfect participle in CG (mood)

Genre/Author/Text	IMP	IND	INF	OPT	PART	SUBJ
Drama	0	77	1	4	3	6
Aeschylus (b. 525/4 BC?)	0	18	0	0	0	0
Sophocles (b. 496/5 BC?)	0	14	0	2	0	2
Euripides (b. 480s BC?)	0	19	1	2	1	2
Aristophanes (b. 460/50 BC?)	0	26	0	0	2	2
Historiography	0	214	10	100	2	36
Herodotus (b. 484 BC?)	0	62	2	31	0	9
Thucydides (b. 460/55 BC?)	0	35	1	4	1	0
Xenophon (b. c.430 BC)	0	118	7	65	2	27
Philosophy	52	420	68	185	21	140
Plato (b. c.429 BC)	14	124	24	110	3	42
Aristotelian corpus (IV BC)	38	296	44	75	18	98
Scientific prose	7	55	9	9	12	103
Oratory	0	280	12	71	2	30
Lysias (b. 459/8 BC?)	0	35	1	8	1	0
Isocrates (b. 436 BC)	0	47	2	8	0	2
Isaeus (b. c.420 BC)	0	24	0	7	0	1
Demosthenes (b. 384 BC)	0	138	9	40	1	26

Key: 'IMP' = imperative; 'IND' = indicative; 'INF' = infinitive; 'OPT' = optative; 'PART' = participle; 'SUBJ' = subjunctive.

Several scholars have suggested that the use of εἰμί with the perfect participle first became established in the subjunctive and optative moods, and only later (in Post-Classical Greek) arose in the indicative

---

[103] For the frequent use of the anterior perfect in oratory, cf. also Chantraine (1927: 175); Willi (2010: 133, 2016).

mood.[104] Table 3.3 shows that this is incorrect: the use of εἰμί with the perfect participle in the subjunctive and optative mood became established only in later writers such as Plato, Xenophon, Demosthenes, and Aristotle;[105] in dramatic texts, there are remarkably few examples. Remarkable in this context is the relatively frequent use of the subjunctive in scientific prose (that is, the Hippocratic corpus), which goes back to a relatively early date. However, we must take into account the following: (a) a large part of the examples are resultatives, and in these 'adjectival' examples εἰμί may take the subjunctive mood more easily; (b) in the work of Herodotus, too, examples in the subjunctive and optative mood are relatively well attested; there may have been dialectal differences, Ionic being more prone to use εἰμί with the perfect participle in moods other than the indicative; (c) the Hippocratic corpus is quite heterogeneous, and also contains texts from a later date.

A less well-known use of the construction is in the imperative mood, as in (84):

(84) τὰ δὲ ὀθόνια καὶ τὰ ἄλλα πλατύτερά τινι ἐσχισμένα ἔστω, ἢ εἰ μὴ ἕλκος εἶχεν· καὶ ᾧ ἂν πρώτῳ ἐπιδέηται, συχνῷ ἔστω τοῦ ἕλκεος πλατύτερον (Hippoc., *Fract.* 26.7–10)

'The bandages and other dressings should be torn in rather broader strips than if there was no wound, and the one first used should be a good deal wider than the wound.' (tr. Withington)

The author discusses how fractures with an external wound should be bandaged. The use of ἔστω with a regular adjective (πλατύτερον 'broader') indicates that ἐσχισμένα ἔστω 'let it be torn' should be taken as having a resultative value, as is the case in various other examples.[106] This is to be expected from the point of view of transitivity (cf. the parameter of 'mode'): examples in the imperative do not express an event that has happened or is happening, so they are of

---

[104] See e.g. Palm (1955: 93, 95).

[105] Cf. Aerts (1965: 40): 'in 5th century Greek...the periphrased perfect subjunctive and optative is also an extremely seldom-used construction...only in the writers of the fourth century B.C. (Xenophon, Plato, Demosthenes) is the use of the perfect subjunctive and optative (almost always periphrastic) somewhat less infrequent'. Aerts (1965: 48–9) notes that synthetic perfect subjunctives and optatives are infrequent in the fourth century BC.

[106] See e.g. Aristot., *Hist. an.* 635a, *Ph.* 233a, *Phgn.* 808a, *Pol.* 1323b; Hippoc., *Prorrh.* 2.7, 2.14; Pl., *Leg.* 951d, 956b.

Perfect Aspect 137

lower transitivity. In some examples, however, a past event does become more foregrounded through the use of an agent, an adverb(ial) of manner, or a past-tense adverb(ial), as in (85), where Aristotle notes that he will not go further into a certain subject since he has already discussed it elsewhere:[107]

(85) ἔστω δὲ περὶ τούτων ἡμῖν τεθεωρημένον ἐν τοῖς περὶ τὰς αἰσθήσεις δεικνυμένοις (Aristot., Mete. 372b)
'However, we must accept the account we have given of these things in the investigation of sensation.' (tr. Webster)

The presence of the agent (ἡμῖν 'by us') and the locative adverbial (ἐν τοῖς περὶ τὰς αἰσθήσεις δεικνυμένοις 'in the investigation of sensation') suggest that an anterior interpretation is to be adopted: 'let there have been theorized'.

Two other morphological categories where the use of εἰμί with the perfect participle expands, especially in the fourth century BC, are *tense* and *person*: the construction also comes to be used as a future perfect[108] and in persons other than the third.[109]

3.3.3 Anterior Subfunctions

As I noted in this chapter's introduction, some scholars have hypothesized that the anterior subfunctions that are commonly recognized from a synchronic point of view—that is, 'perfect of current relevance', 'experiential perfect', 'perfect of persistence', and 'perfect of recent past',[110] also have diachronic relevance: the experiential perfect and the perfect of persistence would form an intermediate

---

[107] For similar examples, see e.g. Aristot., *Ph.* 195b, 265a, *Poet.* 1449a, *Pol.* 1274b, 1327b.

[108] Compare Chantraine (1927: 144) on the synthetic perfect: 'la langue a fait entrer le futur à redoublement dans le système du parfait. Il y a une tentative du grec pour donner au parfait un futur. Cette tentative était conforme à l'évolution de la langue, mais elle n'a pas complètement abouti' ('the language has made the redoubled future enter the perfect system. There is a tentative of Greek to give a future to the perfect. This tendency was in accordance with the development of the language, but it has not entirely succeeded'). For some examples from Aristotle, see e.g. *Cael.* 271b, 272b, 273a; *Gen. corr.* 327a; *Eth. Nic.* 1124b, 1133a, 1142b, 1144b; *Ph.* 192a, 225b, 232a, 233b; *Top.* 102a, 108b, 129b, 130a.

[109] This is particularly noteworthy in Demosthenes. See e.g. Dem. 4.42, 4.50, 15.8, 21.104, 23.122, 27.36, 27.67, 31.14, 33.24, 35.56, 41.9, 47.41, 52.2, 62.44.

[110] Cf. §1.4.1.3.

stage between the resultative perfect and the perfect of current relevance, and the perfect of recent past between the perfect of current relevance and the perfective past. In the present section, I investigate to what extent this claim is upheld by the Ancient (Classical) Greek evidence, concentrating on the use of εἰμί with the perfect participle as an experiential perfect / perfect of persistence, a construction which, as we have seen, was far more frequently used than ἔχω with the aorist participle.

Before analysing the evidence from Ancient Greek, however, it is worth referring to the work of Carey (1994, 1995, 1996), who explains why from a logical-semantic point of view the experiential perfect and the perfect of persistence can be thought of as 'intermediate'. Carey describes the development from resultative to anterior in terms of a shift of 'locus of relevance': with the resultative perfect the locus of relevance is the subject (as in 'the door is closed'), while with the anterior perfect, specifically the perfect of current relevance, the focus is the here-and-now of the discourse context (as in 'I've written a letter to the mayor about this issue').[111] This distinction is reflected in the choice of lexical verbs:[112] as we have seen, resultative perfects are typically limited to telic content verbs, whose final ('result') state is predicated as a property of the subject (e.g. 'the car is washed', or alternatively 'I have the car washed').[113] Perfects of current relevance, on the other hand, also combine with atelic content verbs, which are typically not construed as producing a result (e.g. 'I have spoken to him'): here it is the entire process, rather than the final state that is construed as relevant.[114] Related to this shift in locus of relevance is a shift in 'event-salience': with the resultative perfect the past event

---

[111] See e.g. Carey (1996: 39): 'the "result" in the case of the [anterior] perfect is any present effect that the speaker construes as related to the anterior events'. Compare Duhoux (2000: 427) on the development of the synthetic perfect in Archaic/Classical Greek: 'désormais, l'état rendu par le parfait n'est plus nécessairement celui du sujet verbal, mais peut être considéré en soi, comme une situation globale' ('by now, the state expressed by the perfect is no longer necessarily that of the subject, but can be considered in itself, as an overall situation').

[112] Cf. Carey (1994: 49–50).

[113] As one of the reviewers notes, the rephrasing of resultative perfects such as 'the car is washed' as 'I have the car washed' is unfelicitous in modern-day English, as the latter has a causative meaning.

[114] As Carey (1994: 50) notes with regard to English, the fact that perfects of current relevance can be combined with dummy subjects (as in 'it has rained') clearly shows that with this type of perfect the locus of relevance need not be the subject.

remains non-salient, while with the perfect of current relevance it becomes more salient.[115]

Iterative and durative contexts provide a bridge between these two types, as they involve a relatively low degree of event salience (e.g. 'I have been there three times' or 'I have been coughing since Tuesday'), and are still more subject-oriented than perfects of current relevance.[116] Within the transitivity-framework, it could be said that the shift from resultative to anterior (perfect of current relevance) is one of increasing transitivity ('transitivization'), and that the experiential perfect and the perfect of persistence constitute less transitive 'intermediary' stages (cf. the *kinesis*-parameter).

As for the use of εἰμί with the perfect participle with one of these subfunctions, consider Table 3.4:

Table 3.4. Distribution of εἰμί with the perfect participle in CG (aspect)

Genre/Author/Text	EXP	CURR	PERS
Drama	10	25	0
Aeschylus (b. 525/4 BC?)	2	5	0
Sophocles (b. 496/5 BC?)	2	6	0
Euripides (b. 480s BC?)	1	7	0
Aristophanes (b. 460/50 BC?)	5	7	0
Historiography	44	146	0
Herodotus (b. 484 BC?)	16	43	0
Thucydides (b. 460/55 BC?)	5	18	0
Xenophon (b. *c.*430 BC)	23	85	0
Philosophy	80	253	13
Plato (b. *c.*429 BC)	40	85	6
Aristotelic corpus (IV BC)	40	168	7
Scientific prose	4	20	0
Oratory	84	185	4
Lysias (b. 459/8 BC?)	15	18	0
Andocides (b. *c.*440 BC)	5	4	0
Isocrates (b. 436 BC)	10	30	0
Isaeus (b. *c.*420 BC)	3	22	1
Aeschines (b. *c.*397 BC)	5	4	0
Demosthenes (b. 384 BC)	40	97	3

Key: 'EXP' = experiential perfect; 'CURR' = perfect of current relevance; 'PERS' = perfect of persistence.

---

[115] Cf. Carey (1996: 33).

[116] It is interesting to note in this regard that Chantraine (1927: 13) considers experiential perfects as in our previous example (65) stative ('on employait le parfait pour désigner un ensemble d'actions qui aboutissent à un état présent' ('the perfect was used to refer to a group of actions resulting in a present state')).

140   *Verbal Periphrasis in Ancient Greek*

This table shows that while εἰμί with the perfect participle was most often used as a perfect of current relevance in the Classical period, its use as an experiential perfect was significant, while its use as perfect of persistence much less so.[117] Especially in oratory—where, as we have seen, εἰμί with the perfect participle fully developed as an anterior perfect—its use as an experiential perfect was widespread. Although it cannot be said to have diachronically preceded the use of εἰμί with the perfect participle as a perfect of current relevance,[118] it certainly did play an important role when it comes to the establishment of the construction as an anterior perfect in the Classical period. It would be worth investigating in this regard to what extent the synthetic perfect was used as an experiential perfect: interestingly, some of the earliest (Archaic) examples (as in (65)) are used with the experiential subfunction. Both Chantraine (1927: 13) and Friedrich (1974: 17) have argued that these 'facilitated' the creation of a 'resultative'[119] perfect.

Distinguishing the use of the periphrastic construction as an experiential perfect versus a perfect of current relevance is not always an easy matter,[120] so it may be useful to discuss some of the contexts in which the former use can be found. First, in a number of examples the periphrastic construction is combined with an adverb(ial) of frequency, which indicates repeated occurrence in the past. Consider the following two examples:[121]

(86) δεῖ τοίνυν ὑμᾶς κἀκεῖνο σκοπεῖν, ὅτι πολλοὶ τῶν Ἑλλήνων πολλάκις εἰσὶν ἐψηφισμένοι τοῖς νόμοις χρῆσθαι τοῖς ὑμετέροις, ἐφ' ᾧ φιλοτιμεῖσθ' ὑμεῖς, εἰκότως (Dem. 24.210)

'You ought also to consider this point, that many Hellenic nations have often resolved by vote to adopt your laws; and in this you take an honorable pride, naturally.' (tr. Murray)

(87) {Κλ.} εἰ δ' ἦν τεθνηκὼς ὡς ἐπλήθυνον λόγοι, / τρισώματός τἂν Γηρυὼν ὁ δεύτερος / [πολλὴν ἄνωθεν, τὴν κάτω γὰρ οὐ λέγω,] / χθονὸς τρίμοιρον χλαῖναν ἐξηύχει λαβεῖν, / ἅπαξ ἑκάστῳ κατθανὼν μορφώματι (Aesch., *Ag.* 869–73)

---

[117] With the synthetic perfect too, this subfunction is uncommon. See Slings (1988).
[118] Compare Squartini & Bertinetto (2000: 419–20).
[119] Note that the term 'resultative' is used here in the Wackernagel-Chantraine sense.
[120] Compare Carey (1994: 68).
[121] For similar examples, see e.g. Aristot., *Metaph.* 1021a, *Pol.* 1287b, *Rhet.* 1383a, *Soph. el.* 179b; Dem. 23.122; Hdt. 7.214.3; Pl., *Leg.* 958a; Xen., *An.* 7.8.21, *Hell.* 3.2.14.

'Clytaemnestra. Or if he had died as often as reports claimed, then truly he might have had three bodies, a second Geryon, and have boasted of having taken on him a triple cloak of earth [ample that above, of that below I speak not], one death for each different shape.' (tr. Smyth)

The first of these two examples is quite straightforward: the prosecutor, arguing against Timocrates and the new law he introduced, stresses that the jury must keep in mind that Athenian laws have a reputation to uphold, as they have often been adopted by others. The repetition of the past event is quite clearly indicated by πολλάκις 'often', as well as the plural subject, πολλοί 'many'. In example (87), repetition must be inferred on the basis of the phrase ὡς ἐπλήθυον λόγοι 'as (often) as reports claimed'. Normally, experientials cannot be formed on the basis of verbs that are inherently non-repeatable, such as 'to die'.[122] Here, however, we are dealing with a contrafactual situation in the past, uttered by Clytaemnestra about her husband Agamemnon.

A second context where the experiential use of εἰμί with the perfect participle can often be found is with a plural subject, indicating that multiple persons have undertaken a certain action in the past.[123] Consider examples (88) and (89):[124]

(88) τῆς δὲ νυκτὸς τῷ Νικίᾳ καὶ Δημοσθένει ἐδόκει, ἐπειδὴ κακῶς σφίσι τὸ στράτευμα εἶχε τῶν τε ἐπιτηδείων πάντων ἀπορίᾳ ἤδη, καὶ <u>κατατετραυματισμένοι ἦσαν</u> πολλοὶ ἐν πολλαῖς προσβολαῖς τῶν πολεμίων γεγενημέναις, πυρὰ καύσαντας ὡς πλεῖστα ἀπάγειν τὴν στρατιάν (Thuc. 7.80.1)

'This night it was concluded by Nicias and Demosthenes, seeing the miserable estate of their army, and the want already of all necessaries, and that many of their men had been wounded in many assaults of the enemy, to lead away the army as far as they possibly could.' (tr. Hobbes, slightly modified)

(89) {Χρ.} τέχναι δὲ πᾶσαι διὰ σὲ καὶ σοφίσματα / ἐν τοῖσιν ἀνθρώποισίν ἐσθ' ηὑρημένα (Aristoph., *Plut.* 160–1)

'Chremylus. It is in you that every art, all human inventions, have had their origin.' (tr. O'Neill)

---

[122] Cf. Mittwoch (2008: 327).

[123] Note, however, that the presence of a multiple subject does not always bring forth an experiential interpretation. See e.g. Hdt. 6.44.1, 7.229.1, 8.110.2; Isaeus 3.60; Lys. 12.22.

[124] For similar examples, see e.g. Dem. 19.2, 21.182, 57.58; Hdt. 7.139.3, 9.26.7; Isoc. 21.20; Lys. 20.15, 22.20, 29.12; Pl., *Leg.* 699e; Thuc. 2.49.3; Xen., *Hell.* 4.3.1.

In (88), Thucydides describes how Nicias and Demosthenes decided to retreat, given that the army was in such a poor state, in part because many persons had been wounded in multiple attacks. Both πολλοί 'many' and ἐν πολλαῖς προσβολαῖς 'in many assaults' indicate that we are dealing with an experiential perfect, referring to multiple occurrences in the past. The same is true in (89), where Chremylus notes that Plutus lies at the basis of every art and human invention. The presence of this multiple subject, together with the knowledge that the τέχναι and σοφίσματα have not all been invented at the same time, suggests an interpretation of the periphrastic construction as an experiential perfect.

A third relevant context is where the periphrastic construction is combined with a plural object, indicating that a certain action in the past affected multiple persons. Consider the following two examples:[125]

(90) ἐγὼ γὰρ οἶδ᾽ ὅτι πολλοὶ πολλὰ κἀγάθ᾽ ὑμᾶς εἰσιν εἰργασμένοι, οὐ κατὰ τὰς Μειδίου λῃτουργίας, οἱ μὲν ναυμαχίας νενικηκότες, οἱ δὲ πόλεις εἰληφότες, οἱ δὲ πολλὰ καὶ καλὰ ὑπὲρ τῆς πόλεως στήσαντες τρόπαια (Dem. 21.169)

'For I know that there are many men who have done you great and useful service—though not after the style of Meidias! Some have won naval victories, others have captured cities, others have set up many glorious trophies to the credit of the State.' (tr. Murray)

(91) ἔχων γὰρ βασιλείαν ἀσφαλεστάτην καὶ μεγίστην, ἐν ᾗ πολλὰ καὶ καλὰ διαπεπραγμένος ἦν καὶ κατὰ πόλεμον καὶ περὶ διοίκησιν τῆς πόλεως, ἅπαντα ταῦθ᾽ ὑπερεῖδεν (Isoc. 12.128)

'For although he [Theseus] ruled over the securest and greatest of kingdoms and in the exercise of this power had accomplished many excellent things both in war and in the administration of the state, he disdained all this.' (tr. Norlin)

In (90), Demosthenes notes that many people have done many good deeds for the city, unlike Meidias. There is not only a multiple subject (πολλοί), but also a multiple object (πολλὰ κἀγάθ᾽), leading to an experiential interpretation of εἰσιν εἰργασμένοι 'they have done'. The multiple object is specified in the next sentence: naval victories, the capturing of cities, etc. In (91), Isocrates praises Theseus because he

---

[125] For similar examples, see e.g. And. 1.129; Aristoph., *Plut.* 867; Dem. 36.6, 37.19, 57.66; Lys. 16.19, 18.10, 25.6; Pl., *Menex.* 240a; Xen., *Hell.* 7.1.9.

Perfect Aspect

decided to give the state to the people to govern, even though he had accomplished everything. Here, too, the presence of the object πολλὰ καὶ καλά 'many excellent things' indicates that διαπεπραγμένος ἦν 'he had accomplished' is to be taken as an experiential perfect.

Finally, we consider those examples where negation indicates that a multiple event has not occurred, but the context makes it clear that this might well have been the case. Consider the following example:[126]

(92) καὶ εἰς τοσοῦτόν εἰσι τόλμης ἀφιγμένοι ὥσθ' ἥκουσιν ἀπολογησόμενοι, καὶ λέγουσιν ὡς οὐδὲν κακὸν οὐδ' αἰσχρὸν εἰργασμένοι εἰσίν (Lys. 12.22)
'And they have carried audacity to such a pitch that they come here ready to defend themselves, and state that they are guilty of no vile or shameful action.' (tr. Lamb)

Although the defendants deny that anyone has done anything wrong there is a sense that several persons *could* have done something wrong, as the speaker claims in fact happened.

As Table 3.4 indicates, the use of εἰμί with the perfect participle as a perfect of persistence is rare. As a result, there are no 'typical' contexts in which this use can be found. In example (93), from Plato, the context explicitly indicates that the event denoted by the periphrastic construction started in the past and continues up to the present. Socrates enters the grammar school of Dionysius, and sees two young men disputing. He wants to know what they are discussing, and therefore asks a bystander:

(93) ἦ που μέγα τι καὶ καλόν ἐστι περὶ ὃ τοσαύτην σπουδὴν πεποιημένω ἐστόν; (Pl., Am. 132b)
'Is it then something great and fine, about which they have been showing such great zeal?'

Since the event of disputing is still ongoing at the time when Socrates asks his question, the periphrastic perfect can only be interpreted as a perfect of persistence: 'they have been doing/showing'.

In the following example, the periphrastic form is accompanied by a durative adverbial, πολλοῦ χρόνου 'for a long time':

---

[126] For some examples, see e.g. And. 1.63; Aristot., *Hist. an.* 591a, *Soph. el.* 183b; Dem. 18.178, 20.127, 30.31; Lys. 1.45, 4.19; Pl., *Leg.* 698d, *Menex.* 240c, *Phd.* 109d.

144   *Verbal Periphrasis in Ancient Greek*

(94) ἐπειδὴ γὰρ ἔδει τῷ ὀρφανῷ τὰ χρήματα ἀποδιδόναι, ὁ δ' οὐκ εἶχεν ὁπόθεν ἀποδῷ, τόκοι δὲ πολλοῦ χρόνου <u>συνερρυηκότες ἦσαν</u> αὐτῷ, τὸ χωρίον ἐπώλει (Isaeus 2.28)
'When it became necessary to pay back the money to the orphan, and Menecles did not possess the requisite sum, and interest had accumulated against him over a long period, he was for selling the land.' (tr. Forster)

We read how Menecles wanted to sell his land, since he had to repay a certain orphan but had no money, and interest on the debt had been accumulating over a long period. Here, too, it seems that the periphrastic form is best taken as a perfect of persistence, indicating that the accumulation of interest started at some point in the past, continuing up until the moment he decided to sell his land.

As we have already seen with regard to Archaic Greek (ex. (66)), in cases where the periphrastic form is accompanied by a negation it may be understood as a perfect of persistence, indicating that an event has not yet occurred during a time period that extends up to a certain point in time. Consider, in this regard, (95):[127]

(95) καὶ ταῦθ' ὁ σχέτλιος καὶ ἀναιδὴς οὗτος ἐτόλμα λέγειν ἐφεστηκότων τῶν πρέσβεων καὶ ἀκουόντων, οὓς ἀπὸ τῶν Ἑλλήνων μετεπέμψασθε ὑπὸ τούτου πεισθέντες, ὅτ' οὔπω <u>πεπρακὼς</u> αὐτὸν <u>ἦν</u> (Dem. 19.16)
'This speech the shameless reprobate found courage to make while the ambassadors, whom you summoned from the Greek cities at his own suggestion, when he had not yet sold himself, were standing at his elbow and listening to what he said.' (tr. Vince & Vince)

Demosthenes describes how Aeschines had dared to speak against opposing Philip, even in the presence of the ambassadors who were summoned at his own suggestion, when he had not yet been bribed by Philip. The periphrastic form can be taken as a perfect of persistence, indicating that Aeschines' being bribed had not yet occurred extending from the point when Philip first came on the scene up until the summoning of the ambassadors.

To conclude, I shall briefly discuss to what extent εἰμί with the perfect participle functioned as a 'perfect of recent past'. As I mentioned in the introduction to this chapter, the perfect-of-recent-past function has been considered by some as an intermediate stage

---

[127] For similar examples, see e.g. Aristot., *Pol.* 1317a, *Top.* 113b; Dem. 48.16; Pl., *Plt.* 268c.

between the perfect of current relevance and the perfective past, whereby the construction no longer functions as a 'true' perfect.[128] In a few examples, the periphrastic form is accompanied by an adverb(ial) that indicates recency, as in (96):[129]

(96) ὀλίγον δὲ πρὶν ἡμᾶς ἀπιέναι μάχη ἐγεγόνει ἐν τῇ Ποτειδαίᾳ, ἣν ἄρτι ἦσαν οἱ τῇδε πεπυσμένοι (Pl., Chrm. 153b)
'Shortly before we came away there had been a battle at Potidaea, of which the people here had only just had news.' (tr. Lamb)

Socrates has returned from Potideia, and the people having just heard that there was a battle there want to know whether he participated. The adverb ἄρτι 'only just' clearly indicates the recency of the event that the periphrastic form denotes.

Particularly interesting is the following example:

(97) {Ερ.} ἰηῦ ἰηῦ ἰηῦ, / ὅτ' οὐδὲ μέλλεις ἐγγὺς εἶναι τῶν θεῶν· / φροῦδοι γάρ· ἐχθές εἰσιν ἐξῳκισμένοι (Aristoph., Pax 195-7)
'Hermes. Haw haw haw! You aren't even going to get near the gods. They're gone; they moved out yesterday.' (tr. Henderson)

Trygaeus asks Hermes to call the gods, but the latter answers that this will not be possible, since the gods moved the day before. It is generally stressed that (present) perfects cannot be accompanied by adverb(ial)s that express a definite time,[130] since adverb(ial)s of this nature focus attention entirely on the past event, rather than its current relevance. Nevertheless, in this example the periphrastic form is combined with ἐχθές 'yesterday' (indicating a recent past), which may be a first step towards the further semantic extension of the construction.

Several scholars have posited that already in Classical Greek the synthetic perfect could function as a perfective past, a topic that will

---

[128] This is a development which the synthetic perfect underwent, as will be discussed in §3.4.1.

[129] In Plato, several examples can also be found of ἄρτι with the synthetic perfect. See e.g. Pl., Alc. 2, 145e, Grg. 448a, 469d, Leg. 635b, 679c, 714b, Plt. 305d, Prt. 316a. For further observations on recency and the synthetic perfect, see Slings (1994: 245); Sicking & Stork (1996: 155-7); Ruijgh (2004: 34-6).

[130] See e.g. Comrie (1976: 54) with regard to English. With regard to Ancient (New Testament) Greek, Fanning (1990: 109) notes, however, that 'the Greek perfect has no restrictions on occurring with adverbs denoting a time separate from the time of speaking'.

be discussed at greater length in §3.4.1. Whether the same can be said for periphrastic εἰμί with the perfect participle seems disputable. If one of the typical characteristics of a perfective past is that it denotes *sequentiality* rather than anteriority, two examples may be considered. The first of these comes from a speech of Isocrates, where Isocrates describes how he was doubting whether a speech of his should be destroyed, and decided to ask his former pupils:

(98) τούτων γνωσθέντων οὐδεμίαν διατριβὴν ἐποιησάμην, ἀλλ᾽ εὐθὺς παρεκέκληντο μέν, οὓς εἶπον, προειρηκὼς δ᾽ ἦν αὐτοῖς ἐφ᾽ ἃ συνεληλυθότες ἦσαν, ἀνέγνωστο δ᾽ ὁ λόγος, ἐπῃνημένος δ᾽ ἦν καὶ τεθορυβημένος καὶ τετυχηκὼς ὧνπερ οἱ κατορθοῦντες ἐν ταῖς ἐπιδείξεσιν (Isoc. 12.233)

'Having so resolved, I lost no time; they whom I have mentioned were summoned at once; I announced to them beforehand the object of their coming together; the speech was read aloud, was praised and applauded and accorded even such a reception as is given to successful declamations.' (tr. Norlin)

In this example, the periphrastic past perfects, together with the synthetic forms παρεκέκληντο and ἀνέγνωστο, seem to denote temporally sequential events: [they were summoned] > I announced > [it was read aloud] > it was praised > it was applauded > it was given a great reception.[131] Note, however, that συνεληλυθότες ἦσαν 'they had come together' is used as a regular anterior perfect. In several of the standard grammars, this example is listed as an illustration of the 'pluperfect of rapid relative completion', which can also be found with synthetic past perfects.[132] While Isocrates may be deploying a 'special' perfect of current relevance in order to create a certain effect, it is to be noted that the same phenomenon has been observed in other languages as well,[133] where it has been connected with the process of aoristic drift.

---

[131] Note that some scholars take Isocrates as the subject of ἐπῃνημένος δ᾽ ἦν καὶ τεθορυβημένος καὶ τετυχηκώς, rather than the speech.

[132] See Gildersleeve (1980 [1900–11]): 102–3). Cf. also Kühner & Gerth (1976 [1898]: 152–3); Smyth (1984 [1920]: 435).

[133] Compare e.g. Bertinetto (2010: 10) with regard to the pluperfect in Italian and German: 'the AOR/PPFs [aoristic pluperfects, KB] ... suggest a sort of "immediate completion" of the event, producing an effect of sudden acceleration in the thread-of-discourse. It is as though the plot underwent, so to say, an abrupt forward-jump, such that the reader suddenly finds himself at a slightly more advanced stage than expected, based on the perceived speed of the previous course-of-events. In other words, the reader is biased, so to say, to detect a temporally adjacent R [reference point, KB], directly following the completion of the event.'

The second example, from Demosthenes' oration against Pantaenetus, is more straightforward:

(99) μισθοῦται δ' οὗτος παρ' ἡμῶν τοῦ γιγνομένου τόκου τῷ ἀργυρίῳ, πέντε καὶ ἑκατὸν δραχμῶν τοῦ μηνὸς ἑκάστου. καὶ τιθέμεθα συνθήκας, ἐν αἷς ἥ τε μίσθωσις <u>ἦν γεγραμμένη</u> καὶ λύσις τούτῳ παρ' ἡμῶν ἔν τινι ῥητῷ χρόνῳ (Dem. 37.5)

'And the plaintiff leased them from us at a rent equal to the interest accruing on the money, a hundred and five drachmae a month. We drew up an agreement in which the terms of the lease were stated, and the right was given the plaintiff of redeeming these things from us within a given time.' (tr. Murray)

The speaker describes how he and Evergus had decided to lend Pantaenetus one hundred and five *minae* on the security of a mining property in Maroneia and thirty slaves, which Pantaenetus leased from them at a rent equal to the interest accruing on the money (a hundred and five drachmae a month). The historic present τιθέμεθα συνθήκας 'we drew up an agreement' denotes a foregrounded event, of which ἦν γεγραμμένη 'it was stated' forms a specification, which must be taken as temporally sequential (rather than anterior) to τιθέμεθα.

3.3.4 ἔχω with the (Medio-passive) Perfect Participle

The construction of ἔχω with medio-passive perfect participle[134] is typically referred to as a feature peculiar to Post-Classical Greek. As we saw in §3.2.1, however, the construction can already be found in Archaic Greek.[135] In Classical Greek the construction is attested relatively often, a fact which has never been noted.[136] Consider Table 3.5:

---

[134] There are some instances of this construction with the active perfect participle (see e.g. exx. (100) and (101)), but these occur much less frequently. For ease of reference, I shall refer to this construction as 'ἔχω with the medio-passive perfect participle' in the remainder of this chapter.

[135] It is interesting to note in this respect that in Hittite a similar construction can be found. See e.g. Benveniste (1962, ch. 3); Hoffner & Melchert (2008: 311–12).

[136] Cf. Moser (1988: 239): 'as regards the ἔχω + Medio-passive Perfect Participle (agreeing with the object), there are no instances of it quoted till the late Koine'.

Table 3.5. Distribution of ἔχω with the (medio-passive) perfect participle in CG

Genre/Author/Text	TOT	NRO	TTR
Historiography	26	0.39	0.85
Herodotus (b. 484 BC?)	6	0.32	1
Xenophon (b. c.430 BC)	20	0.62	0.85
Philosophy	63	0.40	0.67
Plato (b. c.429 BC)	4	0.07	1
Aristotelic corpus (IV BC)	59	0.58	0.68
Scientific prose	15	0.41	0.73
Oratory	5	0.08	1
Isocrates (b. 436 BC)	4	0.36	1
Demosthenes (b. 384 BC)	1	0.03	1

Key: 'TOT' = total; 'NRO' = normed rate of occurrence (per 10,000 words); 'TTR' = type/token ratio.

As the data indicate, the construction occurs with some frequency in Classical Greek, especially in fourth-century authors, although no examples are found in drama. The construction can also be found in Herodotus and the Hippocratic corpus.[137] Overall, notwithstanding the four examples in Isocrates, it appears that the construction is mainly limited to works of a lower register, most of which are of a scientific (especially biological) nature (e.g. Aristotle's *Parts of Animals, Generation of Animals, History of Animals*).

The use of ἔχω with the medio-passive perfect participle in all of these works fulfils an exclusively resultative function. Most examples can be classified as instances of Carey's (1994) 'resultant state object construction',[138] as in the following two cases:[139]

(100) ἔτη δὲ ζῶσι πολλά, καὶ ὁ ληφθεὶς λέων χωλὸς πολλοὺς τῶν ὀδόντων εἶχε κατεαγότας, ᾧ τεκμηρίῳ ἐχρῶντό τινες ὅτι πόλλ' ἔτη ζῶσιν· τοῦτο γὰρ οὐκ ἂν συμπεσεῖν μὴ πολυχρονίῳ ὄντι (Aristot., *Hist. an.* 629b)

---

[137] This mostly concerns early writings such as *On Fractures, On Joints, Prognostics,* and *On the Nature of Man.*

[138] Cf. §3.3.2.1.

[139] For similar examples, see e.g. Aristot., *Hist. an.* 489b, 497b, 503a, 520a, 533a, 591a, 627a, *Part. an.* 656b, 657a, 660a, 666b, 671b, 693a, *Poet.* 1450b, *Pol.* 1335b; Hdt. 1.60.1, 1.98.6, 4.183.2; Hippoc., *Aer.* 15.13, *Epid.* 2.2.19, 5.1.40, *Fract.* 7.34, *Prorrh.* 2.32, 2.35, *Progn.* 3.3; Xen., *An.* 1.8.21, *Cyn.* 10.4, *Cyr.* 3.3.27, 5.2.6, 5.2.21, 5.4.15, *Hell.* 5.3.1, *Mem.* 2.1.22.

Perfect Aspect

'They [the lions] live to a good old age. The lion who was captured when lame, had a number of his teeth broken; which fact was regarded by some as a proof of the longevity of lions, as he could hardly have been reduced to this condition except at an advanced age.' (tr. Thompson)

(101) τῇ τεσσαρεσκαιδεκάτῃ ἐξέπεσεν ἐκ τῆς γαστρὸς τὸ παιδίον τεθνεός, ἔχον τὸν δεξιὸν βραχίονα προσπεφυκότα τῇ πλευρῇ (Hippoc., Epid. 5.1.13)

'On the fourteenth day the child fell out of the uterus, dead, having the right arm attached to its side.'

In both examples, a physical state is described: in (100) the broken teeth of the lion and in (101) the deformation of the stillborn child. While there is an external object in both cases, there remains no question of possession: the point is not that the lion has teeth or the child an arm. Thus, the participle can be thought of as obligatory, and the target of 'HAVE' must be the stative relation between the object and the participle.

In the above-mentioned examples, the subject of ἔχω should not be considered the agent of the event expressed by the participle. This is true of most examples, and there are no attested cases with verbs of mental state or of communication, where such an inference is almost automatically made (cf. Carey's 'resultant state process construction').[140] One example worth considering in this regard is the following:

(102) Κῦρος δὲ ὡρμᾶτο ἐκ Σάρδεων, φρουρὰν μὲν πεζὴν καταλιπὼν πολλὴν ἐν Σάρδεσι, Κροῖσον δὲ ἔχων, ἄγων δὲ πολλὰς ἁμάξας πολλῶν καὶ παντοδαπῶν χρημάτων. ἧκε δὲ καὶ ὁ Κροῖσος γεγραμμένα ἔχων ἀκριβῶς ὅσα ἐν ἑκάστῃ ἦν τῇ ἁμάξῃ (Xen., Cyr. 7.4.12)

'But Cyrus, leaving behind a large garrison of foot-soldiers, started from Sardis in company with Croesus; and he took with him many wagons loaded with valuables of every sort. And Croesus also had come having written down accurately what was in each wagon.' (tr. Miller, slightly modified)

Xenophon describes how Cyrus decided to leave Sardis, taking with him both Croesus and a large number of wagons, of which Croesus had an accurate inventory. In this particular case, γεγραμμένα ἔχων 'having written down' could be taken as a resultative perfect with an anterior inference (Croesus being the agent of the event denoted by

---

[140] Cf. §3.3.2.1.

γεγραμμένα), although it seems unlikely[141] that Croesus would make such an inventory himself.

As was noted for resultative εἰμί with the perfect participle, various examples can be found where the participle is coordinated with an adjective, as in ὁ μὲν οὖν ἄνθρωπος ἀπολελυμένην τε καὶ μαλακωτάτην ἔχει μάλιστα τὴν γλῶτταν (Aristot., *Part. an.* 660a) 'man most of all has his tongue detached and very soft' or διηρθρωμένους δ' ἔχει καὶ χωριστοὺς <τοὺς> δακτύλους (Aristot., *Hist. an.* 504a) 'it has its fingers articulated and separate'. In this regard, it seems likely that the origins of the construction lie with ἔχω + object + adjective, which was extended to the perfect participle, perhaps after the example of εἰμί with the perfect participle, which originated from εἰμί with adjective.[142] Other constructions which may have served as a model are ἔχω + object + prepositional phrase, and ἔχω + object + adverb. Consider the following examples:

(103) πολὺ γὰρ δήπου μᾶλλον οἱ προδιδόντες τι τῶν κοινῶν, οἱ τοὺς γονέας κακοῦντες, οἱ μὴ καθαρὰς τὰς χεῖρας ἔχοντες, εἰσιόντες δ' εἰς τὴν ἀγοράν, ἀδικοῦσιν (Dem. 24.60)

'Surely men who are traitors to the commonwealth, men who maltreat their own parents, men who enter the market-place having their hands unclean, offend far more heinously.' (tr. Murray, slightly modified)

(104) κἢν μέλλῃ ὤνθρωπος ἀποθνήσκειν καὶ ἄλλως ἐκ τοῦ τρώματος, ἐν τῷ ὄπισθεν τῆς κεφαλῆς ἔχων τὸ τρῶμα, ἐν πλέονι χρόνῳ ἀποθανεῖται (Hippoc., *Cap. vuln.* 2.29–31)

'And if a man is going to die anyhow from his wound, having the wound in the back of his head, he will die in a longer interval of time.'

(105) ὦ ἄνδρες στρατιῶται, ἐμοὶ δὲ οὐδὲν φαῦλον δοκεῖ εἶναι τὸ πρᾶγμα, εἰ ἡμῖν οὕτως ἔχων τὴν γνώμην Κλέανδρος ἄπεισιν ὥσπερ λέγει (Xen., *An.* 6.6.12)

'Fellow soldiers, it seems to me it is no trifling matter if Cleander is to go away having his intention toward us such as he has expressed.' (tr. Brownson, slightly modified)

It is interesting to note in this regard that ἔχω can occasionally be found combined with the present participle of lexically stative verbs, which presents an interesting parallel to what occurs with the

---

[141] Or even 'scarcely credible', as one of the reviewers puts it.
[142] Cf. §3.3.2.2.

Perfect Aspect 151

constructions of εἰμί with the perfect and present participle.[143] That both types of participles have a semantically related value can be seen in the following example, where Isocrates notes the following about some of his speeches:

(106) οὗτοι μὲν γὰρ τὸ λεγόμενον ὁμολογούμενον ἀεὶ τῷ προειρημένῳ καὶ συγκεκλειμένον ἔχουσιν (Isoc. 15.68)
'For in them each part is always in accord and in logical connection with that which goes before.' (tr. Norlin)

The present participle ὁμολογούμενον 'in accord' and the perfect participle συγκεκλειμένον 'connected closely together' are coordinated, both with a stative value. Since the construction of ἔχω with the stative present participle cannot have given rise to an anterior perfect, it will not be further discussed in this chapter.[144]

To conclude, I mention the semantic difference between resultative εἰμί with the perfect participle and resultative ἔχω with the perfect participle. While the former construction directly predicates a property of its subject, the latter denotes a property of someone/something that can be situated in the sphere of the subject, which is animate in the large majority of the examples. Only when εἰμί with the perfect participle is accompanied by an accusative of respect or a possessive pronoun are the two constructions semantically comparable. Compare, for example, (107) and (108):

(107) ἔχει δὲ καὶ ἡ φώκη ἐσχισμένην τὴν γλῶτταν (Aristot., Hist. an. 508a)
'The seal too has its tongue split.'

(108) ἐν δὲ τῷ ὄρει τῷ Ἐλαφώεντι καλουμένῳ, ὅ ἐστι τῆς Ἀσίας ἐν τῇ Ἀργινούσῃ, οὗ ἐτελεύτησεν Ἀλκιβιάδης, αἱ ἔλαφοι πᾶσαι τὸ οὖς ἐσχισμέναι εἰσίν (Aristot., Hist. an. 578b)
'In the mountain called Deer Mountain, which is in Arginussa in Asia Minor—the place where Alcibiades died—all the hinds have one ear split (lit. are split with regards to the ear).' (tr. Thompson)

In both cases, the passive perfect participle of the verb σχίζω 'I split' is used to denote a bodily property of a type of animal, but in the first example it is accompanied by the verb ἔχω while in the second by εἰμί. The latter expression is much more uncommon though.[145]

---

[143] See further §4.3.   [144] But see §3.6.3 for an innovative use.
[145] For a similar example from Aristotle, see Mete. 374b.

3.3.5 'Minor' Periphrastic Constructions

One of the typical characteristics of perfect periphrases in the period analysed here is the occurrence of various 'minor' periphrastic constructions, only some of which become more successful over time (compare e.g. the use of εἰμί with the perfect participle in Archaic and Classical Greek). In the Classical period, only one such 'minor' construction can be found, that is ἔχω with the perfect participle.[146] The construction can be thought of as an extension of ἔχω with the aorist participle, which, as we have seen in §3.3.2.1, became frequently employed during the Classical period. In addition, the extension of the aorist to the perfect participle may have been stimulated by the rise of εἰμί with the perfect participle. As an example of the construction, consider (109):[147]

(109) {Ιο.} πρὸς θεῶν δίδαξον κἄμ᾽, ἄναξ, ὅτου ποτὲ / μῆνιν τοσήνδε πράγματος στήσας ἔχεις / {Οι.} ἐρῶ· σὲ γὰρ τῶνδ᾽ ἐς πλέον, γύναι, σέβω· / Κρέοντος, οἷά μοι βεβουλευκὼς ἔχει (Soph., OT 698–701)
'Iocaste. I beg you my lord, explain to me also what matter has caused you to build up such great anger. Oedipus. I will, for I have more respect for you, lady, than I have for these. It was Creon, such has been his plot against me!' (tr. Lloyd-Jones)

Iocaste enters the scene, and asks Oedipus to explain why he is so angry. ἔχω is used twice in a periphrastic perfect construction, first with the aorist participle, and afterwards with the perfect participle. Both instances refer to a past event (the building up of anger, Creon's plotting against Oedipus), which has relevance at the time of speaking.

3.4 EARLY POST-CLASSICAL GREEK (III–I BC)

3.4.1 Overall Changes in the Verbal System

Before going further into the history of the periphrastic perfect constructions, I shall briefly outline a number of changes that the

---

[146] Cf. Thielmann (1898: 301); Aerts (1965: 158–9).
[147] For similar examples, see e.g. Pl., *Tht.* 200a; Soph., *Phil.* 600; Xen., *An.* 1.3.14.

Perfect Aspect 153

verbal system underwent during the Post-Classical and Byzantine periods. These changes were quite profound, and are likely to have affected the development of perfect periphrases as well.[148] As Evans (2001: 54) and Dickey (2009: 154-7) among others have noted, in general, the verbal system tended towards simplification, which may be partially the result of language contact.

Perhaps the most important development for our present purposes is the disappearance of the synthetic perfect. This development is generally attributed[149] to the functional overlap between the aorist and the perfect[150] when the latter became an anterior perfect. While initially the synthetic perfect indicated the current relevance of a past event, its use seems to have been extended, whereby it came to be employed as a perfective past.[151] The date of this functional merger has been the subject of some discussion: Chantraine (1927: 164ff.) finds its first traces already in the Classical period; McKay (1965) and Porter (1989: 273) have advanced a much later date, as late as the fourth or fifth century AD. In a similar vein, Rijksbaron (1984: 409-11) has argued that the perfect maintained its value at least until the Hellenistic period.

At the heart of this discussion is the question as to which criteria can be used to identify perfect forms that are used perfectively. Mandilaras (1972: 17) has suggested three criteria: (a) 'when the perfect is connected with an aorist syntactically'; (b) 'when the context demonstrates no relationship of the past action to present time'; (c) 'when there is an indication of past time'. Criterion (c)

---

[148] For further discussion, see esp. Mirambel (1961, 1966); Browning (1983); Joseph (1987); Horrocks (2007, 2010).

[149] See e.g. Chantraine (1927, ch. 8); Mandilaras (1972: 16); Moser (1988: 225); Haspelmath (1992: 217-21); Duhoux (2000: 430-1); Dickey (2009: 155); Horrocks (2010: 176-7).

[150] In this context, some scholars have suggested that Latin may have had an influence (see e.g. Robertson 1915: 359; Dubuisson 1985: 240-5). Contrast, however, Thumb (1974 [1901]: 153), Hilhorst (1976: 59), and most recently Horrocks (2010: 176): 'Latin can have done no more than promote a trend that was already under way.' Other scholars have suggested that the disappearance of the perfect should be attributed to phonological change, making the distinction between the perfect and the aorist difficult. I agree with Moser (1988: 216), however, who notes that 'radical as the change in the phonology of greek may have been, the claim that it was the cause of the loss of the synthetic forms of the perfect cannot stand up to any serious criticism. The similarity of the endings of some perfects to those of some aorists is hardly a sufficient reason for the loss of a whole class of forms.'

[151] Compare our observations on 'aoristic drift' in §3.1.

corresponds to what we have called 'definite time specification' in §3.3.3, while criterion (a) has some affinity with what we have called 'temporal sequentiality'; however, while syntactic coordination is an important indicator of sequentiality, this is not necessarily the case.[152] Criterion (b) seems to be less straightforward, as it is often difficult to ascertain, as Mandilaras (1972: 48) himself recognizes.

When it comes to temporal sequentiality, an early example may be found in the so-called Ptolemaeus archive:[153]

(110) [ἐ]υθὺ ἶδον μίαν αὐτῶν ἐρχομένην πρὸς τό τι[ν]ος εἰς <σ>κοτινὸν τόπον καὶ καθιζάνει ὀροῦσα. εἶδον εὐθὺ ὅτ[ι] μίαν αὐτῶν ἀποκεκάθισται. εἶπα Ἁρμάεις πι . . . . [ἐ]λθῖν αὐτόν. καὶ ἄλλα τινὰ εἶδον πολλὰ καὶ πάλιν ἠξίωκα τὸν Σάραπιν καὶ τὴν Ἶσιν (UPZ.1.78, ll. 18–23 (159 BC))

'At once I saw one of them go to a dark place in someone's house, and she sits down and makes water. I saw at once that the other of them had been sitting off to one side; I told Harmaïs to let[?] him come. I also saw much more, and I again implored Sarapis and Isis.' (tr. Lewis)

In this papyrus, which is composed in low-register Greek (as indicated by the orthographical mistakes), Ptolemaeus recounts dreams he had on several days, many of which involve the twin sisters Thaues and Taous. He narrates that he saw several things ((ἐ)ἶδον), that he addressed a certain Harmaïs (εἶπα), and that he implored Sarapis and Isis (ἠξίωκα). For this last event, a perfect form is used, seemingly functioning as a perfective past; note, however, that ἠξίωκα may be a 'mixed' form, whereby an aorist form is combined with a perfect ending.[154] Such mixed forms are quite frequently attested (e.g. ἐκτέθεικαν (UPZ.1.41, l. 16; 161–160 BC), from the same archive),[155] and are often taken to reflect the functional merger of aorist and perfect. Other scholars,[156] however, note that the existence of such forms should be situated within a broader process of simplification and regularization of the verbal paradigm, as can be seen in forms such as ἐλαμβάνεσαν 'they were receiving' (UPZ.1.54, l. 30 (161

---

[152] Cf. McKay (1965: 16–17).
[153] I borrow this example from Dieterich (1898: 235).
[154] Such morphological confusion may also be the case in P.Tebt.2.283 (93 or 60 BC), where δέδωκα (for δέδωκε) is used to narrate a temporally sequential event. Cf. also Kapsomenakis (1938: 127–8).
[155] I borrow this example from Dieterich (1898: 236). Cf. also Helbing (1907: 67–8); Mihevc (1959: 27–8); Mandilaras (1972: 12–14); Horrocks (2010: 177–8).
[156] See e.g. Hesseling (1928: 14); Evans (2001: 151).

BC)) and εἴχαμεν 'we had' (UPZ.1.18, l. 26 (163 BC)),[157] where aorist and imperfect morphology are confused.[158] Forms with a distinct perfect stem that denote temporally sequential events become more frequent in the Middle Post-Classical period: several examples can be found in the New Testament, the apocryphal Acts, and the Greek novels.[159] Mihevc (1959: 7) even cites an example from Plutarch, noting that certain classes of frequently occurring verbs seem to have been more prone to be used as aoristic perfects (verbs of movement, verbs of perception, verbs of communication, etc.; Mihevc 1959: 8). Various examples can also be found in the Roman papyri.[160]

Examples of perfects being used with definite time specification can be found at an earlier date. Mandilaras (1972: 18), who stresses the value of this criterion, mentions several such examples from the Early Post-Classical period, as in τῆι δὲ ιθ τοῦ αὐτοῦ μηνὸς ἤλκυσμαι λαμπαδάρχης (BGU.6.1256, ll. 10–11 (II BC)) 'on the nineteenth of the same month I was compelled to serve as λ.'; ἀπέσταλκα αὐτὸν πρὸς σὲ τῆι ς τοῦ Φαρμοῦθι (P.Petr.2.2, 2, ll. 5–6 (222 BC)) 'I sent him to you on the sixth of Pharmouthi'; τῆι κ τοῦ Φαῶφι τοῦ ε (ἔτους) . . . τ[ὰ] ἐν τῆι ἑαυτοῦ γῆι ὕδατα κατακέκλυκεν (P.Tebt.1.49, ll. 4–8 (113 BC)) 'on the twentieth of Phaophi in the fifth year he let out the water on his own land'.[161]

In conclusion, it seems that the functional merger of the perfect and the aorist already started in the Early Post-Classical period, as is indicated by the use of perfects with definite time specification, but that it became more prevalent in the Middle Post-Classical period, as is indicated by the use of perfects to denote temporally sequential events. The disappearance of the perfect, which resulted from this functional merger, was gradual: scholars have noted that the past and future perfect disappeared before the present perfect,[162] and that the

---

[157] For further discussion and examples, see e.g. Dieterich (1898: 231–48).

[158] Note in this regard the use of εἶπα, as well as the correct usage of ἀποκεκάθισται in (110).

[159] See Moulton (1908: 142–7); Jannaris (1897: 439–40); Ghedini (1937: 460–2); Papanikolaou (1973: 71–4); Hilhorst (1976: 58). As noted by Moulton (1908: 142) among others, some caution is needed in evaluating these examples.

[160] See Mihevc (1959: 20).

[161] I borrow these examples from Mandilaras (1972: 18).

[162] See Mihevc (1959: 60); Mandilaras (1973: 229); Duhoux (2000: 440). With regard to the past perfect, Mihevc (1959: 25) notes that no more examples can be found in the papyri after the fourth century AD.

medio-passive forms remained in use longer than the active forms.[163] Exactly why the perfect disappeared, after its increase in frequency during the Early Post-Classical period,[164] rather than the aorist, remains unclear. Lindstedt (2000: 373) suggests that 'the morphological type of the perfect—periphrastic vs. inflectional—may have some bearing on its propensity to displace a simple past tense'. Another factor that may have played a role is the fact that the aorist was morphologically better integrated into the paradigm;[165] several Greek dialects (including Tsakonian), however, preserve an 'aorist' in -κα-.[166]

A second change in the paradigm was the disappearance of the optative mood during the Post-Classical period. While some accounts attribute the loss of the optative to phonetic changes,[167] others have noted that the optative disappeared at a relatively early date, before vowel shifts due to iotacism brought about the identity of some optative and subjunctive endings (as in λέγοις – λέγῃς).[168] These scholars draw attention to the 'syntactic weakness' of the optative, being replaceable both in its main- and subordinate-clause uses by a number of variant expressions. Functionally, the optative disappeared gradually: of the three main uses of the optative—volition and potentiality in main clauses, and historic sequence in subordinate clauses—the last of these was the first to be lost, while its use in volitional constructions was retained the longest.[169] In higher-register works, however, the optative continued to be used, as well as in stereotype phrases such as (μὴ) γένοιτο 'may it (not) happen', (μὴ) εἴη 'may it (not) be', and χαίροις 'may you rejoice'.[170]

A third and final change, which is crucial for the present study, concerns the decline of the participle. This decline was gradual. Mirambel (1961: 50) situates it between the first and the thirteenth century AD. As he notes (1961: 47–8), of the rich participial system of

---

[163] See Mihevc (1959: 18, 61).
[164] Cf. Slings (1994: 245–6); Duhoux (2000: 431); Dickey (2009: 155).
[165] Compare Mihevc (1959: 3); Moser (1988: 225).
[166] See Hesseling (1928: 19–24); Mihevc (1959: 47); Horrocks (2010: 178). As Horrocks (2010: 178) notes, even in Standard Modern Greek -κα- is used as an aorist suffix in certain verbs, as well as in the passive voice.
[167] See e.g. Allinson (1902); Mirambel (1966: 172).
[168] See Schwyzer (1950: 337); Evans (2001: 177, fn. 9).
[169] Cf. Jannaris (1897: 561–5); Schwyzer (1950: 338); Mandilaras (1973: 277–8); McKay (1993: 27); Evans (2001: 176–7); Horrocks (2007: 625).
[170] See Mandilaras (1973: 277).

Perfect Aspect 157

Ancient Greek, the modern language only retains three forms, the medio-passive present participle, as in λυνόμενος '(being) released', the medio-passive perfect participle, as in λυμένος 'released', and the indeclinable active present participle (also called gerund), as in λύνοντας '(while) releasing'. This formal and functional reduction of the use of participles is generally attributed to the complexity of participial morphology:[171] most participle forms, including the active present, aorist, and perfect participle, and the passive aorist participle, follow both the first and third declension, the latter of which eventually disappeared.[172] Difficulties in the formation of the participle are reflected in examples such as τῶν νῦν δοθεν σοι παρ' ἐμοῦ χρυσίνων (P.Lond.1.113, 1, l. 89 (VI AD)) 'the golden coins that have now been given by me to you' (with δοθεν for δοθέντων) and ἡμεῖν . . . εὖ βιουντες (P.Mert.2.91, l. 6 (316 AD)) 'for us, who live well' (with βιουντες for βιοῦσι).[173] Another factor that may have played a role is the preference for analytic expression, through either subordination or parataxis, which provided a clearer mode of expression.[174] This factor also played a part in the loss of the infinitive, which, unlike the participle, disappeared entirely except in its use in periphrases of the type ἔχω γράψει 'I have written'.[175] It seems that this took place at a later date: according to Mirambel (1961: 46), the infinitive disappeared from the living usage in the tenth century, and Joseph (1987: 432) notes that there are indications that 'it was maintained until approximately the sixteenth century as at least a marginal category'.

3.4.2 Decrease in Usage of εἰμί with the Perfect Participle?

What impact did the changes in the verbal system outlined in §3.4.1 have on the use of perfect periphrases, particularly εἰμί with the perfect participle? In general, scholars stress the increasing importance (frequency) of periphrastic constructions in the Post-Classical

---

[171] See Jannaris (1897: 505); Horrocks (2010: 181–3). For an alternative account, see Manolessou (2005).
[172] See e.g. Jannaris (1897: 121–2).
[173] I borrow these examples from Dieterich (1898: 207–8) and Horrocks (2010: 183). Cf. also Mirambel (1961: 51).
[174] Given that formal agreement was no longer always maintained, and that the (subordinative) conjunct participle could be employed with a variety of uses. See Jannaris (1897: 504–5); Joseph (1987: 433–4); Horrocks (2010: 94, 181).
[175] Cf. Mirambel (1961: 48); Joseph (1987: 432).

158 Verbal Periphrasis in Ancient Greek

(and Byzantine) period.[176] Moser (1988: 229), for example, notes with regard to εἰμί with the perfect participle that:

> It is ... well attested that this analytic form became far more widely used in the Koine, following the generalised trend of that period towards extensive use of analytic forms in the language.

Somewhat surprisingly, my own corpus-based analysis shows that the frequency of the construction does not *increase*, but rather *decreases*. Consider Table 3.6:

Table 3.6. Distribution of εἰμί with the perfect participle in EPG

Genre/Author/Text	TOT	NRO
Biography/hagiography	206	3.13
Septuagint (III–II BC)	200	3.10
Apocalypse of Enoch (II–I BC)	4	(4.63)
Life of Adam and Eve (I BC–I AD)	2	(4.34)
Historiography	115	1.84
Polybius (b. c.200 BC)	48	1.46
Dionysius of Halicarnassus (b. c.60 BC)	67	2.26
Scientific prose	116	2.85
Archimedes (b. c.287 BC)	77	7.17
Strabo (b. c.64 BC)	39	1.30
Papyri	284	/
Letters	65	/
Petitions	155	/

Key: 'TOT' = total; 'NRO' = normed rate of occurrence (per 10,000 words)

This table shows that the construction is most frequently used in biography/hagiography and scientific prose. The construction is especially frequently used in the work of Archimedes,[177] though much less so in that of Strabo (which is of an entirely different nature). When we make the comparison with Classical Greek,[178] the decrease in frequency in historiography is quite noticeable (NRO 5.5 instances per 10,000 words in CG, vs. 1.8 in EPG).[179]

---

[176] Cf. Jannaris (1897: 492); Robertson (1915: 1119); Chantraine (1927: 222); Mihevc (1959: 47–8); Moulton & Turner (1963: 81); Browning (1983: 32); Gerö & von Stechow (2003: 283); Dickey (2009: 155); Moser (2009: 650). Contrast Aerts (1965: 91) specifically with regard to εἰμί with the perfect participle in 'the Koine' (the period from 300 BC to 1000 AD): 'the frequency of the perfect participle periphrases is rather low'.
[177] It has a low type/token ratio, however. See Table 3.8.
[178] Compare Table 3.2.
[179] Cf. Palm (1955: 94), who notes with regard to Dionysius of Halicarnassus that 'die Anzahl der Fälle ist nich gerade erstaunlich' ('the number of cases is not particularly impressive').

Perfect Aspect 159

This finding is also surprising given that scholars have established a steady increase in the use of the synthetic perfect during this period,[180] which the periphrastic construction obviously does not follow. One of the main reasons for the overall decrease in frequency of εἰμί with the perfect participle concerns the fact that morphologically the construction is used in a much smaller number of contexts, as shown in Table 3.7:

Table 3.7. Distribution of εἰμί with the perfect participle in EPG (mood)

Genre/Author/Text	IMP	IND	INF	OPT	PART	SUBJ
Biography/hagiography	14	173	2	5	0	12
Septuagint (III–II BC)	14	167	2	5	0	12
Apocalypse of Enoch (II–I BC)	0	4	0	0	0	0
Life of Adam and Eve (I BC–I AD)	0	2	0	0	0	0
Historiography	1	88	5	12	2	7
Polybius (b. *c.*200 BC)	0	31	3	6	1	7
Dionysius of Halicarnassus (b. *c.*60 BC)	1	57	2	6	1	0
Scientific prose	19	70	4	7	5	11
Archimedes (b. *c.*287 BC)	19	45	2	0	1	10
Strabo (b. *c.*64 BC)	0	25	2	7	4	1
Papyri	0	203	3	4	0	74
Letters	0	53	1	1	0	10
Petitions	0	106	1	3	0	45

Key: 'IMP' = imperative; 'IND' = indicative; 'INF' = infinitive; 'OPT' = optative; 'PART' = participle; 'SUBJ' = subjunctive.

When we compare this Table to our previous Table 3.3, it becomes clear that the construction is much less often attested outside the indicative: while in the former period 54% (1049/1933) of the examples are used in the indicative, in EPG this amounts to as much as 74% (534/721). The early disappearance of the optative in particular[181] had a clear impact on the use of the construction (representing 19% (369/1933) of the examples in CG, versus 4% in EPG (28/721)). This may be contrasted with the view of Browning (1983: 33) among others, who believes that the construction was first used in the subjunctive and optative, and only afterwards extended to the indicative: 'common in classical Greek in subjunctive and optative, this periphrasis [εἰμί + perfect participle, KB] is

[180] See fn. 164. Duhoux (2000: 431) provides precise statistical data.
[181] See §3.4.1.

160 *Verbal Periphrasis in Ancient Greek*

extended by Koine to the indicative, but never becomes really common.'

As for the use of the construction in terms of aspect, consider Table 3.8:

Table 3.8. Distribution of εἰμί with the perfect participle in EPG (aspect, voice)

Genre/Author/Text	RES (RES)	TTR (RES)	RES (ACT)	RES (MED/PASS)	ANT (ANT)	TTR (ANT)	ANT (ACT)	ANT (MED)	ANT (PASS)
Biography/hagiography	167	0.53	38	129	39	0.82	16	9	14
Septuagint (III–II BC)	161	0.54	37	124	39	0.82	16	9	14
Apocalypse of Enoch (II–I BC)	4	1	1	3	0	0	0	0	0
Life of Adam and Eve (I BC–I AD)	2	0.50	0	2	0	0	0	0	0
Historiography	54	0.70	14	40	61	0.74	26	9	26
Polybius (b. c.200 BC)	25	0.88	5	20	23	0.87	9	5	9
Dionysius of Halicarnassus (b. c.60 BC)	29	0.66	9	20	38	0.71	17	4	17
Scientific prose	93	0.53	12	81	23	0.74	4	4	15
Archimedes (b. c.287 BC)	65	0.40	5	60	12	0.58	2	2	8
Strabo (b. c.64 BC)	28	0.86	7	21	11	1	2	2	7
Papyri[182]	29	0.86	2	27	254	0.31	117	38	99
Letters	14	0.86	0	14	51	0.76	13	18	20
Petitions	4	0.75	0	4	150	0.17	89	8	53

Key: 'RES' = resultative; 'TTR' = type/token ratio; 'ACT' = active; 'MED' = medium; 'PASS' = passive; 'ANT' = anterior.

This table shows that there is a tendency for εἰμί with the perfect participle to be used as a resultative perfect: in biography/hagiography resultatives make up 81% (167/206) of the total number of examples, and in scientific prose 82% (93/116). In historiographical texts, however, the construction is slightly more often used as an anterior perfect, and in the papyri there is a clear predominance of anteriors. This tendency is to some extent genre-related: as we have seen in Classical Greek, genres such as scientific prose have 'information' as their dominant discourse mode, so that resultatives can be expected to occur frequently. That in the LXX the construction is also predominantly used as a resultative perfect is, to some extent,

---

[182] In P.Tebt.3.1.793, 8, l. 12 (183 BC) the construction seems periphrastic, but it is difficult to determine aspectual function due to a lack of context.

Perfect Aspect 161

surprising, though we have to keep in mind that it represents a diverse group of texts, not all of which are predominantly narrative in character. The LXX also resembles scientific prose in terms of its relatively low type/token ratio, which indicates that the frequent occurrence of some verbs also has a role to play in the predominance of resultatives.

A second important observation that can be made on the basis of Table 3.8 is that εἰμί with the perfect participle is predominantly passive. Object-oriented resultatives with active endings cease to be found. Active resultative perfects are essentially limited to a few verb classes: verbs of motion and verbs of assuming a position (e.g. ἵσταμαι 'I stand' and its compounds, πίπτω 'I fall'), psych-verbs and mental state verbs (e.g. γιγνώσκω 'I know', πείθομαι 'I trust', οἶδα 'I know'), and verbs of appearance and disappearance (e.g. τελευτάω 'I die', θνῄσκω 'I die'). Verbs of change of state (e.g. ἀλλάσσω 'I alter', ἀνοίγνυμι 'I open'), which, as we have seen, can take either active or medio-passive endings depending on whether the base verb is causative or non-causative, are mostly formed with the latter endings.[183] Anterior perfects, too, are to a large extent formed in the passive voice, which in part constitutes a reverse development of what we have seen in Classical Greek (where anteriors first occur in the passive voice, and only at a later stage in the active voice).[184] The exact reason for this movement of εἰμί with the perfect participle towards the passive voice is unclear: it might form a parallel with the synthetic perfect, which, as I noted in §3.4.1, was retained the longest in the passive voice. However, this does not accord with the generally assumed chronology, according to which the synthetic perfect was not in decline yet during the EPG.[185] That the decline of the participle would have exerted an influence at this early stage seems unlikely, although a large-scale investigation of the use of the participle in this period could shed more light on the matter.

So far, I have said little about the papyri. As Table 3.6, Table 3.7, and Table 3.8 indicate, the papyrological evidence is not entirely in

---

[183] Compare Schwyzer (1934: 779), who notes with regard to the synthetic perfect that 'intransitive aktive Perfekta wurden im Spätgriechischen durch passive ersetzt' ('intransitive active perfect forms are in later Greek replaced by passive forms'). Note, however, that γίγνομαι is still found in both the active and the passive voice.

[184] See §3.3.2.2.

[185] Moreover, Duhoux (1996: 61) notes that in the New Testament active forms are (still) in the majority. Contrast, however, Chantraine (1927: 218–21).

agreement with what has been observed in the previous paragraphs, since εἰμί with the perfect participle occurs quite frequently in the Ptolemaic papyri, with 284 instances,[186] in moods outside the indicative (the subjunctive in particular), often with an anterior function, and in the active voice. Moreover, in the indicative mood, the construction is quite often used as a future perfect,[187] contrary to what is the case with literary texts, where the construction is predominantly used in the present and the past tense. It has to be noted, however, that a large part of the examples can be found in closing formulas of the type illustrated in (111):

(111) διὸ ἐπιδίδωμί σοι τὸ ὑπόμνημα, ἀξιῶι ἐὰν φαίνηται τὸν προγεγραμμένον Πατῦνιν ἀσφαλίσασθαι. τούτου δὲ γενομ[έ]νου ἔσομαι τετευχὼς [τῆ]ς παρὰ σοῦ ἀντιλήμψεως (P.Tebt.2.283, ll. 16–22 (93/60 BC))
'I therefore present this notice, begging you, if you please, to secure the aforesaid Patynis; for if this is done I shall have gained succor from you' (tr. Grenfell & Hunt)

Taarmiysis, daughter of Tasuthis, addresses the epistatês of Tebtunis. She narrates how a certain Patunis had attacked her mother, 'giving her numerous blows upon various parts of the body'. She asks that Patunis be taken into custody, noting that if the request has been fulfilled, she will have gained help. The periphrastic perfect, ἔσομαι τετευχὼς ἀντιλήμψεως, expresses a future event (gaining help), with relevance at a later point in the future. Such a closing formula occurs in a great deal of petitions.[188] Next to the verb τυγχάνω 'I obtain', which is particularly often used,[189] one often finds a verb of helping (mostly in the passive voice) such as ἀντιλαμβάνω, 'I assist', βοηθέω 'I help', εὐγνωμονέω 'I reward', φιλανθρωπέω 'I treat kindly', and χαρίζω 'I show someone favour'.[190] Occasionally, we also find verbs of injuring, which are then negated, such as ἀδικέω 'I do wrong', λυπέω 'I grieve', and παροράω 'I overlook'.[191]

---

[186] Compare e.g. with the MPG period, for which only 195 examples can be found, although, as noted in fn. 29 (Introduction), in general much more papyri can be found during this period.
[187] Cf. Mayser (1926: 2.1.225).
[188] Cf. White (1972: xi–xii), who considers it a structural part of petitions.
[189] As reflected in the extremely low TTR in Table 3.8.
[190] For some examples, see e.g. BGU.4.1138, l. 23 (19 BC); BGU.16.2601, ll. 26–7 (12–1 BC); P.Oxy.7.1061, l. 20 (22 BC); PSI.4.424, l. 8 (III BC); UPZ.1.108, l. 36 (99 BC).
[191] For some examples, see e.g. BGU.8.1830, l. 6 (51 BC); P.Eleph.27, ll. 24–5 (223 BC).

Perfect Aspect   163

Despite the frequent occurrence of εἰμί with the perfect participle in such formulaic expressions, it has to be noted that the construction is quite productively used in all sorts of documents, including contracts, letters (private, business, and official), petitions, accounts, etc., both in its resultative and anterior function.[192] Consider the following passage from a private letter:

(112) σὺ οὖν καλῶς ποήσεις σαυτῆς ἐπιμελομένη μέχρι τοῦ παραγενέσθαι με ⟦ϵπις⟧ ἐπὶ σὲ συντόμως. τὰ δὲ κατὰ σαυτὴν ἀσφάλισαι ὡς μετελεύσῃ μεθ' ἡμῶν, ⟦τϱὺς⟧ οἱ γὰρ ἄνθρωποι <u>ὑποδεδεγμένοι εἰσίν</u> με ἡδέως (P. Mich.15.750, ll. 14–24 (172 BC))

'Please look after yourself until my forthcoming arrival. Secure your things as you'll be moving with us; for the people received me in a friendly fashion.' (tr. Sijpesteijn)

ὑποδεδεγμένοι εἰσίν 'they have received' fulfils an anterior function:[193] it expresses the relevance of the past reception at the time of writing.

In §3.4.1 it was noted that already in the Ptolemaic papyri there are examples of the synthetic perfect combined with adverb(ial)s indicating a definite time. A parallel may exist in some sowing reports from Tebtunis, as illustrated in (113):[194]

(113) <u>ἐσπαρμέναι ἦσαν ἐν τῶι γ (ἔτει)</u> γῆς (ἄρουραι) Αϱογ ∠ δ' ὧν ἐκφό(ριον) Δχξε [γ' ιβ',] (P.Tebt.1.71, ll. 4–5 (114 BC))

'In year 3 there had been sown $1,193^{3/4}$ ar., yielding rents of $4,665^{5/12}$ art.' (tr. Lewis)

In this papyrus, Menches, the village clerk, gives an overview of the goods that have (already) been sown in the fourth year. He begins his report by giving an overview of what was sown in the third year, and what rents that yielded. While the periphrastic form is accompanied here by an adverbial that refers to a specific time, it seems that ἐν τῶι γ (ἔτει) 'in year 3' indicates a time during which multiple sowing-events

---

[192] Cf. Mayser (1926: 2.1.224–5).
[193] For similar examples of εἰμί with the perfect participle in its anterior function, see e.g. BGU.4.1141, l. 45 (14–13 BC?); BGU.6.1253, ll. 6–7 (II BC); P.Enteux.47, l. 7 (221 BC); P.Enteux.55, l. 9 (222 BC); P.Hal.1, 6, ll. 131–2 (259 BC); P.Tebt.1.16, l. 7 (114 BC); P.Tebt.3.1.740, l. 24 (113 BC); SB.3.7267, l. 3 (184 BC); UPZ.1.6, ll. 29–30 (163 BC).
[194] For similar examples, see P.Tebt.1.66, l. 2 (120 BC), P.Tebt.1.67, l. 3 (117 BC), P.Tebt.1.68, l. 3 (116 BC), P.Tebt.1.69, l. 4 (113 BC), P.Tebt.1.70, l. 3 (110 BC), P.Tebt.1.89, l. 5 (113 BC), P.Tebt.4.1129, l. 6 (123 BC), P.Tebt.4.1130, l. 5 (114 BC).

164 *Verbal Periphrasis in Ancient Greek*

occurred: in other words, ἐσπαρμέναι ἦσαν 'there had been sown' fulfils an experiential function. This also seems to be suggested by Lewis (1986: 113–14), who notes that Menches probably had to submit sowing-reports every ten days, until the sowing season was completed.

3.4.3 ἔχω with the (Medio-passive) Perfect Participle

The construction of ἔχω with the (medio-passive) perfect participle continues to be used in EPG, as shown in Table 3.9:

Table 3.9. Distribution of ἔχω with the (medio-passive) perfect participle in EPG

Genre/Author/Text	TOT	NRO	TTR
Biography/hagiography	4	0.06	0.75
Septuagint (III–II BC)	4	0.06	0.75
Historiography	22	0.35	0.72
Polybius (b. *c.*200 BC)	7	0.21	1
Dionysius of Halicarnassus (b. *c.*60 BC)	15	0.51	0.60
Scientific prose	27	0.66	0.93
Archimedes (b. *c.*287 BC)	2	0.19	1
Strabo (b. *c.*64 BC)	25	0.83	0.92
Papyri	1	/	1
Letters	1	/	1

Key: 'TOT' = total; 'NRO' = normed rate of occurrence (per 10,000 words); 'TTR' = type/token ratio.

This table shows that ἔχω with the (medio-passive) perfect participle is used with more or less the same frequency as in Classical Greek,[195] most often in scientific and historiographical texts (more in particular the work of Dionysius of Halicarnassus and Strabo). Note that there is also an isolated instance from the papyri.[196]

Most cases can be classified under Carey's (1994) 'resultant state object construction',[197] whereby the participle is an obligatory

---

[195] Compare Table 3.5.
[196] SB.5.8754, l. 31 (77 BC?). Mihevc (1959: 51) also considers PSI.4.420, ll. 21–4 (III BC) periphrastic, but in this example the participle may be substantivized.
[197] Cf. §3.3.2.1.

Perfect Aspect

constituent, and the target of HAVE is the stative relationship between the object and the participle. In various such examples, an anterior inference is possible, whereby the subject of ἔχω can be taken as the agent of the event denoted by the participle. In EPG, this occurs with particular frequency in Dionysius of Halicarnassus' *Roman Antiquities* with verbs of combining and attaching, mostly in a military context (as in συντεταγμένην ἔχων τὴν δύναμιν 'having his army drawn up').[198] An anterior inference can also be made in the following example:

(114) τοιαῦτα διαλεχθείς, ἐπικελεύσαντος αὐτῷ τοῦ δήμου μεγάλῃ βοῇ τὸν νόμον εἰσφέρειν, ἔχων αὐτὸν ἤδη γεγραμμένον ἀνεγίνωσκε καὶ ψῆφον δίδωσι τῷ πλήθει περὶ αὐτοῦ παραχρῆμα ἐπενεγκεῖν (Dion. Hal., *Ant. Rom.* 7.17.4)

'When he had thus spoken and the people had cried out to him with a great shout to introduce the law, Sicinius, who had it already drawn up, read it to them and permitted the people to vote upon it immediately.' (tr. Cary)

In this passage, a certain Sicinius addresses the people at the Forum, proposing to enact a law stating that no one can oppose or interrupt a tribune delivering his opinion to the people. As Sicinius already has the law he proposes in writing, he invites the people to vote immediately upon it. Here, it may well be the case that Sicinius has himself written the law, in other words with an anterior inference (ἔχων [τὸν νόμον] γεγραμμένον 'having written down the law').

3.4.4 'Minor' Periphrastic Constructions

As Browning (1983: 32) notes, during the Post-Classical and Byzantine period several alternative 'patterns' (that is, periphrastic constructions) co-existed, many of which played a minor role in terms of frequency. This is a situation that, to some extent, already existed in Classical Greek. However, partly due to the larger developments described in §3.4.1, the number of these constructions does seem to increase in Post-Classical and Early Byzantine Greek.

---

[198] See e.g. Dion. Hal., *Ant. Rom.* 1.46.4, 3.51.1, 6.31.2, 8.19.3, 9.14.7, 9.19.2. Compare Str. 10.4.8, 14.2.24.

One of these constructions is ἔχω with the aorist participle.[199] That this construction still occurs in EPG may come as a surprise: as was noted in §3.3.1, the construction disappeared during the fourth century BC, following the expansion of the synthetic perfect. However, in EPG the construction occurs very infrequently, and is virtually limited to the work of a single author, Dionysius of Halicarnassus, who is known for writing in a higher register, where such Archaic features may be retained. Moreover, in various cases, ἔχω is combined with a verb of change of possession such as λαμβάνω 'I take, receive', making it unclear whether we are in fact dealing with periphrasis: in these examples, the participle could well be taken as a conjunct participle.[200] In the following example, however, ἔχω is combined with a verb of communication, and here periphrasis seems unquestionable (compare Carey's 1994 'resultant state process construction'):[201]

(115) διηγησαμένου δὲ αὐτοῦ πάντα ὡς ἐπράχθη, Ἄγε δή, φησὶν ὁ βασιλεύς, ἐπειδὴ ταῦτ' ἀληθεύσας ἔχεις, φράσον ὅπου νῦν ἂν εὑρεθεῖεν (Dion. Hal., *Ant. Rom.* 1.82.6)

'And when the other [Faustulus] had given him [king Amulius] a full account of everything as it had happened, the king said: "Well then, since you have spoken the truth about these matters, say where they may now be found."' (tr. Cary)

The shepherd Faustulus tries to bring the basket in which Romulus and Remus were put (and then thrown into the Tiber) to Numitor as a proof of their story, and is caught at the city gates. He is brought to King Amulius, who wants to know whether Romulus and Remus are alive, and in what way they have been saved. The form ἀληθεύσας ἔχεις 'you have spoken the truth' is used as an anterior perfect: Faustulus' agreeing to tell the truth has relevance for the order that follows it, that is, to explain where the children are.

A second construction to consider is εἰμί with the aorist participle. The development of this construction can be related to the functional merger of the synthetic perfect and the aorist:[202] in periphrastic constructions too, the perfect participle came to be replaced by the

---

[199] Contrast Bruno (2012: 369): 'no traces of this pattern remain after that century [the fifth century BC, KB].'

[200] Compare our observations on Archaic Greek in §3.2.1. For some examples, see e.g. Dion. Hal., *Ant. Rom.* 8.47.3, 10.31.1, 10.32.2, 11.6.4. Compare P.Sorb.1.13, l. 3 (260 BC).

[201] Cf. §3.3.2.1.   [202] Cf. §3.4.1.

Perfect Aspect 167

aorist participle. This is a process which is generally dated to the MPG period,[203] but for which some isolated examples may already be found in EPG. In Archimedes' *On the sphere and cylinder*, for example, several times we encounter the technical expression ἐστι δοθείς, meaning 'it is given',[204] which can be seen as an extension from the attributive use of δοθείς in combination with γραμμή '[given] line', γωνία '[given] angle', etc.[205] For the use of the construction in a less standardized context, consider the following two examples:

(116) ὅτι οἱ περὶ τὸν Σέξτον προάγοντες ἐκ τῆς Ῥώμης εἰς τὴν Πελοπόννησον ἀπήντησαν τοῖς περὶ τὸν Θεαρίδαν, οἵ(περ) ἦσαν πρεσβευταὶ πεμφθέντες ὑπὸ τῶν Ἀχαιῶν παραιτησόμενοι καὶ διδάξοντες τὴν σύγκλητον (Pol. 38.10.1–2)

'Sextus Iulius and his colleagues on their way from Rome to the Peloponnesus met the envoys headed by Thearidas who had been sent by the Achaeans to excuse themselves and to inform the senate.' (tr. Paton)

(117) ἦσαν δ' ὑπ' αὐτῶν ἀποδειχθέντες ὕπατοι Σπόριος Ποστόμιος Ἀλβῖνος καὶ Κόιντος Σερουίλιος Πρίσκος τὸ δεύτερον. ἐπὶ τούτων ἔδοξαν Αἰκανοὶ παραβαίνειν τὰς πρὸς Ῥωμαίους νεωστὶ γενομένας ὁμολογίας ἀπὸ τοιαύτης αἰτίας (Dion. Hal., *Ant. Rom.* 9.60.1)

'The consuls named by them were Spurius Postumius Albinus and Quintus Servilius Priscus, the latter for the second time. In their consulship the Aequians were held to be violating the agreements lately made with the Romans, and this for the following reason.' (tr. Cary)

In (116), Polybius narrates how Sextus Iulius and his colleagues, sent by the Roman senate to the Achaeans, met some other envoys. ἦσαν πεμφθέντες may be taken periphrastically, with the value of an anterior perfect: 'they had been sent'. However, an alternative interpretation is also possible, whereby πεμφθέντες is taken as a conjunct participle: 'they were envoys, sent . . .'.

In (117), it is noted that the Aequians were considered to be violating some agreements made with the Romans. As in (116), ἦσαν . . . ἀποδειχθέντες occurs in a clause which provides background information. The form can be taken with the value of an anterior perfect: 'they had been appointed'. Again, however, an alternative interpretation

---

[203] See e.g. Björck (1940: 77); Aerts (1965: 81, 90).
[204] See e.g. *Sph. cyl.* 1.103.12, 1.109.28, 1.112.16, 1.116.20–1.
[205] Cf. Mugler (1958: 138–9); Schironi (2010: 346).

is possible, taking ἀποδειχθέντες as a conjunct participle: '...were consuls, appointed by them'.[206] Since, however, ἀποδειχθέντες precedes ὕπατοι, this reading seems less likely than in (116).[207]

Another noteworthy example can be found in the *Life of Adam and Eve*:[208]

(118) καὶ περιπεσὼν εἰς νόσον, καὶ βοήσας φωνῇ μεγάλῃ εἶπεν· ἐλθέτωσαν πρός με οἱ υἱοί μου πάντες, ὅπως ὄψομαι αὐτοὺς πρὶν ἢ ἀποθανεῖν με. καὶ συνήχθησαν πάντες· <u>ἦν</u> γὰρ <u>οἰκισθεῖσα</u> ἡ γῆ εἰς τρία μέρη (*V. Adam* 5.2–5)

'And he fell sick and cried with a loud voice and said, "Let all my sons come to me that I may see them before I die." And all assembled, for the earth was divided into three parts.' (tr. Charles)

Having lived nine hundred and thirty years, Adam has become sick and has called together all his sons. These have to come from different regions, as the earth is divided into different parts. Contrary to what we saw in our two previous examples, ἦν... οἰκισθεῖσα 'it was divided' seems quite clearly periphrastic: its value can be compared with that of the resultative perfect, expressing a stable property about the earth—that is, being divided into three parts.

3.5 MIDDLE POST-CLASSICAL GREEK (I–III AD)

3.5.1 Functional Opposition of εἰμί with the Aorist and Perfect Participle

As noted in §3.4.1, the functional merger of the aorist and perfect became more general in the Middle Post-Classical period (I–III AD), the effects of which can also be observed with regard to verbal periphrasis. During this period, the 'minor' construction of εἰμί with the aorist participle[209] becomes much more frequent, and is

---

[206] Palm (1955: 95) does not find any instances of εἰμί with the aorist participle in the work of Dionysius of Halicarnassus.
[207] Cf. Rijksbaron (2002: 132–3).
[208] Note, however, that the date of this *Vita* is contested, some scholars dating it between the second and the fourth centuries AD.
[209] Cf. §3.4.4.

Perfect Aspect 169

attested in a broader range of texts. Consider the data presented in Table 3.10:

Table 3.10. Distribution of εἰμί with the aorist participle in MPG

Genre/Author/Text	TOT	NRO	TTR
Biography/hagiography	18	0.23	0.94
Plutarch (b. c.50 AD)	1	0.02	1
New Testament (I AD)	1	0.07	1
Acts of Andrew (II AD)	1	(1.04)	1
Acts of John (II AD)	1	0.78	1
Gospel of Peter (II AD)	2	(16.86)	1
Acts of Thomas (III AD)	9	3.02	0.89
Acts of Xanthippe and Polyxena (III AD)	2	(2.07)	1
Gospel of Bartholomew (III AD)	1	(2.41)	1
Greek novel	11	0.55	1
Achilles Tatius (II AD)	9	2.07	1
Heliodorus (III AD)	2	0.25	1
Historiography	3	0.06	1
Cassius Dio (b. c.164 AD)	3	0.08	1
Scientific prose	3	0.08	1
Galen (b. 129 AD)	1	0.06	1
Pausanias (II AD)	2	0.09	1
Papyri	23	/	0.96
Letters	16	/	0.94
Petitions	3	/	1

Key: 'TOT' = total; 'NRO' = normed rate of occurrence (per 10,000 words); 'TTR' = type/token ratio.

This table shows that the construction became more frequently attested especially in the second and third centuries AD. It was particularly often employed in works written in a lower register, such as the *Acts of Andrew*, the *Gospel of Peter*, and the *Acts of Thomas*.[210] Calculated per 10,000 words, the construction occurs most frequently in the Greek novel. This, however, is due to the fact that Plutarch's *Parallel Lives* (which, together, comprise over 500,000 words) are also included under 'biography/hagiography'. Had Plutarch's work not been included, the frequency of the construction in the biographical/hagiographical texts would be 0.61 instances per 10,000 words. Nevertheless, it is surprising to find a relatively high number of

---

[210] See e.g. *A. Thom.* 9.14–15, 16.10, 16.11, 27.4, 91.17–18; *A. Xanthipp.* 26.25, 34.4; *Ev. Barth.* 4.6; *Ev. Petr.* 23.2, 51.2.

instances of the construction in the Greek novel, particularly Achilles Tatius.[211] This seems to confirm the observation made in §1.3.3.4 that the language of the novels is not uniformly higher-register language. The lower-register profile of the construction is also clearly indicated by the fact that in the papyri, where the construction is quite well attested, the majority of the examples occur in (private) letters (15/23 = 65%).[212]

Interestingly, εἰμί with the aorist participle is never employed with a perfective value, as may have been the case during the Classical period.[213] Rather, the construction renders perfect aspect, as in the following example:

(119) ἐάν σοι ἀβαρὲς ᾖ, ἄδελφε, σκῦλαι σεαυτὸν καί, ἐὰν δύνῃ, τὸ ἐλαιωνίδιον ἡμῶν πότισον καὶ <u>ἔσῃ</u> χάριν μεγάλην <u>πο[ι]ήσας</u> (P.Bad.2.33, ll. 5–10 (II AD))

'If it is not burdensome, brother, trouble yourself, and if possible, water our olive-yard and you will have done a great favour.'

In this early example (also from a private letter), we see that even in formulaic expressions of the type discussed in §3.4.2, where future gratitude is expressed when this or that will have been done (in this case the watering of the olive-yard), the aorist participle[214] comes to be used instead of the perfect participle.[215] As in most examples, the construction is used with an anterior value, expressing the relevance of a future event at a later point in the future. The same use can be found in our literary texts, where the construction is mostly employed as a present or past perfect. Consider the following example:

(120) εἶχε δὲ ὁ Σάτυρος τοῦ φαρμάκου λείψανον, ᾧ τὸν Κώνωπα <u>ἦν κατακοιμίσας</u>· τούτου διακονούμενος ἡμῖν ἐγχεῖ λαθὼν κατὰ τῆς κύλικος τῆς τελευταίας, ἣν τῇ Πανθείᾳ προσέφερεν (Ach. Tat., Leuc. et Clit. 2.31.1)

---

[211] See e.g. Ach. Tat., Leuc. et Clit. 6.8.3, 7.1.5, 7.2.2, 7.4.3, 7.9.12, 7.11.6, 7.12.4, 8.9.8. Cf. also Papanikolaou (1973: 79).

[212] For some examples, see e.g. P.Flor.2.175, l. 14 (255 AD); P.Lond.3.948v, ll. 3–4 (257 AD); P.Oxy.42.3067, ll. 11–12 (III AD); P.Oxy.58.3919, l. 11 (188 AD); P.Tebt.2.423, l. 18 (III AD); PSI.12.1248, l. 28 (235 AD); P.Stras.1.73, ll. 20–1 (III AD?); SB.3.6262, ll. 16–17 (III AD?).

[213] See Chapter 5 for further discussion.

[214] For a similar example, see BGU.1.48, ll. 7–8 (II/III AD).

[215] Compare with P.Bon.43, ll. 10–11 (I AD): ἐὰν τοῦτο ποιήσεις, ἔσῃ μοι μεγάλην χάριτα πεποιηκ(ώς) 'if you will do this, you will have done me a great favour.'

Perfect Aspect 171

'Satyrus had some of the drug with which he had put Conops to sleep left over, and when he was ministering to us he secretly poured some into the last cup, which he took to Pantheia.' (tr. Whitmarsh, slightly modified)

Satyrus, using the same drug that he gave to Conops, drugs Pantheia so that she falls asleep. The periphrastic form ἦν κατακοιμίσας functions as an anterior perfect: it refers to a past event, the putting to sleep of Conops, that is relevant at a later point in the narrative, when the drug is given to Pantheia.

Even in these early examples, εἰμί with the aorist participle has a relatively high transitivity profile: it is predominantly used as an anterior perfect, mostly in the active voice, often with a volitional subject (as in (119) and (120)) and an affected object (as in (120)), generally expressing a single, rather than a repeated event. In the light of the grammaticalization path described in the introduction to this chapter, this observation may come as a surprise: perfect periphrases typically develop from resultatives to anteriors, or in other words, from expressing lower to higher transitivity. That the construction was nevertheless used as an anterior perfect right away must be attributed to the development of the synthetic perfect and aorist: the aorist primarily took over the anterior perfect function, and this influence can also be felt in the development of the periphrastic tenses.

In a limited number of examples, however, εἰμί with the aorist participle is used with the value of a resultative perfect (cf. also our earlier example (118)). Consider, for example (121):

(121) τοὺς τῷ βασιλεῖ μου ὑπηρετοῦντας σεμνοὺς καὶ καθαροὺς χρὴ εἶναι καὶ πάσης λύπης καὶ φροντίδος ἀπαλλαγέντας, τέκνων τε καὶ πλούτου ἀνωφελοῦς καὶ ταραχῆς ματαίας (A. Thom. 126.10–13)

'They who serve my king must be reverend and pure and free from all grief and care of children and unprofitable riches and vain trouble.' (tr. James)

Judas observes that just as a king does not want his soldiers to be filthy, so those who serve God must be pure. ἀπαλλαγέντας 'freed (from)' is coordinated with the true adjectives σεμνούς 'reverend' and καθαρούς 'pure', which strongly suggests the resultative value of the construction.

During MPG, the construction of εἰμί with the perfect participle is still the dominant perfect periphrasis, both for the anterior and resultative perfect function. Some of the tendencies that were observed with regard to EPG persist, however. Consider Table 3.11:

Table 3.11. Distribution of εἰμί with the perfect participle in MPG

Genre/Author/Text	TOT	NRO
Biography/hagiography	254	3.18
Plutarch (b. c.50 AD)	107	2.06
New Testament (I AD)	106	7.23
Greek novel	56	2.81
Achilles Tatius (II AD)	22	5.06
Chariton (II AD)	12	3.17
Xenophon of Ephesus (II–III AD)	11	6.40
Heliodorus (III AD)	9	1.12
Historiography	67	1.31
Flavius Iosephus (b. 37/8 AD)	11	0.85
Cassius Dio (b. c.164 AD)	56	1.47
Scientific prose	298	7.55
Galen (b. 129 AD)	52	3.06
Pausanias (II AD)	246	10.95
Papyri	195	/
Letters	37	/
Petitions	114	/

Key: 'TOT' = total; 'NRO' = normed rate of occurrence (per 10,000 words).

This table shows that compared to EPG εἰμί with the perfect participle occurs roughly with the same frequency. The construction can be found with particular frequency, however, in the New Testament and Pausanias' *Description of Greece*.[216] This may be partly related to genre, since in both cases most of the examples are resultatives (see Table 3.12), and the discourse mode 'description' plays a prominent role in both texts.[217] Register may also play a role, however: the novelists and especially the historiographers use the construction infrequently.

As was noted with regard to EPG, the overall decline in frequency can be (at least partly) explained by morphological factors, most importantly the disappearance of the optative mood. Perhaps unsurprisingly, examples in this mood predominantly occur in the work of authors writing in a higher register, such as Plutarch, Cassius Dio, Achilles Tatius, and Xenophon of Ephesus.[218] The same observation can be made with regard to the construction of εἰμί with the aorist

---

[216] On Pausanias' use of the construction, see also Strid (1976: 96–7).

[217] In the case of the New Testament a description of the people involved, while in that of Pausanias' *Description of Greece* works of art are described.

[218] For some examples, see e.g. Ach. Tat., *Leuc. et Clit.* 4.4.8, 7.1.4, 7.2.1; Cassius Dio, *Hist. Rom.* 36.52.4, 37.8.2, 39.45.3; 41.41.5; Plut., *Alex.* 27.5, 60.9, *Mar.* 8.5; Xen., *Eph.* 2.2.4.

Perfect Aspect 173

participle, which also almost never occurs in the optative.[219] It is also apparent that future perfects have become much less prominent. In the MPG papyri, for example, only five examples can be found,[220] versus one hundred in the EPG papyri. In formulaic expressions, the subjunctive mood (introduced by ἵνα) has now become predominant.

As to the use of εἰμί with the perfect participle in terms of aspect, consider Table 3.12:

Table 3.12. Distribution of εἰμί with the perfect participle in MPG (aspect, voice)

Genre/Author/Text	RES	TTR (RES)	RES (ACT)	RES (MED/PASS)	ANT	TTR (ANT)	ANT (ACT)	ANT (MED)	ANT (PASS)
Biography/hagiography	176	0.63	20	156	78	0.71	23	10	45
Plutarch (b. c.50 AD)	63	0.68	10	53	44	0.82	13	7	24
New Testament (I AD)	77	0.65	9	68	29	0.83	9	3	17
Greek novel	36	0.81	5	31	20	0.95	3	9	8
Achilles Tatius (II AD)	14	0.93	3	11	8	1	2	3	3
Chariton (II AD)	7	1	0	7	5	1	0	1	4
Xenophon Eph. (II–III AD)	10	0.8	1	9	1	1	0	1	0
Heliodorus (III AD)	3	1	0	3	6	0.83	1	4	1
Historiography	28	0.86	7	21	39	0.87	25	6	8
Flavius Iosephus (b. 37/8 AD)	6	1	2	4	5	1	1	1	3
Cassius Dio (b. c.164 AD)	22	0.86	5	17	34	0.91	24	5	5
Scientific prose	216	0.40	27	189	81	0.59	21	14	46
Galen (b. 129 AD)	37	0.78	1	36	15	0.87	7	2	6
Pausanias (II AD)	179	0.35	26	153	66	0.56	14	12	40
Papyri[221]	25	0.68	3	22	163	0.21	17	8	138
Letters	9	1	2	7	23	0.78	8	6	8
Petitions	4	1	0	4	110	0.05	2	0	108

Key: 'RES' = resultative perfect; 'TTR' = type/token ratio; 'ACT' = active; 'MED' = middle; 'PASS' = passive; 'ANT' = anterior perfect.

---

[219] Various examples occur in Achilles Tatius, e.g. *Leuc. et Clit.* 6.8.3, 7.2.2, 7.4.3, 7.9.12. Two examples can also be found in the papyri (both in official documents), P.Oxy.10.1252, ll. 29–30 (289/90 AD) and P.Lond.3.1168, l. 43 (44 AD).

[220] See BGU.2.596, ll. 12–13 (84 AD); P.Bon.43, ll. 10–11 (I AD); P.Mert.2.62, l. 10 (7 AD); P.Oxy.38.2857, l. 6 (134 AD); P.Princ.3.162, ll. 12–13 (89 AD). Cf. Mandilaras (1973: 240), who notes that 'the periphrastic future perfect ... appears to have been dropped from the Roman and Byzantine papyri'.

[221] In a number of papyri the construction seems to be clearly periphrastic, but it is difficult to determine aspectual function due to a lack of context. These include

We see that the construction more and more fulfils a resultative perfect function, thus acquiring an increasingly less transitive profile. This use is attested particularly often in Pausanias, although there is a low type/token ratio of the construction in his *Description of Greece*. The historiographical texts, particularly Cassius Dio, go against this general trend, but perhaps this should not surprise us too much, since these texts are written in a higher register, and are known for their resistance to ongoing change. In the papyri, anterior perfects are quite often attested, but we must again take into account the influence of formulaic language.[222]

Table 3.12 furthermore shows that this functional specialization also concerns voice: while the construction with the aorist participle is predominantly used as an anterior in the active voice, the construction with the perfect participle is predominantly used as a resultative in the medio-passive voice. As in EPG, active resultatives are essentially limited to a few verb classes, including verbs of motion and assuming a position (mainly ἵσταμαι 'I stand'), psych-verbs, and verbs of mental state (πείθομαι 'I trust', γιγνώσκω 'I know', ζηλόω 'I am jealous', σπουδάζω 'I am eager').

Even in its anterior function, εἰμί with the perfect participle is now predominantly used in the passive voice. This is most clear in the papyri, where 85% (= 138/163) of the anterior examples are expressed in the passive voice, versus only 39% (= 99/254) in EPG; again, historiographical works do not follow this general tendency, which can be attributed to the higher register adopted. This may be connected with the disappearance of the synthetic perfect: when the functional merger of and ensuing competition between the synthetic perfect and aorist took place, the former most likely first disappeared in the active voice as an anterior, and subsequently in the middle and passive voice as an anterior, and only in a last stage in the medio-passive as a resultative. This hypothesis is confirmed by Mihevc (1959: 62) to some extent, but is in need of further investigation.

BGU.2.624, l. 5 (284–305 AD); P.Cair.Preis.1, l. 16 (II AD); P.Mich.8.480, l. 10 (II AD); P. Rain.Cent.73, l. 3 (III–IV AD); P.Ryl.2.440, l. 9 (III AD?); P.Wash.Univ.1.4, l. 3 (198/9 AD?); SB.14.11899, l. 15 (II AD).

[222] Even though in many cases the perfect participle occurs in the passive voice, the presence of agent expressions shows that we are dealing with an anterior perfect. See e.g. BGU.2.454, ll. 20–1 (193 AD); P.Flor.3.382, ll. 66–7 (222/3 AD); P.Gen.2.1.28, l. 27 (137 AD); P.Kron.2, ll. 18–19 (127–128 AD); P.Lips.2.146, ll. 16–17 (189 AD); P.Meyer.8, l. 18 (151 AD); P.Mich.6.422, l. 37 (197 AD); P.Tebt.2.332, ll. 20–1 (176 AD).

3.5.2 Language Contact and the Development of ἔχω with the Medio-passive Perfect Participle

As recent studies have shown, language contact can stimulate the grammaticalization of constructions, whereby 'minor-use patterns' become 'major-use patterns'.[223] In this context, scholars have observed the existence of parallel developments in Greek and Latin,[224] drawing attention to the presence of two structurally similar constructions, Greek ἔχω with the medio-passive perfect participle and Latin *habeo* with the passive perfect participle.

Both Horrocks (2010: 131–2) and Bruno (2012) have recently argued that Greek must have borrowed this pattern (HAVE + passive perfect participle) from Latin during the MPG period.[225] In support of this hypothesis, they note that (a) ἔχω with the medio-passive perfect participle does not appear in previous stages of the language (the first examples being attested in Diodorus Siculus),[226] and (b) the construction is predominantly used 'in authors prone to Latinisms', such as Diodorus Siculus and Plutarch.[227] Closer inspection reveals, however, that both arguments cannot hold. It has been shown that the construction can already be found in CG and EPG,[228] especially in texts with a 'scientific' character (the Aristotelic corpus, the Hippocratic corpus and Strabo's *Geography*).[229] As in EPG, the construction can also be found in lower registers in MPG, including the papyri.

---

[223] See e.g. Heine & Kuteva (2005). 'Minor use patterns' are constructions that occur relatively infrequently; 'major use patterns' occur relatively frequently.

[224] See e.g. Bonfante (1960); Coleman (1975); Dubuisson (1985, 1992); Adams (2003); Rochette (2010).

[225] Cf. also Bubenik (2010: 34–5), who notes that 'the post-classical Latin "pseudo-possessive" construction of the type *habeo* + object + perfect participle (in agreement with the object) appears to have been calqued in Greek'.

[226] See esp. Horrocks (2010: 131). On Diodorus Siculus, see further Palm (1955: 95). Cf. similarly Mihevc (1959: 51); Coleman (1975: 115); Browning (1983: 33); Kramer (2004: 136).

[227] Horrocks (2010: 131) further specifies that the construction does not occur in low-level literary or subliterary texts, nor in Atticistic works.

[228] Cf. §3.3.4 and §3.4.3.

[229] Compare Mihevc (1959: 53): 'la naissance de la même périphrase en latin . . . n'a pas pu, à mon avis, exercer une influence remarquable sur le développement en grec, car dans la langue grecque ce mode d'expression était possible déjà assez tôt . . . tandis qu'en latin elle n'était encore longtemps assez stabilisée pour pouvoir influencer un phénomène analogue dans une langue voisine' ('the birth of the same periphrasis in Latin has not, to my mind, exerted a serious influence on the development in Greek, since in the Greek language this type of expression was possible already at an early

176 *Verbal Periphrasis in Ancient Greek*

A full overview of the use and frequency of ἔχω with the (medio-passive) perfect participle is given in Table 3.13:

Table 3.13. Distribution of ἔχω with the (medio-passive) perfect participle in MPG

Genre/Author/Text	TOT	NRO	TTR
Biography/hagiography	54	0.68	0.74
Plutarch (b. *c*.50 AD)	35	0.67	0.77
New Testament (I AD)	10	0.68	0.70
Greek novel	7	0.35	1
Chariton (II AD)	3	0.79	1
Heliodorus (III AD)	1	0.12	1
Historiography	18	0.35	1
Flavius Iosephus (b. 37/8 AD)	6	0.46	1
Cassius Dio (b. *c*.164 AD)	12	0.31	1
Scientific prose	40	1.01	0.70
Galen (b. 129 AD)	20	1.18	0.90
Pausanias (II AD)	20	0.89	0.55
Papyri	7	/	1
Letters	3	/	1
Petitions	2	/	1

Key: 'TOT' = total; 'NRO' = normed rate of occurrence (per 10,000 words); 'TTR' = type/token ratio.

This table shows that ἔχω with the medio-passive perfect participle occurs only slightly more frequently than in CG and EPG.[230] While it is true that many examples originate from Plutarch's *Parallel Lives*, various examples can also be found in texts written in a lower register, including biographical/hagiographical texts and scientific prose. Consider the following example from the papyri:[231]

(122) ὥστε πληγ[ῆ]ναι μέν με ἐσθέσθ[αι] [-ca.?- κινδυνεύον-]τος μου κα[ὶ] παρ' αὐτοῦ διαφωνῆ[σαι -ca.?-] δυσας με ἥν <u>εἶχον ἐνδεδυμέν[ην</u> -ca.?-]σας με ἐβάστασεν (P.Flor.1.59, ll. 4–7 (225/241 AD?))

'... so that I felt that I was hit, while I was in danger of even perishing by his hand (?) ... having taken off the clothes which I had put on ... he carried me off (raped me?).'

---

stage ... while in Latin it had not been established for a long enough time to be able to influence an analogous phenomenon in a neighbouring language').
[230] Compare Table 3.5 and Table 3.9.
[231] For similar examples, see e.g. A.Thom. 59.5–6, 63.6, 114.4–5; Heb. 5.14; Lc. 14.18, 14.19, 19.20; Mc. 3.1, 8.17; 2Pet. 2.14; Prec. Josephi 3.10, 27.8; P.Fam.Tebt.24-dupl, 3, l. 79 (124 AD); P.Oxy.50.3555, l. 19 (I/II AD).

While this petition is badly preserved, it is not difficult to make sense of its content: a woman has been attacked, subsequently raped, and asks the (unknown) addressee for a doctor to examine her condition, so that the attacker can be brought to justice. Interestingly, this document, which appears to be poorly written, as a number of orthographical mistakes indicate, also contains an example of ἔχω with the medio-passive perfect participle: ἣν εἶχον ἐνδεδυμέν[ην] 'which I had put on'. While the agreement between the participle with the object indicates that we are dealing with a resultative construction, an anterior inference is certainly not excluded.

Both Horrocks (2010: 131–2) and Bruno (2012) seem to limit their discussion to the use of the construction with an anterior inference, which they formulate in terms of voice.[232] Bruno notes that 'diathetic neutralization'[233] is a feature typical for Latin (which only had the passive participle in the perfect), and notes that this may have been calqued into Greek. She provides the following illustration from Diodorus:

(123) ἐπύθετο τοὺς Γανδαρίδας ἔχειν τετρακισχιλίους ἐλέφαντας πολεμικῶς κεκοσμημένους (Diod. Sic., *Bibl. Hist.* 2.37.3)
'He learned that the Gandaridae had four thousand elephants equipped for war.' (tr. Oldfather, slightly modified)

When Alexander the Great learns that the people of the Gandaridae have four thousand elephants at their disposal, he decides to give up his campaign against them. Bruno (2012: 370) notes that the construction in this example possesses a number of peculiarities, including the fact that the participle is 'diathetically inert': 'it is, in particular, the diathetic neutralization of *-ménos*—a necessary requirement for a reanalysis of the original structure—that appears especially notable in Greek'. As long as there is concord between the object and the participle, however, such 'diathetic neutralization' cannot be taken for granted. In fact, in this example we may not even be dealing with an instance of Carey's (1994) 'resultant state

---

[232] Horrocks (2010: 131) speaks of the use of the construction 'in an active, transitive sense'. Bruno (2012: 370–1) refers to 'active perfects', where the participle is 'diathetically inert'.

[233] With 'diathetic neutralization', Bruno refers to the apparent loss of the passive value of the perfect participle in *-tus* in examples of the type *cognitum habemus* 'we have understood'.

object construction',²³⁴ since ἔχω seems to retain a strong sense of possession.²³⁵ In other words, I do not believe there is much reason to stress the peculiarity of examples such as (123), which at all times remain close to the purely resultative use of the construction.

Recently, a more complex scenario has been argued for by Drinka (2003a, 2003b, 2007), who suggests that language contact must have been *bidirectional* when it comes to the use of HAVE-perfects. She starts from the observation that a HAVE-perfect, namely ἔχω with the aorist participle,²³⁶ was first introduced by the Greeks in the fifth century BC. This construction, she argues, was calqued into Latin by well-educated Romans, who 'had the means and the motivation to bring Greek elements into their language'.²³⁷ Since Latin was more restricted in its use of the participle,²³⁸ however, the (active) aorist participle was replaced by the (medio-passive) perfect participle, as a result of which '[the Romans, KB] were forced to stretch the semantic range of their own participle, causing it to move towards subject-orientation and possible interpretation as an active'.²³⁹ At a later stage, Greeks may have in turn imitated prestigious Romans in their use of *habeo* with the passive perfect participle.

While Drinka's proposal is subtle and well elaborated, it contains a number of problems. First, if we assume that the use of Greek as a second language spread among upper-class Romans beginning only in the third century BC,²⁴⁰ then we must assume that ἔχω with the aorist participle was calqued on the basis of literary works such as those of the tragedians. Even if this would have been the case—and this may be questionable since the construction was never used with a high frequency (with the exception of Sophocles)—we must ask ourselves to what extent the target audience would have recognized this literary reference through the use of *habeo* with the passive perfect participle. Second, it is questionable whether speakers of a language are able to simply 'stretch the semantic range' of the participle, and whether this is also what happened. Most scholars assume a process of gradual development, whereby, according to the grammaticalization process described in the introduction to this chapter, the construction

---

[234] Cf. §3.3.2.1.
[235] For similar examples, see e.g. *Apoc. Joh.* 10.2; Charit. 5.2.2; Lc. 13.6; Plut., *Alex.* 12.1, *Artax.* 25.1, *Caes.* 63.9, *Cam.* 16.3, *Cat. Mi.* 10.2; Xen., *Eph.* 1.8.3.
[236] Cf. §3.3.2.1.   [237] Drinka (2007: 103).
[238] In terms of voice, and by extension aspect.
[239] Drinka (2007: 103).   [240] See e.g. Bruno (2012: 359).

Perfect Aspect

developed from a resultative to an anterior through the process of pragmatic inference.[241] Third, Drinka's account assumes, like Bruno's and Horrocks', that examples of ἔχω with the perfect participle cannot be found at an early stage,[242] but this is manifestly untrue, as we have seen. Already in Classical Greek (especially the fourth century BC) the construction occurs next to ἔχω with the aorist participle.

In conclusion, it seems that the use of ἔχω with the medio-passive perfect participle was not substantially influenced by Latin with regard to frequency or semantics. Rather, I believe we are dealing here with independent parallel developments in genetically related languages. A similar position is taken by Coleman (1975: 117), who notes that 'the primary motivation in each language came... from within its own morphosyntactic system'. Contrary to Coleman, however, I do not believe that ἔχω with the medio-passive perfect participle should be considered a 'replacement' of ἔχω with the aorist participle, which is diachronically untenable. Rather, the starting point for the former was the use of ἔχω with an object and an adjective, prepositional expression, or adverb, examples of which can already be found at an early stage.[243]

3.5.3 'Minor' Periphrastic Constructions

As in EPG, next to εἰμί with the perfect and aorist participle, and ἔχω with the (medio-passive) perfect participle, there are various alternative perfect periphrases, which can be thought of as 'minor' in terms of frequency. During the MPG period, most of these are formed with ἔχω.

A first construction is ἔχω with the aorist participle, which is always used with an anterior function. As in EPG, the construction can only be found in texts written in the high register, like the works of Cassius Dio, Heliodorus, and Plutarch, where it is used in imitation of the Classical authors.[244] Interestingly, the construction is not entirely absent from the papyri:

(124) [ἔ]χω μὲν ὑμῖν καὶ δι' ἑτέρ[ων] μου γραμμάτων προστάξας πεφροντισμ[έ]ν[ως] [τὴ]ν τῶν λῃστῶν ἀναζήτησ[ιν] ποιήσασθαι, κίνδυνον

---

[241] For a recent study, see e.g. Napoli (2007).
[242] Cf. Drinka (2007: 115).   [243] Cf. §3.3.4.
[244] See e.g. Cassius Dio, *Hist. Rom.* 42.20.1, 67.18.1, 75.13.3; Heliod., *Aeth.* 1.8.5, 5.16.4; Plut., *Alex.* 28.2, *Cat. mi.* 45.5, *Dion* 11.6.

ὑμῖν ἐπαρτήσας εἰ ἀμ[ε][λε]ῖτε, καὶ νῦν δὲ διατάγματ[ι. β]εβαιῶσαί μου τὴν γνώμην ἠθέλησα (P.Oxy.12.1408, ll. 12–14 (212–214 AD))

'I have already in a previous letter ordered you to search out robbers with every care, warning you of the peril of neglect, and now I wish to confirm my decision by a decree.' (tr. Grenfell & Hunt)

In this circular from the prefect Iuncinus to the strategi of the Heptanomia and Arsinoïte nomes concerning the suppression of robbers, the construction [ἔ]χω ... προστάξας 'I have ordered' is used as an anterior perfect, expressing the fact that the prefect has given a certain order in the past. Given the formal tone of the message, and the high social status of its author, the appearance of this construction is not entirely surprising.

A second construction with ἔχω, which is only used as a resultative, is ἔχω with the passive aorist participle. This construction can be seen as an analogical extension of ἔχω with the passive perfect participle, whereby the perfect participle is replaced by the aorist participle, perhaps after the example of εἰμί with the perfect and aorist participle.[245] At this stage, only a single example can be found:

(125) καὶ τότε ἡ Κασία περιεζώσατο καὶ <u>ἔσχεν τὴν καρδίαν ἀλλοιωθεῖσαν</u> ὡς μηκέτι ἐνθυμεῖσθαι τὰ κοσμικά (T. Job 49.1)

'Then the other daughter, Kassia by name, put on the girdle, and she had her heart transformed, so that she no longer wished for worldly things.' (tr. James, slightly modified)

Here we read how Job gives one of his daughters a girdle, and her heart is changed. This is expressed by means of a periphrastic form, ἔσχεν τὴν καρδίαν ἀλλοιωθεῖσαν 'she had her heart transformed', which expresses the stative relation between the heart and its altered state.

During the MPG period we also find an entirely new construction, which is formed by ἔχω and a present or aorist participle and a temporal adjunct. Consider example (126):[246]

---

[245] Cf. §3.5.1.
[246] For similar examples, see e.g. A. Thom. 43.19–20 (with the present participle), 150.9 (with the aorist participle).

(126) κάθηται ἐπὶ τῆς κοπρίας ἔξω τῆς πόλεως· <u>ἔχει</u> γὰρ εἴκοσι ἔτη μὴ <u>ἀνελθών</u> ἐν τῇ πόλει (T. Job 28.8)
'He is sitting upon the dung-hill outside of the city for he has not entered the city for seven years.' (tr. James)

Four kings, after hearing of Job's bad physical condition, decide to visit him, and ask where he can be found. They are told that he is sitting on a dung-hill outside the city, which he has not visited in seven years. The γάρ-clause contains a periphrastic form, ἔχει... ἀνελθών 'he has gone up', which can be interpreted as a perfect of persistence: for a period of seven years a certain action has not taken place up until the present. Formally, this construction has some affinity with ἔχω with the aorist participle,[247] but the fact that this construction can be found in a low-register text such as the *Testament of Job* shows that we are dealing here with two separate constructions. Functionally, too, the constructions differ, since ἔχω with the aorist participle is mostly used as a perfect of current relevance, while ἔχω with a present or aorist participle and a temporal adjunct is always used as a perfect of persistence.

One final construction to consider is εἰμί with the present participle. In principle, the possibility that this construction would be used as a perfect periphrasis seems excluded, given that the present participle expresses imperfective aspect. However, in several examples where the present participle of lexically telic verbs is used in the passive voice, the value of the construction seems to approach that of a resultative or even anterior perfect. For instance, in the papyri we find several examples of the following type:[248]

(127) ἐπεὶ οὖν ὁ κύριος ἡμῶν Ἀδριανὸς ... ἐκούφισεν τῶν ἐνχωρίων τὰ βάρη καθολικῶς διὰ προγράμματος, ἀξιῶ ... ἀπολυθῆναι ... ἵν' <u>ὦ</u> [ἐκ τῶ]ν τοῦ κ[υ]ρίου ἐντολῶν <u>προν[οο]ύμενο[ς]</u> (P.Giss.7, 2, ll. 10–22 (117 AD))
'Since now our lord Hadrian generally lightened the loads of the locals through an edict, I demand ... to be acquitted, so that I will have been taken care of by the edict of our lord.'

In this petition addressed to the strategus Apollonius, a peasant asks on the basis of an edict by Hadrian for ἀπόλυσις for half of his land.

---

[247] Note that Mihevc (1959: 48) discusses this construction together with regular instances of ἔχω with the aorist participle.
[248] For a similar example, see P.Mil.Vogl.2.71, l. 26 (172–175 AD).

When granted, he will have been taken care of by Hadrian's edict. As we have seen, in EPG closing formulas of this type were formed predominantly in the active voice, with a perfect participle. In MPG, the passive perfect participle comes to be more often employed (often with an explicit agent), or in the active voice the aorist participle. Quite exceptionally, we also find the present participle, apparently with an anterior value similar to that of the perfect and aorist participle. Most likely, this innovation can be attributed to the overall changes regarding the participle discussed in §3.4.1.

Another example in which we see strong indications that εἰμί with the present participle may be used as a perfect periphrasis is the following:

(128) καὶ οἱ δάκτυλοι τῶν ποδῶν μέρος μέν τι σιδηροῦν μέρος δέ τι ὀστράκινον, μέρος τι τῆς βασιλείας ἔσται ἰσχυρὸν καὶ ἀπ' αὐτῆς ἔσται συντριβόμενον (Dan. (Theodot.) 2.42)

'And the toes of the feet, partly of iron but partly of earthenware: part of the kingdom will be strong and some of it will be broken.' (NETS)

King Nebuchadnezzar has had a dream, in which he saw a gigantic image, which had its feet partly of iron and partly of earthenware. Daniel explains to the king that this means that the kingdom will be partly strong and partly broken. In the version by Theodotion (second century AD), ἰσχυρόν is coordinated with the passive present participle συντριβόμενον. However, an earlier version exists of this same passage (the so-called 'Old Greek version'), where the perfect participle συντετριμμένον is used. In both cases, a property of the kingdom is indicated, its being partly broken.

3.6 LATE POST-CLASSICAL AND EARLY BYZANTINE GREEK (IV-VIII AD)

3.6.1 εἰμί with the Perfect and Aorist Participle: A Shift in Dominance

In his historical grammar, Jannaris (1897: 498) observes that:

> Since B [Byzantine times, that is, 600–1000 AD, KB], if not earlier, Greek speech formed the compound tenses (perfect, pluperfect, future perfect) by means of ἔχω and εἶμαι ... with the participle perfect passive ... as in

Perfect Aspect 183

modern languages, ἔχω serves for the active, and εἶμαι... for the passive and neuter voice.

As we shall see in the final section of this chapter, this situation, which is reminiscent of many modern European languages, is certainly not yet the case in the Late Post-Classical (IV–VI AD) and Early Byzantine (VII–VIII AD) period: the main opposition is that between εἰμί with the perfect participle and εἰμί with the aorist participle. While to some extent this was already the case in MPG, the opposition now becomes firmly established, as is shown in Table 3.14:

Table 3.14. Distribution of εἰμί with the perfect and the aorist participle in LPG & EBG

Genre/Author/Text	TOT (εἰμί + perf. part.)	NRO (εἰμί + perf. part.)	TOT (εἰμί + aor. part.)	NRO (εἰμί + aor. part.)
Biography/hagiography	237	2.47	178	1.86
Acts of Philip (IV AD)	12	5.50	4	1.83
Life of Pachomius (V AD)	10	3.85	6	2.31
John Moschus (b. *c*.550 AD)	7	1.37	22	4.31
Life of Symeon Stylites the Younger (VI AD)	22	4.05	3	0.55
Pope Zacharias (b. 679 AD)	12	6.57	12	6.57
George of Syceon (VII AD)	25	4.74	19	3.60
Leontius of Naples (VII AD)	10	2.58	36	9.28
Miracles of St. Artemius (VII AD)	13	6.31	2	0.97
Historiography	117	1.50	118	1.51
Theodoretus of Cyrrhus (b. *c*.393 AD)	11	1.57	3	0.43
John Malalas (b. *c*.491 AD)	13	1.42	55	6.03
Sozomenus (V AD)	14	1.27	4	0.36
Zosimus (V AD)	18	2.88	7	1.12
Paschal Chronicle (VII AD)	17	1.34	18	1.42
Theophanes Confessor (b. *c*.760 AD)	20	1.48	25	1.85
Scientific prose	76	1.97	19	0.49
John Philoponus (b. *c*.490 AD)	15	2.32	4	0.62
Cosmas Indicopleustes (VI AD)	23	2.59	5	0.56
Paul of Aegina (VII AD)	38	1.84	5	0.24
Papyri	21	/	19	/
Letters	7	/	10	/
Petitions	2	/	6	/

Key: 'TOT' = total; 'NRO' = normed rate of occurrence (per 10,000 words).

184   *Verbal Periphrasis in Ancient Greek*

The data in this table suggest that the opposition between the two constructions exists mainly with respect to biography/hagiography and historiography: in these genres, εἰμί with the aorist participle becomes more frequent especially during the Early Byzantine period, in the work of writers such as Pope Zacharias, Leontius of Naples, and George of Syceon.[249]

The distribution of the two constructions can be connected in part to genre and register: as in MPG, εἰμί with the perfect participle, which is mostly used as a resultative perfect,[250] occurs frequently in biographical/hagiographical texts, where the 'descriptive' discourse mode plays an important role. Rather surprisingly, however, authors of scientific texts, where both 'description' and 'information' are important modes of discourse, do not seem particularly prone to the use of the construction. As for εἰμί with the aorist participle, its use is almost entirely limited to texts written in a lower register—that is, biographical and hagiographical ones. In historiography, too, the construction almost exclusively occurs in lower-register chronicles such as those by John Malalas and Theophanes Confessor. That the construction does not occur more frequently in scientific prose, which is also written in a lower register, can be explained by the fact that the construction is predominantly used with an anterior aspectual function,[251] which is not often called for in scientific texts.

Somewhat surprisingly, the rise of εἰμί with the aorist participle is not observed in the papyri, where the construction actually occurs less frequently than in MPG (nineteen examples in LPG and EBG vs. twenty-three in MPG), though in a wider range of documents: it no longer occurs predominantly in private letters. However, we must take into account the lesser availability of papyrus documents in LPG and especially EBG.[252] The same observation must be made with regard to εἰμί with the perfect participle in the LPG and EBG papyri, where we observe a quite spectacular decrease in frequency (twenty-one examples in LPG and EBG, vs. 195 in MPG).

As discussed in §3.5.1, the functional opposition between εἰμί with the perfect participle and εἰμί with the aorist participle can be conceived of in terms of aspect: the former construction is predominantly used with a resultative aspectual function, which is indicative of low

---

[249] Also note the high frequency in John Malalas and John Moschus.
[250] See Table 3.15.   [251] See Table 3.16.   [252] Cf. fn. 29 (Introduction).

Perfect Aspect

transitivity. This can be seen in the many examples where the perfect participle is coordinated with a regular adjective, as in (129):[253]

(129) ὁ γὰρ αὐτὸς πρᾶός τε ἦν καὶ δραστήριος, σώφρων, δίκαιος, ἀνδρεῖος, σοφὸς καὶ πρὸς πᾶν τῆς ἀρετῆς κάλλος ἀπεξεσμένος (Gr. Presb., V. Gr. Naz. 20.15–17)
'For he himself was mild and efficacious, prudent, just, brave, wise, and polished towards all the beauty of virtue.'

Gregory the Presbyter narrates how a church council had convened to elect the new bishop of Constantinople. At the head of the council is a certain Meletius, who is described as being mild, prudent, brave, etc.

εἰμί with the aorist participle, on the other hand, is predominantly employed in contexts of higher transitivity as an anterior perfect; however, it is nowhere used with a perfective aspectual function. It can be found very often in clauses containing γάρ 'for', less often οὖν 'therefore', providing background information. In the works of John Moschus, John Malalas, and Leontius of Naples, for example, out of a total of seventy-four main-clause anterior examples, the construction can be found in forty-six cases with γάρ (= 62%). Alternatively, it can be found in relative subordinate clauses, which often have a similar 'explanatory' function. Consider (130) and (131):

(130) ἐν δὲ τῷ μεταξὺ συνέβη ἀσθενῆσαι τὸν θειότατον Ἰουστῖνον ἐκ τοῦ ἕλκους οὗ εἶχεν ἐν τῷ ποδί· ἦν γὰρ λαβὼν ἐν τῷ τόπῳ σαγίτταν ἐν πολέμῳ, καὶ ἐξ αὐτοῦ ὁ κίνδυνος τῆς ζωῆς αὐτοῦ ἐγένετο (Jo. Mal., Chron. 424.14–17)
'Meanwhile the most sacred Justin became ill from the ulcer which he had on his foot, for he had been struck there in battle by an arrow and that is what caused the danger to his life.' (tr. Jeffreys et al.)

(131) καταλαβόντες οὖν τοὺς ἁγίους τόπους καὶ εὐξάμενοι ἔρχονται καὶ ἐπὶ τὴν ἔρημον τῆς Νεκρᾶς θαλάσσης, εἰς ἣν καὶ ἦσαν ὑπαναχωρήσαντες οἱ ἀείμνηστοι Ἰωάννης καὶ Συμεών (Leont. N., V. Sym. 86.20-2)
'Thereupon they came to the Holy Places, and after they had prayed, they went also to the desert of the Dead Sea, to which John and Symeon of everlasting memory had withdrawn themselves.' (tr. Krueger, slightly modified)

---

[253] For similar examples, see e.g. Cyr. S., V. Euthym. 37.18; Eus., H.E. 1.7.10, 6.31.1, V.C. 4.29.5; Geo. Syc., V. Theod. Syc. 102.3, Gr. Nyss., V. Macr. 4.14–15, 19.5, V. Mos. 2.174; Marc. Diac., V. Porph. 85.4; Thdt., H.E. 318.17–19; V. Pach. 117.2.

In the first example John Malalas narrates how Justin became ill because of an ulcer on his foot. This ulcer, we read in a γάρ-clause, is the result of an injury he had suffered in battle. Periphrastic ἦν...λαβών 'he had gotten' refers to a past event, his being struck by an arrow, which is relevant at a later time in the past, his becoming sick. In the second example we read how two monks cannot agree on a question and decide to bring the matter to the monks of the desert of the holy Jordan, who apparently have a great reputation. They visit the Holy Places, and afterwards go to the desert of the Dead Sea. About this desert further information is provided in the relative clause—that is, that at an earlier time John and Symeon had withdrawn themselves to this place (ἦσαν ὑπαναχωρήσαντες 'they had withdrawn themselves'). This information proves to be relevant for what is to come, since the two monks then find Father John, who has achieved a high level of virtue.

As we saw in §3.5.1, to a large extent the functional opposition between the two constructions is not only one of aspect but also of voice. Consider Table 3.15 with regard to εἰμί with the perfect participle. Table 3.15 confirms that εἰμί with the perfect participle was mainly used as a resultative perfect in LPG and EBG, especially in biography/hagiography (with 179/237 = 78%). In all genres, resultatives are predominantly expressed in the mediopassive voice: active resultatives can only be found with a number of verb classes, such as verbs of motion (e.g. ἵσταμαι 'I stand'), psych-verbs, and mental state verbs (e.g. θαρρέω 'I feel confident', οἶδα 'I know', πείθομαι 'I trust'), verbs of appearance and disappearance (e.g. θνήσκω 'I die'), and verbs of change of state (e.g. γηράσκω 'I grow old', σήπομαι 'I become rotten'). The table furthermore shows that the construction could also be used as an anterior perfect. As in MPG, such examples can be found most often in historiography; even in higher-register texts, anteriors are mainly expressed in the passive voice.

Now consider Table 3.16, which shows the distribution of εἰμί with the aorist participle in terms of aspect and voice. Table 3.16 confirms that εἰμί with the aorist participle primarily functioned as an anterior perfect, mostly in the active voice. That there are still so many examples in the active voice may be somewhat surprising, since, as noted in §3.4.1, the active participle slowly started to decay, and this also had its effect on the use of

Table 3.15. Distribution of εἰμί with the perfect participle in LPG & EBG (aspect, voice)

Genre/Author/Text	RES	TTR (RES)	RES (ACT)	RES (MED/PASS)	ANT	TTR (ANT)	ANT (ACT)	ANT (MED)	ANT (PASS)
Biography/hagiography									
Acts of Philip (IV AD)	179	0.60	22	157	58	0.72	24	6	28
Life of Pachomius (V AD)	11	0.91	1	10	1	1	0	0	1
John Moschus (b. c.550 AE)	9	1	0	9	1	1	1	0	0
Life of Symeon Stylites the Younger (VI AD)	6	1	1	5	1	1	0	0	1
	22	0.77	3	19	0	0	0	0	0
Pope Zacharias (b. 679 AD)	6	0.83	0	6	6	1	4	0	2
George of Syceon (VII AD)	20	0.45	6	14	5	1	5	0	0
Leontius of Naples (VII AD)	6	1	0	6	4	1	2	0	2
Miracles of St. Artemius (VII AD)	9	0.88	2	7	4	0.75	2	0	2
Historiography	76	0.71	13	63	41	0.78	12	1	28
Theodoretus of Cyrrhus (b. c.393 AD)	8	1	1	7	3	1	2	1	0
John Malalas (b. c.491 AD)	10	0.90	3	7	3	0.67	0	0	3
Sozomenus (V AD)	7	0.43	1	6	7	0.86	1	0	6
Zosimus (V AD)	10	0.90	3	7	8	0.75	1	0	7
Paschal Chronicle (VII AE)	16	0.81	3	13	1	1	1	0	0
Theophanes Confessor (b. c.760 AD)	13	1	1	12	7	1	3	0	4
	62	0.84	11	51	14	0.64	6	3	5
Scientific prose									
John Philoponus (b. c.490 AD)	15	0.73	1	14	0	0	0	0	0
Cosmas Indicopleustes (VI AD)	18	0.78	1	17	5	0.80	1	0	4
Paul of Aegina (VII AD)	29	0.97	9	20	9	0.56	5	3	1
	13	0.92	1	12	8	0.86	4	2	2
Papyri									
Letters	6	1	1	5	1	1	0	1	0
Petitions	0	0	0	0	2	2	1	0	1

Key: 'RES' = resultative; 'TTR' = type/token ratio; 'ACT' = active; 'MED' = middle; 'PASS' = passive; 'ANT' = anterior.

Table 3.16. Distribution of εἰμί with the aorist participle in LPG & EBG (aspect, voice)

Genre/Author/Text	RES	TTR (RES)	RES (ACT)	RES (MED/PASS)	ANT	TTR (ANT)	ANT (ACT)	ANT (MED)	ANT (PASS)
Biography/hagiography									
Acts of Philip (IV AD)	25	1	0	25	149	0.72	90	36	23
Life of Pachomius (V AD)	0	0	0	0	4	0.75	2	2	0
John Moschus (b. c.550 AD)	2	1	0	2	4	1	1	1	2
Life of Symeon Stylites the Younger (VI AD)	4	1	0	4	18	0.83	10	6	2
Pope Zacharias (b. 679 AD)	1	1	0	1	2	1	2	0	0
George of Syceon (VII AD)	1	1	0	1	10	0.80	9	0	1
Leontius of Naples (VII AD)	6	1	0	6	12	1	8	4	0
Miracles of St. Artemius (VII AD)	2	1	0	2	34	0.88	26	5	3
	0	0	0	0	2	1	2	0	0
Historiography									
Theodoretus of Cyrrhus (b. c.393 AD)	8	0.75	0	8	110	0.66	71	21	18
Sozomenus (V AD)	0	0	0	0	3	1	3	0	0
John Malalas (b. c.491 AD)	0	0	0	0	4	1	1	1	2
Zosimus (V AD)	4	0.75	0	4	51	0.67	34	8	9
Paschal Chronicle (VII AD)	0	0	0	0	7	1	5	2	0
Theophanes Confessor (b. c.760 AD)	1	1	0	1	17	0.94	9	3	5
	3	1	0	3	22	0.86	15	5	2
Scientific prose									
John Philoponus (b. c.490 AD)	5	0.60	0	5	14	0.87	12	0	2
Cosmas Indicopleustes (VI AD)	3	0.33	0	3	0	0	0	0	0
Paul of Aegina (VII AD)	0	0	0	0	2	1	1	0	1
	2	1	0	2	3	1	3	0	0
Papyri									
Letters	0	0	0	0	18	0.72	12	0	6
Petitions	0	0	0	0	10	1	7	0	3
	0	0	0	0	5	0.60	5	0	0

Key: 'RES' = resultative; 'TTR' = type/token ratio; 'ACT' = active; 'MED' = middle; 'PASS' = passive; 'ANT' = anterior.

periphrastics.[254] According to Giannaris (2011a: 11), the fact that we do not see any traces of rigidification of the participle[255] can be attributed to the fact that 'the majority of the Early Medieval texts represent a middle register Greek rather than the spoken language of the period.'

There are various examples in which the aorist participle takes the passive voice. These may be anteriors, as in (132):[256]

(132) καὶ τὸ δὲ λεγόμενον Στρατήγιον ἀνενέωσεν ὁ αὐτὸς Σέβηρος· πρῴην γὰρ ἦν κτισθὲν ὑπὸ Ἀλεξάνδρου τοῦ Μακεδόνος, ὅτε κατὰ Δαρείου ἐπεστράτευσεν, ὃς καὶ ἐκάλεσε τὸν τόπον Στρατήγιον (Jo. Mal., Chron. 292.15–17)

'Severus also reconstructed what is known as the Strategion, which had been built formerly by Alexander of Macedon when he campaigned against Dareios. He had named the place Strategion.' (tr. Jeffreys et al.)

John Malalas describes how Severus reconstructed a building called the Strategion. About this building further information is provided in a γάρ-clause, which, as we have seen, is a typical environment for the construction of εἰμί with the aorist participle. Since the periphrastic construction in this example is accompanied by an agent (ὑπὸ Ἀλεξάνδρου τοῦ Μακεδόνος 'by Alexander of Macedon') in principle it is not less transitive than what we have seen in (130) and (131), although it can be thought of as a less prototypical representation of the past event.

Alternatively, εἰμί with the passive aorist participle also seems to have been used as a resultative perfect on a larger scale than previously thought,[257] thus encroaching upon the domain of εἰμί with the medio-passive perfect participle. This is a use that occurs exclusively

---

[254] The same observation is made by Horrocks (2010: 131): 'but as the use of the inflected participles of the 3rd declension (i.e. present/future/aorist active, and aorist passive) began to wither away, in part because of their morphological complexity... the periphrasis with the perfect passive participle, which deployed a combination of "regular" 2nd- and 1st-declension endings... emerged as the major survivor in popular Greek of the medieval period. *None the less, the use of the past tense of "be" with an aorist active participle... is also well attested as a pluperfect substitute* (my emphasis, KB).'

[255] In the sense that the participle lost more and more ground morphologically.

[256] For similar examples, see e.g. A. Barn. 7.8–9; Chron. Pasch. 622.12–13; Gr. Presb., V. Gr. Naz. 3.16; Jo. Mal., Chron. 55.18, 389.13–14, 445.14–15, 463.2–3; Leont. N., V. Jo. Eleem. 353.29; Soz., H.E. 9.9.1; Thphn., Chron. 420.20.

[257] Björck (1940: 74ff.) does not seem to take this use into account. Aerts (1965: 87) only briefly mentions the phenomenon.

in lower-register texts, i.e. biography/hagiography and chronicles. Consider (133):[258]

(133) παρέστη ἄγγελος τοῦ Θεοῦ ἔχων κρατῆρα καὶ ἔριφον αἰγῶν καὶ μάχαιραν, καὶ λαβὼν ἔσφαξεν ἐνώπιόν μου καὶ ὑπεδέξατο τὸ αἷμα ἐν τῷ κρατῆρι, καὶ εἶδον τὸ αἷμα καὶ ἰδοὺ <u>ἦν πεπηγὸς</u> καὶ <u>τυρωθὲν</u> ὡς γάλα
(V. Sym. Styl. J. 166.5–8)
'An angel of the Lord presented itself holding a bowl, a young goat, and a dagger, and having taken [the dagger] he slaughtered [the goat] before my eyes, and he collected the blood in the bowl, and I saw the blood and behold it was coagulated and curdled as milk.'

In this passage, a vision that Simeon the Stylite had when he was young is narrated: an angel came to him, slaughtered a goat, and collected its blood in a crater. The blood has some special properties: it is coagulated (πεπηγός) and curdled (τυρωθέν) as milk. This is a particularly interesting example, since the coordination of the (active) perfect participle and the passive aorist participle quite strongly indicates the resultative character of the latter. There are also some examples attested where the construction is accompanied by a durative adverbial,[259] or where the aorist participle is coordinated with a regular adjective,[260] pointing in the same direction.

With regard to εἰμί with the aorist participle, Björck (1940: 78–80) and Aerts (1965: 76–7) have observed that the construction occurs predominantly in the indicative imperfect.[261] Thus, they suggest that it was a substitute for the synthetic past perfect,[262] which, as we have noted in §3.4.1, disappeared at an earlier time than the present perfect.[263] While my own research confirms this observation (with 90% (300/334) of the examples being used in the imperfect), a number of other factors may play an important role when it comes to this observation: (a) at the time of its greatest extension, the indicative was the main mood in which εἰμί with the aorist participle appeared; (b) the texts in which most of the examples of εἰμί with the

---

[258] For similar examples, see e.g. Eustrat., V. Eutych. 1390; Geo. Syc., V. Theod. Syc. 72.32–3, 81.2–3, 106.14–5, 154.30, 161.145, 167.78; Jo. Mal., Chron. 410.6–8; Leont. N., V. Jo. Eleem. 343.10–11; Pall., H. Laus. 44.4; Thphn., Chron. 481.30–1; V. Syncl. 90, 104, 147–8, 1145; Zach. Papa, V. Bened. 28.7.
[259] See e.g. Geo. Syc., V. Theod. Syc. 167.78
[260] See e.g. Jo. Mal., Chron. 410.6–8.
[261] Without mentioning any specific numbers.
[262] Cf. also Mihevc (1959: 50); Moser (1988: 231); Horrocks (2010: 131).
[263] Though at a later time than the future perfect.

Perfect Aspect

aorist participle are found by Björck (1940), Aerts (1965), and others are primarily of a narrative character,[264] since we find almost no instances in the papyri;[265] (c) the construction was predominantly used as an anterior perfect and was functionally opposed to εἰμί with the perfect participle. All three factors seem to have stimulated the use of εἰμί with the aorist participle as a past perfect, which is confirmed by an analysis of εἰμί with the perfect participle as an anterior perfect in the indicative mood. Consider Table 3.17 (based on literary texts):

Table 3.17. Distribution of εἰμί with the perfect participle from CG to EBG (aspect, tense)

	ANT	IND	IMPF	%IMPF/IND
CG	867	481	204	42%
EPG	123	94	62	66%
MPG	218	157	94	60%
LPG & EBG	113	83	64	77%

Key: 'ANT' = anterior perfect; 'IND' = indicative; 'IMPF' = imperfect.

This table shows that in the indicative mood anterior εἰμί with the perfect participle, too, was predominantly used in the imperfect tense. This is not the case for Classical Greek, for which the corpus also contains non-narrative texts. Two more elements should also be kept in mind. First, the use of εἰμί with the aorist participle in the present or future tense is attested, contrary to what Björck (1940) and Aerts (1965) seem to suggest: examples of its use as a present perfect are attested in John Malalas, Leontius of Naples, and the Paschal Chronicle among others,[266] and a few examples of its use as a future perfect can be found in formulaic expressions in the papyri (as in our example (119)),[267] though not in LPG/EBG. Second, if εἰμί with the aorist participle really functioned as a substitute for the synthetic past perfect, we would expect it to be used with both resultative and anterior aspectual functions. This, however, as shown in Table 3.16, does not seem to have been the case. In conclusion, it seems that εἰμί with the aorist participle is best characterized as a general (that is,

---

[264] Contrary to Classical Greek, for which we also have speeches.
[265] At least partly due to a decline in the total number of texts available.
[266] See *Chron. Pasch.* 327.1, Jo. Mal., *Chron.* 131.14; Leont. N., *V. Sym.* 86.15 16.
[267] Cf. also P.Oxy.42.3067, ll. 11–12 (III AD).

192 *Verbal Periphrasis in Ancient Greek*

present/past/future) perfect periphrasis, even though it was predominantly used as a past anterior.

3.6.2 Constructions with ἔχω

Some disagreement exists in the scholarly literature regarding the use of HAVE-perfects in general and ἔχω with the medio-passive perfect participle in particular in LPG and EBG. While scholars such as Jannaris (1897: 498)[268] stress the importance of the construction at an early time, Horrocks (2010: 131–2) has more recently noted that after a sudden rise in the MPG period,

> It [ἔχω with the medio-passive perfect participle, KB] quickly disappeared even from stylistically middle-brow compositions, and eventually reappears in popular varieties of Greek only after the 'Latin' conquest of much of the Byzantine empire after the capture of Constantinople by the fourth crusade in 1204.[269]

The truth seems to lie somewhere in the middle: the construction continues to be found with more or less the same frequency as in MPG (with an average NRO of 0.45 instances per 10,000 words, based on literary works), but it is nowhere used as Carey's (1994) 'resultant state process construction',[270] let alone as a true anterior perfect construction. Various characteristics indicate the resultative character of the construction, such as the combination of the construction with durative adverbs,[271] its use with inanimate subjects,[272] the presence of an external agent phrase,[273] and the coordination of the perfect participle with regular adjectives.[274]

The construction predominantly occurs in biographical/hagiographical texts (NRO 0.56 instances per 10,000 words) and scientific texts (NRO 0.52 instances per 10,000 words). Especially in the former does

---

[268] Cf. §3.6.1.
[269] Compare also Mihevc (1959: 51); Browning (1983: 33); Moser (1988: 240). Mihevc (1959: 52) notes that the construction did not become frequent until the fourteenth/fifteenth century.
[270] Cf. §3.3.2.1. For instances of this use in later Byzantine Greek, see Moser (1988: 241).
[271] See e.g. M. Pion. 22.1; Soz., H.E. 7.28.2; V. Sym. Styl. J. 153.1–2.
[272] See e.g. Cyr. S., V. Euthym. 53.11–12.
[273] See e.g. V. Alex. Acoem. 697.12–13; V. Sym. Styl. J. 75.1–2.
[274] See e.g. Jo. Mosch., Prat. 70.15–16; Soz., H.E. 2.4.4; V. Sym. Styl. J. 153.1–2.

the construction get used often to describe the (bad) physical state of the main subjects: their abdomen, eyes, feet, flesh, hands, heart, tongue, sight, even their testicles.[275] An example is given in (134):

(134) ἄλλον ἄγροικον ὀνόματι Τρύφωνα ἤνεγκαν σεσηπότα ἔχοντα τὸν πόδα πρὸς τὸ θεραπευθῆναι αὐτὸν ὑπὸ τοῦ ἁγίου (Call., V. Hyp. 40.17)
'They brought another person, a countryman named Tryphon, who had his foot gangrened, so that he could be healed by the saint.'

Here, rustic Tryphon's bad condition is expressed through a periphrasis: σεσηπότα ἔχοντα τὸν πόδα 'having his foot gangrened'. Examples such as these can be compared with those of εἰμί with the medio-passive perfect participle. The latter can also be used to express a state, but offers a different construal of the scene.[276] Compare (134) with a phrase from the same work: ὁ γὰρ μηρὸς αὐτοῦ ὅλος ἦν σεσηπώς (Call., V. Hyp. 28.1) 'for his thigh was entirely suppurated'. Here the body part constitutes the syntactic subject, rather than the object, the participle is in the nominative, and the possessor is in the genitive.

Examples of ἔχω with the medio-passive perfect participle also occur in the papyri, but mostly within the formulaic expression ἐρρωμένην/ ἐρρωμένας ἔχοντες τὴν διάνοιαν / τὰς διανοίας / τὰς φρένας 'having the mind in good health'. This phrase is used in contracts or wills[277] as an affirmation that the person signing the document is sane.

As in all of the previous stages, there are also a limited number of examples where an anterior inference is possible, though not necessary. Such examples do not seem to increase in frequency. An example is given in (135):

(135) ἐς τοῦτο ὑπετύφετο μεγαλαυχίας ὥστε ἐτύγχανε μὲν ὅμηρον τὸν ἑαυτοῦ δεδωκὼς υἱόν, ἕως ἂν ἀποδῷ τοὺς αἰχμαλώτους, οὓς ἐκ τῆς καταδρομῆς εἶχε συνηρπασμένους, τούτους δὲ οὐκ ἀποδιδοὺς ἀπῄτει τὸν ὅμηρον, πολλὰ ἀπειλῶν, εἰ μὴ λάβοι (Eunap., Fragm. 1.221.18-22)

---

[275] See e.g. A. Phil. 12.3; Call., V. Hyp. 40.17; Geo. Syc., V. Theod. Syc. 91.4, 157.34-5; Jo. Mosch., Prat. 47.48-9; Marc. Diac., V. Porph. 90.4-5; xlv mir. Artem. 39.10, 72.25-6, 74.20; Sophr. H., Mir. Cyr. et Jo. 46.14; V. Marth. 71.8, 11-12; V. Sym. Styl. J. 142.2-3, 153.1-2.
[276] Cf. our earlier observations in §3.3.4.
[277] See e.g. P.Cair.Masp.3.67312, l. 12 (567 AD); P.Lond.1.77, l. 11 (VIII AD); P. Lond.5.1727, l. 18 (584 AD); P.Muench.1.8, l. 8 (c.540 AD); P.Oxy.20.2283, l. 8 (586 AD); Stud.Pal.1.1, ll. 2-3 (480 AD).

'He burned with such a measure of arrogance that, when he handed over his own son as hostage until he returned the captives whom he had taken in his raid, he demanded the return of the hostage even though he had not restored the captives, making many threats if this were not done.' (tr. Blockley, slightly modified)

The German Vadomar is presented as an arrogant person. To illustrate his arrogance, Eunapius narrates how, when Vadomar had handed over his son as a hostage until he returned certain captives, he demanded to have his son back before actually returning the captives. While εἶχε συνηρπασμένους could perhaps be interpreted as referring to a past event, with Vadomar as the agent, as Blockley in his translation seems to, the use of ἐκ τῆς καταδρομῆς 'from the raid' (rather than ἐν τῇ καταδρομῇ 'in the raid', which would refer to the actual past event) suggests that a resultative interpretation is to be preferred.

One HAVE-perfect construction that does seem to increase, albeit slightly, in frequency is ἔχω with the present/aorist participle and a temporal adjunct,[278] occurring with an NRO of 0.19 instances per 10,000 words. As already mentioned, this construction is used with one specific anterior subfunction—that is, as a perfect of persistence, which could also be expressed by the synthetic perfect or present/imperfect,[279] or periphrastic εἰμί with the perfect participle.[280] It denotes an event that has started in the past and is ongoing until the time of speaking (in the case of the present perfect), as in (136):

(136) ἰδοὺ τοσούτους χρόνους ἔχω καταναλίσκων τὸ ἔθνος τῶν Χριστιανῶν καὶ οὐκ ἐπάγη ἐν ἐμοὶ βέλος (V. Sym. Styl. J. 186.16–17)

'Behold I have been destroying the Christian people for so many years and there has not been stuck any arrow in me.'

Various scholars have argued that this construction should not be considered periphrastic,[281] suggesting that the accusative of time ought to be considered an object, and that the participle should be understood as an 'explicative' element. In this context, Aerts (1965: 164) draws attention to examples such as the following, which show that the participle could be 'replaced by other ways of expression':

---

[278] For the first instances of this construction, see §3.5.3.
[279] Cf. Smyth (1984 [1920]: 422–4).   [280] See §3.3.3.
[281] See Tabachovitz (1943: 24); Aerts (1965: 164–6); Porter (1989: 490–1).

(137) ἓν ἐξ αὐτῶν ἰδού τέσσαρες μῆνας ἔχει ἐξ ὅτε ἀπέθανεν
(P.Oxy.16.1862, ll. 16–18 (*c.*624 AD))
'Behold, one of them (the horses) died four months ago (lit. it has four months since it died).'

And yet, from a diachronic point of view it is not uncommon for two elements of a construction to be functionally and syntactically autonomous to some extent. A scenario whereby the accusative came to be reanalysed as an accusative of time, and ἔχω together with the present or aorist participle as a periphrasis, is not implausible. As noted by Aerts (1965: 65–6), in one example ἔχω is accompanied by ἐξ ἧς 'since' rather than an accusative, which can be taken as a sign of reanalysis.

One context that may have stimulated such a process of form-function reanalysis is where ἔχω is accompanied by a temporal element, a locative element, and a participle, as in (138):[282]

(138) ἰδοὺ ὡς ὁρᾷς με γέροντα ἄνθρωπον· τεσσαρακοστὸν ἔτος <u>ἔχω</u> ἐν ταύτῃ τῇ κέλλῃ <u>φροντίζων</u> τῆς ἐμαυτοῦ σωτηρίας (Pall., *H. Laus.* 23.3)
'As you see, I am an old man now. I have been concerned with my salvation for a period of forty years in this very cell.' (tr. Meyer)

Palladius describes how he came across a certain monk Pachon, who is about sixty years old and advanced in the practice of asceticism. Palladius informs this monk of his troubled mind, whereupon the monk notes that he has spent forty years in a cell. In contexts such as these the main complement of ἔχω could be either temporal τεσσαρακοστὸν ἔτος or locative ἐν ταύτῃ τῇ κέλλῃ (that is, either '[I have (am) the fortieth year] [in this cell] or '[I am in this cell] [the fortieth year]): both the transitive use and the intransitive use of ἔχω are well established. However, there is an additional ambiguity, since the locative element in turn could be taken with or without the participle (φροντίζων) [I am considering in this cell] [the fortieth year] vs. [I am in this cell] [considering] [the fortieth year]).

That such locative contexts would play a part in the process of reanalysis would not be surprising: functionally, the perfect of persistence function is located in between perfect and imperfective aspect, as it expresses an event that started in the past and is ongoing up until the present (compare English 'I have been coughing since

---

[282] For a similar example, see *Hist. Mon. Aeg.* 14.28–9.

196 *Verbal Periphrasis in Ancient Greek*

Tuesday').[283] As we shall see in the fourth chapter, periphrases in the domain of imperfective aspect often have their origins in locative constructions.[284]

With respect to diachrony, the construction has not yet spread to higher-register texts, and exclusively occurs in lower-register biographical/hagiographical and historiographical texts. Two examples can also be found in the papyri, one of which is the following:[285]

(139) ὡς γὰρ ἔμαθον δύο <u>ἔχει</u> μόν[ας] ἡμέρας <u>ἀπαιτῶν</u> ὁ Φιλόξενος ἐλθὼν ἀφ' Ἡρακλέως καὶ τὰ ζητούμενα ὁλοκότ'τινα πολλά ἐστιν ὡς οἶδέν σου ἡ ἀρετή (P.Mert.1.46, ll. 4–6 (V–VI AD))

'For, as I learnt, Philoxenus, who has come from Heracleopolis, has been only two days collecting and, as your Excellence knows, the number of solidi required is considerable.' (tr. Bell & Roberts)

In this letter, a tax-collector addresses his superior, stressing how hard it is to collect the required taxes. Periphrastic ἔχει... ἀπαιτῶν 'he has been collecting' expresses an event which started in the past, namely collecting taxes, and continues up to the time of writing.

As was already mentioned in §3.5.3, the construction could either be formed with a present or aorist participle (the former being used in the majority of the cases—that is, 63% (= 26/41)). This seems to correlate to some extent with the presence of a negation. Consider the following example:

(140) παρακαλῶ ὑμᾶς τοὺς ξένους ἄνδρας τοὺς ἐλθόντας εἰς τὴν πόλιν ταύτην πάντως ἐμοῦ ἕνεκα καὶ διὰ τὴν πήρωσιν τὴν οὖσαν ἐν ἐμοί, ἵνα κἀγὼ ἰαθῶ. ἰδοὺ γὰρ τρεῖς ἡμέρας <u>ἔχω</u> ὀνείρους <u>βλέπων</u> παραδόξους, καὶ τεσσαράκοντα ἔτη μὴ <u>θεασάμενος</u> τὸ φῶς τοῦ ἡλίου (A. Phil. 14.2)

'I call upon you, strangers who have come to this city, certainly for my sake and because of the disability which is in me, in order that I also may be cured. Look, for three days I have been seeing strange dreams, and I have not seen the light of the sun for forty years.' (tr. Bovon, slightly modified)

A certain Stachys, formerly a persecutor of strangers and Christians, has been blind for forty years. When he hears Philip and his followers

---

[283] This is also indicated by the fact that the perfect of persistence function could be expressed in Ancient Greek by either the synthetic perfect or synthetic present/imperfect (next to the periphrastic constructions discussed in this study).
[284] See further §4.3.2.
[285] For the second example, see P.Oxy.16.1855, ll. 9–10 (VI/VII AD).

have come to his city, he decides to ask them to help him with his illness, noting that, although he has been ill for so many years, recently he has been seeing strange dreams. This is an interesting example, because the present and aorist participle (both of a verb of perception) are successively used in combination with ἔχω as perfects of persistence, the former without the negation and the latter with it. Further investigation confirms that in case of negation the aorist participle is used in 82% (= 9/11) of the examples. This can be explained in terms of prototypicality, in the sense that the present participle is used for the more prototypical cases of the perfect of persistence, denoting events that are ongoing up to a certain point in time. The aorist participle, on the other hand, is mostly used for less prototypical cases of the perfect of persistence, denoting events that have not happened and continue not to happen. Similarly, we find that the aorist participle is used in another less prototypical context, to express that a person has been dead for a given period of time.[286]

Another element of variation is the way the temporal adjunct, which is ubiquitous in the examples from LPG and EBG, is expressed. Mostly we get an exact number accompanied by ἡμέραν 'day', μῆνα 'month', ἔτη 'years', or χρόνους 'years'. The number itself, however, can be expressed either as an ordinal or a cardinal number,[287] as shown in (141) and (142):

(141) καὶ ἀπεκρίθη ὁ ὑπουργός· Ὄντως καὶ ἐγὼ εἰκοσιοκτὼ ἔτη ἔχω ὑπουργῶν καὶ οὐδέποτε τοιοῦτόν τι ἐθεασάμην (xlv mir. Artem. 31.16–17)
'And the assistant replied: "Indeed I too have been an assistant for twenty-eight years and I have never witnessed such a thing."' (tr. Crisafulli)

(142) τετάρτην γὰρ ἔχω ἡμέραν μὴ φαγών, καὶ παραμένει μοι ὀχλοῦσα ἡ γαστὴρ καὶ ζητοῦσα τὸ σύνηθες χρέος οὗ ἄνευ ζῆσαι οὐ δύναμαι (Pall., H. Laus. 37.7)
'For it is the fourth day that I have not eaten, and my stomach continues to trouble me and to seek its usual need without which I cannot live.'

---

[286] See e.g. Anton. Hag., V. Sym. Styl. 29.23; Jo. Mosch., Prat. 87.6, 89.51. Note that the present participle is also used with stative lexical verbs. In these cases, however, the state is ongoing during the lifetime of the subject (e.g. to be sick in V. Pach. 115.2-3, to be a doctor in xlv mir. Artem. 31.15).

[287] Out of thirty-five examples with an exact number, eighteen are with a cardinal number and seventeen with an ordinal number.

The semantic difference between the two expressions seems to be that expressions with a cardinal number describe the entire period during which an event has been ongoing, while those with an ordinal number lay greater emphasis on the final day/month/year during which the event has been ongoing: in (141) the long carreer of the assistant who watches the patient is emphasized, while in (142) the fact that it is already the fourth day in a row that the subject has not eaten is stressed. We also find more general expressions such as πολλὴν ὥραν 'for a long time', τοσούτους χρόνους 'for so many years', and πολλὰ ἔτη 'for many years',[288] which semantically/pragmatically resemble the expressions with cardinal numbers.

3.6.3 'Minor' Periphrastic Constructions

As in all of the previous periods, there are also a number of minor periphrastic perfect constructions. As in MPG, these are mostly formed with the verb ἔχω.

One such construction is ἔχω with the active or middle aorist participle. This is a construction that, as we have seen, goes back to Classical Greek,[289] and in EPG and MPG is mainly used in imitation of the Classical authors. The same is true for LPG and EBG, although the construction occurs less frequently.[290] An interesting example can also be found in a fourth-/fifth-century papyrus document:

(143) εἰδοὺ εἰς δύο μῆνας ἡμερῶν ἔχω σοι πέμψας τὴν πᾶσαν ἀπόκρησείν σου καὶ ξενίζομε μέχρει τῆς σήμερον ἡμέρας πῶς... (P.Stras.1.35, ll. 5–7 (IV–V AD))

'Behold it's been two months since I have sent you the entire loan, and I am astonished until today that...'.

It is rather surprising to find a construction such as this in a business letter, which was sent by an estate manager to his lord (probably the leader of a church or monastery). Clearly no attempt is made at writing in a high register, as shown by the manifold orthographical mistakes, and the use of a phrase such as εἰς δύο μῆνας ἡμερῶν to denote 'two months ago'. As Ghedini (1937: 273–4) writes, 'parebbe

---

[288] See e.g. Anton. Hag., V. Sym. Styl. 24.4–5; Geo. Syc., V. Theod. Syc. 159.22; V. Sym. Styl. J. 186.16.
[289] Cf. §3.3.2.1.   [290] See e.g. Soz., H.E. 3.15.10.

Perfect Aspect

che il greco fosse poco familiare allo scrivente'.[291] Preisigke (1912: 129) among others has suggested that he was a Copt. Though Coptic seems to have had a number of periphrastic constructions,[292] a HAVE-perfect does not seem to have been one of them.

Another minor construction, which we first encountered in MPG, is ἔχω with the passive aorist participle. While, as noted in §3.5.3, this construction still occurs very infrequently at this stage, in LPG and EBG it becomes more frequently attested, undoubtedly stimulated by the increased use of εἰμί with the aorist participle, even in the domain of resultative aspect. Consider (144):

(144) ἐγένετο τινα κατασαπεῖσαν ἔχοντα τὴν δεξιὰν χεῖρα ἀνελθεῖν πρὸς τὸν ἅγιον τοῦ Θεοῦ δοῦλον καὶ ἰαθέντα ἀναλῦσαι ἐν τῷ ἰδίῳ οἴκῳ αὐτοῦ
(V. Sym. Styl. J. 234.1–3)
'It happened that someone who had his hand suppurated went up to the holy servant of the Lord, and that when he was healed he returned to his own home.'

In this sentence, which opens the paragraph, an unnamed subject is said to have visited Symeon the Stylite. A periphrastic form is used to specify the reason for his visit: his hand is suppurated (κατασαπεῖσαν ἔχοντα τὴν δεξιάν 'having the right hand suppurated').[293] In the few instances we have of this construction,[294] an anterior inference seems impossible.

Mention can also be made of ἔχω with the medio-passive present participle.[295] In various cases where the verb is lexically telic, the present participle seems to assume the value of a perfect participle fulfilling a resultative function. To what extent the present participle has lost its imperfective (i.e. progressive) aspectual value is difficult to say, however. Consider the following example:[296]

---

[291] 'It seems that the author was not very familiar with Greek'.
[292] See Layton (2004: 342–3).
[293] Compare §3.6.2 for examples of εἰμί with the perfect participle and ἔχω with the medio-passive perfect participle with the same verb (σήπομαι 'I become rotten').
[294] See e.g. Ath., V. Anton. 48.13; Thdr. Stud., Laud. Theoph. Conf. 7.11; V. Syncl. 1038–9.
[295] Cf. also Wolf (1912: 56), who compares the use of εἶχε [τὸ πῦρ] φυλαττόμενον 'he kept guarded' in John Malalas (Chron. 38.8) to Latin habebat (tenebat) asservatum.
[296] For similar examples, see e.g. Call., V. Hyp. 28.7; Sophr. H., Mir. Cyr. et Jo. 30.135 6, 66.48.

(145) μεμυκῶτα γὰρ ἔσχε τὰ ὄμματα, καὶ μηδαμῶς ἀνοιγόμενα (Sophr. H., Mir. Cyr. et Jo. 46.14)

'For he had his eyes closed, and not at all opened.'

In this example, the coordination of the present and the perfect participle, both of which are combined with ἔσχε 'he had', invites us to identify the two semantically: in both cases a state of the eyes is expressed (though note that the latter is accompanied by the negation). Possibly though the use of the perfect vs. present participle is motivated by the fact that closing one's eyes requires less effort than opening them.[297]

The same observation can be made for εἰμί with the passive present participle, which also seems to be used with the value of a resultative (or even anterior) perfect.[298] In the papyri, an example is again attested where a present (rather than perfect or aorist) participle is used in a closing formula to express future gratitude.[299] In this context, Mandilaras has argued that εἰμί (ἔσομαι) with the present participle ἐπιστάμενος 'knowing'[300] is also used with the value of a future perfect.[301] Consider the following example:[302]

(146) ἔσῃ γὰρ ἐπιστάμενος ὡς ἐὰν εὕρωμέν τινα ἀγοράσαντα ἄνωθεν τῆς λεχθείσης κοπῆς ἡκόντων συ γραμμάτων ἡμῶν ἀποδίδουμέν σοι ἀνταπόδοσιν βλάπτουσάν σε (P.Ross.Georg.4.8, ll. 8–10 (710 AD))

'You should be aware that (you will have learnt that?) if we discover anyone who has bought things for more than the tariff stated in our orders, we are going to give you a harmful reprisal in return.' (tr. <http://papyri.info>)

---

[297] From the point of view of transitivity, progressives typically require a higher degree of volitionality.
[298] Cf. §3.5.3.
[299] See P.Herm.9, ll. 11–13 (IV AD).
[300] Similar examples can be found with the active participle γιγνώσκων in P. Lond.4.1394, l. 23 (708–709 AD) and SB.10.10453, l. 20 (709 AD).
[301] Cf. Mandilaras (1973: 240): 'in papyri of the Arab period a periphrasis of ἔσομαι (in the second person singular) with ἐπιστάμενος appears to be equivalent to a sentence such as "you will have learnt (heard)."'
[302] For further examples, see P.Lond.4.1332dupl, l. 12 (708 AD); P.Lond.4.1333-dupl, ll. 13–14 (708 AD); P.Lond.4.1339, l. 17 (709 AD); P.Lond.4.1344, l. 6 (710 AD); P. Lond.4.1346, l. 16 (710 AD); P.Lond.4.1349, l. 31 (710 AD); P.Lond.4.1356, ll. 24–5 (710 AD); P.Lond.4.1362, l. 12 (710 AD); P.Lond.4.1370, ll. 13–14 (710 AD); P.Ross.Georg.4.1, ll. 8–9 (710 AD); P.Ross.Georg.4.6, l. 25 (710 AD); P.Ross.Georg.4.15, l. 10 (710 AD); SB.3.7241, l. 50 (710 AD).

Perfect Aspect

In this letter sent by the governor of Egypt, Kurrah ben Sharik, the pagarch Basil is admonished to instruct the people in his district not to sell any materials at a higher price than he has ordered. If the pagarch should fail to do so, he will be given a harmful reprisal. Whether we are really dealing here with a future perfect seems questionable: since ἐπίσταμαι 'I know' is a stative content verb, it seems much more evident to simply take ἔσῃ... ἐπιστάμενος as a stative periphrasis, with the future tense conferring an imperative-like value ('be aware that...').

For an illustration of this construction from our literary texts, consider (147):[303]

(147) οὐ γὰρ ἐγίνωσκον ἀκριβῶς, ὅτι ἦν ἐκ τοῦ μαγειρείου καὶ τῆς νηστείας ἡ ὄψις αὐτοῦ ἀλλοιουμένη (Leont. N., V. Jo. Eleem. 371.10–11)
'For they did not recognize him entirely, for his appearance was altered because of his job as a cook and the fasting.' (tr. Festugière (originally in French))

In this passage, a collector of customs, Peter, decides to change his life, and become a slave. A certain day, some of Peter's compatriots visit Peter's master and partly recognize him. Periphrastic ἦν... ἀλλοιουμένη seems to be used with the value of a resultative perfect, expressing the altered state of Peter's appearance. The cause of this altered state is explicitly indicated—that is, ἐκ τοῦ μαγειρείου καὶ τῆς νηστείας 'because of the kitchen and the fasting'.

3.7 CONCLUSION

In the functional domain of perfect aspect, εἰμί was the predominant auxiliary throughout the entire period covered in this chapter. During the Classical period, a single construction, εἰμί with the perfect participle, developed, first being used as a resultative perfect and afterwards also as an anterior perfect. This development, which is in accordance with what has been observed by cross-linguistic studies, can be interpreted as a process of transitivization: the construction became used in increasingly more transitive contexts when it comes

---

[303] For similar examples, see e.g. Jo. Mal., Chron. 367.7–8; Thphn., Chron. 17.30, V. Marth. 24.11.

to the number of participants, the volitionality of the subject, the affectedness of the object, the kinesis of the event (single vs. repeated), etc. The construction occurred next to the synthetic perfect to compensate for a paradigmatic gap, and was even extended to morphological contexts that were also covered by the synthetic perfect.

In time, however, stimulated by the functional convergence of the synthetic perfect with the aorist, and its subsequent retreat from the verbal system (its 'desystematization', as Browning 1983: 32 calls it), a functional opposition arose (especially in MPG and LPG/EBG): εἰμί with the perfect participle became used in less transitive contexts (that is, as a resultative perfect), while a new periphrasis, εἰμί with the aorist participle, became used in more transitive ones (that is, as an anterior perfect). To a large extent, this functional opposition was also one of voice, εἰμί with the perfect participle mainly being used in the medio-passive voice, while εἰμί with the aorist participle in the active voice.

To some extent, the situation described above may come as a surprise, given that (a) to express possession, ἔχω was frequently used next to ἔστι μοι, and over time even came to dominate,[304] and (b) that in many European languages BE and HAVE are used as auxiliaries next to each other,[305] a phenomenon which is known as 'split auxiliarization'.[306] In her recent work, Bruno (2012, 2014) notes that while in Ancient Greek the structural premises for such split auxiliarization were also present (both BE and HAVE being well-established in non-periphrastic uses), the fact that a HAVE-perfect did not develop more fully may be attributed to the complex participial system of Ancient Greek:[307] she argues that a system of periphrastics can either be 'centred upon the lexical contrast of auxiliary forms in diathetically opposed clauses',[308] or display 'patterns in which invariant auxiliary forms apply to variable auxiliated items'.[309] The situation in Ancient Greek resembles that in Modern Greek in the sense that it is mainly centred upon a single auxiliary. In Standard Modern Greek, however, ἔχω has become dominant, and is

---

[304] See e.g. Kulneff-Eriksson (1999: 151): 'ἔχω seems to increase as time passes at the cost of ἔστι μοι in constructions denoting "have".'
[305] For an overview, see Drinka (2003b: 4).
[306] See e.g. Shannon (1995), who makes an interesting connection with transitivity.
[307] Bruno (2014: 50).
[308] e.g. HAVE + passive participle vs. BE + passive participle.
[309] e.g. BE + active participle vs. BE + passive participle.

combined with the 'ἀπαρέμφατο' (as in ἔχει γράψει 'he has written' vs. ἔχει γραφθεί 'it has been written').

Bruno's typological generalizations offer some insight, but at the same time they must be nuanced, as Bruno also recognizes: during the entire period under analysis, we find various alternative constructions, both with ἔχω and with εἰμί, some of which occur more frequently than others. Two main HAVE-constructions are (anterior) ἔχω with the aorist participle and (resultative) ἔχω with the (medio-passive) perfect participle. Another element that should be stressed is that aspect and voice are in principle independent. As we have seen, there is a natural similarity between anteriors and the active voice, and resultatives and the medio-passive voice. However, the former could also be used in the passive voice: during the Classical period, for example, anterior εἰμί with the perfect participle was first used in the passive voice, and only over time also in the active voice.

4

Imperfective Aspect

> If we set aside the expressive use of periphrasis by the poets and the even freer use of the same construction in Herodotus, we see that periphrasis in classical prose as in Homer is essentially a construction with perfect participles. The use with present participles is infrequent; with aorist forms it is so rare as to be practically negligible.
>
> (Kahn 1973: 141–2)

> Ainsi, le grec ancien connaît la périphrase qui consiste à employer le verbe ἐσ- 'être' avec le participe parfait: type ἡ θύρα κεκλησμένη ἐστί 'la porte *est fermée*'. Dans cette expression, la valeur statique est soulignée. Pour les autres thèmes temporels, une telle périphrase ne se trouve guère, du moins en grec homérique et classique (Aerts 1965).
>
> (Ruijgh 1991: 208)[1]

4.1 INTRODUCTION

We can now proceed to the analysis of periphrases formed with εἰμί and ἔχω in the functional domain of imperfective aspect. One important difference between periphrases in the perfect and imperfective

---

[1] 'Ancient Greek has a periphrastic construction which consists of the verb ἐσ- "to be" with the perfect participle: type ἡ θύρα κεκλησμένη ἐστί "the door is closed". In this expression, the static value is emphasized. For the other temporal themes, such a periphrastic construction is almost not attested, at least not in Homeric and Classical Greek (Aerts 1965).'

domains concerns the diachrony of the present theme.[2] As noted by Joseph (1987: 431), the present theme formed part of a stable opposition with the aorist theme during the entire history of the Ancient Greek language, and was not subject to change like the perfect theme.[3] As a result, imperfective periphrases are almost always formed with the present participle, although, as a result of the confusion surrounding the formation of the participle,[4] occasionally the aorist participle is used with a progressive value.

While in English the periphrastic construction of 'be V-ing' eventually came to replace the simple present and past for the expression of progressive aspect, in Ancient Greek εἰμί with the present participle never supplanted synthetic forms to that extent, not even in Post-Classical and Byzantine Greek. Although the decline of the participle is likely to have played a major role in the decline of this and other participial periphrases,[5] Browning (1983: 32) may be right that the strong opposition between the present and aorist theme, or more precisely between the synthetic present/imperfect and aorist, may have exerted an influence as well:

> The opposition between continuous and momentary action is one of those expressed by the distinction between present and aorist theme in late Koine, medieval and modern Greek. So the periphrasis with the present participle never succeeds in replacing the present and imperfect indicative in Koine Greek.

One interesting exception is the Tsakonian Greek dialect:[6] in this dialect, where the present participle persists in three genders, the periphrastic construction has replaced the synthetic present and imperfect in the indicative mood.

The use and development of εἰμί with the present participle has been the subject of much discussion. While Aerts (1965) maintains that the construction was limited to a stative aspectual function in Classical Greek, and in Post-Classical/Byzantine Greek was used with

---

[2] On the notion of theme or verb stem, see e.g. Rijksbaron (2002: 1), who distinguishes between a present stem, an aorist stem, a perfect stem, a future stem, and a future perfect stem.

[3] For similar observations, see Verboomen (1992: 12); Bubenik (1997: 249); Gerö & Ruge (2008: 106–17).

[4] See §3.4.1.

[5] With regard to εἰμί with the present participle, see e.g. Björck (1940: 66); Aerts (1965: 98); Caragounis (2004: 179–80); Gerö & Ruge (2008: 114).

[6] Cf. Aerts (1965: 97–8, 102–9); Browning (1983: 32); Giannaris (2011c: 206).

a progressive value only in imitation of the New Testament, Björck (1940) and Dietrich (1973a, 1973b) allege that its use was much more widespread. These latter scholars find instances of the progressive use of the construction in Classical Greek,[7] and claim that its use with such a function in Post-Classical/Byzantine Greek was much more widespread than Aerts (1965) suggests. Another point of debate concerns the extension of this progressive function: while Porter (1989: 480) renders an example such as ἦν γὰρ ἔχων κτήματα πολλά (Mt. 19.22),[8] where εἰμί is combined with the lexically stative ἔχω 'I have', with an uneasy 'for he was in progress possessing many things', Björck (1940) and Aerts (1965) categorize such examples under the heading of 'adjectival periphrasis'.[9]

In order to re-evaluate the evidence at hand, I again draw on recent typological research. To be more specific, Pier Marco Bertinetto and his colleagues[10] have recently proposed a developmental pathway consisting of five stages, called 'PROG imperfective drift'. A general outline of their proposal is presented in Table 4.1:

Table 4.1. Developmental stages of Bertinetto et al.'s PROG imperfective drift

STAGE	Pure locativity	Progressivity I	Progressivity II	Progressivity III	Pure imperfectivity
SEMANTICS	Locative	Locative + durative	Durative progressive	Focalized progressive	Imperfective (+ habitual)

According to this proposal, progressive 'grams' (short for 'grammatical morphemes') originate from a locative construction,[11] and after a stage of ambiguity (the progressivity I-stage) come to develop a progressive function (the progressivity-II and progressivity-III stages). In a final stage, the construction is no longer restricted to progressive contexts, but can also be used in habitual ones, 'thus

---

[7] Dietrich (1973a, 1973b) even in Archaic Greek.
[8] This phrase is used to characterize a young man who has difficulty with Jesus' precept that 'if you want to be perfect, go and sell all you have and give the money to the poor, and you will have riches in heaven' (GNB).
[9] Cf. Chapter 2.
[10] See Bertinetto (1995); Bertinetto (2000); Bertinetto et al. (2000).
[11] Cf. also Comrie (1976: 98–103); Bybee et al. (1994: 136).

behaving like a typically general-purpose imperfective tense such as the Romance Imperfect'.[12]

Unlike the process of 'aoristic drift' discussed in Chapter 3, this proposal for a 'PROG imperfective drift' is not generally accepted yet, and has not been tested on a broad sample of languages. Bertinetto (1995: 54) himself states:

> Tout cela ne constitue, au niveau actuel de la recherche, qu'une série d'hypothèses raisonnablement fondées sur les données, mais destinées à être précisées et intégrées par les recherches futures.[13]

It seems likely that Ancient Greek—with its long history of written sources—has much to contribute in this regard.

4.2 ARCHAIC GREEK (VIII–VI BC)

4.2.1 εἰμί with the Present Participle as an Innovative Periphrasis?

Unlike εἰμί with the perfect participle, the existence of εἰμί with the present participle as a periphrastic construction in Archaic Greek is not undisputed: a number of scholars[14] maintain that no instances of the construction can be found at this stage, while others mention the use of the construction as a progressive periphrasis. This would be the case in examples such as (148) and (149), where εἰμί is combined with the present participle of the verb κίω 'I go':

(148) ἀλλ' ὅτε δὴ σχεδὸν ἦα κιὼν νεὸς ἀμφιελίσσης, / καὶ τότε τίς με θεῶν ὀλοφύρατο μοῦνον ἐόντα (Hom., Od. 10.156–7)

'But when, as I went, I was near to the curved ship, then some god took pity on me in my loneliness.' (tr. Dimock-Murray)

(149) ἤδη ὑπὲρ πόλιος, ὅθι Ἑρμαιος λόφος ἐστίν, / ἦα κιών, ὅτε νῆα θοὴν ἰδόμην κατιοῦσαν / ἐς λιμέν' ἡμέτερον (Hom., Od. 16.471–3)

'I was now above the city, as I went on my way, where the hill of Hermes is, when I saw a swift ship putting in to our harbor.' (tr. Dimock-Murray)

---

[12] Bertinetto et al. (2000: 540).
[13] 'In the current state of research, all this constitutes but a series of hypotheses reasonably based on the data, destined to be further specified and integrated by future research'.
[14] See e.g. Aerts (1965: 14); Kahn (1973: 131); Fanning (1990: 312).

Amenta (2003: 75–6)[15] has recently suggested that we interpret these examples as progressives: 'ma quando stavo andando alla nave ricurva'[16] (*Od.* 10.156) and 'già fuori dalla città, dove sorge il colle di Ermes, stavo andando quando vidi una nave veloce che entrava nel nostro porto' (*Od.* 16.472).[17] Interestingly, and quite contrary to the predictions made by the grammaticalization path proposed by Bertinetto et al., in both cases we would be dealing with a focalized progressive.[18] In (149), εἰμί with the present participle would provide background to the main action—that is, a god taking pity on Odysseus (announced by καὶ τότε 'and then'). Similarly, in (150) the construction would provide background for the main action, Eumaeus seeing a swift ship putting into the harbour.

Both examples are rather problematic, however, for two reasons: first, it is unclear whether σχεδόν 'near' and ὑπὲρ πόλιος 'above the city' should be taken with ἦα (with κιών functioning as a conjunct participle) or rather with ἦα κιών as a whole. Dimock-Murray, in any case, suggest that the former would be the case: 'as I went, I was near/above the city.' Second, it is unclear whether κιών should be treated as a present participle: Lasso de la Vega (1955: 173), among others, considers it an aorist participle, though noting that 'al no oponerse al aoristo un tema de presente, la interpretación de sus formas, como de presente o de aoristo, debía de ser ambigua'.[19] The former difficulty can also be encountered in another formulaic phrase, ὅτε δὴ σχεδὸν ἦσαν ἐπ' ἀλλήλοισιν ἰόντες 'when they had come near, as they advanced against each other' (tr. Wyatt-Murray).[20] This phrase, which none of the scholars who recognize a periphrastic progressive in Archaic Greek mention, occurs even more frequently. Here, too, the periphrastic construction would

---

[15] Cf. similarly Dietrich (1973a: 189–90); Porter (1989: 457).
[16] 'But when I was going to the curved ship.'
[17] 'I was already going out of the city, where the hill of Hermes rises, when I saw a swift ship which was entering our harbour.'
[18] That is, progressives of the type '*I was reading* when he came in', which temporally overlap with another, foregrounded event, with which they are narrowly connected. See §1.4.1.1.
[19] 'As there is no opposition of the aorist with a present theme, the interpretation of its forms, as present or aorist, must have been ambiguous.'
[20] See Hom., *Il.* 3.15, 5.14, 5.630, 5.850, 6.121, 11.232, 13.604, 16.462, 20.176, 21.148, 22.248, 23.816.

occur in the so-called 'incidence scheme',[21] that is, with εἰμί with the present participle in the subordinate clause (introduced by ὅτε 'when'), and the event interrupting it (serving as 'focalization point') in the main clause.

For another possible example of progressivity, consider (150):[22]

(150) ἡμῖν δ' εἴνατός ἐστι περιτροπέων ἐνιαυτὸς / ἐνθάδε μιμνόντεσσι
(Hom., Il. 2.295-6)

'But for us the ninth year is at its turn, and we are still here.' (tr. Wyatt-Murray)

Odysseus addresses the assembly and notes how the Greeks have every right to be impatient, since they have been away from home for nine years. In this example, a non-periphrastic interpretation seems difficult: given the position of the participle περιτροπέων vis-à-vis ἐνιαυτός, it is easy to see its function as attributive[23] ('it is the ninth revolving year'),[24] whereby περιτροπέω 'I revolve' is taken as an activity-verb, without an inherent endpoint. As Kirk (1985: 147) notes, however, this seems to be excluded on contextual grounds: in Il. 2.134 we learn that nine years have already gone by. In other words, here we do seem to be dealing with a genuine durative-progressive example, expressing the occurrence of an event without there being any narrow connection to another event serving as focalization point. Kirk (1985: 147) proposes the translation 'it is the ninth year that is turning', which can be compared to the translation proposed by Wyatt-Murray.

In the literature, no mention is made of the occurrence of stative εἰμί with the present participle in Archaic (Homeric) Greek. However, it seems that this use is not entirely absent, as shown in (151):

(151) ὦ φίλοι ἥρωες Δαναοὶ θεράποντες Ἄρηος / ἑσταότος μὲν καλὸν ἀκούειν, οὐδὲ ἔοικεν / ὑββάλλειν· χαλεπὸν γὰρ ἐπισταμένῳ περ ἐόντι
(Hom., Il. 19.78-80)

'My friends, Danaan warriors, attendants of Ares, it is good to give ear to him who stands to speak, nor is it right to break in on his words; troublesome would that be even for one well skilled.' (tr. Wyatt-Murray)

---

[21] Cf. fn. 107 (Chapter 1).
[22] This example is also mentioned by Dietrich (1973a: 189), Porter (1989: 455) and Amenta (2003: 68).
[23] Cf. Rijksbaron (2002: 132-3).
[24] See Liddell & Scott (1968: 1391) for this interpretation.

Achilles has just addressed the Greeks, informing them that he will put an end to the strife between himself and Agamemnon. Agamemnon gives his reply from the place where he is seated, asking them to hear him in silence, since even an experienced speaker has difficulty when interrupted. While it could be argued that ἐπισταμένῳ is substantivized, 'an experienced speaker',[25] it seems more likely that ἐπισταμένῳ ἐόντι should be taken as as a stative periphrasis, 'being experienced'.[26]

Moreover, the participle ἀκέων '(being) silent' can be found twice in combination with εἰμί,[27] but it is unclear whether these examples qualify as periphrastic: in these examples, ἀκέων is an indeclinable form, as there is no concord between the subject (Athena) and the participle. Nevertheless, the late formation of the optative ἀκέοις in Apollonius of Rhodes (1.765) shows that ἀκέω 'I am silent' was still felt to be a verb. A similar problem surrounds the form ἀλιτήμενος (Hom., Od. 4.807), which Aerts (1965: 14) considers 'insufficiently elucidated'. Liddell & Scott (1968: 66-7) note that the form constitutes an aorist participle of ἀλιταίνω 'I sin against' (aorist infinitive ἀλιτέσθαι),[28] and that it can have an adjectival meaning comparable to ἀλιτρός 'sinful' (with a dative expressing the person in whose eyes one is sinful, in this case the gods).[29] Chantraine (1942: 190), on the other hand, considers it a perfect form, comparing the accent to that in other (perfect) forms such as ἐσσύμενος 'eager' and κεκλήγοντες 'shrieking'.[30]

4.3 CLASSICAL GREEK (V-IV BC)

4.3.1 εἰμί with the Present Participle as a Stative Periphrasis

During the Classical period, εἰμί with the present participle becomes much more frequently employed, with over 1600 examples in the

---

[25] Compare Björck (1940: 93) on Archil., Fragm. 1.
[26] Cf. Edwards (1991: 245), who compares ἐπιστάμενος to ἐπιστήμων.
[27] See Hom., Il. 4.22, 8.459.
[28] Tichy (1977: 168) notes that the (aorist) participle reads ἀλιτήμενος rather than *ἀλιτούμενος because of the analogical influence of ἀλιτήμων 'sinning'.
[29] Tichy (1977: 168) compares with Hom., Il. 20.347: φίλος ἀθανάτοισι θεοῖσι 'dear to the immortal gods' and Hes., Theog. 766. ἐχθρύς ... θεοῖσιν 'hateful to the gods'.
[30] Cf. similarly Lasso de la Vega (1955: 174, 180).

corpus. Many of these examples are low in transitivity in terms of number of participants, volitionality of the subject, affectedness of the object, etc.: the construction is predominantly used with a stative aspectual function, denoting a property that remains stable over time.

The specific impetus for the dramatic increase in use of the construction in the Classical period must have been analogy: following the establishment of εἰμί with the perfect participle in the domain of perfect (resultative) aspect, in the domain of imperfective aspect, too, a periphrastic construction came to be more frequently employed. Alongside this analogical process, εἰμί with the present participle may have been influenced by the construction of εἰμί with a regular adjective, with which it has a semantic affinity, as noted by Rosenkranz (1930: 163):

> Da aber die Verbindung Adjektiv + εἶναι durchaus geläufig war, konnte natürlich jeden Augenblick die Verbindung Partizip + εἶναι gebildet werden.[31]

The importance of Heine's (1993: 31) 'equation schema' (formulated as 'X is (like) a Y')[32] is confirmed by many examples in which εἰμί with the present participle is coordinated with a regular adjective. As with εἰμί paired with the perfect participle,[33] we find various examples in which the participle expresses a notion that is opposite to that of the adjective with which it is paired, as in οὐ γὰρ ἀναγκαῖον ἢ τυφλὸν ἢ ὄψιν ἔχον εἶναι (Aristot., *Cat.* 13a) 'for it is not necessary that it is blind or has sight'; ἄν τε γὰρ ὦσιν ἀδιάφοροι αἱ μονάδες ἄν τε διαφέρουσαι ἑκάστη ἑκάστης (Aristot., *Metaph.* 1081b) 'for whether the units are undifferentiated or each differs from each' (tr. Ross); πλουσίαν δὲ ἢ πενομένην ἀνάγκη τὴν τυραννουμένην πόλιν εἶναι; (Pl., *Resp.* 577e) 'and must the tyrannized city be either rich or poor?'; ἀνάρμοστον δ' ἐστὶ τὸ αἰσχρὸν παντὶ τῷ θείῳ, τὸ δὲ καλὸν ἁρμόττον (Pl., *Symp.* 206d) 'the ugly is discordant with whatever is divine, whereas the beautiful is accordant' (tr. Fowler). In many other cases, the participle complements one or more regular adjectives, as for example in τοῦτο δ' ἔστω γνώριμον καὶ ὁμολογούμενον (Aristot., *An. post.* 87a) 'let this be well-known and agreed upon'; διαθέσεις δὲ λέγονται ἅ ἐστιν εὐκίνητα καὶ ταχὺ μεταβάλλοντα (Aristot., *Cat.* 8b)

---

[31] 'Since the combination adjective + εἶναι was very familiar, the combination participle + εἶναι could be built at any moment.' Cf. similarly Dover (1968: 87–8).
[32] Cf. §1.5.2. [33] Cf. §3.3.2.2.

'dispositions, however, are qualities easy to move or to change' (tr. Cooke); πειθὼ δὲ κοῦφόν ἐστι καὶ νοῦν οὐκ ἔχον (Aristoph., *Ran.* 1396) 'persuasion is but light, and makes no sense' (tr. Dillon); μὴ γὰρ οἴεσθέ με οὕτως ἀπόπληκτον εἶναι καὶ παντελῶς μαινόμενον (Dem. 34.16) 'do not think I am so senseless and absolutely crazy'.

For a more detailed overview of the distribution of stative εἰμί with the present participle, consider Table 4.2:

Table 4.2. Distribution of εἰμί with the present participle in CG (stative)

Genre/Author/Text	STAT	NRO	TTR	STAT (ACT)	STAT (MED)	STAT (PASS)
Drama	44	1.19	0.64	39	2	3
Aeschylus (b. 525/4 BC?)	7	1.63	0.71	6	1	0
Sophocles (b. 496/5 BC?)	17	2.66	0.76	16	0	1
Euripides (b. 480s BC?)	9	0.57	0.67	8	1	0
Aristophanes (b. 460/50 BC?)	11	1.03	0.91	9	0	2
Historiography	107	1.61	0.36	79	10	18
Herodotus (b. 484 BC?)	67	3.54	0.33	45	6	16
Thucydides (b. 460/55 BC?)	9	0.59	0.78	8	1	0
Xenophon (b. *c*.430 BC)	31	0.96	0.65	26	3	2
Philosophy	740	4.69	0.19	469	181	90
Plato (b. *c*.429 BC)	331	5.83	0.27	232	58	41
Aristotelic corpus (IV BC)	409	4.05	0.21	237	123	49
Scientific prose	49	1.33	0.86	36	8	5
Oratory	125	2.03	0.32	95	15	15
Lysias (b. 459/8 BC?)	4	0.68	0.75	4	0	0
Isocrates (b. 436 BC)	29	2.62	0.48	22	2	5
Isaeus (b. *c*.420 BC)	7	2.12	0.57	2	1	4
Demosthenes (b. 384 BC)	68	2.31	0.41	54	10	4

Key: 'STAT' = stative; 'NRO'= normed rate of occurrence (per 10,000 words); 'TTR' = type/token ratio; 'ACT' = active; 'MED' = middle; 'PASS' = passive.

This table shows that the construction is by far the most often used in philosophical texts, with an NRO of almost five instances per 10,000 words.[34] This shows that Kahn's (1973: 141) and Ruijgh's (1991: 208) statements (the introductory quotes to this chapter), which downplay the importance of periphrasis in the domain of imperfective aspect (at least in the Classical period), must be nuanced.

---

[34] This rate of occurrence can be compared to that of εἰμί with the perfect participle (cf. §3.3.2.2). Note, however, that the construction with the present participle has a very low type/token ratio in Plato and Aristotle.

A second observation that can be made on the basis of Table 4.2 is that the construction could also be used in the passive voice. Some typical expressions in this regard are καλούμενός ἐστι 'it is called', λεγόμενός ἐστι 'it is told', and ὁμολογούμενός ἐστι 'it is agreed upon'.[35] Perhaps the presence of these 'statal passives' can be attributed to the analogical influence of resultative εἰμί with the perfect participle, which, as we have seen in Chapter 3, was also expressed predominantly in the passive voice.[36]

As we observed for the perfect participle,[37] in some cases the value of the passive present participle seems to approach that of a verbal adjective, as in the following example, where the author observes how it is useful for quadrupeds to have ears that stand out free from the head and are moveable:[38]

(152) οὕτω δὲ τὸ πλεῖστον κινουμένων χρήσιμα μετεωρότερά τε <u>ὄντα</u> καὶ <u>κινούμενα</u> (Aristot., *Part. an.* 657a)

'And as they are usually in this posture when in motion, it is useful for them to have their ears well up in the air, and also movable.' (tr. Peck)

As we have already seen in Chapter 2, 'adjectival periphrasis' with the present participle does not form a homogeneous category. A basic distinction can be made between examples with the present participle of lexically *stative* verbs and those with the present participle of lexically *dynamic* verbs. When it comes to the former group, a number of impersonal verbs are very frequently employed, e.g. δεῖ 'it is necessary', ἐνδέχεται 'it is possible', πρέπει 'it is fitting', προσήκει 'it is befitting', and συμφέρει 'it is expedient'. Such verbs, together with a number of less frequently employed verbs such as ἄπειμι 'I am absent', ζάω 'I am alive', δύναμαι 'I am able', etc., can be classified as 'verbs with lexicalized predication of qualities', following Fanning (1990: 135). Two other very frequently employed stative verbs are εἰμί 'I am' and ἔχω 'I have'. The former is almost exclusively used in the philosophical works of Plato and Aristotle, as in (153), where Aristotle discusses the relationship between 'being' and 'not being':[39]

---

[35] See e.g. Aristot., *Ph.* 226a; Hdt. 2.79.2, Pl., *Leg.* 961d (καλούμενος); Aristot., *Mag. mor.* 1.30.2; Hdt. 2.48.3, 7.150.1, 7.167.1; Pl., *Leg.* 881b, *Ti.* 90e (λεγόμενος); Aristot., *Metaph.* 1042a; Dem. 30.32; Isaeus 2.40 (ὁμολογούμενος).
[36] Compare Table 3.2.   [37] Cf. fn. 17 (Chapter 3).
[38] Compare also Aristot., *Mag. mor.* 1.30.2, *Sens.* 439a.
[39] For an exceptional example outside of philosophy, see Hippoc., *Ars med.* 5.7.

(153) εἰ δὲ καὶ ἔστι τὸ μὴ ὂν μὴ ὄν, οὐδ' οὕτως ὁμοίως εἴη ἂν τὸ μὴ ὂν τῷ [μὴ] ὄντι· τὸ μὲν γάρ ἐστι μὴ ὄν, τὸ δὲ καὶ ἔστιν ἔτι (Aristot., MXG 979b)

'But even if what is not is not, yet it does not follow that what is not is in a similar way to what is; for the former is something that is not, while the latter actually is as well.' (tr. Loveday & Forster)

Examples with ἔχω, on the other hand, are used in a much broader range of contexts and can be found in all the genres listed in Table 4.2, including drama: compare, for example, χροιὰν τίνα / ἔχουσ' ἂν εἴη δαίμοσιν πρὸς ἡδονὴν / χολή (Aesch., PV 493–5) 'what color the gall must have to please the gods' (tr. Smyth); ἔστι γὰρ ἔχων στόμα εὐμέγεθες (Aristot., Phgn. 809b) 'he [the lion] has a good-sized mouth' (tr. Loveday & Forster); ἦν δὲ σπλῆνα μέγαν ἔχων (Hippoc., Epid. 2.2.7) 'he had a big spleen'; ἦν ἄνδρας πολλοὺς καὶ μαχίμους ἔχουσα (Xen., An. 7.8.13) 'it had a considerable force of warlike defenders' (tr. Brownson); ἔστι δὲ τοῦθ' οὑτωσὶ μὲν ἀκοῦσαι λόγον τιν' ἔχον (Dem. 20.18) 'at first hearing, the plea seems to have some weight' (tr. Vince & Vince). In other examples, ἔχων is accompanied by an adverb, rather than an accusative object.

Least frequent is the use of εἰμί with the present participle of a dynamic verb. As mentioned in §2.4.4, in this context 'detransitivizing' elements can often be found, such as the coordination of the participle with a regular adjective, the use of εἰμί in the present tense, the presence of an inanimate subject, or the omission of the object.

Constructions with a dynamic verb correspond most closely to what in the literature are called 'generics'.[40] Three main uses can be distinguished in this regard,[41] differing in degree of what Lanérès (1994) calls 'actualization'.[42]

First, the construction can be used to make general, more or less empirically based observations, as in (154), where the author

---

[40] As Declerck (1986: 182) notes, many scholars do not consider sentences with stative predicates generic.

[41] On subtypes of genericity from a general linguistic point of view, see e.g. Declerck (1986); Krifka et al. (1995).

[42] Cf. Lanérès (1994: 378): 'linguistiquement, *actualiser* un énoncé consiste à lui conférer une réalité en l'insérant dans un contexte qui en marque le degré d'existence' ('linguistically, *to actualize* an utterance means to confer to it a reality by inserting it in a context which marks its degree of existence'). Lanérès defines a number of 'actualisateurs' such as adverbs of time and space, demonstratives, personal and possessive pronouns, the definite article, certain adjectives (e.g. 'recent', 'far', 'distant'), etc.

discusses how the medicine *caricum* is made, listing a number of ingredients:

(154) ἢν βούλῃ ὑγρῷ χρέεσθαι, καὶ τὸ καρικὸν φάρμακον ἐπαλείφειν, ἐπιδεῖν δὲ ὥσπερ τὰ πρότερα γέγραπται κατὰ τὸν αὐτὸν λόγον. Ἔστι δὲ ἐκ τῶνδε τὸ φάρμακον ποιεύμενον (Hippoc., *Ulc.* 16.1-3)

'If you wish to use a liquid application, the medicine called caricum may be rubbed in, and the bandages may be applied as formerly described upon the same principle. The medicine is prepared of the following ingredients.' (tr. Potter)

Various examples of this type can be found in all genres: for example, in historiography to describe the Scythian boundaries (Hdt. 4.99.4), in philosophy to describe different types of people (Pl., *Phd.* 82a), in oratory to describe a harmful course of action (Dem. 3.34), and in drama to assert that a certain insight can be found in Aesop's fables (Aristoph., *Av.* 652).

Second, the construction can be used to characterize persons or things that can be situated at a more specific time and place. This resembles the first use of εἰμί with the present participle just discussed, although the focus lies on a particular property of the subject in question: in other words, there is a higher degree of 'actualization'. Consider the following example:[43]

(155) ἄπειρος εἶ τοῦ ἀνδρός, ὦ Ἱππία, ὡς σχέτλιός ἐστι καὶ οὐδὲν ῥᾳδίως ἀποδεχόμενος (Pl., *Hp. mai.* 289e)

'You don't know the man, Hippias, what a wretch he is, and how certain not to accept anything easily.'

The purpose of this statement is not to offer some very general empirical observation, but rather to characterize the subject.

Long ago, Wifstrand (1934: 41) noted that periphrastic εἰμί with the present participle could be used 'um darzulegen, wie die eine oder andere Person in der referierten Rede, Schrift, dem Gedicht, Brief, usw. auftritt oder sich äussert'.[44] One of Wifstrand's examples is the following:

---

[43] For similar examples, see e.g. Aristoph., *Ach.* 428-9; Dem. 19.312, 29.13; Isoc. 15.57; Pl., *Leg.* 765a, 932b, *Phdr.* 239b, *Resp.* 556a; Xen., *An.* 2.6.7.

[44] 'To explain how one or the other person appears or expresses himself in the speech, writing, poem, letter, etc. referred to.'

(156) καὶ πάντ' ἀναδεχόμενος καὶ εἰς αὑτὸν ποιούμενος τὰ τούτων ἁμαρτήματ' ἐστίν (Dem. 19.36)
'And he takes upon himself everything and takes responsibility for their delinquencies.'

Demosthenes describes how a letter was read aloud to the Athenians, in which Philip excuses himself and takes responsibility for the delay of the embassy. Philip's attitude is described with the periphrasis ἀναδεχόμενος καὶ εἰς αὑτὸν ποιούμενος . . . ἐστιν. Examples of this type can be compared with others that characterize persons or things (as in (155)), so that there is no need to classify them under a separate subtype.

Third, the construction could be used for what grammars typically call 'gnomic' statements. Of the three 'generic' uses outlined here, this is the least common one: the nominal sentence, the gnomic aorist, or the generic present tense constitute the more regular expressions.[45] These examples too resemble our first use discussed, although there is a lower degree of 'actualization'. One example would be the following (= (53)):

(157) ἀλλ' ἔστιν, ἔστιν ἡ λίαν δυσπραξία / λίαν διδοῦσα μεταβολάς, ὅταν τύχηι (Eur., IT 721–2)
'Great misfortune can offer great reversals, when it is fated; it can indeed.' (tr. Potter)

Orestes has arrived at the temple of Artemis in Tauris, where Iphigeneia serves as a priestess of the goddess, ritually sacrificing any foreigners who pass by. It seems that Orestes, too, will be sacrificed, and his friend Pylades, who has travelled along with Orestes, notes that 'great misfortune can offer great reversals', in order to console him.[46]

Examples of εἰμί with the present participle are predominantly used in the indicative mood, but examples in the optative are also found.[47] More interestingly, the construction appears frequently in the imperative mood (forty-seven examples),[48] which presents an interesting

---

[45] Cf. §1.4.1.1, §1.4.1.2.

[46] The repetition of ἔστιν is quite noticeable. Flagg (1889: 119) argues that the use of this 'energetic formula', which occurs elsewhere, motivated the use of periphrasis.

[47] Björck (1940: 33) connects this to the avoidance of hiatus. Cf. §1.2.1.

[48] Contrast Porter (1989: 465), who notes that 'the imperative of εἰμί + present participle is found very infrequently in ancient Greek.'

parallel to the use of resultative εἰμί with the perfect participle:[49] in both cases we are dealing with combinations that are low in transitivity. As the following three examples show, this occurs in a number of contexts:

(158) ὅτι μὲν οὖν τὰ πρῶτα ἀρχὰς καὶ στοιχεῖα καλῶς ἔχει λέγειν, <u>ἔστω συνομολογούμενον</u> (Aristot., *Gen. corr.* 329a)
'Let us, then, be agreed that the primary materials... are rightly described as "sources" and "materials".' (tr. Forster)

(159) ὅριον, οἷσι μὲν ὑγιὲς καταλείπεται, κάτω ὑφιεμένης τῆς προφάσιος, ἢ <u>καθαίρων</u>, ἢ <u>ἀποδέων</u>, ἢ <u>ἐκβάλλων</u>, ἢ <u>ἀποτάμνων</u>, ἢ <u>ἀποκαίων ἔσο</u>· οἷσι δὲ μή, οὔ (Hippoc., *Epid.* 6.6.6)[50]
'A distinction: if a healthy area remains when you have removed the cause below, purge, bind off, expel, excise or cauterise. If it does not, not.' (tr. Smith)

(160) <u>ἔστω</u> δὴ <u>λεγόμενον</u> τὸ μετὰ τοῦτο τῇδε (Pl., *Leg.* 881b)
'So the next pronouncement shall run thus.' (tr. Bury)

Example (158) illustrates a common usage in the work of Aristotle: a certain assumption is made, which the reader must take for granted, in this particular case that the primary materials are best described as 'sources' and 'elements'. In (159), on the other hand, we find a surgical precept: when a healthy area remains, one is allowed to perform a series of actions to preserve the healthy tissue. The sentence in (160) follows a discussion of how great a crime it is to lay hands on one's father or mother. Through the use of the imperative it is announced that a certain pronouncement (which is to follow immediately) shall stand expressed in a certain way.[51]

4.3.2 The Progressive Use of εἰμί with the Present Participle

Whether εἰμί with the present participle was used as a progressive periphrasis during the Classical period has been subject to much

---

[49] Cf. §3.3.2.2.

[50] Note that ἔσο is not printed in the Loeb edition by Smith (1994), although the phrase is translated as a series of imperatives.

[51] Compare Alexander's (1883: 303–4) discussion of this passage: 'there is no emphasis on the *act*, but to an abiding condition, "Let the next topic stand expressed in the following way".'

discussion. Both before and after Aerts' (1965) study, which still forms the standard work on the subject, scholars have answered the question affirmatively,[52] a finding of which Aerts (1965) is very critical.[53]

It is true that many of the forms that are suggested as 'progressive' in the literature prove otherwise under close scrutiny. For example, of the four 'clearly progressive' examples that de Foucault (1961) mentions in his short contribution 'La forme progressive existe-t-elle en grec classique', two[54] would be classified as stative within the present framework. Although these examples are formed with dynamic predicates, they are used in generic contexts as discussed under §4.3.1, and are low in transitivity. Dietrich (1973a: 190–203) and Porter (1989: 455–66) also seem to recognize examples with stative verbs as progressive, a possibility which is rejected by most scholars.

Many other forms are ambiguous, a fact that, as was also the case with Archaic Greek, is not always duly recognized.[55] For example, the locative ambiguity which is predicted by Bertinetto *et al.* in stage two of their PROG imperfective drift[56] frequently appears, as in the following excerpt from Herodotus:

(161) ὁ μὲν δὴ πρεσβύτερος τῶν παίδων τῷ Κίμωνι Στησαγόρης <u>ἦν</u> τηνικαῦτα παρὰ τῷ πάτρῳ Μιλτιάδῃ <u>τρεφόμενος</u> ἐν τῇ Χερσονήσῳ
(Hdt. 6.103.4)

'Stesagoras, the elder of Cimon's sons, was then being brought up with his uncle Miltiades in the Chersonese.' (tr. Godley)

Herodotus narrates how the Athenians went to Marathon to rescue their land. Some background information is given about Cimon, the father of the Athenian general Miltiades: he was killed while his elder son, Stesagoras, was staying with his brother (also named Miltiades). Porter (1989: 459) suggests a periphrastic (progressive) interpretation ('the elder son S. was being reared at this time in C. with his uncle M.'),

---

[52] See e.g. Björck (1940: 71–2); de Foucault (1961: 12–13); Dietrich (1973a: 190–203); Porter (1989: 455–66); Ceglia (1998: 28–9); Amenta (2003: 66–84).

[53] See e.g. Aerts (1965: 26): 'so-called progressive periphrases are very rare.' Cf. similarly Fanning (1990: 311–12); Rijksbaron (2002: 127–8). Cobb (1973) argues that the progressive periphrasis was first introduced by Aristotle.

[54] Pl., *Phd.* 82a; Xen., *Cyr.* 5.5.26.

[55] As for example in Dietrich's (1973a, 1973b) and Porter's (1989) treatment of the construction.

[56] See §4.1.

but this is uncertain, for as Aerts (1965: 24) and Dietrich (1973a: 192) note, a non-periphrastic interpretation is just as well possible ('Stesagoras was then with his uncle, being brought up').

While the locative ambiguity is by far the most frequent,[57] we also find other types of ambiguity, that is, when εἰμί has a possessive or existential value. Consider two more examples from Herodotus:

(162) ἦν γάρ τις καὶ τοῦτον ἄχαρις συμφορὴ λυπέουσα παιδοφόνος (Hdt. 7.190.1)

'For some terrible misfortune was tormenting him, too, namely of having killed his son.'

(163) νικώντων δὲ τὰ δύο τῶν Περινθίων, ὡς ἐπαιώνιζον κεχαρηκότες, συνεβάλοντο οἱ Παίονες τὸ χρηστήριον αὐτὸ τοῦτο εἶναι καὶ εἶπάν κου παρὰ σφίσι αὐτοῖσι· «Νῦν ἂν εἴη ὁ χρησμὸς ἐπιτελεόμενος ἡμῖν, νῦν ἡμέτερον τὸ ἔργον» (Hdt. 5.1.3)

'The Perinthians were victorious in two of the combats and raised the cry of "Paean" in their joy. The Paeonians reasoned that this was what the oracle had spoken of and must have said to each other, "This is surely the fulfillment of the prophecy; now it is time for us to act".' (tr. Godley)

In both cases, scholars have suggested that we are dealing with progressive periphrasis, while others disagree. In the first case, Herodotus narrates a shipwreck, and how a certain Ameinocles became very wealthy from this because he found much gold and silver on the shore. He, however, was also unhappy, as he had accidentally killed his son. While Dietrich (1973a: 192) considers ἦν ... λυπέουσα periphrastic ('was tormenting'), Aerts (1965: 12) suggests that ἦν has an existential value ('there was namely ... '). In the second example, we read how the Paeonians march against the Perinthians. As an oracle had told them to attack when the Perinthians started shouting, they do so when the latter raise 'the cry of paean'. Dietrich (1973a: 192) again takes νῦν ἂν εἴη ἐπιτελεόμενος as periphrastic ('[maintenant] semble bien pour nous en voie d'accomplissement'),[58] but Aerts (1965: 24) notes that a non-periphrastic 'nominal construction' may also be possible ('now we can have the fulfillment of the oracle').

---

[57] For similar examples, see e.g. Aristoph., *Eccl.* 1094, *Ran.* 36; Dem. 19.294; Eur., *Or.* 60–1; Hdt. 8.37.1, 8.37.3, 8.107.2; Soph., *Phil.* 1219; Thuc. 2.67.1, 2.93.3; Xen., *An.* 1.2.21, 4.5.15, 7.2.21, *Cyr.* 6.3.10, *Hell.* 3.5.20.

[58] '[Now] it seems for us in the process of being accomplished.'

Imperfective Aspect 221

Note the relationship among examples (161), (162), and (163): in all three of them we find the verb 'to be' (εἰμί), possibly with a non-copulative meaning (locative in (161), existential in (162), and possessive in (163)), roughly at the beginning of the clause, with its subject immediately preceding or following and the participle following later on in the sentence. Examples (161) and (163) in particular resemble each other: in both cases the subject is definite, and there is a dative expressing the 'possessor' in a broad sense. In (162), on the other hand, the subject is indefinite and introduces new information. Following Clark (1978), who stresses the similarity between existential, locative, and possessive constructions in many languages, we can speak of a single, 'locational' source-construction. In contexts such as these, a form-function reanalysis of εἰμί in combination with the present participle as a progressive is likely to have taken place (as in '[he was there] [being brought up]' > '[he was being brought up there]'). Contrary to Aerts' (1965) objections, this process must have already taken place during the Classical period,[59] as is suggested by examples such as (164), which summarizes the events happening at Miletus:

(164) ταῦτα δὲ ἦν γινόμενα ἐν Μιλήτῳ (Hdt. 1.147.1)
'These things were happening in Miletus.'

Karleen (1980) has suggested that progressive examples such as (164) may have been built after the example of εἰμί with the perfect participle, which he accords a 'durative' nature:

> One suspects that the durative periphrastic with some tenses (not the aorist), may have been due to the perfect participle's durative nature as a stative, i.e., *estin gegrammenon* was viewed as denoting a durative condition. Perhaps this characteristic of the perfect periphrastic participle came to be viewed as potentially possible for other tenses used in the periphrastic participle.
>
> (Karleen 1980: 117)

While there is some similarity between durativity and stativity/resultativity, there are also some major differences (in terms of transitivity). Thus, I do not consider the scenario *resultative εἰμί with the perfect participle → progressive εἰμί with the present participle* very likely. If anything, such a process would have happened through the

---

[59] And perhaps even earlier: see our Homeric example (150).

intermediary of *stative* εἰμί *with the present participle*.[60] However, the evidence for such a process—that is, examples that are ambiguously situated between stative and progressive interpretations—seems scanty.[61] More relevant is that anterior εἰμί with the perfect participle underwent a process of form-function reanalysis similar to that discussed in the preceding paragraphs.[62] It is therefore possible that the reanalysis of the construction with the perfect participle as an anterior perfect stimulated the reanalysis of that with the present participle as a progressive,[63] although there is a difference in context: anteriors mainly arise in possessive constructions, while progressives in locative ones.

Table 4.3 shows the distribution of progressive εἰμί with the present participle in Classical Greek:

Table 4.3. Distribution of εἰμί with the present participle in CG (progressive)

Genre/Author/Text	PROG	NRO	TTR	DUR PROG	FOC PROG	PROG (ACT)	PROG (MED)	PROG (PASS)
Drama	13	0.35	1	7	6	10	1	2
Sophocles (b. 496/5 BC?)	4	0.63	1	2	2	4	0	0
Euripides (b. 480s BC?)	6	0.38	1	4	2	4	1	1
Aristophanes (b. 460/50 BC?)	3	0.28	1	1	2	2	0	1
Historiography	21	0.32	0.86	16	5	8	6	7
Herodotus (b. 484 BC?)	14	0.74	0.93	9	5	4	4	6
Thucydides (b. 460/55 BC?)	2	0.13	1	2	0	0	2	0
Xenophon (b. c.430 BC)	5	0.16	1	5	0	4	0	1
Philosophy	15	0.10	0.67	12	3	8	1	6
Plato (b. c.429 BC)	10	0.18	0.90	7	3	3	1	6
Aristotelic corpus (IV BC)	5	0.05	0.40	5	0	5	0	0
Scientific prose	2	0.05	1	0	2	1	1	0
Oratory	1	0.02	1	1	0	0	0	0
Demosthenes (b. 384 BC)	1	0.03	1	1	0	1	0	0

Key: 'PROG' = progressive; 'NRO' = normed rate of occurrence (per 10,000 words); 'TTR' = type/token ratio; 'DUR' = durative; 'FOC' = focalized; 'ACT' = active; 'MED' = middle; 'PASS' = passive.

---

[60] As seems to be suggested by Amenta (2003: 30) and Giannaris (2011b: 257–62).

[61] One example would be Thuc. 2.80.3, where it is not entirely clear whether ἦσαν δὲ Κορίνθιοι ξυμπροθυμούμενοι 'and the Corinthians were sharing in eagerness with' is best conceived of as stative or progressive. Contrast e.g. Björck (1940: 25) (adjectival) with Dietrich (1973a: 198) (progressive).

[62] Cf. §3.3.2.2.

[63] On the affinity between progressive and anterior, see also Cohén (1989: 96–100).

Imperfective Aspect 223

This table shows that the use of εἰμί with the present participle with a progressive aspectual function occurs infrequently in all genres. Particularly noteworthy is its absence in oratory, with only a single clearly periphrastic example in Demosthenes.[64] The construction occurs most frequently in drama and historiography[65] (with a normed rate of occurrence of about 0.3 instances per 10,000 words), which seems to be motivated by genre:[66] dramatical texts offer an occasion to specify what is going on at the moment of speaking, or to recount what happened at a time in the past, while historiographical texts to narrate what events form the background for other main events.

Table 4.3 furthermore shows that, as predicted by the grammaticalization path outlined by Bertinetto *et al.*, examples of the durative progressive type are the most frequent. These durative progressives generally appear in main clauses, mostly in the imperfect tense, denoting an event that is happening in a relatively broad timeframe, without there being any temporal connectivity with another event that might serve as a focalization point. Consider example (165):[67]

(165) ἐχόντων δὲ τὸν πόνον τοῦτον τῶν βαρβάρων, Ἀτταγῖνος ὁ
Φρύνωνος ἀνὴρ Θηβαῖος παρασκευασάμενος μεγάλως ἐκάλεε ἐπὶ ξείνια
αὐτόν τε Μαρδόνιον καὶ πεντήκοντα Περσέων τοὺς λογιμωτάτους,
κληθέντες δὲ οὗτοι εἵποντο· ἦν δὲ τὸ δεῖπνον <u>ποιεύμενον</u> ἐν Θήβῃσι
(Hdt. 9.16.1)

'While the barbarians were engaged in this task, Attaginus son of Phrynon, a Theban, made great preparations and invited Mardonius with the fifty most notable of the Persians to be his guests at a banquet. They came as they were bidden; the dinner was being held at Thebes.'
(tr. Godley, slightly modified)

Herodotus narrates how Mardonius and his men arrive in the land of the Thebans, and are pressed by the need to make a defence for their camp. While they are making this camp, Attaginus decides to invite

---

[64] Dem., *Exord.* 55.2.
[65] Contrast with de Foucault (1961: 13), who finds that 'il semble que le tour domine dans les dialogues philosophiques et scientifiques de Platon' ('it seems that the expression dominates in Plato's philosophical and scientific dialogues').
[66] Compare Dietrich (1973a: 190) with regard to Herodotus.
[67] For similar examples, see e.g. Eur., *Cyc.* 381, *Hec.* 120, *IT* 1368; Hdt. 1.152.1, 2.155.3, 7.190.1; Pl., *Resp.* 490a, *Ti.* 26b.

Mardonius for a banquet. This banquet, it is specified through a periphrastic construction, is held in Thebes. ἦν ... ποιεύμενον 'it was being held' specifies the background for the events that are to follow, but in a very broad manner: there is no strong semantic/pragmatic connectivity between the dinner being held at Thebes and any other specific event.

Alternatively, the construction can be used in the present tense:[68]

(166) εἰ δ' αὖ τις τοῦτ' ἐνθυμεῖται, πῶς ἐπειδὰν πολλοὶ ἐργάται γένωνται, πολλοὶ φανοῦνται καὶ οἱ μισθωσόμενοι, ἐκεῖνο κατανοήσας θαρρείτω, ὅτι πολλοὶ μὲν τῶν κατεσκευασμένων προσμισθώσονται τοὺς δημοσίους (πολλὰ γάρ ἐστι τὰ ὑπάρχοντα), πολλοὶ δ' <u>εἰσὶ</u> καὶ αὐτῶν τῶν ἐν τοῖς ἔργοις <u>γηράσκοντες</u> (Xen., Vect. 4.22)[69]

'But, one may ask, when labour is abundant, how will a sufficient number of persons be found to hire it? Well, if anyone feels doubtful about that, let him comfort himself with the thought that many men in the business will hire the state slaves as additional hands, since they have abundance of capital, and that among those now working in the mines many are growing old.' (tr. Marchant & Bowersock)

In *On Revenues*, Xenophon suggests that the state should become the owner of public slaves, which can then be let out to work in the mines. Xenophon then discusses the question as to whether enough people will be found to hire these public slaves, noting that many of those working in the mines at the time of writing are growing old. It is clear that εἰσι ... γηράσκοντες 'they are growing old' does not denote an event that is narrowly connected to the time of speaking: the growing old happens in a broader time-frame, and may be conceived as occurring repeatedly.[70]

In this context, it is also worth mentioning that several examples approach the value of the 'perfect of persistence': they denote an event that has started in the past and continues in the present.[71] Consider the following example:[72]

---

[68] For similar examples, see e.g. Aristoph., Equ. 468; Aristot., Metaph. 1017a; Eur., Hec. 1179; Soph., OT 847; Xen., An. 3.3.2.

[69] Note that some editions have γηρασκόντων, which destroys the periphrasis.

[70] What some scholars refer to as 'iterative' durative progressive, cf. §1.4.1.1.

[71] On this aspectual subtype being located in between perfect and imperfective aspect, cf. §3.6.2.

[72] For similar examples, see e.g. Soph., Aj. 1320; Pl., Thg. 128d.

(167) μέχρι μὲν τούτου ὄψις τε ἐμὴ καὶ γνώμη καὶ ἱστορίη ταῦτα <u>λέγουσά</u> <u>ἐστι</u>, τὸ δὲ ἀπὸ τοῦδε αἰγυπτίους ἔρχομαι λόγους ἐρέων κατὰ [τὰ] ἤκουον (Hdt. 2.99.1)
'Hitherto my own observation and judgment and inquiry are the vouchers for that which I have said (lit. have been saying these things); but from this point onwards I am about to tell the history of Egypt according to that which I heard.' (tr. Macaulay)

At the beginning of *Histories* 2.99, Herodotus notes that while so far he has been speaking about Egypt on the basis of his own experience, from this point forward he will base his account on what he has heard from other people. λέγουσά ἐστι 'it has been speaking' refers to a durative event that has started in the past (when Herodotus' first started talking about Egypt) and continues up until the present point in the narration (specified by μέχρι . . . τούτου 'hitherto').[73]

Focalized progressives, while rarer than durative progressives, do occur in our corpus. A number of these can be found in drama and Plato's dialogues, with the time of speaking serving as focalization point. Consider example (168):[74]

(168) ἐννοεῖς αὖ, ὦ Μένων, οὗ <u>ἐστιν</u> ἤδη <u>βαδίζων</u> ὅδε τοῦ ἀναμιμνῄσκεσθαι; ὅτι τὸ μὲν πρῶτον ᾔδει μὲν οὔ, ἥτις ἐστὶν ἡ τοῦ ὀκτώποδος χωρίου γραμμή, ὥσπερ οὐδὲ νῦν πω οἶδεν, ἀλλ' οὖν ᾤετό γ' αὐτὴν τότε εἰδέναι, καὶ θαρραλέως ἀπεκρίνετο ὡς εἰδώς, καὶ οὐχ ἡγεῖτο ἀπορεῖν· νῦν δὲ ἡγεῖται ἀπορεῖν ἤδη, καὶ ὥσπερ οὐκ οἶδεν, οὐδ' οἴεται εἰδέναι (Pl., *Men.* 84a)
'There now, Meno, do you observe what progress he has already made in his recollection? At first he did not know what is the line that forms the figure of eight feet, and he does not know even now: but at any rate he thought he knew then, and confidently answered as though he knew, and was aware of no difficulty; whereas now he feels the difficulty he is in, and besides not knowing does not think he knows.' (tr. Lamb)

In order to prove to Meno that there is no teaching but only recollection, Socrates investigates one of Meno's attendants. The attendant arrives at a state of *aporia*, whereupon Socrates notes to Meno that the attendant is making progress inasmuch as it is much better not to know and not to think one knows, than not to know and to think one

---

[73] For alternative interpretations, see Björck (1940: 91) (substantival); Aerts (1965: 24) (adjectival); Porter (1989: 455) (progressive: 'they are speaking').
[74] For similar examples, cf. Aristoph., *Pax* 334, *Plut.* 368; Pl., *Leg.* 736b, *Phdr.* 249d.

knows, with ἐστιν ... βαδίζων 'he is going' referring to an event that is actually going on at the time of speaking, with which it is narrowly connected (contrast with (166)).

We also find examples in the so-called 'incidence scheme', whereby the periphrastic construction occurs in a subordinate clause, and the main clause contains the event that serves as the focalization point.[75] Consider the following example from the Hippocratic corpus:[76]

(169) ἐνάτῃ, πρωΐ ἐξανέστη, ψόφου περὶ τὴν κοιλίην ἄνευ ὀδύνης γενομένου· ὡς ἀφοδεύων δὲ ἦν, ὑπῆλθεν αἵματος πλέον ἢ χοεὺς προσφάτου, καὶ μικρὸν ἐπισχόντι, καὶ τρίτον, πεπηγότες θρόμβοι (Hippoc., Epid. 7.1.10)

'On the ninth morning early, he got up with noise in his intestines, without pain. But as he sat at stool there came forth more than a choeus of fresh blood, and after he waited a brief time a third of a choeus; and there were blood clots' (tr. Smith)

The author describes an enteric illness of a certain Chartades, particularly how the patient excreted 'an impossible amount of blood'[77] (a choeus of blood being the equivalent of six pints of blood). ἀφοδεύων ... ἦν 'he was sitting at stool' serves as the immediate background for the main event, ὑπῆλθεν 'there came forth'.

A noticeable characteristic of progressive εἰμί with the present participle, as also shown by Table 4.3, is that it often occurs in the passive voice, as in the following example:[78]

(170) ἐπειδὴ ἐνταῦθα λόγου γεγόναμεν, ἀναλάβωμεν τὰ πρῶτα λεχθέντα, δι' ἃ δεῦρ' ἥκομεν. ἦν δέ που λεγόμενον λυσιτελεῖν ἀδικεῖν τῷ τελέως μὲν ἀδίκῳ, δοξαζομένῳ δὲ δικαίῳ· ἢ οὐχ οὕτως ἐλέχθη; (Pl., Resp. 588b)

'Let us take up again the statement with which we began and that has brought us to this pass. It was, I believe, averred that injustice is profitable to the completely unjust man who is reputed just. Was not that the proposition?' (tr. Shorey)

After a digression, Socrates proposes to take up the original statement. This statement is described by means of a periphrasis: ἦν ... λεγόμενον

---

[75] This is mostly expressed in the aorist.
[76] As noted by Rydbeck (1967: 199), the presence of progressive examples in the Hippocratic corpus has been completely overlooked by the standard accounts. For similar examples, cf. Eur., HF 313, IT 1339.
[77] Note that this is Smith's assessment of the amount.
[78] For similar examples, see e.g. Aristoph., Equ. 468; Eur., IT 1368; Hdt. 1.152.1, 3.134.4, 5.1.3; Pl., Ti. 26b, Resp. 490a.

'it was [being] said'. Note how the construction lays explicit emphasis on the duration of this saying, while ἐλέχθη 'it was proposed' simply recapitulates.

The fact that many examples occur in the passive voice, without an explicit agent, evidences low transitivity. It forms an interesting parallel to anterior εἰμί with the perfect participle, which, as we saw in §3.3.2.2, also predominantly occurred in the passive voice at an early stage. Low transitivity is also indicated by the fact that even when used in the active voice, the construction almost never occurs with an affected object, and is mostly used with verb classes which only take one participant, such as verbs of movement (as in (168) and (169)).[79]

4.3.3 Functional Competition Between εἰμί and τυγχάνω with the Present Participle?

While Dietrich (1973a: 202) is right that the occurrence of progressive εἰμί with the present participle is not as infrequent as Aerts (1965) and other scholars would have us believe, the normed rate of occurrence of the construction is nevertheless low,[80] especially when we compare its NRO with that of other constructions. That it occurs so infrequently is surprising: if we assume that stative εἰμί with the present participle developed after resultative εἰμί with the perfect participle, and that εἰμί with the perfect participle underwent a process of transitivization in the Classical period,[81] whereby it came to be used as an anterior perfect, one could expect εἰμί with the present participle to undergo a similar process and further development (as a progressive, that is). Several suggestions have been made in this regard. Dietrich (1973a: 190), for example, has noted that genre may have played a role: he observes that the construction occurs most frequently in Herodotus, which he attributes to a particular 'Sprachstil':

> Herodot ist einer der Autoren, die eine große Anzahl partialisierender Verbalperiphrasen aufweisen. Das hängt mit seinem Sprachstil zusammen; die breite Erzählweise gibt Gelegenheit zur Schilderung von Situationen.[82]

---

[79] Cf. also Giannaris (2011b: 151–2, 2011c: 206–7).
[80] Cf. Table 4.3.   [81] Cf. §3.3.2.2.
[82] 'Herodotus is one of the authors who frequently use partializing verbal periphrases. This can be connected with his style; his broad manner of narrating allows for the description of situations.'

Philosophical texts, on the other hand, contain much less 'Erzähl-situationen',[83] and in dramatic texts 'wird eher räsoniert als einfach "erzählt".'[84] While it indeed seems likely that genre plays a role, Dietrich's suggestion does not explain (a) why the construction does not occur more frequently in the work of other historiographers such as Thucydides and Xenophon, and (b) why even in those genres where the construction can be expected to occur frequently it occurs relatively infrequently.[85]

Alternatively, Rydbeck (1969: 194) has suggested that *dialect* may have exerted an influence:[86]

> Diese Art von Periphrase ist später außer Gebrauch gekommen, was sich dadurch erklärt, daß man im Laufe von nur einigen Generationen das Gefühl für eine solche feine Unterscheidung verloren haben kann. Die Attiker—vielleicht mit Ausnahme von dem Individualisten Platon—zeigten wenig Interesse für die Periphrasen des Jonischen.[87]

Rydbeck builds on the work of Rosén (1957), who attempted to demonstrate that the use of εἰμί with the present participle is semantically/pragmatically motivated.[88] More specifically, Rosén argues that the construction should be considered a dedicated argument structure construction that signals constituent focus.[89] Rydbeck (1969) argues that while εἰμί with the present participle was used partly with such a function in Ionic, as represented by Herodotus and the Hippocratic corpus, Attic writers did not accept 'ein so wildgewachsenes und schwieriges Produkt wie die herodotische

---

[83] Dietrich (1973a: 199).

[84] Dietrich (1973a: 202). 'There is argued more than there is "narrated".'

[85] This primarily concerns historiography. In drama, oratory, and Plato's philosophical dialogues, we would also expect focalized progressives, taking the time of speaking as focalization point.

[86] On the difference between the use of periphrasis in Ionic and Attic, cf. also Lasso de la Vega (1955: 170).

[87] 'At a later stage, this type of periphrasis fell into disuse, which can be explained by the fact that in the course of only a few generations the feel for such a sharp distinction was lost. The Atticians—perhaps with the exception of the individualist Plato—showed little interest in the Ionic periphrases.'

[88] Rydbeck (1969: 188–91) is critical of Rosén's (1957) proposal, however, and notes that 'seine Thesen nicht ohne weiteres hingenommen werden können' ('his hypotheses cannot be readily adopted').

[89] Cf. §1.2.3.

Periphrase'[90] and limited the construction to a number of stereotyped uses such as πρέπον ἐστί 'it is fitting'. Rydbeck's suggestion is problematic, however, since (a) it is doubtful whether εἰμί with the present participle was really limited to a number of 'stereotyped' uses in Attic prose, and (b) Rosén's theory, as Rydbeck (1969) recognizes,[91] is not valid for all instances of εἰμί with the present participle, even in Herodotus.[92] In other words, it is unclear whether the construction really would have been considered 'difficult'. A more likely scenario seems to be that the progressive construction originated in the low-register Ionic of Herodotus (as also attested in the Hippocratic corpus), and was afterwards 'picked up' by the tragedians. Note in this regard that the distribution of the construction shows a striking similarity to that of ἔχω with the aorist participle.[93]

A third suggestion that Rydbeck (1969: 193–4) and Dietrich (1973a: 203) have made concerns a possible functional overlap with other periphrastic constructions, particularly τυγχάνω with the present participle.[94] As Table 4.4[95] shows, the participial construction with τυγχάνω was very frequently used, especially with the present participle.[96]

---

[90] 'Such a wildly-grown and difficult product as Herodotean periphrasis.' Rydbeck (1969: 199).

[91] Cf. also the observations by Gonda (1959).

[92] This is not to say that there is no correlationship whatsoever between εἰμί with the present participle and constituent focus, especially at this stage of the language. I believe this can be attributed to two main factors: (a) that εἰμί with the present participle expresses imperfective aspect; scholars in general have noted a correlation between imperfective aspect and constituent focus (see e.g. Sicking 1991, 1996); (b) that the construction is in an early stage of grammaticalization, and in general has a low transitivity profile. Metslang (1995) notes a similar use of the periphrastic progressive in Estonian, which is also in an early stage of development, and presents the following 'componential' analysis: 'in the componential semantic structure of the relatively young Estonian progressive, the component of state is foregrounded and the component of ongoing activity or process is backgrounded' (Metslang 1995: 180).

[93] Compare Table 4.3 to Table 3.1.

[94] Two other relevant constructions would be γίγνομαι with the present participle and ὑπάρχω with the present participle.

[95] The data in this table are taken from the older study by Wheeler (1891), so they must be handled with some caution. There are also some examples with τυγχάνω as infinitive or participle, but these occur much less frequently.

[96] Compare the NRO of τυγχάνω with the perfect participle: drama: 0.22, historiography: 0.68, philosophy: 0.58, oratory: 1.02; τυγχάνω with the aorist participle: drama: 0.62, historiography: 0.35, philosophy: 0.28, oratory: 0.30.

Table 4.4. Distribution of τυγχάνω with the present participle in CG (indicative)

Author/genre	PRES	IMPF	AOR	TOT	NRO
Drama	52	12	19	83	2.24
Aeschylus (b. 525/4 BC?)	1	0	2	3	0.70
Sophocles (b. 496/5 BC?)	9	3	1	13	2.03
Euripides (b. 480s BC?)	25	7	7	39	2.48
Aristophanes (b. 460/50 BC?)	17	2	9	28	2.63
Historiography	72	101	92	265	3.99
Herodotus (b. 484 BC?)	37	17	9	63	3.32
Thucydides (b. 460/55 BC?)	4	20	43	67	4.37
Xenophon (b. c.430 BC)	31	64	40	135	4.20
Philosophy	276	37	27	340	5.99
Plato (b. c.429 BC)	276	37	27	340	5.99
Oratory	152	38	29	219	3.71
Antiphon (b. c.480 BC)	0	3	2	5	2.68
Lysias (b. 459/8 BC?)	14	9	2	25	4.27
Andocides (b. c.440 BC)	6	0	0	6	3.34
Isocrates (b. 436 BC)	109	8	4	121	10.94
Isaeus (b. c.420 BC)	6	5	5	16	4.85
Aeschines (b. c.397 BC)	3	2	3	8	1.74
Lycurgus (b. c.390 BC)	1	2	0	3	2.67
Demosthenes (b. 384 BC)	13	9	13	35	1.19

Key: 'PRES' = present (indicative); 'IMPF' = imperfect; 'AOR' = aorist (indicative); 'TOT' = total; 'NRO' = normed rate of occurrence (per 10,000 words).

While Björck (1940: 63–4) also recognizes the possibility of a partial functional overlap between the two constructions in Classical and Post-Classical Greek, he remains critical of the suggestion:

> Zu einem reinen Ausdruck der Progressivität ist τυγχάνειν mit Partizip m. W. nie geworden. Sobald 'zufällig', 'einmal' oder wenigstens 'gerade' nicht hinzugedacht werden kann, weil es sich vielmehr um etwas handelt, was durchaus zu der gegebenen Zeit zu erwarten war, so ist τυγχάνειν unbrauchbar.[97]

The history of the participial construction with τυγχάνω still needs to be written, but given what we know it seems very likely that such an overlap did occur at some point: (a) Jannaris (1897: 493) points

---

[97] 'As far as I know, τυγχάνειν with the participle never fully came to express purely progressive aspect. As soon as "by coincidence", "once", or at least "just" cannot be added, that is, when we are dealing with something that can be expected at the given time, τυγχάνω cannot be used.'

Imperfective Aspect 231

out that the participial construction with τυγχάνω disappears in Greco-Roman times (that is, the period from 150 BC to 300 AD). This is confirmed by my own research, which shows that in biographical/hagiographical texts of the middle register (such as the Septuagint, the New Testament, etc.) the construction occurs rarely.[98] In texts of the higher register, however, the construction continues to be used with some frequency; (b) Ljungvik (1926: 45) notes with regard to the apocryphal gospels that τυγχάνω is used with the meaning of 'to be':[99] 'τυγχάνειν hat, wie es scheint, die Bedeutung der Zufälligkeit u. dgl. ganz eingebüsst und wurde wohl fast nur als ein volleres "sein" empfunden'.[100]

The most likely scenario is that in the Post-Classical period τυγχάνω with the present participle fully lost its modal meaning and coincided with the periphrastic constructions of εἰμί with the present and perfect participle, which were (or, in the case of εἰμί with the present participle, *became*) firmly established during this period. A similar scenario is suggested by Rydbeck (1969: 193), who notes with regard to the absence of the construction in the New Testament:[101]

τυγχάνειν braucht das Zufällige durchaus nicht so besonders scharf zu unterstreichen, sondern kann in seiner Nuance recht verblaßt sein. Vermutlich ist es so, daß die anderen Periphrasenmöglichkeiten im NT *auf die eine oder andere Weise* die Periphrase mit τυγχάνειν überflüssig gemacht haben.[102]

The more difficult question for us to answer is to what extent this functional overlap already existed in the Classical period. As a lexical

---

[98] In the Septuagint, for example, virtually all examples occur in 2Macc. (3.9, 4.32, 9.1), a work which is known for its elevated register.

[99] Note that Phrynichus (Phryn. 242) rejects this usage. For some examples from the papyri, see e.g. P.Cair.Isid.62, l. 5 (296 AD); P.Cair.Isid.77, ll. 19-20 (320 AD); P.Mert.2.91, l. 4 (316 AD); P.Mich.6.426, l. 9 (199/200 AD?); SB.24.16252, ll. 3-4 (163 AD).

[100] 'τυγχάνειν has, it seems, completely lost the meaning of coincidence and the like, and is almost exclusively used as a fuller expression of "to be".'

[101] That the direct competitor for τυγχάνω with the present participle would have been εἰμί with the aorist participle, as Rydbeck (1969: 193) suggests, seems very unlikely, both from a synchronic (functional) and a diachronic point of view.

[102] 'τυγχάνειν does not need to particularly stress the coincidental, but it can be bleached in its nuance. It is probably so that the other periphrastic means in the NT made the periphrasis with τυγχάνειν unnecessary.'

verb, τυγχάνω has a number of uses,[103] as can be seen in the following examples:[104]

(a) 'to encounter someone' (with genitive)

(171) τυχοῦσαι δ' ἀγαθῶν ἀνδρῶν ὁμοίας ἐκτήσαντο τὰς ψυχὰς τῇ φύσει (Lys. 2.5)

'But having met with valiant men they found their spirit now was like to their sex.' (tr. Lamb)

(b) 'to obtain something' (with genitive)

(172) ὧν δέ σου τυχεῖν ἐφίεμαι / ἄκουσον (Soph., Phil. 1315–16)

'But hear what I desire to gain from you.' (tr. Jebb)

(c) 'to find oneself in a certain place by coincidence'

(173) μὴ σύ γε κεῖθι τύχοις, ὅτε ῥυβδήσειεν (Hom., Od. 12.106)

'May you not be there when she sucks it down.' (tr. Dimock-Murray)

(d) 'to happen to one' (with dative)

(174) γεγήθει δὲ φρένα Νηλεύς, / οὕνεκά μοι τύχε πολλὰ νέῳ πόλεμον δὲ κιόντι (Hom., Il. 11.683–4)

'And Neleus rejoiced at heart, since much booty had fallen to me when I went to war as a stripling.' (tr. Wyatt-Murray)

There are a number of semantic connections between these uses: uses (a) and (b), for example, both take a complement, and both have an animate first participant. Uses (c) and (d), on the other hand, are both 'intransitive' in the traditional sense of the word; note, however, that in (c) the first participant is animate, while in (d) it is inanimate. Uses

---

[103] See Bailly (1903: 1972-4); Liddell & Scott (1968: 1832-3); de la Villa (2008: 274-7). Clarke (2010: 123) criticizes this subdivision of uses, since (a) and (b) 'center on the deliberate, the well-aimed, that which strikes a target', while (c) and (d) revolve 'around the idea of coincidence, of the fortuitous coming-together of events'. That these two groups of uses are 'at loggerheads with each other' does not seem to be true though. The absence of control may be considered a unifying factor, as noted by de la Villa (2008: 275) with regard to uses (a) and (b): 'en ambos casos, estamos ante la descripción de una situación en la que, independientemente del control que ejerza el elemento que aparece como sujeto en la iniciación de la acción, siempre el hecho se produce de una forma azarosa y fuera del control del propio sujeto' ('In both cases, we are dealing with the description of a situation, which, regardless of the control exercised by the element which appears as subject in the initiation of the action, is random and beyond the control of the subject himself').

[104] I borrow these examples from Liddell & Scott (1968: 1832-3).

Imperfective Aspect

(a) and (d) also have a particular connection (as brought forward in the more archaic translations suggested by Liddell & Scott 'to fall in with persons' and 'to befall to someone'), and here we may be dealing with an instance of the transitive alternation which is well attested in other languages (e.g. 'John opens the door' vs. 'the door opens well').[105] More generally, the semantic feature that seems to unify all four uses is the absence of control.[106]

When it comes to the origins of the participial construction (which is already attested in Homer),[107] use (c) seems to have particular relevance:[108] we might imagine a diachronic process whereby τυγχάνω is combined with a locative adjunct and a conjunct participle, and in time comes to be reanalysed as a periphrastic construction.[109] Such an ambiguity can be found in the following early example:

(175) ὁ δ' Ἀστύοχος ὡς τότε ἐν τῇ Χίῳ <u>ἔτυχε</u> διὰ τὴν προδοσίαν τοὺς ὁμήρους <u>καταλεγόμενος</u> τούτου μὲν ἐπέσχεν, ἐπειδὴ ᾔσθετο τάς τε μετὰ Θηριμένους ναῦς ἠκούσας καὶ τὰ περὶ τὴν ξυμμαχίαν βελτίω ὄντα (Thuc. 8.31.1)

'Astyochus was at Chios selecting hostages as a precaution against the betrayal of the island to Athens, but when he heard of the reinforcements which Theramenes had brought, and of the improved prospects of the allies, he desisted.' (tr. Jowett)

Thucydides describes how Astyochus is at Chios, selecting hostages as a precautionary measure.[110] ἐν τῇ Χίῳ ἔτυχε . . . καταλεγόμενος is ambiguous: καταλεγόμενος 'selecting' may function as a conjunct participle, or alternatively be taken with ἐν τῇ Χίῳ ἔτυχε 'he was in

---

[105] See de la Villa (2008: 277–80).

[106] With regard to the use of τυγχάνω in Homeric war-context, De Boel (1988: 132) notes that 'τυγχάνω . . . denotes the success of an intentional action'. Of course, the notions of 'control' and 'intentionality' are not equivalent, control referring both to (a) intentionality, and (b) attainment of one's goal. Cf. Jiménez (1999: 60) on the use of τυγχάνω in Homer: 'τυγχάνω legt den Erfolg des Angriffs nicht fest, da es sowohl den Kontakt mit dem beabsichtigten Ziel als auch den Kontakt mit einem anderen Punkt bezeichnen kann' ('τυγχάνω does not establish the result of the attack, as it can denote both contact with the intented goal as contact with another point').

[107] See Hom., *Od.* 14.334, 19.291.

[108] Clarke's (2010: 129–30) recent discussion seems to suggest an alternative scenario, whereby the participial construction is seen as an extension of the transitive uses (a) and (b): 'τυγχάνω contracts a relationship with the participle of another verb and characterizes the action in that verb as a fortuitous or accidental coming-together of events.'

[109] Compare our observations in §4.3.2.   [110] Cf. Thuc. 8.24.6.

Chios'. While Wheeler (1891: 146) considers this an instance of the participial construction, word order seems to indicate that a non-periphrastic interpretation may be preferable.

In many of the Classical examples, τυγχάνω with the present participle contains a notion of 'coincidence', in accordance with its etymology (> τύχη 'fortune'). By its very nature, 'coincidence' presumes the coming-together of two events, between which temporal coherence exists:[111] it is over this relation, which is somehow 'unexpected', that the subject of the event expressed by τυγχάνω with the present participle does not exercise any control. The coherence between these two events can be either narrow or broad.[112] Consider, in this regard, examples (176) and (177):

(176) ἔτυχε δὲ διαρρέων διὰ τοῦ χωρίου ποταμὸς Σελινοῦς. καὶ ἐν Ἐφέσῳ δὲ παρὰ τὸν τῆς Ἀρτέμιδος νεὼν Σελινοῦς ποταμὸς παραρρεῖ (Xen., An. 5.3.8)

'As it chanced, there flowed through the plot a river named Selinus; and at Ephesus likewise a Selinus river flows past the temple of Artemis.' (tr. Brownson)

(177) προϊόντος δὲ τοῦ χρόνου κατανοήσας ὁ Στρούθας ὅτι Θίβρων βοηθοίη ἑκάστοτε ἀτάκτως καὶ καταφρονητικῶς, ἔπεμψεν ἱππέας εἰς τὸ πεδίον καὶ καταδραμόντας ἐκέλευσε περιβαλλομένους ἐλαύνειν ὅ τι δύναιντο. ὁ δὲ Θίβρων ἐτύγχανεν ἐξ ἀρίστου διασκηνῶν μετὰ Θερσάνδρου τοῦ αὐλητοῦ (Xen., Hell. 4.8.18)

'As time went on, however, Struthas, who had observed that the raiding expeditions of Thibron were in every case carried out in a disorderly and disdainful fashion, sent horsemen to the plain and ordered them to rush upon the enemy and surround and carry off whatever they could. Now it chanced that Thibron, having finished breakfast, was engaged in throwing the discus with Thersander, the flute-player.' (tr. Brownson)

In example (176), Xenophon narrates how he bought a plot of ground to build an altar and a temple for the goddess Artemis. By coincidence, a river called 'Selinus' runs through this plot: at Ephesus a river with the same name flows past the temple of Artemis. The coherence between buying a plot of ground and a river flowing through this plot

---

[111] I take it that it is this anticipation of coincidence with another event which Coseriu (1975: 13-14) refers to when he notes that τυγχάνω can be conceived of as 'εἰμί + momentan'. Cf. similarly Rydbeck (1969: 193), who notes that the use of τυγχάνω with the present participle gives the present theme 'aoristic' aspect.

[112] Compare with our 'durative' and 'focalized' progressive.

is not narrow: the river did not start flowing through the plot at the very moment when Xenophon buys it. This may be contrasted with (177), where we have narrow coherence: Struthas decides to attack the enemy right at a time when their commander, Thibron, was playing the discus; thus, he was killed first. Here the coincidence is not that the subject is engaged in a certain activity, but rather that he is doing so at the very moment when another event happens.

When it comes to functional overlap, τυγχάνω with the present participle resembles progressive εἰμί with the present participle only to some extent: the latter construction does not always indicate overlap, and the co-occurrence with another event is not necessarily unexpected or out of control of the subject. Moreover, τυγχάνω with the present participle also occurs with stative verbs, with a somewhat different effect than εἰμί with the present participle.[113] However, in cases of increased likelihood of control, we also find an increase in similarity between the two constructions. Such contexts include (a) the present tense, (b) the first or second person, and (c) dynamic verbs (especially verbs of communication). Consider the following example:

(178) σκέψαι δ᾽ ὅτι σε τυγχάνω παρακαλῶν ἐξ ὧν ποιήσει τὰς στρατείας
οὐ μετὰ τῶν βαρβάρων ἐφ᾽ οὓς οὐ δίκαιόν ἐστιν, ἀλλὰ μετὰ τῶν Ἑλλήνων
ἐπὶ τούτους πρὸς οὓς προσήκει τοὺς ἀφ᾽ Ἡρακλέους γεγονότας πολεμεῖν
(Isoc. 5.115)

'And mark that I am summoning you to an undertaking in which you will make expeditions, not with the barbarians against men who have given you no just cause, but with the Hellenes against those upon whom it is fitting that the descendants of Heracles should wage war.' (tr. Norlin)

When τυγχάνω is used in the present tense, the temporal overlap is typically between the time of speaking and the event denoted by the participle (in this case summoning). In this particular example, however, it is clear that the speaker has consciously chosen to address his audience: there seems to be little reason why he would consider his summoning the Athenians a matter of coincidence. The semantics of the construction in examples such as these can be described as 'in the given circumstances it is the case that I . . .': τυγχάνω with the present participle provides a more forceful way of asserting a durative event.

---

[113] Compare Adrados (1992a: 452) who notes that τυγχάνω with the present participle is not 'ambiguous' with regard to the stative meaning of the participle.

Examples of this type are found with particular frequency in oratory,[114] and it is quite striking that it is exactly in this context that progressive εἰμί with the present participle virtually never occurs. Frequent use of the construction with such an 'assertive' value is likely to have led to the further bleaching of the semantics of τυγχάνω to the point that it becomes synonymous with εἰμί.[115] An indication of the approximation between the two is also given by the fact that τυγχάνω can be found with regular adjectives, perhaps through the intermediary of the construction τυγχάνω + ὤν + adjective, whereby ὤν was gradually felt to be omissible. In Plato, for example, we find cases such as τυγχάνει καλή (Hp. mai. 300a) 'it is beautiful' and ῥᾴδιον τυγχάνει (Alc. 1, 129a) 'it is easy'.[116]

4.3.4 'Minor' Periphrastic Constructions

As I noted in the introduction to this chapter, we find much less variation between periphrastic constructions in the domain of imperfective aspect. This low variability has to do with the fact that the present and aorist themes formed an aspectual opposition which remained stable throughout the history of the Ancient Greek language.

Additionally, that ἔχω is much less often used as an auxiliary in the domain of imperfective aspect may be related to the fact that as a lexical verb it is mainly used to express possession, whereas εἰμί can be used in a broader range of contexts, including possession, existence, and most importantly location. As a number of scholars have pointed out, there is an intimate connection between perfect aspect and possession.[117] Benveniste (1960: 127) puts it as follows:[118]

---

[114] For similar examples from Isocrates, see e.g. Isoc. 5.28, 113, 8.9, 101, 11.47, 12.29, 172, 205, 206, 15.12.

[115] As indicated by Smyth (1984 [1920]: 467): 'τυγχάνω often loses the idea of chance, and denotes mere coincidence in time (*I am just now, I was just then*) or simply *I am (was)*.'

[116] For a criticial discussion of these and other cases, see Lorimer (1926).

[117] This is not to say that 'have'-verbs never become more general in meaning. In French, for example, *avoir* also expresses notions of existence and location (as in 'il y a', compare Modern Greek ἔχει). See e.g. Meillet (1923: 11, 13); Kulneff-Eriksson (1994: 4); Bauer (2000: 124–6).

[118] Cf. similarly Vendryes (1937: 89).

Imperfective Aspect 237

Que le parfait soit dans ces langues lié à l'emploi des auxiliaires être et avoir, qu'il n'ait pas d'autre expression possible que être ou avoir avec le participe passé du verbe, et que cette forme périphrastique constitue une conjugaison complète, c'est là un ensemble de traits qui éclairent la nature profonde du parfait. *C'est une forme où la notion d'état, associée à celle de possession, est mise au compte de l'auteur de l'action; le parfait présente l'auteur comme possesseur de l'accomplissement* [my emphasis, KB].[119]

But, as was mentioned in §3.6.2, it is not entirely accurate that ἔχω was limited to expressing possession: it could also be used in combination with adverbs or adjuncts of place, with a value that comes close to that of εἰμί (as in οὕτως ἔχει 'it is so' and εἶχε κατ' οἴκους (Hdt. 6.39.2) 'he was at home'). In periphrases, too, ἔχω was not limited to the perfect and aorist participle (in other words, to perfect aspect): in Euripides' *Trojan Women*, we find an exceptional example of ἔχω with the present participle:

(179) ἐπεὶ σύ, μᾶτερ, †ἐπὶ δάκρυσι καὶ† / γόοισι τὸν θανόντα πατέρα πατρίδα τε / φίλαν <u>καταστένουσ' ἔχεις</u>, / ἐγὼ δ' ἐπὶ γάμοις ἐμοῖς / ἀναφλέγω πυρὸς φῶς / ἐς αὐγάν, ἐς αἴγλαν (Eur., *Tro.* 315–21)

'Since you, mother, continually weep and lament, mourning my father who died, and our cherished country, it is I who make the torch fire blaze out at my own wedding.' (tr. Barlow)

Cassandra enters the scene, carrying a flaming torch in either hand. She addresses Hymenaeus, noting that since her mother is entirely absorbed in mourning, she herself must kindle the torch at her own wedding. The periphrasis καταστένουσ' ἔχεις denotes a durative event, that is, the lamenting of Hecuba. Its use can be thought of as a complex case of analogy: following the extension of εἰμί with the perfect participle (perfect aspect) to εἰμί with the present participle (imperfective aspect), ἔχω with the aorist participle (perfect aspect) was extended to ἔχω with the present participle (imperfective aspect). Contrary to Dietrich (1973b: 210), I do not believe the construction should be considered aspectually the same as ἔχω with the

---

[119] 'That the perfect in these languages is related to the use of the auxiliaries be and have, that there is no other expression possible than be or have with the past participle of the verb, and that this periphrasis forms a full conjugation, these are a number of traits which clarify the real nature of the perfect. This is a form where the notion of state, associated with that of possession, is attributed to the author of the action; the perfect presents the author as possessor of the accomplishment.'

present/aorist participle and a temporal adjunct, a construction that we identified in §3.6.2 as functioning as a 'perfect of persistence'.

As regards this passage in Euripides, commentators note that the use of the periphrasis may be semantically motivated: they suggest translating καταστένουσ' ἔχεις as 'you keep lamenting/wailing for'[120] and compare with the use of the participle ἔχων with a finite verb to express duration (as in ληρεῖς ἔχων (Aristoph., Ran. 512) 'you keep on speaking foolishly').[121] In this regard, Lee (1997: 128–9) suggests that 'perhaps the roles of part. and verb are reversed here as sometimes happens with λανθάνω and φθάνω'.[122] A more direct comparison may be made with a passage in Sophocles' Philoctetes (ἐκέλευσ' ἐμοί σε ποῦ κυρῶν εἴης φράσαι (Soph., Phil. 544) 'I told [him] to tell me where you were' (tr. Lloyd-Jones)), of which Aerts (1965: 19) suggests that an inversion of the more regular κυροίης ὤν has taken place because the present optative κυροίην was uncommon.

4.4 EARLY POST-CLASSICAL GREEK (III–I BC)

4.4.1 εἰμί with the Present Participle in the Septuagint

While the Septuagint (LXX) contains a considerable number of examples of εἰμί with the present participle, it has been given surprisingly little scholarly attention so far.[123] As in the Archaic and Classical Greek periods, where stative examples predominate, in the LXX the stative function of εἰμί with the present participle is still prominent, representing 34% of the examples (76/228). As in Classical Greek, these statives do not form a homogeneous group. In the large majority of the cases, they are formed with lexically stative verbs. This includes the earlier mentioned 'verbs of lexicalized predication of properties', as in ἔστωσαν ἐγγίζοντες (3Reigns 8.59) 'let them be near', δέον ἐστὶν καὶ πρέπον (1Macc. 12.11); 'it is necessary and fitting'; ἦν ἐνδεχόμενα (2Macc. 11.18) 'it was possible'; οὐκ ἔσονται

---

[120] See e.g. Thielmann (1891: 301); Tyrrell (1897: 70); Dietrich (1973b: 210).
[121] Cf. Tyrrell (1897: 70).
[122] On such inversions, see Schwyzer (1950: 389): Kühner & Gerth (1976 [1904]: 98–9).
[123] For some discussion, see Dietrich (1973a: 204–9); Verboomen (1992: 25–71); Evans (2001: 230–48); Hauspie (2011).

Imperfective Aspect

δὲ ὁμονοοῦντες (Dan. 2.43) 'they will not be united'. However, we also find participles which are less prototypically adjectival: these may be based on stative verbs, but take an object, as in ἦν γινώσκων οὐθέν (Gen. 39.23) 'he knew nothing'; ἦν τὸν τρόπον ἔχουσα τοῦτον (2Macc. 1.24) 'it (the prayer) had this manner'; ἐπιστήμων ἦν καὶ σοφὸς καὶ ὑπερέχων πάντας τοὺς σοφοὺς (Dan. 5.11) 'he was prudent and wise and surpassed all the sages' (NETS).

Less often, stative examples are based on lexically dynamic verbs. Consider (180):[124]

(180) δὸς ὑψίστῳ κατὰ τὴν δόσιν αὐτοῦ καὶ ἐν ἀγαθῷ ὀφθαλμῷ καθ' εὕρεμα χειρός· / ὅτι κύριος <u>ἀνταποδιδούς ἐστιν</u> καὶ ἑπταπλάσια ἀνταποδώσει σοι (Sir. 35.9–10)

'Give unto the most High according as he has enriched thee; and as thou hast gotten, give with a cheerful eye. For the Lord makes recompense, and will give thee seven times as much.' (KJV)[125]

The reader is encouraged to be generous when offering to the Lord, for God 'makes recompense and will give you seven times as much'. In order to characterize the Lord, a periphrastic form is used, ἀνταποδιδούς ἐστιν, expressing a stable property (compare our earlier ex. (155)). Note the presence of what we have called 'de-transitivizing' elements, namely the use of the present tense and the absence of an object.

As in the Classical period, various examples can also be found with the participle in the passive voice ('statal passives'), as in οὐκ ἦν ἀργύριον λογιζόμενον (2Chron. 9.20) 'silver was not held in any account' (NETS). In some cases, the present participle seems to have a semantic affinity with the perfect participle. Consider the following example:

(181) ἐν τῇ ἡμέρᾳ ἐκείνῃ ἔσται πᾶς τόπος <u>διανοιγόμενος</u> ἐν τῷ οἴκῳ Δαυιδ (Zach. 13.1)

'On that day every place will be opened for the house of David.'

---

[124] For similar examples, see e.g. Eccles. 8.11; Judg. 20.31; 1Reigns 11.7; 3Reigns 20.5.
[125] Perhaps it should not be entirely excluded that the participle ἀνταποδιδούς is used attributively: 'for he is a god who makes recompense.' It should be noted, however, that the absence of the article with κύριος in the LXX is not uncommon. Compare e.g. καὶ ἐπορεύθη Αβραμ, καθάπερ ἐλάλησεν αὐτῷ κύριος (Gen. 12.4) 'and Abraham went, as the Lord had told him to' (NETS).

Zechariah has a message from the Lord, namely that Jerusalem will be attacked on a certain day, a day on which 'every house will be opened'.[126] In this example, a perfect participle (e.g. ἀνεῳγμένος 'opened') could very well have been used instead of the present participle. The use of a present participle where we would expect a perfect participle may have been stimulated by developments elsewhere in the verbal system, in particular the breakdown of the participial system and the loss of the synthetic perfect.[127] However, it should be noted that the use of the passive voice plays an important role in giving the present participle a resultative-like meaning.[128]

Another characteristic of statives, which we have also encountered in Classical Greek,[129] is the use of the imperative: in the LXX various examples can be found of εἰμί with the present participle in the imperative, expressing various sorts of commands, as in ἔστω τὸ οὖς σου προσέχον (2Esd. 11.11) 'let your ear be attentive'.

The most noteworthy examples in the LXX of εἰμί with the present participle are those that fulfil a progressive function. While progressive examples occur relatively infrequently in Classical Greek, they abound in the LXX (137/228 = 60%). As Rydbeck (1969: 187) notes:

> Es ist nicht übertrieben, wenn man behauptet, daß die Septuaginta mehr Periphrasen von Björcks so bezeichnetem 'progressivem' Typus enthält als die ganze übrige vorchristliche Literatur zusammen.[130]

This suggests that the use of progressives may have been influenced by the Hebrew original, an issue that will be further addressed in §4.4.2.

In most cases, εἰμί with the present participle is used in its durative progressive function (117/137 = 85%). It typically denotes the occurrence of an event in a broad time-frame, which is often indicated by the adverb(ial)s accompanying the periphrasis, such as τρία ἔτη (2Chron. 36.5a) 'three years'; τρεῖς ἑβδομάδας (Dan. 10.2) 'three

---

[126] Note that the Masoretic text has a slightly different reading: 'in that day there shall be a fountain opened to the house of David.'

[127] Cf. §3.4.1.

[128] On the affinity of the passive voice with the perfect (resultative) function, see e.g. Sicking & Stork (1996: 169). Compare Haverling (2009: 350, 360–1, 407–8) on the use of the Latin passive (synthetic) present.

[129] Cf. §4.3.1.

[130] 'It is not exaggerated to say that the Septuagint contains more periphrases of Björck's so-called "progressive" type than the entire pre-Christian literature combined.'

weeks'; ἡμέρας ἑκατὸν εἴκοσι (Jth. 1.16) 'hundred and twenty days'; ἡμέρας πλείους (Jth. 4.13) 'many days'; ἐπὶ μῆνας τρεῖς (Jth. 16.20) 'for three months'; τεσσαράκοντα ἔτη (Num. 14.33) 'forty years'. Often such a broad time-frame, whether specified by a temporal adverb(ial) or not, brings with it a sense of iteration, as in (182):[131]

(182) Σιμων δὲ ἦν ἐφοδεύων τὰς πόλεις τὰς ἐν τῇ χώρᾳ καὶ <u>φροντίζων</u> τῆς ἐπιμελείας αὐτῶν (1Macc. 16.14)
'Now Simon was making a tour of the cities that were in the country, and taking care for the good ordering of them.' (BGS, slightly modified)

We read how Simon was going from town to town in Judea, trying to help the people. The phrase ἦν ἐφοδεύων 'he was visiting' expresses a durative event, which is also iterative, given that Simon visits multiple towns.

As in Classical Greek, we also find examples where εἰμί with the present participle denotes an event that started in the past and continues up to a later point in time, what we have called a 'perfect of persistence'. Consider the following example:

(183) <u>ἦσαν</u> οἱ υἱοὶ Ισραηλ καὶ οἱ υἱοὶ Ιουδα μόνοι <u>ποιοῦντες</u> τὸ πονηρὸν κατ' ὀφθαλμούς μου ἐκ νεότητος αὐτῶν (Jer. 39.30)
'For the children of Israel and the children of Judah have been doing only that which was evil in my sight from their youth.' (ASV, slightly modified)

In answer to Jeremiah's prayer, God says that he will give Jerusalem to King Nebuchadnezzar of Babylonia and his army, as the people of Israel and of Judah have displeased him from the very beginning. Periphrastic ἦσαν ... ποιοῦντες 'they were doing' denotes an event which started in the past (ἐκ νεότητος αὐτῶν 'from their youth') and continues up to the time of God's answering Jeremiah.

Durative progressives denoting the continuation of an event in a more narrow time-frame (without any repetition) are (still) uncommon at this stage. One such example would be (184), where the periphrastic construction, quite surprisingly, pushes the plotline forward (i.e. it denotes a temporally sequential event):[132]

---

[131] For similar examples, see e.g. Gen. 26.35; 1Chron. 18.14; 2Chron. 30.10, 36.16; 2Esd. 16.14; 1Macc. 5.53; 4Reigns 17.25.
[132] For similar examples, see e.g. Dan. 1.16; 2Esd. 12.13; 3Reigns 5.24; 4Reigns 17.25, 17.28.

(184) καὶ παρῆλθον ἐπὶ πύλην τοῦ Αιν καὶ εἰς κολυμβήθραν τοῦ βασιλέως, καὶ οὐκ ἦν τόπος τῷ κτήνει παρελθεῖν ὑποκάτω μου. καὶ <u>ἤμην ἀναβαίνων</u> ἐν τῷ τείχει χειμάρρου νυκτὸς καὶ <u>ἤμην συντρίβων</u> ἐν τῷ τείχει. καὶ <u>ἤμην</u> ἐν πύλῃ τῆς φάραγγος καὶ ἐπέστρεψα (2Esd. 12.14–15)

'And I passed on to the fountain gate, and to the king's pool; and there was no room for the beast to pass under me. And I went up by the wall of the brook by night, and mourned over the wall, and passed through the gate of the valley, and returned.' (BGS)

In such examples, εἰμί with the present participle is used in imitation of the Hebrew *wayehi qotel*-structure,[133] which stresses the duration of consecutive ('accomplished') events (with הָיָה (*hāyāh*) 'be' in the inverted imperfect). In Ancient Greek, we usually find the synthetic aorist in these circumstances.[134] It has been suggested that in this and other cases the aspectual function of εἰμί with the present participle should be called 'ingressive' rather than (durative) progressive.[135] I consider that these are more precisely labelled 'durative progressives', whose left temporal boundary is contextually stressed (in the LXX through the use of the periphrastic construction in contexts typical for the Hebrew *wayehi qotel*-structure).[136]

In some cases, the durative event expressed by the periphrastic construction can be related to another, foregrounded event, which typically occurs in another main clause. However, the relationship between these two events is a very general one: in other words, to use Givón's (1995) terminology, there is weak semantic/pragmatic 'connectivity'. Consider the following example:

(185) καὶ βασιλεὺς Συρίας <u>ἦν πολεμῶν</u> ἐν Ισραηλ καὶ ἐβουλεύσατο πρὸς τοὺς παῖδας αὐτοῦ λέγων Εἰς τὸν τόπον τόνδε τινὰ ελμωνι παρεμβαλῶ (4Reigns 6.8)

'And the king of Syria was waging war with Israel and he took counsel with his servants, saying, "I will encamp at this certain place, Elmoni".' (NETS, slightly modified)

There is no narrow connection between ἦν πολεμῶν 'he was waging war' and ἐβουλεύσατο 'he took counsel': the periphrastic construction

---

[133] See Cohén (1984: 323); Verboomen (1992: 25ff.).
[134] Not always, though. See Rijksbaron (2002: 17–19).
[135] Cf. Ceglia (1998: 30–3, 35–6), and Joüon & Muraoka (1991: 412) with regard to Hebrew.
[136] Note that already in Classical Greek we find some cases where the context has a similar effect. See e.g. Eur., *Cyc.* 381; Soph., *OT* 847.

Imperfective Aspect

specifies the very general circumstances under which the foregrounded event takes place, that is, the king was waging war and at a certain point in time decided to consult his servants.

In other examples, a foregrounded event serves as point of interruption or 'focalization point'. Here we can speak, in other words, of 'focalized progressives'. It should be stressed, however, that these occur still much less frequently than statives and durative progressives, representing only 9% (= 20/228) of the total number of examples. This finding is in accordance with the grammaticalization path provided by Bertinetto *et al.*, according to which, from a diachronic point of view, durative progressivity becomes established before focalized progressivity.

In the majority of the examples we find the syntactic configuration illustrated in (186), whereby two clauses are coordinated, the first containing the backgrounded event, and the second the foregrounded event that serves as a focalization point:

(186) καὶ ἦν ὁ βασιλεὺς Ισραηλ διαπορευόμενος ἐπὶ τοῦ τείχους, καὶ γυνὴ ἐβόησεν πρὸς αὐτόν (4Reigns 6.26)
'And the king of Israel was passing by on the city wall, and a woman cried out to him.' (NETS)

In this example, the backgrounded event is expressed by periphrastic ἦν ... διαπορευόμενος 'he was passing by', while the foregrounded event by the aorist ἐβόησεν 'she shouted'. Note how there is both temporal overlap and strong connectivity between the two events: right at the time when the king of Israel was walking on the wall, a woman shouted at him.

In a number of other examples, the focalization point (in the aorist) precedes the periphrastic progressive[137] or is pragmatically provided (with εἰμί in the present tense, accompanied by ἰδού).[138]

It may be clear that the progressive use of εἰμί with the present participle, as illustrated in examples (182) to (186) is much higher in transitivity than the stative use of the same construction:[139] in terms of the kinesis-parameter, they denote an event rather than a state. Clauses containing such a progressive form often have a volitional

---

[137] See e.g. Bel 21; 2Esd. 23.22.
[138] See e.g. Judg. 8.5; 3Reigns 1.25; 4Reigns 17.26.
[139] Though note that in absolute terms they are both indicative of lower transitivity.

first participant. Moreover, contrary to what we have seen in Classical Greek, where either verbs in the passive voice or intransitive verbs in the active voice were used, we also often find a second participant, who may be affected by the event expressed by the participle.[140] For example, we find the construction used with (telic) destroy-verbs such as ἀποκτέννω (4Reigns 17.25) 'I kill', and psych-verbs such as παροξύνω (Deut. 9.22) 'I irritate', παροργίζω (4Reigns 21.15) 'I provoke to anger', and φοβερίζω (2Esd. 16.14) 'I terrify'. Thus, I would argue that in the domain of imperfective aspect too we are dealing with an instance of *transitivization*, which can be compared to the increase in transitivity observed for εἰμί with the perfect participle in the Classical period.[141]

It must be noted, however, that there are also progressive examples that are lower in transitivity. In terms of the kinesis-parameter, for example, we have observed that there are many cases that denote a repeated event (so-called 'iterative durative progressives'). Various examples are attested in the future tense[142] (e.g. Αβρααμ δὲ γινόμενος ἔσται εἰς ἔθνος μέγα (Gen. 18.18) 'Abraham will become a great nation') or the imperative mood (e.g. δαπάνη ἔστω διδομένη (2Esd. 6.8) 'let money be given'), which are lower in transitivity in terms of *mode*. While attested with less frequency than in Classical Greek, examples in the passive voice (without an expressed agent) are also found (e.g. ἦν προσφερόμενον τὸ θυμίαμα (Jth. 9.1) 'the incense was (being) offered').

Moreover, we often find εἰμί combined with lexical verbs that are stative-like in that they denote long temporal duration, low volitionality of the subject, or a combination of both. For example, we find examples with postural verbs such as εἰρηνεύω (Dan. 4.4) 'I live in peace', κατοικέω (Gen. 14.12) 'I inhabit', κρεμάννυμαι (Josh. 10.26) 'I hang', νέμω (Num. 14.33) 'I live in the open', οἰκέω (2Esd. 13.26) 'I live', and παροικέω (2Reigns 4.3) 'I live near', next to psychological

---

[140] Of course, as long as the verb is used with imperfective aspect the object will not be totally affected. Cf. Naess (2007: 119).

[141] Cf. §3.3.2.2.

[142] Compare Ceglia (1998: 37) on the use of the future tense with the progressive periphrasis: 'in effetti le forme di questo tempo presentano un carattere semi-modale che poteva, forse, difficilmente conciliarsi con quello aspettuale che la perifrasi esprime, o quantomeno renderlo meno perspicuo' ('in fact, the forms of this tense have a semi-modal character, which, perhaps, could be difficult to reconcile with the aspectual value expressed by the periphrasis, or at least render it less perspicuous').

Imperfective Aspect 245

verbs such as μισέω (Deut. 19.6) 'I hate', θάλπω (3Reigns 1.4) 'I cherish, keep warm', and ὑποβλέπομαι (1Reigns 18.9) 'I look askance at'.

Interestingly, we also find instances where εἰμί with the present participle seems to fulfil a habitual aspectual function. Differentiating these examples from durative progressives is, however, not entirely simple. Consider example (187):

(187) καὶ ἦν Σαουλ ὑποβλεπόμενος τὸν Δαυιδ ἀπὸ τῆς ἡμέρας ἐκείνης καὶ ἐπέκεινα (1Reigns 18.9)
'And Saul was eyeing David with suspicion from that day and beyond.'
(NETS)

After David has killed Goliath and the battle between the Philistines and Israelites is over, the Israelites praise David more than Saul. Saul becomes jealous and no longer trusts David, as is expressed by the periphrastic form ἦν ὑποβλεπόμενος 'he was eyeing'. Contrary to Verboomen (1992: 40), I do not think this form is best considered habitual. As noted in §1.4.1.1, two main semantic differences between (iterative durative) progressives and habituals are that (a) habituals typically refer to a more extensive period of time,[143] and (b) habituals typically emphasize the separate subevents to a greater extent.[144] While ἦν ὑποβλεπόμενος does refer to an extensive period of time, there is no emphasis on the separate subevents, since no mention is made of place and time, and the participants of the event remain the same.

In an example such as (187), the fact that there is little emphasis on the separate events can be explained by the fact that the lexical verb on which the participle is based is atelic.[145] When a telic verb such as δίδωμι 'I give' is used, as in (188), a habitual interpretation comes

---

[143] Compare Oldsjö (2001: 225): 'the main difference between the two iterative types is that habitual situations refer to sequences that are repeated for a much longer period of time than the normal iterative. This can be formulated as a difference between situations that are iterated for a limited period of time and habits and customs that are always performed under certain conditions.' Of course, what constitutes an 'extended period of time' remains open to interpretation (Fanning 1990: 212).

[144] Compare Xrakovskij (1997: 58): 'habitual utterances normally include actants and circonstants denoting place, time and manner of action which constitute the semantic field of the habitual.'

[145] Compare Wood (2007: 243): 'repetition of an atelic event (without pauses or change in participants) creates a "plural" event with no non-arbitrary subevents, and thus no basis for identifying multiple distinct events.'

much more naturally, since such verbs possess an inherent temporal boundary:

(188) καὶ ἐποίησεν αὐτῷ γαζοφυλάκιον μέγα, καὶ ἐκεῖ ἦσαν πρότερον διδόντες τὴν μαναα καὶ τὸν λίβανον καὶ τὰ σκεύη καὶ τὴν δεκάτην τοῦ σίτου καὶ τοῦ οἴνου καὶ τοῦ ἐλαίου (2Esd. 23.5)
'And he had prepared for him a great chamber, where aforetime they laid the meat offerings, the frankincense, and the vessels, and the tithes of the corn, the new wine, and the oil.' (KJV)

Tobiah is given a great chamber, where offerings used to be laid. The phrase ἦσαν . . . διδόντες 'they were giving' refers to events that occurred repeatedly in the past, that is, the giving of offerings. In comparison with (187), greater emphasis is put on the subevents, since we are dealing with different participants giving different offerings. Note, however, that the adverb πρότερον 'aforetime' refers to an indefinite time period, rather than specifying the occasions on which the repeated event occurred.[146]

That such habitual examples should occur at this stage is unexpected on the basis of the grammaticalization path proposed by Bertinetto *et al.*, according to which the habitual function follows the focalized progressive one. Given that (a) there is a clear semantic affinity between durative progressives and habituals, and (b) that focalized progressives still occur infrequently, a change to the grammaticalization path may tentatively be suggested, according to which both habituals and focalized progressives can independently develop from durative progressives.[147] A similar suggestion has been made by Bybee *et al.* (1994: 158–9) with regard to habituals:

> Both habitual and iterative [i.e. iterative durative progressive, KB] indicate that an action is repeated, but in the case of iterative, the action is repeated on the same occasion, while habitual means that the different occurrences are on separate occasions. Our theory would lead us to expect that one of these specific meanings is the earlier meaning of the gram, and the other is added as the meaning of the gram generalizes.

---

[146] In general, iterative adverb(ial)s co-occur infrequently with periphrastic forms in the LXX. In a number of examples we find the expression πάσας τὰς ἡμέρας (e.g. Deut. 28.29; 3Reigns 5.15; 1Macc. 3.12) 'every day', but this expression seems to emphasize the continuity of the action. Perhaps the clearest example would be εἰς ἡμέραν μίαν (2Esd. 15.18) 'day by day'.

[147] With habituals perhaps resulting from iterative durative progressive examples, while focalized progressives resulting from non-iterative durative progressive ones.

We do not have direct evidence concerning the directionality of this development, that is, whether iterative generalizes to include habitual or habitual generalizes to include iterative. However, it is possible to infer that iterative is probably the earlier more specific meaning of these grams, using formal and semantic evidence.

4.4.2 Language Contact: From Minor to Major Use Pattern

In §4.4.1, I suggested that the use of εἰμί with the present participle in the LXX, especially in its (durative) progressive function, may have been influenced by the Hebrew model. In the present section, we shall try to determine the extent of this influence. In order to do so, use can be made of recent work by Evans (2001: 220–57), who in his book on verbal syntax in the Greek Pentateuch recognizes a number of degrees of structural motivation when it comes to verbal periphrasis. More specifically, Evans (2001: 249–55) proposes to distinguish between three broad translation-technical categories. The first of these is most clear, and comprises Hebrew constructions that bear an obvious structural affinity to periphrastic εἰμί: Hebrew הָיָה (hāyāh) 'be' with the participle, and also a Hebrew pronoun or particle (e.g. הִנֵּה (hinnēh) 'behold') combined with the participle.[148] The second category mostly consists of Hebrew הָיָה (hāyāh) with a noun or adjective, next to the participle without הָיָה (hāyāh), while the third refers to freely used Greek periphrases. Consider the following examples:

Category 1

(189) וּמֹשֶׁה הָיָה רֹעֶה אֶת־צֹאן יִתְרוֹ (Exod. 3.1)
umōseh hāyāh rō 'eh 'et-ṣōn yitrōw
καὶ Μωυσῆς ἦν ποιμαίνων τὰ πρόβατα Ιοθορ
'Now Moses was keeping the flock of Jethro.' (WEB)

Category 2

(190) וְהָיִיתָ אַךְ שָׂמֵחַ (Deut. 16.15)
wehāyītā ak sāmēaḥ
καὶ ἔσῃ εὐφραινόμενος
'(Then) you shall be joyful.' (NETS)

---

[148] Constructions consisting of a Hebrew pronoun or particle combined with a participle already show a lesser degree of structural affinity with Ancient Greek εἰμί with the present participle.

Category 3

(191) וְאָרְנָן דָּשׁ חִטִּים (1Chron. 21.20)
we'ornān dāš ḥiṭṭīm
καὶ Ορνα ἦν ἀλοῶν πυρούς
'Now Ornan was threshing wheat.' (WEB)

In (189), we encounter the highest degree of structural similarity:[149] Hebrew הָיָה רֹעֶה (*hāyāh rō'eh*) (with imperfect 3SG of הָיָה (*hāyāh*) 'be' and the active participle of רָעָה (*rā'āh*) 'to tend a flock') is translated by Greek ἦν ποιμαίνων 'he was herding' (with imperfect 3SG of εἰμί and the present participle of ποιμαίνω 'I herd'). Example (190) is representative of the second category,[150] with a lesser degree of structural affinity: Hebrew וְהָיִיתָ שָׂמֵחַ (*wehāyītā sāmēaḥ*) (with perfect 2SG of הָיָה (*hāyāh*) 'be' and the adjective שָׂמֵחַ (*sāmēaḥ*) 'joyful') is translated by Greek ἔσῃ εὐφραινόμενος 'you will be joyful' (with future 2SG of εἰμί and the present participle of the verb εὐφραίνομαι 'I rejoice'). The third category is illustrated in (191):[151] here the synthetic Hebrew form דָּשׁ (*dāš*) (perfect 3SG of the verb דּוּשׁ (*dūš*) 'to thresh') is translated by the periphrastic Greek form ἦν ἀλοῶν 'he was threshing' (with imperfect 3SG of εἰμί and the present participle of ἀλοάω 'I thresh').

Having compared all Greek periphrastic forms to their Hebrew equivalent (so not taking into account the deuterocanonical/apocryphal books included in the Greek Septuagint), I find that 104 out of a total of 178 examples, or 58%, are directly influenced by the Hebrew original (corresponding to Evans' first category). I have found forty-two examples (= 24%) where there is some structural affinity (corresponding to Evans' second category), and a further thirty-two (= 18%) that show no structural influence whatsoever (corresponding to Evans' third category). In other words, as much as 82% (146/178) of the examples are structurally influenced (to a greater or lesser degree), while only 18% are freely employed. Of these 82% structurally influenced forms, only 26% (38/146) are stative, while of the 18% freely employed ones, 56% (18/32) are stative.

---

[149] For similar examples, see e.g. Dan. 1.16, 10.2; Deut. 19.6, 28.29; Exod. 25.20; Gen. 4.17, 14.12; Jer. 4.24; Lev. 15.19.

[150] For similar examples, see e.g. 2Chron. 9.20, 18.7; Gen. 9.3, 26.35, 39.23; Jer. 39.30; Num. 35.23; Ps. 91.15; 4Reigns 17.32, 17.41.

[151] For similar examples, see e.g. 1Chron. 21.20, 23.26, 29.15; 2Chron. 15.16, 36.15; Gen. 13.10; Ezech. 1.12, 16.7, 23.29; Isa. 22.24.

Imperfective Aspect

These findings confirm that the main area of influence of Hebrew lies in the employment of εἰμί with the present participle in its (durative) progressive function. While progressive examples can be found in Classical Greek, they constitute what Heine & Kuteva (2005: 44) call a 'minor use pattern'. Under situations of contact, such a minor use pattern may develop into a 'major use pattern' (on the model of another language), which is what we find in the LXX.

4.4.3 Other EPG Testimonies

εἰμί with the present participle is well attested in other EPG texts too, primarily in its stative aspectual function. Consider Table 4.5 (for ease of comparison, data from the LXX have been included):

Table 4.5. Distribution of εἰμί with the present participle in EPG (stative)

Genre/Author/Text	STAT	NRO	TTR	STAT (ACT)	STAT (MED)	STAT (PASS)
Biography/hagiography	79	1.20	0.67	57	14	8
Septuagint (III–II BC)	76	1.18	0.68	55	13	8
Apocalypse of Enoch (II–I BC)	2	(2.31)	1	1	1	0
Life of Adam and Eve (I BC–I AD)	1	(2.17)	1	1	0	0
Historiography	122	1.96	0.30	89	12	21
Polybius (b. c.200 BC)	76	2.32	0.24	61	3	12
Dionysius of Halicarnassus (b. 60 BC)	46	1.55	0.52	28	9	9
Scientific prose	86	2.11	0.52	47	16	23
Archimedes (b. c.287 BC)	35	3.26	0.34	11	9	15
Strabo (b. c.64 BC)	51	1.70	0.67	36	7	8
Papyri	36	/	0.33	26	6	4
Letters	14	/	0.50	10	2	2
Petitions	3	/	0.67	2	1	0

Key: 'STAT' = stative; 'NRO' = normed rate of occurrence (per 10,000 words); 'TTR' = type/token ratio; 'ACT' = active; 'MED' = middle; 'PASS' = passive.

This table shows that the stative use of the construction remains more or less stable vis-à-vis Classical Greek. Note that this use is also not more frequent in the LXX than in the other texts. As in Classical Greek, combinations with participles of 'verbs with lexicalized predication of qualities' occur very frequently, such as δέον ἐστί 'it is necessary' (forty five instances), προσῆκόν ἐστι 'it is seemly' (fourteen instances), πρέπον ἐστί 'it is fitting' (ten instances), ὁμολογούμενόν ἐστι 'it is acknowledged' (eleven instances) and συμφέρον ἐστί 'it is expedient' (eight instances).[152] Combinations with other stative verbs, or with dynamic verbs, can also be found. Consider the following example:

(192) ὅσα δὲ ἂν ἦι τιμὰς οὐχ ἐστη[κ]υίας ἔχοντα, ἐπὶ δὲ τοῖς ἐργαζομένοις [ἐσ]τὶν τ[άσ]ϙειν \ᾶς/ ἂν βο[ύ]λωνται, ἐξεταζέσ[θ]ω καὶ τοῦτο μὴ παρέργως (P.Tebt.3.1.703, ll. 176–9 (c.210 BC))

'Make also a careful investigation of those goods which have no fixed prices and on which the dealers may put what prices they like.' (tr. Hunt & Smyly)

In this memorandum, the διοικητής (financial official) gives instructions to a subordinate concerning a number of matters. Among others, the latter is instructed to carefully investigate 'those goods which have no fixed price', which are referred to by means of a stative periphrastic form, ἦι ... ἔχοντα 'it has'.

While in this type of construction the participle occurs predominantly in the active voice, in scientific prose and historiography various 'statal passives' can be found. This can be explained—to some extent—by the presence of stereotype expressions such as the earlier mentioned ὁμολογούμενόν ἐστι 'it is acknowledged'. In addition, we find examples in Dionysius of Halicarnassus that are reminiscent of Herodotus (of the type ἔστι δέ τις ... λεγόμενος λόγος 'some story is told', Ant. Rom. 2.49.4), and that may well constitute conscious borrowings. In scientific prose, Archimedes in particular, the passive voice is often used in assumptions of the following type:[153]

(193) ἔστω τμᾶμα τὸ ΒΘΓ περιεχόμενον ὑπὸ εὐθείας καὶ ὀρθογωνίου κώνου τομᾶς (Archim., Quad. Parab. 2.178.2-3)

'Let the segment ΒΘΓ be encompassed by a straight line and a parabola.'

Archimedes starts his discussion by assuming the existence of a segment, which is encompassed by a parabola and a straight line. In this passage, which is reminiscent of what we find in Aristotle, a passive periphrasis is used, ἔστω ... περιεχόμενον 'let it be encompassed'.

---

[152] These figures do not include the LXX.
[153] For similar examples, see e.g. Archim., Aren., 2.146.19–20, Con. sph. 1.170.18–19, Eratosth. 3.86.11, 100.1, Quad. parab. 2.181.4, 2.182.14.

Imperfective Aspect 251

The use of εἰμί with the present participle in more transitive contexts, that is, as a durative/focalized progressive, is also attested in other EPG texts, though much less frequently. Consider Table 4.6 (for ease of comparison, data from LXX have again been included):

Table 4.6. Distribution of εἰμί with the present participle in EPG (progressive)

Genre/Author/Text	PROG	NRO	TTR	DUR PROG	FOC PROG	PROG (ACT)	PROG (MED)	PROG (PASS)
Biography/hagiography	150	2.28	0.73	127	23	103	35	12
Septuagint (III–II BC)	137	2.13	0.74	117	20	94	33	10
Apocalypse of Enoch (II–I BC)	11	(12.73)	0.91	8	3	8	1	2
Life of Adam and Eve (I BC–I AD)	2	(4.34)	1	2	0	1	1	0
Historiography	21	0.34	0.95	18	3	7	6	8
Polybius (b. c.200 BC)	4	0.12	1	4	0	2	0	2
Dionysius of Halicarnassus (b. 60 BC)	17	0.57	0.94	14	3	5	6	6
Scientific prose	0	0.00	0	0	0	0	0	0
Papyri	7	/	0.86	4	3	4	2	1
Letters	4	/	1	4	0	3	0	1

Key: 'PROG' = progressive; 'NRO' = normed rate of occurrence (per 10,000 words); 'TTR' = type/token ratio; 'DUR' = durative; 'FOC' = focalized; 'ACT' = active; 'MED' = middle; 'PASS' = passive.

As the table shows, the use of εἰμί with the present participle with a durative or focalized progressive function is to a large extent limited to the LXX, which again suggests the importance of Hebrew as a model. In the *Apocalypse of Enoch* and the *Life of Adam and Eve* various progressive examples are found,[154] but given the Jewish background of these texts perhaps this should not surprise us too much. Interestingly, we also find some isolated instances of progressive examples in our other literary texts, contrary to what is often claimed.[155] These are generally of the durative progressive type, in accordance with the predictions made by the grammaticalization path provided by Bertinetto *et al.* Note that in scientific prose progressive

---

[154] See e.g. *Apoc. En.* 10.19, 10.21, 14.14, 94.3, 95.2; *V. Adam* 13.12, 39.8. Note that in the Apocalypse of Enoch almost all examples occur in the future tense.
[155] See further §4.5.3.

examples are entirely absent, which is very likely to be influenced by genre.

Progressive examples occur relatively frequently in historiography at least partly due to the presence of a specific syntactic pattern, that is, πολὺς εἰμί + present participle 'I am very much V-ing'. Consider the following example:

(194) ἔνθα δὴ πολὺς ὁ Ταρκύνιος <u>ἦν</u> ἐπιορκίαν τε καὶ ἀπιστίαν τοῖς Ῥωμαίοις <u>ἐγκαλῶν</u>, καὶ τὸν βασιλέα <u>παροξύνων</u> (Dion. Hal., Ant. Rom. 5.33.2)

'Then indeed Tarquinius was vehement in accusing the Romans of a breach of their oaths and of perfidy, and in goading the king.' (tr. Cary)

The Romans have sent an embassy to king Porsena, asking him to serve as a judge between the Tarquinii and themselves. When the hostages accompanying the ambassadors flee, Tarquinius accuses the Romans of perfidy, πολὺς ἦν . . . ἐγκαλῶν 'he was accusing' expressing his repeated accusal. This (sub)construction, which does not occur in the LXX, accounts for 43% (10/23) of the progressive examples in Polybius and Dionysius of Halicarnassus.[156] In general, this can be considered a relatively high-transitivity construction, since it takes a volitional subject, often includes two participants, and almost exclusively occurs in the imperfect tense.[157] Instances can also be found in Herodotus (with πολλός),[158] and as such we may again be dealing with a case of conscious imitation, especially in Dionysius of Halicarnassus, in whose work the majority of the examples can be found (8/10).

Whether this construction can be considered equivalent to the other examples discussed in this chapter is unclear: the construction may be related to the more well-known type δῆλός εἰμι + participle 'it is clear that I am V-ing', which is not usually considered periphrastic. As Jannaris (1897: 494) indicates, the latter construction gradually disappears in Post-Classical Greek, a process which is likely to have taken place first in the lower register: thus, such a relationship may explain why the construction of πολὺς ἦν + present participle only occurs in higher-register historiographical texts.

---

[156] See e.g. Dion. Hal., Ant. Rom. 4.65.4, 7.54.6, 10.58.3; Pol. 16.6.9.
[157] The function of πολύς could be called 'intensifying'.
[158] See Hdt. 1.98.1, 9.91.1. Kühner & Gerth (1976 [1904]: 58) also mention the construction.

And yet regular progressive examples of εἰμί are found, even in the papyri.[159] Dietrich (1973a: 211–12) cites in this context ἐνοχλού[μενος πρὸ]ς τῶι σπόρωι εἰμί (P.Hamb.1.27, ll. 18–19 (250 BC)) 'I am occupied by / involved in sowing' and καλῶς δ' ἂν ποιήσαις ὑποζύγιον δοὺς ἐὰν ἦι σχολάζον (PSI.5.530, ll. 5–8 (III BC)) 'you will do well giving me the beast, if it might be free'.[160] I believe both examples are best considered stative, however. A more interesting case is the following:

(195) ὁ δ' ἀποσταλεὶς οὐκ ἀποδέδωκ[εν] αὐτῶι τὰ γράμμα\τα/, ἀλλ' ἔστι ἐν Ἀλεξανδρείαι <u>σκηνῶν</u> ἐν τοῖς Ἀριστοβούλου \φθειρόμενος·/ ... ἵνα οὖν μηθὲν αὐτῶι γένηται \τῶν φιλανθρώπων·/ ἔστι γὰρ ἀλλότριος καὶ <u>διαβάλλων</u> ὡς διὰ τού\του/ τὰ περὶ Δάναον γέγονεν (P.Cair.Zen. 1.59037, ll. 5–7; 10–12 (258 BC))

'But the emissary has not delivered the letters to him, but is living in Alexandria in the house of Aristoboulos, following evil ways ... Therefore (take care) that he [Pankris] obtains no favours, for he is hostile and spreading the word that the trouble about Danaos happened because of him [Apollonios].' (tr. Bagnall & Derow)

In this memorandum to Zenon, an unknown friend provides information about a financial scandal in which Danaus was involved. The son of Danaus had sent a letter to the διοικητής Apollonius to settle the matter. This letter, however, had never arrived to its destination, because the emissary, who was staying in the house of Apollonius' political opponent, Aristobulus, had not delivered it. While ἔστι ... σκηνῶν 'he is living' could perhaps be interpreted non-periphrastically, the use of φθειρόμενος 'following evil ways' as a conjunct participle, without καί between the two participles, seems to indicate that we are dealing with a periphrastic form (cf. also the translation by Bagnall & Derow). Zenon is furthermore asked not to give any favours to a certain Pankris, who has shown a hostile attitude, saying that the scandal involving Danaus was the fault of Apollonius. As in some of our previous examples, ἔστι ... διαβάλλων 'he is spreading the word' expresses an event that occurs repeatedly in a broad time-frame.

Various other examples can be found in the papyri, typically in lower-register documents such as accounts of dreams (καθημέν' ἦν καὶ οὐ κινοῦσα (UPZ.1.79, ll. 12–13 (after 159 BC)) 'she was sitting and

---

[159] Contrast Aerts (1965. 56).
[160] Cf. also Porter (1989: 455); Amenta (2003: 34).

254   *Verbal Periphrasis in Ancient Greek*

not moving'), business letters (ἐάν που ἦι πωλούμενος ἐπίστειλον ἡμῖν (P.Cair.Zen.5.59814, l. 6 (257 BC)) 'if it (the seed) is being offered for sale somewhere, write to us'), and a deposition (ἦν καθημένη (P.Hib.2.200, ll. 6–7 (246–221 BC)) 'she was sitting').

4.5 MIDDLE POST-CLASSICAL GREEK (I–III AD)

4.5.1 The Expansion of the (Focalized) Progressive in the New Testament

Ever since Björck's (1940) seminal study, scholars have considered the use of εἰμί with the present participle as fulfilling a progressive function characteristic of the New Testament's idiom. As my own data show, there is not only an increase in productivity vis-à-vis CG,[161] but also with regard to EPG: in the LXX the progressive construction has an NRO of 2.13 instances per 10,000 words, while in the NT it has one of 4.98 instances per 10,000 words.

Before going into the progressive use of εἰμί with the present participle in greater detail, I shall again draw attention to the existence of examples of this periphrasis that fulfil a stative function. As mentioned in the introduction to this chapter, the relationship of statives and progressives has not always been properly understood. Porter (1989), for example, translates cases such as ἦν συγκύπτουσα καὶ μὴ δυναμένη ἀνακύψαι (Lc. 13.11), ἔσῃ σιωπῶν καὶ μὴ δυνάμενος λαλῆσαι (Lc. 1.20), and ἦν δὲ θυμομαχῶν Τυρίοις καὶ Σιδωνίοις (Acts 12.20) with 'and she was already bending over and not being able to straighten up or raise her head',[162] 'you will be in progress being silent and unable to speak'[163] and 'he was in progress being very angry with the residents of T. and S.'[164] respectively. While undoubtedly meant as working translations, I find such renderings misleading (as well as ungrammatical in English): these examples, which are low on the transitivity scale, should not be considered progressive.

In terms of the threefold distinction of statives introduced in §4.3.1, examples from all three groups can be found. Next to cases where the participle is based on a lexically stative content verb, as in

---

[161] Cf. Ceglia (1998: 29–30).   [162] Porter (1989: 481).
[163] Porter (1989: 483).   [164] Porter (1989: 482).

ἦν συνομοροῦσα (Acts 18.7) 'it was bordering on', ἦν θέλων ἰδεῖν αὐτὸν (Lc. 23.8) 'he wanted to see her', ἦσαν ἀγανακτοῦντες (Mc. 14.4) 'they were angry', and ἦν ἔχων κτήματα (Mc. 10.22) 'he had money', we also find examples where a verb of dynamic content is used,[165] as in (196):

(196) οὐκ ἔστιν αὕτη ἡ σοφία ἄνωθεν <u>κατερχομένη</u>, ἀλλὰ ἐπίγειος, ψυχική, δαιμονιώδης (James 3.15)

'Such wisdom does not come down from heaven; it belongs to the world, it is unspiritual and demonic.' (GNB)

James advises his audience to show that they are wise by living right and being humble, and by not bragging or lying. Using a periphrastic form (ἔστιν ... κατερχομένη 'it comes down'), James adds the gnomic statement that the latter kind of 'wisdom' does not come from above, but rather is earthly. Note the presence of various of what we have called 'de-transitivizing' elements, such as the use of an inanimate subject (σοφία 'wisdom'), the present tense, and the coordination with regular adjectives.

As regards progressives in the NT, the increase in productivity involves both durative and focalized progressives. The durative progressives found in the NT resemble those encountered in the LXX. Again we find durative progressives used to denote the occurrence of an event in a broad time-frame, with a sense of repetition, as in (197):[166]

(197) ὁ μὲν οὖν Πέτρος ἐτηρεῖτο ἐν τῇ φυλακῇ· προσευχὴ δὲ ἦν ἐκτενῶς <u>γινομένη</u> ὑπὸ τῆς ἐκκλησίας πρὸς τὸν θεὸν περὶ αὐτοῦ (Acts 12.5)

'Peter therefore was kept in the prison, but constant prayer was made by the assembly to God for him.' (WEB)

King Herod has caused suffering for the Christians by ordering that James' head be cut off and that Peter be jailed. During this period, the Christians pray continually for Peter. Periphrastic ἦν ... γινομένη 'it was happening' refers to various occasions, but since there is no

---

[165] One type of example which I do not consider periphrastic (*contra* Porter 1989: 455; Fanning 1990: 312) is that where the participle μεθερμενευόμενον (or any of its alternatives) has an explicative function, as in καὶ κρατήσας τῆς χειρὸς τοῦ παιδίου λέγει αὐτῇ, Ταλιθα κουμ, ὅ ἐστιν μεθερμηνευόμενον Τὸ κοράσιον, σοὶ λέγω, ἔγειρε (Mc. 5.41) 'and taking the damsel by the hand, he said to her: *Talitha cumi*, which is, in translation: Damsel (I say to you) arise.'

[166] For similar examples, see e.g. Acts 9.28, 14.7; John 3.23, 10.40; Lc. 4.44.

particular emphasis on the subevents, the example is best considered iterative, rather than habitual.

Although it occurs mostly in the imperfect tense (32/41 = 78%), we also encounter future forms of εἰμί with the present participle. This pairing may be thought of as less transitive, in the sense that an event is denoted that neither is actually taking place nor has taken place (cf. the mode-parameter). Consider the following example:[167]

(198) καὶ οἱ ἀστέρες ἔσονται ἐκ τοῦ οὐρανοῦ πίπτοντες, καὶ αἱ δυνάμεις αἱ ἐν τοῖς οὐρανοῖς σαλευθήσονται (Mc. 13.25)
'And the stars shall be falling from heaven, and the powers that are in the heavens shall be shaken.' (ASV)

Jesus tells his disciples what will happen at the second coming: among other events, stars will be falling and the powers in the sky will be shaken. The periphrastic form ἔσονται ... πίπτοντες 'they will be falling' expresses a durative event that is situated in the future. Just as in (197), here there is a sense of repetition (iteration), which is connected to the plural subject.

Various scholars[168] have suggested that the occurrence of such future periphrases should be connected to the synthetic future, which was slowly disappearing in Post-Classical Greek (in part, because of phonological reasons),[169] and moreover was aspectually neutral between perfective and imperfective aspect.[170] In this respect, constructions such as the one found in (198) provide the language user with an expressive alternative that can explicitly mark durative aspect in the future. Alternatively, Aerts (1965: 59–60) argues that we are not dealing with a 'natural' phenomenon; rather, he believes that the construction should be considered a Semitism, which was largely restricted to the LXX and the NT.[171] In the remainder of this chapter, I shall argue that Aerts' claim must be dismissed.

---

[167] For similar examples, see e.g. 1Cor. 14.9; Lc. 5.10, 21.17, 21.24; Mt. 10.22, 24.9; Mc. 13.13.

[168] See e.g. Jannaris (1897: 444); Robertson (1915: 889).

[169] See e.g. Dieterich (1898); Tonnet (1982).

[170] Note, however, that there is some discussion with regard to the opposition between the sigmatic middle future and the future in -(θ)η. Some scholars have suggested that this opposition may be aspectual (e.g. Kühner & Gerth 1976 [1898]: 114; Smyth 1984 [1920]: 395; Allan 2003: 178–202), a view which is rejected by others (e.g. Magnien 1912: 278–80; Hartmann 1934; Schwyzer 1950: 266).

[171] Cf. similarly Fanning (1990: 317–18); Ceglia (1998: 37–8).

In comparison with the LXX, the NT's durative progressive is more often used for non-iterative events, occurring in a narrower timeframe. This is the case in examples such as (199), where the left boundary of the event is contextually emphasized:[172]

(199) καὶ ὁ Πέτρος ἀπὸ μακρόθεν ἠκολούθησεν αὐτῷ ἕως ἔσω εἰς τὴν αὐλὴν τοῦ ἀρχιερέως, καὶ ἦν συγκαθήμενος μετὰ τῶν ὑπηρετῶν καὶ θερμαινόμενος πρὸς τὸ φῶς (Mc. 14.54)
'Peter followed from a distance and went into the courtyard of the High Priest's house. There he sat down with the guards, keeping himself warm by the fire.' (GNB)

Jesus is arrested and brought to the High Priest's house, where the chief priests and the council look for someone to accuse Jesus. Peter has followed from a distance into the courtyard, where he is sitting down with the guards and keeping himself warm. While both ἦν συγκαθήμενος 'he was siting' and ἦν . . . θερμαινόμενος 'he was warming' express events in progress, the left boundary of these events is stressed,[173] due to two factors: (a) the occurrence of a lexically perfective verb (ἀκολουθέω (εἰς) 'I follow (to)'), bringing about a change of state and thus creating the appropriate conditions for the occurrence of another event/series of events;[174] (b) pragmatic knowledge, which tells us that the relationship between following, sitting, and warming oneself will be one of *consequentiality*,[175] rather than temporal overlap.

As with the LXX, in the NT we find a number of examples that can be classified as habitual, though these are rather infrequent.[176] Consider the following example:[177]

---

[172] What some call an 'ingressive' value. For similar examples, see Acts 14.7; Lc. 1.22, 2.51, 4.44. Cf. also Ceglia (1998: 36), though I do not completely agree with his selection of examples (in Mc. 14.4 the construction has a stative function, and Lc. 3.23 is best taken non-periphrastically).

[173] An alternative interpretation, suggested by one of the reviewers, would be that the left boundary is simply omitted: 'Peter followed from a distance and went into the ... house. There he was sitting with the guards ...'. Under this interpretation, the narrator moves to the ensuing state following the situation change which remains implicit (compare Rijksbaron's 2002: 17–18 'immediative imperfect').

[174] ἠκολούθησεν (εἰς τὴν αὐλὴν) possesses what Caenepeel (1989: 70) calls a 'contingency structure'.

[175] Cf. Caenepeel (1995: 226).

[176] Cf. Amenta (2003: 73–4).

[177] For a similar example, see Lc. 4.31.

(200) καὶ ἦν διδάσκων τὸ καθ' ἡμέραν ἐν τῷ ἱερῷ. οἱ δὲ ἀρχιερεῖς καὶ οἱ γραμματεῖς ἐζήτουν αὐτὸν ἀπολέσαι καὶ οἱ πρῶτοι τοῦ λαοῦ (Lc. 19.47)
'And he taught daily in the temple. But the chief priests and the scribes and the chief of the people sought to destroy him.' (KJV)

Jesus arrives in Jerusalem, goes to the temple, and drives out the merchants. Afterwards, he teaches daily in the temple. While periphrastic ἦν διδάσκων 'he was teaching' denotes an event in progress, the circumstances under which this event are repeated are quite clear in terms of location and time (τὸ καθ' ἡμέραν 'every day', ἐν τῷ ἱερῷ 'in the temple'), so that we can classify the event as habitual.[178]

Undoubtedly the most innovative aspect of the use of the progressive construction in the NT (with respect to both CG and EPG) is the increased frequency of the focalized progressive type: such examples represent 44% (32/73) of the total number of progressive cases, while they represent only 15% (20/137) in the LXX. It seems that Björck (1940: 41ff.) in his treatment of εἰμί with the present participle in the NT specifically had this use in mind, as he explicitly draws a comparison with the English 'I am V-ing' construction, which is almost always used as a focalized progressive.[179] Björck (1940: 44) notes that:

> Die Beschreibung der englischen Progressivform als 'ein umgebender Rahmen' passt weitgehend auf den Gebrauch der Periphrase im griechischen N.T.[180]

As we have already seen with regard to the LXX, focalized progressives can occur in a number of syntactic frames. Two important criteria in this regard are whether the periphrastic construction occurs in a *main* or *subordinate* clause,[181] and whether it *precedes* or *follows* its focalization point. Given the extension of the focalized progressive use of εἰμί with the present participle in the NT, it is

---

[178] Compare Amenta (2003: 73).
[179] Cf. similarly Aerts (1965: 52): 'a new form of application appears, namely that which we shall call the progressive periphrasis ... this can conveniently be compared with the use of the progressive form in modern English.'
[180] 'The description of the English progressive as "encompassing another event" fits to a large extent the use of the periphrasis in the Greek NT.'
[181] Compare Pollak (1976: 293): 'ce schéma d'incidence peut asusi se produire entre deux propositions indépendantes' ('this scheme of incidence can also occur with two independent propositions').

Imperfective Aspect

worth giving a general overview of these syntactic frames.[182] Five main types can be distinguished:[183]

- **Type 1**: *PROG used in the main clause with the time of speaking serving as FP*

With this first (rather marginal) type, the event denoted by the periphrastic progressive is not narrowly connected to another, foregrounded event, but rather to the time of speaking. Consider (201):

(201) παραγενόμενος δέ τις ἀπήγγειλεν αὐτοῖς ὅτι Ἰδοὺ οἱ ἄνδρες οὓς ἔθεσθε ἐν τῇ φυλακῇ <u>εἰσὶν</u> ἐν τῷ ἱερῷ <u>ἑστῶτες</u> καὶ <u>διδάσκοντες</u> τὸν λαόν (Acts 5.25)

'And there came one and told them, Behold, the men whom ye put in the prison are in the temple standing and teaching the people.' (ASV)

The High Priest and the Sadducees have arrested the apostles. The following day, the council is summoned, and people are sent to bring the apostles before them. However, an angel of the Lord has already opened the doors of the jail, and ordered the apostles to preach to the people in the temple. This news is reported to the council by an unnamed individual, who notes that at the very time he is reporting the news the apostles are preaching. Note that εἰσὶν... διδάσκοντες 'they are teaching' is ambiguous: it is not pellucid as to whether it is periphrastic or non-periphrastic,[184] due to the occurrence of the locative adjunct ἐν τῷ ἱερῷ 'in the temple' in between the component parts of the verbal group (εἰσίν and διδάσκοντες).

- **Type 2**: *PROG used in the main clause preceding a foregrounded event serving as FP*

By far the most frequently occurring syntactic frame is that where the periphrastic construction is used in the main clause, setting the stage, and is followed by an aorist form. This is illustrated in (202):[185]

---

[182] For a fuller discussion, see Bentein (2013b).
[183] In what follows, I use the abbreviations 'PROG' for periphrastic progressive, and 'FP' for focalization point.
[184] According to Regard (1918: 119), though, 'la nuance "en train de" est particulièrement sensible dans cet exemple'.
[185] For similar examples, see e.g. Acts 10.30, 11.5 (ambiguous), 19.14; Lc. 1.21; Mc 2.6 (ambiguous), 10.32; Mt. 8.30 (ambiguous).

(202) ἦν δὲ Σίμων Πέτρος ἑστὼς καὶ θερμαινόμενος. εἶπον οὖν αὐτῷ, Μὴ καὶ σὺ ἐκ τῶν μαθητῶν αὐτοῦ εἶ; (John 18.25)
'Now Simon Peter was standing and warming himself. They said therefore to him, "You aren't also one of his disciples, are you?"' (WEB)

As in example (199), Peter is standing with the servants and warming himself. In this particular example, however, the progressive event is connected with another foregrounded event—that is, the servants addressing Peter. In other words, the aorist form εἶπον 'they said' serves as the focalization point for periphrastic ἦν ... θερμαινόμενος 'he was warming himself'.

- **Type 3**: *PROG used in the subordinate clause preceding a foregrounded event serving as FP*

This third type is much like the second, except for the fact that the periphrastic construction occurs in a subordinate clause, as shown in (203):

(203) καὶ ὡς ἀτενίζοντες ἦσαν εἰς τὸν οὐρανὸν πορευομένου αὐτοῦ, καὶ ἰδοὺ ἄνδρες δύο παρειστήκεισαν αὐτοῖς ἐν ἐσθήσεσι λευκαῖς (Acts 1.10)
'While they were looking steadfastly into the sky as he went, behold, two men stood by them in white clothing.' (WEB)

The apostles are watching Jesus being conveyed to heaven. As they are watching, suddenly two men are standing beside them. In this particular example, the focalization point is not specified by a verb in the aorist, but rather by the focalizing particle ἰδού 'behold',[186] introducing a new participant on the scene.[187]

While this third type may seem more 'natural' than the second in the sense that a subordinate clause is a typical syntactic environment for background information, it occurs relatively infrequently. This could be due to the fact that parataxis was increasingly preferred in the lower registers.[188] In fact, Björck (1940: 64–5) has even suggested that the 'schwach entwickelte Periodisierung des volkstümlichen Erzählungsstiles'[189] may have stimulated the rise of the progressive

---

[186] As Matt Newman (p.c.) observes, however, ἰδού is in origin an aorist form.
[187] As Johannessohn (1942: 36, 48, 55) notes, the use of ἀνήρ as subject and ἵστημι as predicate after ἰδού are typical for Luke (ἵστημι especially in Acts).
[188] See e.g. Jannaris (1897: 400–2; 451).
[189] 'The weakly developed periodization of the popular narrative style.'

Imperfective Aspect 261

construction as an alternative means of indicating background information.

- **Type 4**: *PROG used in the main clause following a foregrounded event serving as FP*

With this fourth type, the progressive construction does not precede, but follows its focalization point. This is illustrated in (204):

(204) τῇ δὲ ἐπαύριον εἰσῆλθεν εἰς τὴν Καισάρειαν· ὁ δὲ Κορνήλιος <u>ἦν προσδοκῶν</u> αὐτούς, συγκαλεσάμενος τοὺς συγγενεῖς αὐτοῦ καὶ τοὺς ἀναγκαίους φίλους (Acts 10.24)

'On the next day they entered into Caesarea. Cornelius was waiting for them, having called together his relatives and his near friends.' (WEB)

Peter and some of the Lord's followers are invited by Cornelius to come to Caesarea, so that he can hear Peter's words. When they arrive, Cornelius is expecting them. The periphrastic progressive, ἦν προσδοκῶν 'he was expecting', follows its focalization point, εἰσῆλθεν 'he entered', and can be said to have an 'explicative' function: it specifies the circumstances under which Peter arrives.

- **Type 5**: *PROG used in the subordinate clause following a foregrounded event serving as FP*

With the fifth and final type we find the progressive construction used in a subordinate clause following a foregrounded event. Consider (205) (= (5)):

(205) συνιδών τε ἦλθεν ἐπὶ τὴν οἰκίαν τῆς Μαρίας τῆς μητρὸς Ἰωάννου τοῦ ἐπικαλουμένου Μάρκου, οὗ <u>ἦσαν</u> ἱκανοὶ συνηθροισμένοι καὶ <u>προσευχόμενοι</u> (Acts 12.12)

'Thinking about that, he came to the house of Mary, the mother of John whose surname was Mark, where many were gathered together and were praying.' (WEB)

Peter is kept in jail, but is rescued by an angel sent by the Lord. He then goes to the house of Mary, where many people are gathered in prayer. ἦσαν ... προσευχόμενοι 'they were praying' expresses a durative event which can be connected to foregrounded ἦλθεν 'he went'. Here again, the progressive construction is not so much used to set the stage for the main event, but rather to specify the circumstances during which it occurs.

To conclude this section, it may be clear that the development we are witnessing in the NT is the progression to the next stage of Bertinetto et al.'s PROG imperfective drift. In §4.4.1, I suggested that the general development from stative to progressive can be characterized in terms of transitivization, the construction being used in increasingly transitive contexts. The development from durative progressivity to focalized progressivity also fits within this general development, in the sense that durative progressives often refer to a repeated event occurring in a broad time-frame (cf. the kinesis-parameter), while focalized progressives always refer to a single event which is narrowly connected to another, foregrounded event (and hence necessarily of shorter duration).

4.5.2 The Use of εἰμί with the Present Participle in Other MPG Texts

A summary of the stative use of εἰμί with the present participle in the other MPG texts is given in Table 4.7 (for ease of comparison, data from the NT have been included):

Table 4.7. Distribution of εἰμί with the present participle in MPG (stative)

Genre/Author/Text	STAT	NRO	TTR	STAT (ACT)	STAT (MED)	STAT (PASS)
Biography/hagiography	121	1.51	0.55	88	16	17
Plutarch (b. c.50 AD)	63	1.21	0.54	42	8	13
New Testament (I AD)	32	2.18	0.75	27	4	1
Greek novel	13	0.65	1	8	3	2
Achilles Tatius (II AD)	7	1.61	1	5	1	1
Heliodorus (III AD)	3	0.37	1	2	1	0
Historiography	64	1.25	0.44	55	5	4
Flavius Iosephus (b. 37/8 AD)	8	0.62	0.75	7	1	0
Cassius Dio (b. c.164 AD)	56	1.47	0.45	48	4	4
Scientific prose	76	1.93	0.50	52	9	15
Galen (b. 129 AD)	26	1.53	0.65	14	7	5
Pausanias (II AD)	50	2.23	0.50	38	2	10
Papyri	69	/	0.17	66	1	2
Letters	21	/	0.29	21	0	0
Petitions	11	/	0.27	11	0	0

Key: 'STAT' = stative; 'NRO' = normed rate of occurrence (per 10,000 words); 'TTR' = type/token ratio; 'ACT' = active; 'MED' = middle; 'PASS' = passive.

Imperfective Aspect 263

This table shows that the construction continues to be used with a stative aspectual function with more or less the same frequency as in the previous periods discussed in this chapter. The construction appears most frequently in biography and scientific prose, which can be connected to genre: in these types of texts, the discourse-modes information and description are more frequently employed. The construction is least often employed in the Greek novels, but this does not seem to be due to register: in Cassius Dio, who also employs the higher register, the construction occurs with some frequency.

The large majority of these stative examples are combinations of low transitivity, formed mostly with neuter participles such as ἀρέσκον 'pleasing', δέον 'necessary', ἐξόν 'possible', καθῆκον 'proper', λυσιτελοῦν 'beneficiary', παρόν 'present' and προσῆκον 'fitting'.[190] This is particularly noticeable in the papyri, where forty-five out of sixty-nine examples are formed with δέον.

Fernández Marcos (2000: 335; referring to Tabachovitz 1956: 41–7) has recently noted that the expression ἦν γὰρ ἔχων κτήματα πολλά (Mc. 10.22) 'for he had many possessions' cannot have been used in imitation of the LXX, as Hebrew did not have a verb 'have'; thus it must have been 'an analogical construction from similarity with many other periphrastic constructions of the LXX (although not with ἔχων) typical of translation Greek', by which she presumably means those with a progressive function.[191] While I do not want to exclude the possibility that the increased usage of the progressive periphrasis in the NT may indeed have stimulated the use of εἰμί with the present participle with a stative function, it is the case that in texts from both the low and high register stative examples such as ἔχων ἐστί occur quite regularly,[192] as in (206) (which is one out of ten instances in Cassius Dio's *Roman Histories*):[193]

(206) καὶ <u>ἦν</u> μὲν καὶ τοῦτο τὴν ἴσην τῷ ἑτέρῳ ἰσχὺν <u>ἔχον</u> (Cassius Dio, *Hist. Rom.* 57.7.5)

'And this method too had the same effectiveness as the other.' (tr. Cary)

---

[190] Compare Blass & Debrunner (1979: 286): 'die Umschreibung der Impersonalia durch das adj. Ptz. ist nicht nur allgemein hellenistisch, sondern auch schon attisch' ('periphrasis of impersonal verbs through the adjectival participle is not just generally Hellenistic, but also Attic').
[191] Cf. also Tabachovitz (1956: 47).
[192] I count thirty-seven clearly periphrastic instances with ἔχων in my corpus, not including the NT.
[193] For similar examples, see e.g. Ach. Tat., *Leuc. et Clit.* 4.12.7; Cassius Dio, *Hist. Rom.* 46.49.3, 51.9.2, 73.6.2; Paus. 5.19.3, 8.11.9, 8.31.4; BGU.13.2349, l. 14 (II AD).

Cassius Dio describes how Tiberius would either speak after a few others or even last, or not speak his mind directly, in order not to take away freedom of speech. Both methods proved to be as effective, as expressed by the stative periphrasis ἦν . . . ἔχον 'it had'.

As for the use of εἰμί with the present participle with a progressive function, consider Table 4.8 (for ease of comparison, data from the NT have again been included):

Table 4.8. Distribution of εἰμί with the present participle in MPG (progressive)

Genre/Author/Text	PROG	NRO	TTR	DUR PROG	FOC PROG	PROG (ACT)	PROG (MED)	PROG (PASS)
Biography/hagiography	129	1.61	0.69	72	57	76	46	7
Plutarch (b. c.50 AD)	11	0.21	1	5	6	5	6	0
New Testament (I AD)	73	4.98	0.70	41	32	41	25	7
Greek novel	8	0.40	1	8	0	6	2	0
Achilles Tatius (II AD)	2	0.46	1	2	0	1	1	0
Heliodorus (III AD)	5	0.62	1	5	0	4	1	0
Historiography	5	0.10	1	4	1	2	1	2
Flavius Iosephus (b. 37/8 AD)	5	0.39	1	4	1	2	1	2
Scientific prose	32	0.81	0.81	32	0	24	7	1
Pausanias (II AD)	30	1.34	0.80	30	0	22	7	1
Papyri	11	/	0.91	9	2	4	4	3
Letters	6	/	1	5	1	2	1	3
Petitions	1	/	1	0	1	0	1	0

Key: 'PROG' = progressive; 'NRO' = normed rate of occurrence (per 10,000 words); 'TTR' = type/token ratio; 'DUR' = durative; 'FOC' = focalized; 'ACT' = active; 'MED' = middle; 'PASS' = passive.

This table shows that εἰμί with the present participle is predominantly used with a progressive function in biographical/hagiographical texts, the NT in particular. Examples with a durative progressive function are most often used in texts from this register, although focalized progressives become much more frequently attested than what we have seen in CG and EPG. An example of the latter use is given in (207):[194]

(207) καὶ ὡς ἦν ταῦτα λέγουσα, καὶ πλείονα τούτων, ὁ ὄρθρος ἐπανῆλθεν, καὶ ἡ λέαινα παρεγένετο ἀπὸ τῆς θήρας αὐτῆς (A. Xanthipp. 27.1-3)

---

[194] For similar examples, see e.g. A. Andr. 14.7-8; A. Jo. 56.1; Protev. 37a.12, 38.7-8; T. Abr. A. 5.19.

Imperfective Aspect 265

'And as she was saying these words, and more than these, the morning dawned, and the lioness came from her hunting.' (tr. James)

Polyxena has fled in fear, and unintentionally walked into the empty den of a lioness. She is talking to herself, when the lioness returns. As in our previous example (203), the periphrastic progressive is used in a subordinate clause, providing the immediate background for the foregrounded events ἐπανῆλθεν 'it dawned' and παρεγένετο 'she arrived', which are expressed in the aorist.

In the other genres, progressive examples occur much less frequently. In authors such as Chariton, Longus, and Cassius Dio, for example, the construction is conspicuously absent. This is not to say, however, that no examples can be found. In this context, it is worth mentioning Pausanias' *Description of Greece*, where as many as thirty examples can be found.[195] These examples all have a similar profile: Pausanias uses the construction to describe works of art[196] as in the following example:[197]

(208) πεποίηται δὲ καὶ Θέτις παρθένος, λαμβάνεται δὲ αὐτῆς Πηλεύς, καὶ ἀπὸ τῆς χειρὸς τῆς Θέτιδος ὄφις ἐπὶ τὸν Πηλέα ἐστὶν ὁρμῶν. Αἱ δὲ ἀδελφαὶ Μεδούσης ἔχουσαι πτερὰ πετόμενον Περσέα εἰσὶ διώκουσαι (Paus. 5.18.5)

'There is also a figure of Thetis as a maid; Peleus is taking hold of her, and from the hand of Thetis a snake is darting at Peleus. The sisters of Medusa, with wings, are chasing Perseus, who is flying.' (tr. Jones)

Pausanias describes a scene represented in the temple of Olympian Hera. Twice the periphrastic progressive is used, to describe how a snake is darting at Peleus (ἐστὶν ὁρμῶν), and how the sisters of Medusa are chasing Perseus (εἰσὶ διώκουσαι).

Strid (1976: 96), following Wifstrand (1945: 14), makes a comparison with the use mentioned under §4.3.1, whereby εἰμί with the present participle denotes how a person expresses himself or acts in

---

[195] The frequent use of the construction in Pausanias (which presents an interesting parallel to his frequent use of εἰμί with the perfect participle; see Table 3.11) seems to have been overlooked by all standard accounts. It is worth mentioning that there are many more ambiguous examples in Pausanias. This ambiguity is caused by the fact that Pausanias always indicates where the action is taking place, using a locative adjunct (see for example Paus. 1.22.6).

[196] Cf. Wifstrand (1945: 14); Strid (1976: 96–7).

[197] For similar examples, see e.g. Paus. 3.18.11, 3.18.13, 5.17.3, 6.16.3, 10.25.3, 10.27.3, 10.27.4, 10.31.9.

a letter, book, poem, etc. (as in our example (156)). I believe this comparison is warranted only to some extent: this latter use is best classified as stative, since what is described is not an event in progress, but rather a particular attitude, a characterizing property of a person in a certain context.[198] In examples such as (208), on the other hand, Pausanias is actually describing an event that is unfolding in a work of art.

In such examples, εἰμί is always used in the present tense; therefore, one could wonder whether we might be dealing with focalized progressives, taking the time of speaking (that is, the time of Pausanias' description) as focalization point. While this may be the case, I prefer to interpret these examples as durative progressives, whereby the action is described from a more general point of view, and not necessarily connected only to Pausanias' time of observing.

For examples of progressive εἰμί with the present participle in a narrative context, we can turn to the Greek novel and historiography.[199] Consider the following example from Flavius Iosephus:

(209) ὃς ἐπειδὴ καὶ τότε τὸν Ἀντίγονον ἐθεάσατο παριόντα διὰ τοῦ ἱεροῦ, πρὸς τοὺς γνωρίμους ἀνέκραγεν, ἦσαν δ' οὐκ ὀλίγοι <u>παρεδρεύοντες</u> αὐτῷ τῶν μανθανόντων (Flav. Ios., *Bell. Iud.* 1.78)

'On this occasion, seeing Antigonus passing through the court of the temple, he [Judas] exclaimed to his acquaintances—a considerable number of his disciples were sitting beside him...' (tr. Thackeray, slightly modified)

Judas is characterized as one whose predictions have never proved false. When he sees Antigonus passing by he exclaims 'ah me' to the acquaintances who are sitting nearby, since he had predicted that Antigonus would be slain that day. ἦσαν παρεδρεύοντες 'they were sitting by' can be considered a focalized progressive; ἀνέκραγεν 'he exclaimed' functions as the focalization point, the periphrastic construction further specifying the circumstances.[200]

As shown in Table 4.8, some examples can also be found in Plutarch. A number of these are accompanied by πολύς (or a semantically similar adjective), however.[201]

---

[198] Two examples of this use in Pausanias are 4.3.2 and 10.29.10.
[199] For the Greek novels, cf. Papanikolaou (1973: 77–82).
[200] Compare with the fourth type discussed in §4.5.1, in particular example (204), where we also find the particle δέ.
[201] See e.g. Plut., *Brut.* 14.7, *Cam.* 7.4, *Pelop.* 25.7.

Imperfective Aspect 267

In the papyri some progressive examples can also be found.[202] Interestingly, we find constructions with εἰμί in the future tense, which Aerts (1965: 59–60), as mentioned in §4.5.1, considers a Semitism, mainly limited to the LXX and the NT. Examples such as the following undermine Aerts' claim:[203]

(210) ἀντὶ δὲ τῶν τόκων τοῦ αὐτοῦ ἀργυρίου ἔσται τελῶν ὁ Ἀθθαῖος τῶι Λυσίαι κατ' ἔτος, ἀπὸ ληνοῦ, οἴνου κεράμια δεκαδύο καὶ ἥμισυ ἀπὸ τοῦ ἐνεστῶτος χρόνου μέχρι τῆς τοῦ ἀργυρίου ἀποδόσεως (P.Dura.23, ll. 6–10 (133 AD))

'And instead of the interest on the above silver, the above Aththaeus will continue delivering to the above Lysias, each year, from the vat, twelve and a half keramia of wine, from the present time until the repayment of the silver.' (tr. Perkins)

In this second-century contract, Aththaeus promises to deliver twelve and a half keramia of wine instead of the interest on the silver which Lysias has lent. The act of delivering the wine is expressed by a durative progressive with a future form of εἰμί: ἔσται τελῶν 'he will be delivering'.

4.5.3 Motivating the Expansion of the Periphrastic Progressive in the New Testament

What motivated the considerable increase in frequency of εἰμί with the present participle in its progressive function in the NT is a much-debated issue. In what follows, I give an overview of the three dominant views, accompanied by a critical discussion of them on the basis of my own corpus-based findings. Before doing so, I stress that what is of interest is not the use of εἰμί with the present participle in all of its aspectual functions, but specifically the progressive function. As Aerts (1965: 61) notes, not distinguishing between the stative and the progressive functions of the periphrastic construction has led to much confusion in the literature.

---

[202] See e.g. P.Bad.2.41, ll. 12–13 (108 AD); P.Giss.Apoll.8, ll. 3–4 (115 AD); P.Mich.5.229, ll. 7–8 (48 AD); P.Oxy.55.3808, ll. 6–7 (I/II AD); PSI.14.1419, l. 9 (III AD); P.Vind.Sijp.27, l. 13 (III/IV AD).
[203] Compare P.Dura.20, l. 15 (121 AD); P.Dura.21, ll. 2–3 (II AD).

4.5.3.1 The progressive periphrasis as a 'Semitism'

Since a periphrastic progressive construction with הָיָה (*hāyāh*) 'be' can be found both in Hebrew (especially later Biblical Hebrew) and in Aramaic,[204] many scholars have held that the increased usage of a structurally similar construction in the NT must be attributed to the influence of one or both of these Semitic languages.[205] While Mussies (1971: 306) believes it difficult to attribute the presence of εἰμί with the present participle (in its progressive function) to specifically Hebrew or Aramaic, Rosén (1967, 1979) stresses that we must turn to Aramaic.

Several arguments can be raised against this hypothesis. What is most often marshalled as evidence against Aramaic influence is the fact that the progressive construction appears most frequently in Luke, who was not of Jewish descent and had a good mastery of Greek.[206] Furthermore, it has been pointed out that most of Luke's Semitisms must be considered 'Hebraisms' ('Septuagintalisms' to be more specific, see §4.5.2), rather than Aramaisms.[207] From a syntactic point of view, it has been noted that while in the NT the periphrastic progressive construction generally has the order *finite verb – participle*,[208] in Aramaic the construction takes a different order—that is, *participle – finite verb*.[209] Finally, it is worth mentioning that while in the NT the construction is used both with a durative and a focalized progressive function (see §4.5.1), in both Hebrew and Aramaic the character of the construction is predominantly durative.[210]

4.5.3.2 The progressive periphrasis as a 'Septuagintalism'

A second hypothesis was brought forward by Tabachovitz (1956: 41–7), and afterwards adopted in studies such as those by Aerts

---

[204] See e.g. Waltke & O'Connor (1990: 629); Sáenz-Badillos (1993: 144).
[205] See e.g. Robertson (1915: 888); Blass & Debrunner (1979: 286); Voelz (1984: 962).
[206] Cf. Aerts (1965: 57). Mussies (1971: 306), however, writes that 'the non-Jewish ancestry of St. Luke is . . . by no means certain'.
[207] See Sparks (1950: 26); Verboomen (1992: 19–22).
[208] Cf. Amenta (2003: 78).
[209] See Johannessohn (1942: 54–5); Verboomen (1992: 20–1).
[210] See Cohén (1984: 298–458) for an in-depth treatment of the semantics of the construction in both Semitic languages. In his treatment, Cohén (1984) refers to the distinction between the focalized and durative progressive type with the terms 'concomitant' and 'non-concomitant' respectively.

(1965), Rydbeck (1969), Fanning (1990), Verboomen (1992), and Fernández Marcos (2000). On the basis of the above-mentioned observation that Luke, though not being of Jewish birth and having a good knowledge of Greek, used the progressive construction most often, Tabachovitz concludes that Luke must have drawn on sources translated into Greek, that is, the LXX (which constituted a 'source for linguistic inspiration', as Fernández Marcos 2000: 332 notes). In other words, the construction was consciously employed as a so-called 'Septuagintalism', as part of a 'judeo-christian Kunstsprache' which Luke tried to imitate/elaborate.[211]

One of the weaknesses of this theory is that it focuses almost exclusively on Luke: while the high frequency of the construction in Luke is an important observation, Mussies (1971: 306) rightly notes that the occurrence of the construction in Matthew and Mark (and elsewhere) cannot be ignored outright.

Another critique concerns the fact that, with the exception of Aerts (1965: 61), scholars adhering to this hypothesis tend to consider all instances of εἰμί with the present participle (both with a progressive and a stative function) 'Septuagintalisms'.[212] This may go back to Tabachovitz, according to whom a multi-word expression such as that of εἰμί with the present participle had a certain 'solemn ring'. The most extreme example of this view is Ceglia (1998: 32), who describes the construction as a stylistic 'wild card': in his opinion, employment of this construction was not motivated by any particular aspectual choice, but rather by the desire to write in a style which is suited for the words of God, and similar to the Hebrew model. Together with Hartman (1963: 26), I believe this view must be rejected: Mark and Luke did not simply use the construction 'as occasion arose'. If this were the case, then, as Hartman points out, it would be remarkable that Luke in some passages does not take the opportunity of adopting Mark's periphrasis.

In support of this second hypothesis, a number of arguments have been adduced alongside the fact that the construction occurs most frequently in Luke. Aerts (1965: 56), for example, claims that the construction does not occur in what he calls 'common koine-usage', and that the examples in the early Christian texts are motivated by the

---

[211] See Verboomen (1992: 71).
[212] Compare with what we have noted in §4.5.2 on the use of a stative construction such as ἔχων ἐστί in Mark.

wish to imitate the NT.²¹³ It may be clear on the basis of our treatment in §4.5.2 that Aerts overstates his case: while it is undeniably true that progressive examples occur most often in biographical/hagiographical texts of a Christian origin, examples can also be found in pagan texts such as Pausanias' *Description of Greece*, as well as the papyri.

Verboomen (1992: 77) approaches the problem differently. He observes that in Luke the periphrastic progressive is often accompanied by (other) 'Septuagintalisms' such as καὶ ἐγένετο 'and it happened', ἐν τῷ 'while', καὶ ἰδού 'and behold', and καὶ αὐτός 'and he', as illustrated in (211):

(211) καὶ ἐγένετο ἐν τῷ ἐλθεῖν αὐτὸν εἰς οἶκόν τινος τῶν ἀρχόντων [τῶν] Φαρισαίων σαββάτῳ φαγεῖν ἄρτον καὶ αὐτοὶ ἦσαν παρατηρούμενοι αὐτόν. καὶ ἰδοὺ ἄνθρωπός τις ἦν ὑδρωπικὸς ἔμπροσθεν αὐτοῦ (Lc. 14.1-2)
'And it came to pass, when he went into the house of one of the rulers of the Pharisees on a sabbath to eat bread, that they were watching him. And behold, there was before him a certain man that had the dropsy.' (ASV)

Regrettably, Verboomen does not discuss the value of this observation as an argument in favour of the second hypothesis: are all words surrounding such Semitisms (Septuagintalisms) necessarily of the same nature? Moreover, it seems that three of these supposedly 'random'²¹⁴ Semitisms are functionally related to the progressive construction (καὶ ἐγένετο and ἐν τῷ being backgrounding elements and καὶ ἰδού specifying the focalization point).

Finally, it has been argued that the use of εἰμί with the present participle in the New Testament resembles that of the Septuagint.²¹⁵ After giving a brief overview of some examples in the Septuagint (mostly focalized progressives), Tabachovitz concludes (1956: 43):

Man wird wohl kaum fehlgehen, wenn man annimmt, dass solche Stellen das Vorbild abgegeben haben für die ähnlich stilisierten neutestamentlichen Sätze.²¹⁶

---

²¹³ See further §4.6.2.   ²¹⁴ Cf. Verboomen (1992: 77).
²¹⁵ See Tabachovitz (1956: 42-4).
²¹⁶ 'It would not be wrong to assume that such [Septuagintal, KB] passages have set the example for the similarly stylized New Testamental sentences.'

Imperfective Aspect 271

This statement must be nuanced: while focalized progressives are rather marginal in the LXX, they become much more prominent in the NT.

4.5.3.3 The progressive periphrasis as a 'vulgarism'

Various other authors have attached less importance to direct or indirect Semitic influences. Björck argues that the construction can be found particularly often in the synopticists because of the 'special character' of their writings as 'Volkserzählung'.[217] That the construction does not appear more frequently in the papyri can be attributed to the fact that these documents are 'unergiebig . . . schon weil sie naturgemäss nicht sehr oft eine ausführliche Schilderung von Episoden enthalten.'[218] While Björck's findings have been much criticized, my own corpus-based research confirms the importance of register and genre: in high-register narrative texts such as historiography or the Greek novel the progressive construction is almost unattested, while in middle-register ones it occurs much more frequently. In texts that are not primarily narrative, such as the papyri and scientific texts, the construction also occurs infrequently. Pausanias is an exception to this tendency: he employs elaborate descriptions when discussing works of art. While Pausanias' language should not be equated with that of the New Testament, it is not Atticistic either.[219]

One of the few scholars to have followed Björck (1940) is Dietrich (1973a, 1973b). Dietrich further explores the relationship suggested by Björck between periphrasis and genre, suggesting that aspectual periphrases in general, not just those constructed with εἰμί, are typical for a narrative 'Erzählungsmanier'.[220] While the papyri contain only a few truly narrative passages,[221] Dietrich considers the Christian texts to occupy a 'Sonderstellung' in Hellenistic literature because of their new way of narrative, favouring the use of

---

[217] Björck (1940: 67). Cf. Caragounis (2004: 177).
[218] '[They are] unproductive . . . because in accordance with their nature they do not very often contain a detailed description of episodes'. Björck (1940: 66–7).
[219] See e.g. Hutton (2005: 189–90): 'Pausanias knew what the Attic forms were and could use them properly, but made what must have been a conscious and mostly successful effort to keep his text free of them.'
[220] Dietrich (1973a: 202–3), (1973b: 203–4).
[221] Dietrich (1973a: 211), (1973b: 204).

periphrasis.[222] While there may be some truth in the relationship Dietrich proposes between Erzählungsmanier, periphrasis, and Christian texts, it remains unclear (a) exactly what is meant by the concept of 'Erzählungsmanier', and (b) whether such an 'Erzählungsmanier' is indeed characteristic for Christian texts.[223]

Perhaps the concept of 'Erzählungsmanier' could be taken to resemble that of 'narrative pace'[224] adopted in more recent narratological works. Since background tenses such as the imperfect and perfect (whether periphrastic or synthetic) are typical for a slow narrative pace, while a foreground tense such as the aorist is typical for a quick narrative pace,[225] and since periphrastic constructions are typically formed in functional domains such as the progressive and the perfect (next to the future), there seems to be a natural connection between periphrasis and a slow narrative pace.[226] However, this still leaves us with the question as to whether all Christian texts can really be characterized in terms of such a slow narrative pace: recent research by Oldsjö (2001) on Latin historiography has demonstrated that within one genre authors can choose to adopt either one of these paces—Caesar maintains a slow narrative pace, while Velleius Paterculus' pace is much quicker—and that there may be considerable variation between different parts of one and the same text as well. In my view, the differences in use between narrative genres such as

---

[222] Dietrich (1973b: 204, 209).
[223] For a critique, see also Verboomen (1992: 6–7).
[224] Oldsjö (2001: 274) defines narrative pace in terms of the relation between what is traditionally called 'erzählte Zeit' and 'Erzählzeit' (for example, one author can dedicate fifty pages to one historical year, while another author can deal with the same events in one page; the latter author will have the quickest narrative pace). I assume that such a narrative pace can be 'quick' or 'slow', though a continuum-view is perhaps more realistic.
[225] Compare Oldsjö (2001: 281) on Latin: 'if we compare the distribution of the tense forms to the pace of the narratives, we see that there is a connection. The quicker the pace of the narrative, the higher the percentage of the perfect tense form and, accordingly, the lower the percentage of the imperfect. On the basis of such observations we have good reason to state that the narrative pace and the distribution of the tense forms stand in proportion to one another—or, more exactly, that there is a reciprocity between the narrative pace and the choice between the perfective and the imperfective aspect.'
[226] Of course, we should not take this argument too far: periphrastic perfects may become perfective past tenses, so that these will also show up in texts with a quick narrative pace.

biography/hagiography, novel, and historiography are best accounted for in terms of *register*.[227]

To conclude, I believe scholars who adhere to this third hypothesis are correct in stressing the continuity between Classical and Post-Classical Greek. As my own corpus-based research confirms, it should no longer be maintained that progressive εἰμί with the present participle should exclusively be viewed as a 'Semitism' or a 'Septuagintalism'. This is not to say, however, that language contact and especially the influence of the LXX as a linguistic model had no role to play whatsoever, as can be seen in the very high frequency of occurrence of the construction in the NT.[228] Thus, there may be some truth in Rundgren's (1965: 466) statement that the origins of the progressive construction in the NT actually are threefold.

4.5.4 'Minor' Periphrastic Constructions

As I mentioned in §3.4.1, the changes in the participial system led to confusion between the different types of participle,[229] as a result of which even εἰμί with the aorist participle could occasionally be used with a stative or progressive force. Examples of this type may be found as early as the second-century *Acts of Andrew*.[230] Consider the following example:

(212) καὶ ἦν ἡ τοιαύτη ἀγαλλίασις αὐτῶν ἐπὶ ἡμέρας ἱκανὰς γενομένη, ἐν αἷς οὐκ ἔσχεν ὁ Αἰγεάτης ἔννοιαν ἐπεξελθεῖν τὴν κατὰ τὸν ἀπόστολον αἰτίαν. Ἐστηρίζοντο οὖν ἑκάστοτε ἐπὶ τὴν τοῦ κυρίου ἐλπίδα· καὶ συλλεγόμενοι πάντες ἀφόβως εἰς τὸ δεσμωτήριον ἅμα τῇ Μαξιμίλλῃ καὶ τῇ Ἰφιδάμᾳ καὶ τοῖς λοιποῖς ἀδιαλείπτως ἔχουσιν περισκεπόμενοι τῇ περιβολῇ καὶ χάριτι τοῦ κυρίου (A. Andr. 34.6–11)

'And there was among them rejoicing after this sort for many days, while Aegeates took not thought to prosecute the accusation against the Apostle. Every one of them then was confirmed at that time in hope toward the Lord, and they assembled without fear in the prison, with

---

[227] See further §4.6.3.
[228] For a similar view, cf. Amenta (2003: 65–6).
[229] See e.g. Ghedini (1937: 460) and Browning (1983: 64) with regard to the aorist participle in general, and Mirambel (1966: 181) more specifically with regard to εἰμί with the aorist participle.
[230] A. Andr. 2.10 and 25.1 may be similar, but in these examples it is unclear whether we are dealing with periphrasis to begin with.

Maximilla, Iphidamia, and the rest, continually, being sheltered by the protection and grace of the Lord.' (tr. James)

Immediately before this passage, we read how Andrew in prison preaches to the brethren, thereby strengthening their faith. Among his audience is Maximilla, the wife of the Roman proconsul Aegeates, who has been healed by Andrew and is no longer interested in her husband. After some days of rejoicing, however, Aegeates goes to his wife and proposes that she choose between himself and Andrew. While it may be possible to interpret ἦν ... γενομένη as an anterior perfect (meaning 'it had happened'), situating the days of rejoicing before the moment that Aegeates makes his proposal to Maximilla, it seems more likely that ἦν ... γενομένη expresses the rejoicing that is ongoing after Andrew's preaching.[231] The imperfect form ἐστηρίζοντο 'they were confirmed' would then resume ἦν ... γενομένη, giving a more precise expression to the joy they felt.

A second type of innovative periphrastic construction is ἔχω with the present participle, which we have also encountered in Classical Greek. This construction is not mentioned by Aerts (1965), but Papanikolaou (1973: 81–2) mentions its use in the Greek novel without discussing it further. Consider the following example:

(213) «ἔστιν ἡμῖν» ἔφη «χρήματα» λάθρα πρὸς τὸν Καλάσιριν ἡ Χαρίκλεια «καὶ ἐπάγγειλαι πλῆθος ὁπόσον βούλει· τὸν ὅρμον ὃν οἶσθα διασῴζω καὶ <u>ἔχω φέρουσα</u>» (Heliod., Aeth. 5.11.5)
'"I have money," said Charicleia softly to Calasiris. "Promise as much as you like. I have kept safe and carry with me the jewels you know of."' (tr. Hadas)

Calasiris the Egyptian has found Charicleia, and is informed that her lover Theagenes was taken captive. They realize that they will need money to free Theagenes, at which point Charicleia says that she carries jewels with her. Whether ἔχω φέρουσα is truly periphrastic seems debatable: the example has some similarity with the earlier-mentioned cases of the type ἔχω λαβών in Homer,[232] where ἔχω denotes possession and the participle functions as a conjunct participle. More interesting in this regard is the following example:

---

[231] Bonnet (1898: 38) has proposed the conjecture γινομένη.
[232] Cf. §3.2.1.

(214) συνέλθετε εἰ δοκεῖ πρὸς τὸ συνέδριον εἰς αὔριον δημοσίᾳ δι' ὑμᾶς ἐσόμενον καὶ γνώσεσθε αὐτήν τε ὁμολογοῦσαν καὶ ὑπὸ τῶν συνειδότων οὓς ἔχω φρουροῦσα διελεγχομένην (Heliod., Aeth. 8.9.18)

'Come, all of you, and attend, if you please, at the council meeting to be held tomorrow in public for your satisfaction, when you will witness her confession, and her conviction on the evidence of the accomplices which I am holding in custody.' (tr. Lamb)

Charicleia is sentenced to be burned alive, but carrying out the punishment turns out to be impossible, as the flames retreat wherever Charicleia stands. The people believe they are witnessing a divine intervention, at which point Arsace addresses them, and asks them not to have mercy. They are all invited to the council meeting, where Charicleia will confess, and her accomplices will be shown. In this particular case it seems less evident to interpret ἔχω φρουροῦσα non-periphrastically: ἔχω can be used of keeping people in captivity, but this interpretation would render the combination with the participle pleonastic (φρουρέω meaning 'I hold in subjection, custody'). Rather, we may be dealing here with a conscious imitation of Euripides' use of the construction as a progressive periphrasis.[233] This can be compared to the use of ἔχω with the aorist participle in Post-Classical Greek,[234] although this is a much more noticeable case of imitation, since there is only a single instance of the construction in the Classical period.

To conclude, it is also worth mentioning ἀδιαλείπτως ἔχουσιν περισκεπόμενοι in our previous example (212). This is a rather complex case: James in his translation seems to take ἀδιαλείπτως ἔχουσιν as a dative participle with ἅμα τῇ Μαξιμίλλῃ καὶ τῇ Ἰφιδάμᾳ καὶ τοῖς λοιποῖς 'together with Maximilla, Iphidamia, and the rest', but contextually this does not seem to make much sense, and it leaves the sentence without a main verb. Prieur (1989: 484), on the other hand, seems to take the construction periphrastically, with ἔχουσιν as an indicative present: 'ils ne cessaient jamais d'être gardés par la protection et la grâce du Seigneur.'[235] However, this has the disadvantage that in the given context, we would expect a past, rather than a

---

[233] Cf. our previous ex. (179). Heliodorus is known to have been influenced by Euripides. See e.g. Feuillatre (1966: 116–21).
[234] See e.g. §3.4.4.
[235] 'They never stopped being guarded by the protection and the grace of the Lord.'

276   *Verbal Periphrasis in Ancient Greek*

present tense form (as also indicated by Prieur's translation).[236] It is interesting to note in this regard that Bonnet (1898: 39) suspects a lacuna before ἔχουσιν (which he considers corrupt), which is nevertheless rejected by Prieur (1989: 484).

4.6 LATE POST-CLASSICAL AND EARLY BYZANTINE GREEK (IV–VIII AD)

4.6.1 Rise or Decline of εἰμί with the Present Participle?

Opinions differ greatly as to the further use of εἰμί with the present participle in LPG and EBG. While some scholars maintain that the construction was in decline in these periods, others claim that it was actually quite frequently employed. Rosén (1979: 64), for example, believes that the forms were already in decline at the time of the NT, and at a later stage were virtually non-existent:

> En réalité, les formes périphrastiques étaient mourantes en grec à notre époque; après le Nouveau Testament, on n'en trouve que très peu de traces dans quelque emploi que ce soit, seule la langue néotestamentaire a pu les maintenir jusqu'en pleine époque de la κοινή tardive grâce à l'appui apporté par l'araméen.[237]

Björck (1940: 66) relates the development of the progressive periphrasis to the decline of the participial forms,[238] and notes that while after the NT the construction can be found in Christian 'Volksliteratur' and Byzantine chronicles, 'die Frequenz ist ... im Ganzen eine abnehmende'.[239] Dietrich (1973b: 207), on the other hand, takes a much more positive stance and stresses that:

> Ausserordentlich lebendig ist die Periphrase der Winkelschau [i.e. the progressive periphrasis, KB] in der vom NT abhängigen Literatur

---

[236] For a non-periphrastic interpretation which also takes ἔχουσιν as an indicative present, see MacDonald (2005: 92): 'they were almost always with Maximilla and Iphidama and the others, because they were screened by the covering and grace of the Lord.'

[237] 'In reality, the periphrastic forms were dying out in the Greek of our time; after the New Testament one can find very few traces of them in whatever use; only the New Testamental language has been able to maintain them until the late κοινή thanks to the support given by Aramaic.'

[238] Cf. §3.4.1.   [239] 'On the whole, the frequency ... is decreasing.'

der Apostolischen Väter, Kirchenväter und der apokryphen Schriften zum NT.[240]

Remarkably, however, none of these authors base their views on corpus-based findings. Rather, it seems that in formulating these and other claims, most scholars are guided by their view on the use of the construction in the NT: if one claims that the use of periphrastic construction in the NT is entirely the result of imitation of the LXX, as Aerts does (1965), it would be difficult to argue for the liveliness of the construction elsewhere. Moreover, most authors fail to specify whether the periphrastic construction disappears in its entirety, or only in one of its aspectual functions.

An overall summary of my own findings is given in Fig. 4.1, where I have represented the development of εἰμί with the present participle in the Post-Classical and Byzantine periods (note that these data do not include the papyri):

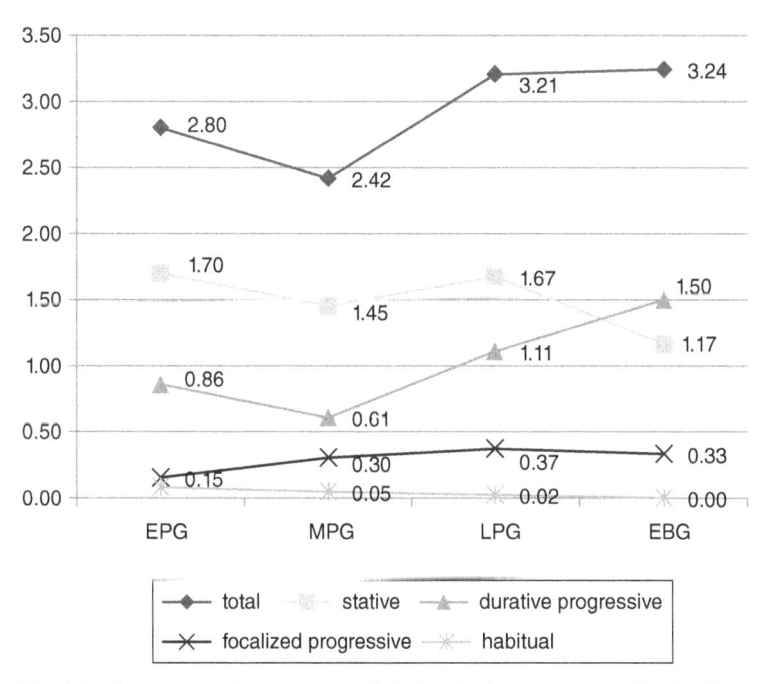

Fig. 4.1. Frequency of occurrence of εἰμί with the present participle (from EPG to EBG)

---

[240] 'The progressive periphrasis is exceptionally vivid in the literature dependent on the New Testament, that is, the Apostolic Fathers, the Church Fathers, and the apocryphal New Testament writings.'

A figure such as this must be approached with some caution, since the relative weight of texts from different genres may differ over time, and thus influence statistics (e.g. the presence of the Greek novel in MPG). At the very least, however, the figure shows that it cannot be upheld that the construction of εἰμί with the present participle was 'dying out', as Rosén (1979: 64) would have it: the overall frequency of the construction even seems to increase in LPG and EBG. A second general observation concerns the fact that the construction remains in use in all of its aspectual functions. In what follows, I briefly discuss each of these (including evidence from the papyri).

Statives remain more or less stable throughout the entire period under analysis (with a small increase in frequency in LPG, and a decrease in EBG). In almost each stage of the language, this is the predominant aspectual function of εἰμί with the present participle. As in all of the previous periods, the construction is most often used with lexically stative verbs, in particular 'adjectival' participles such as δέον 'necessary', ἐξόν 'possible', καθῆκον 'proper', πρέπον 'fitting', and συμφέρον 'useful'.[241] In John Malalas, the participle is also often combined with εἰμί in long enumerations of properties such as the following:

(215) παραλαβὼν δὲ τὴν χώραν καὶ τὴν πόλιν ὁ Ἀχιλλεὺς τὸν Φόρβαντα φονεύει καὶ λαμβάνει πάντα <τὰ> τῆς βασιλείας αὐτοῦ καὶ τὴν θυγατέρα αὐτοῦ Διομήδαν ἄγει· ἦν δὲ ἡ κόρη λευκή, στρογγυλόψις, γλαυκή, τελεία, ὑπόξανθος, ὑπόσιμος, <u>οὖσα</u> ἐνιαυτῶν κβ΄, παρθένος (Jo. Mal., Chron. 100.5–10)

'Capturing the district and the city, Achilles killed Phorbas and seized all his empire's possessions, and carried off his daughter Diomeda. The girl was fair-skinned, round-faced, grey-eyed, well-grown, with fairish hair and a slightly upturned nose; she was 22 years old and a virgin.' (tr. Jeffreys et al.)

John Malalas narrates how Achilles kills Phorbas and takes all his possessions, including his daughter Diomeda. The latter's many good qualities are then enumerated, the present participle οὖσα being used to denote her age.[242]

---

[241] Note, however, that these expressions are much less often attested in EBG, which partly explains the decrease in frequency observed in Fig. 4.1.

[242] Compare our earlier ex. (4).

Less frequent are combinations with lexically dynamic verbs, as in (216):

(216) τί αὐτῷ ποιήσωμεν; ὅτι ἠκούσαμεν πεποιηκέναι αὐτὸν σημεῖα καὶ θαυμάσια εἰς τὰς ἄλλας πόλεις, καὶ οὐδεὶς ἠδυνήθη κακῶσαι αὐτόν. ἡ δὲ διδασκαλία αὐτοῦ ἐστιν διαχωρίζουσα ἄνδρας καὶ γυναῖκας (A. Phil. 5.5)
'What should we do to him? For we have heard that he has done signs and wonders in other cities, and no one was able to harm him. But his teaching is that husbands and wives should separate.' (tr. Bovon)

When Philip approaches Nicatera the leaders of the city are distressed, because they fear the consequences of Philip's arrival. Among others, they note that Philip's teaching separates husbands and wives. This separation is expressed by a periphrastic form, ἐστιν διαχωρίζουσα 'it separates'.

As far as the progressive function is concerned, Fig. 4.1 shows that the focalized progressive type does not expand in this period of the language, as we might have expected, but the durative progressive type does. This is not to say, however, that focalized progressives are entirely absent, as some scholars have claimed. Since the focalized progressive type is discussed in greater detail in §4.6.2, I concentrate on durative progressives in what follows.

As in the previous two periods, durative progressives can denote the occurrence of either a single or multiple events. In both cases the periphrastic construction is often accompanied by an adverb(ial) stressing the continuity of the event, such as ἀδιαστάτως 'without intermission' (Geo. Syc., V. Theod. Syc. 26.31); δι' ὅλης τῆς νυκτός 'the entire night' (Jo. Damasc., Artem. 50.9); ἐπὶ ἱκανὸν καιρόν 'for a considerable time' (xlv mir. Artem. 66.4); ἐπὶ πολλὰς ἡμέρας 'for many days' (V. Alex. Acoem. 682.18); ἕως θανάτου 'until death' (V. Steph. Jun. 69.14); λοιπόν 'henceforward' (V. Aux. 161-2); ὅλην τὴν ἡμέραν ἐκείνην καὶ τὴν δευτέραν 'this entire day as well as the second' (V. Pach. 52.3).

When the durative event is repeated, the time-frame is usually broad. Consider the following example:[243]

---

[243] For similar examples, see e.g. Chron. Pasch. 243.14–15; Eus., H.E. 4.11.9; Geo. Syc., V. Theod. Syc. 59.10, 131.7–8, 154.17–18; Jo. Mal., Chron. 161.7–8; Thdt., H.E. 268.7–8; V. Alex. Acoem. 664.2; V. Aux. 112.

(217) πολλά τε θαύματα ἦν ἐργαζόμενος διὰ τῆς θεόθεν δωρηθείσης αὐτῷ χάριτος κατὰ πάσης μὲν νόσου καὶ μαλακίας, ἐξαιρέτως δὲ κατὰ τῶν ἀκαθάρτων πνευμάτων τὰς ἐντεύξεις ποιούμενος (Geo. Syc., V. Theod. Syc. 40.1-4)

'Because of the grace which had been given to him by God, Theodore was not only doing many miracles against all illness and sickness, but above all he interceded against impure spirits.' (tr. Festugière, slightly modified, originally in French)

George of Syceon notes how Saint Theodore of Syceon worked many miracles because of the grace given to him by God. Periphrastic ἦν ἐργαζόμενος 'he was doing' refers to an event that is ongoing, with a sense of repetition (due to the multiple object). This clearly is an event of long duration, and the statement seems to be intended as a summarizing one.

In other cases, the repeated event occurs in a more narrow timeframe. Consider (218):[244]

(218) ἐβάπτιζεν δὲ ὁ Φίλιππος τοὺς ἄνδρας, ἡ δὲ Μαριάμνη τὰς γυναῖκας· καὶ πάντες δὲ οἱ ὄχλοι ἐθαύμαζον σφόδρα, ὅτι λεόπαρδος καὶ ἔριφος τῶν αἰγῶν ἦσαν ἐπιλέγοντες τὸ ἀμήν (A. Phil. 12.9)

'Philip was baptizing the men and Mariamne the women, and all the crowds were exceedingly amazed because the leopard and the kid of the goat were pronouncing the amen' (tr. Bovon)

In this scene it is narrated how Philip, together with Mariamne, is baptizing the people in Hierapolis. Miraculously, the animals also contribute: a leopard and a young goat are saying 'amen'. Since there is a plural subject and multiple people are being baptized, we can assume that the event of 'saying amen' is repeated several times. As there is no clear separation of these events, it is best to consider ἦσαν ἐπιλέγοντες 'they were pronouncing' an iterative durative progressive.

As already mentioned, examples such as these can be considered less transitive than those where there is no sense of repetition. Another type of less transitive context is that where εἰμί is used in the future tense, since an event is not actually occurring, or has occurred (cf. the transitivity-parameter of mode).[245] The presence of

---

[244] For similar examples, see e.g. A. Phil. 4.1; Eustrat., V. Eutych. 1312; Jo. Damasc., Artem. 50.9-10; V. Sym. Styl. J. 188.36-7, xlv mir. Artem. 9.9, 30.16.

[245] See e.g. Anton. Hag., V. Sym. Styl. 4.17; Chron. Pasch. 129.12; Ignat. Diac., V. Greg. Dec. 46.8; Jo. Mosch., Prat. 69.40-1, 143.29; Leont. N., V. Jo. Eleem. 396.8-9.

such examples confirms our earlier observation that this subconstruction should not be considered a 'Semitism', confined to the LXX and NT, as Aerts (1965: 59) would have it.

One can also find more transitive durative examples, that is, where εἰμί denotes the continuation of a single event, without the event being interpreted in connection with a focalization point. Consider (219):[246]

(219) ἀράμεναι δὲ αὐτὴν ἥ τε Ἰουλιανὴ καὶ ἡ ἀδελφὴ αὐτῆς ἥκασι πρὸς αὐτόν, ῥῖψαι αὐτὴν ἐνώπιον αὐτοῦ. Καὶ οὐκ ἦν αὐτῇ γινομένη βοήθεια, πταῖσμα ἐχούσης τῆς μητρὸς αὐτῆς (V. Sym. Styl. J. 101.13–16)
'Juliana and her sister took her, came to him, and threw her before him. No help was happening for her, because her mother had committed a sin.'

While St Symeon the Stylite healed both Juliana and her sister, no such help occurs for the latter's daughter, who is possessed by a demon. This absence of aid is expressed by the periphrastic form οὐκ ἦν γινομένη 'it was not happening'. In examples such as these, the left boundary of the event denoted by the periphrastic construction is contextually emphasized (what some call an 'ingressive' nuance). Two contextual factors are of major importance in this regard:[247] (a) the occurrence of an aspectually perfective verb (ῥῖψαι 'having thrown'), bringing about a change of state and thus creating the appropriate conditions for the occurrence of another event/series of events; and (b) pragmatic knowledge, which tells us that the relationship between throwing a person before a holy man and being healed is one of *consequentiality*, rather than temporal overlap.

In texts from the higher register, we again find various examples where εἰμί is combined with πολύς (or the like) and a participle. In these, there can be a sense of repetition, but not necessarily: πολύς 'intensifies', either through repetition ('continually') or through increased effort ('vehemently').[248]

---

[246] For similar examples, see e.g. Ath., V. Anton. 5.35–6; A. Phil. 11.1; Geo. Syc., V. Theod. Syc. 162.19–20; Thphyl., Hist. 1.6.2; V. Pach. 77.12, 125.8–9, 137.5–6.
[247] Compare §4.5.1.
[248] See e.g. Ath., V. Anton. 82.13–14; Gr. Presb., V. Gr. Naz. 10.32; Ign. Diac., V. Taras. 5.26 7; Soz., H.E. 8.2.11; Thphyl., Hist. 8.6.1; Zos., H.N. 4.8.5.

282 *Verbal Periphrasis in Ancient Greek*

Finally, Fig. 4.1 shows that habituals are least frequently employed,[249] which is in accordance with the grammaticalization path proposed by Bertinetto *et al.*, according to which the habitual function is acquired only at the last stage.

4.6.2 Imitating the New Testament? The Focalized Progressive in LPG and EBG

As I have already mentioned, there is no general[250] increase in frequency of focalized progressives in LPG and EBG—perhaps contrary to what one would expect. As various scholars have noted, however, such forms do appear with some frequency in Christian (biographical/hagiographical/historiographical) texts.[251] In view of his hypothesis that the use of εἰμί with the present participle (in its (focalized) progressive function) in the NT should be considered a 'Septuagintalism', Aerts (1965: 55–6)—after a brief survey of Post-Classical examples—has made the bold claim that the use of the focalized progressive in these Christian texts should equally be considered imitative:

> The reminiscences of the Biblical model can clearly be discerned in all the writings mentioned, even if there is a slight difference here and there.

In the present section, I intend to show that while there are indeed indications of imitation, Aerts' view cannot be upheld. In §4.6.3, I present an alternative perspective, which is based on the notion of 'register' and also takes into account the durative progressive, for which we do observe such a general increase in frequency.[252]

In Table 4.9, some examples are given where εἰμί with the present participle is likely to have been employed in imitation of the LXX or the NT:

---

[249] See e.g. Ath., *V. Anton.* 47.3–4; *V. Pach.* 29.5.
[250] That is, manifested in the entire corpus.
[251] See e.g. Aerts (1965: 55): 'the number of instances of this form is rather limited... they almost all originate from what might be called the Christian vulgar speech.'
[252] See again Fig. 4.1.

Imperfective Aspect

Table 4.9. Some passages (possibly) imitating the LXX/NT

Passage from LPG/EBG	(Possible) parallel from LXX/NT
ἦν ἀγαπώμενος ὑπὸ τοῦ θεοῦ (Ath., V. Anton. 85.15–16)	ἀγαπώμενος τῷ θεῷ ἦν (2Esd. 23.26)
ἦν γὰρ ὁ Φίλιππος διδάσκων αὐτούς (A. Phil. 7.4)	ἦν γὰρ διδάσκων αὐτούς (Mt. 7.29)
ὡς οὖν ἦσαν οἱ ὄχλοι ἀτενίζοντες, ἔλεγον (A. Phil. 4.1)	πάντων οἱ ὀφθαλμοὶ ἐν τῇ συναγωγῇ ἦσαν ἀτενίζοντες αὐτῷ (Lc. 4.20)
ὡς ἦν ταῦτα διανοούμενος, ἰδοὺ παιδίον εὔμορφον ἐφάνη τῷ Φιλίππῳ (A. Phil. 4.2)	καὶ ὡς ἀτενίζοντες ἦσαν εἰς τὸν οὐρανὸν πορευομένου αὐτοῦ, καὶ ἰδοὺ ἄνδρες δύο παρειστήκεισαν αὐτοῖς (Acts 1.10)
ὁ δὲ Φίλιππος ἦν ἐννεύων τῷ λεοπάρδῳ (A. Phil. 11.1)	καὶ αὐτὸς ἦν διανεύων αὐτοῖς (Lc. 1.22)
ἔστιν θεὸς ἀποδιδοὺς ἑκάστωι τὰ πρὸς ἀξίαν (Cyr. S., V. Euthym. 81.5)	κύριος ἀνταποδιδούς ἐστιν (Eccles. 35.10)
ἦν γὰρ καὶ ὁ λαὸς προσδοκῶν αὐτόν, ὅτι πάντες ἐπεθύμουν βλέπειν αὐτόν (Eustrat., V. Eutych. 2585–6)	καὶ ἦν ὁ λαὸς προσδοκῶν τὸν Ζαχαρίαν (Lc. 1.21)
πᾶσα γὰρ δόσις ἀγαθὴ καὶ πᾶν δώρημα τέλειον ἄνωθέν ἐστι καταβαῖνον (Eustrat., V. Eutych. 314–16)	οὐκ ἔστιν αὕτη ἡ σοφία ἄνωθεν κατερχομένη (James 3.15)
ἦσαν γὰρ οἱ τῶν ἐκεῖσε ἀγνοοῦντες αὐτόν (Geo. Syc., V. Theod. Syc. 64.3)	ἤμην δὲ ἀγνοούμενος τῷ προσώπῳ ταῖς ἐκκλησίαις τῆς Ἰουδαίας ταῖς ἐν Χριστῷ (Gal. 1.22)
ἦν γὰρ λοιπὸν τὰ τελευταῖα πνέων καὶ πυρετῷ συνεχόμενος (Jo. Eleem., V. Tych. 24.23–4)	πενθερὰ δὲ τοῦ Σίμωνος ἦν συνεχομένη πυρετῷ μεγάλῳ (Lc. 4.38)
ἔφη εἰς τὸν κανόνα μόνον λαλῶν, ἔξωθεν δὲ τοῦ κανόνος σιωπῶν τὸ παράπαν (Jo. Mosch., Prat. 143.43–4)	ἔσῃ σιωπῶν καὶ μὴ δυνάμενος λαλῆσαι (Lc. 1.20)
ἦν δὲ πάλιν ἅπαξ καθήμενος μετὰ ἀδελφῶν καὶ θερμαινόμενος πλησίον τοῦ καμινίου τοῦ ὑελοψοῦ (Leont. N., V. Sym. 97.7–8)	ἦν συγκαθήμενος μετὰ τῶν ὑπηρετῶν καὶ θερμαινόμενος πρὸς τὸ φῶς (Mc. 14.54)
καὶ ἐκεῖ ἦν εὐαγγελιζόμενος καὶ διδάσκων τὰ περὶ τῆς βασιλείας τοῦ Θεοῦ (V. Aux. 112–13)	κἀκεῖ εὐαγγελιζόμενοι ἦσαν (Acts 14.7)
ἦν ὑποτασσόμενος ὁ μαθητὴς τῷ διδασκάλῳ ἐν πᾶσιν (V. Aux. 340–1)	καὶ κατέβη μετ' αὐτῶν καὶ ἦλθεν εἰς Ναζαρέθ, καὶ ἦν ὑποτασσόμενος αὐτοῖς (Lc. 2.51)
καὶ ἦν εἰσπορευόμενος καὶ ἐκπορευόμενος, τοῦ δαίμονος ἐπὶ ἡμέρας κολαζομένου (V. Sym. Styl. J. 219.45–6)	καὶ ἦν μετ' αὐτῶν εἰσπορευόμενος καὶ ἐκπορευόμενος εἰς Ἰερουσαλήμ (Acts 9.28)
ἦν συγκύπτων καὶ μὴ δυνάμενος ἀνανεῦσαι (V. Sym. Styl. J. 145.2)	ἦν συγκύπτουσα καὶ μὴ δυναμένη ἀνακύψαι (Lc. 13.11)

What is perhaps most noticeable about this table is the predominance of parallel passages from the NT (rather than the LXX), next to the fact that the imitation found in these examples does not just concern the progressive function of εἰμί with the present participle.

While in all of these examples there is a direct lexical parallel (which is the most easily recognizable kind of imitation), Aerts takes his claim for imitation one step further by arguing that the progressives found in later Post-Classical Greek are used in roughly the same syntactic frames as in the NT. With regard to (220), for example, Aerts (1965: 56) refers to similar New-Testamental passages where the periphrastic progressive is followed by the particle ἰδού (e.g. Acts 1.10,[253] where we also find the progressive in a subordinate clause).

(220) ὡς δὲ ταῦτα ἦν λέγων ὁ Φίλιππος, καὶ ἰδοὺ Ἰωάννης εἰσῆλθεν εἰς τὴν πόλιν ὡς συμπολίτης αὐτῶν (A. Phil. (Vat. Gr. 824) 128.1-2)
'When Philip was saying these things, behold John entered the city as a fellow-citizen of them.' (tr. James)

Aerts' claim has been contradicted by Dietrich (1973a: 224), who writes with regard to the progressive examples in his corpus that:

Ihre Volkstümlichkeit, die man aus der großen Verbreitung und Variierung dieser Schriften schließen darf, spricht trotz der Abhängigkeit dieser Schriften vom NT für die Lebendigkeit der Kategorie der Winkelschau, da sie zum großen Teil frei, d.h. in Kombinationen realisiert wird, für die bisher kein Vorbild bestand.[254]

Regrettably, however, Dietrich does not provide us with any further commentary, limiting himself to giving an overview of Post-Classical examples.

The typology of the focalized progressive in the New Testament which I introduced in §4.5.1 allows us to explicitly compare examples from LPG and EBG with those found in the NT. When going through the eighty examples of focalized progressives, we can make three

---

[253] Our example (203).
[254] 'Their popular nature, which one can infer from the great circulation and variation of these writings, is—despite their dependency on the NT—an argument in favour of the vividness of the progressive periphrasis, which is mostly used freely, that is, in combinations for which there is no example.'

main observations: first, the first type, where the time of speaking serves as the focalization point, is still infrequent,[255] owing in part to the fact that the corpus mainly consists of narrative texts; second, examples of the second type are still predominant, (representing 36% (29/80) of the total number of focalized progressives), though less so than in the NT (where the second type represents 66% (21/32) (!) of the total number of focalized progressives);[256] and third, what is most surprising is the increase in frequency of examples of the third, fourth, and fifth types, which are rather marginal in the NT. A particularly noteworthy trend,[257] which concerns the third and fifth types, is the use of the periphrastic progressive in the subordinate clause. In almost all cases, the periphrastic progressive is found in a temporal clause introduced by ὡς 'when'.[258] This development is a sign of tighter event integration,[259] and could be taken as a sign of the further grammaticalization of the focalized progressive use.

In conclusion, while there does seem to be some affinity between the use of the focalized progressive in the NT on the one hand and that in LPG and EBG Christian texts on the other—especially with regard to the second syntactic type—Aerts' claim of syntactic imitation cannot be upheld.

4.6.3 Register and Diachrony: The Spread of the Durative Progressive Type

Since Aerts' claim about the occurrence of the focalized progressive in Christian texts cannot be upheld, not to mention the fact that it does not explain why durative progressives increase in frequency,

---

[255] See e.g. A. *Phil. pass.* 34.12; Cosm. Ind., *Top.* 1.15.
[256] Note, however, that with this second syntactic type in LPG and EBG the focalization point is often expressed in the form of a conjunct participle (see e.g. Geo. Syc., *V. Theod. Syc.* 168.52-3; *Hist. Mon. Aeg.* 8.198-9; Thphn., *Chron.* 349.6-7), which is less often the case in the NT.
[257] This is referred to by Aerts (1965: 56) as 'a slight difference here and there'.
[258] See e.g. Ath., *V. Anton.* 61.14; *A. Phil* 4.2, 5.4; Geo. Syc., *V. Theod. Syc.* 136.9; *Hist. Mon. Aeg.* 10.159; Jo. Mal., *Chron.* 358.19; Pall., *H. Laus.* 37.5; *V. Sym. Styl. J.* 178.17, 214.32; *xlv mir. Artem.* 7.17, 11.23.
[259] Cf. Givón (1995).

I propose taking an alternative perspective towards the distribution of the construction by means of the concept *register*.²⁶⁰ The relevance of this concept has also been stressed by Markopoulos (2009) in his recent work on the history of the Ancient Greek future periphrases with ἔχω 'I have', θέλω 'I want', and μέλλω 'I am about to'. Markopoulos observes that:

> The rise in the frequency of use and the establishment of a construction in a specific register almost without exception follows the demise of another in the same register, so that a situation whereby two or more AVCs [= auxiliary verb ('periphrastic') constructions] are equally frequent in a genre or in all contexts in a period never obtains.
> (Markopoulos 2009: 226)

Markopoulos furthermore posits a so-called 'fifth, sociolinguistic, parameter of grammaticalization', which predicts that 'the further grammaticalized an AVC becomes, the higher up it rises in terms of sociolinguistic (register) acceptability'.²⁶¹ These findings tie in with recent advancements in sociolinguistics and socio-historical linguistics,²⁶² which has shown that the propagation of innovations typically happens in an orderly way: first, the variant becomes used by other individuals within the same speech community²⁶³ (at this stage, the innovation acquires a social significance: it comes to serve as a social marker).²⁶⁴ It is only at a later stage that the innovation *may* spread to other speech communities, in which case it becomes conventionalized.²⁶⁵

Now consider the use of εἰμί with the present participle as a durative and focalized progressive in the Post-Classical and Early Byzantine periods:

---

²⁶⁰ On register and diachrony, see further Bentein (2013a).
²⁶¹ Markopoulos (2009: 232). Cf. §1.5.4.3.
²⁶² See e.g. Milroy (1992).
²⁶³ Speech communities can be defined in terms of (social) domains (e.g. school, family, friends) or shared expertise (e.g. linguistics, cooking, informatics). Since each individual typically belongs to multiple speech communities, each with their own code, (s)he will speak multiple codes (known as the individual's *repertoire*).
²⁶⁴ Cf. Milroy (1992: 83).
²⁶⁵ When this happens, one or more alternative constructions may be eliminated, or become (functionally/ pragmatically) specialized.

Table 4.10. Distribution of εἰμί with the present participle in LPG and EBG (progressive)

Genre/Author/Text	PROG	NRO	TTR	DUR PROG	FOC PROG	PROG (ACT)	PROG (MED)	PROG (PASS)
Biography/hagiography								
Acts of Philip (IV AD)	282	2.94	0.67	217	65	181	66	35
Life of Alexander (V AD)	31	14.20	0.90	17	14	24	7	0
Life of Pachomius (V AD)	13	13.83	0.92	11	2	9	1	3
John Moschus (b. c.550 AD)	18	6.92	0.94	17	1	13	4	1
Life of Symeon Stylites the Younger (VI AD)	7	1.37	0.86	5	2	5	2	0
John of Damascus (b. c.675 AD)	21	3.86	0.81	15	6	10	5	6
George of Syceon (VII AD)	7	2.41	1	5	2	4	3	0
xIv miracles of Artemius (VII AD)	39	7.39	0.67	30	9	23	12	4
Ignatius the Deacon (b. c.770/80 AD)	14	6.80	1	5	9	11	2	1
Stephen the Deacon (VIII–IX AD)	8	1.87	1	8	0	5	3	0
	7	3.09	1	7	0	4	0	3
Historiography								
Theodoretus of Cyrrhus (b. c.393 AD)	53	0.68	0.89	46	7	33	13	7
John Malalas (b. c.491 AD)	5	0.71	1	5	0	3	0	2
Sozomenus (V AD)	7	0.77	0.86	6	1	5	2	0
Zosimus (V AD)	3	0.27	1	3	0	2	0	0
Paschal Chronicle (VII AD)	3	0.48	1	3	0	2	0	1
Theophylact Simocotta (VII AD)	13	1.02	0.77	11	2	10	3	0
Theophanes Confessor (b. c.760 AD)	4	0.61	1	4	0	2	2	0
	12	0.89	1	10	2	6	4	2
Scientific prose								
Cosmas Indicopleustes (VI AD)	8	0.21	1	6	2	4	3	1
	6	0.68	1	4	2	3	2	1
Papyri	5	/	1	2	3	1	2	2
Letters	3	/	1	1	2	1	1	1

Key: 'PROG' = progressive; 'NRO' = normed rate of occurrence (per 10,000 words); 'TTR' = type/token ratio; 'DUR' = durative; 'FOC' = focalized; 'ACT' = active; 'MED' = middle; 'PASS' = passive.

Table 4.10 does not show the role of the stative and habitual functions of εἰμί with the present participle, but as was already mentioned the former was well established in all registers at all times, while the latter remained marginal in all registers at all times.

When it comes to the progressive use of the construction, we can see that it becomes more frequent than in MPG, even when the NT is included.[266] This particularly concerns the durative progressive function in biographical/hagiographical texts from the middle register such as the *Acts of Philip*, the *Life of Alexander* and George of Syceon's *Life of Theodore of Syceon*. It is interesting to make a comparison in this regard with the spread of (anterior) εἰμί with the aorist participle,[267] which is attested in the same sorts of texts.[268] However, while (anterior) εἰμί with the aorist participle never spread to texts from the high register, in EBG we see that the durative progressive use of εἰμί with the present participle is also more frequently attested in higher-register (biographical/hagiographical) texts such as the works of John of Damascus, Ignatius the Deacon, and Stephen the Deacon. That this aspectual function has become sociolinguistically acceptable to writers adopting the high register explains the general increase we have noted in Fig. 4.1. As for focalized progressives, these are attested with some frequency in texts from the middle register, but remain marginal in texts from the high register. This progressive function does not seem to have become sociolinguistically acceptable in the high register, which explains why we did not note a general increase in frequency in Fig. 4.1.[269] In the papyri and scientific texts, both progressive functions are infrequent, which may be explained by reference to genre.

To conclude, it should be noted that the register-based view advocated here does not exclude an influence from the NT: it is hardly unimaginable that the use of the periphrastic progressive was indeed a social marker connoting membership in the Christian community (i.e. used by a sub-group of authors adopting the middle register),[270] but to confirm this, we would need middle-register pagan texts with a predominantly narrative character.

---

[266] Compare Table 4.8.   [267] See Table 3.16.

[268] Note, however, that John Moschus and John Malalas do not seem to use the construction with particular frequency (contrary to what is the case for εἰμί with the aorist participle).

[269] Cf. Milroy (1992: 169) on resistance to incipient changes.

[270] Cf. Amenta (2003: 17); Drinka (2011: 41).

4.6.4 'Minor' Periphrastic Constructions

Occasionally, we find some 'minor' alternative periphrastic constructions in LPG and EBG. As in MPG, εἰμί with the aorist participle sometimes seems to be used with a progressive (or less frequently stative) value, due to the changes in the participial system. Consider (221):[271]

(221) παριόντων γὰρ ἡμῶν διά τινος τόπου εἰς τὰς Νιτρίας κοιλάς τις ἦν κατὰ τὴν χώραν ὕδατος γέμουσα, ἐν ᾗ <u>ἐναπομείναντες</u> κροκόδειλοι πολλοὶ <u>ἦσαν</u> τοῦ ὕδατος ἐκ τῶν χωρῶν ὑποχωρήσαντος (Hist. Mon. Aeg. 27.44)
'As we went to Nitria, we passed by a certain place where there was a hollow in the land full of water; many crocodiles were staying there, because the water had receded from the surrounding countryside.' (tr. Festugière, originally in French)

The author narrates how the journey he has undertaken to visit the Desert Fathers was full of dangers. On one occasion, he came by a certain place where crocodiles were staying. Being interested, he goes to have a look, when suddenly the crocodiles attack. In this example it seems more evident to accord ἐναπομείναντες ... ἦσαν a progressive ('they were staying', compare Festugière's 's'y tenaient à demeure') rather than an anterior value ('they had stayed'), since the crocodiles are obviously still present when they attack.

4.7 CONCLUSION

Finally, I want to draw attention to the diachronic similarities that exist between the two periphrastic constructions that are dominant in the functional domains of perfect and imperfective aspect—that is, εἰμί with the perfect and the present participle. Both constructions undergo a development that can be understood in terms of transitivization, the construction being used in increasingly transitive contexts (in terms of volitionality, participants, kinesis, etc.). As with anterior aspect, we see that progressive aspect itself develops

---

[271] For similar examples, see Call., *V. Hyp.* 22.8; Geo. Syc., *V. Theod. Syc.* 124.10-11; *V. Alex. Acoem.* 683.3; Zach. Pap., *V. Bened.* 28.14.

gradually, with the earlier examples often denoting a repeated action, sometimes in the passive voice. A third important similarity concerns the diachronic sources: two source-constructions are particularly relevant, that is the locational construction (accompanied by a conjunct participle), and εἰμί with a regular adjective. Especially in the case of stative εἰμί with the present participle, it seems likely that (resultative) εἰμί with the perfect participle exerted an analogical influence.

Contrary to what was the case with perfect periphrases, we have mainly concentrated on a single periphrastic construction in this chapter, εἰμί with the present participle. Particularly with regard to the use of this construction with a progressive function, attention was drawn to the connection that exists with genre and register. In the period of its greatest extension, Post-Classical and Early Byzantine Greek, the construction was first used with a durative progressive function in the low and especially middle register, and starting from MPG with a focalized progressive function in these same registers. In the higher register, the construction was used with much less frequency until EBG, when the construction becomes used with a durative progressive function. That the construction does not occur with particular frequency in low-register documentary texts can be related to genre, as the discourse modes description and narration occur less frequently. This provides an alternative approach to the much-discussed 'Semitic' character of the progressive construction, although it should be stressed that in the earliest period, EPG, language contact is likely to have provided an important stimulus.

While the grammaticalization path provided by Bertinetto and his colleagues provided an important guiding principle for the diachronic description of εἰμί with the present participle, the evidence reviewed in this chapter suggests that some modifications may be necessary. When it comes to the diachronic sources, it seems insufficient to concentrate entirely on the locative construction, even though this construction plays a particularly important role.[272] Second, I noted that examples with a habitual function are semantically closer to those with a (iterative) durative progressive function than those with a focalized progressive function. Thus,

---

[272] Compare Bertinetto *et al.* (2000: 553, fn. 16); Killie (2008: 85–6).

Imperfective Aspect 291

I suggest that the grammaticalization path provided by Bertinetto *et al.* should allow for multiple branching, as demonstrated in Fig. 4.2:

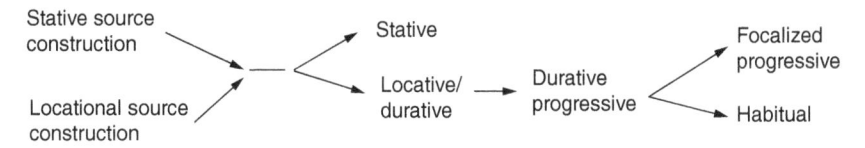

```
Stative source                    Stative                        Focalized
construction  ↘                  ↗                               progressive
               — <                              Durative       ↗
              ↗                  ↘ Locative/ →  progressive   
Locational source                   durative                   ↘ Habitual
construction
```

Fig. 4.2. PROG-imperfective drift (revised)

It should be stressed, however, that the proposal made in Fig. 4.2 is only a suggestion and needs to be confirmed by extensive further research on other languages that use a progressive periphrasis.

5

Perfective Aspect

> In the treatment of εἶναι + present participle it appeared relatively easy on the whole to determine the pattern of meaning and the manner of occurrence. The use of the aorist participle in periphrasis presents the interpreter with problems that are difficult to solve.
>
> (Aerts 1965: 27)

5.1 INTRODUCTION

So far, we have not dealt with the use of εἰμί with the aorist participle in the Classical period. This construction, which appears in writers as early as Herodotus, constitutes an interesting case: if the synthetic perfect and aorist did not enter into functional competition yet, or at least not to the extent that they did in the Post-Classical period, εἰμί with the aorist participle may have been used as a perfective periphrasis.

While scholars such as Björck (1940: 83–4) argue that εἰμί with the aorist participle served as a periphrastic perfect already in Classical Greek,[1] other scholars emphasize that 'the aorist periphrases in ancient Greek all fall within the framework of the aorist aspect and do not occur as substitution for any other function of aspect whatsoever'.[2] Porter (1989: 476) adds that Björck's theory leaves 'the Aorist without an equivalent periphrasis and the Perfect with an unnecessary duplicate set of forms to serve the same function'; in view of the multiplicity of perfect periphrases considered in Chapter 3, this

---

[1] Cf. similarly Gildersleeve (1980 [1900–11]: 125); Ceglia (1998: 25–6).
[2] Aerts (1965: 35).

argument is not entirely convincing, however. By extension, scholars have debated whether there is any continuity between Classical and Post-Classical εἰμί with the aorist participle: as was noted in the third chapter, the latter was never used with a perfective value.

This short last chapter intends to explore the aspectual semantics of the construction, and to put its appearance into historical perspective. Unlike in the previous chapters, no grammaticalization path is available: as mentioned in §1.5.2, from a cross-linguistic point of view, periphrases in the domain of perfective aspect are rare.

5.2 FUNCTIONAL COMPLEXITY OF εἰμί WITH THE AORIST PARTICIPLE IN THE CLASSICAL PERIOD

Here I provide an overview of the use of εἰμί with the aorist participle. Combinations of εἰμί with the aorist participle are not unattested in the Archaic period, but at this stage they are either non-periphrastic or ambiguous, as in the following example:[3]

(222) ἀλλ' ἄγε τῷδ' ἔφες ἀνδρὶ βέλος Διὶ χεῖρας ἀνασχών / ὅς τις ὅδε κρατέει καὶ δὴ κακὰ πολλὰ ἔοργε / Τρῶας, ἐπεὶ πολλῶν τε καὶ ἐσθλῶν γούνατ' ἔλυσεν· / εἰ μή τις θεός ἐστι κοτεσσάμενος Τρώεσσιν / ἱρῶν μηνίσας (Hom., Il. 5.174–8)

'Come now, lift up your hands in prayer to Zeus, and let fly a shaft at this man, whoever he is that so prevails and has done the Trojans much harm, since he has loosed the knees of many noble men; unless indeed he is some god who is resentful of the Trojans, angered because of sacrifices.' (tr. Wyatt-Murray)

Although he has already been hit once by Pandarus, Diomedes keeps killing many Trojans. When Aeneas sees this, he exhorts Pandarus to aim an arrow at the man, and to stop him once and for all. This is on condition, of course, that he is not a god who is angry with the Trojans. It seems clear that εἰ μή τις θεός ἐστι κοτεσσάμενος should not be taken as 'if not some god has become enraged': rather, we can assume continuity of subject (that is, Diomedes), with κοτεσσάμενος as a conjunct participle.

---

[3] For similar examples, see Hom., Il. 4.211, 5.191, 13.764. Cf. also Lasso de la Vega (1955: 172–4). Note that Porter (1989: 477) and Giannaris (2011b: 127–8) consider Il. 4.211 periphrastic.

Perfective Aspect 295

In the Classical period, on the other hand, we do find clearly periphrastic examples. The distribution of the construction is given in Table 5.1:

Table 5.1. Distribution of εἰμί with the aorist participle in CG

Genre/Author/Text	TOT	NRO	TTR	ACT	MED	PASS
Drama	9	0.24	1	5	0	4
Aeschylus (b. 525/4 BC?)	1	0.23	1	0	0	1
Sophocles (b. 496/5 BC?)	6	0.94	1	4	0	2
Euripides (b. 480s BC?)	2	0.13	1	1	0	1
Historiography	3	0.05	1	1	1	1
Herodotus (b. 484 BC?)	3	0.16	1	1	1	1
Philosophy	23	0.16	0.57	4	10	9
Plato (b. c.429 BC)	15	0.26	0.73	2	4	9
Aristotelic corpus (IV BC)	8	0.08	0.38	2	6	0
Scientific prose	2	0.05	1	1	1	0
Oratory	4	0.07	1	3	1	0
Antiphon (b. c.480 BC)	1	0.54	1	1	0	0
Lysias (b. 459/8 BC?)	2	0.34	1	1	1	0
Demosthenes (b. 384 BC)	1	0.03	1	1	0	0

Key: 'TOT' = total; 'NRO' = normed rate of occurrence (per 10,000 words); 'TTR' = type/token ratio; 'ACT' = active; 'MED' = middle; 'PASS' = passive.

Interestingly, this table shows that the distribution of the construction is similar to that of progressive εἰμί with the present participle,[4] and to a lesser extent with anterior ἔχω with the aorist participle:[5] it occurs in the dramatists, Herodotus, the Hippocratic corpus, Plato, and Aristotle. There may be a connection with register, although in the case of the dramatists, other factors may have played a role.[6] Some scholars have stressed the particular preference Ionic had for periphrasis,[7] but in the case of εἰμί with the aorist participle, there does not seem to be a noticeable difference in frequency among Herodotus, the Hippocratic corpus, and other texts.

The use of the construction is quite complex. As Aerts (1965) notes, 'the aorist periphrases do not form a well-defined category.' Perhaps one of the clearest realizations of the perfective value would be in the future tense. Since the future may be considered aspectually

---

[4] Compare Table 4.3.   [5] Compare Table 3.1.

[6] Cf. Aerts (1965: 34), who notes that in the large majority of the examples periphrases occur at the end of the verse. Note that the participle almost always precedes the finite verb, and that in half of the examples the future form ἔσῃ occurs at the end of the verse, immediately preceded by the participle.

[7] Cf. Lasso de la Vega (1955: 170).

neutral,[8] constructions such as these allowed the speaker to express a punctual future event,[9] as in the following example:

(223) {Xo.} ἐκ τῶνδε τοίνυν, ἴσθι, μηχανὴ καλή / {Ba.} λέξον· τίν' αὐδὴν τήνδε γηρυθεῖσ' ἔσῃι; (Aesch., *Supp.* 459-60)
'Chorus. Well, these [girdles and belts], I tell you, give us a fine method— Pelasgus. Say what words these are that you are going to utter.' (tr. Sommerstein)

The Danaids have come to Argus, asking king Pelasgus for protection. They threaten Pelasgus (to hang themselves, as becomes clear a few verses later), and the king wants to know what their threat is. A periphrasis is used, γηρυθεῖσ' ἔσῃι, referring to a bounded future event: 'you are going to say'. This use of the construction is almost entirely limited to the dramatists (Sophocles in particular),[10] in whose work Aerts (1965: 33) considers the construction 'asseverating or solemnly assuring'. An isolated instance can also be found in Lysias and perhaps Herodotus.[11]

The construction can be used with a perfective value in tenses other than the future, too: it enables a very specific expression of thought. These periphrases can be observed in Plato, among others,[12] who makes relatively frequent use of the construction, especially in the passive voice. Consider the following example:

(224) {Σω.} ἀλλὰ τὰ μὲν ἔμπροσθέν σοι ἦν πρὸς τοῦτον ῥηθέντα ὥσπερ ἄνευ μαρτύρων λεγόμενα· νυνὶ δὲ ἐμὲ ποίησαι μάρτυρα, καὶ ἐναντίον ἐμοῦ κάτειπε τίς ἐστιν αὕτη ἡ σοφία ἧς ἐπιθυμεῖς (Pl., *Thg.* 123a)
'Socrates. Well, what you said to him before was spoken, as it were, without witnesses; but now you shall take me as a witness, and declare before me what is this wisdom that you desire.' (tr. Lamb)

Demodocus has come with his son Theages to Athens, so that the latter can learn 'wisdom'—that is, how to govern free citizens with their consent. Socrates asks Theages what kind of knowledge he hopes

---

[8] Cf. our observations with regard to ἔσομαι with the present participle in §4.5.1.
[9] Cf. Jannaris (1897: 443); Gildersleeve (1980 [1900-11]: 125); Moorhouse (1982: 205). Contrast Björck (1940: 87-8), who considers the construction a future (anterior) perfect.
[10] See further Soph., *Ant.* 1067, *OC* 816, *OT* 1146, *Trach.* 1113.
[11] See Hdt. 7.194.3; Lys. 2.13. Note that in the Herodotean passage some editors prefer the reading περιέσεσθαι.
[12] Cf. Aerts (1965: 30-1).

to acquire. Theages replies that he has often told his father, but Socrates encourages him to say it again, this time with Socrates as a witness. A periphrasis is used to refer to the previous occasions: ἦν ... ῥηθέντα 'it was spoken'. Note that the construction is not used as a past anterior, since there is no other past event before which it can situated.[13]

The following is a similar example, which seems to have been overlooked by previous accounts:

(225) <u>νομίσαντα</u> δ' <u>εἶναι</u> χρὴ τὸν γαμοῦντα ταῖν οἰκίαιν ταῖν ἐν τῷ κλήρῳ τὴν ἑτέραν οἷον νεοττῶν ἐγγέννησιν καὶ τροφήν, χωρισθέντα ἀπὸ πατρὸς καὶ μητρὸς τὸν γάμον ἐκεῖ ποιεῖσθαι καὶ τὴν οἴκησιν καὶ τὴν τροφὴν αὐτοῦ καὶ τῶν τέκνων (Pl., Leg. 776a)

'He that has marriage in mind must think of one of the two homesteads on his own actual lot as a nest and nursery for his chicks, must leave father and mother and hold his nuptials there, and there keep house and home for himself and his children.' (tr. Hamilton et al.)

In his *Laws*, Plato notes that whoever is getting married must decide which of the two pieces of his allotment (cf. *Leg.* 745c–d) he will consider his 'nest'. The aorist participle (νομίσαντα) is formed on the basis of a lexically stative verb, resulting in an ingressive reading.[14] This is a shade of meaning that would be impossible to express with either the present or perfect participle.[15]

In the following, quite perplexing example from Herodotus, εἰμί with the aorist participle also seems to have quite a distinctive value:

(226) ἐγὼ οὐδένα κω ἀνθρώπων δείσας ἔφυγον οὔτε πρότερον οὔτε νῦν σὲ φεύγω· οὐδέ τι νεώτερόν <u>εἰμι ποιήσας</u> νῦν ἢ καὶ ἐν εἰρήνῃ ἐώθεα ποιέειν (Hdt. 4.127.1)

'I never ran from any man before out of fear, and I am not running from you now; I am not doing any differently now than I am used to doing in time of peace, too.' (tr. Godley)

The Persian king Darius has come to the land of the Scythians. Rather than fighting an open battle, however, the Scythians continually

---

[13] Cf. similarly Aerts (1965: 31).
[14] Cf. the French translation by Chambry: 'que celui qui se marie se mette dans l'esprit que ...'.
[15] Cf. similarly Eur., *Alc.* 465. In Eur., *Supp.* 511 we also have a lexically stative verb, but here the ingressiveness is much less obvious. Aerts (1965: 34) suspects that the construction was used for metrical reasons.

retire, driving away the cattle and filling the wells with earth, and leading the Persians to their neighbouring enemies. Darius grows tired of this, and sends a messenger to ask the Scythian king Idanthyrsus why they flee on every single occasion. Idanthyrsus replies that the Scythians' behaviour is similar to that in times of peace. Various suggestions have been made for periphrastic εἰμι ποιήσας, ranging from 'I have done nothing new'[16] to 'I am doing nothing new'[17] and 'I will do nothing new'.[18] I agree with Aerts (1965: 27), who notes that 'the periphrasis serves more or less as unaugmented aorist indicative' and that 'the point in question here is an explanation of Idanthyrsus's behaviour, not the ascertainment of what he is, or of the circumstances in which he finds himself'. To be more specific, the aspectual function of εἰμι ποιήσας can be considered habitual, with νῦν referring to an extensive period of time during which Idanthyrsus undertook the action of fleeing when approached by Darius (cf. Hdt. 4.126.1, where we read πολλὸν τοῦτο ἐγίνετο καὶ οὐκ ἐπαύετο 'this went on for a long time and did not cease).[19]

In a number of other examples, the aorist participle seems to have an 'adjectival' value when combined with εἰμί. This is most evident in Aristotle, where γενόμενος is quite frequently used with the meaning of 'generated', always in contrast with the true adjectives ἀγέννητος 'ungenerated' or ἀΐδιον 'eternal'.[20]

As we saw in Chapter 2, like combinations of εἰμί with the present participle of lexically dynamic verbs, in exceptional cases the aorist participle is used in coordination with one or more regular adjectives. Consider example (227) in this regard:

(227) οὕτω τοίνυν οὗτός ἐστ᾽ ἀσεβὴς καὶ μιαρὸς καὶ πᾶν ἂν ὑποστὰς εἰπεῖν καὶ πρᾶξαι, εἰ δ᾽ ἀληθὲς ἢ ψεῦδος ἢ πρὸς ἐχθρὸν ἢ φίλον ἢ τὰ τοιαῦτα, ἀλλ᾽ οὐδ᾽ ὁτιοῦν διορίζων, ὥστ᾽ ἐπαιτιασάμενός με φόνου καὶ τοιοῦτο πρᾶγμ᾽ ἐπαγαγών, εἴασε μέν μ᾽ εἰσιτητήρι᾽ ὑπὲρ τῆς βουλῆς ἱεροποιῆσαι (Dem. 21.114)

---

[16] Björck (1940: 84); Ceglia (1998: 25).
[17] Aerts (1965: 28). Cf. also the translation provided by Godley.
[18] Rosén (1957: 139).
[19] Aerts (1965: 27) notes that 'the present participle cannot express this shade of meaning, nor, obviously, can the perfect participle'. This, I believe, is only partly true: durative εἰμί with the present participle can, as we have seen, also refer to multiple occasions. With the present participle, however, the multiple occasions are construed as interconnected to a greater extent.
[20] See e.g. Aristot., *MXG* 975a, 979a, 979b, *Top.* 104b.

'This man, then, is so impious, so abandoned, so ready to say or do anything, without stopping for a moment to ask whether it is true or false, whether it touches an enemy or a friend, or any such question, that after accusing me of murder and bringing that grave charge against me, he suffered me to conduct initiatory rites for the Council.' (tr. Murray)

In his famous speech *Against Meidias*, Demosthenes narrates how he has been treated by Meidias in the past. Among other malfeasances, he notes how Meidias has accused him of murder, while not objecting to Demosthenes performing public functions. A periphrasis is used to characterize Meidias, ἐστι ... ἂν ὑποστάς 'he would consent'. Note how the construction is combined with the particle ἄν, situating the event denoted by the participle in a modal sphere of potentiality, without any particular emphasis on duration.

A more complex instance of 'adjectival periphrasis' can be found in (228) (= (50)):

(228) {Οἰ.} ἔστιν δὲ ποῖον τοὔπος; οὔτε γὰρ θρασύς / οὔτ' οὖν <u>προδείσας εἰμὶ</u> τῷ γε νῦν λόγῳ (Soph., *OT* 89–90)
'Oedipus. But what is the oracle? So far, I am neither bold nor fearing prematurely by your words.'

Thebes is in mourning, since the city has been struck by the plague. King Oedipus has sent Creon to the oracle, to find out how he can protect the city. When Creon returns, he starts by saying rather enigmatically that 'troubles hard to bear, if they chance to turn out well, can bring good fortune'. Oedipus asks Creon to be more specific, noting that his words so far neither frighten nor encourage.

Normally, when perfective aspect is used with stative verbs, this results in an ingressive reading, as we have observed in (225). In this particular case, however, ingressiveness is backgrounded, since we are dealing with what could be called a 'tragic aorist',[21] expressing Oedipus' immediate reaction at Creon's words. A form such as προδείσας εἰμί 'I am fearing prematurely' is admittedly a somewhat unusual tragic aorist, since it does not occur in the past tense.[22] This,

---

[21] Cf. Aerts (1965: 34); Kamerbeek (1967: 47); Rijksbaron (2002: 128).
[22] Three other typical characteristics of tragic aorists are (a) use of a verb of judgement, emotion, saying, ordering, or advising; (b) use of the first person; (c) use of aoristic aspect (cf. Bary 2009: 122). On the tragic aorist, see e.g. Kühner & Gerth (1976 [1898]: 163–5); Smyth (1984 [1920]: 432); Moorhouse (1982: 195–6); Lloyd (1999); Duhoux (2000: 393–5); Rijksbaron (2002: 29–30).

however, should be considered within its larger context. As Bary (2009: 121–32) notes, for so-called 'performatives' (denoting completed action at the time of speaking, as in 'I swear') 'a form for aoristic aspect and present tense... would be the optimal form'. In the absence of such a form, a speaker of Ancient Greek could opt for one of two 'suboptimal' forms: either the synthetic present, in which case present tense is given primacy and perfective aspect is taken for granted, or the synthetic aorist, in which case perfective aspect is given primacy and past tense is taken for granted. The use of the periphrastic form (not mentioned by Bary) allows a combination of the two features, and in this regard can be considered more 'optimal', though little use seems to have been made of the construction.

In some other examples, the use of εἰμί with the aorist participle can be compared to that of (anterior) εἰμί with the perfect participle.[23] Given that the synthetic aorist could be used with a value similar to that of the (anterior) perfect,[24] perhaps the occurrence of these examples should not surprise use too much. Consider (229):[25]

(229) ἀλλὰ γὰρ ψευσάμενοί εἰσιν οἱ ἄνθρωποι τῶν ἁλμυρῶν ὑδάτων πέρι δι' ἀπειρίην, καὶ ὅτι νομίζεται διαχωρητικά (Hippoc., Aer. 7.68–70)
'People have deceived themselves with regard to salt waters, from inexperience, for they think these waters purgative.' (tr. Darwin Adams)

In a discussion of which types of water are best for cooking, the author of *On Airs, Waters, and Places*, one of the earlier works in the Hippocratic corpus, perhaps composed by Hippocrates himself, notes that people have often mistaken themselves when it comes to salt water: they consider it purgative (laxative), while it actually is the opposite. Periphrastic ψευσάμενοί εἰσιν 'they have deceived themselves' refers to multiple occasions in the past, which can be situated before the time of speaking, and can be compared to what we have called an 'experiential (anterior) perfect' in Chapter 3.[26]

A similar example can be found in Herodotus, with the aorist participle in the passive voice:

---

[23] Cf. Björck (1940: 83–4).   [24] Cf. §1.4.1.2
[25] Cf. similarly Hippoc., *Prorrh.* 2.1; Lys. 20.1; Thuc. 1.138.3, 4.54.3.
[26] See esp. §3.3.3.

(230) οἱ δὲ ἔφραζον ὥς σφι θεὸς <u>εἴη φανεὶς</u> διὰ χρόνου πολλοῦ ἐωθὼς ἐπιφαίνεσθαι καὶ ὡς, ἐπεὰν φανῇ, τότε πάντες Αἰγύπτιοι κεχαρηκότες ὀρτάζοιεν (Hdt. 3.27.3)

'The rulers told him that a god, wont to appear after long intervals of time, had now appeared to them; and that all Egypt rejoiced and made holiday whenever he so appeared.' (tr. Godley)

Having lost large part of his army, Cambyses arrives in Memphis, where the Egyptians are in a festive mood. Cambyses wants to know whether there is a connection between his loss and the festivities. The Egyptians explain that a god, Apis, had appeared to them, and that they always behaved this way when he appeared. Periphrastic εἴη φανείς 'he had appeared' refers to an event which occurred before the time of speaking, the appearance of the god, and as such has an anterior value.

Aerts (1965: 28-9) notes that in examples such as (230) avoidance of the perfect form may underlie the use of periphrasis (the forms πεφηνὼς εἴη, πεφασμένος εἴη, and πεφήνοι being uncommon), and here εἰμί with the aorist participle can be compared to the use of ἔχω with the aorist participle. Whether εἰμί with the aorist participle should also be characterized as a 'perfect periphrasis'—at least in these examples—is a moot point. Keil (1963: 31-2) notes with regard to the synthetic aorist that it could signal implicitly what the perfect signals explicitly—'der Aor. drückt zwar das Resultat aus, die andauernde Wirkung muß jedoch aus dem Zusammenhang erschlossen werden'[27]—and perhaps the semantic difference between anterior εἰμί with the aorist and εἰμί with the perfect participle is best thought of in similar terms. ἔχω with the aorist participle is different, since this periphrasis explicitly stresses the state that is the result of the past action, through the presence of ἔχω.[28] Consider the following example:

(231) {Νε. Σω.} ταῦτ' <u>ἔστω</u> ταύτῃ <u>λεχθέντα</u>· πάντως γὰρ ἱκανῶς δεδήλωται (Pl., Plt. 265d)

'Younger Socrates. Assume that I have said that; for you have made it perfectly clear' (tr. Fowler)

---

[27] 'The aorist expresses the result, but the lasting effect must be inferred from the context.'
[28] Cf. Thielmann (1891: 299); Moorhouse (1982: 206).

Young Socrates is in discussion with a Stranger about the subclassification of the art of tending animals: a first distinction is made between aquatic-herding vs. land-herding, then land-animals are further divided into flying and walking animals, and walking animals into those with and without horns. Young Socrates is ordered by the Stranger to define this last subdistinction further, but has to ask the Stranger for help, who gives the answer. Young Socrates then asks the Stranger to assume that *he* has given the answer. ἔστω... λεχθέντα lit. 'let it have been said' is used to refer to a past event which is *assumed* to have taken place before the time of speaking, and in this respect may be contrasted with δεδήλωται 'it has been made clear', as well as instances of ἔστω with the passive perfect participle.[29]

To conclude this section, it must be stressed that εἰμί with the aorist participle was used in a broad range of contexts, with an aspectual value that can be considered perfective in some contexts, and more perfect-like in others. Given this functional complexity, there seems to be little reason to assume any continuity between the Classical and the Post-Classical periods. Rather, as Keil (1963: 45) argues, the construction is best considered an innovative periphrasis, following the establishment of εἰμί with the perfect and the present participle in the Classical period:

> Während sich im 5. Jahrhundert die überkommenen Möglichkeiten der Umschreibung von Tempora ausweiten, kommt ein neuer Typ auf: εἶναι mit Part. Aor. Diese Erscheinung ist ein weiteres Zeichen für die Suche dieser Zeit nach neuen Ausdrucksmöglichkeiten.[30]

5.3 TRANSITIVITY AND THE DIACHRONY OF PERIPHRASIS IN CLASSICAL (ANCIENT) GREEK

In the two previous chapters, we saw how the two 'dominant' constructions—εἰμί with the perfect participle in the domain of perfect aspect and εἰμί with the present participle in the domain of

---

[29] See e.g. ex. (85).
[30] 'While during the fifth century BC the possibilities of periphrastic expression are expanding, a new type can be found: εἶναι with the aorist participle. The appearance of this construction constitutes another sign of the search of this time for new expressive possibilities.'

imperfective aspect—underwent a process of transitivization, meaning that they were used in increasingly transitive contexts. With regard to εἰμί with the perfect participle, I noted that the construction was used increasingly often with a volitional first participant and a second, possibly affected, participant. Moreover, the construction came to be used increasingly often in the active voice, resembling the expression of a prototypical transitive event. With regard to εἰμί with the present participle, I showed that the construction came to be used with a volitional first participant, and possibly with a second participant. While initially the construction tended to denote iteration, over time it more and more often expressed a single event.

Whether the same process of transitivization occurred for εἰμί with the aorist participle during the Classical period is difficult to say: the construction is much less often attested, and its different uses are also much more diverse. More interesting, however, is the role the appearance of this perfective periphrasis plays for our understanding of the development of periphrasis in Classical Greek, and by extension Ancient Greek. If we consider the parameter of 'aspect' an overarching transitivity-parameter, and maintain that unbounded (imperfective) aspect is less transitive than bounded (perfective) aspect, and that perfect aspect is in turn less transitive than imperfective aspect, since it does not actually express an action, but the state which may be the result of this action, we can say that periphrasis over time became more transitive: it first appeared in the domain of perfect aspect (with εἰμί with the perfect participle and ἔχω with the aorist participle), afterwards in the domain of imperfective aspect (with εἰμί with the present participle), and only in a final stage in the domain of perfective aspect.[31]

The development individuated here, that is, transitivization, has not run its entire course, and the perfective periphrasis was soon lost. Due to the changes elsewhere in the verbal system, εἰμί with the aorist participle came to be employed as a replacement for the more transitive use of εἰμί with the perfect participle (that is, as an anterior perfect), while εἰμί with the perfect participle retained its earlier

---

[31] One of the reviewers questions this overall development, noting that 'a perfective PC [periphrastic construction] was present in Classical Greek just as the other PCs'. While it is true that perfect, imperfective, and perfective periphrases can all be found in the Classical period, the perfective periphrasis is not attested in the Archaic period, and occurs much less frequently than imperfective and perfect periphrases in the Classical period.

resultative aspectual function. In other words, in the case of εἰμί with the perfect participle, we can speak of both transitivization and detransitivization. It should also be noted with regard to the use of εἰμί with the aorist participle as a perfective periphrasis during the Classical period that none of its uses can be considered prototypically perfective (or, in other words, highly transitive)—that is, to denote a past event with a volitional first participant and an affected second participant, in the active voice (which on the textual level would be reflected in the foregrounding of the clause). Rather, we find that the construction is used in non-prototypical contexts, such as the future tense, in the passive voice, coordinated with adjectives, referring to multiple occasions, etc.

In his monograph on the verb 'be' in Ancient Greek, Kahn (1973: 137–8) has brought forward a somewhat similar perspective: he notes that εἰμί with the perfect participle is most frequently used, εἰμί with the present participle somewhat less frequently, and εἰμί with the aorist participle least frequently,[32] which he explains in terms of a 'convergence of static tendencies':

> The static aspect of the verb and the adjective-like predicate syntax of the participle reinforce one another, since a predicate adjective usually describes a lasting quality or state of the subject. I suggest that it is this convergence of static tendencies in the periphrastic construction which explains the preference for perfect periphrasis in Greek, from Homer to the present. (Kahn 1973: 138)

Kahn's view presents a number of distinct disadvantages, however, which have come to light in the previous chapters: (a) while it is true that εἰμί on some occasions has a stative value, and that the participle can show adjective-like behaviour, in principle there is no reason why the finite verb or the participle should have retained this feature; (b) Kahn's observations in terms of frequency are not entirely accurate: εἰμί with the present participle did come to be used quite frequently; and (c) that εἰμί with the perfect and the present participle remained stative throughout their history, a view which is also advanced by Aerts and a number of other scholars, is oversimplified.

---

[32] Kahn (1973: 141–2).

Conclusion to Verbal Periphrasis in Ancient Greek

> A pervasive structural-semantic feature like that presented above [transitivity, KB] might be expected to play a role in language change.
> (Hoppper & Thompson 1980: 279)

In this study, I have analysed the use and development of periphrastic constructions that are built with the verbs εἰμί and ἔχω, in an attempt to answer a number of questions of both synchronic and diachronic relevance. Here I summarize some of the main conclusions I have drawn.

From a synchronic point of view, one of my objectives was to clarify which constructions that consist of a finite verb and a participle qualify as 'periphrastic'. While various constructions whose finite member is a verb of state, movement, or phase are considered 'periphrastic' in the literature, previous attempts to define verbal periphrasis have been unsatisfying. In this book, I advanced an alternative, which is based on the view that categories are 'prototypically' organized: I suggested that useful phonological, functional, and morpho-syntactic criteria can be derived from Grammaticalization Theory in order to identify prototypical periphrastic constructions.

A second synchronic objective was to clarify how the notion of 'adjectival' periphrasis relates to that of 'verbal' periphrasis. While some scholars have introduced the former notion to distinguish constructions of the type πρέπον ἐστί 'it is fitting' or ἀνεῳγμένον ἐστί 'it is open(ed)' from 'truly' periphrastic constructions, I argued that a binary opposition between 'adjectival' and 'verbal' periphrasis cannot be upheld. The morpho-syntactic criteria advanced for such a view are problematic, and almost exclusively oriented towards the present participle. As a result, it is unclear whether the adjectival perfect and aorist participles should also be considered 'adjectivized'. Alternatively, adjectival periphrasis, too, can be thought of as a prototypically organized notion, whereby the adjectival (or more correctly 'property-referring') participle is located on a continuum with an adjective-like and a verb-like side.

In terms of semantics, the notion of adjectival periphrasis can be connected with that of scalar transitivity: sentences containing 'adjectival' periphrases are typically low in transitivity. This allows one to make a distinction between participles where a property reading comes natural versus those where this is much less the case: with the perfect participle and the present participle of lexically stative verbs (which are inclined towards low transitivity) a property reading constitutes the 'default construal', while it constitutes the 'non-default construal' with the aorist participle and the present participle of lexically dynamic verbs (which are inclined towards higher transitivity).

In what forms the main part of this book, I analysed the diachronic development of periphrastic constructions with εἰμί and ἔχω. I described three main 'functional domains': perfect aspect (Chapter 3), imperfective aspect (Chapter 4), and perfective aspect (Chapter 5).

The variety of periphrastic constructions in these different domains, as well as their overall frequency, differs considerably. In the domain of perfect aspect, three 'major' constructions can be identified: εἰμί with the perfect participle occurs throughout the entire period analysed, ἔχω with the aorist participle only occurs with some frequency in the Classical period, and εἰμί with the aorist participle only occurs in the Post-Classical/Byzantine period. Next to these three major constructions, there are also numerous 'minor' perfect constructions. Periphrasis in the domain of imperfective aspect is almost entirely limited to a single construction, εἰμί with the present participle, which occurs with much higher frequency than was previously thought. Perfective periphrases are rare: εἰμί with the aorist participle is used as such only in the Classical period, and to a very limited extent. One interesting similarity across these different domains is that εἰμί constitutes the dominant auxiliary in terms of frequency: there is no 'split auxiliarization' comparable to what we see in many European languages.

In order to describe the development of periphrastic constructions with εἰμί and ἔχω, the notion of 'grammaticalization paths'—universal semantic paths along which relevant forms can develop—proved instrumental, particularly in the functional domains of perfect and imperfective aspect. For example, I argued that the construction of εἰμί with the perfect participle follows the commonly attested path of development RESULTATIVE > ANTERIOR, a development which took place already in the Classical period. εἰμί with the present participle also follows a generally attested path of development, that is, STATIVE > PROGRESSIVE. This development took place at a later stage though: some early progressive examples can be found in the Classical period, but they become much more common in the Post-Classical period. Not all constructions necessarily undergo these paths of development: ἔχω with the medio-passive perfect participle remains limited to a resultative aspectual function during the entire period under analysis, and εἰμί with the aorist participle is typically used with an anterior function in the Post-Classical/Byzantine period.

Following up on earlier studies that draw attention to the role of the presence of an (affected) object when it comes to the development of the synthetic perfect, I argued that next to (or better, in combination with) the above-mentioned grammaticalization paths the notion of 'transitivity' provides additional insight in the diachronic development of periphrastic constructions; however, I argued that transitivity is best understood in a 'scalar' sense, whereby a number of parameters should be taken into account, including participants, kinesis, aspect, volitionality, mode, and affectedness of the object. To be more specific, I drew attention to the fact that periphrastic constructions with εἰμί tend to become used in more transitive contexts, a process for which I devised the term 'transitivization'. For example, the development from 'resultative' to 'anterior' undergone by εἰμί with the perfect participle is one whereby two participants become central, one of which is often an agent and the other a patient. Other elements emphasizing the action, such as adverbs of manner, in time also become employed. Similarly, in the development from 'stative' to 'progressive', as evidenced by εἰμί with the present participle, a second participant often becomes more prominent, and the action is frequently carried out by an agent.

The concept of transitivization has further relevance for periphrasis with εἰμί. At a detailed level of analysis, an interesting similarity can be observed between the development of anterior εἰμί with the perfect participle and progressive εἰμί with the present participle: early examples are often expressed in the passive voice (often without an agent), and frequently denote a repeated, rather than a single event. Increased transitivity can also be recognized from a much more general point of view: if we take it that imperfective aspect is less transitive than perfective aspect (cf. the aspect-parameter), and that perfect aspect is less transitive than imperfective aspect (cf. the kinesis-parameter), we can say that periphrasis in general becomes more transitive, first being attested in the functional domain of perfect aspect, afterwards in that of imperfective aspect, and only in a final stage in that of perfective aspect.

While this study has focused exclusively on Ancient Greek, its findings are also of relevance from a more general point of view. Perhaps most important in this regard are the observations and adaptations made concerning the above-mentioned grammaticalization paths. With regard to 'aoristic drift', for example, I noted that the occurrence of εἰμί with the perfect participle as an 'experiential perfect' and/or a 'perfect of persistence' should not be considered a *necessary* intermediary stage between its use as a resultative perfect and a perfect of current relevance, as some scholars have suggested. With regard to PROG imperfective drift, I argued that the construction of εἰμί with the present participle has multiple origins, and that the habitual function is best considered a continuation of the durative (iterative) progressive function, rather than the focalized progressive function.

Another issue that I have advanced in this book, which was also stressed by Markopoulos (2009) in his study of future periphrases, is the importance of integrating diachronic research with a social dimension. While such a socio-historical perspective has not been particularly popular within Grammaticalization Theory, I believe it holds great promise to refine our analysis further. Particularly with regard to Post-Classical and Early Byzantine Greek, the notion 'register' proved to be of relevance: the functional specialization of εἰμί with the perfect participle, for example, first takes place in the middle register in Middle Post-Classical Greek, which is also where we first find the diffusion of εἰμί with the aorist participle. Similarly, the diffusion of εἰμί with the present participle with a durative progressive function first occurs in the middle register in Early Post-Classical Greek, and only at a later stage (Late Post-Classical Greek) in the high register. While in need of further research, these findings indicate that the above-mentioned grammaticalization paths can be considered multi-layered, in the sense that the use of a given construction may be further advanced on the grammaticalization path in one register than in the other.

A third and final issue which may be of a more general importance is that of studying the development of periphrastic constructions in their context. Next to the language-external context (that is, language contact with Latin and Hebrew), particular attention was drawn in this study to language-internal factors. In the functional domain of perfect aspect, for example, I drew attention to the effect of the development and decline of the synthetic perfect on periphrastic perfect constructions. In the functional domain of imperfective aspect, I suggested that the frequent use of the construction of τυγχάνω may have blocked the further development of progressive εἰμί with the present participle. Such language-internal relations are not necessarily confined to a single functional domain: we have seen that εἰμί with the present participle in its stative aspectual function is likely to have been influenced by resultative εἰμί with the perfect participle, and that εἰμί with the aorist participle in the Classical period can be considered an innovative extension of the more common constructions of εἰμί with the perfect and the present participle.

APPENDIX

Archaic Greek (VIII–VI BC)

Epic poetry

Iliad	Homer	VIII BC	T.W. Allen. 1931. *Homeri Ilias*, vols. 2–3. Oxford: Clarendon Press.
Odyssey	Homer	VIII BC	P. von der Mühll. 1962. *Homeri Odyssea*. Basel: Helbing & Lichtenhahn.
Theogony	Hesiod	VIII–VII BC	M.L. West. 1966. *Hesiod. Theogony*. Oxford: Clarendon Press.
Works and Days	Hesiod	VIII–VII BC	F. Solmsen. 1970. *Hesiodi opera*. Oxford: Clarendon Press.
Homeric Hymns		VIII–VI BC	T.W. Allen, W.R. Halliday, and E.E. Sikes. 1936. *The Homeric hymns*, 2nd edn. Oxford: Clarendon Press.

Classical Greek (V–IV BC)

Drama

Tragedies	Aeschylus	VI–V BC	D.L. Page. 1972. *Aeschyli septem quae supersunt tragoedias*. Oxford: Clarendon Press.
Tragedies	Euripides	V BC	J. Diggle. 1981–94. *Euripidis fabulae*, vols. 1–3. Oxford: Clarendon Press.
Tragedies	Sophocles	V BC	H. Lloyd-Jones and N.G. Wilson. 1990. *Sophoclis fabulae*. Oxford: Clarendon Press.
Comedies	Aristophanes	V–IV BC	N.G. Wilson. 2007. *Aristophanis Fabulae*, vols. 1–2. Oxford: Oxford University Press.

Historiography

Histories	Herodotus	V BC	Ph.-E. Legrand. 1932–54. *Hérodote. Histoires*, 9 vols. Paris: Les Belles Lettres.

Histories	Thucydides	V BC	H.S. Jones and J.E. Powell. 1942. *Thucydidis historiae*, 2 vols. Oxford: Clarendon Press.
Agesilaus	Xenophon	V–IV BC	E.C. Marchant. 1920. *Xenophontis opera omnia*, vol. 5. Oxford: Clarendon Press.
Anabasis	Xenophon	V–IV BC	E.C. Marchant. 1904. *Xenophontis opera omnia*, vol. 3. Oxford: Clarendon Press.
Apology	Xenophon	V–IV BC	E.C. Marchant. 1921. *Xenophontis opera omnia*, vol. 2, 2nd edn. Oxford: Clarendon Press.
Cyropaedia	Xenophon	V–IV BC	E.C. Marchant. 1910. *Xenophontis opera omnia*, vol. 4. Oxford: Clarendon Press.
Economics	Xenophon	V–IV BC	E.C. Marchant. 1921. *Xenophontis opera omnia*, vol. 2, 2nd edn. Oxford: Clarendon Press.
Hellenica	Xenophon	V–IV BC	E.C. Marchant. 1900. *Xenophontis opera omnia*, vol. 1. Oxford: Clarendon Press.
Hiero	Xenophon	V–IV BC	E.C. Marchant. 1920. *Xenophontis opera omnia*, vol. 5. Oxford: Clarendon Press.
Memorabilia	Xenophon	V–IV BC	E.C. Marchant. 1921. *Xenophontis opera omnia*, vol. 2, 2nd edn. Oxford: Clarendon Press.
On hunting	Xenophon	V–IV BC	E.C. Marchant. 1920. *Xenophontis opera omnia*, vol. 5. Oxford: Clarendon Press.
On revenues	Xenophon	V–IV BC	E.C. Marchant. 1920. *Xenophontis opera omnia*, vol. 5. Oxford: Clarendon Press.
On the art of horsemanship	Xenophon	V–IV BC	E.C. Marchant. 1920. *Xenophontis opera omnia*, vol. 5. Oxford: Clarendon Press.
On the Athenian republic	Xenophon	V–IV BC	E.C. Marchant. 1920. *Xenophontis opera omnia*, vol. 5. Oxford: Clarendon Press.

On the cavalry commander	Xenophon	V–IV BC	E.C. Marchant. 1920. *Xenophontis opera omnia*, vol. 5. Oxford: Clarendon Press.
On the constitution of the Lacedaemonians	Xenophon	V–IV BC	E.C. Marchant. 1920. *Xenophontis opera omnia*, vol. 5. Oxford: Clarendon Press.
Symposium	Xenophon	V–IV BC	E.C. Marchant. 1921. *Xenophontis opera omnia*, vol. 2, 2nd edn. Oxford: Clarendon Press.

Philosophy

Dialogues	Plato	V–IV BC	J. Burnet. 1900–1907. *Platonis opera*, vols. 1–5. Oxford: Clarendon Press.
Categories	Aristotelic corpus	IV BC	L. Minio-Paluello. 1949. *Aristotelis categoriae et liber de interpretatione*. Oxford: Clarendon Press.
Constitution of the Athenians	Aristotelic corpus	IV BC	H. Oppermann. 1928. *Aristotelis Ἀθηναίων Πολιτεία*. Leipzig: Teubner.
Divisions	Aristotelic corpus	IV BC	H. Mutschmann. 1906. *Divisiones quae vulgo dicuntur Aristoteleae*. Leipzig: Teubner.
Economics	Aristotelic corpus	IV BC	B.A. van Groningen and A. Wartelle. 1968. *Aristote. Économique*. Paris: Les Belles Lettres.
Eudemian ethics	Aristotelic corpus	IV BC	F. Susemihl. 1884. *Aristotelis ethica Eudemia*. Leipzig: Teubner.
Generation of animals	Aristotelic corpus	IV BC	H.J. Drossaart Lulofs. 1965. *Aristotelis de generatione animalium*. Oxford: Clarendon Press.
History of animals	Aristotelic corpus	IV BC	P. Louis. 1964–69. *Aristote. Histoire des animaux*, vols. 1–3. Paris: Les Belles Lettres.

Magna moralia	Aristotelic corpus IV BC	F. Susemihl. 1935. *Aristotle*, vol. 18. Cambridge, MA: Harvard University Press.
Mechanics	Aristotelic corpus IV BC	I. Bekker. 1831. *Aristotelis opera*, vol. 2. Berlin: Reimer.
Metaphysics	Aristotelic corpus IV BC	W.D. Ross. 1924. *Aristotle's metaphysics*, 2 vols. Oxford: Clarendon Press.
Meteorology	Aristotelic corpus IV BC	F.H. Fobes. 1919. *Aristotelis meteorologicorum libri quattuor*. Cambridge, MA: Harvard University Press.
Movement of animals	Aristotelic corpus IV BC	W. Jaeger. 1913. *Aristotelis de animalium motione et de animalium incessu. Ps.-Aristotelis de spiritu libellus*. Leipzig: Teubner.
Nicomachean ethics	Aristotelic corpus IV BC	I. Bywater. 1894. *Aristotelis ethica Nicomachea*. Oxford: Clarendon Press.
On breath	Aristotelic corpus IV BC	W. Jaeger. 1913. *Aristotelis de animalium motione et de animalium incessu. Ps.-Aristotelis de spiritu libellus*. Leipzig: Teubner.
On colours	Aristotelic corpus IV BC	I. Bekker. 1831. *Aristotelis opera*, vol. 2. Berlin: Reimer.
On divination by dreams	Aristotelic corpus IV BC	W.D. Ross. 1955. *Aristotle. Parva naturalia*. Oxford: Clarendon Press.
On dreams	Aristotelic corpus IV BC	W.D. Ross. 1955. *Aristotle. Parva naturalia*. Oxford: Clarendon Press.
On generation and corruption	Aristotelic corpus IV BC	C. Mugler. 1966. *Aristote. De la génération et de la corruption*. Paris: Les Belles Lettres.
On indivisible lines	Aristotelic corpus IV BC	I. Bekker. 1831. *Aristotelis opera*, vol. 2. Berlin: Reimer.

On interpretation	Aristotelic corpus	IV BC	L. Minio-Paluello. 1949. *Aristotelis categoriae et liber de interpretatione*. Oxford: Clarendon Press.
On length and shortness of life	Aristotelic corpus	IV BC	W.D. Ross. 1955. *Aristotle. Parva naturalia*. Oxford: Clarendon Press.
On marvellous things heard	Aristotelic corpus	IV BC	I. Bekker. 1831. *Aristotelis opera*, vol. 2. Berlin: Reimer.
On Melissus, Xenophanes, and Gorgias	Aristotelic corpus	IV BC	H. Diels. 1900. *Aristotelis qui fertur de Melisso Xenophane Gorgia libellus*. Berlin: Reimer.
On memory and recollection	Aristotelic corpus	IV BC	W.D. Ross. 1955. *Aristotle. Parva naturalia*. Oxford: Clarendon Press.
On respiration	Aristotelic corpus	IV BC	W.D. Ross. 1955. *Aristotle. Parva naturalia*. Oxford: Clarendon Press.
On sleep	Aristotelic corpus	IV BC	W.D. Ross. 1955. *Aristotle. Parva naturalia*. Oxford: Clarendon Press.
On sophistical refutations	Aristotelic corpus	IV BC	W.D. Ross. 1958. *Aristotelis topica et sophistici elenchi*. Oxford: Clarendon Press.
On the heavens	Aristotelic corpus	IV BC	P. Moraux. 1965. *Aristote. Du ciel*. Paris: Les Belles Lettres.
On the soul	Aristotelic corpus	IV BC	W.D. Ross. 1964. *Aristotle. De anima*. Oxford: Clarendon Press.
On the universe	Aristotelic corpus	IV BC	W.L. Lorimer. 1933. *Aristotelis qui fertur libellus de mundo*. Paris: Les Belles Lettres.
On things heard	Aristotelic corpus	IV BC	I. Bekker. 1831. *Aristotelis opera*, vol. 2, 2nd edn. Berlin: Reimer.
On virtues and vices	Aristotelic corpus	IV BC	I. Bekker. 1831. *Aristotelis opera*, vol. 2. Berlin: Reimer.
On youth and old age	Aristotelic corpus	IV BC	W.D. Ross. 1955. *Aristotle. Parva naturalia*. Oxford: Clarendon Press.

Parts of animals	Aristotelic corpus	IV BC	P. Louis. 1956. *Aristote. Les parties des animaux.* Paris: Les Belles Lettres.
Physics	Aristotelic corpus	IV BC	W.D. Ross. 1950. *Aristotelis physica.* Oxford: Clarendon Press.
Physiognomonics	Aristotelic corpus	IV BC	I. Bekker. 1831. *Aristotelis opera*, vol. 2. Berlin: Reimer.
Poetics	Aristotelic corpus	IV BC	R. Kassel. 1965. *Aristotelis de arte poetica liber.* Oxford: Clarendon Press.
Politics	Aristotelic corpus	IV BC	W.D. Ross. 1957. *Aristotelis politica.* Oxford: Clarendon Press.
Prior & posterior analytics	Aristotelic corpus	IV BC	W.D. Ross. 1964. *Aristotelis analytica priora et posteriora.* Oxford: Clarendon Press.
Problems	Aristotelic corpus	IV BC	I. Bekker. 1831. *Aristotelis opera*, vol. 2. Berlin: Reimer.
Progression of animals	Aristotelic corpus	IV BC	W. Jaeger. 1913. *Aristotelis de animalium motione et de animalium incessu. Ps.-Aristotelis de spiritu libellus.* Leipzig: Teubner.
Protreptic	Aristotelic corpus	IV BC	I. Düring. 1961. *Aristotle's protrepticus.* Stockholm: Almqvist & Wiksell.
Rhetoric	Aristotelic corpus	IV BC	W.D. Ross. 1959. *Aristotelis ars rhetorica.* Oxford: Clarendon Press.
Sense and sensibilia	Aristotelic corpus	IV BC	W.D. Ross. 1955. *Aristotle. Parva naturalia.* Oxford: Clarendon Press.
The situations and names of winds	Aristotelic corpus	IV BC	I. Bekker. 1831. *Aristotelis opera*, vol. 2. Berlin: Reimer.
Topics	Aristotelic corpus	IV BC	W.D. Ross. 1958. *Aristotelis topica et sophistici elenchi.* Oxford: Clarendon Press.

Oratory

Orations	Antiphon	V BC	L. Gernet. 1923. *Antiphon. Discours*. Paris: Les Belles Lettres.
Orations	Andocides	V–IV BC	G. Dalmeyda. 1930. *Andocide. Discours*. Paris: Les Belles Lettres.
Orations	Isaeus	V–IV BC	P. Roussel. 1960. *Isée. Discours*, 2nd edn. Paris: Les Belles Lettres.
Orations	Isocrates	V–IV BC	É. Brémond and G. Mathieu. 1929–62. *Isocrate. Discours*, vols. 1, 2 & 4. Paris: Les Belles Lettres; G. Mathieu. 1942. *Isocrate. Discours*, vol. 3. Paris: Les Belles Lettres.
Orations	Lysias	V–IV BC	U. Albini. 1955. *Lisia. I discorsi*. Florence: Sansoni.
Orations	Aeschines	IV BC	G. de Budé and V. Martin. 1927–8. *Eschine. Discours*, vols. 1–2. Paris: Les Belles Lettres.
Orations	Demosthenes	IV BC	S.H. Butcher. 1903–7. *Demosthenis orationes*, vols. 1 & 2.1. Oxford: Clarendon Press; W. Rennie. 1921–31. *Demosthenis orationes*, vols. 2.2 & 3. Oxford: Clarendon Press.
Orations	Hyperides	IV BC	C. Jensen. 1917. *Hyperidis orationes sex*. Leipzig: Teubner.
Orations	Lycurgus	IV BC	N.C. Conomis. 1970. *Lycurgi oratio in Leocratem*. Leipzig: Teubner.
Orations	Dinarchus	IV–III BC	N.C. Conomis. 1975. *Dinarchi orationes cum fragmentis*. Leipzig: Teubner.

Scientific prose

Aphorisms	Hippocratic corpus	V–IV BC	É. Littré. 1844. *Oeuvres complètes d'Hippocrate*, vol. 4. Paris: Baillière.

Epidemics	Hippocratic corpus	V–IV BC	É. Littré. 1840–6. *Oeuvres complètes d'Hippocrate*, vols. 2–3, 5. Paris: Baillière.
Mochlicon	Hippocratic corpus	V–IV BC	É. Littré. 1844. *Oeuvres complètes d'Hippocrate*, vol. 4. Paris: Baillière.
On affections	Hippocratic corpus	V–IV BC	É. Littré. 1849. *Oeuvres complètes d'Hippocrate*, vol. 6. Paris: Baillière.
On airs	Hippocratic corpus	V–IV BC	É. Littré. 1849. *Oeuvres complètes d'Hippocrate*, vol. 6. Paris: Baillière.
On airs, waters, and places	Hippocratic corpus	V–IV BC	É. Littré. 1840. *Oeuvres complètes d'Hippocrate*, vol. 2. Paris: Baillière.
On aliment	Hippocratic corpus	V–IV BC	É. Littré. 1861. *Oeuvres complètes d'Hippocrate*, vol. 9. Paris: Baillière.
On anatomy	Hippocratic corpus	V–IV BC	É. Littré. 1853. *Oeuvres complètes d'Hippocrate*, vol. 8. Paris: Baillière.
On ancient medicine	Hippocratic corpus	V–IV BC	É. Littré. 1839. *Oeuvres complètes d'Hippocrate*, vol. 1. Paris: Baillière.
On critical days	Hippocratic corpus	V–IV BC	É. Littré. 1861. *Oeuvres complètes d'Hippocrate*, vol. 9. Paris: Baillière.
On decorum	Hippocratic corpus	V–IV BC	É. Littré. 1861. *Oeuvres complètes d'Hippocrate*, vol. 9. Paris: Baillière.
On dentition	Hippocratic corpus	V–IV BC	É. Littré. 1853. *Oeuvres complètes d'Hippocrate*, vol. 8. Paris: Baillière.
On diseases	Hippocratic corpus	V–IV BC	É. Littré. 1849–51. *Oeuvres complètes d'Hippocrate*, vols. 6–7. Paris: Baillière.
On fistulae	Hippocratic corpus	V–IV BC	É. Littré. 1849. *Oeuvres complètes d'Hippocrate*, vol. 6. Paris: Baillière.

On fleshes	Hippocratic corpus	V–IV BC	É. Littré. 1853. *Oeuvres complètes d'Hippocrate*, vol. 8. Paris: Baillière.
On fractures	Hippocratic corpus	V–IV BC	É. Littré. 1841. *Oeuvres complètes d'Hippocrate*, vol. 3. Paris: Baillière.
On hemorrhoids	Hippocratic corpus	V–IV BC	É. Littré. 1849. *Oeuvres complètes d'Hippocrate*, vol. 6. Paris: Baillière.
On injuries of the head	Hippocratic corpus	V–IV BC	É. Littré. 1841. *Oeuvres complètes d'Hippocrate*, vol. 3. Paris: Baillière.
On internal affections	Hippocratic corpus	V–IV BC	É. Littré. 1851. *Oeuvres complètes d'Hippocrate*, vol. 7. Paris: Baillière.
On joints	Hippocratic corpus	V–IV BC	É. Littré. 1844. *Oeuvres complètes d'Hippocrate*, vol. 4. Paris: Baillière.
On purgative medicines	Hippocratic corpus	V–IV BC	H. Schöne. 1924. Hippokrates. Περὶ φαρμάκων. *Rheinisches Museum* 73, 440–3.
On regimen	Hippocratic corpus	V–IV BC	É. Littré. 1849. *Oeuvres complètes d'Hippocrate*, vol. 6. Paris: Baillière.
On regimen in acute diseases	Hippocratic corpus	V–IV BC	É. Littré. 1840. *Oeuvres complètes d'Hippocrate*, vol. 2. Paris: Baillière.
On semen, On the nature of the child, On diseases iv	Hippocratic corpus	V–IV BC	É. Littré. 1851. *Oeuvres complètes d'Hippocrate*, vol. 7. Paris: Baillière.
On superfoetation	Hippocratic corpus	V–IV BC	É. Littré. 1853. *Oeuvres complètes d'Hippocrate*, vol. 8. Paris: Baillière.
On the art of medicine	Hippocratic corpus	V–IV BC	É. Littré. 1849. *Oeuvres complètes d'Hippocrate*, vol. 6. Paris: Baillière.
On the crises	Hippocratic corpus	V–IV BC	É. Littré. 1861. *Oeuvres complètes d'Hippocrate*, vol. 9. Paris: Baillière.

On the diseases of women	Hippocratic corpus	V–IV BC	É. Littré. 1853. *Oeuvres complètes d'Hippocrate*, vol. 8. Paris: Baillière.
On the diseases of young women	Hippocratic corpus	V–IV BC	É. Littré. 1853. *Oeuvres complètes d'Hippocrate*, vol. 8. Paris: Baillière.
On the eighth months child	Hippocratic corpus	V–IV BC	É. Littré. 1851. *Oeuvres complètes d'Hippocrate*, vol. 7. Paris: Baillière.
On the excision of the foetus	Hippocratic corpus	V–IV BC	É. Littré. 1853. *Oeuvres complètes d'Hippocrate*, vol. 8. Paris: Baillière.
On the glands	Hippocratic corpus	V–IV BC	É. Littré. 1853. *Oeuvres complètes d'Hippocrate*, vol. 8. Paris: Baillière.
On the heart	Hippocratic corpus	V–IV BC	É. Littré. 1861. *Oeuvres complètes d'Hippocrate*, vol. 9. Paris: Baillière.
On the humors	Hippocratic corpus	V–IV BC	É. Littré. 1846. *Oeuvres complètes d'Hippocrate*, vol. 5. Paris: Baillière.
On the nature of man	Hippocratic corpus	V–IV BC	É. Littré. 1849. *Oeuvres complètes d'Hippocrate*, vol. 6. Paris: Baillière.
On the nature of the bones	Hippocratic corpus	V–IV BC	É. Littré. 1861. *Oeuvres complètes d'Hippocrate*, vol. 9. Paris: Baillière.
On the nature of the woman	Hippocratic corpus	V–IV BC	É. Littré. 1851. *Oeuvres complètes d'Hippocrate*, vol. 7. Paris: Baillière.
On the physician	Hippocratic corpus	V–IV BC	É. Littré. 1861. *Oeuvres complètes d'Hippocrate*, vol. 9. Paris: Baillière.
On the places in man	Hippocratic corpus	V–IV BC	É. Littré. 1849. *Oeuvres complètes d'Hippocrate*, vol. 6. Paris: Baillière.
On the sacred disease	Hippocratic corpus	V–IV BC	É. Littré. 1849. *Oeuvres complètes d'Hippocrate*, vol. 6. Paris: Baillière.

On the seven months child	Hippocratic corpus	V–IV BC	É. Littré. 1851. *Oeuvres complètes d'Hippocrate*, vol. 7. Paris: Baillière.
On the use of liquids	Hippocratic corpus	V–IV BC	É. Littré. 1849. *Oeuvres complètes d'Hippocrate*, vol. 6. Paris: Baillière.
On the weeks	Hippocratic corpus	V–IV BC	W.H. Roscher. 1913. *Die hippokratische Schrift von der Siebenzahl.* Paderborn: Schöningh.
On ulcers	Hippocratic corpus	V–IV BC	É. Littré. 1849. *Oeuvres complètes d'Hippocrate*, vol. 6. Paris: Baillière.
On vision	Hippocratic corpus	V–IV BC	É. Littré. 1861. *Oeuvres complètes d'Hippocrate*, vol. 9. Paris: Baillière.
Precepts	Hippocratic corpus	V–IV BC	É. Littré. 1861. *Oeuvres complètes d'Hippocrate*, vol. 9. Paris: Baillière.
Prognostics	Hippocratic corpus	V–IV BC	É. Littré. 1840. *Oeuvres complètes d'Hippocrate*, vol. 2. Paris: Baillière.
Prorrhetics	Hippocratic corpus	V–IV BC	É. Littré. 1846–61. *Oeuvres complètes d'Hippocrate*, vols. 5 and 9. Paris: Baillière.
Regimen in health	Hippocratic corpus	V–IV BC	É. Littré. 1849. *Oeuvres complètes d'Hippocrate*, vol. 6. Paris: Baillière.
The coan praenotions	Hippocratic corpus	V–IV BC	É. Littré. 1846. *Oeuvres complètes d'Hippocrate*, vol. 5. Paris: Baillière.
The Hippocratic oath	Hippocratic corpus	V–IV BC	É. Littré. 1844. *Oeuvres complètes d'Hippocrate*, vol. 4. Paris: Baillière.
The law	Hippocratic corpus	V–IV BC	É. Littré. 1844. *Oeuvres complètes d'Hippocrate*, vol. 4. Paris: Baillière.
The physician's establishment	Hippocratic corpus	V–IV BC	É. Littré. 1841. *Oeuvres complètes d'Hippocrate*, vol. 3. Paris: Baillière.

Early Post-Classical Greek (III–I BC)

Biography/hagiography

Septuagint	III/II BC	A. Rahlfs. 1935. *Septuaginta*, 9th edn. Stuttgart: Württemberg Bible Society.
Apocalypse of Enoch	II/I BC	M. Black. 1970. *Apocalypsis Henochi Graece*. Leiden: Brill.
Life of Adam and Eve	I BC / I AD	C. Tischendorf. 1866. *Apocalypses apocryphae*. Leipzig: Mendelssohn.

Historiography

Histories	Polybius	III/II BC	T. Büttner-Wobst. 1882–1904. *Polybii historiae*. Leipzig: Teubner.
Roman Antiquities	Dionysius of Halicarnassus	I BC	K. Jacoby. 1885–1905. *Dionysii Halicarnasei antiquitatum Romanarum quae supersunt*. Leipzig: Teubner.

Scientific prose

Book of lemmas	Archimedes	III BC	C. Mugler. 1971. *Archimède*, vol. 3. Paris: Les Belles Lettres.
Measurement of a circle	Archimedes	III BC	C. Mugler. 1970. *Archimède*, vol. 1. Paris: Les Belles Lettres.
On conoids and spheroids	Archimedes	III BC	C. Mugler. 1970. *Archimède*, vol. 1. Paris: Les Belles Lettres.
On floating bodies	Archimedes	III BC	C. Mugler. 1971. *Archimède*, vol. 3. Paris: Les Belles Lettres.
On spirals	Archimedes	III BC	C. Mugler. 1971. *Archimède*, vol. 2. Paris: Les Belles Lettres.
On the equilibrium of planes	Archimedes	III BC	C. Mugler. 1971. *Archimède*, vol. 2. Paris: Les Belles Lettres.
On the sphere and the cylinder	Archimedes	III BC	C. Mugler. 1970. *Archimède*, vol. 1. Paris: Les Belles Lettres.
The method	Archimedes	III BC	C. Mugler. 1971. *Archimède*, vol. 3. Paris: Les Belles Lettres.

The quadrature of the parabola	Archimedes	III BC	C. Mugler. 1971. *Archimède*, vol. 2. Paris: Les Belles Lettres.
The sand-reckoner	Archimedes	III BC	C. Mugler. 1971. *Archimède*, vol. 2. Paris: Les Belles Lettres.
Geography	Strabo	I BC / I AD	A. Meineke. 1877. *Strabonis geographica*, 3 vols. Leipzig: Teubner.

Middle Post-Classical Greek (I–III AD)

Biography/hagiography

Apocalypse of Baruch	I AD	J.C. Picard. 1967. *Apocalypsis Baruchi Graece*. Leiden: Brill.
New Testament	I AD	K. Aland, M. Black, C. M. Martini, B.M. Metzger & A. Wikgren. 1968. *The Greek New Testament*, 2nd edn. Stuttgart: Württemberg Bible Society.
Testament of Abraham	I AD	M.R. James. 1892. *The testament of Abraham*. Cambridge: Cambridge University Press.
Parallel lives	Plutarch I/II AD	B. Perrin. 1914–26. *Plutarch's lives*, vols. 1, 4, 5 & 11. Cambridge, MA: Harvard University Press; K. Ziegler. 1964–71. *Plutarchi vitae parallelae*, vols. 1.1 (4th edn.), 1.2 (3rd edn.), 2.1 (2nd edn.), 2.2 (2nd edn.), 3.1 (2nd edn.). Leipzig: Teubner.
Acts of Andrew	II AD	J.-M. Prieur. 1989. *Acta Andreae*. Turnhout: Brepols.
Acts of John	II AD	M. Bonnet.1898. *Acta apostolorum apocrypha*. Leipzig: Mendelssohn.
Acts of Paul	II AD	C. Schmidt & W. Schubart. 1936. *Acta Pauli*. Glückstadt: Augustin.
Acts of Paul and Thecla	II AD	R.A. Lipsius. 1891. *Acta apostolorum apocrypha*. Leipzig: Mendelssohn.

Acts of the Scillitan martyrs	II AD	J.A. Robinson. 1891. *The passion of S. Perpetua.* Cambridge: Cambridge University Press.
Apocalypse of John	II AD	C. Tischendorf. 1866. *Apocalypses apocryphae.* Leipzig: Mendelssohn.
Bel et Draco (Theodotion)	II AD	A. Rahlfs. 1935. *Septuaginta,* 9th edn. Stuttgart: Württemberg Bible Society.
Confession and prayer of Aseneth	II AD	M. Philonenko. 1968. *Joseph et Aséneth.* Leiden: Brill
Daniel (Theodotion)	II AD	A. Rahlfs. 1935. *Septuaginta,* 9th edn. Stuttgart: Württemberg Bible Society.
Gospel of Peter	II AD	M.G. Mara. 1973. *Évangile de Pierre.* Paris: Éditions du Cerf.
Gospel of the Ebionites	II AD	E. Klostermann. 1910. *Apocrypha II. Evangelien,* 2nd edn. Bonn: Marcus & Weber.
Gospel of Thomas	II AD	E. Klostermann. 1910. *Apocrypha II. Evangelien,* 2nd edn. Bonn: Marcus & Weber.
Martyrdom of Paul	II AD	R.A. Lipsius. 1891. *Acta apostolorum apocrypha.* Leipzig: Mendelssohn.
Martyrdom of Peter	II AD	L. Vouaux. 1922. *Les actes de Pierre.* Paris: Letouzey & Ané.
Proto-evangelium of James	II AD	É. de Strycker. 1961. *La forme la plus ancienne du protévangile de Jacque.* Brussels: Société des Bollandistes.
Susanna (Theodotion)	II AD	A. Rahlfs. 1935. *Septuaginta,* 9th edn. Stuttgart: Württemberg Bible Society.
Testament of Job	II AD	S.P. Brock. 1967. *Testamentum Jobi.* Leiden: Brill.
Acts of Justin	II/III AD	H. Musurillo. 1972. *The acts of the Christian martyrs.* Oxford: Clarendon Press.

Acts of the Alexandrines		II/III AD	H. Musurillo. 1961. *Acta Alexandrinorum*. Leipzig: Teubner.
Acts of Thomas		III AD	M. Bonnet. 1903. *Acta apostolorum apocrypha*, vol. 2.2. Leipzig: Mendelssohn.
Acts of Xanthippe and Polyxena		III AD	M.R. James. 1893. *Apocrypha anecdota*. Cambridge: Cambridge University Press.
Gospel of Bartholomew		III AD	G.N. Bonwetsch. 1897. Die apokryphen Fragen des Bartholomäus. *Nachrichten von der königlichen Gesellschaft der Wissenschaften, Philol.-hist. Kl.*. Göttingen, 9–29.

Greek novel

Daphnis and Chloe	Longus	II AD	G. Dalmeyda. 1934. *Longus. Pastorales (Daphnis et Chloé)*. Paris: Les Belles Lettres.
Callirhoe	Chariton	II AD	B.P. Reardon. 2004. *Charitonis Aphrodisiensis de Callirhoe narrationes amatoriae*. Munich-Leipzig: K.G. Saur.
Leucippe and Clitophon	Achilles Tatius	II AD	E. Vilborg. 1955. *Achilles Tatius. Leucippe und Clitophon*. Stockholm: Almqvist & Wiksell.
Ephesian tale	Xenophon	II/III AD	G. Dalmeyda. 1926. *Xénophon d'Éphèse. Les Éphésiaques ou le roman d'Habrocomès et d'Anthia*. Paris: Les Belles Lettres.
Ethiopian story	Heliodorus	III AD	T.W. Lumb, J. Maillon, and R.M. Rattenbury. 1960. *Héliodore. Les Éthiopiques (Théagène et Chariclée)*, 3 vols., 2nd edn. Paris: Les Belles Lettres.

Appendix

Historiography

Jewish war	Flavius Iosephus	I AD	B. Niese. 1895. *Flavii Iosephi opera*, vol. 6. Berlin: Weidmann.
Roman Histories	Cassius Dio	II/III AD	U.P. Boissevain. 1895–1901. *Cassii Dionis Cocceiani historiarum Romanarum quae supersunt*. Berlin: Weidmann.

Scientific prose

On antidotes	Galen	II AD	C.G. Kühn. 1827. *Claudii Galeni opera omnia*, vol. 14. Leipzig: Knobloch.
On semen	Galen	II AD	C.G. Kühn. 1822. *Claudii Galeni opera omnia*, vol. 4. Leipzig: Knobloch.
On the natural faculties	Galen	II AD	G. Helmreich, J. Marquardt, and I. Müller. 1893. *Claudii Galeni Pergameni scripta minora*, vol. 3. Leipzig: Teubner.
On the preservation of health	Galen	II AD	K. Koch. 1923. *Galeni de sanitate tuenda libri vi*. Leipzig: Teubner.
The art of medicine	Galen	II AD	C.G. Kühn. 1821. *Claudii Galeni opera omnia*, vol. 1. Leipzig: Knobloch.
Description of Greece	Pausanias	II AD	F. Spiro. 1903. *Pausaniae Graeciae descriptio*, 3 vols. Leipzig: Teubner.

Late Post-Classical Greek (IV–VI AD)

Biography/hagiography

Acts of Philip		IV AD	F. Amsler, B. Bouvier, and F. Bovon. 1999. *Acta Philippi*. Turnhout: Brepols.
Collection of ancient martyrdoms	Eusebius	IV AD	J.-P. Migne. 1857–66. *Patrologiae cursus completus (series Graeca) (MPG)* 20. Paris: Migne.

Encomium on the holy forty martyrs	Ephraem the Syrian	IV AD	K.G. Phrantzoles. 1998. *Ὁσίου Ἐφραίμ τοῦ Σύρου ἔργα*, vol. 7. Thessalonica: To Perivoli tis Panagias.
Lausaic history	Palladius	IV AD	G.J.M. Bartelink. 1974. *Palladio. La storia Lausiaca*. Verona: Fondazione Lorenzo Valla.
Life of Antony	Athanasius	IV AD	G.J.M. Bartelink. 2004. *Athanase d'Alexandrie, Vie d'Antoine*. Paris: Éditions du Cerf.
Life of St Macrina	Gregory of Nyssa	IV AD	P. Maraval. 1971. *Grégoire de Nysse. Vie de sainte Macrine*. Paris: Éditions du Cerf.
Life of Constantine	Eusebius	IV AD	F. Winkelmann. 1975. *Eusebius Werke, Band 1.1: Über das Leben des Kaisers Konstantin*. Berlin: Akademie Verlag.
Martyrium of Pionius the presbyter and his comrades		IV AD	H. Musurillo. 1972. *The acts of the Christian martyrs*, 136–66. Oxford: Clarendon Press.
On Gordius the Martyr	Basil of Caesarea	IV AD	J.-P. Migne. 1857–66. *Patrologiae cursus completus (series Graeca) (MPG)* 31. Paris: Migne.
On the life of blessed Abraham and his granddaughter Maria	Ephraem the Syrian	IV AD	K.G. Phrantzoles. 1998. *Ὁσίου Ἐφραίμ τοῦ Σύρου ἔργα*, vol. 7. Thessalonica: To Perivoli tis Panagias.
On the life of Gregory the wonderworker	Gregory of Nyssa	IV AD	J.-P. Migne. 1857–66. *Patrologiae cursus completus (series Graeca) (MPG)* 46. Paris: Migne.
On the life of Moses	Gregory of Nyssa	IV AD	J. Danielou. 1968. *Grégoire de Nysse. La vie de Moïse*, 3rd edn. Paris: Éditions du Cerf.
On the martyrs of Palestine	Eusebius	IV AD	G. Bardy. 1958. *Eusèbe de Césarée. Histoire ecclésiastique*, vol. 3. Paris: Éditions du Cerf.

On those who in Euphratesia and the Osrhoene region, Syria, Phoenicia and Cilicia live the monastic life	Theodoretus of Cyrrhus	IV/V AD	J.-P. Migne. 1857–66. *Patrologiae cursus completus (series Graeca) (MPG)* 83. Paris: Migne.
Acts of Barnabas		V AD	M. Bonnet. 1903. *Acta apostolorum apocrypha*, vol. 2.2. Leipzig: Mendelssohn.
Encomium on John the Baptist	Chrysippus of Jerusalem	V AD	A. Sigalas. 1937. *Des Chrysippos von Jerusalem Enkomion auf den hl. Johannes den Täufer*. Athens: Verlag der Byzantinisch-neugriechischen Jahrbücher.
Encomium on St Theodorus	Chrysippus of Jerusalem	V AD	A. Sigalas. 1921. *Des Chrysippos von Jerusalem Enkomion auf den heiligen Theodoros Teron*. Leipzig: Teubner.
History of the monks in Egypt		V AD	A.-J. Festugière. 1971. *Historia monachorum in Aegypto*. Brussels: Société des Bollandistes.
Laudation on mother Mary	Proclus	V AD	F.J. Leroy. 1967. *L'homilétique de Proclus de Constantinople*. Vatican City: Biblioteca Apostolica Vaticana.
Life of Alexander		V AD	E. de Stoop. 1911. *Vie d' Alexandre l' Acémète*. Turnhout: Brepols.
Life of Pachomius		V AD	F. Halkin. 1982. *Le corpus athénien de saint Pachome*. Genève: Cramer.
Life of Porphyry bishop of Gaza	Mark the Deacon	V AD	H. Gregoire & M.-A. Kugener. 1930. *Marc le Diacre. Vie de Porphyre, évêque de Gaza*. Paris: Les Belles Lettres.
Life of St Hypatius	Callinicus	V AD	G.J.M. Bartelink. 1971. *Callinicos. Vie d'Hypatios*. Paris: Éditions du Cerf.

Appendix 329

Life of St Syncletica	Pseudo-Athanasius	V AD	L. Abelarga. 2002. *The Life of Saint Syncletica. Introduction-Critical Text-Commentary.* Thessalonica: Centre for Byzantine Research.
Life of Symeon Stylites the Elder	Antony the Hagiographer	V AD	H. Lietzmann. 1908. *Das Leben des heiligen Symeon Stylites.* Leipzig: Hinrichs.
Passion of Gregory the Illuminator	Agathangelus	V AD	G. Garitte. 1946. *Documents pour l' étude du livre d' Agathange.* Rome: Bibliotheca Apostolica Vaticana.
Laudation of Theodorus Graptus	Theophanes of Caesarea	VI AD	J. Featherstone. 1980. The praise of Theodore Graptos by Theophanes of Caesarea. *Analecta Bollandiana* 98, 104–50.
Life of Abramius	Cyril of Scythopolis	VI AD	E. Schwartz. 1939. *Kyrillos von Skythopolis.* Leipzig: Hinrichs.
Life of Cyriacus	Cyril of Scythopolis	VI AD	E. Schwartz. 1939. *Kyrillos von Skythopolis.* Leipzig: Hinrichs.
Life of Euthymius	Cyril of Scythopolis	VI AD	E. Schwartz. 1939. *Kyrillos von Skythopolis.* Leipzig: Hinrichs.
Life of John the Silentiary	Cyril of Scythopolis	VI AD	E. Schwartz. 1939. *Kyrillos von Skythopolis.* Leipzig: Hinrichs.
Life of Sabas	Cyril of Scythopolis	VI AD	E. Schwartz. 1939. *Kyrillos von Skythopolis.* Leipzig: Hinrichs.
Life of Symeon Stylites the Younger		VI AD	P. van den Ven. 1962. *La vie ancienne de S. Syméon Stylite le jeune (521–592).* Brussels: Société des Bollandistes.
Life of Theodosius	Cyril of Scythopolis	VI AD	E. Schwartz. 1939. *Kyrillos von Skythopolis.* Leipzig: Hinrichs.
Life of Eutychius	Eustratius the Presbyter	VI/VII AD	C. Laga. 1992. *Eustratii presbyteri vita Eutychii patriarchae Constantinopolitani.* Turnhout: Brepols.
Life of Golinduch	Eustratius the Presbyter	VI/VII AD	A. Papadopoulos-Kerameus. 1897–8. Ἀνάλεκτα Ἱεροσολυμιτικῆς σταχυολογίας, vol. 4/5. St Petersburg: Kirschbaum.

Life of Martha the mother of Simeon Stylites the Younger		VI/VII AD	P. van den Ven. 1970. *La vie ancienne de S. Syméon Stylite le jeune*, vol. 2. Brussels: Société des Bollandistes.
Life of Tycho	John the Merciful	VI/VII AD	H. Usener. 1907. *Sonderbare Heilige I. Der heilige Tychon*. Leipzig: Teubner.
Spiritual Meadow	John Moschus	VI/VII AD	J.-P. Migne. 1857–66. *Patrologiae cursus completus (series Graeca) (MPG)* 87.3. Paris: Migne.

Historiography

Ecclesiastical history	Eusebius	IV AD	G. Bardy. 1952–8. *Eusèbe de Césarée. Histoire ecclésiastique*. Paris: Éditions du Cerf.
Historical fragments	Eunapius	IV/V AD	L. Dindorf. 1870. *Historici Graeci minores*, vol. 1. Leipzig: Teubner.
Ecclesiastical history	Theodoretus of Cyrrhus	IV/V AD	L. Parmentier & F. Scheidweiler. 1954. *Theodoret. Kirchengeschichte*, 2nd edn. Berlin: Akademie Verlag
Ecclesiastical history	Sozomenus	V AD	J. Bidez & G.C. Hansen. 1960. *Sozomenus. Kirchengeschichte*. Berlin: Akademie Verlag.
New history	Zosimus	V AD	F. Paschoud. 1971–89. *Zosime. Histoire nouvelle*, vols. 1–3.2. Paris: Les Belles Lettres.
Chronography	John Malalas	VI AD	L. Dindorf. 1831. *Ioannis Malalae chronographia*. Bonn: Weber.

Scientific prose

Exposition of astronomical hypotheses	Proclus	V AD	C. Manitius. 1909. *Procli Diadochi hypotyposis astronomicarum positionum*. Leipzig: Teubner.
Christian topography	Cosmas Indicopleustes	VI AD	W. Wolska-Conus. 1968–73. *Cosmas Indicopleustès. Topographie chrétienne*, 3 vols. Paris: Éditions du Cerf.

| On the creation of the world | John Philoponus | VI AD | W. Reichardt. 1897. *Joannis Philoponi de opificio mundi libri vii*. Leipzig: Teubner. |

Early Byzantine Greek (VII–VIII AD)

Biography/hagiography

Apocalypse	Pseudo-Methodius	VII AD	A.C. Lolos. 1976. *Die Apokalypse des Ps.-Methodios*. Meisenheim am Glan: Hain.
Laudation of St Anastasius the Persian	George Pisida	VII AD	B. Flusin. 1992. *Saint Anastase le Perse et l'histoire de la Palestine au début du VIIe siècle*, vol. 1. Paris: Centre National de la Recherche Scientifique.
Laudation of St John Chrysostomus	John of Damascus	VII AD	P.B. Kotter. 1988. *Die Schriften des Johannes von Damaskos*, vol. 5. Berlin & New York: De Gruyter.
Laudation of St martyr Anastasia	John of Damascus	VII AD	P.B. Kotter. 1988. *Die Schriften des Johannes von Damaskos*, vol. 5. Berlin & New York: De Gruyter.
Laudation of St martyr Barbara	John of Damascus	VII AD	P.B. Kotter. 1988. *Die Schriften des Johannes von Damaskos*, vol. 5. Berlin & New York: De Gruyter.
Life of John the Merciful	Leontius of Naples	VII AD	A.-J. Festugière & L. Rydén. 1974. *Léontios de Néapolis, Vie de Syméon le Fou et Vie de Jean de Chypre*. Paris: Geuthner.
Life of St Auxibius		VII AD	J. Noret. 1993. *Hagiographica Cypria*. Turnhout: Brepols.
Life of St Gregory the Theologian	Gregory the Presbyter	VII AD	X. Lequeux. 2001. *Gregorii Presbyteri vita Sancti Gregorii Theologi*. Turnhout: Brepols.
Life of St Symeon the fool	Leontius of Naples	VII AD	A.-J. Festugière & L. Rydén. 1974. *Léontios de Néapolis, Vie de Syméon le Fou et Vie de Jean de Chypre*. Paris: Geuthner.

Life of St Theodore of Syceon	George of Syceon	VII AD	A.-J. Festugière. 1970. *Vie de Théodore de Sykeôn*, vol. 1. Brussels: Société des Bollandistes.
xlv miracles of St Artemius		VII AD	A. Papadopoulos-Kerameus. 1909. *Varia graeca sacra*. St Petersburg: Kirschbaum.
Miracles of St Demetrius	John of Thessalonica	VII AD	P. Lemerle. 1979. *Les plus anciens recueils des miracles de saint Démétrius et la pénétration des Slaves dans les Balkans*, vol. 1. Paris: Centre National de la Recherche Scientifique.
Narration of the miracles of Sts. Cyrus and John	Sophronius	VII AD	N. Fernández Marcos. 1975. *Manuales y anejos de 'Emérita'* 31, 243–400. Madrid: Instituto 'Antonio de Nebrija'.
Passion of the great martyr Artemius	John of Damascus	VII AD	P.B. Kotter. 1988. *Die Schriften des Johannes von Damaskos*, vol. 5. Berlin & New York: De Gruyter.
Two shorter lives of Theodore of Syceon		VII AD	A.-J. Festugière. 1970. *Vie de Théodore de Sykeôn*, vol. 1. Brussels: Société des Bollandistes.
Passion of St Parasceva	John of Euboea	VII/VIII AD	F. Halkin. 1966. *La Passion de Sainte Parascève par Jean d'Eubée*. Heidelberg: Winter.
Life of St Benedictus	Pope Zacharias	VIII AD	G. Rigotti. 2001. *Vita di s. Benedetto nella versione greca di papa Zaccaria*. Alessandria, Italy: Edizioni dell'Orso.
Martyrium of Julian and Basilissa		VIII AD	F. Halkin. 1980. La passion ancienne des saints Julien et Basilisse. *Analecta Bollandiana* 98, 243–96.
Laudation of John Chrysostomus	Cosmas Vestitor	VIII/IX AD	C.I. Dyobouniotes. 1940. Κοσμᾶ Βεστίτωρος ἀνέκδοτον ἐγκώμιον εἰς Ἰωάννην τὸν Χρυσόστομον. Ἐπετηρὶς Ἑταιρείας Βυζαντινῶν Σπουδῶν 16, 151–5.

Appendix 333

Laudation of St Mocius	Michael Syncellus	VIII/IX AD	H. Delehaye. 1912. Saints de Thrace et de Mésie. *Analecta Bollandiana* 31, 176–87.
Laudation of Theophanes Confessor	Theodorus Studites	VIII/IX AD	S. Efthymiadis. 1993. Le panégyrique de S. Théophane le Confesseur par S. Théodore Stoudite (BHG 1792b). *Analecta Bollandiana* 111, 268–84.
Life of Gregory the Decapolite	Ignatius the Deacon	VIII/IX AD	G. Makris. 1997. *Ignatios Diakonos und die Vita des Hl. Gregorios Dekapolites*. Stuttgart: Teubner.
Life of Nicephorus	Ignatius the Deacon	VIII/IX AD	C. de Boor. 1880. *Nicephori archiepiscopi Constantinopolitani opuscula historica*. Leipzig: Teubner.
Life of St Andrew of Crete	Nicetas the Patrician	VIII/IX AD	A. Papadopoulos-Kerameus. 1888. Ἀνάλεκτα ἱεροσολυμιτικῆς σταχυολογίας ἢ συλλογὴ ἀνεκδότων, vol. 5, 169–79.
Life of Stephan the Younger	Stephan the Deacon	VIII/IX AD	M.-F. Auzépy. 1997. *La Vie d' Étienne le Jeune par Étienne le Diacre*. Aldershot/Brookfield: Variorum.
Life of Tarasius the Patriarch	Ignatius the Deacon	VIII/IX AD	S. Efthymiadis. 1998. *The Life of the Patriarch Tarasios by Ignatios the Deacon*. Aldershot, England: Ashgate.
Three laudations on St Zacharias	Cosmas Vestitor	VIII/IX AD	F. Halkin. 1987. Zacharie, père de Jean Baptiste. Trois panégyriques par Cosmas Vestitor. *Analecta Bollandiana* 105, 252–63.

Historiography

Histories	Theophylact Simocatta	VII AD	C. de Boor. 1887. *Theophylacti Simocattae historiae*. Leipzig: Teubner.
Paschal Chronicle		VII AD	L. Dindorf. 1832. *Chronicon paschale*, vol. 1. Bonn: Weber.

| Chronography | Theophanes Confessor | VIII/IX AD | C. de Boor. 1883. *Theophanis chronographia*, vol. 1. Leipzig: Teubner. |

Scientific prose

| Medical compendium in seven books | Paul of Aegina | VII AD | J.L. Heiberg. 1921–4. *Paulus Aegineta*, 2 vols. Leipzig: Teubner. |

Note

A full overview of the printed editions of the papyri included in the *Duke Databank of Documentary Papyri* is available at <http://library.duke.edu/rubenstein/scriptorium/papyrus/texts/clist_papyri.html>.

Glossary

Accomplishment	One of four verb categories proposed by Vendler (1957). Accomplishment verbs such as 'to paint (a picture)' have an inherent endpoint and involve an action that lasts for an interval of time.
Achievement	One of four verb categories proposed by Vendler (1957). Achievement verbs such as 'to reach' have an inherent endpoint, and involve an action that is punctual.
Actionality	A property of the verb and its complements (also called 'Aktionsart' or 'lexical aspect'). Vendler (1957) has proposed to distinguish between four main verb classes: 'accomplishments', 'achievements', 'activities', and 'states'.
Activity	One of four verb categories proposed by Vendler (1957). Activity verbs such as 'to walk' do not have an inherent endpoint, and involve an action that lasts for an interval of time.
Adjectival periphrasis	A term coined by Björck (1940), Aerts (1965) and others to distinguish 'adjectival' constructions of the type ἀνεῳγμένον ἐστί 'it is opened' or πρέπον ἐστί 'it is fitting' from truly periphrastic constructions. In this book, I argue that no binary distinction can be made between 'adjectival' and 'verbal' periphrasis; rather, some participles have more adjectival characteristics than others.
Affectedness	One of Hopper & Thompson's (1980) transitivity parameters. Participants can be affected by the verbal event; if so, they are 'patients' (e.g. 'Paul' in 'he murdered Paul').
Analytic language	See synthetic language
Anterior perfect	A subtype of perfect aspect, denoting a past event with relevance at a later point in time (compare 'perfect of current relevance').

Aspect	A property of the clause, which is traditionally described in terms of temporality. The event 'to walk in the park', for example, can be conceptualized as temporally bounded ('he walked in the park') (perfective aspect) or temporally unbounded ('he was walking in the park') (imperfective aspect). Alternatively, aspect can be described in terms of 'transitivity'.
Categorial status	The status of a word in terms of word class. 'Table' for example, has the categorial status 'noun', while 'easy' has the categorial status 'adjective'.
Connectivity	The degree of dependency between two events/ clauses. For example, in 'I want to eat', there is strong connectivity between 'I want' and 'to eat', whereas in 'I put my coat on. It was cold', connectivity is weaker. Dependency relations of the first type are often called 'semantic', whereas those of the latter are 'pragmatic', but the distinction is somewhat arbitrary.
Daueradjektivierung	A term coined by Björck (1940), referring to participles that are frequently 'adjectivized' and so used for 'adjectival' periphrasis (e.g. συμφέρον ἐστί 'it is expedient').
Decategorialization	One of the parameters of grammaticalization, whereby e.g. nouns and verbs lose their canonical nominal/verbal properties.
Default construal	The more typical usage of a word or construction. For example, 'off' is typically used as a preposition, rather than a verb (as in 'to off someone'). The less typical usage is called the 'non-default' construal.
Discourse mode	Within a text (discourse), different types of passages can be distinguished, e.g. narrative versus descriptive passages. Smith (2001, 2003) recognizes five general 'modes' of discourse: 'narrative', 'report', 'description', 'information', and 'argument'.
Durative progressive aspect	Subtype of progressive aspect. Durative progressives refer to an event that is not evaluated with regard to a single point in time

Glossary

	and that typically occurs in a broad time-frame, as in 'he was baptizing people for three weeks' (contrast focalized progressive aspect). With durative progressives, there is often a sense of iteration ('iterative durative progressives'), but this is not necessarily the case (as in 'yesterday, she was playing for three hours').
Durativity	Semantic notion used in Vendler's (1957) classification of actionality, referring to the duration vs. non-duration of an event (e.g. 'to eat' vs. 'to arrive').
Dynamicity	Semantic notion used in Vendler's (1957) classification of actionality, referring to whether an event is stative or non-stative/dynamic (contrast e.g. 'to like' with 'to hit').
Event	A general category subsuming all aspectual types, including states.
Experiential perfect	Subtype of anterior perfect aspect. Experiential perfects denote an event that took place repeatedly in the past, rather than just once, and has relevance at a later point in time, as in 'I have spoken with the professor on several occasions'.
Focalization point	The point of interruption with focalized progressives. For example, in a sentence such as 'he was reading, when I came in', 'I came in' functions as the focalization point.
Focalized progressive aspect	Subtype of progressive aspect. Focalized progressives refer to an event that overlaps with another, foregrounded event, with which it is narrowly connected (e.g. 'she was reading, when he said...') (contrast durative progressive aspect).
Form-function reanalysis	A mechanism of diachronic change, involving a reanalysis of the 'mapping' between form and meaning. An example would be the 'be going to'-construction in cases such as '[I am going] [to buy cake]': the semantic feature of future intention may be analysed as inherent in the construction and that of spatial motion dropped: '[I am going to buy cake]'.

Gelegenheitsadjektivierung	A term coined by Björck (1940), referring to participles that are infrequently 'adjectivized' and so used for 'adjectival' periphrasis (e.g. κακουργοῦσά ἐστιν 'it injures') (contrast *Daueradjektivierung*).
Generalization	One of the functional parameters of grammaticalization, referring to the generalization of meaning of a grammaticalizing element.
Grammaticalization	'The change whereby lexical items and constructions come in certain linguistic contexts to serve grammatical functions and, once grammaticalized, continue to develop new grammatical functions' (Hopper & Traugott 2003: xv). Grammaticalization is typically conceived of as a set of concurrent phonological, functional, and morpho-syntactic processes.
Grammaticalization path	A commonly attested path of development. For example, verbs denoting 'movement towards' frequently develop into future markers, as in English 'going to' or French 'aller'.
Grammaticalization Theory	A functionalist theory of language change centred around the notion of 'grammaticalization'.
Idiomaticization	One of the parameters of grammaticalization, referring to the process whereby the informational contribution of the grammaticalizing elements becomes less transparent (e.g. *go*, *-ing*, and *to* in the 'going to V-' construction).
Imperfective aspect	One of three main types of aspect, next to 'perfective' and 'perfect' aspect. Imperfective aspect can be defined in terms of temporal unboundedness, meaning that no explicit attention is paid to the boundary transition phases of the event (as in 'he was writing').
Kinesis	One of Hopper & Thompson's (1980) parameters of transitivity, referring to whether a transfer of energy occurs from one participant to another (contrast e.g. 'I kissed the girl' with

	'I loved the girl': actions are kinetic, while states are non-kinetic). Also relevant for the kinesis-parameter is whether the action occurs once, or repeatedly.
Mode	One of Hopper & Thompson's (1980) parameters of transitivity, referring to the distinction between 'realis' and 'irrealis', or more broadly the occurrence versus non-occurrence of an actual event (e.g. 'I ate the sandwich' vs. 'I will eat the sandwich').
Non-default construal	See 'default construal'.
Normed rate of occurrence	'The rate at which a feature occurs in a fixed amount of text' (Biber & Conrad 2009: 62). In this book, normed rate of occurrence is calculated for amounts of text of 10,000 words.
Obligatorification	One of the parameters of grammaticalization, referring to the process whereby a construction becomes the sole expression for a certain function.
Paradigmaticization	One of the parameters of grammaticalization, referring to the process whereby a construction becomes integrated into the grammatical paradigm.
Participants	One of Hopper & Thompson's (1980) parameters of transitivity, referring to the number of participants to the verbal event (contrast e.g. 'he died' (one participant) with 'he saw the man' (two participants)).
Perfect aspect	One of three main types of aspect, next to 'perfective' and 'imperfective' aspect. Perfect aspect constitutes an intermediate category in terms of boundedness: perfects typically refer to both a bounded (past) event and the unbounded situation resulting from this event, and either of these components may be highlighted (as in 'the door is closed' vs. 'he has closed the door').
Perfect of current relevance	Subtype of anterior perfect aspect. Perfects of current relevance denote an event that occurred in the past and has relevance at a later point in time, as in 'I've studied this book thoroughly', said at the time of an exam.

Perfect of persistence	Subtype of anterior perfect aspect. Perfects of persistence denote an event that started in the past and continues up to a later point in time (often the time of speaking), as in 'he has been coughing since Tuesday'.
Perfect of recent past	Subtype of anterior perfect aspect. Perfects of recent past denote an event that has occurred very recently (hence a certain emphasis), as in 'I've just seen him!'.
Perfective aspect	One of three main types of aspect, next to 'imperfective' and 'perfect' aspect. Perfective aspect can be defined in terms of temporal boundedness, meaning that explicit attention is paid to the boundary transition phases of the event (as in 'he saw a film').
Progressive aspect	Subtype of imperfective aspect. Progressives denote the continuation of an event, as in 'I was speaking to him'. Two subtypes can be distinguished: 'focalized' progressives and 'durative' progressives.
Prototype Theory	A theory of categorization that is centred around the notion of 'prototypicality'. This theory, which forms an alternative to the classical, criterial-attribute model of linguistic categorization, claims that (a) necessary and sufficient conditions for category membership cannot always be defined, (b) some entities may be better examples of the category than others, and (c) category boundaries may be blurred at the edges or 'fuzzy'.
Register	'A variety of language defined according to its use in social situations' (Crystal 1991: 295). With regard to written language, for example, one can distinguish between low-, middle-, and high-register texts, depending on who the author and the audience of the text are, and what their relationship is.
Resultative perfect	A subtype of perfect aspect. Resultatives highlight the situation resulting from a past event, as in 'the door is closed' (contrast with 'I've closed the door', where emphasis lies on the past event causing the situation).

Glossary 341

Rigidification	One of the morpho-syntactic parameters of grammaticalization, whereby linear order becomes more rigid.
Semantic integration	A notion which refers to the semantic contribution made by the component parts of a construction: when both component parts make a substantial semantic contribution, there is a low degree of semantic integration, and vice versa (contrast e.g. 'I love to eat' with 'I'm going to eat').
Statal passive	A term used to refer to stative events in the passive voice, as in 'it is agreed upon'.
State	One of four verb categories proposed by Vendler (1957). Stative verbs such as 'to like' last for an interval of time, do not involve an action, and do not have an inherent endpoint.
Stative aspect	A subtype of imperfective aspect, not to be confused with stative actionality. Statives denote temporally stable events, as in 'John smokes cigars, not cigarettes', or 'he loves that movie'.
Synthetic language	A synthetic language has a high *morpheme-per-word* ratio, while an analytic language has a low *morpheme-per-word* ratio. Contrast, for example, the Ancient Greek form λυθήσομαι with its English counterpart *I will be released*.
Telicity	Semantic notion used in Vendler's (1957) classification of actionality, referring to the presence or absence of a natural endpoint (contrast e.g. 'to walk' with 'to drown').
Transitivity	Traditionally, the notion of transitivity refers to the presence of two arguments in the clause (subject and object, coded as nominative and accusative in Ancient Greek). Hopper & Thompson (1980) argue that a clause is not simply 'transitive' or 'intransitive': they view transitivity as a prototypical concept, and argue that a clause can be more or less transitive. To evaluate the degree of transitivity of a clause, they propose a set of parameters, including not only 'participants', but also 'kinesis', 'volitionality', 'mode', affectedness', etc.

Type/token ratio	Type/token ratio specifies the ratio of the number of different non-finite verbs (the 'types') to the total number of non-finite verbs (the 'tokens') appearing in each construction.
Verbal periphrasis	In this book, I argue that verbal periphrasis is best understood as a prototypical category. In order to identify prototypical periphrastic constructions, phonological, functional, and morpho-syntactic criteria can be derived from Grammaticalization Theory (the so-called 'parameters of grammaticalization').
Volitionality	One of Hopper & Thompson's (1980) parameters of transitivity, referring to whether an act is done purposefully or non-purposefully (e.g. 'I wrote your name' versus 'I forgot your name').

Bibliography

Aarts, B. 2006. Conceptions of categorization in the history of linguistics. *Language Sciences* 28, 361–85.
Adams, J.N. 2003. *Bilingualism and the Latin language*. Cambridge: Cambridge University Press.
Adrados, F.R. 1992a. *Nueva sintaxis del griego antiguo*. Madrid: Gredos.
Adrados, F.R. 1992b. La lengua de Sócrates y su filosofía. *Méthexis* 5, 29–52.
Adrados, F.R. 2005. *A history of the Greek language: From its origins to the present*. Leiden: Brill.
Aerts, W.J. 1965. *Periphrastica: An investigation into the use of εἶναι and ἔχειν as auxiliaries or pseudo-auxiliaries in Greek from Homer up to the present day*. Amsterdam: Hakkert (diss. Amsterdam).
Alexander, W.J. 1883. Participial periphrases in Attic prose. *American Journal of Philology* 6, 291–308.
Allan, R.J. 2003. *The middle voice in ancient Greek: A study in polysemy*. Amsterdam: J.C. Gieben.
Allinson, F.G. 1902. On causes contributory to the loss of the optative etc. in later Greek. In: *Studies in honor of Basil L. Gildersleeve*, 353–56. Baltimore: John Hopkins Press.
Ameis, K.F. & C. Hentze. 1920[13]. *Homers Odyssee. Erster Band / Erstes Heft, Gesang I–VI*. Leipzig & Berlin: B.G. Teubner.
Ameis, K.F. & C. Hentze. 1922[12]. *Homers Odyssee. Erster Band / Zweites Heft, Gesang VII–XII*. Leipzig & Berlin: B.G. Teubner.
Amenta, L. 2003. *Perifrasi aspettuali in greco e in latino. Origini e grammaticalizzazioni*. Milano: Franco Angeli.
Auwera, J. van der. 1999. Periphrastic 'do': Typological prolegomena. In: A. J. Tops, B. Devriendt & S. Geukens (eds.), *Thinking English grammar: To honour Xavier Dekeyser*, 457–70. Leuven: Peeters.
Bailey, N.A. 2009. *Thetic constructions in Koine Greek*. PhD thesis, VU-University Amsterdam.
Bailly, A. 1903. *Dictionnaire grec-français*. Paris: Hachette.
Bakker, E. 1997. Verbal aspect and mimetic description in Thucydides. In: E. Bakker (ed.), *Grammar as interpretation. Greek literature in its linguistic contexts*, 7–54. Leiden: Brill.
Bakker, E. 2001. Similes, augment, and the language of immediacy. In: J. Watson (ed.), *Speaking volumes: Orality and literacy in the Greek and Roman World*, 1–23. Leiden: Brill.
Bakker, E. 2006. Contract and design: Thucydides' writing. In: A. Rengakos & A. Tsakmakis (eds.), *Brill's companion to Thucydides*, 109–29. Leiden: Brill.

Barbelenet, D. 1913. *De la phrase à verbe être dans l'ionien d' Hérodote*. Paris: H. Champion.
Bary, C., 2009. *Aspect in Ancient Greek. A semantic analysis of the aorist and imperfective*. PhD thesis, Nijmegen University.
Basset, L. 1979. *Les emplois périphrastiques du verbe grec ΜΕΛΛΕΙΝ: Étude de linguistique grecque et essai de lingistique générale*. Lyon: Maison de l'Orient.
Bauer, B. 2000. *Archaic syntax in Indo-European: The spread of transitivity in Latin and French*. Berlin: Mouton de Gruyter.
Beekes, R.S. & L. van Beek. 2010. *Etymological dictionary of Greek*. Leiden: Brill.
Bentein, K. 2012a. Verbal periphrasis in Ancient Greek. A state of the art. *Revue Belge de Philologie et d'Histoire* 90, 5–56.
Bentein, K. 2012b. The periphrastic perfect in Ancient Greek. A diachronic mental space analysis. *Transactions of the Philological Society* 110, 171–211.
Bentein, K. 2013a. Register and the diachrony of Post-classical and Byzantine Greek. *Revue Belge de Philologie et d'Histoire* 91, 5–44.
Bentein, K. 2013b. The syntax of the periphrastic progressive in the Septuagint and the New Testament. *Novum Testamentum* 55, 168–92.
Bentein, K. 2013c. Adjectival periphrasis in Ancient Greek: The categorial status of the participle. *Acta Classica* 56, 1–28.
Bentein, K. 2014a. Tense and aspect from Hellenistic to Early Byzantine. In: G. Giannakis, V. Bubenik, E. Crespo, C. Golston, A. Lianeri, S. Luraghi & S. Matthaios (eds.), *Encyclopedia of Ancient Greek Language and Linguistics*, volume 3, 379–82. Brill: Leiden.
Bentein, K. 2014b. Perfect. In: G. Giannakis, V. Bubenik, E. Crespo, C. Golston, A. Lianeri, S. Luraghi & S. Matthaios (eds.), *Encyclopedia of Ancient Greek Language and Linguistics*, volume 3, 46–9. Brill: Leiden.
Bentein, K. 2015a. Aspectual choice with *verba dicendi* in Herodotus' *Histories*. *Emerita* 83, 221–45.
Bentein, K. 2015b. The Greek documentary papyri as a linguistically heterogeneous corpus: The case of the *katochoi* of the Sarapeion-archive. *Classical World* 108, 721–53.
Bentein, K. 2016. Aspectual choice and the presentation of narrative. An application to Herodotus' *Histories*. *Glotta* 92, 24–55.
Benveniste, E. 1960. 'être' et 'avoir' dans leurs fonctions linguistiques. *Bulletin de la Société Linguistique de Paris* 55, 113–34.
Benveniste, E. 1962. *Hittite et indo-européen; études comparatives*. Paris: A. Maisonneuve.
Bergs, A. & G. Diewald. 2008. *Constructions and language change*. Berlin: Mouton de Gruyter.

Bertinetto, P.M. 1990. Perifrasi verbali italiane, criteri di identificazione e gerarchie di perifrasticità. In: G. Bernini & A. Giacalone Ramat (eds.), *La temporalità nell'acquisizione di lingue seconde*, 331–50. Milano: Franco Angeli.
Bertinetto, P.M. 1995. Vers une typologie du progressif dans les langues d'Europe. *Modèles Linguistiques* 16, 37–61.
Bertinetto, P.M. 1997. *Il dominio tempo-aspettuale: Demarcazioni, intersezioni, contrasti*. Torino: Rosenberg & Sellier.
Bertinetto, P.M. 2000. The progressive in Romance, as compared with English. In: Ö. Dahl (ed.), *Tense and aspect in the languages of Europe*, 559–604. Berlin & New York: de Gruyter.
Bertinetto, P.M. 2010. Non-conventional uses of the Pluperfect in the Italian (and German) literary prose. *Quaderni del Laboratorio di Linguistica* 9. Downloaded at <http://linguistica.sns.it/%20QLL/QLL10/Bertinetto.pdf> (last accessed September 7, 2012).
Bertinetto, P.M., K.H. Ebert & C. de Groot. 2000. The progressive in Europe. In: Ö. Dahl (ed.), *Tense and aspect in the languages of Europe*, 517–58. Berlin & New York: de Gruyter.
Biber, D. & S. Conrad. 2009. *Register, genre, and style*. Cambridge: Cambridge University Press.
Binnick, R.I. 1991. *Time and the verb: A guide to tense and aspect*. Oxford: Oxford University Press.
Björck, G. 1940. *Ἤν διδάσκων. Die periphrastischen Konstruktionen im Griechischen*. Uppsala: Almqvist & Wiksell (diss. Uppsala).
Blass, F. & A. Debrunner. 1979[15]. *Grammatik des neutestamentlichen Griechisch. Bearbeitet von Friedrich Rehkopf*. Göttingen: Vandenhoeck & Ruprecht.
Bohnemeyer, J. & M. Swift. 2004. Event realization and default aspect. *Linguistics and Philosophy* 27, 263–96.
Bonfante, G. 1960. Les rapports linguistiques entre la Grèce et l'Italie. In: *Hommages à Léon Herrmann*, 171–83. Bruxelles: Latomus.
Bonnet, M. 1898. *Passio Andreae / Ex actis Andreae / Martyria Andreae / Acta Andreae et Matthiae / Acta Petri Andreae / Passio Bartholomaei / Acta Joannis / Martyrium Matthaei*. Leipzig: Mendelssohn.
Boogaert, R. 2004. Aspect and Aktionsart. In: G. Booij, C. Lehmann & J. Mugdan (eds.), *Morphology: An international handbook on inflection and word-formation*, vol. 2, 1165–80. Berlin & New York: Mouton de Gruyter.
Borer, H. 1990. V + ing: It walks like an adjective, it talks like an adjective. *Linguistic Inquiry* 21, 95–103.
Boyer, J.L. 1984. The classification of participles: A statistical study. *Grace Theological Journal* 5, 163–79.

Bowie, E.L. 1985. The Greek novel. In: P.E. Easterling & B.M.W. Knox (eds.), *The Cambridge history of classical literature, vol. 1: Greek literature*, 683-99. Cambridge: Cambridge University Press.

Brandwood, L. 1990. *The chronology of Plato's dialogues*. Cambridge: Cambridge University Press.

Brinton, L.J. 1988. *The development of English aspectual systems: Aspectualizers and post-verbal particles*. Cambridge: Cambridge University Press.

Browning, R. 1978. The language of Byzantine literature. In: S. Vryonis (ed.), *The 'past' in medieval and modern Greek culture*, 103-33. Malibu, CA: Undena.

Browning, R. 1983². *Medieval and modern Greek*. Cambridge: Cambridge University Press.

Bruno, C. 2012. On a Latin-Greek diachronic convergence: The perfects with Latin habeo/Greek échō and a participle. In: C. Chamoreau & I. Léglise (eds.), *Dynamics of contact-induced language change*, 359-76. Berlin: Mouton de Gruyter.

Bruno, C. 2014. Ἔχω-perfects in Greek: A diachronic view. In: A. Bartolotta (ed.), *The Greek verb. Morphology, syntax and semantics*, 43-52. Louvain-la-Neuve: Peeters.

Bubenik, V. 1997. From Ancient to Modern Greek. In: J. Hewson & V. Bubenik, *Tense and aspect in Indo-European languages: Theory, typology, diachrony*, 24-45. Amsterdam & Philadelphia: John Benjamins.

Bubenik, V. 2010. Hellenistic Koine in contact with Latin and Semitic languages during the Roman period. *Studies in Greek Linguistics* 30, 32-54.

Bybee, J.L. 1985. *Morphology: A study of the relation between meaning and form*. Amsterdam: John Benjamins.

Bybee, J.L. 2003a. Cognitive processes in grammaticalization. In: M. Tomasello (ed.), *The new psychology of language: Cognitive and functional approaches to language structure*, vol. 2, 145-67. Mahwah, NJ: Erlbaum.

Bybee, J.L. 2003b. Mechanisms of change in grammaticalization: The role of frequency. In: B.D. Joseph & R.D. Janda (eds.), *The handbook of historical linguistics*, 602-23. Malden, MA: Blackwell.

Bybee, J.L. 2006. From usage to grammar: The mind's response to repetition. *Language* 82, 711-33.

Bybee, J.L. 2007. Diachronic linguistics. In: D. Geeraerts & H. Cuyckens (eds.), *The Oxford handbook of Cognitive Linguistics*, 945-87. Oxford: Oxford University Press.

Bybee, J.L. 2009a. Language universals and usage-based theory. In: M. Christiansen, C. Collins & S. Edelman (eds.), *Language universals*, 17-39. Oxford: Oxford University Press.

Bybee, J.L. 2009b. Grammaticization: Implications for a theory of language. In: J. Guo, E. Lieven, S. Ervin-Tripp, N. Budwig, S. Ozcaliskan & K. Nakamura (eds.), *Crosslinguistic approaches to the psychology of language: Research in the tradition of Dan Isaac Slobin*, 345–55. New York: Taylor & Francis Group, LLC.
Bybee, J.L. 2010. *Language, usage and cognition*. Cambridge: Cambridge University Press.
Bybee, J.L. & Ö. Dahl. 1989. The creation of tense and aspect systems in the languages of the world. *Studies in Language* 13, 51–103.
Bybee, J.L., W. Pagliuca & R.D. Perkins. 1991. Back to the future. In: E. C. Traugott & B. Heine (eds.), *Approaches to grammaticalization*, vol. 2, 17–58. Amsterdam & Philadelphia: John Benjamins.
Bybee, J.L., R.D. Perkins & W. Pagliuca. 1994. *The evolution of grammar: Tense, aspect, and modality in the languages of the world*. Chicago, IL: University of Chicago Press.
Caenepeel, M. 1995. Aspect and text structure. *Linguistics* 33, 213–53.
Campbell, L. 1894. On Plato's use of language. In: B. Jowett & L. Campbell, *Plato's Republic: The Greek text. II: Essays*, 165–340. Oxford: Clarendon Press.
Campbell, L. 2001. What's wrong with grammaticalization? *Language Sciences* 23, 113–61.
Campbell, L. & R. Janda. 2001. Introduction: Conceptions of grammaticalization and their problems. *Language Sciences* 23, 93–112.
Campbell, C. 2008. *Verbal aspect and non-indicative verbs*. New York: Lang.
Caragounis, C. 2004. *The development of Greek and the New Testament: Morphology, syntax, phonology, and textual transmission*. Tübingen: Mohr Siebeck.
Carey, K. 1994. *Pragmatics, subjectivity and the grammaticalization of the English perfect*. PhD dissertation, University of California, San Diego.
Carey, K. 1995. Subjectification and the development of the English Perfect. In: D. Stein & S. Wright (eds.), *Subjectivity and subjectivisation*, 83–102. Cambridge: Cambridge University Press.
Carey, K. 1996. From resultativity to current relevance. In: A.E. Goldberg (ed.), *Conceptual structure, discourse and language*, 31–48. Stanford: CSLI Publications.
Castelnovo, W. 1993. Progressive and actionality in Italian. *Rivista di Linguistica* 5, 3–29.
Ceglia, L. 1998. L'evoluzione della costruzione perifrastica verbale nel greco del Nuovo Testamento. *Archivio Glottologico Italiano* 83, 20–44.
Chanet, A-M. 1986. Sur l'aspect verbal. *Cratyle* 5, 1–51.
Chantraine, P. 1927. *L'histoire du parfait grec*. Paris: Champion.
Chantraine, P. 1942. *Grammaire Homérique*, vol. 1. Paris: Klincksieck.

Christidis, A.-F. 2007. General introduction: Histories of the Greek language. In: A.-F. Christidis (ed.), *A history of Ancient Greek: From the beginnings to Late Antiquity*, 1-23. Cambridge: Cambridge University Press.
Clark, E.V. 1978. Locationals: Existential, locative, and possessive constructions. In: J.H. Greenberg, C.A. Ferguson & E.A. Moravcsik (eds.), *Universals of Human Language, vol. 4: Syntax*, 85-126. Stanford: Stanford University Press.
Clarke, M. 2010. Semantics and vocabulary. In: E.J. Bakker (ed.), *A companion to the Ancient Greek language*, 120-33. Oxford: Wiley-Blackwell.
Cloud, F.L. 1910. *Use of the perfect tense in the attic orators*. Norristown, PA: Press of the Herald publishing co.
Cobb, R.A. 1973. The present progressive periphrasis and the metaphysics of Aristotle. *Phronesis* 18, 80-90.
Cohén, D. 1984. *La phrase nominale et l'évolution du système verbal en sémitique: Études de syntaxe historique*. Leuven: Peeters.
Cohén, D. 1989. *L'aspect verbal*. Paris: Presses Universitaires de France.
Coleman, R. 1975. Greek influence on Latin syntax. *Transactions of the Philological Society* 74, 101-56.
Comrie, B. 1976. *Aspect: An introduction to the study of verbal aspect and related problems*. Cambridge: Cambridge University Press.
Conti, L. 2014. Transitivity. In: G. Giannakis, V. Bubenik, E. Crespo, C. Golston, A. Lianeri, S. Luraghi & S. Matthaios (eds.), *Encyclopedia of Ancient Greek Language and Linguistics*, volume 3, 423-7. Brill: Leiden.
Conybeare, F.C. & S.G. Stock. 1995 [1905]. *Grammar of Septuagint Greek*. Boston, MA: Hendrickson Publishers.
Cook, J.A. 2012. Detecting development in Biblical Hebrew using diachronic typology. In: C. Miller-Naudé & Z. Zevit (eds.), *Diachrony in Biblical Hebrew*, 83-95. Winona Lake: Eisenbrauns.
Cooreman, A., B. Fox & T. Givón. 1983. The discourse definition of ergativity. *Studies in Language* 8, 1-34.
Coseriu, E. 1971. Das Problem des griechischen Einflusses auf das Vulgärlatein. In: G. Narr (ed.), *Griechisch und Romanisch*, 1-15. Tübingen: Fotodruck Präzis.
Coseriu, E. 1975. Der periphrastische Verbalaspekt im Altgriechischen. *Glotta* 53, 1-25.
Coseriu, E. 1977. El aspecto verbal perifrástico en griego y sus reflejos románicos. In: *Estudios de Lingüística románica*, 231-63. Madrid: Credos.
Crespo, E., L. Conti & H. Maqueira. 2003. *Sintaxis del griego clásico*. Madrid: Gredos.
Croft, W. 1991. *Syntactic categories and grammatical relations*. Chicago, IL: University of Chicago Press.
Croft, W. 2000. *Explaining language change. An evolutionary approach*. Harlow: Longman.

Croft, W. 2001. *Radical construction grammar: Syntactic theory in typological perspective*. Oxford: Oxford University Press.
Croft, W. 2012. *Verbs: Aspect and causal structure*. Oxford: Oxford University Press.
Croft, W. & D.A. Cruse. 2004. *Cognitive Linguistics*. Cambridge: Cambridge University Press.
Croke, B. 2010. Uncovering Byzantium's historiographical audience. In: R. Macrides (ed.), *History as literature in Byzantium*, 42–50. Aldershot: Ashgate.
Crudden, M. 2001. *The Homeric hymns*. Oxford: Oxford University Press.
Crystal, D. 1991. *A dictionary of linguistics and phonetics*. Oxford: Basil Blackwell.
Dahl, Ö. & E. Hedin. 2000. Current relevance and event reference. In: Ö. Dahl (ed.), *Tense and aspect in the languages of Europe*, 385–402. Berlin: de Gruyter.
Dawe, R.D. 2006. *Oedipus Rex*. Cambridge: Cambridge University Press.
Dawsey, J.M. 1986. *The Lukan voice: Confusion and irony in the Gospel of Luke*. Macon: Mercer University Press.
De Boel, G. 1987. Aspekt, Aktionsart und Transitivitat. *Indogermanische Forschungen* 92, 33–57.
De Boel, G. 1988. *Goal accusative and object accusative in Homer: A contribution to the theory of transitivity*. Brussel: Koninklijke akademie voor wetenschappen, letteren en schone kunsten van Belgie.
De Boel, G. 1991. Aspect en lexicale betekenis van het Griekse werkwoord. *Kleio*, 383–99.
De Boel, G. 2004. Van dingen die overgaan... De Griekse herkomst en gebruik van de term en het concept 'transitiviteit'. In: *Taeldeman, man van de taal, schatbewaarder van de taal: Liber amicorum Johan Taeldeman*, 249–56. Ghent: Academia Press.
Declerck, R. 1986. The manifold interpretations of generic sentences. *Lingua* 68, 149–88.
Declerck, R. 1997. *When-clauses and temporal structure*. London: Routledge.
Delancey, S. 1987. Transitivity in grammar and cognition. In: R. Tomlin (ed.), *Coherence and grounding in discourse*, 53–68. Amsterdam: John Benjamins.
Desclés, J.P. 1998. Transitivité sémantique, transitivité syntaxique. In: A. Rousseau (ed.), *La transitivité*, 162–80.Villeneuve-d'Ascq: Presses universitaires du Septentrion.
Dickey, E. 2003. Latin influence on the Greek of documentary papyri: An analysis of its chronological distribution. *Zeitschrift für Papyrologie und Epigraphik* 145, 249–57.
Dickey, E. 2009. The Greek and Latin languages in the papyri. In: R.S. Bagnall (ed.), *Oxford handbook of papyrology*, 149–69. New York: Oxford University Press.

Dieterich, K. 1898. *Untersuchungen zur Geschichte der griechischen Sprache: Von der hellenistischen Zeit bis zum 10. Jahrhundert n. Chr.* Leipzig: Teubner.

Dietrich, W. 1973a. *Der periphrastische Verbalaspekt in den romanischen Sprachen.* Tübingen: Niemeyer. Translated into Spanish (1983): *El aspecto verbal perifrástico en las lenguas románicas.* Madrid: Gredos.

Dietrich, W. 1973b. Der Periphrastische Verbalaspekt im Griechischen und Lateinischen. *Glotta* 51, 188–228.

Dixon, R.M. 1977. Where have all the adjectives gone? *Studies in Language* 1, 19–80.

Doiz-Bienzobas, A. 2002. The preterite and the imperfect as grounding predications. In: F. Brisard (ed.), *Grounding: The epistemic footing of deixis and reference*, 299–347. Berlin: de Gruyter.

Dover, K.J. 1968. Review: W.J. Aerts, Periphrastica. *Gnomon* 40, 87–8.

Dover, K.J. 1987. The colloquial stratum in Classical Attic prose. In: K. J. Dover (ed.), *Greek and the Greeks, collected papers*, vol. 1, 16–30. Oxford: Basil Blackwell.

Dover, K.J. 2003. Hiatus. In: S. Hornblower & A. Spawforth (eds.), *The Oxford Classical Dictionary*, third edition, 703–4. Oxford: Oxford University Press.

Drinka, B. 2003a. The formation of periphrastic perfects and passives in Europe: An areal approach. In: B. Blake & K. Burridge (eds.), *Historical Linguistics 2001*, 105–28. Amsterdam & Philadelphia: John Benjamins.

Drinka, B. 2003b. Areal factors in the development of the European periphrastic perfect. *Word* 54, 1–38.

Drinka, B. 2007. The development of the HAVE perfect: Mutual influences of Greek and Latin. In: R. Aranovich (ed.), *Split auxiliary systems: A cross-linguistic perspective*, 101–21. Amsterdam: John Benjamins.

Drinka, B. 2009. The *-to-/-no- construction of Indo-European: Verbal adjective or past passive participle? In: V. Bubenik, J. Hewson & S. Rose (eds.), *Grammatical change in Indo-European languages*, 141–58. Amsterdam: John Benjamins.

Drinka, B. 2011. The sacral stamp of Greek: Periphrastic constructions in New Testament translations of Latin, Gothic and Old Church Slavonic. In: E. Welo (ed.), *Indo-European syntax and pragmatics: Contrastive approaches, Oslo Studies in Language* 3, 41–73.

Dubuisson, M. 1985. *Le latin de Polybe: Les implications historiques d'un cas de bilinguisme.* Paris: Klincksieck.

Dubuisson, M. 1989. Le contact linguistique gréco-latin. Problemes d'interférences et d'emprunts. *Lalies* 10, 91–109.

Duhoux, Y. 1996. La fréquence décroissante du médio-passif au parfait depuis le Ve s. avant. J.-C.: Une caractéristique de l'attique et de la koiné? *Historische Sprachforschung / Historical Linguistics* 109, 53–72.

Duhoux, Y. 2000². *Le verbe grec ancien. Éléments de morphologie et de syntaxe historiques*. Louvain-la-Neuve: Peeters.
Edwards, M. 1991. *The Iliad: A commentary. Volume V: Books 17–20*. Cambridge: Cambridge University Press.
Edwards, M. 1994. *The Attic orators*. London: Bristol Classical Press.
England, E.B. 1883. *The Iphigeneia among the Tauri of Euripides*. London: MacMillan & Co.
Efthymiadis, S. 2011. Hagiography from the 'Dark Age' to the age of Symeon Metaphrastes (eighth–tenth centuries). In: S. Efthymiadis (ed.), *The Ashgate research companion to Byzantine hagiography, volume 1: Periods and places*, 95–142. Farnham & Burlington, VT: Ashgate.
Eijk, P.J. van der. 1997. Towards a rhetoric of ancient scientific discourse. In: E.J. Bakker (ed.), *Grammar as interpretation. Greek literature in its linguistic contexts*, 77–129. Brill: Leiden.
Evans, T.V. 2001. *Verbal syntax in the Greek Pentateuch: Natural Greek usage and Hebrew interference*. Oxford: Oxford University Press.
Evans, T.V. & D.D. Obbink. 2010. Introduction. In: T.V. Evans & D.D. Obbink (eds.), *The language of the papyri*, 1–12. Oxford: Oxford University Press.
Evans, V. & M. Green. 2006. *Cognitive Linguistics: An introduction*. Edinburgh: Edinburgh University Press.
Fanning, B. 1990. *Verbal aspect in New Testament Greek*. Oxford: Clarendon Press.
Farrar, F.W. 1867. *A brief Greek syntax and hints on Greek accidence*. London: Longmans.
Faulkner, A. 2008. *The Homeric hymn to Aphrodite*. Oxford & New York: Oxford University Press.
Fernández Marcos, N. 2000. *The Septuagint in context: Introduction to the Greek versions of the bible*. Leiden: Brill.
Feuillatre, E. 1966. *Études sur les Éthiopiques d'Héliodore*. Paris: Presses Universitaires de France.
Fischer, O. 2007. *Morphosyntactic change: Functional and formal perspectives*. Oxford: Oxford University Press.
Fischer, O. 2008. On analogy as the motivation for grammaticalization. *Studies in Language* 32, 336–82.
Fischer, O. & A. Rosenbach 2000. Introduction. In: O. Fischer, A. Rosenbach & D. Stein (eds.), *Pathways of change: Grammaticalization in English*, 1–37. Amsterdam: John Benjamins.
Flagg, I. 1889. *Euripides: Iphigenia among the Taurians*. Boston, MA & London: Ginn & Company.
Fleischman, S. 1989. Temporal distance: A basic linguistic metaphor. *Studies in Language* 13, 1–51.
Fleischman, S. 1990. *Tense and narrativity: From medieval performance to modern fiction*. Austin: University of Texas Press.

Fleischman, S. 2000. Methodologies and ideologies in historical linguistics: On working with older languages. In: S.C. Herring, P. van Reenen & L. Schøsler (eds.), *Textual parameters in older languages*, 33–58. Amsterdam: John Benjamins.

Foucault, de M.J. 1961. La forme progressive existe-t-elle en grec classique? *Revue des Études Grecques* 74, 12–13.

Fox, B. 1983. The discourse function of the participle in Ancient Greek. In: F. Klein-Andreu (ed.), *Discourse perspectives on syntax*, 23–41. New York: Academic Press.

Friedrich, P. 1974. On aspect theory and Homeric aspect. *International Journal of American Linguistics* 40, 1–44.

Galton, A. 1997. Verb aspect and prototype theory. In: *Proceedings of the European Conference on Cognitive science (ECCS '95)*, 121–8. Downloaded at <http://citeseerx.ist.psu.edu/viewdoc/download?doi=10.1.1.48.329&rep=rep1&type=pdf> (last accessed April 4, 2014).

García Hernández, B. 1980. El desarrollo de la expresión analítica en latín vulgar. Planteamiento general. *Revista Española de Lingüística* 10, 307–30.

Gautier, L. 1911. *La langue de Xénophon*. Genève: Georg.

Geeraerts, D. 2006 [1989]. Prospects and problems of prototype theory. In: D. Geeraerts (ed.), *Cognitive linguistics: Basic readings*, 141–66. Berlin: Mouton de Gruyter.

Gelderen, E. van. 2013. The linguistic cycle and the language faculty. *Language and Linguistics Compass* 7, 233–50.

George, C.H. 2005. *Expressions of agency in Ancient Greek*. Cambridge: Cambridge University Press.

Gerö, E.-C. & A. von Stechow. 2003. Tense in time: The Greek perfect. In: R. Eckardt, K. von Heusinger & C. Schwarze (eds.), *Words in time: Diachronic semantics from different points of view*, 251–94. Berlin: de Gruyter.

Gerö, E.-C. & H. Ruge. 2008. Continuity and change: The history of two Greek tenses. In: F. Josephson & I. Söhrman (eds.), *Interdependence of diachronic and synchronic analyses*, 105–29. Amsterdam: John Benjamins.

Ghedini, G. 1923. *Lettere Cristiane: Dai papiri greci del III e IV secolo*. Milano: Aegyptus.

Ghedini, G. 1937. La lingua dei vangeli apocrifi greci. In: *Studi dedicati alla memoria di Paolo Ubaldi*, 443–80. Milano: Vita e pensiero.

Giannaris, A. 2011a. Pluperfect periphrases in Medieval Greek: A perspective on the collaboration between linguistics and philology. *Transactions of the Philological Society* 109, 232–45.

Giannaris, A. 2011b. Οι περιφράσεις 'εἰμί/εἴμαι + μετοχή' στην Ελληνική. Διαχρονική προσέγγιση. PhD thesis, University of Athens.

Giannaris, A. 2011c. The diachrony of 'BE + present participle' in Greek and Old English: Multiple paths in language change. In: E. Kitis, N. Lavidas,

N. Topintzi & T. Tsangalidis (eds.) *Selected papers from the 19th international symposium on theoretical and applied linguistics* (19th ISTAL, April 2009), 205-12. Thessaloniki: Monochromia.
Gignac, F.T. 1985. The papyri and the Greek language. *Yale Classical Studies* 28, 155-65.
Gildersleeve, B.L. 1980 [1900-11]. *Syntax of classical Greek*. Groningen: Bouma.
Givón, T. 1979. *On understanding grammar*. New York, NY: Academic Press.
Givón, T. 1984. *Syntax*, vol. 1. Amsterdam: John Benjamins.
Givón, T. 1989. *Mind, code and context: Essays in pragmatics*. Hillsdale, NJ: Erlbaum.
Givón, T. 1995. Coherence in text vs. coherence in mind. In: M. A. Gernsbacher & T. Givón (eds.), *Coherence in spontaneous text*, 59-115. Amsterdam: John Benjamins.
Givón, T. 2001. *Syntax: An introduction*, 2 vols. Amsterdam: John Benjamins.
Goldberg, A.E. 2003. Constructions: A new theoretical approach to language. *Trends in Cognitive Sciences* 7, 219-24.
Gonda, J. 1959. A remark on 'periphrastic' constructions in Greek. *Mnemosyne* 12, 97-112.
Greenberg, J.H. 1960 [1954]. A quantitative approach to the morphological typology of language. *International Journal of American Linguistics* 26, 178-94.
Habermann, W. 1998. Zur chronologischen Verteilung der papyrologischen Zeugnisse. *Zeitschrift für Papyrologie und Epigraphik* 122, 144-60.
Hackstein, O. 2010. The Greek of epic. In: E.J. Bakker (ed.), *The Blackwell companion to the ancient Greek language*, 401-23. Oxford: Blackwell.
Hagège, C. 1993. *The language builder*. Amsterdam: John Benjamins.
Haiman, J. 1994. Ritualization and the development of language. In: W. Pagliuca (ed.), *Perspectives on grammaticalization*, 3-28. Amsterdam: John Benjamins.
Halliday, M.A.K. 1978. *Language as social semiotic: The social interpretation of language and meaning*. London: Arnold.
Hamann, C. 1991. Adjectival semantics. In A. von Stechow & D. Wunderlich (eds.), *Semantics: An international handbook of contemporary research*, 657-73. Berlin: de Gruyter.
Harris, A.C. & L. Campbell. 1995. *Historical syntax in cross-linguistic perspective*. Cambridge: Cambridge University Press.
Harris, M.B. 1982. The 'past simple' and the 'present perfect' in Romance. In: N. Vincent & M.B. Harris (eds.), *Studies in the Romance verb*, 42-70. London: Croom Helm.
Harry, J.E. 1905. The perfect subjunctive, optative and imperative in Greek. *The Classical Review* 19, 347-54.

Harry, J.E. 1906. The perfect forms in later Greek from Aristotle to Justinian. *Transactions and Proceedings of the American Philological Association* 37, 53–72.
Hartmann, F. 1934. Zur Frage der Aspektbedeutung beim griechischen Futurum. *Zeitschrift für vergleichende Sprachforschung auf dem Gebiete der indogermanische Sprachen* 62, 116–31.
Hartman, L. 1963. *Participial constructions in the synoptic gospels.* Lund: Gleerup.
Haspelmath, M. 1992. From resultative to perfect in Ancient Greek. In: J.L. Iturrioz Leza (ed.), *Nuevos estudios sobre construcciones resultativos* (= Función 11–12), 187–224. Universidad de Guadalajara: Centro de Investigación de Lenguas Indígenas.
Haspelmath, M. 1999. Why grammaticalization is irreversible. *Linguistics* 37, 1043–68.
Haspelmath, M. 2000. Periphrasis. In: G. Booij, C. Lehmann & J. Mugdan (eds.), *Morphology. An international handbook on inflection and word formation,* vol. 1, 654–64. Berlin: de Gruyter.
Haspelmath, M. 2003. The geometry of grammatical meaning. In: M. Tomasello (ed.), *The new psychology of language,* vol. 2, 211–43. New York: Lawrence Erlbaum Associates Publishers.
Haspelmath, M. & T. Müller-Bardey. 2004. Valency change. In: G. Booij (ed.), *Morphology: A handbook on inflection and word formation,* vol. 2, 1130–45. Berlin: de Gruyter.
Haug, D. 2008. From resultatives to anteriors in Ancient Greek: On the role of paradigmaticity in semantic change. In: T. Eythórsson (ed.), *Grammatical change and linguistic theory,* 285–305. Amsterdam: John Benjamins.
Hauspie, K. 2011. Periphrastic tense forms with *eimi* and *gignomai* in the Septuagint of Ezekiel. In: E. Bons & T.J. Kraus (eds.), *Et sapienter et eloquenter: Studies on rhetorical and stylistic features of the Septuagint,* 127–52. Göttingen: Vandenhoeck & Ruprecht.
Haverling, G. 2009. Actionality, tense, and viewpoint. In: P. Cuzzolin & P. Baldi (eds.), *New perspectives on historical Latin syntax, vol. 2: Constituent syntax: adverbial phrases, adverbs, mood, tense,* 277–523. Berlin & New York: de Gruyter.
Heine, R. 1972. Vermutungen zum lateinischen Partizip. *Gymnasium* 79, 209–38.
Heine, B. 1993. *Auxiliaries: Cognitive forces and grammaticalization.* New York: Oxford University Press.
Heine, B. 1997. *Possession: Cognitive sources, forces, and grammaticalization.* Cambridge: Cambridge University Press.
Heine, B. 2002. On the role of context in grammaticalization. In: I. Wischer & G. Diewald (eds.), *New reflections on grammaticalization,* 83–101. Amsterdam: John Benjamins.

Heine, B. 2003. Grammaticalization. In R. Janda & B. Joseph (eds.) *The handbook of historical linguistics*, 575–601. Oxford: Blackwell.
Heine, B., U. Claudi & F. Hünnemeyer. 1991. *Grammaticalization: A conceptual framework*. Chicago, IL: University of Chicago Press.
Heine, B. & T. Kuteva. 2005. *Language contact and grammatical change*. Cambridge: Cambridge University Press.
Helbing, R. 1907. *Grammatik der Septuaginta, Laut- und Wortlehre*. Göttingen: Vandenhoeck & Ruprecht.
Hesseling, D.C. 1928. *Het perfectum in het postklassieke Grieks: Overblijfsels in de taal van heden*. Amsterdam: Koninklijke akademie van wetenschappen.
Hettrich, H. 1976. *Kontext und Aspekt in der altgriechischen Prosa Herodots*. Göttingen: Vandenhoeck & Ruprecht.
Hewson, J. 1997. Tense and aspect: Description and theory. In: J. Hewson & V. Bubenik, *Tense and aspect in Indo-European languages: Theory, typology, diachrony*, 1–23. Amsterdam & Philadelphia: John Benjamins.
Hilhorst, A. 1976. *Sémitismes et latinismes dans le Pasteur d'Hermas*. Nijmegen: Dekker en van de Vegt.
Hodge, C.T. 1970. The linguistic cycle. *Language Sciences* 13, 1–7.
Hoffner, H.A. & H.C. Melchert. 2008. *A grammar of the Hittite language*. Winona Lake, IN: Eisenbrauns.
Høgel, C. 2002. *Symeon Metaphrastes: Rewriting and canonisation*. Copenhagen: Museum Tusculanum Press.
Hopper, P.J. & S.A. Thompson. 1980. Transitivity in grammar and discourse. *Language* 56, 251–99.
Hopper, P.J. & S.A. Thompson. 1984. The discourse basis for lexical categories in universal grammar. *Language* 60, 703–52.
Hopper, P.J. & E.C. Traugott. 2003². *Grammaticalization*. Cambridge: Cambridge University Press.
Horrocks, G.C. 1997. *Greek: A history of the language and its speakers*. London: Longmann.
Horrocks, G.C. 2007. Syntax: From Classical Greek to the Koine. In: A.P. Christidis (ed.), *A history of Ancient Greek*, 618–31. Cambridge: Cambridge University Press.
Horrocks, G.C. 2010². *Greek: A history of the language and its speakers*. Oxford & Malden, MA: Wiley-Blackwell.
Horsley, G.H.R. 1994. Papyrology and the Greek Language. A fragmentary ABECEDARIUS of desiderata for future study. In: A. Bülow-Jacobsen (ed.), *Proceedings of the 20th international congress of papyrologists*, 48–70. Copenhagen: Museum Tusculanum.
Hudson, G. 2000. *Essential introductory linguistics*. Malden, MA: Blackwell Publishers.
Humbert, J. 1972³. *Syntaxe grecque*. Paris: Éditions Klincksieck.

Humboldt, W. 1979 [1827-9]. Über die Verschiedenheit des menschlichen Sprachbaues und ihren Einfluss auf die geistige Entwickelung des Menschengeschlechts. In: A. Flitner & K. Giel (eds.), *Werke in fünf Bänden / Wilhelm von Humboldt*, vol. 3. Stuttgart: Cotta.

Hunter, R.L. 1983. *A study of Daphnis & Chloe*. Cambridge: Cambridge University Press.

Hutton, W. 2005. *Describing Greece: Landscape and literature in the Periegesis of Pausanias*. Cambridge: Cambridge University Press.

Isebaert, L. 1991. L'aspect en grec à la lumière des recherches recentes: Le cas du parfait. In: M. Biraud (ed.), *Études de syntaxe du grecque classique: Recherches linguistiques et applications didactiques*, 99-112. Paris: Publications de la Faculté des Lettres et Sciences Humaines de Nice.

Jäger, A. 2006. *Typology of periphrastic 'do' constructions*. Bochum: Brockmeyer.

James, P. 2008. *Complementary participles and infinitives with verbs of perception and declaration in the Roman and Byzantine documentary papyri*. PhD dissertation, Cambridge University.

James, P. 2014. Papyri, language of. In: G. Giannakis, V. Bubenik, E. Crespo, C. Golston, A. Lianeri, S. Luraghi & S. Matthaios (eds.), *Encyclopedia of Ancient Greek Language and Linguistics*, vol. 3, 11-14. Brill: Leiden.

Janda, R. 2001. Beyond 'pathways' and 'unidirectionality': On the discontinuity of language transmission and the counterability of grammaticalization. *Language Sciences* 23, 265-340.

Jannaris, A. 1897. *An historical Greek grammar chiefly of the Attic dialect*. Hildesheim: Olms.

Jiménez, L.C. 1999. Zur Bedeutung von *tunchano* und *hamartano* bei Homer. *Glotta* 75, 50-62.

Johannessohn, M. 1942. Das biblische καὶ ἰδού in der Erzählung samt seiner hebräischen Vorlage. *Zeitschrift für vergleichende Sprachforschung auf dem Gebiet der indogermanischen Sprachen* 67, 30-84.

Jones, M.A. 1996. *Foundations of French syntax*. Cambridge: Cambridge University Press.

Joseph, B.D. 1987. Greek. In: B. Comrie (ed.), *The world's major languages*, 410-39. London: Croom Helm.

Joseph, B.D. 2001. Is there such a thing as 'grammaticalization'? *Language Sciences* 23, 163-86.

Joseph, B.D. 2004. Rescuing traditional historical linguistics from grammaticalization theory. In: O. Fischer, M. Norde & H. Perridon (eds.), *Up and down the cline—The nature of grammaticalization*, 45-71. Amsterdam: John Benjamins.

Joseph, B.D. 2009. Review article. Theodore Markopoulos: The future in Modern Greek: From Ancient to Medieval. *Journal of Greek Linguistics* 9, 195-214.

Jouanna, J. 1992. *Hippocrate*. Paris: Fayard.
Joüon, P. & T. Muraoka. 1991. *A grammar of Biblical Hebrew*. Roma: Pontificio Istituto Biblico.
Kahn, C.H. 1973. *The verb Be and its synonyms: Philosophical and grammatical studies. 6: The verb Be in Ancient Greek*. Dordrecht: Reidel.
Kamerbeek, J.C. 1967. *The plays of Sophocles, commentaries. Part 4: The Oedipus tyrannus*. Leiden: Brill.
Kapsomenakis, S.G. 1938. *Voruntersuchungen zu einer Grammatik der Papyri der nachchristlichen Zeit: Beiträge zur Herstellung und Deutung einzelner Texte*. München: Beck.
Karleen, P.S. 1980. *The syntax of the participle in the Greek New Testament*. PhD thesis, University of Pennsylvania.
Kavčič, J. 2014. Notes on the transitivity of the aorist and the perfect in Classical Greek. In: A. Bartolotta (ed.), *The Greek verb. Morphology, syntax and semantics*, 183–200. Louvain-la-Neuve: Peeters.
Keil, F. 1963. Untersuchungen zum Perfektgebrauch Herodots. *Glotta* 41, 10–51.
Kemmer, S. & A. Verhagen. 1994. The grammar of causatives and the conceptual structure of events. *Cognitive Linguistics* 5, 115–56.
Killie, K. 2008. From locative to durative to focalized? The English progressive and 'PROG imperfective drift'. In M. Gotti, M. Dossena & R. Dury (eds.), *English historical linguistics 2006*, 69–88. Amsterdam: John Benjamins.
Kimball, S.E. 1991. The origin of the Greek κ-perfect. *Glotta* 69, 141–53.
Kirk, G.S. 1985. *The Iliad: A commentary. Vol. 1: Books 1–4*. Cambridge: Cambridge University Press.
Kirk, G.S. 1985b. The epic tradition after Homer and Hesiod: The Homeric Hymns. In: P.E. Easterling & B.M.W. Knox (eds.), *The Cambridge history of classical literature, vol. 1: Greek literature*, 110–16. Cambridge: Cambridge University Press.
Kittilä, S. 2002a. Remarks on the basic transitive sentence. *Language Sciences* 24, 107–30.
Kittilä, S. 2002b. *Transitivity: Toward a comprehensive typology*. Åbo: Åbo Akademiska Tryckeri.
Kontos, K.S. 1898. Φιλολογικαὶ παρατηρήσεις. *Ἀθηνᾶ* 10, 269–306; 307–24.
Kramer, J. 2004. Das Griechische und das Lateinisch-Romanische auf dem Wege vom synthetischen zum analytischen Sprachtyp? In: U. Hinrichs (ed.), *Die europäischen Sprachen auf dem Weg zum analytischen Sprachtyp*, 127–46. Wiesbaden: Harrossowitz.
Krifka, M., F.J. Pelletier, G.N. Carlson, A. ter Meulen, G. Link & G. Chierchi. 1995. Genericity: An introduction. In: G.N. Carlson & F.J. Pelletier (eds.), *The generic book*, 1–124. Chicago: University of Chicago Press.

Kühner, R. & B. Gerth. 1976 [1898–1904]³. *Ausführliche Grammatik der griechischen Sprache. Zweiter Teil: Satzlehre.* Hannover: Verlag Hahnsche Buchhandlung.

Kühner, R. & F. Blass. 1983 [1892]³. *Ausführliche Grammatik der griechischen Sprache. Erster Teil: Elementar- und Formenlehre.* Hannover: Verlag Hahnsche Buchhandlung.

Kulneff-Eriksson, K. 1999. *On 'have' in Ancient Greek. An investigation on echo and the construction einai with a dative as expressions for 'have'.* Lund: Lund University Press.

Kuteva, T. 1998. Large linguistic areas in grammaticalization: Auxiliation in Europe. *Language Sciences* 20, 289–311.

Labov, W. 1973. The boundaries of words and their meanings. In: C.-J. N. Bailey & R.W. Shuy (eds.), *New ways of analysing variation in English*, 340–73. Washington: Georgetown University Press.

La Roche, J. 1893. *Beiträge zur griechischen Grammatik.* Leipzig: B.G. Teubner.

Lakoff, G. 1977. Linguistic gestalts. *Chicago Linguistic Society* 13, 236–87.

Lakoff, G. 1987. *Women, fire, and dangerous things: What categories reveal about the mind.* Chicago, IL: University of Chicago Press.

Lanérès, N. 1994. *La forme de la phrase nominale en grec ancien: Étude sur la langue de l'Iliade.* Lille: Université Charles-de-Gaulle-Lille III.

Langacker, R.W. 1987. *Foundations of cognitive grammar. Vol. 1: Theoretical prerequisites.* Stanford: Stanford University Press.

Langacker, R.W. 1991. *Foundations of cognitive grammar. Vol. 2: Descriptive application.* Stanford: Stanford University Press.

Langacker, R.W. 1995. Viewing in cognition and grammar. In: P. Davis (ed.), *Alternative Linguistics: Descriptive and theoretical modes*, 153–212. Amsterdam: John Benjamins.

Langacker, R.W. 2005. Integration, grammaticization, and constructional meaning. In M. Fried & H.C. Boas (eds.), *Grammatical constructions: Back to the roots*, 157–90. Amsterdam: John Benjamins.

Lasso de la Vega, J.S. 1955. *La oración nominal en Homero.* Madrid: Instituto Antonio de Nebrija.

Layton, B. 2004. *A Coptic grammar: With chrestomathy and glossary.* Wiesbaden: Harrassowitz.

Lazard, G. 2002. Transitivity revisited as an example of a more strict approach in typological research. *Folia Linguistica* 36, 141–90.

Lee, J.A.L. 1985. Some features of the speech of Jesus in Mark's Gospel. *Novum Testamentum* 27, 1–26.

Lee, J.A.L. 2007. Ἐξαποστέλλω. In: J. Joosten & P.J. Tomson (eds.), *Voces Biblicae: Septuagint Greek and its significance for the New Testament*, 99–113. Leuven: Peeters.

Lee, J.A.L. 2013. The atticist grammarians. In: S.E. Porter & A.W. Pitts (eds.), *The language of the New Testament: Context, history and development*, 283–308. Leiden: Brill.
Lee, K.H. 1997. *Troades / Euripides; edited with introduction and commentary*. London: Bristol Classical Press.
Lehmann, C. 1985. Grammaticalization: Synchronic and diachronic change. *Lingua e Stile* 20, 303–18.
Lehmann, C. 1995 [1982]. *Thoughts on grammaticalization*. München: LINCOM Europa.
Létoublon, F. 1982. Les verbes de mouvement en grec: De la métaphore à l'auxiliarité? *Glotta* 60, 178–96.
Levin, B. 1993. *English verb classes and alternations: A preliminary investigation*. Chicago, IL: University of Chicago Press.
Lewis, N. 1986. *Greeks in Ptolemaic Egypt: Case studies in the social history of the Hellenistic world*. Oxford: Clarendon Press.
Liddell, H.G. & R. Scott. 1968[9]. *A Greek-English lexicon*. Oxford: Clarendon Press.
Lindstedt, J. 2000. The perfect—aspectual, temporal and evidential. In: Ö. Dahl (ed.), *Tense and aspect in the languages of Europe*, 365–83. Berlin & New York: de Gruyter.
Lindstedt, J. 2001. Tense and Aspect. In: M. Haspelmath, E. König, W. Österreicher & W. Raible (eds.), *Language typology and language universals*, vol.1, 768–83. Berlin: de Gruyter.
Ljungvik, H. 1926. *Studien zur Sprache der apokryphen Apostelgeschichten*. Uppsala: Lundequistska bokhandeln.
Lloyd, M. 1999. The tragic aorist. *The Classical Quarterly* 49, 24–25.
Long, A.A. 1985. Aristotle. In: P.E. Easterling & B.M.W. Knox (eds.), *The Cambridge history of classical literature, vol. 1: Greek literature*, 527–40. Cambridge: Cambridge University Press.
Longacre, R.E. 1989. Two hypotheses regarding text generation and analysis. *Discourse processes* 12, 413–60.
Longacre, R.E. 1996[2]. *The grammar of discourse*. New York: Plenum.
López Eire, A. 1986. La lengua de la comedia Aristofanica. *Emerita* 54, 237–74.
Lorimer, W.L. 1926. ΤΥΤΧΑΝΩ for ΤΥΓΧΑΝΩ ΩΝ in Attic Prose. *Classical Quarterly* 20, 195–200.
Luraghi, S. 1993. Il concetto di prototipicità in linguistica. *Lingua e Stile* 28, 511–30.
Luraghi, S. 1995. The pragmatics of verb initial sentences in some ancient Indo-Europen languages. In: P. Downing & M. Noonan (eds.), *Word order in discourse*, 355–86. Amsterdam: John Benjamins.
MacDonald, D.R. 2005. *Acts of Andrew*. Santa Rosa, CA: Polebridge Press.
Magnien, V. 1912. *Le futur grec*, vol. 2. Paris: H. Champion.

Malchukov, A.L. 2006. Transitivity parameters and transitivity alternations: Constraining co-variation. In: L. Kulikov, A. Malchukov & P. de Swart (eds.), *Case, valency and transitivity*, 329–59. Amsterdam: John Benjamins.

Mandilaras, B.G. 1972. *Studies in the Greek language. Some aspects of the development of the Greek language up to the present day*. Athens: N. Xenopoulos Press.

Mandilaras, B.G. 1973. *The verb in the Greek non-literary papyri*. Athens: Hellenic Ministry of Culture and Sciences.

Manolessou, I. 2005. From participles to gerunds. In: M. Stavrou & A. Terzi (eds.), *Advances in Greek generative syntax*, 241–83. Amsterdam: John Benjamins.

Marchello-Nizia, C. 2006. *Grammaticalisation et changement linguistique*. Bruxelles: De Boeck.

Markopoulos, T. 2009. *The future in Greek. From Ancient to Medieval*. Oxford: Oxford University Press.

Maslov, Y.S. 1985. An outline of contrastive aspectology. In: Y.S. Maslov (ed.), *Contrastive studies in verbal aspect: in Russian, English, French and German; translated and annotated by James Forsyth in collaboration with Josephine Forsyth*, 1–44. Heidelberg: J. Groos.

Mateos, J. 1977. *El aspecto verbal en el Nuevo Testamento*. Madrid: Ed. Cristianidad.

Mayser, E. 1926–38. *Grammatik der griechischen Papyri aus der Ptolemäerzeit*. Berlin & Leipzig: de Gruyter.

McKay, K.L. 1965. The use of the Ancient Greek perfect down to the end of the second century AD. *Bulletin of the Institute of Classical Studies* 12, 1–21.

McKay, K.L. 1980. On the perfect and others aspects in the Greek non-literary papyri. *Bulletin of the Institute of Classical Studies* 27, 23–49.

McKay, K.L. 1993. The declining optative: Some observations. *Antichthon* 27, 21–30.

McKay, K.L. 1994. *A new syntax of the verb in New Testament Greek*. New York: Peter Lang.

McMahon, A. 1994. *Understanding language change*. Cambridge: Cambridge University Press.

Meillet, A. 1921 [1912]. L'évolution des formes grammaticales. In: É. Champion (ed.), *Linguistique historique et linguistique générale*, 130–48. Paris: Librairie Ancienne Honoré Champion.

Meillet, A. 1923. Le développement du verbe avoir. In: *Festschrift Jacob Wackernagel zur Vollendung des 70. Lebensjahres*, 9–13. Göttingen: Vandenhoeck & Ruprecht.

Meiser, G. 2004. Die Periphrase im Urindogermanischen. In: A. Hyllested, A.R. Jørgensen, J.H. Larsson & Th. Olander (eds.), *Per Aspera ad Asteriscos*.

Studia Indogermanica in honorem E.J. Rasmussen, 343–53. Innsbruck: Institut für Sprachen und Literaturen der Universität Innsbruck.

Metslang, H. 1995. The progressive in Estonian. In: P.M. Bertinetto, V. Bianchi, Ö. Dahl & M. Squartini (eds.), *Temporal reference, aspect and actionality, vol. 2: Typological perspectives*, 169–83. Torino: Rosenberg & Sellier.

Michaelis, L.A. 1998. *Aspectual grammar and past-time reference*. London: Routledge.

Mihevc, E. 1959. *La disparition du parfait dans le grec de la basse époque.* Ljubljana: Slovenka Akademija znanosti in umetnosti. Razred filološke in literarne vede.

Milroy, J. 1992. *Linguistic variation and change: On the historical sociolinguistics of English*. Oxford: Blackwell.

Mirambel, A. 1961. Participe et gérondif en grec médiéval et moderne. *Bulletin de la Société Linguistique de Paris* 56, 46–79.

Mirambel, A. 1966. Essai sur l'évolution du verbe en grec byzantin. *Bulletin de la Société Linguistique de Paris* 61, 167–90.

Mitchell, B. 1985. *Old English syntax*, vol. 1. Oxford: Clarendon Press.

Mittwoch, A. 2008. The English resultative perfect and its relationship to the experiential perfect and the simple past tense. *Linguistics and Philosophy* 31, 323–51.

Moorhouse, A.C. 1982. *The syntax of Sophocles*. Leiden: Brill.

Moser, A. 1988. *A history of the perfect periphrases in Greek*. PhD thesis, University of Cambridge.

Moser, A. 2008. The changing relationship of tense and aspect in the history of Greek. *Language Typology and Universals* (STUF) 61, 5–18.

Moser, A. 2009. Restructuring the system: the case of the Greek aorist and perfect. In: Ἀντιφίλησις: *Studies on Classical, Byzantine and Modern Greek literature and culture, in honour of professor John-Theophanes A. Papademetriou*, 648–56. Stuttgart: Franz Steiner Verlag.

Moulton, J.H. 1908³. *A grammar of New Testament Greek. Vol. 1: Prolegomena*. Edinburgh: T. & T. Clark.

Moulton, J.H. & N. Turner. 1963. *A grammar of New Testament Greek. Vol. 3: Syntax*. Edinburgh: T. & T. Clark.

Mugler, C. 1958. *Dictionnaire historique de la terminologie géométrique des Grecs*. Paris: Klincksieck.

Mussies, G. 1971. *The morphology of Koine Greek as used in the Apocalypse of St. John. A study in bilingualism*. Leiden: Brill.

Naess, A. 2007. *Prototypical transitivity*. Amsterdam: John Benjamins.

Napoli, M. 2006. *Aspect and actionality in Homeric Greek. A contrastive analysis*. Milano: FrancoAngeli.

Napoli, M. 2007. Latino habeo più participio perfetto passivo. Riflessioni su grammatica e lessico. *Archivio Glottologico Italiano* 92, 3–50.

Nedjalkov, V. & S.J. Jaxontov. 1988. The typology of resultative constructions. In: V.P. Nedjalkov (ed.), *Typology of resultative constructions*, 3–62. Amsterdam: John Benjamins.

Nedjalkov, V. 2001. Resultative constructions. In: M. Haspelmath (ed.), *Language typology and universals. An International Handbook*, vol. 2, 928–40. Berlin & New York: de Gruyter.

Nevalainen, T. & M. Palander-Collin. 2011. Grammaticalization and sociolinguistics. In: H. Narrog & B. Heine (eds.), *The Oxford handbook of grammaticalization*, 118–28. Oxford: Oxford University Press.

Newmeyer, F.J. 1998. *Language form and language function*. Cambridge, MA: MIT Press.

Newmeyer, F.J. 2001. Deconstructing grammaticalization. *Language Sciences* 23, 187–229.

Norde, M. 2013. *Degrammaticalization*. Oxford: Oxford University Press.

Núñez-Pertejo, P. 2003. Adjectival participles or present participles? On the classification of some dubious examples from the Helsinki Corpus. In: J.L. Bueno Alonso, J. Figueroa Dorrego, D. González Álvarez, J. Pérez Guerra & M. Urdiales Shaw (eds.), *Nothing but papers, my lord. Studies in Early Modern English language and literature (SEDERI XIII)*, 141–53. Vigo: Universidade de Vigo.

O'Donnell, M.B. 2000. Designing and compiling a register-balanced corpus of Hellenistic Greek for the purpose of linguistic description and investigation. In: S.E. Porter (ed.), *Diglossia and other topics in New Testament linguistics*, 255–97. Sheffield: Sheffield Academic Press.

Oesterreicher, W. 2001. Historizität—Sprachvariation, Sprachverschiedenheit, Sprachwandel. In: M. Haspelmath, E. König, W. Oesterreicher & W. Raible (eds.), *Language typology and language universals / La typologie des langues et les universaux linguistiques / Sprachtypologie und sprachliche Universalien*, vol. 2, 1554–95. Berlin & New York: Walter.

Oldsjö, F. 2001. *Tense and aspect in Caesar's narrative*. Uppsala: Uppsala University Library.

Olsen, M.J. 1994. *A semantic and pragmatic model of lexical and grammatical aspect*. PhD thesis, Northwestern University.

Oreal, E. 2000. Détermination et indétermination: Un paramètre du fonctionnement de l'aspect en grec ancien. In: B. Jacquinod (ed.), *L'aspect verbal chez Platon*, 285–302. Saint Etienne: Mémoires du Centre Jean Palerne.

Palm, J. 1955. *Über Sprache und Stil des Diodoros von Sizilien: Ein Beitrag zur Beleuchtung der hellenistischen Prosa*. PhD thesis, University of Lund.

Palme, B. 2009. The range of documentary texts: Types and categories. In: R.S. Bagnall (ed.), *Oxford handbook of papyrology*, 358–94. New York: Oxford University Press.

Palmer, L.R. 1980. *The Greek language*. London & Boston, MA: Faber & Faber.

Papanikolaou, A.D. 1973. *Chariton-Studien: Untersuchungen zur Sprache und Chronologie der griechischen Romane*. Göttingen: Vandenhoeck & Ruprecht.
Pinkster, H. 1987. The strategy and chronology of the development of future and perfect tense auxiliaries in Latin. In: M. Harris & P. Ramat (eds.), *The historical development of auxiliaries*, 193–223. Berlin: de Gruyter.
Pollak, W. 1976. Un modèle explicatif de l'opposition aspectuelle: Le schéma d'incidence. *Le français moderne* 44, 289–311.
Pompei, A. 2006. Participles as a non prototypical word class. In: E. Crespo, J. de la Villa & A.R. Revuelta (eds.), *Word classes and related topics in Ancient Greek*, 361–88. Louvain-la-Neuve: Peeters.
Porter, S.E. 1988. Vague verbs, periphrastics, and Matt 16: 19. *Filologia Neotestamentaria* 1, 155–73.
Porter, S.E. 1989. *Verbal aspect in the Greek of the New Testament, with reference to tense and mood*. New York: Peter Lang (diss. Sheffield).
Porter, S.E. 1999^2. *Idioms of the Greek New Testament*. Sheffield: Sheffield Academic Press.
Pouilloux, J. 1957. Une particularité sophocléenne: La périphrase du participe aoriste et de ἔχω. In: *Mélanges offerts à Octave et Melpo Merlier à l'occasion du 25e anniversaire de leur arrivée en Grèce*, 117–35. Athènes: Institut Français d'Athènes.
Preisigke, F. 1912. *Griechische Papyrus der Kaiserlichen Universitäts- und Landesbibliothek zu Strassburg*. Leipzig: Hinrichs.
Prieur, J.-M. 1989. *Acta Andreae*. Turnhout: Brepols.
Pusch, C.D. 2003. Aspectuality and focality—Reflections on semantics-pragmatics relations and isomorphism in Romance progressive periphrases. In: C.D. Pusch & A. Wesch (eds.), *Verbalperiphrasen in den (ibero-)romanischen Sprachen*, 179–92. Hamburg: Buske.
Pustet, R. 2003. *Copulas: Universals in the categorization of the lexicon*. Oxford: Oxford University Press.
Regard, P.F. 1918. *La phrase nominale dans la langue du Nouveau Testament*. Paris: Leroux.
Rice, S.A. 1987. *Towards a Cognitive model of transitivity*. PhD dissertation, University of California, San Diego.
Rijksbaron, A. 1984. Het Griekse perfectum: Subject contra object. *Lampas* 17, 403–20.
Rijksbaron, A. 1988. The discourse function of the imperfect. In: A. Rijksbaron et al. (eds.), *In the footsteps of Raphaël Kühner*, 237–54. Amsterdam: Gieben.
Rijksbaron, A. 2002^3. *The syntax and semantics of the verb in Classical Greek*. Amsterdam: Gieben.
Ringe, D. 1984. Εἴληφα and the aspirated perfect. *Glotta* 62, 125–41.
Risselada, R. 1987. Voice in Ancient Greek: Reflexives and passives. In: J. van der Auwera & L. Goossens (eds.), *Ins and outs of the predication*, 123–36. Dordrecht: Foris.

Robertson, A.T. 1915². *A grammar of the Greek New Testament in the light of historical research*. New York: Hodder & Stoughton, George H. Doran company.
Rochette, B. 2010. Greek and Latin bilingualism. In: E.J. Bakker (ed.), *A companion to the Ancient Greek language*, 281–93. Oxford: Wiley-Blackwell.
Ronnet, G. 1951. *Étude sur le style de Démosthène dans les discours politiques*. Paris: E. de Boccard.
Ros, J.S.J. 1938. *Die metabolē (variatio) als Stilprinzip des Thukydides*. Paderborn: F. Schöningh.
Rosch, E. 1978. Principles of categorization. In: E. Rosch & B.B. Lloyd (eds.), *Cognition and categorization*, 27–48. Hillsdale: Lawrence Erlbaum Associates.
Rosemeyer, M. 2012. How to measure replacement: Auxiliary selection in Old Spanish bibles. *Folia Linguistica Historica* 46, 135–74.
Rosén, H.B. 1957. Die 'zweiten' Tempora des Griechischen: Zum Prädikatsausdruck beim griechischen Verbum. *Museum Helveticum* 14, 133–54.
Rosén, H.B. 1967. HN *ΔΙΔΑΣΚΟΝ* et questions apparentées. Mises au point sur les contacts linguistiques néotestamentaires. *Bulletin de la Société de Linguistique de Paris* 62, xxi–xxvi.
Rosén, H.B. 1975. Gedanken zur Geschichte des griechischen Satzbaus. *Die Sprache* 21, 23–36.
Rosén, H.B. 1979. *L'hébreu et ses rapports avec le monde classique: Essai d'évaluation culturelle*. Paris: Geuthner.
Rosén, H.B. 1987. Rhème et non-rhème: entités de langue. Pour une typologie des moyens d'expression formels. *Bulletin de la Société Linguistique de Paris* 82, 135–62.
Rosén, H.B. 1992. *Die Periphrase. Wesen und Entstehung*. Innsbruck: Institut für Sprachwississenschaft.
Rosenkranz, B. 1930. Der lokale Grundton und die persönliche Eigenart in der Sprache des Thukydides und der älteren attischen Redner. *Indogermanische Forschungen* 48, 129–79.
Rosenqvist, J.O. 2007. *Die byzantinische Literatur: Vom 6. Jahrhundert bis zum Fall Konstantinopels 1453*. Berlin & New York: de Gruyter.
Ross, J.R. 1972. The category squish: Endstation Hauptwort. In: *Papers from the eighth regional meeting of the Chicago Linguistic Society*, 316–28. Chicago, IL: University of Chicago.
Rowe, G.O. 1983. Demosthenes' use of language. In: J.J. Murphy (ed.), *Demosthenes' On the crown: A critical case study of a masterpiece of ancient oratory*, 175–99. Davis, CA: Hermagoras Press.
Ruijgh, C.J. 1970. Review: E. Coseriu, El aspecto verbal perifrástico. *Lingua* 25, 75–6.
Ruijgh, C.J. 1985. L'emploi 'inceptif' du thème du présent du verbe grec. Esquisse d'une theorie de valeurs temporelles des thèmes temporels. *Mnemosyne* 38, 1–61.

Ruijgh, C.J. 1991. Les valeurs temporelles des formes verbales en grec ancien. In: J. Gvozdanovic & T. Janssen (eds.), *The function of tense in texts*, 197–217. Amsterdam: North-Holland.
Ruijgh, C.J. 2004. Over de gebruikswijzen van het Griekse perfectum. Met speciale aandacht voor Plato's Politeia. *Lampas* 37, 24–45.
Ruipérez, M.S. 1979 [1954]. *Structure du système des aspectes et des temps du verbe en grec ancien: Analyse fonctionelle synchronique*. Paris: Les Belles-lettres.
Rundgren, F. 1965. The synoptic gospels as language. *Biblica* 46, 465–9.
Rutherford, R. 2010. The Greek of Athenian tragedy. In: E.J. Bakker (ed.), *The Blackwell companion to the Ancient Greek Language*, 441–54. Oxford: Blackwell.
Rydbeck, L. 1967. *Fachprosa, vermeintliche Volkssprache und Neues Testament: Zur Beurteilung der sprachlichen Niveauunterschiede im nachklassischen Griechisch*. Uppsala: Almquist & Wiksell.
Rydbeck, L. 1969. Bemerkungen zu Periphrasen mit εἶναι + Präsens Partizip bei Herodot und in der Koine. *Glotta* 47, 186–200.
Rydbeck, L. 1991. On the question of linguistic levels and the place of the New Testament in the contemporary language milieu. In: S.E. Porter (ed.), *The language of the New Testament: Classic essays*, 191–204. Sheffield: Sheffield Academic Press.
Sáenz-Badillos, A. 1993. *A history of the Hebrew language*. Cambridge: Cambridge University Press.
Salonius, A.H. 1927. *Zur Sprache der griechischen Papyrusbriefe*. Helsingfors: Akademische Buchhandlung.
Sandbach, F.H. 1985. Plato and the Socratic work of Xenophon. In: P.E. Easterling & B.M.W. Knox (eds.), *The Cambridge history of classical literature, vol. 1: Greek literature*, 478–97. Cambridge: Cambridge University Press.
Sapir, E. 1921. *Language: An introduction to the study of speech*. New York: Harcourt & Brace.
Sasse, H.-J. 2002. Recent activity in the theory of aspect: Accomplishments, achievements, or just non-progressive state? *Linguistic Typology* 6, 199–271.
Sasse, H.-J. 2006. Aspect and Aktionsart. In: K. Brown (ed.), *Encyclopedia of language and linguistics*, vol. 1, 535–8. Boston, MA: Elsevier.
Schick, C. 1956. Appunti per una storia della prosa greca. 3. La Lingua di Erodoto. *Memorie dell'Accademia Nazionale dei Lincei* s. VIII 7, 345–95.
Schironi, F. 2010. Technical languages: Science and medicine. In: E.J. Bakker (ed.), *The Blackwell companion to the Ancient Greek Language*, 338–53. Oxford: Blackwell.
Schwegler, A. 1990. *Analyticity and syntheticity: A diachronic perspective with special reference to Romance languages*. Berlin & New York: Mouton de Gruyter.

Schwenter, S.A. 1994a. The grammaticalization of an anterior in progress: Evidence from a Peninsular Spanish dialect. *Studies in Language* 18, 71-111.
Schwenter, S.A. 1994b. 'Hot news' and the grammaticalization of perfects. *Linguistics* 32, 995-1028.
Schwenter, S.A. & R.T. Cacoullos 2008. Defaults and indeterminacy in temporal grammaticalization: The 'perfect' road to perfective. *Language Variation and Change* 20, 1-39.
Schwyzer, E. 1950^4. *Griechische Grammatik. Zweiter Band: Syntax und syntaktische Stilistik. Vervollständigt und herausgegeben von Albert Debrunner*. München: C.H. Beck.
Schwyzer, E. 1953^6. *Griechische Grammatik. Erster Band: Allgemeiner Teil, Lautlehre, Wortbildung, Flexion*. München: C.H. Beck.
Sevčenko, I. 1981. Levels of style in Byzantine prose. *JÖB* 31, 289-312.
Shain, R. 2009. *Koine Greek aktionsart and the preverb eis-*. Master's Thesis, Ohio State University.
Shannon, T.F. 1995. Toward a cognitive explanation of perfect auxiliary variation: Some modal and aspectual effects in the history of Germanic. *American Journal of Germanic Linguistics and Literatures*, 129-63.
Sicking, C.M.J. 1991. The distribution of aorist and present tense stem forms in Greek, especially in the imperative. *Glotta* 69, 14-43, 154-70.
Sicking, C.M.J. 1996. Aspect choice. Time reference or discourse function? In: C.M.J. Sicking & P. Stork (eds.), *Two studies in the semantics of the verb in Classical Greek*, 1-118. Leiden: Brill.
Sicking, C.M.J. & P. Stork. 1996. The synthetic perfect in Classical Greek. In: C.M.J. Sicking & P. Stork (eds.), *Two studies in the semantics of the verb in Classical Greek*, 119-298. Leiden: Brill.
Slings, S.R. 1988. Het perfectum van Griekse toestandswerkwoorden. In: S.R. Slings & I. Sluiter (eds.), *Ophelos: Zes studies voor D.M. Schenkeveld*, 61-76. Amsterdam: VU Uitgeverij.
Slings, S.R. 1994. Geschiedenis van het perfectum in het oud-Grieks. In: R. Boogaart & J. Noordegraaf (eds.), *Nauwe betrekkingen: Voor Theo Janssen bij zijn vijftigste verjaardag*, 239-47. Amsterdam: Stichting Neerlandistiek VU.
Smith, C.S. 1997^2. *The parameter of aspect*. Dordrecht: Kluwer.
Smith, C.S. 2001. Discourse modes: Aspectual and tense interpretation. *Cahiers de Grammaire* 26, 183-206.
Smith, C.S. 2003. *Modes of discourse: The local structure of texts*. Cambridge: Cambridge University Press.
Smyth, H.W. 1984 [1920]. *Greek grammar*. Harvard: Harvard University Press.
Sparks, H.F. 1950. The semitisms of the Acts. *The Journal of Theological Studies* 1 (n.s.), 16-28.

Squartini, M. & P.M. Bertinetto. 2000. The simple and compound past in Romance languages. In: Ö. Dahl (ed.), *Tense and aspect in the languages of Europe*, 385–402. Berlin: de Gruyter.
Stahl, J.M. 1907. *Kritisch-historische Syntax des griechischen Verbums der klassischen Zeit*. Heidelberg: Winter.
Stein, H. 1962[8]. *Herodotus: Werke*. Berlin: Weidmann.
Stevens, P.T. 1936. Aristotle and the Koine—Notes on the Prepositions. *The Classical Quarterly* 30, 204–17.
Stork, P. 1982. *The aspectual usage of the dynamic infinitive in Herodotus*. Groningen: Bouma.
Strid, O. 1976. *Über Sprache und Stil des Periegeten Pausanias*. Stockholm: Almqvist & Wiksell.
Strunk, K. 1971. Historische und deskriptive Linguistik bei der Textinterpretation. *Glotta* 49, 191–216.
Swain, S. 1996. *Hellenism and empire: Language, classicism, and power in the Greek world, AD 50–250*. Oxford: Clarendon Press.
Tabachovitz, D. 1943. *Études sur le grec de la basse époque*. Uppsala: Almqvist & Wiksell.
Tabachovitz, D. 1956. *Die Septuaginta und das Neue Testament: Stilstudien*. Lund: Gleerup.
Taylor, J.R. 1998. Syntactic constructions as prototype categories. In: M. Tomasello (ed.), *The new psychology of language: Cognitive and functional approaches to language structure*, 177–202. Mahwah, NJ: Erlbaum.
Taylor, J.R. 2003[3]. *Linguistic categorization: Prototypes in linguistic theory*. Oxford: Clarendon Press.
Thesleff, H. 1954. *Studies on intensification in early and classical Greek*. PhD thesis, University of Helsinki.
Thesleff, H. 1966. Scientific and technical style in early Greek prose. *Arctos* 4, 89–113.
Thesleff, H. 1967. *Studies in the styles of Plato*. Helsinki: Suomalaisen Kirjallisuuden Kirjapaino.
Thielmann, P. 1891. Ἔχω mit Particip. In: *Abhandlungen aus dem Gebiet der klassischen Altertums-Wissenschaft*, 294–306. München: Beck.
Thielmann, P. 1898. Über periphrastische Verba im Griechischen. *Blätter für das Gymnasialschulwesen* 34, 55–65.
Thompson, S.A. 1989. A discourse approach to the cross linguistic category 'Adjective'. In: R. Corrigan, F. Eckman & M. Noonan (eds.), *Linguistic categorization*, 245–65. Amsterdam: John Benjamins.
Thompson, S.A. & P.J. Hopper. 2001. Transitivity, clause structure, and argument structure: Evidence from conversation. In: J.L. Bybee & P.J. Hopper (eds.), *Frequency and the emergence of linguistic structure*, 27–60. Amsterdam: John Benjamins.

Tichy, E. 1977. Griech. ἀλειτηρός, νηλειτής und die Entwicklung der Wortsippe ἀλείτης. *Glotta* 55, 160–77.

Thumb, A. 1974 [1901]. *Die Griechische Sprache im Zeitalter des Hellenismus*. Berlin & New York: Walter de Gruyter.

Tomasello, M. 2003. *Constructing a language: A usage-based theory of language acquisition*. Cambridge, MA: Harvard University Press.

Tonnet, H. 1982. Note sur la constitution du futur grec moderne. *Cahiers Balkaniques* 3, 105–19.

Traugott, E. & R. Dasher. 2002. *Regularity in semantic change*. Cambridge: Cambridge University Press.

Traugott, E.C. 2003. Constructions in grammaticalization. In: B.D. Joseph & R.D. Janda (eds.), *A handbook of historical linguistics*, 624–47. Oxford: Blackwell.

Treadgold, W.T. 2007. *The early Byzantine historians*. Basingstoke: Palgrave Macmillan.

Trenkner, S. 1960. *Le style kai dans le récit attique oral*. Assen: Van Gorcum.

Tsunoda, T. 1985. Remarks on transitivity. *Journal of Linguistics* 21, 385–96.

Tyrrell, R.Y. 1897. *The Troades of Euripides. With revised text and notes*. London: Macmillan & Co.

Vendler, Z. 1957. Verbs and time. *Philosophical Review* 66, 143–60.

Vendryes, J. 1937. Sur l'emploi de l'auxiliaire 'avoir' pour marquer le passé. In: *Mélanges de linguistique et de philologie offerts à Jacq. Van Ginneken*, 85–92. Paris: C. Klincksieck.

Verboomen, A. 1992. *L'imparfait périphrastique dans l'Évangile de Luc et dans la Septante*. Louvain & Paris: Peeters.

Verdenius, W. J. 1985. The nature of Aristotle's scholarly writings. In: J. Wiesner (ed.), *Aristoteles—Werk und Wirkung, 1. Band: Aristoteles und seine Schule*, 12–21. Berlin & New York: de Gruyter.

Vester, E. 1977. On the so-called 'participium coniunctum'. *Mnemosyne* 30, 243–85.

Villa, J. de la. 1989. La identificación de la auxiliaridad verbal en Griego. *Cuadernos de Filología Clásica* 22, 195–208.

Villa, J. de la. 2008. La suerte y la sintaxis: sobre las construcciones de τυγχάνω. *Faventia* 30, 271–83.

Villa, J. de la. 2014. Tense/aspect. In: G. Giannakis, V. Bubenik, E. Crespo, C. Golston, A. Lianeri, S. Luraghi & S. Matthaios (eds.), *Encyclopedia of Ancient Greek Language and Linguistics*, vol. 3, 382–9. Brill: Leiden.

Voelz, J.W. 1984. The language of the New Testament. *Aufstieg und Niedergang der römischen Welt* II, 25.2, 894–977.

Wackernagel, J. 1953 [1904]. Studien zum griechischen Perfectum. Programm zur akademischen Preisverteilung, 3–32. Repr. in *Kleine Schriften*, 1000–21. Göttingen: Vandenhoek & Ruprecht.

Wakker, G. 2006. Future auxiliaries or not? In: E. Crespo, J. de la Villa & A.R. Revuelta (eds.), *Word classes and related topics in Ancient Greek*, 237-55. Louvain-la-Neuve: Peeters.
Wakker, G. 2007. Intentions and future realisations in Herodotus. In: R.J. Allan & M. Buijs (eds.), *The language of literature: Linguistic approaches to Classical texts*, 168-87. Leiden: Brill.
Waltke, B.K. & M.P. O'Connor. 1990. *An introduction to Biblical Hebrew syntax*. Winona Lake: Eisenbrauns.
Webster, T.B.L. 1941. A study of Greek sentence construction. *American Journal of Philology* 62, 385-415.
West, M.L. 1980. *Hesiod: Works and days*. Oxford: Clarendon Press.
Weinreich, U., Labov, W. & M. Herzog. 1968. Empirical foundations for a theory of language change. In: W. Lehmann & Y. Malkiel (eds.), *Directions for historical linguistics*, 95-195. Austin: University of Texas Press.
Wheeler, J.R. 1891. The participial constructions with τυγχάνειν and κυρεῖν. *Harvard Studies in Classical Philology* 2, 143-57.
White, J.L. 1972. *The form and structure of the official petition: A study in greek epistolography*. Missoula, MT: Soc. of biblical literature.
Wierzbicka, A. 1986. What's in a noun? (Or, how do nouns differ in meaning from adjectives?). *Studies in Language* 10, 353-89.
Wifstrand, A. 1934. Eine besondere Anwendung der Verbalumschreibung mit εἶναι + Präsenspartizip. *Vetenskaps-Societetens i Lund, Årsbok*, 41-4.
Wifstrand, A. 1945. *Eikota. emendationen und interpretationen zu griechischen prosaikern der kaiserzeit. V: zu den romanschriftstellern*. Lund: Gleerup.
Wifstrand 2005, A. Greek prose style: An historical survey. In: L. Rydbeck & S.E. Porter (eds.), *Epochs and styles: Selected writings on the New Testament, Greek language and Greek culture in the post-classical era*, 81-92. Tübingen: Mohr Siebeck.
Wistrand, E. 1972. *Opera selecta*. Lund: Åström.
Wille, G. 1965. Zu Stil und Methode des Thukydides. In: H. Flashar & K. Gaiser (eds.), *Synusia. Festgabe für Wolfgang Schadewaldt*, 53-77. Pfullingen: Neske.
Willi, A. 2003. *The languages of Aristophanes: Aspects of linguistic variation in Classical Attic Greek*. Oxford: Oxford University Press.
Willi, A. 2010. Register variation. In: E.J. Bakker (ed.), *The Blackwell companion to the Ancient Greek Language*, 297-310. Oxford: Blackwell.
Willi, A. 2016. Register variation and tense/aspect/mood categories in Ancient Greek. Problems and perspectives. In: K. Bentein, M. Janse & J. Soltic (eds.), *Variation and change in Ancient Greek tense, aspect and modality*. Brill: Leiden.
Wolf, K. 1912. *Studien zur Sprache des Malalas*. München: Straub.

Wood, E.J. 2007. *The semantic typology of pluractionality*. PhD thesis, University of California, Berkeley, CA.

Xrakovskij, V.S. 1997. Semantic types of the plurality of situations and their natural classification. In: V.S. Xrakovskij (ed.), *Typology of iterative constructions*, 3–64. München: LINCOM Europa.

Zhang, L. 1995. *A contrastive study of aspectuality in German, English & Chinese*. New York: Peter Lang.

Index locorum

Achilles Tatius (Ach. Tat.)
Leucippe and Clitophon (Leuc. et Clit.)
 2.31.1: 170
 4.4.8: 172
 4.12.7: 263
 6.8.3: 170, 173
 7.1.4: 172
 7.1.5: 170
 7.2.1: 172
 7.2.2: 170, 173
 7.4.3: 170, 173
 7.9.12: 170, 173
 7.11.6: 170
 7.12.4: 170
 8.9.8: 170
Acts of Andrew (A. Andr.)
 2.10: 273
 14.7-8: 264
 25.1: 273
 34.6-11: 273
Acts of Barnabas (A. Barn.)
 7.8-9: 189
Acts of John (A. Jo.)
 56.1: 264
Acts of Philip (A. Phil.)
 4.1: 280, 283
 4.2: 283
 5.5: 279
 7.4: 283
 11.1: 281, 283
 12.3: 193
 12.9: 280
 14.2: 196
 (Vat. Gr. 824) 124.2-3: 87
 (Vat. Gr. 824) 128.1-2: 284
 pass. 34.12: 285
Acts of Thomas (A. Thom.)
 9.14-15: 169
 16.10: 169
 16.11: 169
 27.4: 169
 43.19-20: 180
 59.5-6: 176
 63.6: 176

 91.17-18: 169
 114.4-5: 176
 126.10-13: 171
 150.9: 180
Acts of Xanthippe and Polyxena
 (A. Xanthipp.)
 26.25: 169
 27.1-3: 264
 34.4: 169
Aeschylus (Aesch.)
Agamemnon (Ag.)
 869-73: 140
Prometheus bound (PV)
 493-5: 215
The libation bearers (Cho.)
 239: 96
 696: 95
The suppliants (Supp.)
 459-60: 296
 946: 95
Andocides (And.)
 1.63: 143
 1.129: 142
Antiphon (Antiph.)
 1.8: 128
Antony the Hagiographer (Anton. Hag.)
Life of Symeon Stylites the Elder (V. Sym. Styl.)
 4.17: 280
 24.4-5: 198
 29.23: 197
Apocalypse of Enoch (Apoc. En.)
 10.19: 251
 10.21: 251
 14.14: 251
 94.3: 251
 95.2: 251
Apocalypse of John (Apoc. Joh.)
 10.2: 178
Archimedes (Archim.)
On conoids and spheroids (Con. Sph.)
 1.170.18-19: 250

372 Index locorum

Archimedes (Archim.) (*cont.*)
On the sphere and the cylinder
  (*Sph. Cyl.*)
  1.103.12: 167
  1.109.28: 167
  1.112.16: 167
  1.116.20-1: 167
The method (Eratosth.)
  3.86.11: 250
  3.100.1: 250
The quadrature of the parabola
  (*Quad. Parab.*)
  2.178.2-3: 250
  2.181.4: 250
  2.182.14: 250
The sand-reckoner (Aren.)
  2.146.19-20: 250

Aristophanes (Aristoph.)
Ecclesiazusae (Eccl.)
  1094: 220
  1145-8: 130
Peace (Pax)
  195-7: 145
  334: 225
Thesmophoriazusae (Thesm.)
  77: 95
The Acharnians (Ach.)
  428-9: 216
The Birds (Av.)
  652: 216
The Clouds (Nub.)
  794-6: 130
The Frogs (Ran.)
  36: 220
  512: 238
  1396: 92, 213
The Knights (Equ.)
  468: 224
The Wasps (Vesp.)
  127: 95
Wealth (Plut.)
  49: 85
  160-1: 141
  368: 225
  867: 128, 142

Aristotle (Aristot.)
Categories (Cat.)
  8b: 212
  13a: 212
Economics (Oec.)
  1348b: 128

History of animals (Hist. an.)
  489b: 148
  497b: 148
  503a: 148
  504a: 150
  508a: 151
  520a: 148
  533a: 148
  578b: 95, 151
  591a: 143, 148
  606b: 130
  627a: 148
  629b: 148
  635a: 136
Magna moralia (Mag. mor.)
  1.17.10: 92
  1.30.2: 214
  1.34.3: 93
  2.11.40: 93
Metaphysics (Metaph.)
  1011a: 96
  1017a: 224
  1021a: 140
  1042a: 214
  1081b: 212
Meteorology (Mete.)
  372b: 137
  374a: 95
  374b: 151
Nicomachean ethics (Eth. Nic.)
  1124b: 137
  1133a: 137
  1142b: 137
  1144b: 137
On generation and corruption
  (*Gen. corr.*)
  327a: 137
  329a: 218
On interpretation (De Int.)
  23b: 96
On marvellous things heard (Mir.)
  846b: 93, 95
On Melissus, Xenophanes and
  Gorgias (MXG)
  975a: 94, 298
  979a: 298
  979b: 215, 298
On sophistical refutations (Soph. el.)
  179b: 140
  183b: 143
On the heavens (Cael.)
  271b: 137

Index locorum

272b: 137
273a: 137
280a: 127
On the universe (Mund.)
  391a: 85
Parts of animals (Part. an.)
  656b: 148
  657a: 148, 214
  660a: 82, 148, 150
  666b: 148
  671b: 148
  680a: 81
  693a: 148
Physics (Ph.)
  192a: 137
  195b: 137
  225b: 137
  226a: 214
  232a: 137
  233a: 136
  233b: 137
  265a: 137
Physiognomonics (Phgn.)
  808a: 136
  809b: 215
Poetics (Poet.)
  1449a: 137
  1450b: 148
  1452a: 127
Politics (Pol.)
  1274b: 137
  1278a: 96
  1287b: 140
  1301a: 96
  1317a: 144
  1323b: 136
  1327b: 137
  1335b: 148
Posterior analytics (An. post.)
  87a: 212
Prior analytics (An. pr.)
  51b: 95
Problems (Pr.)
  939a: 101
  953b: 97
Rhetoric (Rhet.)
  1369a: 92
  1370a: 126
  1380b: 128
  1383a: 140
  1419a: 128

Sense and sensibilia (Sens.)
  439a: 214
Topics (Top.)
  102a: 128, 137
  102b: 128
  104b: 298
  108b: 128, 137
  109b: 128
  113b: 144
  129b: 137
  130a: 137
  131b: 128
  143a: 128

Athansius (Ath.)
Life of Antony (V. Anton.)
  5.35–6: 281
  47.3–4: 282
  48.13: 199
  61.14: 285
  82.13–14: 281
  85.15–16: 283

Callinicus (Call.)
Life of St Hypatius (V. Hyp.)
  22.8: 289
  28.1: 193
  28.7: 199
  40.17: 193

Cassius Dio
Roman histories (Hist. Rom.)
  36.52.4: 172
  37.8.2: 172
  39.45.3: 172
  41.41.5: 172
  42.20.1: 179
  46.49.3: 263
  51.9.2: 263
  57.7.5: 263
  67.18.1: 179
  73.6.2: 263
  75.13.3: 179

Chariton (Charit.)
Callirhoe
  5.2.2: 178

Cicero (Cic.)
On the ends of good and evil (Fin.)
  4.11: 118

Confession and prayer of Aseneth (Prec. Josephi)
  3.10: 176

Confession and prayer of Aseneth
(Prec. Josephi) (cont.)
  27.8: 176

Cosmas Indicopleustes (Cosm. Ind.)
Christian topography (Top.)
  1.15: 285

Cyril of Scythopolis (Cyr. S.)
Life of Euthymius (V. Euthym.)
  37.18: 185
  53.11–2: 192
  81.5: 283

Demosthenes (Dem.)
  1.8: 39
  3.7: 61
  3.34: 216
  4.42: 137
  4.50: 137
  7.46: 80
  13.15: 93
  14.20: 17
  15.8: 137
  16.10: 96
  18.178: 143
  19.2: 141
  19.16: 128, 144
  19.36: 217
  19.181: 38
  19.224: 96, 126
  19.288: 13
  19.294: 220
  19.312: 96, 216
  20.10: 62, 65
  20.18: 215
  20.127: 143
  21.104: 137
  21.114: 92, 94, 298
  21.169: 128, 142
  21.182: 141
  21.185: 96
  22.22: 95
  23.122: 137, 140
  23.179: 74
  23.194: 96
  23.209: 128
  24.60: 150
  24.107: 128
  24.210: 12, 140
  27.17: 75
  27.36: 137
  27.67: 137
  29.13: 92, 216
  30.31: 128, 143
  30.32: 214
  31.14: 128, 137
  33.24: 137
  34.11: 129
  34.16: 213
  35.26: 128
  35.31: 129
  35.36: 93, 126, 128
  35.53: 130
  35.56: 137
  36.6: 128, 142
  37.5: 147
  37.19: 142
  41.9: 137
  43.68: 128
  46.11: 126
  47.38: 95
  47.41: 128, 137
  48.16: 144
  48.6: 95
  48.19: 128
  52.2: 137
  55.8: 128
  57.58: 141
  57.66: 128, 142
  58.31: 128
  58.34: 95
  62.44: 137
  Exord. 55.2: 223

Diodorus of Sicily (Diod. Sic.)
The library of history (Bibl. Hist.)
  2.37.3: 177

Dionysius of Halicarnassus
  (Dion. Hal.)
Roman Antiquities (Ant. Rom.)
  1.46.4: 165
  1.82.6: 166
  2.49.4: 250
  3.51.1: 165
  4.65.4: 252
  5.33.2: 252
  6.31.2: 165
  7.17.4: 165
  7.54.6: 252
  8.19.3: 165
  8.47.3: 166
  9.14.7: 165
  9.19.2: 165
  9.60.1: 167
  10.31.1: 166

Index locorum

10.32.2: 166
10.58.3: 252
11.6.4: 166
Eunapius (Eunap.)
Historical fragments (Fragm.)
1.221.18–22: 193
Euripides (Eur.)
Alcestis (Alc.)
465: 297
Andromache (Andr.)
1081–2: 13
Hecuba (Hec.)
120: 223
1179: 224
Helen (Hel.)
92: 2
Heracles (HF)
313: 226
Hippolytus (Hipp.)
185: 2
1413: 97
Ion
230: 116
680: 127
736: 116
Iphigenia at Aulis (IA)
1463: 76
1472–3: 76
Iphigenia in Tauris (IT)
509: 126
721–2: 217
1339: 226
1368: 226
Orestes (Or.)
60–1: 220
The Bacchantes (Bacch.)
471: 96
The cyclops (Cyc.)
381: 223
The Heracleidae (Heracl.)
910–11: 93
The suppliants (Supp.)
511: 297
The Trojan women (Tro.)
315–21: 237
Eusebius (Eus.)
Ecclesiastical history (H.E.)
1,7.10: 185
4.11.9: 279
6.31.1: 185
Life of Constantine (V.C.)
4.29.5: 185

Eustratius the Presbyter (Eustrat.)
Life of Eutychius (V. Eutych.)
314–16: 283
1312: 280
1390: 190
2585–6: 283
Flavius Iosephus (Flav. Ios.)
Jewish war (Bell. Iud.)
1.78: 266
George of Syceon (Geo. Syc.)
Life of St Theodore of Syceon (V. Theod. Syc.)
26.31: 279
40.1–4: 280
59.10: 279
64.3: 283
72.32–3: 190
81.2–3: 190
91.4: 193
102.3: 185
106.14–15: 190
124.10–11: 289
131.7–8: 279
136.9: 285
154.17–18: 279
154.30: 190
157.34–5: 193
159.22: 198
161.145: 190
162.19–20: 281
167.78: 190
168.52–3: 285
Gospel of Bartholomew (Ev. Barth.)
4.6: 169
Gospel of Peter (Ev. Petr.)
23.2: 169
51.2: 169
Gregory of Nyssa (Gr. Nyss.)
Life of St Macrina (V. Macr.)
4 14–15: 185
19.5: 185
On the life of Moses (V. Mos.)
2.174: 185
Gregory the Presbyter (Gr. Presb.)
Life of St Gregory the Theologian (V. Gr. Naz.)
3.16: 189
10.32: 281
20.15–17: 185

Homeric Hymns (H. Hom.)
5.34: 112
5.155–8: 113

Herodotus (Hdt.)
Histories
1.44.2: 128
1.45.1: 128
1.57.1–2: 16, 17
1.60.1: 148
1.63.2: 92
1.83.1: 123
1.86.5: 93
1.92.1: 95
1.98.1: 252
1.98.6: 93, 97, 148
1.102.2: 92
1.206.1: 35
1.133.1: 117
1.147.1: 221
1.152.1: 223, 226
1.194.1: 2
1.199.5: 96
1.206.1: 35
2.40.1: 61, 77
2.48.3: 214
2.51.1: 2
2.63.1: 117
2.79.2: 214
2.99.1: 225
2.134.2: 93, 97
2.152.3: 130
2.155.3: 223
3.27.3: 301
3.64.2: 128
3.119.1: 128
3.134.4: 226
4.14.2: 126
4.66.1: 128
4.99.4: 216
4.127.1: 297
4.136.1: 130
4.183.2: 148
4.204.1: 61
5.1.3: 220, 226
5.124.2: 95
6.23.5: 130
6.39.2: 237
6.44.1: 141
6.103.4: 219
6.126.3: 95
7.11.2: 95
7.68.1: 126
7.95.2: 96
7.150.1: 214
7.167.1: 214
7.190.1: 220, 223
7.194.3: 296
7.214.3: 140
7.229.1: 130, 141
8.23.1: 36
8.26.3: 33
8.35.2: 35
8.37.1: 220
8.37.3: 220
8.47.1: 95
8.107.2: 220
8.110.2: 141
9.16.1: 223
9.27.5: 131
9.60.1: 127
9.76.2: 120
9.91.1: 252

Heliodorus (Heliod.)
Ethiopian story (Aeth.)
1.8.5: 179
5.11.5: 274
5.16.4: 179
8.9.18: 275

Hesiod (Hes.)
Theogony (Theog.)
766: 211
Works and days (Op.)
42–4: 109
533–5: 38

Hippocrates (Hippoc.)
Epidemics (Epid.)
2.2.7: 93, 215
2.2.19: 148
5.1.13: 149
5.1.40: 148
5.1.64: 97
6.6.6: 218
7.1.10: 226
On airs, waters, and places (Aer.)
7.10–11: 127
7.68–70: 300
15.13: 148
On fractures (Fract.)
4.2: 126
7.34: 148
26.7–10: 136
On injuries of the head (Cap. vuln.)
2.29–31: 150

On joints (Art.)
  47.8: 126
On regimen in acute diseases (Acut.)
  1.14: 92
On the art of medicine (Ars Med.)
  5.7: 214
On the diseases of women (Mul.)
  11.15: 127
On the places in man (Loc. Hom.)
  29.4: 126
On the sacred disease (Morb. Sacr.)
  16.10–11: 93
  17.14–16: 120
On the seven months child (Septim.)
  122.17: 126
On ulcers (Ulc.)
  16.1–3: 216
Prognostics (Progn.)
  3.3: 148
Prorrhetics (Prorrh.)
  2.1: 300
  2.7: 136
  2.14: 136
  2.24: 127
  2.32: 148
  2.35: 148

History of the monks in Egypt (Hist. mon. Aeg.)
  14.28–9: 195
  8.198–9: 285
  10.159: 285
  27.44: 289

Homer (Hom.)
Iliad (Il.)
  1.212: 108
  1.356: 109
  1.388: 108
  1.507: 109
  2.240: 109
  2.257: 108
  2.272–3: 112
  2.295–6: 210
  3.15: 209
  4.22: 211
  4.211: 294
  5.14: 209
  5.174–8: 294
  5.191: 294
  5.630: 209
  5.850: 209
  6.121: 209
  6.488: 112
  8.459: 211
  9.111: 109
  9.310: 108
  10.239: 48
  11.232: 209
  11.682–4: 111
  11.683–4: 232
  12.120–2: 110
  13.604: 209
  13.764: 294
  14.196: 108
  15.128–9: 111
  16.462: 209
  18.4: 108
  18.427: 108
  19.78–80: 210
  20.176: 209
  20.347: 211
  21.148: 209
  21.531: 110
  22.248: 209
  23.816: 209
Odyssey (Od.)
  1.18: 112
  4.807: 211
  5.90: 108, 109
  9.452–5: 112
  10.156: 209
  10.156–7: 208
  11.168–9: 47
  11.441–3: 107
  12.106: 232
  14.334: 233
  15.536: 108
  16.440: 108
  16.471–3: 208
  17.163: 108
  17.229: 108
  19.291: 233
  19.309: 108
  19.547: 108
  21.336–9: 108

Ignatius the Deacon (Ign. Diac.)
Life of Gregory the Decapolite (V. Greg. Dec.)
  46.8: 280
Life of Tarasius the Patriarch (V. Taras.)
  5.26–7: 281

Index locorum

Irenaeus (Iren.)
  4.38.3: 66
Isaeus
  2.28: 144
  2.40: 214
  3.40: 128
  3.60: 141
  11.28: 92
Isocrates (Isoc.)
  5.28: 236
  5.110: 96
  5.113: 236
  5.115: 235
  6.14: 96
  6.72: 85
  8.9: 236
  8.101: 236
  11.47: 236
  12.29: 236
  12.128: 128, 142
  12.130: 128
  12.172: 236
  12.205: 236
  12.206: 236
  12.233: 146
  12.263: 95
  14.9: 128
  15.12: 236
  15.57: 81, 100, 216
  15.68: 151
  15.117: 93
  19.44: 128
  21.3: 128
  21.20: 141
John of Damascus
  (Jo. Damasc.)
Passion of the great martyr Artemius (Artem.)
  50.9–10: 279, 280
John the Merciful (Jo. Eleem.)
Life of Tycho (V. Tych.)
  24.23–4: 283
John Malalas (Jo. Mal.)
Chronography (Chron.)
  38.8: 199
  55.18: 189
  100.5–10: 278
  101.16–19: 14
  131.14: 191
  161.7–8: 279
  292.15–17: 189
  358.19: 285
  367.7–8: 201
  389.13–14: 189
  410.6–8: 190
  424.14–17: 185
  445.14–15: 189
  463.2–3: 189
John Moschus (Jo. Mosch.)
Spiritual meadow (Prat.)
  47.48–9: 193
  69.40–1: 280
  70.15–16: 192
  87.6: 197
  89.51: 197
  143.29: 280
  143.43–4: 283
Leontius of Naples (Leont. N.)
Life of John the Merciful (V. Jo. Eleem.)
  343.10–11: 190
  353.29: 189
  371.10–11: 201
  396.8–9: 280
Life of St Symeon the fool (V. Sym.)
  86.15–16: 191
  86.20–2: 185
  97.7–8: 283
Life of Adam and Eve (V. Adam)
  5.2–5: 168
  13.12: 251
  39.8: 251
Life of Alexander (V. Alex. Acoem.)
  664.2: 279
  682.18: 279
  683.3: 289
  697.12–13: 192
Life of St Auxibius (V. Aux.)
  112: 279
  112–3: 283
  161–2: 279
  340–1: 283
Life of Martha the mother of Simeon Stylites the Younger (V. Marth.)
  24.11: 201
  71.8: 193
  71.11–12: 193
Life of Pachomius (V. Pach.)
  29.5: 282
  52.3: 279
  77.12: 281

115.2-3: 197
117.2: 185
125.8-9: 281
137.5-6: 281

Life of Symeon Stylites the Younger
(V. Sym. Styl. J.)
75.1-2: 192
101.13-16: 281
142.2-3: 193
145.2: 283
153.1-2: 192, 193
166.5-8: 190
178.17: 285
186.16: 198
186.16-17: 194
188.36-7: 280
214.32: 285
219.45-6: 283
234.1-3: 199

Life of St Syncletica (V. Syncl.)
90: 190
104: 190
147-8: 190
1038-9: 199
1145: 190

Mark the Deacon (Marc. Diac.)
Life of Porphyry bishop of Gaza
(V. Porph.)
85.4: 185
90.4-5: 193

Martyrium of Pionius the presbyter and his comrades (M. Pion.)
22.1: 192

New Testament (Nov. T.)
1Corinthians (1Cor.)
14.9: 256
2Peter (2Pet.)
2.14: 176
Acts
1.10: 260, 283, 284
2.5: 18
2.6: 18
5.25: 259
9.28: 255, 283
10.24: 261
10.30: 259
11.5: 259
12.5: 255
12.12: 14, 261
12.20: 254
14.7: 65, 255, 257, 283
18.7: 255
19.14: 259
Galatians (Gal.)
1.22: 283
Hebrews (Heb.)
5.14: 176
James
3.15: 255, 283
John
3.23: 255
10.40: 255
16.12: 66
18.25: 260
19.10: 33
Luke (Lc.)
1.20: 254, 283
1.21: 259, 283
1.22: 257, 283
2.41: 34
2.51: 257, 283
3.23: 257
4.20: 283
4.31: 257
4.38: 283
4.44: 255, 257
5.10: 256
13.6: 178
13.11: 254, 283
14.1-2: 270
14.18: 176
14.19: 176
19.20: 176
19.47: 258
21.17: 256
21.24: 256
23.8: 255
24.36: 32
Mark (Mc.)
2.6: 259
3.1: 176
5.41: 255
8,17: 176
10.22: 255, 263
10.32: 62, 259
13.13: 256
13.25: 256
14.4: 255, 257
14.54: 257, 283
Matthew (Mt.)
3.9: 2
7.29: 283

Index locorum

New Testament (Nov. T.) (*cont.*)
  8.30: 259
  10.22: 256
  19.22: 207
  21.27: 2
  24.9: 256

Papyri
BGU
  1.48, ll. 7–8: 170
  2.454, ll. 20–1: 174
  2.596, ll. 12–13: 173
  2.624, l. 5: 174
  4.1138, l. 2: 162
  4.1141, l. 45: 163
  6.1253, ll. 6–7: 163
  6.1256, ll. 10–11: 155
  8.1830, l. 6: 162
  13.2349, l. 14: 263
  16.2601, ll. 26–7: 162
P.Bad.
  2.33, ll. 5–10: 170
  2.41, ll. 12–13: 267
P.Bon.
  43, ll. 10–11: 170
P.Cair.Isid.
  62, l. 5: 231
  77, ll. 19–20: 231
P.Cair.Masp.
  3.67312, l. 12: 193
P.Cair.Preis.
  1, l. 16: 174
P.Cair.Zen.
  1.59037, ll. 5–7; 10–12: 253
  5.59814, l. 6: 254
P.Dura
  20, l. 15: 267
  21, ll. 2–3: 267
  23, ll. 6–10: 267
P.Eleph.
  27, ll. 24–5: 162
P.Enteux.
  47, l. 7: 163
  55, l. 9: 163
P.Fam.Tebt.
  24dupl, 3, l. 79: 176
P.Flor.
  1.59, ll. 4–7: 176
  2.175, l. 14: 170
  3.382, ll. 66–7: 174
P.Gen.
  2.1.28, l. 27: 174
P.Giss.
  7, 2, ll. 10–22: 181

P.Giss.Apoll.
  8, ll. 3–4: 267
P.Hal.
  1, 6, ll. 131–2: 163
P.Hamb.
  1.27, ll. 18–19: 253
P.Herm.
  9, ll. 11–13: 200
P.Hib.
  2.200, ll. 6–7: 254
P.Kron.
  2, ll. 18–19: 174
P.Lips.
  2.146, ll. 16–17: 174
P.Lond.
  1.77, l. 11: 193
  1.113, 1, l. 89: 157
  3.948v, ll. 3–4: 170
  3.1168, l. 43: 173
  4.1332dupl, l. 12: 200
  4.1333dupl, ll. 13–14: 200
  4.1339, l. 17: 200
  4.1344, l. 6: 200
  4.1346, l. 16: 200
  4.1349, l. 31: 200
  4.1356, ll. 24–5: 200
  4.1362, l. 12: 200
  4.1370, ll. 13–14: 200
  4.1394, l. 23: 200
  5.1727, l. 18: 193
P.Mert.
  1.46, ll. 4–6: 196
  2.62, l. 10: 173
  2.91, l. 4, l. 6: 231, 157
P.Meyer
  8, l. 18: 174
P.Mich.
  5.229, ll. 7–8: 267
  6.422, l. 37: 174
  6.426, l. 9: 231
  8.480, l. 10: 174
  15.750, ll. 14–24: 163
P.Mil.Vogl.
  2.71, l. 26: 181
P.Muench.
  1.8, l. 8: 193
P.Oxy.
  7.1061, l. 20: 162
  10.1252, ll. 29–30: 173
  12.1408, ll. 12–14: 180
  16.1855, ll. 9–10: 196
  16.1862, ll. 16–18: 195
  20.2283, l. 8: 193

Index locorum

38.2857, l. 6: 173
42.3067, ll. 11–12: 170, 191
50.3555, l. 19: 176
55.3808, ll. 6–7: 267
58.3919, l. 11: 170
P.Petr.
  2.2, 2, ll. 5–6: 155
P.Rain.Cent.
  73, l. 3: 174
P.Ross.Georg.
  4.1, ll. 8–9: 200
  4.6, l. 25: 200
  4.8, ll. 8–10: 200
  4.15, l. 10: 200
P.Ryl.
  2.440, l. 9: 174
P.Sorb.
  1.13, l. 3: 166
P.Stras.
  1.35, ll. 5–7: 198
  1.73, ll. 20–1: 170
P.Tebt.
  1.16, l. 7: 163
  1.49, ll. 4–8: 155
  1.66, l. 2: 163
  1.67, l. 3: 163
  1.68, l. 3: 163
  1.69, l. 4: 163
  1.70, l. 3: 163
  1.71, ll. 4–5: 163
  1.89, l. 5: 163
  2.283: 154
  2.283, ll. 16–22: 162
  2.332, ll. 20–1: 174
  2.423, l. 18: 170
  3.1.703, ll. 176–9: 250
  3.1.740, l. 24: 163
  3.1.793, 8, l. 12: 160
  4.1129, l. 6: 163
  4.1130, l. 5: 163
P.Vind.Sijp.
  27, l. 13: 267
P.Wash.Univ.
  1.4, l. 3: 174
PSI
  4.420, ll. 21–4: 164
  4.424, l. 8: 162
  5.530, ll. 5–8: 253
  12.1248, l. 28: 170
  14.1419, l. 9: 267
SB
  3.6262, ll. 16–17: 170
  3.7241, l. 50: 200

3.7267, l. 3: 163
5.8754, l. 31: 164
10.10453, l. 20: 200
14.11899, l. 15: 174
24.16252, ll. 3–4: 231
Stud.Pal.
  1.1, ll. 2–3: 193
UPZ
  1.6, ll. 29–30: 163
  1.18, l. 26: 155
  1.41, l. 16: 154
  1.54, l. 30: 154
  1.78, ll. 18–23: 154
  1.79, ll. 12–13: 253
  1.108, l. 36: 162

Palladius (Pall.)
Lausaic history (H. Laus.)
  23.3: 195
  37.5: 285
  37.7: 197
  44.4: 190

Paschal chronicle (Chron. Pasch.)
  129.12: 280
  243.14–15: 279
  327.1: 191
  622.12–13: 189

Pausanias (Paus.)
Description of Greece
  1.22.6: 265
  3.18.11: 265
  3.18.13: 265
  4.3.2: 266
  5.17.3: 265
  5.18.5: 265
  5.19.3: 263
  6.16.3: 265
  8.11.9: 263
  8.31.4: 263
  10.25.3: 265
  10.27.3: 265
  10.27.4: 265
  10.29.10: 266
  10.31.9: 265

Phrynichus (Phryn.)
  242: 231

Plato (Pl.)
Alcibiades 1 (Alc. 1)
  129a: 236
Alcibiades 2 (Alc. 2)
  139d: 97
  140c: 128
  145e: 145

Plato (Pl.) (cont.)
  149b: 85
Apology (Ap.)
  34e: 126
  37a: 39
Charmides (Chrm.)
  153b: 145
Cratylus (Crat.)
  386e: 93
  404c: 123
Critias (Criti.)
  117a: 96
Crito (Crit.)
  44a: 40
Gorgias (Grg.)
  448a: 145
  469d: 126, 145
  502b: 127
  518a: 61
Hippias maior (Hp. Mai.)
  288a: 128
  289e: 216
  300a: 236
Ion
  533c: 77
  541c: 114
Laches (La.)
  188d: 96
Lysis (Ly.)
  207b: 35
Meno (Men.)
  84a: 225
  97d: 93
Menexenus (Menex.)
  240a: 142
  240c: 143
Parmenides (Prm.)
  141a: 93
  144e: 126
Phaedo (Phd.)
  76b: 128
  82a: 216, 219
  106b: 92
  109d: 143
Phaedrus (Phdr.)
  239b: 216
  249d: 225
Protagoras (Prt.)
  316a: 145
  349d: 85
  350b: 95
  358a: 128

Sophist (Soph.)
  229d: 93
Statesman (Plt.)
  261c: 96
  265d: 301
  268c: 144
  305d: 145
Symposium (Symp.)
  206d: 212
Theages (Thg.)
  123a: 296
  128d: 224
Theaetetus (Tht.)
  195a: 93
  200a: 152
The laws (Leg.)
  23b: 96
  631c: 96
  635b: 145
  679c: 145
  696b: 95
  698d: 143
  699e: 141
  711c: 92, 101
  714b: 145
  719d: 96
  723c: 85
  736b: 225
  758e: 96
  759b: 96
  765a: 88, 216
  776a: 297
  793b: 121
  800e: 13
  805c: 96
  840a: 95, 97
  881b: 214, 218
  932b: 216
  951d: 136
  956b: 136
  958a: 123, 140
  961d: 214
The republic (Resp.)
  431e: 95
  490a: 223, 226
  556a: 216
  577e: 212
  588b: 226
The rival lovers (Am.)
  132b: 143
Timaeus (Ti.)
  26b: 223, 226

Index locorum 383

52b: 96
90e: 214
Plutarch (Plut.)
Alexander the Great (Alex.)
  12.1: 178
  27.5: 172
  28.2: 179
  60.9: 172
Artaxerxes (Artax.)
  25.1: 178
Brutus (Brut.)
  14.7: 266
Caesar (Caes.)
  63.9: 178
Camillus (Cam.)
  7.4: 266
  16.3: 178
Cato the Younger (Cat. Mi.)
  10.2: 178
  45.5: 179
Dion
  11.6: 179
Marius (Mar.)
  8.5: 172
Pelopidas (Pelop.)
  25.7: 266
Polybius (Pol.)
Histories (Hist.)
  16.6.9: 252
  38.10.1–2: 167
Pope Zacharias (Zach. Papa)
Life of St Benedictus (V. Bened.)
  28.7: 190
  28.14: 289
Proto-evangelium of James (Protev.)
  37a.12: 264
  38.7–8: 264
Septuagint (LXX)
1Chronicles (1Chron.)
  18.14: 241
  21.20: 248
  23.26: 248
  29.15: 248
1Maccabees (1Macc.)
  3.12: 246
  5.53: 241
  12.11: 238
1Reigns
  11.7: 239
  18.9: 245

2Chronicles (2Chron.)
  9.20: 239, 248
  15.16: 248
  18.7: 248
  30.10: 241
  36.15: 248
  36.16: 241
2Esdras (2Esd.)
  6.8: 244
  11.11: 240
  12.13: 241
  12.14–15: 242
  13.26: 244
  15.18: 246
  16.14: 241, 244
  23.5: 246
  23.22: 243
  23.26: 283
2Maccabees (2Macc.)
  1.24: 239
  11.18: 238
2Reigns
  4.3: 244
3Reigns
  1.4: 245
  1.25: 243
  5.15: 246
  5.24: 241
  8.59: 238
  20.5: 239
4Reigns
  6.8: 242
  6.26: 243
  17.25: 241, 244
  17.26: 243
  17.28: 241
  17.32: 248
  17.41: 248
  21.15: 244
Bel
  21: 243
Daniel (Dan.)
  1.16: 241, 248
  2.43: 239
  4.4: 244
  5.11: 239
  10.2: 240, 248
  (Theodot.) 2.42: 182
Deuteronomy (Deut.)
  9.22: 244
  16.15: 69, 247
  19.6: 245, 248

Septuagint (LXX) (*cont.*)
  28.29: 246, 248
Ecclesiast (Eccles.)
  8.11: 239
  35.10: 283
Exodus (Exod.)
  3.1: 247
  21.23: 69
  25.20: 248
Ezechiel (Ezech.)
  1.12: 248
  16.7: 248
  23.29: 248
Genesis (Gen.)
  3.9: 2
  4.17: 248
  9.3: 68, 248
  12.4: 239
  13.10: 248
  14.12: 244, 248
  15.7: 2
  18.18: 244
  26.35: 241, 248
  30.33: 69
  39.23: 239, 248
Isaiah (Isa.)
  22.24: 248
Jeremiah (Jer.)
  4.24: 248
  39.30: 241, 248
Joshua (Josh.)
  10.26: 244
Judith (Jth.)
  1.16: 241
  4.13: 241
  9.1: 244
  16.20: 241
Judges (Judg.)
  8.5: 243
  20.31: 239
Leviticus (Lev.)
  14.46: 69
  15.19: 248
Numbers (Num.)
  14.33: 241, 244
  35.23: 248
Psalms (Ps.)
  91.15: 248
Sirach (Sir.)
  35.9–10: 239
Zechariah (Zach.)
  13.1: 239

Lycurg.
  1.27: 85, 97
  1.141: 127

Lysias (Lys.)
  1.45: 143
  2.5: 232
  2.13: 296
  4.19: 143
  9.7: 128
  12.17: 35
  12.22: 141, 143
  12.27: 61
  12.82: 128
  16.19: 142
  18.10: 128, 142
  20.1: 300
  20.15: 141
  22.16: 39
  22.20: 141
  25.6: 142
  29.12: 141
  32.18: 128

Sophocles (Soph.)
Ajax (Aj.)
  1042: 48
  1320: 224
  1320–1: 80
  1324: 15
  1330: 92, 95
Antigone (Ant.)
  22: 116
  76–7: 120
  178–81: 75
  1067: 296
  1068: 116
  1270–2: 74
  1350–3: 36
Oedipus at Colonus (OC)
  816: 296
  817: 116
  1472–4: 122
Oedipus the King (OT)
  89–90: 82, 299
  274: 96
  576–7: 122
  577: 116
  580: 93
  698–701: 152
  731: 75, 123
  747: 15, 95
  847: 224, 242

1146: 296
1285: 95
1389: 93, 95
Philoctetes (Phil.)
435: 95
544: 238
600: 152
942–3: 120
1219: 220
1315–16: 232
The women of Trachis (Trach.)
37: 123
247: 126
268: 97
941–2: 95
1113: 296

Sophronius of Jerusalem (Sophr. H.)
Narration of the miracles of Sts. Cyrus and John (Mir. Cyr. et Jo.)
30.135–6: 199
46.14: 193, 200
66.48: 199

Sozomenus (Soz.)
Ecclesiastical history (H.E.)
2.4.4: 192
3.15.10: 17, 198
7.28.2: 192
8.2.11: 281
9.9.1: 189

Strabo (Str.)
10.4.8: 165
14.2.24: 165

Testament of Job (T. Job)
28.8: 181
49.1: 180

Testament of Abraham (T. Abr.)
5.19: 264

The law of the twelve tables (Lex XII Tab.)
3.4: 118

Theodorus Studites (Thdr. Stud.)
Laudation of Theophanes Confessor (Laud. Theoph. Conf.)
7.11: 199

Theodoretus of Cyrrhus (Thdt.)
Ecclesiastical history (H.E.)
268.7–8: 279
318.17–19: 185

Theophanes Confessor (Thphn.)
Chronography (Chron.)
17.30: 201
349.6–7: 285
420.20: 189
481.30–1: 190

Theophylact Simocatta (Thphyl.)
Histories (Hist.)
1.6.2: 281
8.6.1: 281

Thucydides (Thuc.)
Histories
1.69.5: 73
1.138.3: 300
2.49.3: 141
2.67.1: 220
2.80.3: 222
2.91.2: 90
2.93.3: 220
3.52.2: 130
3.52.4: 128
4.54.3: 300
4.109.2: 95
5.7.5: 97
6.29.1: 128
7.51.1: 97
7.80.1: 141
8.24.6: 233
8.31.1: 233

Varro
On the Latin language (L.L.)
5.84: 118

Xenophon (Xen.)
Agesilaus (Ages.)
1.24: 127
Anabasis (An.)
1.2.21: 220
1.3.14: 152
1.4.9: 90
1.8.21: 148
1.9.2: 33
1.10.19: 73
2.2.13: 92
2.6.5: 72
2.6.7: 216
3.1.2: 96
3.1.46: 90
3.3.2: 224
3.4.35: 97

Xenophon (Xen.) (*cont.*)
  4.5.15: 220
  4.8.26: 128
  5.3.1: 95
  5.3.8: 234
  5.6.36: 97, 126
  6.6.12: 150
  6.6.25: 128
  7.2.21: 220
  7.7.1: 130
  7.8.13: 86, 215
  7.8.21: 140
Cyropaedia (Cyr.)
  1.4.18: 93
  1.6.41: 97, 127
  2.1.11: 96
  3.3.27: 148
  4.5.14: 130
  5.2.6: 148
  5.2.21: 148
  5.4.15: 148
  5.5.26: 219
  6.3.10: 220
  7.4.6: 97
  7.4.12: 149
  8.6.9: 96, 126
Economics (Oec.)
  10.5: 97
Hellenica (Hell.)
  1.3.17: 130
  1.5.2: 128
  1.6.31: 93, 97
  3.2.14: 140
  3.5.20: 220
  3.5.23: 95
  4.3.1: 141
  4.8.18: 234
  4.8.35: 128
  5.2.7: 96
  5.2.27: 128
  5.2.38: 128
  5.3.1: 148
  5.3.7: 37
  6.4.10: 127
  7.1.9: 142
Memorabilia (Mem.)
  2.1.22: 148
  2.6.4: 96
  4.3.11: 96
On hunting (Cyn.)
  4.8: 93
  10.4: 148
On revenues (Vect.)
  4.17: 128
  4.22: 224
Symposium (Symp.)
  4.32: 96

Xenophon of Ephesus (Xen.)
Ephesian tale (Eph.)
  1.8.3: 178
  2.2.4: 172

xlv miracles of St Artemius (xlv. mir. Artem.)
  7.17: 285
  9.9: 280
  11.23: 285
  30.16: 280
  31.15: 197
  31.16–17: 197
  39.10: 193
  66.4: 279
  72.25–6: 193
  74.20: 193

Zosimus (Zos.)
New history (H.N.)
  4.8.5: 281

Index nominum et rerum

accomplishment 41–3
achievement 41–3, 44
actionality:
   definition of 40–1
   diagnostic tests 43
   difficulties of application 44–5
   Vendlerian classification 41–2
activity 41–3
actualization 215–17
adjectival periphrasis:
   Daueradjektivierung 81, 85, 99
   definition of 63, 79–82
   Gelegenheitsadjektivierung 81, 99
   prototype approach towards 88–99
   relationship with verbal periphrasis 102–3
Aerts 12, 63, 84, 87, 106, 116, 125, 190–1, 194–5, 206–7, 219, 256, 268–70, 282–5, 293, 296, 298, 301
ambiguity 8, 220
   locative ambiguity, *see* locative
Amenta 82, 83, 84, 86, 88, 209
analyticity 1, 2
   analytic aspect 31
   analytic expression 157
   analytic form 158
   analytic language 1, 2
anterior 38, 39, 51, 75, 106–7, 113, 115, 124, 128–9, 131–2, 133–5, 137–47, 160–1, 171, 173, 174, 181, 185–9, 190–2, 194, 201–3
   experiential perfect 39, 112, 137–43, 308
   perfect of current relevance 39, 109, 181, 308
   perfect of persistence 39, 106, 112, 143–4, 180–1, 194–8, 224–5, 241, 308
   perfect of recent past 39–40, 107, 144–7
aorist:
   competition with the perfect, *see* synthetic perfect
   endings of 25, 29, 154–5
   gnomic 36, 217

   theme, *see* theme
   tragic 299
   synthetic 242, 300, 301
aoristic drift 106–7, 146, 208, 308
aspect:
   aspectual function 9, 30
   aspectual language 30
   aspectual neutrality 256, 295–6
   aspectual subdistinctions 30
   definition of 30–1
   functional approach towards 29–30
   imperfective aspect 31
   non-aspectual language 30
   perfect aspect 37–8
   perfective aspect 35
atelic, *see* telic
Atticism 17, 20, 27, 175, 228, 271
auxiliary 62, 66–7, 68–9, 118, 201–2, 306
auxiliarity 62, 68
auxiliarization, *see* split auxiliarization

background:
   background information 167, 185, 219, 260, 261
   background tense 272
   backgrounded event 16, 18, 209, 223–4, 226, 243, 265
   backgrounding elements 270
Bary 299, 300
Basset 66
Bertinetto 33, 34, 107, 108, 207–8, 209, 246, 262, 290–1
biography/hagiography 25, 158, 159, 160, 164, 169, 172, 173, 176, 183–4, 186–8, 249, 251, 262, 264, 273, 287
Björck 13, 62–3, 80–1, 83, 84, 99, 190–1, 230, 258, 260, 271, 276, 293
Bruno 175, 177, 202–3

Carey 118–19, 138–9
categorial status 79, 87
Ceglia 88, 269
Chantraine 38, 114–16, 117, 126, 132, 134, 140, 153, 211

Christian:
    Christianity 26
    community 288
    literature 26
    texts 269, **271**, 272, 282, 285
coalescence 52, 71
coincidence 232, **234-5**
Coleman 179
connectivity:
    strong 32, 243
    weak 223, 224, 242
consequentiality 257, 281
construal **99-101**, 102, 306
construction:
    definition of 55
    HAVE-construction 110
    innovative, *see* innovation
    locational construction 221, 290, 291
    locative construction, *see* locative
    minor 106, 152, 165-8, 179-82, 198-201, 236-8, 273-6, 289, 306
    possessive construction 118, 121, 131, 221, 222
    resultant state object construction **119**, 120, 121, 131, 148, 164
    resultant state process construction **119**, 121, 149, 166, 192
    secondary predicate construction **119**, 120, 131
control 119, **232-5**
corpus language 7, 30, 44, 52, 85
Croft 52, **89**, 100

dependency 91
διαγίγνομαι, with the present participle 60, 61-2, **72-4**, 75, 78-9
dialect 19, 21
    Attic 23, **228**
    Ionic 22, **136**
    Tsakonian 156, 206
diathetic neutralization 177
Dietrich **64-5**, 207, 227-9, 237, 253, 271-2, 276-7, 284
discourse mode **28**, 48, 134-5, 160, 172, 184, 290
documentary papyri 8, 20, **25**, 28, 155, 158, 159, 160, 161-4, 164, 169, 170, 172-3, 173-4, 176, 179, 181, 183-4, 187, 188, 191, 193, 196, 200, 249, 251, 253-4, 262-3, 264, 267, 270, 271, 287-8
drama **21**, 124, 132, 133, 135-6, 139, 148, 213, 215, 216, 222-3, 225, 228, 230, 295-6
Drinka 118, 131, **178-9**
durativity **41-2**, 221
dynamicity **41**, 91-2, 99

εἰμί 15, 18, 61, 88, 201-3, 306
    with the aorist participle 106, 166, **168-74**, **182-92**, 199, 201-3, **293-304**
    with the perfect participle 65, 76, 103, 106, 107, 112-13, 116, **125-37**, **137-47**, 150-1, 157-64, 171-4, 180, **182-92**, 194, 201-3, 300, 301, 302-4, 306-9
    with the present participle 181-2, 200, 206, **208-11**, **211-27**, **227-36**, 237, **238-54**, **254-73**, **276-89**, **289-91**, 295, 298, 302-4, 306-9
ἔχω 36, 61, 63, 67, 93, 202-3
    with the aorist participle 17, 60, **74-6**, 78-9, 106, 107, 109-10, 113, 116, 117, **118-25**, 131, 166, 178, 179-80, 181, 198-9, 203, 295, 301, 303, 306
    passive 180, 199
    with temporal adjunct 180-1, **194-8**
    with the perfect participle 152
    medio-passive 106, 109-10, **147-51**, 164-5, **175-9**, 192-4, 307
    with the present participle medio-passive 199-200
    with temporal adjunct 180-1, **194-8**
epic poetry **20-1**
ἔρχομαι 59, 61
    with the future participle 2-3, **76-8**, 79
Erzählungsmanier 271-2
Evans **68-9**, 153, 247-8
event schema 54
    equation schema **127-8**, 212

Fanning 101, 145, 269
Fernández Marcos 263, 269

focalization point 33, 210, 223, 225,
    226, 228, 243, 258–62, 266, 270,
    281, 285
foreground:
    foreground tense 272
    foregrounded event 32–3, 137, 147,
        209, 242, 243, 258–62, 265
    foregrounding 47–8, 304
formulaic expression 162–3, 170, 173,
    191, 193
function:
    functional competition 227, 293
    functional complexity 294, 302
    functional domain 31, 51, 105, 201,
        205, 272, 289, 306–9
    functional opposition 65, 168, 184,
        186, 202
    functional overlap 153, 229–31, 235
future 8, 29, 54, 101, 108, 244, 256, 267,
    280–1, 286, 295–6, 304
    future participle 60, 61, 71, 76–8, 79
    future perfect 137, 155, 162, 170, 173,
        191–2, 200, 201
    synthetic future 21, 25, 26

generalization 52, 54, 56, 71, 78–9
generic 34, 36–7, 215–18
genre 19–20, 28–9, 78–9, 125, 160, 172,
    184, 186, 223, 227–8, 252, 263,
    265, 271–2, 288, 290
    narrative genre 272
Giannaris 6, 189
Givón 32, 49, 90–1, 94, 242
grammaticalization 51–3, 72, 77, 79,
    175, 229, 285, 308
    cognitive factors underlying 53–5
    criticism of 55–8
    definition of 52
    gram 54, 77, 207, 246–7
    grammaticalization scale 70
    grammaticalization path 54, 106, 207,
        246–7, 290–1, 294, 306–8
    Grammaticalization Theory 51–2, 53,
        67, 70, 305
    parameters/processes of 52, 58, 65,
        71–2, 286
Greek novel 27, 28–9, 155, 169–70, 172,
    173, 176, 262–3, 264, 266, 271,
    273, 274

habitual 31, 34, 37, 207, 245–7, 257–8,
    282, 288, 290–1, 298, 308

Haspelmath 4, 30, 38, 55–6, 57, 93, 115–16
Heine 53–4, 56, 57, 127–8, 212, 249
historiography 17, 22, 26–7, 124, 133,
    135, 139, 148, 158, 159, 160, 164,
    169, 172, 173–4, 176, 183–4, 186,
    187, 188, 196, 213, 216, 222–3,
    228, 230, 249, 250, 251–2, 262,
    264, 266, 271–3, 282, 287, 295
Hopper & Thompson 45–8, 50–1
    criticism of 48–50
Horrocks 28, 153, 175, 177, 189, 192

imitation 17, 178–9, 198, 206–7, 242,
    252, 263, 269–70, 275, 277, 282–5
imperative 13, 135, 136–7, 159, 201,
    217–18, 240, 244
incidence scheme 32, 210, 226
inference 37, 119, 121, 149, 165, 177,
    179, 193, 199
infinitive 66, 68, 78, 135, 159
    articular 28
    decline of 157
innovation 21, 22, 24, 111–13, 132, 182,
    208–11, 258, 274, 286, 302, 309
iterativity 34, 139, 241, 244, 246–7, 257,
    280, 290–1, 308

Jannaris 182–3, 192, 230–1, 252

Kahn 15, 63–4, 84, 87, 205, 213, 304
Karleen 84–5, 221
Keil 301–2
Kunstsprache 21, 269

language change 70, 119, 305
    approaches towards 51–3
    social dimension of 56, 57–8, 308
language contact 6, 153
    with Aramaic 268
    with Hebrew 247–9, 268, 273
    with Latin 175–9
locative 207, 291
    ambiguity 195, 207, 219, 220, 233, 265
    construction 196, 207, 221–2, 290
    context 195, 259

Malchukov, see transitivity: transitivity
    scale
Mandilaras 153–4, 155, 200–1
Markopoulos 55, 57–8, 72, 286, 308
Meillet 52
Moser 66–7, 105, 106, 125, 153, 158

narrative pace 272
New Testament 206–7, 231, **254–62**, 267–73, **282–5**
normed rate of occurrence 8
noun-to-verb continuum 91, **98–9**, 101, 102–3

obligatorification 72
optative 25, 26, 27, 108, 116, **135–6**, 159, 172–3, 211, 217, 238
　disappearance of **156**, 172
oratory 24, 124–5, 133–5, 139, 148, 213, 216, 222–3, 230, 236, 295

paradigmaticization 52, 72
participle:
　adjectivization **63**, 67, 68–9, 79–82, 100, 102, 306
　criteria for 82–8
　decline of **156–7**, 206, 276
　property-referring 79–82
parts of speech **89**, 91
passive 114–15, 116–17, 123, 130–1, 133–4, 160–1, 173–4, 177, 181–2, 186–8, 189–90, 200, 202–3, 213–14, 222, 226–7, 239–40, 244, 249–50, 251, 262, 264, 287, 290, 295–6, 300, 304, 307
　statal 214, 239, 250
performative 300
philosophical prose **23–4**, 124, 133, 135, 139, 148, 213, 214, 216, 222, 228, 230, 295
πολύς, with εἰμί and the present participle 252, 266, 281
Porter 20, **67–8**, 80, 117, 153, 207, 219, 254, 293–4
Pouilloux 109, **123**
Principles and Parameters 51
productivity 163, 254–5, 271
PROG imperfective drift **207–8**, 219, 262, 291, 308
progressive 15, 28–9, **31–2**, 43, 51, 73, 206–7, 208–10, 218–27, 226–7, 235–6, 240, 251–4, 264–7, 275, 287, 289, 307, 309
　durative progressive **32–3**, 34, 207, 223–5, 240–3, 245, 251, 255–7, 262, 264, 266, 277, 279–81, 285–8, 290–1, 308
　　iterative durative progressive, *see* iterativity

focalized progressive **32**, 207, 225, 228, 243, 246, 258–9, 262, 264, 266, 277, 279, **282–5**, 287–8, 290–1
　types of 258–61
prototypicality 45–6, 50, 51, 197
　periphrastic prototype 78, 305
　prototype model of linguistic categorization 60, 67, **69–70**, 88, 89, 102
　prototypical adjective **89**, 90–1, 93–4
　prototypical noun **89**, 94
　prototypical property 98
　prototypical representation of an event **123**, 189
　prototypical transitive event 303
　prototypical transitivity 93, 100
　prototypical verb **89**, 94, 100
Pustet 91–4, 98–9, 100

reanalysis **118**, 121, 131, 134, 177, 195, 221, 222
register 17, **19–29**, 57–8, 72, 78, 148, 156, 166, 169–70, 172, 174, 175–6, 179, 181, 184, 186, 189–90, 196, 198, 229, 231, 252, 253, 260, 263, 264, 271, 273, 281–2, 290, 295
　definition of 19–20
　register continuum **20**, 21, 22, 58
　tenor vector 19
　spread through **285–8**, 308
resultative 38, 51, 75, 93, 106–7, 108, 110, 111, 113, 114–15, 116, 125, 131, 132, 133–5, 136, 140, 148–51, 160, 161, 168, 171, 172, 173–4, 177–9, 180, 181–2, 184, 186–9, 189–90, 190–2, 194, 199, 200, 201–3, 212, 214, 218, 221, 227, 240, 290, 304, 307–9
　object-oriented 125–8
　subject-oriented 125–8
rigidification **52**, 72, 189
Rijksbaron 12, 15, 35, 73, **114–15**, 128, 153
Rosén 16, 117, **228–9**, 268, 276, 278
Ruijgh 17, **205**, 213
Rydbeck 16, 28, **228–9**, 231, 240, 269

scientific prose **22–3**, 27–8, 124, 133–5, 135–6, 139, 148, 158, 159, 160–1, 164, 169, 172, 173, 176, 183–4,

Index nominum et rerum

187, 188, 213, 222, 249, 250, 251, 262-3, 264, 287, 295
semantic integration **52**, **63**, **71**, **72**, 103
Semitism 256, 267, **268**, 270, 273, 281
Septuagint 16, 160-1, 164, 231, **238-47**, **247-9**, 249, 251
septuagintalism 268-71, 273, 282
social marker 286, 288
socio-historical linguistics 57, 286
sociolinguistic acceptability, *see* grammaticalization: parameters/processes of
split auxiliarization **202**, 306
state 38, **41-3**, 44-5, 49, 92, 95-8, 108, 110, 111-12, 114-15, 119, 138, 149, 180, 193, 200, 201, 237, 301, 303-4
    stative 28-9, **31-4**, 41, 51, 60, 81, 88, 92, 94, 99, 106, 111, 117, 119, 121, 128, 165, 180, 197, 201, 206-7, 210-11, **211-18**, 222, 227, 235, 238-40, 248, 249-50, 254-5, 262-4, 265-6, 269, 273, 277, 278, 288, 289, 290-1, 297, 299, 304, 306-9
subjunctive **116**, 135-6, 156, 159, 162, 173
syntactic frame **258-62**, 284
synthetic perfect 13, 37, 111, 159, 161
    development of 105, **114-17**, 126, 132, 134, 171, 307
    disappearance of 153-6, 174, 240, 309
    formation of **116-17**, 135, 137, 202
    functional merger with the aorist 153, 166, 174, 293
    perfective value of 145-6, 163
syntheticity 2
    synthetic language 1
    synthetic form 11-12, 13, 17-18, 63, 65, 66, 68, 72, 76, 109, 116, 146, 153, 206
    synthetic tense 105

Tabachovitz 263, **268-71**
telic **41-2**, 45, 46, 49, 73, 77, 79, 115, 126, 138, 181, 199, 244, 245
tense 8, 29, 50, 53-4, 101, 117, 137, 156, 162, 190-1, 215, 217, 235, 239, 252, 255, 266, 276, 299, 300, 304
background tense, *see* background

foreground tense, *see* foreground temporality 30-1, 45, 115
theme **206**, 209, 234, 236
Thielmann 109, 116, 124-5
time-frame **32-3**, 224, 240-1, 253, 255, 262, 279
time-stability **90-1**, 94
transience 91, **94-8**, 99
transitivity **45-51**, 93-4, 99, 100, 112, 115, 129, 130, 134, 136-7, 139, 171, 221, 244, **302-4**, **306-8**
    de-transitivising elements **101**, 123, 239, 255
    detransitivization 304
    high 101, 122-3, 171, 185, 243, 252
    low 100, 136-7, 184-5, 212, 218, 219, 227, 229, 244, 263, 306
    transitive context 201-2, 251, 262, 280, 289, 303, 307
    transitive prototype 50
    transitivity hypothesis 47, 48-50
    transitivity parameters **46-7**, 48-9, 51
    transitivity profile 171, 229
    transitivity scale 50, 254
    transitivization 134, 139, 201, 227, 244, 262, 289, 303-7
τυγχάνω 162, **231-3**
    with the present participle 26, 59-61, **227-36**, 309
        assertive value 235-6
        disappearance of 230-1
        functional overlap with εἰμί with the present participle 227-36
        origins of 233-4
type-token ratio **8**, 108

unidirectionality 57
use pattern 175, **247-9**

Vendler, *see* actionality
verbal periphrasis:
    definition of 62-9, **69-72**, 305
    emergent phenomenon 107-10
    motivation for 18, 247
    periphrastic continuum 78-9
    periphrasticity 62, 63, 70
        criteria of 70-2
    relationship with adjectival periphrasis 80-1, **102-3**, **305-6**
    type of **12**, 63
    with phasal verbs 61-2, 71

verbal periphrasis: (cont.)
   with verbs of movement 61, 71
   with verbs of state 60–1, 71
verbal system 66–7, 202
   changes in **152–7**, 240, 303
   desystematization 202

Verboomen 245, 269, **270**
vulgarism 271–3

Wackernagel 38, **114–15**, 129
Wifstrand **216–17**, 265
word order **88**, 234

Lightning Source UK Ltd.
Milton Keynes UK
UKHW010035170223
417038UK00001B/16